FOURTH EDITION

Assessing Learners with Special Needs

An Applied Approach

Terry Overton
University of Texas–Pan American

Upper Saddle River, New Jersey
Columbus, Ohio

Library of Congress Cataloging in Publication Data
Overton, Terry.
Assessing learners with special needs: an applied approach/Terry Overton—4th ed.
p. cm.
Includes bibliographical references and indexes.
ISBN 0-13-094309-6
1. Educational tests and measurements—United States. 2. Special education—United States. 3. Behavioral assessment of children—United States. I. Title.

LB3051.094 2003
371.9--dc21

Vice President and Publisher: Jeffery W. Johnston
Acquisitions Editor: Allyson P. Sharp
Editorial Assistant: Penny Burleson
Production Editor: Sheryl Glicker Langner
Production Coordination: Rebecca K. Giusti, Clarinda Publication Services
Design Coordinator: Diane C. Lorenzo
Photo Coordinator: Cynthia Cassidy
Cover Designer: Ali Mohrman
Cover art: The watercolor cover is by 16-year-old artist David Dow, using his non-dominant left hand. At the age of 10, David had a massive stroke that caused partial paralysis and aphasia due to a rare disease called MoyaMoya. David's art is an inspiration to others as he continues to develop his talent.
Production Manager: Laura Messerly
Director of Marketing: Ann Castel Davis
Marketing Manager: Amy June
Marketing Coordinator: Tyra Cooper

This book was set in Garamond by The Clarinda Company. It was printed and bound by R. R. Donnelley & Sons Company. The cover was printed by Phoenix Color Corp.

Photo Credits:
Scott Cunningham/Merrill: pp. 3, 15, 61, 163, 185, 289, 377; Cheryl Fielding: p. ix; Larry Hammill/Merrill: p. 483; Ken Karp/PH College: p. 199; Anthony Magnacca/Merrill: pp. 97, 437; John Neubauer/PhotoEdit: p. 40; Riverside Publishing Company: p. 128 (© 2001 used with permission); Barbara Schwartz/Merrill: pp. 334, 506; Anne Vega/Merrill: p. 249;

Pearson Education Ltd.
Pearson Education Australia Pty. Limited
Pearson Education Singapore Pte. Ltd.
Pearson Education North Asia Ltd.
Pearson Education Canada, Ltd.
Pearson Educación de Mexico, S.A. de C. V.
Pearson Education—Japan
Pearson Education Malaysia Pte. Ltd.
Pearson Education, *Upper Saddle River, New Jersey*

10 9 8 7 6 5 4 3
ISBN: 0-13-094309-6

For Frank, for your patience and your faith in me.

For Jake, Crissy, and Jackson, may your future be bright.

For Kristy, you are wiser than your years.
Thanks for your guidance.

PREFACE

The process of assessing students with special needs continues to change. The fourth edition of *Assessing Learners with Special Needs: An Applied Approach* was written to reflect the changes in the assessment process.

Like earlier editions, the primary focus of this text is to provide students with a practical applied approach for learning about the complex procedures of the assessment process. This latest revision incorporates the federal regulations for the IDEA 1997 Amendments and includes the following changes:

- Application exercises that reflect increasing consideration of learners from culturally and linguistically diverse backgrounds
- Issues and practices of high-stakes assessment of learners with special needs
- Issues and practices of transition planning for learners with special needs
- Issues and practices of functional behavioral assessment of learners with special needs
- Case examples that provide students with experiences in the interpretation of data from reevaluations and comprehensive evaluations of learners from culturally and linguistically diverse environments
- Case examples that provide students with exercises involving considerations for transition planning, functional behavioral assessment, and educational planning for various ages
- Opportunities for students to participate in team meetings to determine the outcomes for the case examples
- Opportunities for students to complete short-term behaviorally stated objectives or benchmarks and long-term goals for case examples

This text presents complex concepts in a step-by-step manner and provides students with practice exercises for each step. Students also have portions of assessment instruments, protocols, and scoring tables provided as part of their practice exercises. Students will participate in the educational decision-making process using data from norm-referenced instruments, informal assessment data, and functional behavioral assessment data. Students will have the opportunity to plan for appropriate statewide assessment accommodations in application exercises.

The text is divided into four parts. Part 1, "Introduction to Assessment," introduces students to the assessment process and the federal laws and regulations governing that process. Professional standards and ethical considerations are included in Part 1.

Part 2, "Technical Prerequisites of Understanding Assessment," addresses the topics of descriptive statistics, reliability, validity, and the basic mechanics of administering tests. This part also presents both individualized assessment and group assessment, including high-stakes testing.

Part 3, "Assessing Students," includes numerous norm-referenced instruments, informal instruments, techniques for informal assessment, and behavioral assessment. It also covers the issues and practices of assessing young children and youth who are transitioning to adulthood.

Part 4, "Interpreting Assessment for Educational Intervention," discusses interpreting test results for interventions and eligibility decisions, writing test results, and using test results to write short-term objectives and long-term goals. Students using this text will draw on the information in these chapters to conduct team meetings in order to reach educational decisions.

At the end of most chapters the reader will find exercises to review and reinforce the chapter content. Because Chapter 13, "Case Studies," is completely an application chapter, it does not include the end-of-chapter exercise.

ACKNOWLEDGMENTS

I am forever grateful to the faculty and students at the University of Texas–Pan American, especially to Cheryl Fielding, Ph.D., and Ana Rodriguez, Ed.D. Thank you for your continued support and feedback during the development of this revised text. Your motivation, dedication, and persistence are inspirational. I thank the following reviewers, who reviewed this project for Prentice Hall: Greg Conderman, University of Wisconsin–Eau Claire; Charleen Peryon, University of Dubuque; Diane T. Woodrum, West Virginia University; Grace L. Denison, University of Maine at Farmington; and Robert Strosnider, Hood College. And to the graduate students at the University of Texas–Pan American, who provided insight and perspective in the assessment of students from culturally and linguistically diverse backgrounds, thank you.

I would like to express a personal note of thanks to Hilda Medrano, Ph.D., and JoAnn Mitchell, Ph.D., for your encouragement in the development of this text. Your kindness is greatly appreciated.

Discover the Companion Website Accompanying This Book

THE PRENTICE HALL COMPANION WEBSITE: A VIRTUAL LEARNING ENVIRONMENT

Technology is a constantly growing and changing aspect of our field that is creating a need for content and resources. To address this emerging need, Prentice Hall has developed an online learning environment for students and professors alike—Companion Websites—to support our textbooks.

In creating a Companion Website, our goal is to build on and enhance what the textbook already offers. For this reason, the content for each user-friendly website is organized by topic and provides the professor and student with a variety of meaningful resources. Common features of a Companion Website include:

FOR THE PROFESSOR—

Every Companion Website integrates **Syllabus Manager™,** an online syllabus creation and management utility.

- **Syllabus Manager™** provides you, the instructor, with an easy, step-by-step process to create and revise syllabi, with direct links into Companion Website and other online content without having to learn HTML.
- Students may log on to your syllabus during any study session. All they need to know is the web address for the Companion Website and the password you've assigned to your syllabus.

- After you have created a syllabus using **Syllabus Manager™**, students may enter the syllabus for their course section from any point in the Companion Website.
- Clicking on a date, the student is shown the list of activities for the assignment. The activities for each assignment are linked directly to actual content, saving time for students.
- Adding assignments consists of clicking on the desired due date, then filling in the details of the assignment—name of the assignment, instructions, and whether or not it is a one-time or repeating assignment.
- In addition, links to other activities can be created easily. If the activity is online, a URL can be entered in the space provided, and it will be linked automatically in the final syllabus.
- Your completed syllabus is hosted on our servers, allowing convenient updates from any computer on the Internet. Changes you make to your syllabus are immediately available to your students at their next logon.

COMMON COMPANION WEBSITE FEATURES FOR THE STUDENT INCLUDE:

- **Chapter Objectives**—outline key concepts from the text
- **Interactive Self-Quizzes**—complete with hints and automatic grading that provide immediate feedback for students

  After students submit their answers for the interactive self-quizzes, the Companion Website **Results Reporter** computes a percentage grade, provides a graphic representation of how many questions were answered correctly and incorrectly, and gives a question-by-question analysis of the quiz. Students are given the option to send their quiz to up to four email addresses (professor, teaching assistant, study partner, etc.).
- **Web Destinations**—links to www sites that relate to chapter content
- **Learning Network**—the Pearson Learning Network offers a wealth of additional resources to aid in their understanding and application of content
- **Message Board**—serves as a virtual bulletin board to post—or respond to—questions or comments to/from a national audience
- **Chat**—real-time chat with anyone who is using the text anywhere in the country—ideal for discussion and study groups, class projects, etc.

To take advantage of these and other resources, please visit the *Assessing Learners with Special Needs: An Applied Approach,* Fourth Edition, Companion Website at

www.prenhall.com/overton

ABOUT THE AUTHOR

Terry Overton began her career as a teacher of students with special needs. She completed her master's degree at Texas Woman's University and became an educational diagnostician. She completed her doctorate at Texas Woman's University in special education and her post-doctoral training in school psychology at the University of Virginia. Overton currently teaches at the University of Texas–Pan American near the Mexican border, where she serves as the program coordinator of the graduate program in school psychology.

CONTENTS

PART 1

***Introduction to Assessment* 1**

Chapter 1 An Introduction 3

Chapter Focus 4
Assessment: A Necessary Part of Teaching 4
Assessment: A Continuous Process 5
Prereferral 9
Designing An Assessment Plan 20
A Continuous Model of Assessment 23
The Comprehensive Evaluation 27
Assessing the Whole Child: Cultural Considerations 29
Chapter Summary 32
Think Ahead 32

Chapter 2 Laws, Ethics, and Issues 40

Chapter Focus 41
The Law: Public Law 94-142 and IDEA 41
IDEA and Assessment 43
Initial Evaluations 43 • Parental Consent 44 • Nondiscriminatory Assessment 46
Evaluating Children with Specific Learning Disabilities 53
Meeting the Needs of Persons with Attention Disorders 54
IEP Team Evaluation 55
Determining Eligibility 58
Parent Participation 60
Developing the Individualized Education Program 61
Transition Services 64
Due Process 66
Impartial Due Process Hearing 67

Section 504 68
Research and Issues Concerning IDEA 68
Issues of Nondiscriminatory Assessment 72
The Multidisciplinary Team and the Decision-Making Process 75
Least Restrictive Environment 76
Impartial Hearings 78
Ethics and Standards 79
Chapter Summary 85
Think Ahead 85

PART 2

Technical Prerequisites of Understanding Assessment 95

Chapter 3 Descriptive Statistics 97

Chapter Focus 98
Why is Measurement Important? 98
Getting Meaning from Numbers 99
Review of Numerical Scales 100
Descriptive Statistics 101
Measures of Central Tendency 102
Average Performance 103
Measures of Dispersion 110
Standard Deviation 113 • Standard Deviation and the Normal Distribution 115
Mean Differences 117
Skewed Distributions 117
Percentile Ranks and *z* Scores 119
Think Ahead 120

Chapter 4 Reliability and Validity 128

Chapter Focus 129
Reliability and Validity in Assessment 129
Correlation 129
Positive Correlation 130 • Negative Correlation 133 • No Correlation 134
Methods of Measuring Reliability 136
Test-Retest Reliability 137 • Equivalent Forms Reliability 137 • Internal Consistency Measures 138 • Interrater Reliability 139

Which Type of Reliability Is the Best? 140

Reliability for Different Groups 141

Standard Error of Measurement 143

Applying Standard Error of Measurement 146

Estimated True Scores 149

Test Validity 151

Criterion-Related Validity 151 • Content Validity 152 • Construct Validity 153 • Validity of Tests Versus Validity of Test Use 154

Reliability Versus Validity 155

Think Ahead 155

Chapter 5 An Introduction to Norm-Referenced Assessment 163

Chapter Focus 164

How Norm-Referenced Tests Are Constructed 164

Basic Steps in Test Administration 169

Beginning Testing 170 • Calculating Chronological Age 171 Calculating Raw Scores 174 • Determining Basals and Ceilings 175 • Using Information on Protocols 178 • Administering Tests: For Best Results 180 • Obtaining Derived Scores 183

Types of Scores 183

Group Testing: High-Stakes Assessment 184

Accommodations in High-Stakes Testing 187 • Alternate Assessment 188 • Issues in High-Stakes Testing 189

Chapter Summary 189

Think Ahead 190

PART 3

Assessing Students 197

Chapter 6 Tests of Educational Achievement 199

Chapter Focus 200

Achievement Tests 200

Standardized Norm-Referenced Tests Versus Curriculum-Based Assessment 200

The Review of Achievement Tests 201

Woodcock-Johnson III Tests of Achievement 202 • Peabody Individual Achievement Test—Revised 209 • Kaufman Test of Educational Achievement 213 • Wechsler Individual Achievement Test, Second Edition 224 • Wide Range

Achievement Test—Revision 3 228 • *Woodcock-McGrew-Werder Mini-Battery of Achievement* 234 • *Research and Issues* 236

Selecting Academic Achievement Tests 239

Think Ahead 241

Chapter 7 Standardized Diagnostic Testing 249

Chapter Focus 250

When to Use Diagnostic Testing 250

The Review of Diagnostic Tests 251

Keymath—Revised 251 • *Test of Mathematical Abilities—2* 262 • *Woodcock Reading Mastery Tests—Revised* 263

Other Diagnostic Tests 270

Gray Oral Reading Tests—Fourth Edition 270 • *Test of Reading Comprehension—Third Edition* 271 • *Test of Written Language—3* 272 • *Test of Written Spelling—4* 273

Assessing Other Language Areas 274

Peabody Picture Vocabulary Test—Third Edition 275 • *Test of Language Development—Primary: Third Edition* 277 • *Test of Language Development—Intermediate: Third Edition* 278 • *Test of Adolescent and Adult Language—Third Edition* 279

Selecting Diagnostic Instruments 281

Research and Issues 281

Think Ahead 282

Chapter 8 Informal Assessment Techniques 289

Chapter Focus 290

Problems of Norm-Referenced Assessment 290

Criterion-Referenced Assessment 291

The Brigance Inventories 292 • *Teacher-Made Criterion-Referenced Tests* 294

Curriculum-Based Assessment and Direct Measurement 299

Curriculum-Based Measurement 301 • *Cautions* 302

Task Analysis and Error Analysis 304

Teacher-Made Tests 307

Other Informal Methods of Academic Assessment 310

Informal Assessment of Reading 311 • *Informal Assessment of Mathematics* 318 • *Informal Assessment of Spelling* 318 • *Informal Assessment of Written Language* 320

Performance Assessment and Authentic Assessment 324

Portfolio Assessment 325
Think Ahead 327

Chapter 9 Assessment of Behavior 334

Chapter Focus 335
Requirements of the 1997 IDEA Amendments 335
Functional Behavioral Assessments 337

Direct Observation Techniques 338 • Antecedents 338 • Anecdotal Recording 339 • Event Recording 342 • Time Sampling 343 • Interval Recording 343 • Duration Recording 345 • Latency Recording 345 • Interresponse Time 345

Structured Classroom Observations 347

Child Behavior Checklist 347

Other Techniques for Assessing Behavior 348

Checklists and Rating Scales 348 • Questionnaires and Interviews 353 • Sociograms 355 • Ecological Assessment 357

Projective Assessment Techniques 359

Sentence Completion Tests 359 • Drawing Tests 360 • Apperception Tests 362

Computerized Assessment of Attention Disorders 364

Continuous Performance Test 364 • Conners Continuous Performance Test 365

Research and Issues 365
Think Ahead 369

Chapter 10 Measures of Intelligence and Adaptive Behavior 377

Chapter Focus 378
Measuring Intelligence 378
The Meaning of Intelligence Testing 378
Alternative Views of Intellectual Assessment 380
Litigation and Intelligence Testing 382
Use of Intelligence Tests 385
Review of Intelligence Tests 386

Wechsler Intelligence Scale for Children—Third Edition 386 • Wechsler Adult Intelligence Scale—Third Edition • 391 • Woodcock-Johnson III Tests Of Cognitive Abilities 395 • Stanford-Binet Intelligence Scale—Fourth Edition 397 • Kaufman Assessment Battery for Children 400 • Detroit Tests of Learning Aptitude—4 402 • Kaufman Adolescent and Adult Intelligence Test 404 Kaufman Brief Intelligence Test 405

Special Considerations for Students from Culturally and Linguistically Diverse Environments 406

Nonverbal Measures of Intellectual Ability 407 • Comprehensive Test of Nonverbal Intelligence 407 • Test of Noverbal Intelligence—Third Edition 409

Research on Intelligence Measures 410

Assessing Adaptive Behavior 413

Review of Adaptive Behavior Scales 416

Vineland Adaptive Behavior Scales 416 • AAMR Adaptive Behavior Scale—School, Second Edition 423 • Adaptive Behavior Inventory 424

Intelligence and Adaptive Behavior: Concluding Remarks 426

Think Ahead 428

Chapter 11 Special Considerations in Assessment 437

Chapter Focus 438

Legal Guidelines of Early Childhood Education 438

Infants, Toddlers, and Young Children 438

Eligibility 439

Evaluation and Assessment Procedures 439

Issues and Questions about Serving Infants and Toddlers 441

Methods of Early Childhood Assessment 444

Assessment of Infants 444

Assessment of Toddlers and Young Children 446

Mullen Scales of Early Learning: Ags Edition 446 • Wechsler Preschool and Primary Scale of Intelligence—Revised 447 • AGS Early Screening Profiles 449 • Kaufman Survey of Early Academic and Language Skills 452 • Brigance Screens 452 • Developmental Indicators for the Assessment of Learning—Third Edition 453

Techniques and Trends in Infant and Early Childhood Assessment 455

Other Considerations in Assessing Very Young Children 458

Phonemic Awareness 459

Transition and Postsecondary Considerations 464

Assessment of Transition Needs 466 • Transition Planning Inventory 467

Assessing Functional Academics 469

Kaufman Functional Assessment Skills Test 469

Research and Issues Related to Transition Planning 472

Think Ahead 473

PART 4

Interpreting Assessment for Educational Intervention 481

Chapter 12 Interpreting Assessment for Educational Intervention 483

Chapter Focus 484
Interpreting Test Results for Educational Decisions 485
The Art of Interpreting Test Results 487
Intelligence and Adaptive Behavior Test Results 490 • *Educational Achievement and Diagnostic Test Results 491*
Writing Test Results 491
Case Study 492
Writing Educational Objectives 500
IEP Team Meeting Results 500 • *Sve's IEP 501*
Reevaluations 503
Think Ahead 503

Chapter 13 Case Studies 506

Chapter Focus 507
Case 1: Sharon 507
Case 2: Steve 512
Case 3: Alicia 518
Case 4: Travis 523
Case 5: Eric 526
Case 6: Burt 531
Case 7: Lupita 538

Name Index 545
Subject Index 551

Note: Every effort has been made to provide accurate and current Internet information in this book. However, the Internet and information posted on it are constantly changing, so it is inevitable that some of the Internet addresses listed in this textbook will change.

PART 1

Introduction to Assessment

Chapter 1 **An Introduction**
Chapter 2 **Law, Ethics, and Issues**

CHAPTER 1

An Introduction

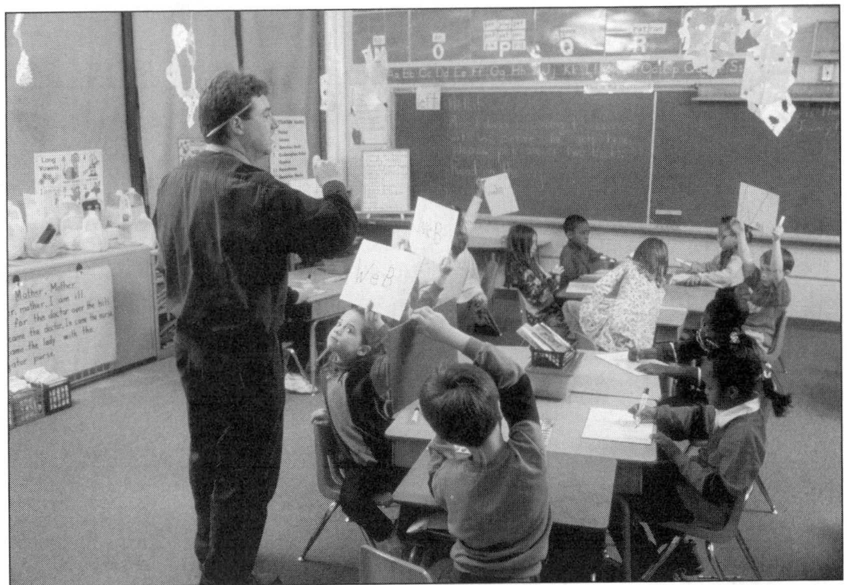

Key Terms

testing
assessment
continuous assessment
curriculum-based assessment
criterion-related assessment
criterion-referenced tests
performance assessment
portfolio assessment
dynamic assessment
error analysis
checklists
high-stakes testing
alternative assessments
informal assessment
teacher assistance team
child study committee
prereferral intervention strategies
overidentification
individualized education program (IEP)
ecological assessment
screening
individual assessment plan
Standards for Educational and Psychological Testing (APA Standards)
norm-referenced tests
standardized tests
individualized education program (IEP) team
eligibility meeting
alternative planning
Individual Family Service Plan (IFSP)

CHAPTER FOCUS

This introductory chapter presents an overview of the assessment process in general education in today's educational environment, reflecting current emphasis on inclusion and accountability of education for all children. The process includes prereferral strategies in the classroom setting, screening and assessment of students who, even with appropriate interventions, require additional support in the general education setting or other special settings. Various types of assessment are presented along with considerations of assessment of the child as a whole.

ASSESSMENT: A NECESSARY PART OF TEACHING

testing A method to determine a student's ability to complete certain tasks or demonstrate mastery of a skill or knowledge of content.

assessment The process of gathering information to monitor progress and make educational decisions if necessary.

Testing is one method of evaluating progress and determining student outcomes and individual student needs. Testing, however, is only one form of **assessment.** Assessment includes many formal and informal methods of evaluating student progress and behavior.

Assessment happens every day in every classroom. A teacher observes the behaviors of a student solving math problems. The teacher then checks the student's answers and determines the student's ability to solve that particular type of math problem. If the student made mistakes, the teacher determines the types of errors and decides what steps must be taken to correct the miscalculations. This is one type of assessment. The teacher observes behavior, gathers information about the student, and makes instructional changes according to the information obtained.

The process of assessment plays an important role in the determination of student outcomes. The IDEA 1997 Amendments and current educational reform place more emphasis on the assessment of all students for the measurement of attainment of educational standards within the general curriculum (Federal Register, 1999; Ysseldyke, Nelson, House, 2000). The effectiveness of earlier special education programs has also been debated in the literature, and such discussions have contributed to the current inclusion movement of students with disabilities in the general education curriculum and setting (Detterman & Thompson, 1997; Detterman & Thompson, 1998; Keogh, Forness, & MacMillan, 1998; Symons & Warren, 1998). Although the percentage of students receiving special education support continues to increase, so has the percentage of students in those programs graduating with regular high school diplomas (U.S. Department of Education, 2000). The increase in the numbers of students receiving special education support services who graduate with regular high school diplomas may reflect the effort to improve accountability of special education services. Educational accountability efforts include improving education and achievement for all students and especially improving the educational outcomes for culturally, linguistically, and ethnically diverse students, who continue to be represented in disproportionate numbers in several categories of special education (U.S. Department of Education, 1999; U.S. Department of Education, 2000). Teachers and other educational personnel must make decisions about the types of evaluations and tests and any accommodations that might be needed for statewide assessments in order to include students receiving special education support in accountability measures (Ysseldyke, Thurlow, Kozleski, & Reschly, 1998).

Assessment of students with disabilities is based on the same principles as assessment of students in general education. Inclusion of students with disabilities within the context of the general education classroom setting, as a mode of service delivery, has increased to more than 46% and will continue to increase due to the IDEA 1997 emphasis on general curriculum (U.S. Department of Education, 1999; Federal Register, 1999). This increase of students with disabilities in the general education environment results in common expectations for educational standards and common assessment (U.S. Department of Education, 1999).

In the assessment of students, behavior is observed, progress is evaluated, and a program is planned. The very best assessment practices, however, must adhere to legal mandates, ethical standards, and basic principles of measurement. Teachers and other educational personnel have a professional responsibility to be accountable for each decision about assessment decision. Therefore, knowledge of the fundamentals of assessment and the various types of assessment is necessary.

ASSESSMENT: A CONTINUOUS PROCESS

Assessment occurs in every classroom. To be aware of progress as students meet state standards for general curriculum goals and to determine if a student is having difficulty mastering skills and meeting goals, the effective teacher continuously monitors students' progress. Research supports the ability of teacher judgment and prediction of individual student progress (Demaray & Elliott, 1998; Taylor, Anselmo, Foreman, Schatschneider, & Angelopoulos, 2000). Teachers are daily observing students' abilities. In other words, the teacher uses **continuous assessment.**

continuous assessment The continuous monitoring of student progress.

When a student fails to progress as expected, the teacher may use several methods in an attempt to discover why progress has not been made as expected. The teacher may develop assessment measures directly from curriculum materials. This type of assessment is **curriculum-based assessment.** Curriculum-based assessment is common and may measure a student's performance within the curriculum.

curriculum-based assessment Using the content from the currently used curriculum to assess student progress.

When students are tested for mastery of a skill or an objective, the assessment is called **criterion-related assessment,** and tests of this type may be labeled **criterion-referenced tests.** Criterion-referenced tests compare the performance of a student to a given criterion. Students may be required to create a product that demonstrates their skills or competency; the assessment of their creation is called **performance assessment.** The assessment of a collection of various types of products or assessments collected over time that demonstrate student progress is known as **portfolio assessment.** When the assessment process includes interaction or teaching and prompting to determine a student's potential to learn a skill, the teacher has used the technique known as **dynamic assessment.**

Learning how the student performs tasks may also provide insight into the nature of the academic or behavioral difficulty. Observing the steps a student takes to solve a problem or complete a task can benefit the teacher as well as the student. The teacher may ask the student to verbalize the steps he takes while reading a paragraph for content or while solving a math equation. The teacher can then note the types or patterns of errors the student made during the process. This type of analysis is known as **error analysis** (e.g., $7 \times 3 = 10$; the student added rather than multiplied the numbers).

Teachers also develop **checklists** to identify students who have mastered skills, tasks, or developmental expectations appropriate to their grade level. Checklists can be found in some commercial materials or school curriculum guides. Placement in the specific curriculum within the general education classroom may be based on a student's performance on skills listed on these commercial checklists or on other curriculum-based assessment results.

Current reform movements in special education and general education emphasize the changing the role of assessment in special education (U.S. Congress, 1993; U.S. Department of Education, 1997). The result of this changing trend is the encouragement of nontraditional methods of assessment and the inclusion of students with disabilities in statewide accountability and competency testing (IDEA Amendments, 1997). Including students with disabilities in district and statewide assessment, or **high-stakes testing,** is necessary to determine the effectiveness of educational programs (Ysseldyke et al., 1998). Students with disabilities who are determined unable to participate in these assessments are to be assessed using **alternative assessments** to measure attainment of standards. Teachers will be required to use a variety of assessment techniques to assess student competency and demonstrate mastery of educational goals and objectives. The model of continuous assessment enables teachers to view assessment as an ongoing process that may result in referral for an evaluation to determine if the student has a disability only when interventions have been unsuccessful.

criterion-related assessment When items of an assessment instrument are related to meeting objectives or passing skill mastery objectives.

criterion-referenced tests Tests designed to accompany and measure a set of criteria or skill-mastery criteria.

performance assessment When a student is required to create a product to demonstrate knowledge.

portfolio assessment Evaluating student progress, strengths, and weaknesses using a collection of different measurements and work samples.

dynamic assessment Assessment in which the examiner prompts or interacts with the student to determine the student's potential to learn a skill.

error analysis Using a student's errors to analyze specific learning problems.

checklists Lists of skills developmentally sequenced and used to monitor student progress.

high-stakes testing Accountability assessment of state or district standards, which may be used for funding or accreditation decisions.

alternative assessments Assessment methods for students with disabilities, designed to measure progress in the general curriculum.

Check Your Understanding

Complete Activity 1.1.

ACTIVITY 1.1

Review the testing terms introduced in the previous paragraphs. Use the following terms to designate the type of assessment described in each statement.

Terms

assessment
error analysis
alternate assessments
curriculum-based assessment
performance assessment
high-stakes testing
criterion-related assessment
checklist
portfolio assessment
criterion-referenced tests
dynamic assessment

1. A teacher wants to determine why a student who can multiply single-digit numbers cannot multiply double-digit numbers. The teacher asks the student to verbally describe the steps she is using in the process of multiplying double-digit numbers. This is ______________.
2. The spelling series used in one classroom contains tests that are directly tied to the spelling curriculum. When the teacher uses these tests, ______________ is being used.
3. A teacher collects class work, quizzes, book reports, and writing assignments to determine the students' strengths and weaknesses in language arts. This is known as ______________.
4. When a teacher assesses a student's potential to learn a new math skill by prompting or cuing the student, ______________ has been used.
5. For a teacher to determine a student's understanding of the solar system, the student is required to create a project that demonstrates the Earth's position relative to designated planets. This is ______________.
6. A classroom teacher along with a team of other educational professionals determined that John, who has multiple disabilities, is not able to participate in the statewide assessment. The team develops ______________ to assess John's attainment of educational goals.

7. A student is not progressing as the teacher believes he should for his age expectancy. The teacher uses teacher-made tests, observation, and criterion-referenced tests to gather information about the student. This teacher is using different methods of ______________ to discover why the student is not making progress.
8. To determine whether a student has mastered a specific skill or objective, the teacher uses ______________.
9. A first-grade student has difficulty with fine motor skills. The teacher is concerned that the student may not have the developmental ability to learn manuscript handwriting. The handwriting series lists skills a student must master before writing letters. Using this device, the teacher has employed a ______________.
10. Assessment devices in a school's language series provide skills and objectives for each level of English, creative writing, and literature. These are ______________.
11. Each year the Mulberry Elementary School tests students to determine which students have mastered state curriculum standards. This testing is known as ______________.

Apply Your Knowledge

Analyze the following sentences written by Roberto. Identify the spelling errors.

1. The yellow kat is very big.
2. The oshun has big waves.
3. The kan was bent.

Your error analysis is that Roberto ______________________________
____.

informal assessment Nonstandardized methods of evaluating progress, such as interviews, observations, and teacher-made tests.

teacher assistance team A team of various professionals who assist the teacher in designing interventions for students who are not making progress.

Informal assessment is used every day without students' awareness of the monitoring of progress by this technique. Informal assessment includes worksheets, written samples of students' work, teacher-made tests and quizzes, oral reading assignments, oral responses, group projects, and class assignments. Informal assessment allows teachers to continually screen all students, including those who are academically at risk and those with special needs. (Informal assessment is discussed further in chapter 8.)

It is usually through informal assessment that a teacher first becomes aware that a student has not progressed as expected. More in-depth classroom assessment and observation techniques can then be used to pinpoint

child study committee A committee of various professionals at the student's school who determine if additional interventions are needed or if the student should be referred for a comprehensive evaluation.

prereferral intervention strategies Methods used by teachers and other team members to observe and modify student behaviors, learning environment, and/or teaching methods before making a formal referral.

the specific area of difficulty. When the in-depth assessment provides little help for the classroom teacher, that teacher may seek help from a special education teacher, school psychologist, educational diagnostician, or school principal. These are educational professionals who are commonly members of the **teacher assistance team** or a **child study committee.** If the student fails to make expected progress following the use of additional interventions by the classroom teacher, the teacher may refer the student to a committee to determine whether additional interventions, called **prereferral interventions,** are needed or whether the student should be referred for a comprehensive evaluation. The comprehensive evaluation is completed by a team of professionals that evaluates students to determine if a disability exists.

PREREFERRAL

Before referring a student for a comprehensive evaluation, a teacher must clearly target the student's learning or behavioral difficulty and attempt to address the difficulty within the classroom setting. Strategies taken by the classroom teacher before considering a referral are called prereferral intervention strategies. A teacher assistance team may be called on to assist in the development of specific strategies to be used in the classroom. Functional assessment of academic performance problems has been suggested as a method of targeting difficulties and implementing specific prereferral strategies (Daly, Witt, Martens, & Dool, 1997). This procedure provides hypotheses for the teacher to test through the use of classroom instructional interventions (see Figure 1.1). Once classroom teachers have documented the area of difficulty, they can systematically implement strategies for correction. Ideally, the prereferral strategies will decrease referrals by resolving some students' learning or behavioral problems within the general education classroom (Nelson, Smith, Taylor, Dodd, & Reavis, 1992).

Prereferral strategies include observation by objective persons, informal assessment techniques, curriculum modifications, environmental (classroom) modifications, and consultation with the parents and other members of the multidisciplinary team. In one statewide study, successful prereferral interventions also included teacher assistance teams, mainstream assistance teams, and collaborative peer problem solving (Nelson et al., 1992). Increasingly, state education agencies are recommending or requiring that educators implement prereferral interventions before referring a student for a comprehensive evaluation (Carter & Sugai, 1989; Nelson et al., 1992). The 1997 Amendments to IDEA begin with *Congressional Findings*, which lists areas that the amendments are seeking to improve, including the use of prereferral interventions. The goal of increasing the use of prereferral inter-

Reasonable Hypotheses	*Possible Interventions*
The student is not motivated to respond to the instructional demands	Increase interest in curricular activities: 1. Provide incentives for using the skill 2. Teach the skill in the context of using the skill 3. Provide choices of activities
Insufficient active student responding in curricular materials	Increase active student responding: 1. Estimate current rate of active responding & increase rate during allocated time
Insufficient prompting and feedback for active responding	Increase rate of complete learning trials: 1. Response cards 2. Choral responding 3. Flash card intervention with praise/error correction 4. Peer tutoring
Student displays poor accuracy in target skill(s)	Increase modeling and error correction: 1. Reading passages to student 2. Use cover-copy-compare 3. Have student repeatedly practice correct response in context for errors
Student displays poor fluency in target skill(s)	Increase practice, drill, or incentives: 1. Have the student repeatedly read passages 2. Offer incentives for beating the last score
Student does not generalize use of the skill to the natural setting or to other materials/settings	Instruct the student to generalize use of the skill: 1. Teach multiple examples of use of the skill 2. Teach use of the skill in the natural setting 3. "Capture" natural incentives 4. Teach self-monitoring
The instructional demands do not promote mastery of the curricular objective	Change instructional materials to match the curricular objective: 1. Specify the curricular objective and identify activities that promote use of the skill in the context in which it is generally used
Student's skill level is poorly matched to the difficulty of the instructional materials	Increase student responding using better matched instructional levels: 1. Identify student's accuracy and fluency across instructional materials and use instructional materials that promote a high rate of responding

Figure 1.1 Academic interventions identified by the presumed function of the behavior. (*Source: School Psychology Review, 26*(4), 558. Copyright 1997 by the National Association of School Psychologists. Reprinted by permission of the publisher.)

ventions is to address the student's needs within the general education classroom and prevent additional assessment. Congress stated:

> Over 20 years of research and experience has demonstrated that the education of children with disabilities can be made more effective by providing incentives for whole school approaches and pre-referral intervention to reduce the need to label children as disabled in order to address their learning needs. IDEA, 20 U.S.C. S1400(c)(5)(F).

The importance of prereferral interventions has become apparent through research studies that identify varying referral practices and recommend reform in the referral process. Research suggests referral practices in the past were inconsistent and may have been contributing to bias in the referral, assessment, and eligibility process. For example, studies found that males are referred more frequently and that students with a previous history of difficulties tend to be referred more often (Del'Homme, Kasari, Forness, & Bagley, 1996); female teachers referred students with behavioral problems more frequently than did male teachers (McIntyre, 1988); teachers referred students with learning and behavioral problems more often than those with behavioral problems alone (Soodak & Podell, 1993); and the teacher referrals were global in nature and contained subjective rather than objective information in more than half the cases (Reschly, 1986; Ysseldyke, Christenson, Pianta, & Algozzine, 1983). According to research, a teacher's decision to refer may be influenced by the student's having a sibling who has had school problems as well as by the referring teacher's tolerance for certain student behaviors; the teacher with a low tolerance for particular behaviors may more readily refer students exhibiting those behaviors (Thurlow, Christenson, & Ysseldyke, 1983).

In another study, it was found that the characteristics of referred students may vary with student age (Harvey, 1991). Males were referred more frequently than female students at all grade levels. In the primary grade levels, younger students (for grade level) were referred more frequently than students who had birth dates farther from the school admission cutoff date (October 31). Students who were referred in the third grade or later had birth dates distributed evenly throughout the year, which suggests that students in the primary grades exhibited developmental differences rather than true learning or behavioral problems. Andrews, Wisnieswski, and Mulick (1997) found that students were referred at a higher rate if their height and weight were greater than average for their grade and gender. This study also found that more African American students were referred for developmental disability services than Caucasian students and that males were referred more frequently for behavioral problems than females (Andrews et al., 1997).

Early research indicated that nationwide more than 90% of the students referred for evaluation were tested. Of those tested, 73% were subsequently found eligible for services in special education (Algozzine, Christenson, & Ysseldyke, 1982). More recently, Del'Homme et al. found that 63% of the students in their study who were referred subsequently received special education services (1996). Students who are referred are highly likely to complete the evaluation process and receive special education services. In another study, 54% of the students referred for assessment were determined to be eligible (Fugate, Clarizio, & Phillips, 1993).

Although effective prereferral strategies have been found to reduce the number of referrals for assessment, one study found that general education teachers had only a vague understanding of specific strategies and how to implement them (Wilson, Gutkin, Hagen, & Oats, 1998). In this study, the participating teachers viewed the prereferral process as a step in the referral process rather than an intervention to prevent assessment. This research illustrates the problems encountered in the referral process and has influenced a move toward more comprehensive and detailed prereferral intervention strategies. The more frequent use of better prereferral intervention is a step forward in the prevention of unnecessary evaluation and the possibility of misdiagnosis and **overidentification** of special education students. Halgren and Clarizio (1993) found that 38% of the students in special education were either reclassified or terminated from special education. This indicates a need for more specific identification of the learning or behavioral problems through referral and initial assessment.

overidentification Describes the phenomenon of identifying students who seem to be eligible for special education services but who are actually not disabled.

Valles (1998) suggested that teacher training in special and general education may be needed to prevent inappropriate referrals of minority and bilingual students. Gopaul-McNicol and Thomas-Presswood caution that often, teachers of students whose primary language is not English consider bilingual education or English as a Second Language (ESL) classes as prereferral interventions (1998). In a study of the referral and assessment practices of Asian American students, it was found that prereferral interventions were limited and did not reflect the approaches needed that may have assisted with language development (Poon-McBrayer & Garcia, 2000). In this study, these students were referred for evaluations when language interventions may have resolved the difficulties. Teachers of students with cultural and linguistic differences should employ prereferral intervention strategies that promote language acquisition in addition to ESL or bilingual curriculum.

Providing consulting services to general education teachers could help resolve student problems before referral (Zins, Graden, & Ponti, 1989). Serna, Forness, and Nielsen (1998) suggest that systemic changes in referral practices are needed at the preservice level of teacher training. This type of prereferral intervention would place team members in a consulting role for a large part of their service time and decrease the time they spent testing. Fuchs (1991) found that several features need to exist in the practice of prereferral interventions. The following list is adapted from this study:

1. Prereferral intervention should be included in the job descriptions of those persons responsible for implementation. This includes both professional and paraprofessional staff.

2. A consultant or team should serve to guide the prereferral effort.
3. All staff involved should receive adequate training in the prereferral strategies.
4. The consultation effort should be efficient and exhibit desired outcomes.
5. Consultants should define the problem behavior, set goals for students and teachers, collect data, and evaluate effectiveness.
6. Interventions should be agreeable to both consultants and teachers.
7. Strategies should be implemented as designed.
8. Data should be collected at multiple intervals. (p. 263)

Check Your Understanding

Complete Activity 1.2.

ACTIVITY 1.2

Refer to the faulty referral practices cited in the research in the previous paragraphs to determine what types of errors have been made in the following cases.

1. Mr. Jones has Billy for fourth and fifth periods each day at Randolph Middle School. Ms. Jarrod stopped by Mr. Jones's room after school one day to tell Mr. Jones that she was going to refer Billy for evaluation for behavioral problems. She said that she cannot tolerate Billy's behavior another day. Mr. Jones remarked that Billy seems to get along fine in his class as long as there is structure and guidance within the class, including telling Billy when his work is completed nicely. According to research, Ms. Jarrod's feelings might be an example of ______________.
2. Mr. Bonderan has just received his class roll for the new school year. His heart sinks when he sees the name Jeffery Dews. Mr. Bonderan knows that he will have to refer Jeffery for a comprehensive evaluation, just as he had to refer Jeffery's older brother Jonathan last year. Mr. Bonderan may be referring Jeffery only because ______________.
3. A referral turned in last Monday by Miss Greene contained the following information: "Susie is just not acting as she should. I think she has a problem. I have been teaching school for 15 years, and I have never had such a stubborn little girl in my class. I don't know what her problem is, but I can't keep her in my class any longer. I think she should be tested right away. I don't want to try any more interventions. I tried moving her closer to the blackboard. She just doesn't want to learn." What problems do you see with Miss Greene's referral? ______________________________.
4. Mrs. Fielding expressed concern to a resource teacher about a student in her class named Emily, who "seems to be a little behind the

others." Emily is slightly overweight and large for her age when compared with the other fifth-grade students. The resource teacher listened patiently and then asked, "Isn't Emily younger than the other students in your class?" This resource teacher may have been concerned that Mrs. Fielding might be making what type of error in considering a referral? ___________

Apply Your Knowledge

Shantel is not making the progress her teacher expected her to make in mathematics. Shantel is able to add single digits fairly consistently, but she has not been successful mastering simple subtraction facts. Some days Shantel seems to answer most of the problems correctly. Other days, she seems to add all of the problems. Her teacher, Mr. Patience, believes that Shantel has the ability to learn this skill. Another teacher suggests that Mr. Patience should refer Shantel to the child study committee. You suggest to Mr. Patience that he ___________.

individualized education program (IEP) A written plan of educational interventions designed for each student who receives special education.

ecological assessment Method of assessing a student's total environment to determine what factors are contributing to learning or behavioral problems.

In the past, a student was referred for testing, evaluated by team members, and, if determined eligible for special education services, given an **individualized education program** (IEP) and placed in a special education setting. Although these steps were reported nationally as those most commonly followed in the evaluation process (Ysseldyke & Thurlow, 1983), they do not include the step of prereferral intervention.

The model proposed by Graden, Casey, and Christenson (1985), however, includes "identifying, defining, and clarifying the problem, analyzing the components of the classroom ecology that affect the problem, designing and implementing interventions, and evaluating intervention effectiveness" (p. 383). As Graden and colleagues have written, this type of prereferral intervention looks at many variables surrounding the student's educational performance rather than assuming first that the difficulty is with the student. This type of assessment, called **ecological assessment,** reflects a major trend toward considering the environment and assessing students in their natural environment (Reschly, 1986).

Messick (1984) proposed a two-phase assessment strategy that emphasizes prereferral assessment of the student's learning environment. The information needed during Messick's first phase includes

1. Evidence that the school is using programs and curricula shown to be effective not just for students in general but for the various ethnic, linguistic, and socioeconomic groups actually served by the school in question.
2. Evidence that the students in question have been adequately exposed to the curriculum by virtue of not having missed too many lessons because of

Prereferral intervention.

absence or disciplinary exclusion from class and that the teacher has implemented the curriculum effectively.

3. Objective evidence that the child has not learned what was taught.
4. Evidence that systematic efforts were or are being made to identify the learning difficulty and to take corrective instructional action, such as introducing remedial approaches, changing the curriculum materials, or trying a new teacher.

Source: From "Assessment in Context: Appraising Student Performance in Relation to Instructional Quality," by S. Messick, 1984, *Educational Researcher, 13,* p. 5. Copyright 1984 by American Educational Research Association. Reprinted by permission of the publisher.

The referring teacher may use a checklist such as the one in Figure 1.2 to determine whether all necessary interventions have been attempted. Using a prereferral checklist not only clarifies areas of concern but also helps the referral-screening committee decide whether the evaluation is necessary, and if so, what types of assessment instruments will be administered. It is no longer considered acceptable to refer students who have difficulty in the regular classroom without prereferral interventions unless they appear to be experiencing severe learning or behavioral problems or are in danger of harming themselves or others.

Prereferral intervention strategies have had positive effects. In schools where a prereferral intervention model was implemented, consultation services increased within the general education classroom, and both testing

Prereferral Checklist

Name of Student ______________________________

Concerned Teacher ______________________________

Briefly describe area of difficulty:

1. Curriculum evaluation:

_________ Material is appropriate for age and/or grade level.
_________ Instructions are presented clearly.
_________ Expected method of response is within the student's capability.
_________ Readability of material is appropriate.
_________ Prerequisite skills have been mastered.
_________ Format of materials is easily understood by students of same age and/or grade level.
_________ Frequent and various methods of evaluation are employed.
_________ Tasks are appropriate in length.
_________ Pace of material is appropriate for age and/or grade level.

2. Learning environment:

_________ Methods of presentation are appropriate for age and/or grade levels.
_________ Tasks are presented in appropriate sequence.
_________ Expected level of response is appropriate for age and/or grade level.
_________ Physical facilities are conducive to learning.

3. Social environment:

_________ Student does not experience noticeable conflicts with peers.
_________ Student appears to have adequate relationships with peers.
_________ Parent conference reveals no current conflicts or concerns within the home.
_________ Social development appears average for age expectancy.

4. Student's physical condition:

_________ Student's height and weight appear to be within average range of expectancy for age and/or grade level.
_________ Student has no signs of visual or hearing difficulties (asks teacher to repeat instructions, squints, holds papers close to face to read).

Figure 1.2 A prereferral checklist to determine whether all necessary interventions have been attempted.

_________ Student has had vision and hearing checked by school nurse or other health official.
_________ Student has not experienced long-term illness or serious injury.
_________ School attendance is average or better.
_________ Student appears attentive and alert during instruction.
_________ Student appears to have adequate motor skills.
_________ Student appears to have adequate communication skills.

5. Intervention procedures (changes in teaching strategies that have been attempted):

_________ Consultant has observed student:

	Setting	***Date***	***Comments***
1.			
2.			
3.			

_________ Educational and curriculum changes were made:

	Change	***Date***	***Comments***
1.			
2.			
3.			

_________ Behavioral and social changes were made:

	Change	***Date***	***Comments***
1.			
2.			
3.			

_________ Parent conferences were held:

	Date	***Comments***
1.		
2.		
3.		

_________ Additional documentation is attached.

Figure 1.2 continued.

and educational placements decreased significantly (Graden, Casey, & Bonstrom, 1985). In a study by Chalfant and Psyh (1989), the inappropriate referral rate decreased to 63%, and interventions were successful in approximately 88% of the cases. Many special education administrators support the use of prereferral intervention models, although some confusion remains about whether special education or general education should control the process (Nelson et al., 1992). Wide use of prereferral intervention would help increase the numbers of students who would experience academic success within the very least restrictive environment, the general education class setting.

Check Your Understanding

Complete Activity 1.3.

ACTIVITY 1.3

Look at the partially completed prereferral checklist that follows. Read the interventions carefully. Before completing a referral form, what suggestions might be included as prereferral interventions? Write your suggestions for intervention strategies in section 5 (ignore "Date" and "Comment" columns) of this form. Answer the questions following the form.

Prereferral Checklist.

Name of Student: Mary Ellen Pollard
Teacher: Ms. J. M. Anderson
Briefly describe area of difficulty:

Mary Ellen has been in my class for 3 months and has not progressed in math. Although she is performing well in reading and spelling, she does not seem to be a happy student. She does not have many friends, and the other children laugh at her and make fun of her during math class.

1. Curriculum evaluation

__yes__ Material is appropriate for age and/or grade level, and linguistic background.
__yes__ Instructions are presented clearly.
__yes__ Expected method of response is within the student's capability.
__yes__ Readability of material is appropriate.
not sure Prerequisite skills have been mastered.
__yes__ Format of materials is easily understood by students of same age and/or grade level and linguistic background.
not sure Frequent and various methods of evaluation are employed.
not sure Tasks are appropriate in length.
__yes__ Pace of material is appropriate for age and/or grade level.

2. Learning environment

__yes__ Methods of presentation are appropriate for age and/or grade level and linguistic background.

__yes__ Tasks are presented in appropriate sequence.
__yes__ Expected level of response is appropriate for age and/or grade level.
__yes__ Physical facilities are conducive to learning.

3. Social environment
   not sure Student does not experience noticeable conflict with peers.
   __no__ Student appears to have adequate relationships with peers.
   __yes__ Parent conference reveals no current conflicts or concerns within the home.
   not sure Social development appears average for age expectancy.
4. Student's physical condition
   __yes__ Student's height and weight appear to be within average range of expectancy for age and/or grade level.
   __yes__ Student has no signs of visual or hearing difficulties (e.g., asks teacher to repeat instructions, squints, holds papers too close to face to read).
   __yes__ Student has had vision and hearing checked by school nurse or other health official.
   not sure Student has not experienced long-term illness or serious injury.
   __no__ School attendance is average or better.
   not sure Student appears attentive and alert during instruction.
   __yes__ Student appears to have adequate motor skills.
   __yes__ Student appears to have adequate communication skills.
5. Intervention procedures (changes in teaching strategies that have been attempted)

Consultant has observed student.

Setting	**Date**	**Comments**
1.		
2.		
3.		

Educational and curriculum changes were made.

Change	**Date**	**Comments**
1.		
2.		
3.		

Behavioral and social changes were made.

Change	Date	Comments
1.		
2.		
3.		

Parent conferences were held.

Date	Comments
1.	
2.	
3.	

Additional documentation is attached.

Apply Your Knowledge

1. After reading this checklist, what areas do you think appear to represent problems for Mary Ellen?
2. If Mary Ellen were your student, what questions would you seek to answer before requesting a comprehensive evaluation?
3. What additional documentation might be beneficial for you to obtain before considering a referral for special education evaluation?

DESIGNING AN ASSESSMENT PLAN

screening A process of reviewing a referral to determine whether a student needs further evaluation by the multidisciplinary team.

Federal law mandates that evaluation measures used during the assessment process are those measures specifically designed to assess areas of concern (IDEA Amendments of 1997). (The specific laws pertaining to the education of individuals with disabilities are discussed in chapter 2.) Through the use of appropriate prereferral intervention strategies, the referring teacher is able to pinpoint specific areas of difficulty, and the assessment team can then design an appropriate assessment plan. At this time, the referring teacher may formally refer the student and begin the **screening** process. A screening committee determines whether the referred student should be evaluated further by a multidisciplinary team. If the committee decides that further assessment is warranted, the student is referred to the evaluation team. The team must then determine which instruments will be administered and which special education professionals are needed to complete the assessment.

Federal law also requires that the instruments selected have been validated for the purpose of intended use. For example, if the student has been referred for problems with reading comprehension, the appropriate assessment instrument would be one of good technical quality that has been designed to measure reading problems, specifically, reading comprehension skills. In addition to requiring selection of the appropriate tests, the law mandates that persons administering the tests be adequately trained to administer those specific tests and that more than a single instrument be used to determine eligibility for special services. To meet these mandates, the educator must design an **individual assessment plan** for each student. Maxam, Boyer-Stephens, and Alff (1986) recommended that each evaluation team follow these specific steps in preparing an assessment plan:

individual assessment plan A plan that lists the specific tests and procedures to be used for a student who has been screened and needs further assessment.

1. Review all of the screening information in each of the seven areas (health, vision, hearing, speech and language skills, intellectual, academic, prevocational/vocational).
2. Determine what area(s) need further evaluation.
3. Determine the specific data-collection procedures to use (interviews, observation of behavior, informal or formal techniques, standardized tests).
4. Determine persons responsible for administering the selected procedures. These persons must be trained or certified if the assessment instrument calls for specific qualifications.

Source: From *Assessment: A Key to Appropriate Program Placement* (Report No. CE 045 407, pp. 11–13) by S. Maxam, A. Boyer-Stephens, and M. Alff, 1986, Columbia, MO: University of Missouri, Columbia, Department of Special Education and Department of Practical Arts and Vocational-Technical Education. (ERIC Document Reproduction Service No. ED 275 835.) Copyright 1986 by the authors. Reprinted by permission.

Check Your Understanding

Complete Activity 1.4.

ACTIVITY 1.4

Read the following case study. Determine what types of assessment might be used to further evaluate the student. Some suggestions from which to choose are listed after the case study.

Referral

Name of Student: George B. Baker, Jr. Grade Placement: 5.7
Referring Teacher: Ms. C. K. Williamson

Reason for Referral

The teacher reported: "George has been experiencing difficulties in reading, spelling, writing, and English. Curriculum changes included using a fourth-grade reader and spelling book, allowing George more time to complete assignments, and providing extra individual attention and peer tutoring. George gets along fine with other students and has no academic problems in other subjects as long as he is not responsible for independently reading material above the third-grade level. His fifth-grade science book is read aloud by other students during class time, and he listens intently. George has not mastered fourth-grade reading and spelling curriculum. I think he has the mental capability, but I'm not sure why he experiences very little success in language arts."

Methods of Assessment

The following methods are available and are administered by the teacher or special education teacher unless indicated otherwise:

1. Curriculum-based assessment in reading, spelling, English, and math
2. Screening test in all academic areas
3. Individual intelligence test (by school psychologist)
4. Diagnostic reading test and math test
5. Developmental spelling and reading checklists
6. Criterion-referenced test by reading series publisher
7. Vision and hearing screening (by school nurse)
8. General individual academic achievement test
9. Interviews with other teachers
10. Informal assessment of class work
11. Classroom observations during language arts class and other classes
12. Informal reading inventory
13. Parent interview
14. Student interview

Using the referral data provided and the types of assessment available, design an assessment plan for George. In the blanks provided, list the appropriate tests and the team members who will administer them. Select the team members from the following: general education teacher, special education teacher, school psychologist, parent, student, school nurse or other medical professional.

Assessment Plan

Name: George B. Baker, Jr.
Team Member Name [you]:
Types of Assessment

1. ______________ by: ______________
2. ______________ by: ______________
3. ______________ by: ______________

4. ______________ by: ______________
5. ______________ by: ______________
6. ______________ by: ______________
7. ______________ by: ______________
8. ______________ by: ______________

Apply Your Knowledge

As George's classroom teacher, you decide it will be beneficial to the team to supply a portfolio of George's classroom work. You would like to show examples representing George's strengths and difficulties. What would you include? ______________________________
____

Standards for Educational and Psychological Testing (APA Standards) Professional and ethical standards that suggest minimum criteria for assessing students.

In addition to federal mandates and recommendations from professionals in the field of special education, the professional organizations of the American Psychological Association, the American Educational Research Association, and the National Council on Measurement in Education have produced the **Standards for Educational and Psychological Testing** (1985), which clearly defines acceptable professional and ethical standards for individuals who test children in schools. (Several of these standards are included in later chapters of this text.) The APA Standards (1985) emphasize the importance of using tests for the purpose intended by the test producer and place ethical responsibility for correct use and interpretation on the person administering and scoring tests in the educational setting. The Code of Fair Testing Practices in Education is included in the appendix. Other professional organizations, such as the Council for Exceptional Children and the National Association of School Psychologists, have ethics and standards about assessment. These are presented in chapter 2.

A student who has been referred for an initial evaluation may be found eligible for services according to the definitions of the various disabling conditions defined in federal law. Figure 1.3 lists the classifications as specified in the Individuals with Disabilities Education Act (IDEA; discussed further in chapter 2).

A CONTINUOUS MODEL OF ASSESSMENT

One proposed model of assessment is illustrated in Figure 1.4. This model incorporates standardized state and district testing, informal assessment, and prereferral intervention strategies before the formal referral and screening processes. A student who continues to have significant difficulty after

Autism	A developmental disability significantly affecting verbal and nonverbal communication and social interaction, generally evident before age 3, that adversely affects a child's educational performance. Other characteristics often associated with autism are engagement in repetitive activities and stereotyped movements, resistance to environmental change or change in daily routines, and unusual responses to sensory experiences. The term does not apply if the child's educational performance is adversely affected primarily because the child has an emotional disturbance.
Deafness	A hearing impairment that is so severe that the child is impaired in processing linguistic information through hearing with or without amplification, which adversely affects educational performance.
Deaf-blindness	Concomitant hearing and visual impairments, the combination of which causes such severe communication and other developmental and educational problems that the child cannot be accommodated in special education programs solely for children with deafness or children with blindness.
Emotional Disturbance	A condition exhibiting one or more of the following characteristics over a long period of time and to a marked degree that adversely affects a child's educational experience: 1. An inability to learn that cannot be explained by intellectual, sensory, or health factors. 2. An inability to build or maintain satisfactory interpersonal relationships with peers and teachers. 3. Inappropriate types of behavior or feelings under normal circumstances. 4. A general pervasive mood of unhappiness or depression. 5. A tendency to develop physical symptoms or fears associated with personal or school problems. Emotional disturbance may include those persons with schizophrenia and does not include students who are socially maladjusted unless it is determined that they are also emotionally disturbed.
Hearing Impairment	Hearing impairment, whether permanent or fluctuating, that adversely affects a child's educational performance but is not included under the definition of deafness.
Mental Retardation	Significantly subaverage general intellectual functioning existing concurrently with deficits in adaptive behavior manifested during the developmental period, which adversely affects the child's educational performance.

Figure 1.3 Disabilities defined in IDEA for which students are eligible for special education services.

Multiple Disabilities	Concomitant impairments (e.g., mental retardation-blindness, mental retardation-orthopedic impairment), the combination of which causes such severe educational problems that the child cannot be accommodated in special education programs solely for one of the impairments; does not include deaf-blindness.
Orthopedic Impairment	Severe orthopedic impairment that adversely affects a child's educational performance. The term includes impairments caused by congenital anomaly (e.g., clubfoot, absence of some member), impairments caused by disease (e.g., poliomyelitis, bone tuberculosis), and impairments from other causes (e.g., cerebral palsy, amputations, and fractures or burns that cause contractures).
Other Health Impairment	Means having limited strength, vitality, or alertness, including a heightened alertness to environmental stimuli, that results in limited alertness with respect to the educational environment, that is due to chronic or acute health problems such as asthma, attention deficit disorder or attention deficit hyperactivity disorder, diabetes, epilepsy, a heart condition, hemophilia, lead poisoning, leukemia, nephritis, rheumatic fever, and sickle-cell anemia, which adversely affects the child's educational performance.
Specific Learning Disability	A disorder in one or more of the basic psychological processes involved in understanding or using language, spoken or written, that manifests itself in the imperfect ability to listen, speak, read, write, spell, or do mathematical calculations. The term includes such conditions as perceptual disabilities, brain injury, minimal brain dysfunction, dyslexia, and developmental aphasia. The term does not include learning problems that are primarily the result of visual, hearing, or motor disabilities; mental retardation, emotional disturbance, or environmental, cultural, or economic disadvantage.
Speech Impairment	A communication disorder, such as stuttering, impaired articulation, a language impairment, or a voice impairment, that adversely affects a child's educational performance.
Traumatic Brain Injury	Means an acquired injury to the brain caused by an external physical force, resulting in total or partial functional disability or psychosocial impairment, or both, that adversely affects a child's educational performance. The term applies to open or closed head injuries resulting in impairments in one or more areas such as cognition, language, memory, attention, reasoning, abstract thinking, judgment, problem-solving, sensory, perceptual, and motor abilities, psychosocial behavior, physical functions, information processing, and speech. The term does not apply to brain injuries that are congenital or degenerative, or to brain injuries induced by brain trauma.
Visual Impairment	Means an impairment in vision that, even with correction, adversely affects a child's educational performance. The term includes both partial sight and blindness.

Figure 1.3 continued.

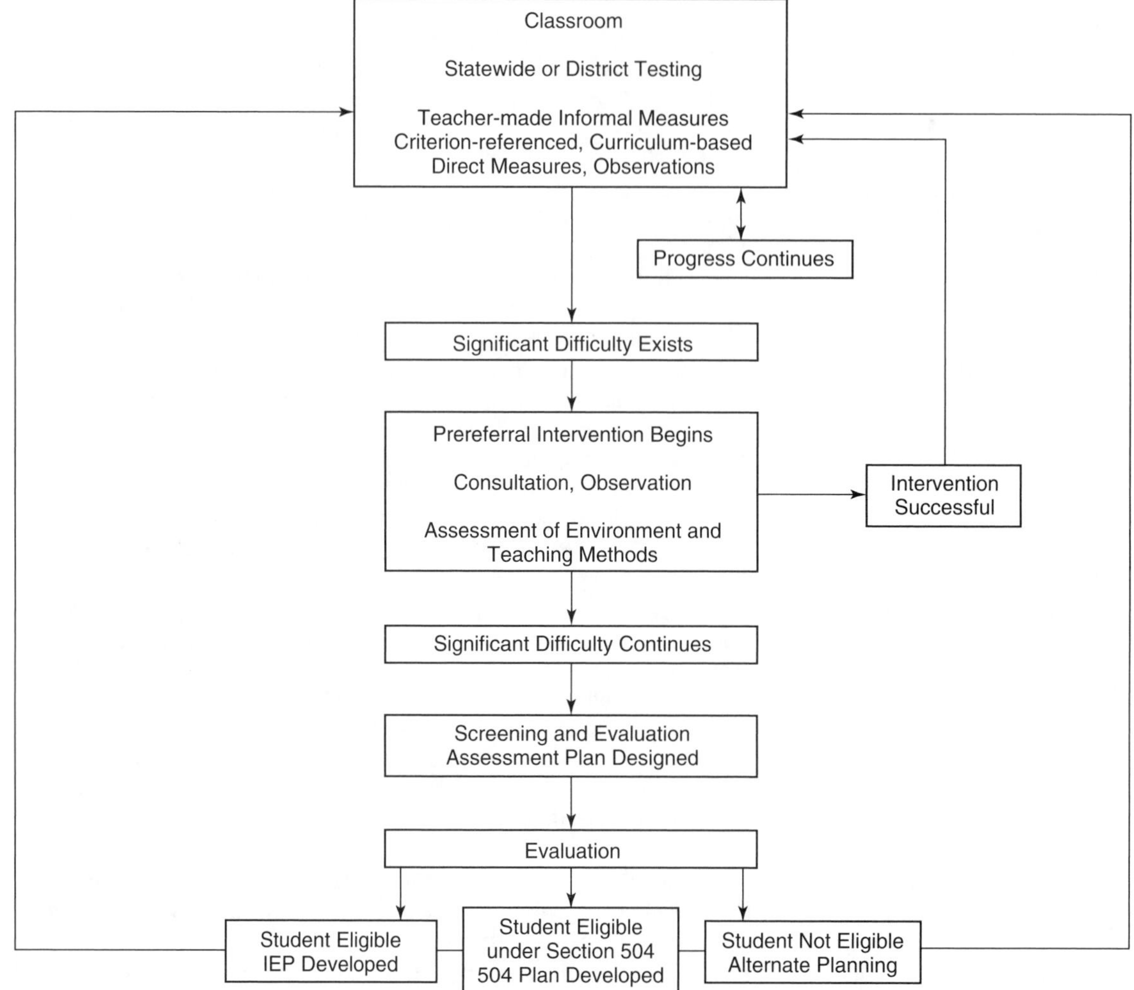

Figure 1.4 Continuous model of assessment.

numerous prereferral interventions usually is referred for a formal evaluation. After being received by the special education team, the referral is screened. During the screening process, the educators may determine that the student needs further assessment. At that time, team members design an individual assessment plan based on the referral information.

Although the professional literature advises careful design of assessment plans, research indicates that problems exist in referral and screening practices. White and Calhoun (1987) found that many special education teachers felt they were "gatekeepers" in the sense of determining which students would be screened and eventually tested for possible special education placement. It also seemed that the formal act of screening affected decisions only when the special education teacher was not certain about the student's eligibility (White & Calhoun, 1987). Ideally, the purpose of the screening process is to determine the need for further testing and the specific types of assessment that may be necessary. Ysseldyke, Algozzine, Richey, and Graden (1982) found that much of the information gathered to use in decision making has very little influence in the assessment process. Failure to rely on relevant referral data and to develop an individual assessment plan could lead to unnecessary testing and misdiagnosis.

The federal laws were designed to serve as a safeguard for students and provide structure in the assessment and educational programming process. Research indicates, however, that local education agencies attempting to comply with federal regulations do not necessarily provide beneficial programming for the students referred (Patton, 1998).

THE COMPREHENSIVE EVALUATION

When a student has not had success in a learning environment after several prereferral strategies have been applied, a formal referral is made. During the screening process, the screening committee, often called a child study committee, makes a decision to recommend a comprehensive evaluation or perhaps an educational alternative, such as a change in classroom teachers. If the committee recommends a comprehensive evaluation, the assessment plan is designed. The appropriate team members are contacted to begin the process. The types of assessment that may be used in a comprehensive evaluation are varied, depending upon the student's needs. Some instruments used are **norm-referenced tests** or assessment devices. These instruments have been developed to determine how a student performs on tasks when compared with students of the same age or grade level. These tests are also **standardized tests.** This means that the tests were developed with very structured and specific instructions, formats, scoring, and interpretation procedures. These specifics, written in the test manual, must be followed to ensure that the tests are used in the manner set forth by the test developers.

norm-referenced tests Tests designed to compare individual students with national averages, or norms of expectancy.

standardized tests Tests developed with specific standard administration, scoring, and interpretation procedures that must be followed precisely to obtain optimum results.

In addition to standardized norm-referenced tests, team members use informal methods such as classroom observations, interviews with teachers and parents, and criterion-referenced instruments. A team of designated professionals and the parents of the student make up the **individualized education program (IEP) team.** The team reviews the results from the assessments in the **eligibility meeting.** This meeting will determine what educational changes may be necessary to provide the best instruction for the student.

individualized education program (IEP) team The team specified in the IDEA amendments to make decisions about special education eligibility and interventions.

eligibility meeting A conference held after a preplacement evaluation to determine if a student is eligible for services.

During the eligibility meeting, the IEP team may determine that the student is eligible for services based on the information collected through the evaluation process. If the student is eligible an IEP, or individual education program, must be written for the student. If, however, the student is not

504 Accommodation Plan

Name of Student ______________________________ Date ________________

1. Describe the concern for this student's achievement in the classroom setting: ______________________________

2. Describe or attach the existing documentation for the disability or concern (if documentation exists). ______________________________

3. Describe how this affects the student's major life activities. ______________________________

4. The Child Study Team/504 Team has reviewed the case and recommends the following checked accommodations:

Physical Characteristics of Classroom or Other Environment

_____ Seat student near teacher.

_____ Teacher to stand near student when instructions are provided.

_____ Separate student from distractors (other students, air-conditioning or heating units, doorway).

Presentation of Instruction

_____ Student to work with a peer during seatwork time.

_____ Monitor instructions for understanding.

_____ Student to repeat all instructions back to teacher.

_____ Provide a peer tutor.

_____ Provide a homework helper.

_____ All written instructions require accompanying oral instructions.

_____ Teacher to check student's written work during working time to monitor for understanding.

_____ Student may use tape recorder during lessons.

Figure 1.5 Sample 504 Plan.

alternative planning A plan designed for educational intervention when a student has been found not eligible for special education services.

Individual Family Service Plan (IFSP) A plan designed for children ages 3 and younger that addresses the child's strengths and needs as well as the family's needs.

eligible for special education services, **alternative planning** should be considered, including educational intervention suggestions for the student. Alternative planning may include a plan for accommodations in the general classroom setting under Section 504. This law (presented in chapter 2) requires that students who have disabilities or needs, who are not eligible to receive services under IDEA, must have accommodations for their needs or disabilities in the regular classroom setting. A 504 accommodation plan is the plan designed to implement those accommodations. A sample 504 accommodation plan is presented in Figure 1.5.

When the referred child is 3 years of age or younger and eligibility for services has been determined, the law requires that an **Individual Family Service Plan** (IFSP) be developed by the team members and parents. The

Assignments

——— Student requires reduced workload.

——— Student requires extended time for assignments.

——— Student requires reduced stimuli on page.

——— Student requires that work be completed in steps.

——— Student requires frequent breaks during work.

——— Student requires use of tape recorder for oral responses.

——— Student requires lower level reading/math problems.

——— No penalty for handwriting errors.

——— No penalty for spelling errors.

——— No penalty for grammatical errors.

Additional Accommodations for Medical Concerns (List)

____

____

Additional Accommodations for Behavioral Concerns (List)

____

____

Additional Resources for Parents (List)

____

____

Participating Committee Members

____

____

____

____

Figure 1.5 continued.

IFSP differs from the IEP in that the family's needs as well as the child's needs are addressed. Early childhood assessment is presented in chapter 11.

ASSESSING THE WHOLE CHILD: CULTURAL CONSIDERATIONS

The 1997 IDEA Amendments (presented in chapter 2) required that state educational systems report the frequency of occurrence of disabilities and the race/ethnicity of students with disabilities. The first reported results of

Disability	American Indian	Asian/ Pacific Islander	Black (non-Hispanic)	Hispanic	White (non-Hispanic)
Specific Learning Disabilities	1.4	1.4	18.3	15.8	63.0
Speech and Language Impairments	1.2	2.4	16.5	11.6	68.3
Mental Retardation	1.1	1.7	34.3	8.9	54.1
Emotional Disturbance	1.1	1.0	26.4	9.8	61.6
Multiple Disabilities	1.4	2.3	19.3	10.9	66.1
Hearing Impairments	1.4	4.6	16.8	16.3	66.0
Orthopedic Impairments	.8	3.0	14.6	14.4	67.2
Other Health Impairments	1.0	1.3	14.1	7.8	75.8
Visual Impairments	1.3	3.0	14.8	11.4	69.5
Autism	.7	4.7	20.9	9.4	64.4
Deaf-Blindness	1.8	11.3	11.5	12.1	63.3
Traumatic Brain Injury	1.6	2.3	15.9	10.0	70.2
Developmental Delay	.5	1.1	33.7	4.0	60.8
All Disabilities	1.3	1.7	20.2	13.2	63.6
Resident Population	1.0	3.8	14.8	14.2	66.2

Figure 1.6 Percentage of ethnic groups in special education. (*Source:* U.S. Department of Education (2001). Twenty-Second Annual Report to Congress on the Implementation of the Individuals with Disabilities Education Act. Washington, DC: Author.)

this accounting are found in the Twenty-Second Annual Report to Congress on the Implementation of the Individuals with Disabilities Education Act (U.S. Department of Education, 2000). As reported in the literature for several years, particular groups of students from cultural and linguistically diverse backgrounds were found to be overrepresented in some categories of disabilities (see Figure 1.6).

It has been observed that the disproportionate rate of occurrence of some students from various ethnic and cultural backgrounds happens in the disability categories that rely heavily on "clinical judgment," such as students with learning disabilities, students within the range of mild mental retardation, and students with emotional disturbances (Harry & Anderson, 1995). Fujiura and Yamaki (2000) reported troubling patterns indicating that students from homes that fall in the range of poverty and that structurally include a single parent are at increased risk for disabilities. While there may be increased risks involved in environments that lack resources and support for single parents, the educational assessment of students from various cultural and linguistic backgrounds must be completed cautiously, fairly, and from the perspective of the child as a whole. Educators must keep the individual child's cultural, ethnic, and linguistic background in the forefront during the evaluation process.

Portes (1996) posed the question, "What is it about culture and ethnicity that accounts for significant differences in response to the schooling process and its outcomes?" (p. 351). Portes further reasons that it is not fixed characteristics of students but more likely the learned behaviors and identities associated with school. An example of such learned behaviors was described by Marsh and Cornell (2001). Marsh and Cornell found that minority students' experiences of school played a more important role in the likelihood of exhibiting at-risk behaviors than ethnicity. Educators must continue to strive for methods of assessment that are fair to all students. Burnette (1998) suggested the following strategies for improving accuracy in the assessment process in order to reduce disproportional representation of minorities in special education:

- Ensure that the staff knows requirements and criteria for referral and is kept abreast of current research affecting the process.
- Check that the student's general education program uses instructional strategies appropriate for the individual, has been adjusted to address the student's area of difficulty, includes ongoing communication with the student's family, and reflects a culturally responsive learning environment.
- Involve families in the decision to refer to special education in ways that are sensitive to the family's cultural background.
- Use only tests and procedures that are technically acceptable and culturally and linguistically appropriate.
- Testing personnel should have had training in conducting these particular assessments and interpreting the results in a culturally responsive manner.
- Personnel who understand how racial, ethnic and other factors influence student performance should be included in the eligibility decision.
- When eligibility is first established, a set of firm standards for the student's progress and readiness to exit special education should be recorded.

Source: Reducing the Disproportionate Representation of Minority Students in Special Education. ERIC/OSEP Digest E566. March 1998.

The early writings of Vygotsky concerning special education students' development and assessment cautioned professionals to be certain that the disability was not in "the imagination of the investigators" (Vygotsky, 1993, p. 38). Vygotsky also emphasized that the qualitative aspect of assessment in determining strengths and weaknesses is important rather than the concern only of quantifiable *deficits* in children. Vygotsky reminded educators that children with disabilities should be viewed in light of their developmental processes in their various environments (Gindis, 1999; Vygotsky, 1993). The way the student adapts to his or her environment, including culture and school, has a profound impact on the student's ability to have a successful school experience.

Today the IDEA Amendments call for educational equity and reform as well as emphasize the use of a variety of prereferral and assessment techniques that will be useful in educational planning rather than assessment only for determining eligibility. The remaining chapters of this text present educators with both formal and informal assessment and evaluation procedures to be used in educational planning and intervention.

CHAPTER SUMMARY

Assessment includes many types of evaluation of student progress. Assessment is necessary to monitor achievement, measure achievement of statewide curriculum standards, screen students who may require comprehensive evaluations to determine eligibility for services for disabilities, and to determine when programs need to be modified. Assessment must consider the student's cultural, linguistic, and ethnic background during the process. Assessment must view the student as a whole.

THINK AHEAD

The steps of the evaluation process are structured by both federal and state laws. The federal mandates are presented in chapter 2. Why do you think it is necessary to have laws that regulate the assessment process in education?

EXERCISES

Part I

Select the correct terms and write them in the blank spaces provided in each statement below:

assessment	checklist
testing	continuous assessment
curriculum-based assessment	overidentification
error analysis	APA Standards
informal assessment	screening
prereferral intervention strategies	IEP
individual assessment plan	alternative planning
norm-referenced test	standardized tests
performance assessment	IFSP
eligibility meeting	dynamic assessment

1. Concerns regarding the ______________ of students from diverse ethnic and cultural backgrounds emphasize the need for collecting assessment data in a variety of ways.
2. In order to assess all areas to obtain a view of the whole child, the ______________ is designed for every individual student.
3. When a teacher wants to determine how a student has solved a problem incorrectly, the teacher completes a(n) ______________.
4. When a child from a different linguistic background is assessed by providing cues or prompts, a form of ______________ has been employed.
5. As a result of the ______________, an IEP or an alternative plan would be developed for a student.
6. ______________ must be given in a specific manner as stated by the publisher, while informal tests include a variety of methods and strategies for collecting data.
7. If ______________ prove to be unsuccessful, the team may conclude that the student requires additional assessment to determine if additional services are needed.
8. A test that compares a student's performance with a national sample of students of the same age or grade is known as a ______________.
9. A student who is found to be eligible for services who is between the ages of 6 and 21 will have an Individualized Educational Program written for her, while a student younger than school age will have a(n) ______________ designed for her.
10. Teachers who design assessment instruments from classroom materials are using ______________.

Part II

Answer the following questions:

1. One way to document that strategies have been attempted before referral is to use a ______________.
2. Why are statewide tests called high-stakes tests? ______________
____.
3. How might high-stakes testing improve the education of all students?
____.
4. The 1997 Amendments to IDEA emphasize that more than 20 years of research indicates that the education of children with disabilities can be made more effective by ______________________________.
5. Summarize the best practice procedures from prereferral to the evaluation process. ______________________________

ANSWER KEY FOR CHECK YOUR UNDERSTANDING

Activity 1.1

1. error analysis
2. curriculum-based assessment
3. portfolio assessment
4. dynamic assessment
5. performance assessment
6. alternate assessments
7. assessment
8. criterion-related assessment
9. checklist
10. criterion-referenced tests
11. high-stakes testing

Apply Your Knowledge. This student has not mastered the spelling of hard and soft *c*.

Activity 1.2

1. A female teacher making a referral that a male teacher may be less likely to make.
2. This may be an example of a teacher making a referral believing that the sibling of a child with difficulty will also have difficulty.
3. This referral seems to be based on subjective information alone, and the teacher appears to be "bothered" by this student's behavior.
4. The teacher may have made the referral thinking that this child was older than her real age. The teacher may think that the child is older and should have advanced skills simply because the child is larger than expected for her age.

Apply Your Knowledge. You suggest that Mr. Patience may want to have Shantel verbalize her strategies. Shantel may be simply overlooking the correct sign (− vs. +) and verbalizing may help Mr. Patience to determine this. Shantel may be confused about the concepts of adding and subtracting. Verbalizing the steps she uses to solve these problems will allow Mr. Patience to determine whether the problem is conceptual or merely a careless error, and Mr. Patience will then be able to assist Shantel with the errors.

Activity 1.3

The prereferral strategies should include consulting with the school psychologist or guidance counselor to determine additional informal methods of assessment of behavior/social factors.

Educational strategies to determine appropriate math placement within the curriculum is a first step. This can be accomplished through use of curriculum-made materials, by reviewing school work and permanent products (homework assignments, class papers), and by completing an error analysis of the math problems Mary Ellen missed. If a pattern of errors is noted, remedial instruction may improve Mary Ellen's performance in math.

School records should also be reviewed to determine significant related factors such as frequent moves, family issues, records of illness, and other events that may be resulting in poor attendance. The school nurse may be able to provide needed information.

An ecological assessment may provide more information. This assessment would analyze the environment in which Mary Ellen works and participates with peers. Noted difficulties should be addressed. As the process of data collection continues, the parents should be contacted to determine whether outside factors or possible physical conditions are causing difficulties with attendance.

Apply Your Knowledge.

1. Mary Ellen appears to have some outside factors contributing to her social/behavioral and attendance problems.
2. It needs to be determined that Mary Ellen has mastered prerequisite skills. Social skills should be determined.
3. In addition to determining these factors, you should look to other sources of information such as the cumulative file (usually kept in the school office). This file contains information such as current address and will provide insight as to frequent moves, changes in the family home (remarriages, siblings, etc.) that may have an impact on Mary Ellen's development. The absentee record across school years, previous disciplinary referrals, and records of other significant events are contained in the cumulative file. The school nurse may have other information that may not yet be known to the classroom teacher. These records may include history of illnesses, eye exams, and medications.

Activity 1.4

Methods of Assessment. The types of assessment that seem to be appropriate for this student should focus on reading, spelling, language arts, and writing.

Although a full evaluation will also include psychological measures, health exam, social evaluation, and so on, the focus of the prereferral assessment should include the assessment methods listed by the following numbers: 1, 5, 6, 7, 8, 10, 11, 12, 13, 14.

Apply Your Knowledge. Samples that would assist the team in understanding George's abilities might include writing samples that vary over time and task (sentences, single words, stories), content-area work such as science and social studies reports, worksheets, and homework; and math assignments. Classroom tests in the various subject areas as well as any projects constructed through the year should be reviewed. Creative examples in areas that appear to indicate strength or problem-solving skills and abilities should also be included.

REFERENCES

Algozzine, B., Christenson, S., & Ysseldyke, J. (1982). Probabilities associated with the referral-to-placement process. *Teacher Education and Special Education, 5,* 19–23.

American Psychological Association. (1985). *Standards for educational and psychological testing.* Washington, DC: Author.

Andrews, T. J., Wisnieswski, J. J., & Mulick, J. A. (1997). Variables influencing teachers' decisions to refer children for psychological assessment services. *Psychology in the Schools, 34,* 239–244.

Barnett, D. W., & Macmann, G. M. (1992). Decision reliability and validity: Contributions and limitations of alternative assessment strategies. *Journal of Special Education, 25,* 431–452.

Burnette, J. (1998 March). Reducing the disproportionate representation of minority students in special education. *ERIC/OSEP Digest E566.*

Carter, J., & Sugai, G. (1989). Survey on prereferral practices: Responses from state departments of education. *Exceptional Children, 55,* 298–308.

Chalfant, J. C., & Psyh, M. (1989). Teachers assistance teams: Five descriptive studies on 96 teams. *Remedial and Special Education, 10*(6), 49–58.

Cronis, T. G., & Ellis, D. N. (2000 Summer). Issues facing special educators in the new millennium. *Education, 120*(4), 639–648.

Daly, E. J., Witt, J. C., Martens, B. K., & Dool, E. J. (1997). A model for conducting a functional analysis of academic performance problems. *School Psychology Review, 26,* 554–574.

Del'Homme, M., Kasari, C., Forness, S. R., & Bagley, R. (1996). Prereferral intervention and students at risk for emotional or behavioral disorders. *Education and Treatment of Children, 19,* 272–285.

Demaray, M. K., & Elliott, S. N. (1998). Teachers' judgment of students' academic functioning: A comparison of actual and predicted performances. *School Psychology Quarterly, 13*(1), 8–24.

Detterman, D. K., & Thompson, L. A. (1997). What is so special about special education? *American Psychologist, 52*(10), 1082–1090.

Detterman, D. K., & Thompson, L. A. (1998). They doth protest too much. *American Psychologist, 53*(10), 1162–1163.

Federal Register. (1992, September 29). Washington, DC: U.S. Government Printing Office.

Federal Register. (1999, March 12). Washington, DC: U.S. Government Printing Office.

Fuchs, D. (1991). Mainstream assistance teams: A prereferral intervention system for difficult to teach students. In Stoner, G., Shinn, M. R., & Walker, H. M. (Eds.), *Interventions for achievement and behavior problems* (pp. 241–267). Silver Spring, MD: National Association of School Psychologists.

Fugate, D. J., Clarizio, H. F., & Phillips, S. E. (1993). Referral-to-placement ratio: A finding in need of reassessment? *Journal of Learning Disabilities, 26*(6), 413–416.

Fujiura, G. T., & Yamaki, K. (2000). Trends in demography of childhood poverty and disability. *Exceptional Children, 66*(2), 187–199.

Gindis, B. (1999). Vygotsky's vision: Reshaping the practice of special education for the 21st century. *Remedial and Special Education, 20,* 333–340.

Gopaul-McNicol, S., & Thomas-Presswood, T. (1998). *Working with linguistically and culturally different children: Innovative clinical and educational approaches.* Boston: Allyn & Bacon.

Graden, J., Casey, A., & Bonstrom, O. (1985). Implementing a prereferral intervention system: Part II. The data. *Exceptional Children, 51,* 487–496.

Graden, J., Casey, A., & Christenson, S. (1985). Implementing a prereferral intervention system: Part I. The model. *Exceptional Children, 51,* 377–384.

Halgren, D. W., & Clarizio, H. F. (1993). Categorical and programming changes in special education services. *Exceptional Children, 59,* 547–555.

Harry, B., & Anderson, M. G. (1995). The disproportionate placement of African American males in special education programs: A critique of the process. *Journal of Negro Education, 63*(4), 602–619.

Harvey, V. (1991). Characteristics of children referred to school psychologists: A discriminant analysis. *Psychology in the Schools, 28,* 209–218.

Individuals with Disabilities Education Act Amendments of 1997, Pub. L. No. 105-17, 105th Congress.

Keogh, B. K., Forness, S. R., & MacMillan, D. L. (1998). The real world of special education. *American Psychologist, 53*(10), 1161–1162.

Mamlin, N., & Harris, K. R. (1998). Elementary teachers' referral to special education in light of inclusion and prereferral: "Every child is here to learn . . . but some of these children are in real trouble." *Journal of Educational Psychology, 90*(3), 385–396.

Marsh, T. Y., & Cornell, D. G. (2001). The contributions of student experiences to understanding ethnic differences in high risk behaviors at school. *Behavior Disorders, 26*(2), 152–163.

Maxam, S., Boyer-Stephens, A., & Alff, M. (1986). Assessment: A key to appropriate program placement. (Report No. CE 045 407, pp. 11–13). Columbia: University of Missouri Columbia, Department of Special Education and Department of Practical Arts and Vocational-Technical Education. (ERIC Document Reproduction Service No. ED 275 835)

McIntyre, L. (1988). Teacher gender: A predictor of special education referral? *Journal of Learning Disabilities, 21,* 382–384.

Messick, S. (1984). Assessment in context: Appraising student performance in relation to instructional quality. *Educational Researcher, 13,* 3–8.

Nelson, J. R., Smith, D. J., Taylor, L., Dodd, J. M., & Reavis, K. (1992). A statewide survey of special education administrators regarding mandated prereferral interventions. *Remedial and Special Education, 13*(4), 34–39.

Patton, J. M. (1998). The disproportionate representation of African Americans in special education: Looking behind the curtains for understanding and solutions. *Journal of Special Education, 32*(1), 25–31.

Poon-McBrayer, F., & Garcia, S. B. (2000). Profiles of Asian American students with leaning disabilities at initial referral, assessment, and placement in special education. *Journal of Learning Disabilities, 33*(1), 61–71.

Portes, P. R. (1996). Ethnicity and culture in educational psychology. In D. C. Berliner & R. C. Calfee (Eds.), *Handbook of Educational Psychology* (pp. 331–357). New York: Simon Schuster McMillan.

Reschly, D. (1986). Functional psychoeducational assessment: Trends and issues. *Special Services in the Schools, 2,* 57–69.

Serna, L. A., Forness, S. R., & Nielsen, M. E. (1998). Intervention versus affirmation: Proposed solutions to the problem of disproportionate minority representation in special education. *Journal of Special Education, 32*(1), 48–51.

Shinn, M., Tindal, G., & Spira, D. (1987). Special education referrals as an index of teacher tolerance: Are teachers imperfect tests? *Exceptional Children, 54,* 32–39.

Soodak, L. C., & Podell, D. M. (1993). Teacher efficacy and student problem as factors in special education referral. *Journal of Special Education, 27*(1), 66–81.

Symons, F. J., & Warren, S. F. (1998). Straw men and strange logic issues and pseudo-issues in special education. *American Psychologist, 53*(10), 1160–1161.

Taylor, H. G., Anselmo, M., Foreman, A. L., Schatschneider, C., & Angelopoulos, J. (2000). Utility of kindergarten teacher judgments in identifying early learning problems. *Journal of Learning Disabilities, 33*(2), 200–210.

Thurlow, M., Christenson, S., & Ysseldyke, J. (1983). *Referral research: An integrative summary of findings* (Research Report No. 141). Minneapolis: University of Minnesota, Institute for Research on Learning Disabilities.

U.S. Congress (1993, March). *Goals 2000: Educate America Act.* Pub. L. No. 103-227, 103rd Congress.

U.S. Department of Education (1997). *Nineteenth annual report to Congress on the implementation of the Individuals with Disabilities Education Act.* Washington, DC: Author.

U.S. Department of Education (1999). *Twenty-first annual report to Congress on the implementation of the Individuals with Disabilities Education Act.* Washington, DC: Author.

U.S. Department of Education (2000). *Twenty-second annual report to Congress on the implementation of the Individuals with Disabilities Education Act.* Washington, DC: Author.

Valles, E. C. (1998). The disproportionate representation of minority students in special education: Responding to the problem. *Journal of Special Education, 32*(1), 52–54.

Vygotsky, L. S. (1993). *The collected works of L. S. Vygotsky: Vol. 2, The fundamentals of defectology (abnormal psychology and learning disabilities* (J. E. Knox & C. B. Stevens, Trans.). New York: Plenum.

White, R., & Calhoun, M. (1987). From referral to placement: Teachers' perceptions of their responsibilities. *Exceptional Children, 5,* 460–468.

Wilson, C. P., Gutkin, T. B., Hagen, K. M., & Oats, R. G. (1998). General education teachers' knowledge and self-reported use of classroom interventions for working with difficult-to-teach students: Implications for consultation, prereferral intervention and inclusive services. *School Psychology Quarterly, 13*(1), 45–62.

Ysseldyke, J., Algozzine, B., Richey, L., & Graden, J. (1982). Declaring students eligible for learning disability services: Why bother with the data? *Learning Disabilities Quarterly, 5,* 37–44.

Ysseldyke, J., Christenson, S., Pianta, B., & Algozzine, B. (1983). An analysis of teachers' reasons and desired outcomes for students referred for psychoeducational assessment. *Journal of Psychoeducational Assessment, 1,* 73–83.

Ysseldyke, J. E., Thurlow, M. L., Kozleski, E., & Reschly, D. (1998). Accountability for the results of educating students with disabilities: Assessment conference report on the new assessment provisions of the 1997 Amendments to the Individuals with Disabilities Education Act. (EC 306929) National Center on Educational Outcomes. (ERIC Document Reproduction Service No. ED 425 588)

Ysseldyke, J. E., Nelson, J. R., & House, A. L. (2000). Statewide and district wide assessments: Current status and guidelines for student accommodations and alternate assessments. In C. F. Telzrow and M. Tankersley (Eds.), *IDEA Amendments of 1997: Practice guidelines for school-based teams*. Bethesda, MD: National Association of School Psychologists.

Ysseldyke, J., & Thurlow, M. (1983). *Identification/classification research: An integrative summary of findings* (Research Report No. 142). Minneapolis: University of Minnesota, Institute for Research on Learning Disabilities.

Zins, J., Graden, J., & Ponti, C. (1989). Prereferral intervention to improve special services delivery. *Special Services in the Schools, 4,* 109–130.

CHAPTER 2

Laws, Ethics, and Issues

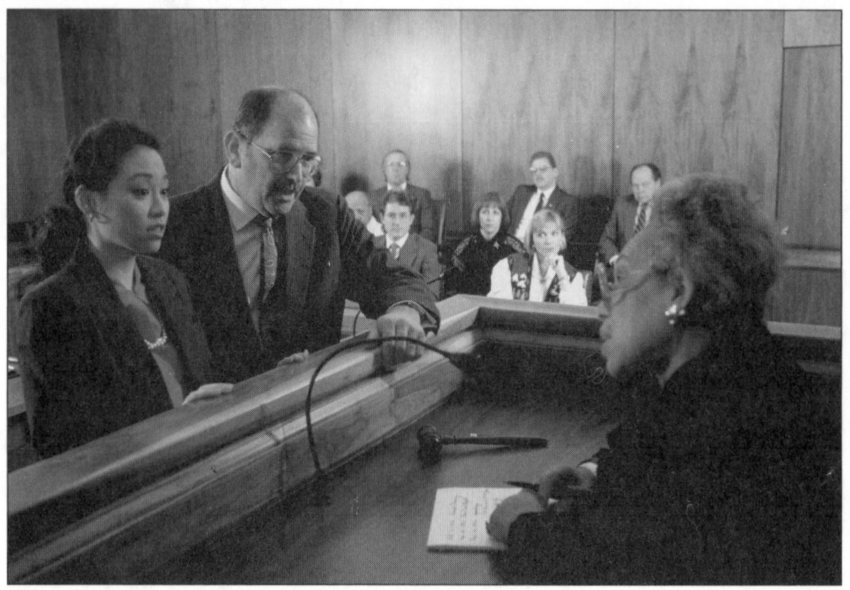

Key Terms

Public Law 94-142
IDEA
IDEA Amendments of 1997
compliance
PL 99-457
due process
initial evaluation
comprehensive educational evaluation
informed consent
surrogate parent
consent form
parents' rights booklet
nondiscriminatory assessment
special education services
related services
grade equivalent
age equivalent
standard scores
annual goals
short-term objectives
least restrictive environment
transition services
procedural safeguards
mediation
independent educational evaluation
impartial due process hearing
impartial hearing officer
Section 504 of the Rehabilitation Act of 1973
minority overrepresentation

CHAPTER FOCUS

This chapter includes the laws and ethical standards governing the use and interpretation of tests used in determining eligibility for special education services. Procedures for implementation of test results for educational interventions and issues of assessment are also included.

THE LAW: PUBLIC LAW 94-142 AND IDEA

Public Law 94-142 Education for All Handicapped Children Act of 1975; guarantees the right to a free and appropriate education in the least restrictive environment; renamed IDEA in 1990.

IDEA Individuals with Disabilities Education Act, passed in 1990 to give new name to PL 94-142.

IDEA Amendments of 1997 Passed in 1997, these amendments make several changes to the original law.

compliance To be operating within the federal regulations, within the confines of the law.

During the 1970s, substantial legal changes for persons with disabilities occurred. Much of the pressure for these changes came from parents and professionals. Another influential source affecting the language of the law was litigation in the civil court system. In 1975, the Education for All Handicapped Children Act, referred to as **Public Law 94-142,** was passed and two years later, the regulations were completed (Education of the Handicapped Act [EHA], 1975; *Federal Register,* 1977). In 1990, under PL 101-476, the act was renamed the Individuals with Disabilities Education Act, or **IDEA.** The regulations were written in 1992 (*Federal Register,* 1992). IDEA contains several major provisions guaranteeing the right to education for persons ages 3 to 21 with disabilities that require special services in the United States. The law grants the right to a free appropriate public education in the least restrictive environment. Many of IDEA's provisions concern the process of assessment. The law mandates that state education agencies (SEAs) ensure that proper assessment procedures are followed (*Federal Register,* 1992).

In 1997, IDEA was amended by the 105th Congress and is referred to as the **Individuals with Disabilities Education Act Amendments of 1997.** Although the original law has been in effect for two decades, professional educators must continue to monitor **compliance** with the mandates within each local education agency (LEA). Informed teachers and parents are the best safeguards for compliance in every school. Even several years after the law was enacted, one study revealed that only 28% of special educators felt they knew special education law (Silver, 1987). Congress noted continued difficulties with the implementation of the original law in the findings section of the law and stated that special education efforts should strive to ensure that students receive an appropriate education and that the rights of children and their parents are protected. The primary goals of Congress in passing the 1997 Amendments were summarized by Yell, Drasgrow, and Ford (2000) and are presented in Table 2.1.

In 1999, the final regulations of the 1997 Amendments were published. The regulations governing assessment, titled Procedures for Evaluation and Determination of Eligibility (*Federal Register,* 1999), include changes to the

Table 2.1 Congressional goals in passing IDEA 1997.

Major Goal	Explanation
Increasing parental participation	Parents must be more fully involved in the special education process through involvement in evaluation, program planning, and placement decisions.
Ensuring student access to the general curriculum	Students with disabilities have opportunity to be involved in the general curriculum and be educated with their nondisabled peers.
Decreasing inappropriate labeling	State education agencies give increased attention to racial, ethnic, and linguistic diversity to prevent inappropriate identification and mislabeling.
Using mediation to resolve disputes	Parents and educators are encouraged to work out their differences using nonadversarial means.
Improving educational results	Unnecessary paperwork requirements reduced to free teachers to focus on teaching and learning. Accountability mechanisms are incorporated in IDEA 97 (e.g., measurable annual goals).
Increasing school safety	IDEA 97 now includes disciplinary requirements.

Source: From *IDEA Amendments of 1997: Practice Guidelines for School-Based Teams* (p. 6). Edited by Cathy F. Telzrow and Melody Tankersley, 2000, Bethesda, MD: National Association of School Psychologists. Copyright 2000 by the National Association of School Psychologists. Reprinted by permission.

original regulations of 1977 as well as sections that remain unchanged. The 1997 Amendments to IDEA and sections of the final regulations are incorporated in the following sections of this chapter.

PL 99-457 IDEA amendments that extend services for special-needs children through infancy and preschool years.

In 1986 the Education for the Handicapped Act Amendments, **PL 99-457,** were passed. The final regulations, written in 1993 (*Federal Register,* 1993), were developed to promote early intervention for preschool children and infants with special needs or developmental delays. Additional changes were added in the 1997 Amendments of IDEA. Specific issues concerning PL 99-457 and the assessment of preschool children are discussed in chapter 11.

This chapter contains sections of the law that directly affect the assessment of children and youth of school age. The IDEA topics presented in this chapter are listed in Table 2.2.

Table 2.2 IDEA Topics Presented in Chapter 2.

- Initial evaluations
- Parental consent
- Procedural safeguards
- Nondiscriminatory assessment
- Determining needed evaluation data
- Evaluating children with specific learning disabilities
- Meeting the needs of persons with ADHD
- Multidisciplinary team evaluations
- The IEP team
- IDEA regular education teacher requirements
- Determining eligibility
- Parent participation
- Developing the IEP
- Considerations of special factors
- Transition services
- Due process
- Impartial due process hearings

IDEA AND ASSESSMENT

due process The right to a hearing to settle disputes; a protection for children with disabilities and their families.

initial evaluation A comprehensive evaluation before receiving special education services.

IDEA is a federal law containing mandates to promote fair, objective assessment practices and **due process** procedures, the foundations for legal recourse when parents or schools disagree with evaluation or placement recommendations. Teachers not only should be aware of the law but also should strive to maintain compliance in testing students, recommending placement, and developing IEPs. Teachers can help their local education agencies comply by following guidelines, meeting time lines, and correctly performing educational functions specified in the law. The first topic presented is the **initial evaluation,** or the first evaluation of a student to determine if special education services are needed.

INITIAL EVALUATIONS

§ 300.320 Initial Evaluations

(A) . . . before the initial provision of special education and related services to a child under this part.

(B) Procedures—Such initial evaluation shall consist of procedures—

(i) to determine if a child is a child with a disability (as defined in section 602(3)); and

(ii) to determine the educational needs of such child. IDEA, 20 U.S.C. § 1414(a)(1)(A&B).

Before a student can receive special education services in a general education classroom or in a special education setting, the members of the multidisciplinary team must complete a comprehensive individual evaluation of the student's needs. This evaluation should reflect consideration of the specific academic, behavioral, communicative, cognitive, motor, and sensory areas of concern. This **comprehensive educational evaluation** must be completed before eligibility can be determined. Reevaluation of a student with a disability occurs every 3 years, or if conditions warrant or if the parent requests another evaluation, it may occur as needed.

comprehensive educational evaluation A complete assessment in all areas of suspected disability.

PARENTAL CONSENT

The initial preplacement evaluation and subsequent reevaluations cannot take place without parental **informed consent.**

informed consent Parents are informed of rights in their native language and agree in writing to procedures for the child; consent may be revoked at any time.

§ 300.505 Parental Consent

(a)(1)(C) Parental consent . . .

(i) In general—The agency proposing to conduct an initial evaluation to determine if the child qualifies as a child with a disability as defined in section 602(3)(A) OR 602(3)(B) shall obtain an informed consent from the parent of such child before the evaluation is conducted. Parental consent for evaluation shall not be construed as consent for placement for receipt of special education and related services.

(ii) Refusal—If the parents of such child refuse consent for the evaluation, the agency may continue to pursue an evaluation by utilizing the mediation and due process procedures under section 615, except to the extent inconsistent with State law relating to parental consent. IDEA, 20 U.S.C. § (a)(1)(C).

According to federal regulations, parental consent means that the parent, guardian, or **surrogate parent** has been fully informed of all educational activities to which he or she is being asked to consent. When a parent gives consent for an initial evaluation, for example, this means that the parent has been fully informed of the evaluation procedures and told why the school personnel believe these measures are necessary, and that the parent has agreed to the evaluation.

surrogate parent Person appointed by the court system to be legally responsible for a child's education.

The 1997 amendments add that parents must be notified of any evaluation the school proposes to conduct. Furthermore, informed consent means that the parent has been informed in his or her native language or mode of communication. If the parent does not speak English, the information must be conveyed verbally or in writing in the parent's native language. In areas where languages other than English are prevalent, education agencies often employ bilingual personnel to translate assessment and placement information as necessary. Additionally, many state education

consent form Written permission form that grants permission for evaluation or placement.

parents' rights booklet Used to convey rights and procedural safeguards to parents.

agencies provide **consent forms** and **parents' rights booklets** in languages other than English. IDEA's statement regarding mode of communication sends a clear message that parents with visual or hearing impairments must be accommodated. The education agency must make every effort to provide sign interpreters for parents with hearing impairments who sign to communicate and large-type or braille materials for parents with visual impairments who read in this fashion.

IDEA Amendments of 1997: Procedural Safeguards

§ 300.507 Procedural Safeguards Notice

The IDEA Amendments of 1997 state that parents must be provided with a copy of procedural safeguards at a minimum—

(A) upon initial referral for evaluation

(B) upon each notification of an individualized education program meeting and upon reevaluation of the child; and

(C) upon registration of a complaint . . . IDEA, 20 U.S.C. § 1415(d)(1)

Parental consent must be obtained before the school releases any student records to a third party. If, for example, the school personnel want the records to be mailed to a psychologist in private practice, the parents must consent in writing to the school to release the records and must know exactly which records are to be mailed and to whom.

Federal law requires that school personnel inform the parents before assessment and before placement that their consent is considered mandatory and may be revoked at any time. Therefore, if the parents had previously agreed to a placement for their child in a special education resource room for 1 hour per day and it is later recommended that the student receive services 3 hours per day, the parents may revoke their consent to approve special education services if they believe it to be in the best interest of their child. Should the parents revoke their consent, they are guaranteed the rights of due process. The school personnel are granted the same rights of due process and may decide to file a complaint against the parents. (Due process is discussed in more depth later in this chapter.)

Check Your Understanding

Complete Activity 2.1.

ACTIVITY 2.1

Use the requirements that concern initial evaluation and informed consent to complete this activity. Choose from the phrases listed to answer the questions that follow the phrases:

initial evaluation
native language
parents' rights booklet

due process
every 3 years
voluntary informed consent
informed of activities
mode of communication
comprehensive evaluation
revoke consent
release of records
reevaluation

1. The consent given by parents indicates that the parents have been ______________ that the school personnel feel are necessary and in the child's best interest.
2. In compliance with IDEA, many parents are informed of their legal rights and responsibilities through the use of a ______________.
3. A teacher would not be allowed to give a student's records to another interested party. Before the ______________, the parents must consent in writing and receive an explanation of who would receive which records.
4. When parents decide that they no longer agree with a school placement or services for their child, they may ______________, and if necessary, they may begin ______________ procedures.
5. For students who are receiving special education services, a ______________ must be completed at least ______________.
6. It is the responsibility of school personnel to provide information to parents in their ______________ or using the parents' ______________ to comply with the federal law.

Apply Your Knowledge

Explain how the requirements regarding release of records affect the day-to-day life of a teacher (including a student teacher) working with special-needs students.

NONDISCRIMINATORY ASSESSMENT

nondiscriminatory assessment Fair and objective testing practices for students from all cultural and linguistic backgrounds.

Many of the requirements that guide professionals in the assessment process are concerned with fair testing practice. The regulations presented on **nondiscriminatory assessment** address the issue of nondiscriminatory assessment consistent with the original regulations. The regulations of 1999 add a statement regarding the assessment of students with limited English proficiency:

Idea Amendments of 1997: Regulations

§ 300.532 Evaluation Procedures

According to the regulations, each public agency shall ensure, at a minimum, that the following requirements are met:

a. 1. Tests and other evaluation materials used to assess a child under Part B of the Act—
   (i) Are selected and administered so as not to be discriminatory on a racial or cultural basis, and
   (ii) Are provided and administered in the child's native language or other mode of communication, unless it is clearly not feasible to do so; and
   2. Materials and procedures used to assess a child with limited English proficiency are selected and administered to ensure that they measure the extent to which the child has a disability and needs special education, rather than measuring the child's English language skills. IDEA, 20 U.S.C. § 1414(b)(3)

Nondiscriminatory assessment is mandated in IDEA to ensure fairness and objectivity in testing. This section requires that the instruments or techniques used in the assessment process are not racially or culturally biased. This section of the law sets forth the minimum criteria for nondiscriminatory assessment practice in special education. The first criterion to ensure fairness in testing is that the tests are presented and administered in the student's language unless it is impossible to do so. This section also requires that the mode of communication used by the student be used in the assessment process. Like the communication standards written for parental consent, this section requires that school personnel find and use such appropriate methods as sign language or braille if necessary to assess the individual's ability in the most fair and objective manner.

The assessment of students with limited proficiency or emerging proficiency in English is especially difficult. The regulations require that assessment personnel make certain that the instruments employed in the assessment of students who have not mastered English, assess skills and abilities other than English skills.

Additional requirements included in the regulations follow.

b. A variety of assessment tools and strategies to gather relevant functional and developmental information about the child, including information provided by the parent, and information related to enabling the child to be involved in and progress in the general curriculum (or for the preschool child, to participate in appropriate activities) that may assist in determining—
   1. Whether the child is a child with a disability under § 300.7; and
   2. The content of the child's IEP. IDEA, 20 U.S.C. § 1414(b)(2)

This section of the Amendments of 1997 clearly indicates that additional measures or strategies other than "tests," as well as parental input, should be considered in the evaluation process. This input should be incorporated in the eligibility decision and in educational interventions for the student. Moreover, information gathered should be for the purpose of enabling the student to participate in the general education curriculum. The assessment information is then to be used to determine if the child is eligible for special education services by meeting the criteria described in the definitions of special education (see chapter 1). In addition, if the student is determined to be eligible for services, the assessment information gathered must directly be related to the components of the student's individualized educational program. This regulation is included as part of the emphasis that all assessment and subsequent evaluations be conducted with the goal of providing functional information that will be of benefit to the student.

This section continues with the following requirements regarding standardized assessment:

> c. 1. Any standardized tests that are given to the child—
> (i) Have been validated for the specific purpose for which they are used;
> (ii) Are administered by trained and knowledgeable personnel in accordance with any instructions provided by the producer of such tests.
>
> 2. If an assessment is not conducted under standard conditions, a description of the extent to which it varied from standard conditions (e.g. the qualifications of the person administering the test, or the method of test administration) must be included in the evaluation report. IDEA, 20 U.S.C. § 1414(b)(3)(b)

In addition to using tests validated for the purpose for which they will be used, schools must ensure that tests are administered by trained personnel in the manner specified by the test producer. Much information regarding the training of personnel and administration of specific tests can be found in the individual test manuals, which the team member should study thoroughly before administration. Examples of errors made by professionals who do not comply with this section include administering tests or sections of a test to a group of students when the test was designed for individual administration, giving instructions to students in writing when the manual specifies oral presentation, or allowing 2 minutes for a test item when the test manual states that the time allowed is 90 seconds. When an examiner fails to follow directions specified by the developer of a standardized test, the results may lead to inaccurate interpretations and poor recommendations. In this regard, the testing has been unfair to the student.

The best and most consistent practice for using standardized instruments in the assessment of students for consideration of special services is to follow specific instructions provided for administration in a standardized manner. There are times, however, when the best practice for determining an *estimate* of the student's ability may require adaptation of the standardized administration. For example, it may be necessary when assessing a very young child who has a high level of anxiety or a child with limited cognitive ability to request that the parent or primary caretaker remain in the room, perhaps with the child sitting on the parent's lap. The parent in such situations may assist with some of the assessment items (such as providing translations if the young child has difficulty with articulation). In such cases, the regulations require that the modifications be explained in the written evaluation report. In such situations, an estimate of the child's ability has been obtained. This would require that additional measures, both standardized and non-standardized, be incorporated into the assessment before making a decision about the student's eligibility.

The regulations governing the assessment of students continue with the following:

> d. Tests and other evaluation materials include those tailored to assess specific areas of educational need and not merely those that are designed to provide a single general intelligence quotient.
>
> e. Tests are selected and administered so as best to ensure that if a test is administered to a child with impaired sensory, manual, or speaking skills, the test results accurately reflect the child's aptitude or achievement level or whatever other factors the test purports to measure, rather than reflecting the child's impaired sensory, manual, or speaking skills (unless those skills are the factors that the test purports to measure).
>
> f. No single procedure is used as the sole criterion for determining whether a child is a child with a disability and for determining an appropriate educational program for the child.
>
> g. The child is assessed in all areas of suspected disability including, if appropriate, health, vision, hearing, social and emotional status, general intelligence, academic performance, communicative status, and motor abilities. 20 U.S.C. § 1414(b)(2)(B&C)

According to the IDEA amendments, the assessment of a student must include multiple measures designed for evaluating specific educational needs rather than using a single instrument. This part of the regulations indicates that no single instrument should be used to determine eligibility. Before the passage of the original law (PL 94-142), numerous students were unfairly discriminated against because of conclusions based on a single IQ score. Often this resulted in very restrictive placement settings, such as institutions or self-contained classrooms, rather than more appropriate educational interventions. In addition to the federal mandates, court cases, such as *Larry P. v. Riles* (1972), have had a significant impact on discriminatory testing practices. This case and others are presented in chapter 10.

Assessment can be discriminatory in other ways. The law mandates that the instruments used to assess one skill or area do not discriminate or unduly penalize a student because of an existing impairment. For example, a student with speech articulation problems who is referred for reading difficulties should not be penalized on a test that requires the student to pronounce nonsense syllables. The student in this case may have incorrectly pronounced sounds because of the speech condition, and the mispronunciations might be counted as reading errors. The reading scores obtained may be substantially lower than the student's actual reading ability because the misarticulations sounded like mispronunciations, or decoding errors, of the nonsense words.

The regulations also require that students are assessed in all areas of suspected disability and that sensory, motor, and emotional areas should be included when appropriate. The addition of considerations of students who have previously been found to have a disability are expanded in the new regulations:

h. In evaluating each child with a disability under §§ 300.531–300.535, the evaluation is sufficiently comprehensive to identify all of the child's special education and related service needs, whether or not commonly linked to the disability category in which the child has been classified.

i. The public agency uses technically sound instruments that may assess the relative contribution of cognitive and behavioral factors, in addition to physical or developmental factors.

These regulations require assessment personnel to consider all possible areas of need, even areas that are not typically thought to be associated or linked with the specific disability category. For example, it may not be uncommon for some students with specific learning disabilities to have difficulties in more than one academic area (e.g., spelling, writing, reading). Assessment personnel must also consider other areas that may require additional evaluation, such as emotional or motor areas. If these areas are determined to require educational interventions, these must be addressed through special education or related services (e.g., counseling or occupational therapy).

It is also required that the tests or instruments employed be psychometrically adequate. Test consumers are therefore required to have an understanding of general testing principles and the accuracy with which inferences about student's cognitive, academic, and behavioral functioning can be made using such instruments.

The final requirements concerning the actual evaluation process stress the need for a thorough evaluation by a group of professionals from various fields.

The regulations encourage the use of a variety of assessment devices and require the participation of several professionals in the decision-making process. Using many and varied assessment materials helps professionals to establish a more holistic view of the student. The professional expertise provided by a multidisciplinary team aids in promoting fair and objective assessment. It is necessary to involve many different professionals to assess all factors, such as vision, emotion, and language, that may need to be evaluated to reach the best educational decision.

These sections include the requirement to assess the student in all areas of suspected disability. In many cases, a referred student is known to have academic difficulty, but the disability might be due to many factors. The best way to determine whether the student truly has a disability—and if so, what type of disability—is to assess all of the suspected areas. For example, a referred student who demonstrated immature social skills and inappropriate behavior also demonstrated developmental and learning problems, but when the referral information was submitted, background information was too limited to determine whether the student was having emotional problems or specific learning problems or possibly was subaverage in intellectual ability. In cases such as this, the law mandates that all areas be assessed to determine whether a disability exists. In this particular case, the young student was found to have a mild hearing impairment and subsequently had developed some behavioral problems. Appropriate audiological and educational interventions prevented further behavioral problems from developing and helped to remediate academic skills.

The regulations emphasize the need for practical and relevant assessment by including the following statement:

> j. The public agency uses assessment tools and strategies that provide relevant information that directly assists persons in determining the educational needs of the child. 20 U.S.C. § 1414(b)(2).

Other discriminatory test practices concerned with test bias, examiner bias, and so on are presented in the section "Research and Issues Concerning IDEA," later in this chapter. The IDEA Amendments of 1997 include additional specific regulations regarding the initial assessment and reevaluation of students that require the consideration of additional data. These regulations concern data that may exist from previous assessments completed by the classroom teacher as well as additional data provided by the parents and other sources.

Check Your Understanding

Complete Activity 2.2.

ACTIVITY 2.2

Read the following statements to determine whether they represent fair testing practice and then check the appropriate blank. If the statement is unfair, write a statement explaining how to correct the situation. If you think the statement is fair, explain why you think so.

1. A screening test may be used to make placement decisions about a student who was referred for special education services.
   _____ Fair _____ Unfair
   Comments: ____.
2. Individuals who administer tests in the Woodlake local education agency are thoroughly trained to use each new instrument through school inservice sessions and graduate courses.
   _____ Fair _____ Unfair
   Comments ____.
3. A special education teacher is asked to test a student who speaks only Japanese. The teacher cannot find a test in that language, so he observes the student in the classroom setting and recommends that the student be placed in special education.
   _____ Fair _____ Unfair
   Comments: ____.

4. A special education teacher is asked to give an educational test to a student from a minority culture. The test has been validated and proven to be culturally nondiscriminatory.
   _____ Fair _____ Unfair
   Comments: ____.
5. A student is referred for an evaluation for possible eligibility for special education. The student has cerebral palsy, and the team member has no knowledge of this disorder. The team member asks the physical therapist to give advice on how to administer the test and requests that the therapist attend and assist during the evaluation. The team member also requests the assistance of the school psychologist to determine how the adaptations affect the psychometrics of the test administration. The team member documents all changes in the reevaluation report.
   _____ Fair _____ Unfair
   Comments: ____.
6. A team decides to use the latest IQ score to make a decision regarding a change in eligibility for a student. The team agreed that no additional testing or data were necessary.
   _____ Fair _____ Unfair
   Comments: ____.

Apply Your Knowledge

According to legal requirements, list the possible circumstances in which you would be required to ask for consultative guidance from other professionals during the assessment process. _______________.

Determining Needed Evaluation Data

§ 300.533 Determination of Needed Evaluation Data

The regulations for the 1997 Amendments of IDEA state that, if appropriate during initial evaluation and for all reevaluations, the team, including the parents, shall—

1. Review existing evaluation data on the child, including—
   (i) Evaluations and information provided by the parents of the child;
   (ii) Current classroom-based assessments and observations; and
   (iii) Observations by teachers and related services providers; and
2. On the basis of that review, and input from the child's parents, identify what additional data, if any, are needed to determine—
   (i) Whether the child has a particular category of disability, as described in § 300.7, or, in case of a reevaluation of a child whether the child continues to have such a disability;
   (ii) The present levels of performance and educational needs of the child;

(iii) Whether the child needs special education and related services, or in the case of a reevaluation of a child, whether the child continues to need special education and related services; and

(iv) Whether any additions or modifications to the special education and related services are needed to enable the child to meet the measurable annual goals set out in the IEP of the child and participate, as appropriate, in the general education curriculum.

The amendments and the regulations of the IDEA amendments call on professionals and parents alike to determine what data may be needed to obtain the most accurate picture of the child's current ability and educational needs. The regulations require that the services are designed to assist the student in meeting the measurable goals of the IEP and, again, the regulations require that as appropriate, the student should participate in the general curriculum.

These requirements indicate that the IEP team may review data from a variety of sources and, in the case of reevaluation, may determine that enough data exist to support continued eligibility. In such cases, the student would not be subjected to additional testing to complete the triennial (3-year) review for continued placement unless the parents request that their child be retested. The student's progress is to be reviewed, although this does not necessarily involve substantial formal testing procedures. The triennial evaluation may consist of the testing considered to be necessary to determine the student's current educational or behavioral functioning. For example, a student who excels in math but has a specific reading disability may not require a reevaluation of math skills.

Additional regulations specify that the IEP team may conduct the review of the existing data without a meeting. Following the review, if additional data are needed, the public agency shall go about administering tests and other instruments in order to obtain the needed data. In the case of reevaluations, if additional data are not needed, the parents are to be notified by the team that no additional data are needed. Parents are also to be informed of the reasoning for the decision and that they have the right to request an assessment. Should the parents request additional assessment, the team is then required to complete the testing before determining that the child should continue receiving special education support. IDEA 70, U.S.C. § 1414(c)(1)(A&B)

EVALUATING CHILDREN WITH SPECIFIC LEARNING DISABILITIES

Federal regulations include specific criteria that must be used when determining the existence of a possible learning disability. The regulations include an operational definition of specific learning disabilities and require that observations be a part of the evaluation process.

IDEA includes specific requirements for the assessment and observation of students who may have learning disabilities. The diagnostic criteria are presented in chapter 12, "Interpreting Assessment for Educational Intervention." The requirements for observing students suspected of having a learning disability state that at least one team member other than the child's general education teacher should observe the child within the regular classroom setting. If the child is not in school because of age or other conditions, the team member is required to observe the child in an age-appropriate environment.

A student may be diagnosed as having an existing learning disability when she is not achieving as expected for her age and ability levels and exhibits a severe discrepancy between achievement and intellectual ability in one or more of the following areas: oral expression, listening comprehension, written expression, basic reading skill, reading comprehension, mathematics calculation, and mathematics reasoning. The student may not be found to have a learning disability if the discrepancy between achievement and intellectual ability is the result of a sensory impairment, mental retardation, emotional disturbance, or environmental or cultural disadvantage.

MEETING THE NEEDS OF PERSONS WITH ATTENTION DISORDERS

When PL 94-142 was revised, attention disorders were studied by the U.S. Department of Education (U.S. Department of Education, 1991) for possible addition as a new disability category to IDEA. The decision was made that attention disorders (such as attention deficit disorder, or ADD) did not need a separate category because students with these disorders were already served, for the most part, in settings for students with learning or behavioral disabilities. If the student did not meet the criteria for either specific learning disabilities or emotional disturbance, he could be served in an appropriate setting under the category of Other Health Impairment "in instances where the ADD is a chronic or acute health problem that results in limited alertness, which adversely affects educational performance" (U.S. Department of Education, 1991, p. 3). The terms *attention deficit disorder* and *attention deficit hyperactivity disorder* (ADHD) are included among those listed in the definition of the category of Other Health Impairment (§ 300.7(c)(9)(i), IDEA, 1997).

In cases where the attention disorder does not significantly impair the student's ability to function in the regular classroom, the student may be served within the regular classroom under the provisions of Section 504 of the Rehabilitation Act of 1973 (discussed later in the chapter). This law requires that students be given reasonable accommodations for their disability in the general education environment.

Students with attention disorders must undergo a comprehensive evaluation by a multidisciplinary team to determine whether they are eligible for services and, if so, whether they would be better served by the provisions of IDEA or of Section 504.

IEP TEAM EVALUATION

To decrease the possibility of subjective and discriminatory assessment, IDEA regulations mandate that the comprehensive evaluation be conducted by the members of a multidisciplinary IEP team. As stated in the federal requirements, each student must be assessed in a variety of areas by a team made up of professionals from various disciplines according to the individual's needs. All areas of suspected disability are assessed. If the team has determined during screening and has specified in the assessment plan that the student needs further evaluation in speech, language, reading, and social/behavioral skills, then a speech-language clinician, a special education teacher or educational diagnostician, and a school psychologist will be members of the assessment team. The team may obtain additional information from the parents, classroom teacher, school nurse, school counselor, principal, and other school personnel. Figure 2.1 describes the responsibilities of the various members who might be on the IEP team.

In compliance with the nondiscriminatory section of the law, team members employ several types of assessment and collect different types of data. Team members select instruments for their validity, technical adequacy, cultural fairness, and objectivity. Because the law requires that a variety of methods be used in assessment, the team should make use of additional classroom observations, informal assessment measures, and parent interviews. Additional data provided by outside sources or from previous assessment should also be considered.

The IDEA amendments specify that an IEP team comprises specific individuals who reach a decision regarding the student's eligibility for services and possible interventions. Each member of the IEP team contributes carefully documented information to the decision-making process.

IDEA Amendments of 1997: IEP Team

§ 300.344 IEP Team

(d)(1)(B) Individualized education program team—The term individualized education program team or IEP team means a group of individuals composed of—

(i) the parents of a child with a disability;

(ii) at least one regular education teacher of such child (if the child is or may be participating in the regular education environment);

(iii) at least one special education teacher, or where appropriate, at least one special education provider of such child;

Team members include, in addition to the child's parents, the following:

Team Member	***Responsibilities***
School nurse	Initial vision and hearing screens, checks medical records, refers health problems to other medical professionals.
Special education teacher	Consultant to regular classroom teacher during prereferral process; administers educational tests, observes in other classrooms, helps with screening and recommends IEP goals, writes objectives, and suggests educational interventions.
Special education supervisor	May advise all activities of special education teacher, may provide direct services, guides placement decisions, recommends services.
Educational diagnostician	Administers norm-referenced and criterion-referenced tests, observes student in educational setting, makes suggestions for IEP goals and objectives.
School psychologist	Administers individual intelligence tests, observes student in classroom, administers projective instruments and personality inventories; may be under supervision of a doctoral-level psychologist.
Occupational therapist	Evaluates fine motor and self-help skills, recommends therapies, may provide direct services or consultant services, may help obtain equipment for student needs.
Physical therapist	Evaluates gross motor functioning and self-help skills, living skills, and job-related skills necessary for optimum achievement of student; may provide direct services or consultant services.
Behavioral consultant	Specialist in behavior management and crisis intervention; may provide direct services or consultant services.
School counselor	May serve as objective observer in prereferral stage, may provide direct group or individual counseling, may schedule students and help with planning of student school schedules.

Figure 2.1 IEP team: Who's who?

Team Member	*Responsibilities*
Speech-language clinician	Evaluates speech-language development, may refer for hearing problems, may provide direct therapy or consultant services for classroom teachers.
Audiologist	Evaluates hearing for possible impairments, may refer students for medical problems, may help obtain hearing aids.
Physician's assistant	Evaluates physical condition of student and may provide physical exams for students of a local education agency, refers medical problems to physicians or appropriate therapists, school social worker, or visiting teacher.
Home-school coordinator; school social worker or visiting teacher	Works directly with family; may hold conferences, conduct interviews, and administer adaptive behavior scales based on parent interviews; may serve as case manager.
Regular education teacher	Works with the special education team, student, and parents to develop an environment that is appropriate and as much like that of general education students as possible; implements prereferral intervention strategies.

Figure 2.1 continued.

(iv) a representative of the local education agency who—

(I) is qualified to provide or supervise the provision of, specially designed instruction to meet the unique needs of children with disabilities;

(II) is knowledgeable about the general curriculum; and

(III) is knowledgeable about the availability of resources of the local education agency;

(v) an individual who can interpret the instructional implications of evaluation results, who may be a member of the team described in clauses (ii) through (vi)

(vi) at the discretion of the parent or the agency other individuals who have knowledge or special expertise regarding the child, including related services personnel as appropriate

(vii) whenever appropriate, the child with a disability . . . IDEA 70 U.S.C. § 1414(d)(1)(B)

The amendments require that at a minimum, the IEP team should include the child's parents, a regular education teacher (if the child is or may be participating in the general education environment), a special education teacher, a supervisor of special education services who is knowledgeable about general curriculum and local resources, and someone who is able to interpret the instructional implications of evaluation results. In many cases, one person may fulfill more than one role on the IEP team. The school or parent may invite others as long as they have knowledge of the child or the services that will be provided. Together, the IEP team and other professionals, as appropriate, determine eligibility based on federal and state criteria.

IDEA Regular Education Teacher Requirements. The regulations include requirements for a general education teacher:

> (C) Requirement with respect to regular education teacher—The regular education teacher of the child, as a member of the IEP Team, shall, to the extent appropriate, participate in the development of the IEP of the child including the determination of appropriate positive behavioral interventions and strategies and the determination of supplementary aids and services, program modifications, and support for school personnel consistent with paragraph (I)(A)(iii),
>
> (B) Requirement with respect to the regular education teacher—The regular education teacher of the child, as a member of the IEP Team, shall, to the extent appropriate, participate in the review and the revision of the IEP of the child. IDEA, 20 U.S.C. § 1414(d)(3)(C)

These sections of the law provide guidance about how to involve general education teachers in the IEP process and encourage the child's teachers to contribute to the review and revision of the program. These regulations also encourage the general education teacher to incorporate necessary behavioral interventions within the general education environment.

DETERMINING ELIGIBILITY

IDEA includes definitions and some fairly global criteria for determining eligibility for services for students with the following disabilities: autism, deaf-blindness, deafness, hearing impairment, mental retardation, multiple disabilities, orthopedic impairment, emotional disturbance, specific learning disability, speech or language impairment, traumatic brain injury, and visual impairment, including blindness. Most states have more specific criteria for determining eligibility for services, and many have different names for the conditions stated in the law. For example, some states use the term *perceptual disability* rather than *learning disability,* or *mental handicap* rather than *mental retardation.*

During the eligibility meeting, all members should, objectively and professionally, contribute data, including informal observations. The decision to provide the student with special education services or to continue in a regular classroom without special education interventions should be based on data presented during the eligibility meeting. Parents are to be active participants in the eligibility meeting. School personnel should strive to make parents feel comfortable in the meeting and should welcome and carefully consider all of their comments and any additional data they submit. If the student has been found eligible for services, the team discusses educational interventions and specific **special education services** and **related services.** The federal requirements recommend that students are educated, as much as possible, with general education students.

special education services Services not provided by regular education but necessary to enable an individual with disabilities to achieve in school.

related services Those services related to special education but not part of the educational setting, such as transportation and therapies.

The regulations of IDEA Amendments of 1997 include statements regarding when a student cannot be found eligible for services. These are stated in the following section.

§ 300.534 Determination of Eligibility

b. A child may not be determined to be eligible under this part if—
   1. The determinant factor for that eligibility determination is—
      (i) Lack of instruction in reading or math; or
      (ii) Limited English proficiency; and
   2. The child does not otherwise meet the eligibility criteria in § 300.7(a). IDEA, 20 U.S.C. § 1414(b)(5)

This special rule for determining eligibility is aimed at preventing students from becoming special education eligible solely on the basis of no instruction or limited instruction in reading or math. Students may not be found eligible solely on the basis of having limited English proficiency. In other words, students who have had these experiences must have other causative factors that result in the need for special education or related services. For example, a student may have had little or no instruction in math and be found eligible for services because of a reading disability if that has been documented through the evaluation.

Check Your Understanding

Complete Activity 2.3.

ACTIVITY 2.3

Using the information from Figure 2.1, assign the appropriate team member to solve the following problems.

1. A student in Ms. Whittle's class has been rubbing his eyes frequently and holding books very close to his face. Ms. Whittle should request the help of ______________.
2. A young student in your class has a difficult time holding a pencil and using scissors. You have tried several procedures to help the student learn how to use these tools, but she continues to have difficulty. You decide to refer the student to ______________.
3. Mr. Powers has a student in his class who seems to be having difficulty staying awake. From time to time, the student appears

to be in a daze. Mr. Powers does not know whether the child has a physical, emotional, or even drug-related problem. He asks you to help because "you know what to do with these problem children." You advise Mr. Powers to contact ______________.

4. Ms. Stewart has a student who just doesn't seem to be learning. She tells you that she has "tried everything," including changing to an easier textbook. She feels sure that the student has a learning disability and should be tested and "taken out of my room so I can spend more time with the other students." You advise Ms. Stewart to consult ______________.
5. Miss Henry has a young male student who exhibits aggressive behaviors in class. She is concerned that the student may harm himself or others. Your advice to her is to contact or refer to ______________.

Apply Your Knowledge

Whom should you consult when you are not certain of the type of problem a student may have, or you are uncertain of the professional who assists with a particular type of problem? ______________.

PARENT PARTICIPATION

Every effort should be made to accommodate the parents so that they may attend all conferences pertaining to their child's education. The federal requirements emphasize the importance of parental attendance.

The importance of parent involvement was underscored in the provisions of PL 99-457. The amendments require that the intervention plan, called the Individual Family Service Plan (IFSP), be designed to include necessary participation of the family members. As mentioned in chapter 1, the IFSP identifies family needs relating to the child's development that, when met, will increase the likelihood of successful intervention. The legislation emphasizes the family and the child with the disability (Turnbull, 1990).

The IDEA Amendments of 1997 further stressed the importance of parent participation by including the parents on the IEP team and by encouraging parents to submit additional information to be used during the eligibility and planning process. These regulations also require that the parent be given a copy of the evaluation report as well as the documentation of eligibility upon completion of administration of tests and other evaluation materials.

Involve parents through parent-teacher conferences.

DEVELOPING THE INDIVIDUALIZED EDUCATION PROGRAM

grade equivalent Grade score assigned to a mean raw score of a group during norming process.

age equivalents Age score assigned to a mean raw score of a group during norming process.

standard scores Scores calculated during norming process of a test; follow normal distribution theory.

annual goals Long-term goals for educational intervention.

short-term objectives Behaviorally stated objectives to plan educational interventions for a short period of time.

Every student receiving special education services must have an individualized education program or plan (IEP) that is written in compliance with the requirements of IDEA. Current levels of educational performance may include scores such as **grade equivalents, age equivalents,** and or **standard scores.** In addition, present level of performance information should include classroom performance measures and classroom behavior. Measurable long-term goals, sometimes called **annual goals,** as well as the **short-term objectives** must be included in the IEP. Short-term objectives are the intermediate steps needed to reach the educational goal. Every area in which special education services are provided must have an annual goal.

The IDEA Amendments of 1997 added requirements for the IEP team to incorporate in the IEP. These requirements, presented in the following section, indicate what should be included in the written individual educational program, a plan for instructional intervention.

§ 300.347 Content of the IEP

(d)(1)(A) Individualized education program—The term individualized education program or IEP means a written statement for each child with a disability that is developed, reviewed, and revised in accordance with this section and that includes—

(i) a statement of the child's present levels of educational performance, including—

(I) how the child's disability affects the child's involvement in the general curriculum; or

(II) for preschool children as appropriate, how the disability affects the child's participation in appropriate activities;

(ii) a statement of measurable annual goals including benchmarks or short-term objectives related to—

(I) meeting the child's needs that result from the disability to enable the child to be involved in and progress in the general curriculum; and

(II) meeting each of the child's other educational needs that result from the child's disability;

(iii) a statement of the special education and related services and supplementary aids to be provided to the child or on behalf of the child, and a statement of the program modifications or supports for school personnel that will be provided for the child—

(I) to advance appropriately toward attaining annual goals;

(II) to be involved in and progress in the general curriculum in accordance with clause (i) and to participate in extracurricular and other nonacademic activities; and

(III) to be educated and participate with other children with disabilities and nondisabled children in the activities described in this paragraph;

(iv) an explanation of the extent, if any, to which the child will not participate with nondisabled children in the regular class and in the activities described in clause (iii);

(v) (I) a statement of any individual modifications in the administration of State or district wide assessments of student achievement that are needed in order for the child to participate in such assessment; and

(II) if the IEP Team determines that the child will not participate in a particular State or district wide assessment of student achievement (or part of such an assessment), a statement of—

(aa) why the assessment is not appropriate for the child; and

(bb) how the child will be assessed. IDEA, 20 U.S.C. § 1414(d)

The first requirement is that the IEP team include a statement of the student's current functioning and, most important, how the child's disability affects the child's ability to be involved with general education students. The 1997 amendments now assume that students with disabilities will be educated with their nondisabled peers unless the IEP team provides reasons why this is not appropriate for the specific student (Huefner, 2000). The previous regulations stated a preference for educating students in the general education environment; however, the language included in the newest regulations is stronger. These IEP requirements focus on inclusion of the student with disabilities within the mainstream environment and with general education students for education and other activities outside the educational setting.

School district decisions should be based on formative data collected throughout the LRE process.

1. Has the school taken steps to maintain the child in the general education classroom?
   - What supplementary aids and services were used?
   - What interventions were attempted?
   - How many interventions were attempted?
2. Benefits of placement in general education with supplementary aids and services versus special education.
   - Academic benefits
   - Nonacademic benefits
3. What are the effects of the education on other students?
   - If the student is disruptive, is the education of the other students adversely affected?
   - Does the student require an inordinate amount of attention from the teacher, thereby adversely affecting the education of others?
4. If a student is being educated in a setting other than the general education classroom, are integrated experiences available with able-bodied peers to the maximum extent possible?
   - In what academic settings is the student integrated with able-bodied peers?
   - In what nonacademic settings is the student integrated with able-bodied peers?
5. Is the entire continuum of alternative services available from which to choose an appropriate environment?

Figure 2.2 Determination of the least restrictive environment. (*Source:* From "Least Restrictive Environment, Inclusion, and Students with Disabilities: A Legal Analysis," by M. L. Yell, 1995, *Journal of Special Education, 28*, 389–404. Copyright by PRO-ED, Inc. Adapted by permission.)

least restrictive environment The environment determined to be the most like that of nondisabled peers.

This part of IDEA is known as the provision of educational services in the **least restrictive environment** (LRE, discussed further later in the chapter).

Several court cases have resulted in interpreting the least restrictive environment requirement of the child's IEP. The movement toward inclusion as a method of providing the least restrictive environment has been found to be appropriate in some situations and not in others. Yell (1995) has offered a method that may assist IEP teams in making the determination of the appropriate educational environment that is based on the results of current interpretation within the judicial system. This method is shown in Figure 2.2.

The team must consider the extent to which the student can participate in statewide assessments. The level of participation in these assessments and any accommodations required must be stated in the IEP. It is clear that meeting the student's needs within the least restrictive environment is a goal of the amendments of 1997.

The IDEA amendments include a section of considerations for students with special factors or conditions. These considerations are presented in the following paragraphs.

(d)(3)(B) Considerations of Special Factors

(i) in the case of a child whose behavior impedes his or her learning or that of others, consider, when appropriate, strategies, including positive behavioral interventions, strategies, and supports to address that behavior;

(ii) in the case of a child with limited English proficiency, consider the language needs of the child as such needs relate to the child's IEP;

(iii) in the case of a child who is blind or visually impaired, provide for instruction in Braille and the use of Braille unless the IEP Team determines, after evaluation of the child's reading and writing skills, needs, and appropriate reading and writing media (including an evaluation of the child's future needs for instruction in Braille or the use of Braille), that instruction in Braille or the use of Braille is not appropriate for the child;

(iv) consider the communication needs of the child and in the case of a child who is deaf or hard of hearing, consider the child's language and communication needs, opportunities for direct communications with peers and professional personnel in the child's language and communication mode, academic level, and full range of needs, including opportunities for direct instruction in the child's language and communication mode; and

(v) consider whether the child requires assistive technology devices and services. IDEA, 20 U.S.C. § 1414(d)(3)(B)

Each of these requirements mandates the IEP team to consider specific needs of individuals, such as students with limited English proficiency and students with various disabilities. These specific needs, which have been determined through effect assessment, should be addressed in the IEP and progress monitored and reviewed, at least annually, by the IEP team.

TRANSITION SERVICES

In the section addressing the content of the IEP, the law addresses the needs of students who are nearing the age when they may make the transition to adult life.

(d)(1)(A)(vii)(I) beginning at age 14, and updated annually, a statement of the transition services needs of the child under the applicable components of the child's IEP that focuses on the child's course of study (such as participation in advanced-placement courses or a vocational education program);

(II) beginning at age 16 (or younger, if determined appropriate by the IEP Team), a statement of needed transition services for the child, including, when appropriate, a statement of the interagency responsibilities or any needed linkages; and

(III) beginning at least one year before the child reaches the age of majority under the State law, a statement that the child has been informed of his or her rights under this title, if any, that will transfer to the child on reaching the age of majority under 615(m). IDEA, 20 U.S.C. § 1414(d)(1)(A)(vii I & II & III)

transition services Services designed to help students make the transition from high school to postsecondary education or work environment.

IDEA stressed the importance of **transition services** to prepare students 16 years or older for a work or postsecondary environment. Where appropriate in educational planning, younger students may also be eligible for such services. The law underscores the importance of early planning and decisions by all members affected, including the student. The planning for the needed transition begins by age 14 or younger, if appropriate.

The IDEA amendments emphasized transition services to a greater extent than did other regulations. They also extended the rights to the student at the age of majority according to individual state laws. The age of majority is the age at which a child is no longer considered to be a minor (in many states, the age is 18). School personnel are responsible for communicating to the student that the rights under the law are now in the hands of the student rather than the parents. Moreover, the law requires that the student be informed of the transfer of rights a year before the student reaches the age of majority.

Check Your Understanding

Complete Activity 2.4.

ACTIVITY 2.4

Read the case study. Using the previous information on parent participation, eligibility, and placement procedures, list the events that are not in compliance with federal regulations.

Case Study

John's teacher, Ms. Nogood, has been having problems with John in class. John will not listen and does not appear to be learning anything. Ms. Nogood has decided that she cannot take John another day, so she refers him for testing to "get him out of my class." The referral is given to Mr. I. Dunno, the special education teacher. Mr. Dunno is a very busy man who does not want to wait to test John. He calls John's parents but gets no answer. Mr. Dunno tells Ms. Nogood that John's parents are not at home and says, "I guess I've tried enough contact, and you can document that for me." Ms. Nogood says, "OK." John is given the Out-of-Date Invalid Screening Test. This test indicates that John is not performing as expected in reading. Mr. Dunno tries to call John's parents that same afternoon; again, no answer. The eligibility meeting is set for the next morning at 7:30. The school psychologist, Mrs. Hurryup, does not attend, nor does the principal, Miss Toobusy. The next morning, Mr. Dunno and Ms. Nogood decide that John will be placed in the resource room with Mr. Fixall.

List the events that are not in compliance with IDEA: ____.

Apply Your Knowledge

Using the scenario in this activity, list the correct steps that Ms. Nogood should follow. ____.

DUE PROCESS

IDEA was influenced to a large degree by parent organizations and court cases involving individuals with disabilities and their right to education. When schools implement the provisions of the law, occasionally differences arise between the schools providing the service and the parents of the student with the disability. Therefore, IDEA contains provisions for parents and schools to resolve their differences. These provisions are called due process provisions.

procedural safeguards Provisions of IDEA designed to protect students and parents in the special education process.

The **procedural safeguards** are inherent throughout the portions of the law concerned with assessment. For example, parental informed consent is considered a procedural safeguard designed to prevent assessment and placement of students without parents' knowledge. Parents may withdraw their consent at any time. Other provisions promote fairness in the decision-making process. Included in these provisions are the parents' right to examine all educational records and the right to seek an independent educational evaluation as well as the right to a hearing to resolve differences.

mediation Process of settling a dispute between parents and schools without a full third-party hearing.

The IDEA Amendments of 1997 include a significant addition in the area of due process. The amendments provide new sections for promoting **mediation** as a method to resolve disagreements between parents and their local school agency. The requirements mandate local education agencies to provide mediation at no cost to the parents. The mediation process is voluntary on the part of the school and the parents. This process cannot be used by a local education agency to delay parental rights to a hearing or to deny any other rights provided in the regulations. The mediation process is to be conducted by qualified and impartial trained mediators who are included on a list maintained by each state.

The parents of a student who has been evaluated by school personnel may disagree with the results obtained during the assessment process.

independent educational evaluation Comprehensive evaluation provided by a qualified independent evaluator.

Should this occur, the parents have the right to obtain an independent evaluation by an outside examiner. The **independent educational evaluation** is provided by a qualified professional not employed with the local education agency. Should the independent evaluation results differ from the evaluation results obtained by school personnel, the school must pay for the evaluation. The exception to this is if the school initiates an impartial due process hearing to resolve the different results and the hearing officer finds in favor of the school. In this case, the parents would be responsible for paying for the independent evaluation. If, however, favor is found with the parents as a result of the hearing, the school is responsible for payment.

IMPARTIAL DUE PROCESS HEARING

impartial due process hearing A hearing by an impartial officer that is held to resolve differences between a school and parents of a student with disabilities.

impartial hearing officer Person qualified to hear disputes between schools and parents; not an employee of school agency.

The parents and school are provided with procedures for filing complaints and requesting an **impartial due process hearing.** In a third-party hearing, the parents and the school may individually explain their side of the disagreement before an **impartial hearing officer.** The impartial hearing officer is a person qualified to hear the case. In some states, third-party hearing officers are lawyers; in other states, the hearing officers are special education professionals, such as college faculty who teach special education courses to prepare teachers.

Parents should be advised before the hearing that although counsel (an attorney) is not required for the hearing, they do have the right to secure counsel as well as experts to give testimony. After hearing each side of the complaint, the hearing officer reaches a decision. On finding in favor of the parents, the school must comply with the ruling or appeal to a state-level hearing. In turn, if favor is found with the school, the parents must comply. If the parents do not wish to comply, they may be able to request a state-level hearing or file an appeal with a civil court.

While the school and parents are involved with due process and hearing procedures, the student remains in the classroom setting in which she was placed before the complaint was filed. This requirement has been called the stay-put provision.

The IDEA Amendments of 1997 provide additional requirements for procedural safeguards in the event of students with disabilities who are removed from school or placed in different settings, such as alternative placements, as the result of disciplinary measures. The regulations are extensive and beyond the scope of this text. One provision that should be noted is the temporary change of placement of a student that may be made under conditions that threaten the safety of the student, other students, or staff. A hearing officer may make a change of placement for 45 days if the current placement will likely result in harm to the student or others. For additional information, refer to PL 105-17, Section 615, Procedural Safeguards.

Table 2.3 Differences between IDEA and 504.

Component	IDEA	Section 504
Purpose of law	• Provides federal funding to states to assist in education of students with disabilities • Substantive requirements attached to funding	• Civil rights law • Protects persons with disabilities from discrimination in programs or services that receive federal financial assistance • Requires reasonable accommodations to ensure nondiscrimination
Who is protected?	• Categorical approach • Thirteen disability categories • Disability must adversely impact educational performance	• Functional approach • Students (a) having a mental or physical impairment that affects a major life activity, (b) with a record of such an impairment, or (c) who are regarded as having such an impairment • Protects students in general and special education
FAPE	• Special education and related services that are provided at public expense, meet state requirements, and are provided in conformity with the IEP • Substantive standard is educational benefit	• General or special education and related aids and services • Requires a written education plan • Substantive standard is equivalency
LRE	• Student must be educated with peers without disabilities to the maximum extent appropriate	• School must ensure that the students are educated with their peers without disabilities

SECTION 504

Section 504 of the Rehabilitation Act of 1973 A civil rights law that includes protection from discrimination and reasonable accommodations.

Section 504 of the Rehabilitation Act of 1973 includes many of the same concepts, such as procedural safeguards and evaluation, as those in IDEA. The law extends beyond the categories listed in IDEA and beyond the public school environment. This law is a civil rights law. Its purpose is to prevent discrimination against individuals with disabilities in programs receiving federal financial assistance. Students with disabilities are protected from discrimination in schools receiving federal financial assistance under Section 504, whether or not they are protected by IDEA. The law extends the educational regulations to include postsecondary environments, such as colleges and universities. It is used to address people with chronic health conditions in the public education setting that may not be addressed through IDEA, such as students with ADHD who do not

Component	IDEA	Section 504
	• Removal from integrated settings only when supplementary aids and services are not successful • Districts must have a continuum of placement available	
Evaluation and placement	• Protection in evaluation procedures • Requires consent prior to initial evaluation and placement • Evaluation and placement decisions have to be made by a multidisciplinary team • Requires evaluation of progress toward IEP goals annually and reevaluation at least every 3 years	• Does not require consent; requires notice only • Requires periodic reevaluation • Reevaluation is required before a significant change in placement
Procedural safeguards	• Comprehensive and detailed notice requirements • Provides for independent evaluations • No grievance procedure • Impartial due process hearing	• General notice requirements • Grievance procedure • Impartial due process hearing
Funding	• Provides for federal funding to assist in the education of students with disabilities	• No federal funding
Enforcement	• U.S. Office of Special Education Programs (OSEP) (can cut off IDEA funds) • Compliance monitoring by state educational agency (SEA)	• Complaint can be filed with Office of Civil Rights (OCR) (can cut off all federal funding) • Complaints can be filed with state's department of education

Source: From *The law and special education,* by M. L. Yell, 1997, Upper Saddle River, NJ: Prentice-Hall. Copyright by Prentice-Hall.

need full special education support because of other significant learning disabilities.

Some notable differences exist between IDEA and Section 504 that were summarized by Yell (1997). These differences are presented in Table 2.3.

For the purposes of assessment and educational planning, Section 504 seeks to meet the needs of students according to how students' conditions affect their functioning within life activities. This places the emphasis of assessment and program planning on a student's current functioning within that activity and calls for reasonable accommodations. For a college student with a specific learning disability, for example, the reasonable accommodations may include taking exams in a quiet room with extended time because of attention deficit disorder or waiving a foreign language requirement because of a specific learning disability in written language.

RESEARCH AND ISSUES CONCERNING IDEA

IDEA states that each school agency shall actively take steps to ensure that parents participate in the IEP process in several ways. First, the parents must agree by informed consent before the initial evaluation and before receiving special education services. The 1997 amendments added the provision that parents must consent prior to the reevaluation. The parents also participate in the decision-making process regarding eligibility. Following the eligibility determination, the parents are to participate in the development of the IEP. Legally, parents have the right to participate in the evaluation and IEP processes, and schools are mandated by the regulations to involve parents.

Informed consent is one of the first ways to ensure parental involvement and procedural safeguards. Informed consent is compounded by issues such as parental literacy, parental comprehension of the meaning of legal terminology, and the lack of time professionals spend with parents explaining testing and special education. Parents' rights materials may be made more difficult to understand because of their use of highly specialized vocabulary. According to an early study involving observation and analysis of interactions in IEP conferences, parents' rights were merely "glossed over in the majority of conferences" (Goldstein, Strickland, Turnbull, & Curry, 1980, p. 283). This suggests that sufficient time may not be allotted to discussing issues of central concern to parents. Recent changes in the 1997 amendments are designed to promote genuine parental involvement in educational assessment and planning.

Katsiyannis (1994) reviewed decisions and reports from the Office of Civil Rights (OCR) concerned with the question of procedural safeguards and parental involvement. Katsiyannis stated that the OCR found that the typical sequence of the referral/screening process denied procedural safeguards at the prereferral stage. Furthermore, parents should be informed of procedural safeguards at the time that the student is screened to determine whether additional assessment will be conducted. Educators should keep in mind that the new regulations stress parental involvement during all stages of the assessment and planning process. These regulations provide the minimum guidelines for professionals while best practice dictates that parents should be involved throughout their child's education (Sheridan, Cowan, & Eagle, 2000).

The provision granted to parents in the IEP process is active participation in the IEP conference by contributing to the formulation of objectives and long-term goals for their children. In the past, traditional IEP conference, parents were found to be passive and to attend merely to receive information (Barnett, Zins, & Wise, 1984; Brantlinger, 1987; Goldstein et al., 1980; Goldstein & Turnbull, 1982; Vaughn, Bos, Harrell, & Lasky, 1988; Weber & Stoneman, 1986). Parents are now considered to be equal team members in the IEP process.

An area of additional concern involves working with parents of culturally, linguistically, or environmentally diverse backgrounds. Professionals should make certain that materials and concepts presented are at the

Table 2.4 Actions reflective of collaborative relationships.

1. Listening to one another's perspective.
2. Viewing differences as a strength.
3. Remaining focused on a mutual interest (e.g., assessment and planning for student needs).
4. Sharing information about the child, the home, the school system, and problems encountered in the system.
5. Asking for ideas and opinions about the child, problems, goals, and potential solutions.
6. Respecting the skill and knowledge of each other related to the student, the disability, and contextual considerations.
7. Planning together to address parents', teachers', and students' needs.
8. Making joint decisions about the child's educational program and goals.
9. Sharing resources to work toward goal attainment.
10. Providing a common message to the student about schoolwork and behavior.
11. Demonstrating willingness to address conflict.
12. Refraining from finding fault, and committing to sharing successes.

Source: From S. M. Sheridan et al. (2000). Partnering with parents in educational programming for students with special needs; in C. F. Telzrow and M. Tankersley (eds.), *IDEA Amendments of 1997: Practice Guidelines for School-Based Teams.* Bethesda, MD: National Association of School Psychologists, p. 316. Copyright 2000 by the National Association of School Psychologists. Reprinted by permission.

appropriate level. Special education or legal concepts are complex for many persons who are not familiar with the vocabulary and process. For persons who do not speak English as a primary language, legal terms and specialized concepts may be difficult even though materials are presented in the individual's native language. These concepts may be different than educational concepts of their original culture. Salend and Taylor (1993) suggested that the parents' level of acculturation be considered, noting that children may become acculturated much more quickly than their parents. In addition, Salend and Taylor have reminded educators to consider the family's history of discrimination and the family structure, since these factors may have an impact on the family's interactions with school personnel. Educational professionals should make every effort to be certain that all parents are familiar with the special education process, services available, and their expected role during the assessment and IEP processes.

Parents and educators working together will be a benefit to the student's educational program. Establishing a positive relationship with parents requires educators to work with parents in a collaborative manner. Sheridan et al. provided a list of actions that may enhance the collaborative nature of the relationship (2000). These actions are presented in Table 2.4.

ISSUES OF NONDISCRIMINATORY ASSESSMENT

minority overrepresentation When the percentage of a culturally different group is greater in special education classes than in the local education agency.

Perhaps no other area in the field of psychoeducational assessment has received more attention than that of nondiscriminatory assessment. Much of the research and controversial issues center around the overrepresentation of minority students in special education classes. **Minority overrepresentation** is found to occur when the percentage of minority students enrolled in particular special education classes is larger than the percentage of minority students enrolled in the local education agency. In other words, if classes for mildly disabled students were made up of 28% minority students yet only 12% of the local education agency was made up of minorities, the local education agency's special education classes would have an overrepresentation of minority students.

The U.S. Department of Education reported that minority overrepresentation in special education continues to be problematic (U.S. Department of Education, 1997). Analyzing data from the Office of Civil Rights, the U.S. Department of Education reported that although African Americans account for 16% of the total population in schools, 32% of the students in settings for persons with mild mental retardation and 29% of the students diagnosed as having moderate mental retardation are African American. In addition to these classifications, African Americans account for 24% of the students within the category of emotional disturbance and 18% of students served as having specific learning disabilities. Concerns expressed in the *Nineteenth Annual Report to Congress on the Implementation of IDEA* (U.S. Department of Education, 1997) include that minority students are placed into more segregated classroom settings and restrictive curricula, which results in lower achievement.

A study examining the relationship between state financial resources and special education categories reported that states with higher numbers of children who are considered living in poverty had lower percentages of students categorized as learning disabled, and states with more financial resources had a higher percentage of students with learning disabilities (McLaughlin & Owings, 1992). Sherman concluded that risk of experiencing developmental delays, emotional disturbance, or learning disabilities increased by 2.4% if the child comes from a family experiencing poverty (Sherman, 1994). Children experiencing poverty are more likely to have health problems, developmental problems, and low achievement, which will require special education support (U.S. Department of Education, 1997).

Much of the blame for the overrepresentation of minorities in special education has been attributed to referral and evaluation practices. The amount of attention given to the assessment process may be due in part to IDEA's emphasis on nondiscriminatory assessment. The law clearly states that educational agencies should use evaluation procedures that are not racially or culturally discriminatory. This can have many implications when assessing students who have linguistic differences and those who may come from culturally different backgrounds or deprived environments. The following list of problems of bias in assessment is adapted from Reynolds, Lowe, and Saenz (1999):

1. Inappropriate content. Students from minority populations may lack exposure to certain items on the assessment instrument.
2. Inappropriate standardization samples. Ethnic minorities were not represented in the normative sample at the time of development of the instrument.
3. Examiner and language. White, English-speaking examiners may intimidate students of color and students from different linguistic backgrounds.
4. Inequitable social consequences. Because of discriminatory assessment practices, minority students may be relegated to lower educational placements, which may ultimately result in lower-paying jobs.
5. Measurement of different constructs. White test developers designed instruments assumed to measure academic or cognitive ability for all students. When used with minority students, however, the instruments may measure only the degree to which the minority students have been able to absorb white middle-class culture.
6. Different predictive validity. Instruments designed to predict the educational or academic outcome or potential for white students might not do so for minority students.
7. Qualitatively distinct minority and majority aptitude and achievement. This suggests that persons from various ethnic groups are qualitatively different and therefore tests designed to measure aptitude in one group cannot adequately measure the aptitude of another group. (Reynolds, Lowe, & Saenz, 1999, pp. 556–557)

Additional problems in biased assessment include overinterpretation of test results. This means that an examiner may report to have assessed a trait, attribute, or characteristic that the instrument is not designed to measure (Flaugher, 1978). For example, an examiner may report a cognitive ability level or a behavioral trait based on the results of a student's academic achievement test. The assessment is inaccurate because the test was designed to measure academic achievement only.

Another problem that may arise in assessment is that of testing students whose dominant language is not English. Although some instruments are published in languages other than English, such as Spanish, the translations may result in different conceptual meanings and influence test performance and test results (Fradd & Hallman, 1983). Lopez (1995) recommended that norm-referenced instruments should not be used with bilingual students. Lopez provides several reasons for this recommendation:

1. Norms are usually limited to small samples of minority children.
2. Norming procedures routinely exclude students with limited English proficiency.

3. Test items tap information that minority children may not be familiar with due to their linguistically and culturally different backgrounds.
4. Testing formats do not allow examiners the opportunity to provide feedback or to probe into the children's quality of responses.
5. The tests' scoring systems arbitrarily decide what are the correct responses based on majority culture paradigms.
6. The standardized testing procedures assume that the children have appropriate test-taking skills (Lopez, 1995, p. 1113).

IDEA mandates that the evaluation of students for possible special education services must involve the use of tests that have been validated for the purpose for which they are used. Regardless of these legal and professional guidelines, most norm-referenced tests used in schools are not diagnostic in nature but rather measure expected academic achievement or intellectual functioning. The developmental process of many instruments gives little attention to validity studies with disabled populations. Fuchs, Fuchs, Benowitz, and Barringer (1987) called for discontinuing use of tests with no validation data on disabled populations if those tests are used for diagnosis and placement of students with disabilities. The movement toward restructuring education and the way that special education services are delivered has resulted in a call for the use of more varieties of tests that measure the student's knowledge and skills as they relate to the curriculum (IDEA Amendments of 1997; Lipsky & Gartner, 1997; U.S. Department of Education, 1997). The use of these devices will require additional research regarding validity, reliability, and generalizability (Burger & Burger, 1994). The regulations that guide the assessment process call for careful selection of assessment instruments and state that the purpose of the assessment is to determine educational needs.

The IDEA regulations contain language requiring that at a minimum, professionals be trained in assessment and, more specifically, that training or expertise is available to enable the examiner to evaluate students with disabilities. Past research has shown that some professionals responsible for the evaluation of students with disabilities lacked competence in test selection, scoring, and interpretations (Bennett, 1981; Bennett & Shepherd, 1982; McNutt & Mandelbaum, 1980; Ysseldyke & Thurlow, 1983). Valles (1998) advocated improving teacher training at the preservice level to decrease the likelihood that minorities are inaccurately diagnosed.

Of all of the controversial areas in nondiscriminatory assessment, the most controversial area remains that of IQ testing for the purpose of determining eligibility for services under the diagnostic category of mental retardation. One professional in the field (Jackson, 1975) called for banning the use of IQ tests. Some state and local education agencies, either by litigation or voluntarily, have discontinued the use of IQ tests with minority students. Evidence indicates, however, that IQ scores continue to be the most influential test score variable in the decision-making process (Sapp, Chissom, & Horton, 1984). MacMillan and Forness (1998) argue that

IQ testing may only be peripheral in placement rather than the determining factor. In their study, they concluded that the use of IQ scores may in fact prevent some students from eligibility who may truly be in need of support services. The trend in assessment to use more functional measures than traditional assessment may be the result of assessment practices viewed as biased.

IDEA and the 1997 amendments require that other data, such as comments from parents and teachers and adaptive behavior measures, be considered in the decision-making process. In calling for a complete reconceptualization of special education and the assessment process, Lipsky and Gartner (1997) posed the following questions:

> Why must children suspected of having a disability undergo a costly, lengthy, and intrusive process in order to receive public education services similar to one that their peers without disabilities receive without such procedures?
>
> Why must parents of children with disabilities be denied opportunities available to parents of children without disabilities to choose the neighborhood school, or "magnet" or "school of choice" programs?
>
> Why must children be certified to enter a special education system if all children are entitled to a free and appropriate education that prepares them effectively to participate in and contribute to the society of which they are a part?
>
> Why must parents and their children in need of special education services lose substantial free-choice opportunities to gain procedural rights?
>
> Are the gains worth the cost? (pp. 28–29)

These questions raise important issues for consideration. In attempting to provide appropriate services that are designed to meet the individual student's needs, it seems that the system may have become cumbersome and may even be unfair for some families. Patton (1998) suggested that the current system is unfair to African American families because of the disproportionate numbers of children placed in special education from these families because of inaccurate diagnoses. Patton further stated that the current practices are not sensitive to minority cultures and behaviors. Others have called for a redirection of special education efforts in assessment and classification, particularly in applying these procedures with students who have emotional and behavioral disorders (Ruehl, 1998; Smith, 1997). These issues need additional investigation as schools implement the IDEA amendments with an emphasis on education of students with special needs in the regular classroom setting.

THE MULTIDISCIPLINARY TEAM AND THE DECISION-MAKING PROCESS

The regulations call for a variety of professionals and the parents of the student to be involved in the assessment and IEP processes. The decision-making process is to include all members of the IEP multidisciplinary team as another method of increasing accuracy of decisions. In a review of analogue research, Huebner (1991) determined that often teacher perceptions disproportionately influence the team's decision. This results in inaccurate decision making and may be considered a form of bias in the assessment process. School psychologists, as members of the IEP multidisciplinary team, may rely on clinical judgment to make eligibility decisions and fail to consistently consider information across cases; such practices, too, may lead to errors in the decision-making process (Ward, Ward, & Clark, 1991).

In other studies, inconsistencies in decisions of eligibility made by teams have been found specifically in determining eligibility of mild disabilities such as learning disabilities (Bocian, Beebe, MacMillan, & Gresham, 1999; MacMillan, Gresham, & Bocian, 1998). These researchers concluded that various forms of evidence, such as behaviors observed by teachers, may have weighed heavily in the decision-making process. Gresham, MacMillan, and Bocian (1998) postulated that eligibility decisions may be based on educational need more than actual legal criteria for students with mild disabilities.

LEAST RESTRICTIVE ENVIRONMENT

IDEA is designed to provide special education support services in the least restrictive environment. In many cases, this means that a student will be served within the general education classroom setting. Macready (1991) proposed that when a decision is made to place a student in an environment other than the general education setting, it should be viewed conceptually as a "foster placement rather than as a placement for adoption" (p. 151). The new regulations of IDEA '97 emphasize that students with disabilities should be educated within the general education environment unless there are justifiable reasons for the student to be educated in a special education setting.

Decisions of appropriate educational environments should be made carefully. Morsink and Lenk (1992) suggested that each decision be made on an individual basis and that the teacher's training and effectiveness in instruction and all environmental factors, such as the impact on other students or limiting environmental factors, be considered. Morsink and Lenk warned that a proposed placement, seen at first as the least restrictive environment, may indeed be an inappropriate environment when these factors are not considered to be favorable.

The provision of least restrictive environment may be implemented in various ways in different states and local education agencies. One study of six states found that finances, parent advocacy, categorically based systems, and varying layers of organizational structure all influenced the way that the least restrictive environment provision was implemented (Hasazi, Johnston, Liggett, & Schattman, 1994). This study found that these variables were complex and interconnected.

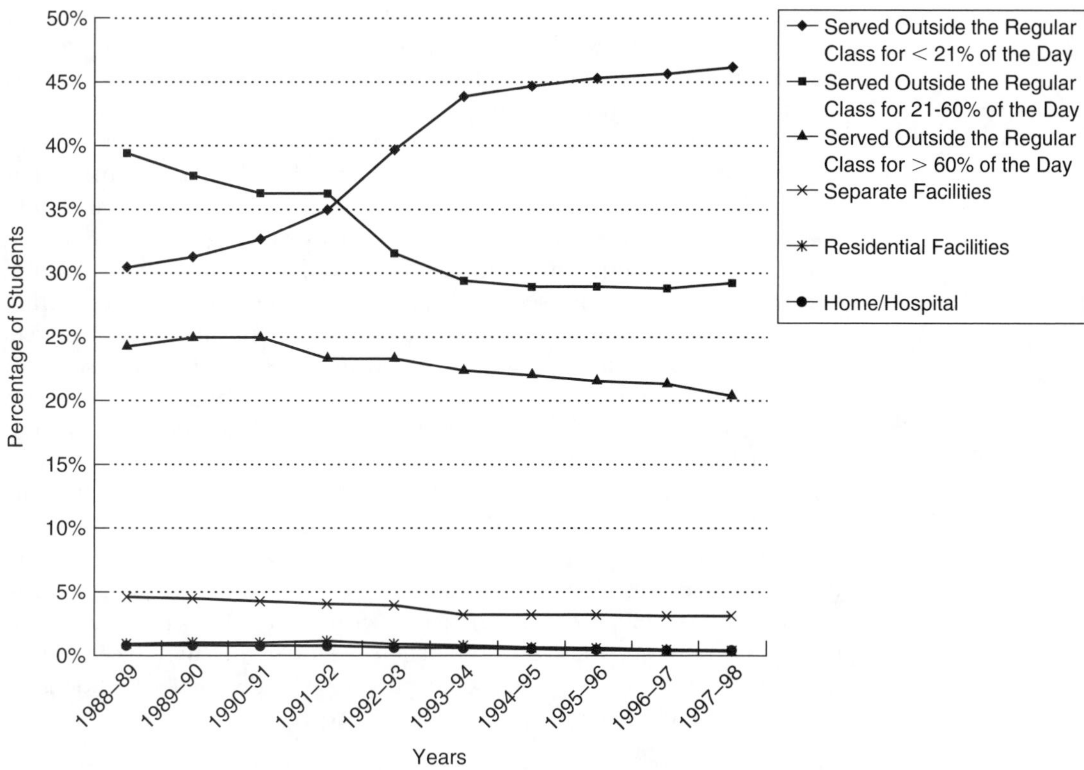

Figure 2.3 Increasing trend of students with disabilities ages 6–21 served in each general education environment: 1988–89 through 1998–99. (*Source:* U.S. Department of Education, Office of Special Education Programs, Data Analysis System [DANS], In *To assure the free appropriate public education of all children with disabilities*, 2000.

The research conducted by the U.S. Department of Education indicates that there has been an increasing trend to serve students in the general education classroom environment for most of the school day (1999). Figure 2.3 illustrates this trend.

The implementation of least restrictive environment and, more specifically, inclusion has been interpreted through litigation in several state and federal courts (Kubicek, 1994; Lipsky & Gartner, 1997; Yell, 1997). In summary, the courts have interpreted that the least restrictive environment decision must first consider placement in a regular education environment with additional supplementary aids if needed. If this arrangement will be equal or better for the student than the special education setting, the student should be placed within the general education environment. The student's academic and nonacademic benefits must be considered in the decision. This includes consideration of the benefits of social interaction in nonacademic activities and environments. The IEP team must also review the effect that the student will have on the teacher in terms of time and attention required and the effect the student may have on the other students in the general classroom. If the educational services required of the student can be provided better and the education is considered superior in the segregated setting, the student may be placed in a special education environment. For additional review, please refer to Lipsky and Gartner (1997) and Yell (1997).

Research has produced interesting results regarding inclusion in general education settings. One study that surveyed secondary students found that more students expressed a desire for a pull-out program for meeting their educational needs but enjoyed inclusion for the social aspects (Klinger, Vaughn, Schumm, Cohen, & Forgan, 1998). Some of the students in this study stated that the general education environment was simply too noisy. Bennett, Lee, and Lueke (1998) state that inclusion decisions should consider the parents' expectations. Their research found that several factors, such as the parents' view of inclusion, may have an impact on the parents' desire to have their child served in a general education setting. Another study of general education teachers' perceptions of inclusion found that more teachers were willing to include students with mild disabilities in the general education setting (Scruggs & Mastropieri, 1996). In this study, only one-third of the teachers believed that they had enough time and training to adequately serve students with disabilities in their general education classrooms. It is clear that placement decisions are complex.

IMPARTIAL HEARINGS

The procedural safeguards provided through due process seek to involve the parents in all stages of the IEP process rather than only during third-party hearings. Due process provisions specify at least 36 grounds for either schools or parents to seek a hearing (Turnbull, Turnbull, & Strickland, 1979). If abused, the process could result in chaos in the operation of school systems. The years since the law was enacted have witnessed a great deal of interpretation of uncertain issues through the judicial system (Turnbull, 1986).

Due process may be discriminatory because its cost may prohibit some families from following this procedure. The cost may involve both financial and human resources. The remaining problems are best summed up by Turnbull (1986):

> Problems remain. The greatest one seems to be the cost of due process. Cost consists of three elements: (1) the actual financial cost of the hearings; preparing for them, hiring attorneys and expert witnesses, paying for the documents required for evidence, and pursuing an appeal; (2) the emotional and psychic cost—the enormous energy and stress involved in a hearing and its appeal; and (3) the cost that consists of time spent and perhaps lost, when the child may (or may not) be receiving an appropriate education. (p. 192)

Because the financial cost may be so burdensome, educators are concerned that due process in IDEA may become yet another vehicle that increases rather than decreases discriminatory practices. Budoff and Orenstein (1981) found that due process hearings were overrepresented by upper-middle-class parents and recommended using mediation without counsel as an alternative to the expensive hearing process. The 1997 amendments that provide specific guidelines for mediation may result in more timely and economical resolutions. Engiles, Fromme, LeResche, and Moses suggested that there are strategies that schools and personnel can implement to increase participation in mediation of parents of culturally and linguistically diverse backgrounds (1999). These authors included strategies, at the system level as well as the practitioner level, to involve parents in mediation. Engiles et al. remind educators that some persons from various cultures do not believe that they should be involved in educational decisions, and others may not welcome the involvement of school personnel in family or personal matters. Increasing parental involvement and communication between parents and schools from the prereferral stage through the decision-making stage may decrease the need for both mediation and third-party hearings.

Should parents or schools exhaust the hearing process without satisfaction, the right remains for either party to take the case through the civil court system. IDEA continues to be interpreted through the judicial system.

ETHICS AND STANDARDS

In addition to the legal requirements of the process of assessment and planning in special and general education, ethical standards for practice have been established by professional organizations. In special education, standards of practice and policies have been set forth by the Council for Exceptional Children. The National Association of School Psychologists has established standards and ethics for professionals in the school psychology field. And the American Educational Research Association, the American Psychological Association, and the National Council on Measurement in Education have established the *Standards for Educational and Psychological Testing* (1999). These professional groups have policies regarding the education and assessment of students from culturally and linguistically diverse backgrounds.

Although professionals in the field of education and educational psychology are required by law to follow the regulations and federal mandates, the standards and ethics are established by professional groups to encourage professionalism and best practice. Sections of the standards, codes, and policies that are relevant to assessment and special education are included in the following pages.

The Standards of Practice set out by the Council for Exceptional Children (CEC) are similar to the federal regulations governing assessment, use of goals and objectives for planning, record keeping and confidential-

- Use assessment instruments and procedures that do not discriminate against persons with exceptionalities on the basis of race, color, creed, sex, national origin, age, political practices, family or social background, sexual orientation, or exceptionality.
- Base grading, promotion, graduation, and/or movement out of the program on the individual goals and objectives for individuals with exceptionalities.
- Provide accurate program data to administrators, colleagues, and parents, based on efficient and objective record keeping practices, for the purpose of decision making.
- Maintain confidentiality of information except when information is released under specific conditions of written consent and statutory confidentiality requirements.

Figure 2.4 CEC standards for professional practice relevant to the assessment and planning process.

ity, and decision-making practices. The standards relevant to assessment are presented in Figure 2.4.

The policies of CEC for students from various ethnic groups and migrant students are designed to assist with the decrease in the overrepresentation of minority students receiving special education support. These policies emphasize nondiscriminatory assessment practice, consideration of language dominance, and understanding of cultural heritage. The policy on migrant students focuses on the special educational needs of students who are from migrant families. This policy statement calls on educational professionals to understand that the assessment and programming procedures used for stationary students are not appropriate for migrant students. It further points out that the frequent disruptions in education affect the students' lives in both educational and social areas. This CEC statement also reminds professional educators that the eligibility requirements and other special education considerations often differ from state to state. The CEC policy statements are presented in Figures 2.5 and 2.6.

The National Association of School Psychologists revised the Professional Conduct Manual in 2000. There are sections that cover all areas of practice for psychologists working within the school setting. The general principles for assessment and intervention and reporting data and conference results are presented in Figure 2.7. The principles are consistent with the legal requirements for assessment and the evaluation process.

The Standards for Educational and Psychological Testing also contain standards for all areas of testing. The standards are also consistent with the federal regulations. For example, the standards include language regarding using multiple measures for reaching decisions about the individual's functioning, following standardized administration procedures, and confidentiality of test results and test instruments. Selected standards are presented in Figure 2.8.

Preamble

The Council believes that all policy statements previously adopted by CEC related to children with and without exceptionalities, as well as children with gifts and talents, are relevant and applicable to both minority and nonminority individuals. In order to highlight concerns of special interest to members of ethnic and multicultural groups, the following policy statements have been developed. (Chapter 08, Para. 1)

Ethnicity and Exceptionality

The Council recognizes the special and unique needs of members of ethnic and multicultural groups and pledges its full support toward promoting all efforts which will help to bring them into full and equitable participation and membership in the total society. (Chapter 08, Para. 2)

Identification, Testing, and Placement

The Council supports the following statements related to the identification, testing, and placement of children from ethnic and multicultural groups who are also exceptional.

a. Child-find procedures should identify children by ethnicity as well as type and severity of exceptionality or degree of giftedness.
b. Program service reporting procedures should identify children by ethnicity as well as exceptionality or degree of giftedness.
c. All testing and evaluation materials and methods used for the classification and placement of children from ethnic and multicultural groups should be selected and administered so as not to be racially or culturally discriminatory.
d. Children with exceptionalities who are members of ethnic and multicultural groups should be tested in their dominant language by examiners who are fluent in that language and familiar with the cultural heritage of the children being tested.
e. Communication of test results with parents of children from ethnic and multicultural groups should be done in the dominant language of those parents and conducted by persons involved in the testing or familiar with the particular exceptionality, fluent in that language, and familiar with the cultural heritage of those parents.

Figure 2.5 CEC policy on ethnic and multicultural groups relevant to the assessment and planning process. (*Source:* CEC Policies for Delivery of Services: Ethnic and Multicultural Groups. *CEC Policy Manual,* Section Three, part 1, pp. 6, 20–21.)

Preamble

Exceptional students who are mobile due to their parents' migrant employment, experience reduced opportunities for an appropriate education and a reduced likelihood of completing their education. Child-find and identification policies and practices, designed for a stationary population, are inadequate for children who move frequently. Incomplete, delayed, or inadequate transfer of records seriously impedes educational continuity. Interstate/provincial differences in special education eligibility requirements, programs and resources, minimum competency testing, and graduation requirements result in repetition of processing formalities, gaps in instruction, delays in the resumption of services, an inability to accumulate credits for graduation, and other serious inequities. In addition to the disruption of learning, mobility disrupts health care, training, teacher-student rapport, and personal relationships.

Figure 2.6 CEC policy on migrant students relevant to the assessment and planning process. (*Source:* CEC Policies for Delivery of Services: Ethnic and Multicultural Groups. *CEC Policy Manual,* Section Three, part 1, pp. 6, 20–21.)

C) Assessment and Intervention

1. School psychologists maintain the highest standard for educational and psychological assessment and direct and indirect interventions.
   a. In conducting psychological, educational, or behavioral evaluations or in providing therapy, counseling, or consultation services, due consideration is given to individual integrity and individual differences.
   b. School psychologists respect differences in age, gender, sexual orientation, and socioeconomic, cultural, and ethnic backgrounds. They select and use appropriate assessment or treatment procedures, techniques, and strategies. Decision-making related to assessment and subsequent interventions is primarily data-based.
2. School psychologists are knowledgeable about the validity and reliability of their instruments and techniques, choosing those that have up-to-date standardization data and are applicable and appropriate for the benefit of the child.
3. School psychologists use multiple assessment methods such as observations, background information, and information from other professionals, to reach comprehensive conclusions.
4. School psychologists use assessment techniques, counseling and therapy procedures, consultation techniques, and other direct and indirect service methods that the profession considers to be responsible, research-based practice.

Figure 2.7 Selected principles from the National Association of School Psychologists Professional Conduct Manual.

5. School psychologists do not condone the use of psychological or educational assessment techniques, or the misuse of the information these techniques provide, by unqualified persons in any way, including teaching, sponsorship, or supervision.
6. School psychologists develop interventions that are appropriate to the presenting problems and are consistent with data collected. They modify or terminate the treatment plan when the data indicate the plan is not achieving the desired goals.
7. School psychologists use current assessment and intervention strategies that assist in the promotion of mental health in the children they serve.

D) Reporting Data and Conference Results

1. School psychologists ascertain that information about children and other clients reaches only authorized persons.
   a. School psychologists adequately interpret information so that the recipient can better help the child or other clients.
   b. School psychologists assist agency recipients to establish procedures to properly safeguard confidential material.
2. School psychologists communicate findings and recommendations in language readily understood by the intended recipient. These communications describe potential consequences associated with the proposals.
3. School psychologists prepare written reports in such form and style that the recipient of the report will be able to assist the child or other clients. Reports should emphasize recommendations and interpretations; unedited computer-generated reports, preprinted "check-off" or "fill-in-the-blank" reports, and reports that present only test scores or global statements regarding eligibility for special education without specific recommendations for intervention are seldom useful. Reports should include an appraisal of the degree of confidence that could be assigned to the information. Alterations of previously released reports should be done only by the original author.
4. School psychologists review all of their written documents for accuracy, signing them only when correct. Interns and practicum students are clearly identified as such, and their work is co-signed by the supervising school psychologist. In situations in which more than one professional participated in the data collection and reporting process, school psychologists assure that sources of data are clearly identified in the written report.
5. School psychologists comply with all laws, regulations, and policies pertaining to the adequate storage and disposal of records to maintain appropriate confidentiality of information.

Figure 2.7 continued.

Standard	
5.1	Test administrators should follow carefully the standardized procedures for administration and scoring specified by the test developer, unless the situation or a test taker's disability dictates that an exception should be made. (p. 63)
5.7	Test users have the responsibility of protecting the security of test materials at all times. (p. 64)
10.1	In testing individuals with disabilities, test developers, test administrators, and test users should take steps to ensure that the test score inferences accurately reflect the intended construct rather than any disabilities and their associated characteristics extraneous to the intent of the measurement. (p. 106)
10.12	In testing individuals with disabilities for diagnostic and intervention purposes, the test should not be used as the sole indicator of the test taker's functioning. Instead, multiple sources of information should be used. (p. 108)
11.3	Responsibility for test use should be assumed by or delegated only to those individuals who have the training, professional credentials, and experience necessary to handle this responsibility. Any special qualifications for test administration or interpretation specified in the test manual should be met. (p. 114)
11.20	In educational, clinical, and counseling settings, a test taker's score should not be interpreted in isolation; collateral information that may lead to alternative explanations for the examinee's test performance should be considered. (p. 117)
12.11	Professionals and others who have access to test materials and test results should ensure the confidentiality of the test results and testing materials consistent with legal and professional ethics requirements. (pp. 132–133)
13.10	Those responsible for educational testing programs should ensure that the individuals who administer and score the test(s) are proficient in the appropriate test administration procedures and scoring procedures and that they understand the importance of adhering to the directions provided by the test developer. (p. 147)
13.13	Those responsible for educational testing programs should ensure that the individuals who interpret the test results to make decisions within the school context are qualified to do so or are assisted by and consult with persons who are so qualified. (p. 148)

Figure 2.8 Selected standards from the Standards for Educational and Psychological Testing. (*Source: Standards for educational and psychological testing,* Washington, DC: American Educational Research Association, 1999.)

CHAPTER SUMMARY

For more than 25 years federal regulations have been in place to provide all students having special needs with a free and appropriate education. In order to receive special education support, assessment and planning procedures, as set out in the regulations, must be completed. The regulations continue to be revised and strive to provide all students with appropriate education within the general education environment. Improvements in the regulations focus on increasing parental involvement and including more considerations for students from culturally and linguistically diverse backgrounds. Ethics and policies of professional organizations encourage educators and assessment personnel to consistently use best practice in assessment and planning procedures.

THINK AHEAD

The procedures used to understand the results of a student's performance on test instruments involve basic statistical methods (presented in chapter 3). Do you think tests using the same numerical scales can easily be compared?

EXERCISES

Part I

Match the following terms with the statements below.

a. Public Law 94-142
b. IDEA
c. IDEA Amendments of 1997
d. compliance
e. PL 99-457
f. due process
g. initial evaluation
h. comprehensive educational evaluation
i. informed consent
j. surrogate parent
k. consent form
l. parents' rights booklet
m. nondiscriminatory assessment
n. special education services
o. related services
p. grade equivalent
q. standard scores
r. annual goals
s. short-term objectives
t. least restrictive environment
u. transition services
v. procedural safeguards
w. mediation
x. independent educational evaluation
y. impartial due process hearing
z. impartial hearing officer
aa. Section 504 of the Rehabilitation Act of 1973
bb. minority overrepresentation

_____ 1. Mary, a student receiving special education services also needs the _____ of occupational therapy and speech therapy in order to benefit from her appropriate educational plan.

_____ 2. During the screening by educational professionals, it is determined that a student has significant educational needs and is therefore referred for a(n) _____.

_____ 3. The 1997 amendments stress that parents and educational personnel employ the method of _____ to resolve disagreements.

_____ 4. It is now required that all _____ included in IEPs be measurable.

_____ 5. A school system that meets appropriate timelines and follows all state and federal regulations is said to be in _____.

_____ 6. Parents who have a preschool-aged child with special needs may find assistance with obtaining educational services for their child through the federal regulations of _____.

_____ 7. In a specific school system, the ethnicity of the population was determined to include 17% of persons of Hispanic origin, yet more than 22% of the students receiving services for learning disabilities were of Hispanic origin. This system may have _____ of persons of Hispanic origin within the category of learning disabilities.

_____ 8. Short-term objectives are designed to assist the student in meeting _____.

_____ 9. A fifth-grade student was recently assessed and was found not eligible to receive special education support. His parents decided that they disagreed with the assessment and therefore requested information to obtain a(n) _____.

_____ 10. During a meeting of the child study team, the members determined that the prereferral intervention strategies employed with a third-grade student were not successful in remediating reading difficulties. The members must now obtain _____ in order to begin the assessment process.

_____ 11. Initially, the federal law that mandated a free and appropriate public education for all children with disabilities was called the Education for All Handicapped Children Act. In 1990, this was renamed _____.

_____ 12. A major principle of IDEA is that all evaluation measures used during the assessment process should yield similar results for children regardless of their ethnicity. This principle is known as _____.

Part II

Answer the following questions.

1. What were the sources of pressure that resulted in substantial legal changes in the 1970s?

   ____

2. According to IDEA, what agency is responsible for ensuring that proper assessment procedures are followed?
   ____
3. When are the local education agencies required to provide parents with procedural safeguards?
   (a) ____________________
   (b) ____________________
   (c) ____________________
   (d) ____________________
4. The nondiscriminatory assessment practices must, as a minimum, ensure that evaluation materials
   (a) ____________________
   (b) ____________________
   (c) ____________________
   (d) ____________________
   (e) ____________________
   (f) ____________________
   (g) ____________________
   (h) ____________________
5. Explain how the transition needs of students with special needs are addressed in IDEA.
6. In the IDEA, how are parents encouraged to participate in the assessment and decision-making process?
   ____
7. What specific evaluation procedures are included in the regulations for students with learning disabilities? ____________________
8. How are students with attention problems served in school?
   ____
   ____
9. How are the federal mandates interpreted over time?
   ____
   ____

Part III

Discuss the following:

1. The changes in the 1997 amendments regarding the resolution of differences between parents and schools in the assessment process.
   ____
   ____
   ____
   ____
   ____

2. Parental consent in the assessment process addressed in the 1997 amendments. ______

3. How students who are eligible for services participate in statewide assessments. ______

4. How students who are eligible for services participate in the general classroom with nondisabled peers or, if necessary, how they do not participate in such settings. ______

Part IV

Summarize the research findings.

1. Summarize the research findings on the IEP team decision-making process. ______

2. Explain how the research regarding third-party hearings may have had an impact on the changes concerning mediation in the 1997 amendments. ______

3. Summarize the difficulties of assessing students from culturally and linguistically diverse backgrounds. ______

ANSWER KEY FOR CHECK YOUR UNDERSTANDING

Activity 2.1

1. informed of activities
2. parents' rights booklet
3. release of records
4. revoke consent, due process
5. reevaluation, every 3 years
6. native language, mode of communication

Apply Your Knowledge. Confidential records and the information contained in the records are not to be released without the parents' consent. Therefore, any information included, such as test scores, family history, and psychological information, cannot be discussed by any person not directly involved with educating that student. Teachers (and student teachers) are thereby legally prohibited from discussing such information with anyone not involved with the professional concerns of the student.

Activity 2.2

1. Unfair—A screening test cannot be used for placement decisions; therefore, an individually administered diagnostic test as well as other educational measures (curriculum-based assessment and other informal measures) should be used to gather information about the student's functioning.
2. Fair—These professionals continue to be trained in the latest assessment methods.
3. Unfair—This assessment does not comply with any of the regulations required. Prereferral interventions should be employed, and the student should be studied extensively before a referral for an evaluation is made.
4. Fair—This test has been especially validated with this specific population and is considered to be nondiscriminatory.
5. Fair—This professional has requested the assistance of the appropriate personnel.
6. Unfair—The decisions made regarding interventions and special education support require the use of multiple measures.

Apply Your Knowledge. You may require the assistance of another professional at any point in the assessment process during which you are uncertain about school policies, procedures, and state and federal guidelines, as well as when you are uncertain about the administration and scoring of an assessment instrument. You may also need to ask for assistance when you encounter a student with a disability with which you are not familiar. In short, whenever in doubt, ask. It is in the best interest of your students to do so.

Activity 2.3

1. school nurse and parent of the student
2. occupational therapist
3. parent of the student and the school nurse
4. a teacher of students with learning disabilities to determine appropriate interventions and in-class assessment strategies
5. school psychologist, school counselor, and parents of student

Apply Your Knowledge. If you are not certain whom to ask for guidance, first ask your school principal or special education supervisor. Many new teachers have a special education mentor who provides guidance during the first two or three years of teaching.

Activity 2.4

At a minimum, the following were out of compliance with the federal regulations:

1. Ms. Nogood referred without any prereferral interventions.
2. There was no child study committee to determine whether assessment was needed.
3. There was no informed consent.
4. An inappropriate measure was used, and only one measure was used.
5. The student was not assessed by a multidisciplinary team.
6. The effort made to have the parents attend was minimal.
7. The placement decision was not made by the IEP team (including the parents as members).

Apply Your Knowledge. Ms. Nogood should study this student and then make prereferral interventions. If needed, additional assessment in the classroom should form the basis for a referral. Following the child study team's recommendation and informed consent of the parents, the student will then be assessed according to an individual assessment plan. The results are shared with the team (including the parents), and a decision is reached by the team. The parents must agree to the services recommended. Only then can the student begin to receive services.

REFERENCES

American Educational Research Association (AERA), American Psychological Association (APA), & National Council on Measurement in Education (NCME) (1999). *Standards for educational and psychological testing.* Washington, DC: AERA.

Barnett, D., Zins, J., & Wise, L. (1984). An analysis of parental participation as a means of reducing bias in the education of handicapped children. *Special Services in the Schools, 1,* 71–84.

Bennett, R. (1981). Professional competence and the assessment of exceptional children. *Journal of Special Education, 15,* 437–446.

Bennett, R., & Shepherd, M. (1982). Basic measurement proficiency of learning disability specialists. *Learning Disabilities Quarterly, 5,* 177–183.

Bennett, T., Lee, H., & Lueke, B. (1998). Expectations and concerns: What mothers and fathers say about inclusion. *Education and Training in Mental Retardation and Developmental Disabilities, 33*(2), 108–122.

Bocian, K. M., Beebe, M. E., MacMillan, D., & Gresham, F. M. (1999). Competing paradigms in learning disabilities classification by schools and the variations in the meaning of discrepant achievement. *Learning Disabilities Research, 14*(1), 1–14.

Brantlinger, E. (1987). Making decisions about special education placement: Do low-income parents have the information they need? *Journal of Learning Disabilities, 20,* 94–101.

Budoff, M., & Orenstein, A. (1981). Special education appeals hearings: Are they fair and are they helping? *Exceptional Education Quarterly, 2,* 37–48.

Burger, S. E., & Burger, D. L. (1994). Determining the validity of performance-based assessment. *Educational Measurement: Issues and Practices, 13,* 9–15.

Council for Exceptional Children (1997–1999). Standards for professional practice. Reston, VA: Author.

Council for Exceptional Children (1993). CEC policies for delivery of services: Ethnic and multicultural groups. *CEC Policy Manual,* section 3, part 1 (pp. 6, 20–21). Reston, VA: Author.

Education of the Handicapped Act (1975, 1977). PL 94-142, 20 U.S.C. §§ 1400–1485, 34 CFR-300.

Engiles, A., Fromme, C., LeResche, D., & Moses, P. (1999). *Keys to access: Encouraging the use of mediation by families from diverse backgrounds.* (Document No. EC 307 554). Consortium for Appropriate Dispute Resolution in Special Education. (ERIC Document Reproduction Service No. ED 436 881)

Federal Register (1977, August 23). Washington, DC: U.S. Government Printing Office.

Federal Register (1992, September 29). Washington, DC: U.S. Government Printing Office.

Federal Register (1993, July 30). Washington, DC: U.S. Government Printing Office.

Federal Register (1999, March 12). Washington, DC: U.S. Government Printing Office.

Flaugher, R. (1978). The many definitions of test bias. *American Psychologist, 33,* 671–679.

Fradd, S., & Hallman, C. (1983). Implications of psychological and educational research for assessment and instruction of culturally and linguistically different students. *Learning Disabilities Quarterly, 6,* 468–477.

Fuchs, D., Fuchs, L., Benowitz, S., & Barringer, K. (1987). Norm-referenced tests: Are they valid for uses with handicapped students? *Exceptional Children, 54,* 263–271.

Goldstein, S., Strickland, B., Turnbull, A., & Curry, L. (1980). An observational analysis of the IEP conference. *Exceptional Children, 46,* 278–286.

Goldstein, S., & Turnbull, A. (1982). Strategies to increase parent participation in IEP conferences. *Exceptional Children, 48,* 360–361.

Gresham, F. M., MacMillan, D. L., & Bocian, K. M. (1998). Agreement between school study team decisions and authoritative definitions in classifications of students at-risk for mild disabilities. *School Psychology Quarterly, 13*(3), 181–191.

Hasazi, S. B., Johnston, A. P., Liggett, A. M., & Schattman, R. A. (1994). A qualitative policy study of the least restrictive environment provision of the Individuals with Disabilities Education Act. *Exceptional Children, 60,* 491–507.

Huebner, E. S. (1991). Bias in special education decisions: The contribution of analogue research. *School Psychology Quarterly, 6*(1), 50–65.

Huefner, D. S. (2000). The risks and opportunities of the IEP requirements under the IDEA '97. *Journal of Special Education, 33*(4), 195–204.

Individuals with Disabilities Education Act (IDEA, 20 U.S.C. § 1400 et seq. (1997).

Individuals with Disabilities Education Act Regulations, 34, CFR. §§ 300 and 303 (1999).

Jackson, G. D. (1975). Another psychological view from the Association of Black Psychologists. *American Psychologist, 30,* 88–93.

Katsiyannis, A. (1994). Prereferral practices: Under Office of Civil Rights scrutiny. *Journal of Developmental and Physical Disabilities, 6,* 73–76.

Klinger, J. K., Vaughn, S., Schumm, J. S., Cohen, P., & Forgan, J. W. (1998). Inclusion or pull-out: Which do students prefer? *Journal of Learning Disabilities, 31,* 148–158.

Kubicek, F. C. (1994). Special education reform in light of select state and federal court decisions. *Journal of Special Education, 28,* 27–42.

Larry P. v. Riles, 343 F. Supp. 1306, aff'd., 502 F.2d 963, further proceedings, 495 F. Supp. 926, aff'd., 502 F.2d 693 (9th Cir. 1984).

Lipsky, D. K., & Gartner, A. (1997). *Inclusion and school reform: Transforming America's classrooms.* Baltimore, MD: Brookes Publishing.

Lopez, E. C. (1995). Best practices in working with bilingual children. In Alex Thomas and Jeff Grimes (Eds.), *Best Practices in School Psychology* (3rd ed.), p. 1113. Bethesda, MD: National Association of School Psychologists.

MacMillan, D. L., & Forness, S. R. (1998). The role of IQ in special education placement decisions: Primary and determinative or peripheral and inconsequential. *Remedial and Special Education, 19,* 239–253.

MacMillan, D. L., Gresham, F. M., & Bocian, K. (1998). Discrepancy between definitions of learning disabilities and school practices: An empirical investigation. *Journal of Learning Disabilities, 32*(4), 314–326.

Macready, T. (1991). Special education: Some thoughts for policy makers. *Educational Psychology in Practice, 7*(3), 148–152.

McLaughlin, M. J., & Owings, M. F. (1992). Relationship among states' fiscal and demographic data and the implementation of P.L. 94-142. *Exceptional Children, 59,* 247–261.

McNutt, G., & Mandelbaum, L. (1980). General assessment competencies for special education teachers. *Exceptional Education Quarterly, 1,* 21–29.

Morsink, C. V., & Lenk, L. L. (1992). The delivery of special education programs and services. *Remedial and Special Education, 13*(6), 33–43.

National Association of School Psychologists (2000). *National Association of School Psychologists Professional Conduct Manual: Principles for professional ethics; guidelines for the provision of school psychologists.* Bethesda, MD: Author.

Patton, J. M. (1998). The disproportionate representation of African Americans in special education: Looking behind the curtain for understanding and solutions. *Journal of Special Education, 32,* 25–31.

Reynolds, C. R., Lowe, P. A., & Saenz, A. L. (1999). The problems of bias in psychological assessment. In C. R. Reynolds & T. Gutkin (Eds.), *The Handbook of School Psychology* (3rd ed.), pp. 556–557. New York: Wiley.

Ruehl, M. E. (1998). Educating the child with severe behavioral problems: Entitlement, empiricism, and ethics. *Behavioral Disorders, 23,* 184–192.

Salend, S. J., & Taylor, L. (1993). Working with families: A cross-cultural perspective. *Remedial and Special Education, 14*(5), 25–32, 39.

Sapp, G., Chissom, B., & Horton, W. (1984). An investigation of the ability of selected instruments to discriminate areas of exceptional class designation. *Psychology in the Schools, 5,* 258–262.

Scruggs, T. E., & Mastropieri, M. A. (1996). Teacher perceptions of mainstreaming/inclusion, 1958–1995: A research synthesis. *Exceptional Children, 63,* 59–74.

Section 504 of the Rehabilitation Act of 1973, 29 U.S.C. § 794 et seq.

Sheridan, S. M., Cowan, P. J., & Eagle, J. W. (2000). Partnering with parents in educational programming for students with special needs. In C.F. Telzrow &

M. Tankersley (Eds.), *IDEA Amendments of 1997: Practice Guidelines for School-Based Teams*. Bethesda, MD: National Association of School Psychologists.

Sherman, A. (1994). *Wasting America's future: The Children's Defense Fund report on the cost of child poverty*. Boston: Beacon Press.

Silver, S. (1987). *Compliance with PL 94-142 mandates: Policy implications*. (ERIC Document Reproduction Service No. ED 284 705)

Smith, C. R. (1997). Advocacy for students with emotional and behavioral disorders: One call for redirected efforts. *Behavioral Disorders, 22*(2), 96–105.

Sontag, J. C., & Schacht, R. (1994). An ethnic comparison of parent and information needs in early intervention. *Exceptional Children, 60,* 422–433.

Telzrow, C. F., & Tankersley, M. (2000). *IDEA: Amendments of 1997: Practice Guidelines for School-Based Teams*. Bethesda, MD: National Association of School Psychologists.

Turnbull, H. R. (1986). *Free and appropriate public education: The law and children with disabilities*. Denver: Love Publishing.

Turnbull, H. R. (1990). *Free and appropriate public education: The law and children with disabilities* (3rd ed.). Denver: Love Publishing.

Turnbull, H. R., Turnbull, A. P., & Strickland, B. (1979). Procedural due process: The two-edged sword that the untrained should not unsheath. *Journal of Education, 161,* 40–59.

U.S. Department of Education (1991). *Memorandum to chief state school officers*. Washington, DC: Author.

U.S. Department of Education. (1997). *Nineteenth annual report to Congress on the implementation of the Individuals with Disabilities Education Act*. Washington, DC: Author.

U.S. Department of Education (1999). *Assistance to states for the education of children with disabilities and the early intervention program for infants and toddlers with disabilities: Final regulations*. Washington DC: Author.

Valles, E. C. (1998). The disproportionate representation of minority students in special education: Responding to the problem. *Journal of Special Education, 32,* 52–54.

Vaughn, S., Bos, C., Harrell, J., & Lasky, B. (1988). Parent participation in the initial placement/IEP conference ten years after mandated involvement. *Journal of Learning Disabilities, 21,* 82–89.

Ward, S. B., Ward, T. J., & Clark, H. T. (1991). Classification congruence among school psychologists and its relationship to type of referral question and professional experience. *Journal of School Psychology, 29,* 89–108.

Weber, J., & Stoneman, Z. (1986). Parental nonparticipation as a means of reducing bias in the education of handicapped children. *Special Services in the Schools, 1,* 71–84.

Yell, M. L. (1995). Least restrictive environment, inclusion and students with disabilities: A legal analysis. *Journal of Special Education, 28,* 389–404.

Yell, M. L. (1997). *The law and special education*. Upper Saddle River, NJ: Prentice-Hall.

Yell, M. L., Drasgow, E., & Ford, L. (2000). The individuals with disabilities education act amendments of 1997: Implications for school-based teams. In Telzrow, C. F., & Tankersley, M. (Eds.), *IDEA: Amendments of 1997: Practice Guidelines for School-Based Teams* (pp. 1–28). Bethesda, MD: National Association of School Psychologists.

Ysseldyke, J., & Thurlow, M. (1983). *Identification/classification research: An integrative summary of findings* (Research Report No. 142). Minneapolis: University of Minnesota, Institute for Research on Learning Disabilities.

PART 2

Technical Prerequisites of Understanding Assessment

Chapter 3 **Descriptive Statistics**

Chapter 4 **Reliability and Validity**

Chapter 5 **An Introduction to Norm-Referenced Assessment**

CHAPTER 3

Descriptive Statistics

Key Terms

raw score
norm-referenced tests
nominal scale
ordinal scale
interval scale
ratio scale
derived scores
standard scores
descriptive statistics
measures of central tendency
normal distribution
frequency distribution
mode
bimodal distribution
multimodal distribution
frequency polygon
median
mean
standard deviation
variability
measures of dispersion
variance
range
skewed
positively skewed
negatively skewed
percentile ranks
z scores

CHAPTER FOCUS

This chapter presents the basic statistical concepts needed to interpret information from standardized assessment.

WHY IS MEASUREMENT IMPORTANT?

Psychoeducational assessment using standardized instruments historically has been applied in the educational decision-making process. To properly use standardized instruments, one must understand test-selection criteria, basic principles of measurement, administration techniques, and scoring procedures. Careful interpretation of test results relies on these abilities. Thus, research that questions the assessment competence of special educators and other professionals is frightening because the educational future of so many individuals is at risk.

Of concern are studies indicating typical types of mistakes made by professionals in the field: Professionals identified students as eligible for services when test scores were within the average range and relied instead on referral information to make decisions (Algozzine & Ysseldyke, 1981). Data presented during educational planning conferences played little if any part in the team members' decisions (Ysseldyke, Algozzine, Richey, & Graden, 1982). Professionals continued to select poor-quality instruments when better tests were available (Davis & Shepard, 1983; Ysseldyke, Algozzine, Regan, & Potter, 1980).

Research by Huebner (1988, 1989) indicated that professionals made errors in the diagnosis of learning disabilities more frequently when scores were reported in percentiles. This reflects inadequate understanding of data interpretation.

Eaves (1985) cited common errors made by professionals during the assessment process. Some of the test examiners' most common errors, adapted from Eaves's research, include

1. Using instruments in the assessment process solely because those instruments are stipulated by school administrators.
2. Regularly using instruments for purposes other than those for which tests have been validated.
3. Taking the recommended use at face value.
4. Using the quickest instruments available even though those instruments may not assess the areas of concern.
5. Using currently popular instruments for assessment.
6. Failing to establish effective rapport with the examinee.
7. Failing to document behaviors of the examinee during assessment that may be of diagnostic value.

8. Failing to adhere to standardized administration rules, which may include
   a. Failing to follow starting rules.
   b. Failing to follow basal and ceiling rules.
   c. Omitting actual incorrect responses on the protocol, which could aid in error analysis and diagnosis.
   d. Failing to determine actual chronological age or grade placement.
9. Making various scoring errors, such as
   a. Making simple counting errors.
   b. Making simple subtraction errors.
   c. Counting items above the ceiling as correct or items below the basal as incorrect.
   d. Entering the wrong norm table, row, or column to obtain a derived score.
   e. Extensively using developmental scores when inappropriate.
   f. Showing lack of knowledge regarding alternative measures of performance.
10. Ineffectively interpreting assessment results for educational program use. (pp. 26–27)

The occurrence of such errors illustrates why educators need a basic understanding of the measurement principles used in assessment. McLoughlin (1985) advocated training special educators to the level of superior practice rather than meeting only minimum competencies of psychoeducational assessment. The *Standards for Educational and Psychological Testing* (APA, 1985) warn that when special educators have little or no training in the basic principles of measurement, assessment instruments could be misused.

Much of the foundation of good practice in psychoeducational assessment lies in a thorough understanding of test reliability and validity as well as basic measurement principles. Borg, Worthen, and Valcarce (1986) found that most teachers believe that understanding basic principles of measurement is an important aspect of classroom teaching and evaluation. Yet research has shown that professionals who were believed to be specialists in working with students with learning problems were able to correctly answer only 50% of the items on a test of measurement principles (Bennett & Shepherd, 1982). As a result, this chapter is designed to promote the development of a basic understanding of general principles of measurement and the application of those principles.

GETTING MEANING FROM NUMBERS

raw score The first score obtained in testing; usually represents the number of items correct.

Any teacher who scores a test, either published or teacher-made, will subtract the number of items a student missed from the number of items presented to the student. This number, known as the **raw score,** is of little value to the teacher unless a frame of reference exists for that number. The frame of reference might be comparing the number of items the student answered correctly with the number the student answered correctly on the previous day (e.g., Monday, 5 out of 10 responses correct; Tuesday, 6 out of 10 responses correct; etc.). The frame of reference might be a national sample of students the same age who attempted the same items in the same manner on a **norm-referenced** standardized test. In all cases, teachers must clearly understand what can and cannot be inferred from numerical data gathered on small samples of behavior known as *tests*.

norm-referenced tests Tests designed to compare an individual student's scores with national averages.

The techniques used to obtain raw scores are discussed in chapter 5. Raw scores are used to obtain the other scores presented in this chapter.

REVIEW OF NUMERICAL SCALES

Numbers can denote different meanings from different scales. The scale that has the least meaning for educational measurement purposes is the **nominal scale.** The nominal scale consists of numbers used only for identification purposes, such as student ID numbers or the numbers on race cars. These numbers cannot be used in mathematical operations. For example, if race cars were labeled with letters of the alphabet rather than with numerals, it would make no difference in the outcome of the race. Numbers on a nominal scale function like names.

nominal scale Numerical scale that uses numbers for the purpose of identification.

When numbers are used to rank the order of objects or items, those numbers are said to be on the **ordinal scale.** An ordinal scale is used to rank the order of the winners in a science fair. The winner has the first rank, or number 1, the runner-up has the second rank, or number 2, and so on. In this scale, the numbers have the quality of identification and indicate greater or lesser quality. The ordinal scale, however, does not have the quality of using equidistant units. For example, suppose the winners of a bike race were ranked as they came in, with the winner ranked as first, the runner-up as second, and the third bike rider as third. The distance between the winner and the second-place bike rider might be 9 seconds, and the difference between the second- and third-place bike riders might be 30 seconds. While the numbers do rank the bike riders, they do not represent equidistant units.

ordinal scale Numerical scale in which numbers are used for ranking.

Numbers that are used for identification that rank greater or lesser quality or amount and that are equidistant are numbers used on an **interval scale.** An example is the scale used in measuring temperature. The degrees on the thermometer can be added or subtracted—a reading of 38°F is 10° less than a reading of 48°F. The interval scale does not have an absolute zero quality. For example, zero degrees does not indicate that there is no temperature. The numbers used on an interval scale also cannot be used in other mathematical operations, such as multiplication. Is a reading of 100°F really four times as hot as 25°F? An interval scale used in assessment is the IQ scale. IQ numbers are equidistant, but they do not possess additional numerical properties. A person with an IQ of 66 cannot be called two-thirds as smart as a person with an IQ of 99.

interval scale A scale that uses numbers for ranking in which numerical units are equidistant.

When numbers on a scale are equidistant from each other and have a true meaning of absolute zero, they can be used in all mathematical operations. This **ratio scale** allows for direct comparisons and mathematical manipulations.

ratio scale Numerical scale with quality of equidistant units and absolute zero.

When scoring tests and interpreting data, it is important to understand which numerical scale the numbers represent and to realize the properties and limitations of that scale. Understanding what test scores represent may decrease errors such as attributing more meaning to a particular score than should be allowed by the nature of the numerical scale.

Check Your Understanding

Complete Activity 3.1.

ACTIVITY 3.1

Use the following terms to complete the sentences and answer the questions.

nominal scale ordinal scale
interval scale ratio scale

1. Measuring with a thermometer is an example of using numbers on the ______________ scale.
2. Which scale(s) can be added and subtracted but not multiplied? ______________
3. The ribbons awarded in a painting contest illustrate which scale? ______________
4. Numbers pinned on the shirts of runners in a marathon are numbers used on the ______________ scale.
5. The ______________ scale has a true meaning of absolute zero.

Apply Your Knowledge

Which of the numerical scales is used to determine your semester GPA? ______________

DESCRIPTIVE STATISTICS

When assessing a student's behavior or performance for the purpose of educational intervention, it is often necessary to determine the amount of difference or deviance that the student exhibits in a particular area from the expected level for his age or grade. By looking at how much difference exists in samples of behavior, educational decision makers and parents can appropriately plan interventions. As previously mentioned, obtaining a raw score will not help with educational planning unless the evaluator has a frame of reference for that score. A raw score may have meaning when

derived scores Scores obtained by using a raw score and expectancy tables.

standard scores Derived scores that represent equal units; also known as *linear scores*.

descriptive statistics Statistics used to organize and describe data.

compared with previous student performance, or a raw score may be used to gain information from another set of scores called **derived scores.** Derived scores may be scores such as percentile ranks, **standard scores,** grade equivalents, age equivalents, or language quotients. Many derived scores obtain meaning from large sets of data or large samples of scores. By observing how a large sample of students the same age or grade level performed on the same tasks, it becomes possible to compare a particular student with the large group to see if that student performed as well as the group, better than the group, or not as well as the group.

Large sets of data are organized and understood through methods known as **descriptive statistics.** As the name implies, these are statistical operations that help educators understand and describe sets of data.

MEASURES OF CENTRAL TENDENCY

measures of central tendency Statistical methods for observing how data cluster around the mean.

normal distribution A symmetrical distribution with a single numerical representation for the mean, median, and mode.

One way to organize and describe data is to see how the data fall together, or cluster. This type of statistics is called **measures of central tendency.** Measures of central tendency are methods to determine how scores cluster—that is, how they are distributed around a numerical representation of the average score.

One common type of distribution used in assessment is called a **normal distribution.** A normal distribution has particular qualities that, when understood, help with the interpretation of assessment data. A normal distribution hypothetically represents the way test scores would fall if a particular test is given to every single student of the same age or grade in the population for whom the test was designed. If educators could administer an instrument in this way and obtain a normal distribution, the scores would fall in the shape of a bell curve, as shown in Figure 3.1.

In a graph of a normal distribution of scores, a very large number of the students tested are represented by all of the scores in the middle, or the "hump" part, of the curve. Because fewer students obtain extremely high or low scores, their scores are plotted or represented on the extreme ends of the curve. It is assumed that the same number of students obtained the higher scores as obtained the lower scores. The distribution is symmetric, or equal, on either side of the vertical line. The normal distribution is dis-

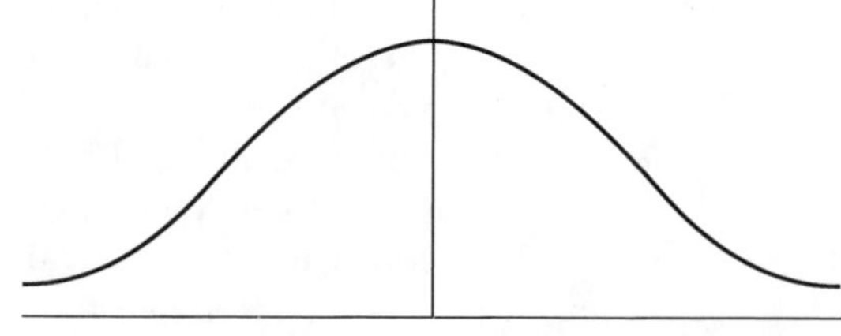

Figure 3.1 Normal distribution of scores, shown by the bell curve.

cussed throughout the text. One method of interpreting norm-referenced tests is to assume the principles of normal distribution theory and employ the measures of central tendency.

AVERAGE PERFORMANCE

Although educators are familiar with the average grade of C on a letter-grading system (interval scale), the numerical ranking of the C grade might be 70 to 79 in one school and 76 to 84 in another. If the educator does not understand the numerical meaning of *average* for a student, the letter grade of C has little value. The educator must know how the other students performed and what type of performance or score indicates average, what score is considered excellent, and what score is considered poor. To determine this, the teacher must determine what is considered average for that specific set of data.

frequency distribution Method of determining how many times each score occurs in a set of data.

One way to look at a set of data is to rank the scores from highest to lowest. This helps the teacher see how the group performed. After ranking the data in this fashion, it is helpful to complete a **frequency distribution** by counting how frequently each score occurred. Here is an example of 39 test scores, which the teacher ranked and then counted to record frequency:

DATA SET A

Score	Tally	Frequency
100	|	1
99	|	1
98	||	2
94	||	2
90	~~||||~~	5
89	~~||||~~ ||	7
88	~~||||~~ ~~||||~~	10
82	~~||||~~ |	6
75	||	2
74	|	1
68	|	1
60	|	1

Check Your Understanding

Complete Activity 3.2.

ACTIVITY 3.2

Place the following set of data in rank order and complete a frequency count.

Data Set B

92, 98, 100, 98, 92, 83, 73, 96, 90, 61, 70, 89, 87, 70, 85, 70, 66, 85, 62, 82

Score	Tally	Frequency	Score	Tally	Frequency
_____			_____		
_____			_____		
_____			_____		
_____			_____		
_____			_____		
_____			_____		
_____			_____		
_____			_____		

Apply Your Knowledge

Which of the numerical scales can be rank ordered? ______________

By arranging the data in this order and tallying the frequency of each score, the teacher can determine a trend in the performance of the class.

mode The most frequently occurring score in a set of scores.

Another way to look at the data is to determine the most frequently occurring score, or the **mode.** The mode can give the teacher an idea of how the group performed because it indicates the score or performance that occurred the most number of times. The mode for data set A (p. 103) was 88 because it occurred 10 times. In data set B (Activity 3.2), the mode was 70.

Check Your Understanding

Complete Activity 3.3.

ACTIVITY 3.3

Rank order the following set of data, complete a frequency count, and determine the mode.

Data Set C

62, 63, 51, 42, 78, 81, 81, 63, 75, 92, 94, 77, 63, 75, 96, 88, 60, 50, 49, 74

Score	Tally	Frequency	Score	Tally	Frequency
_____			_____		
_____			_____		
_____			_____		
_____			_____		
_____			_____		
_____			_____		
_____			_____		
_____			_____		

The mode is _____

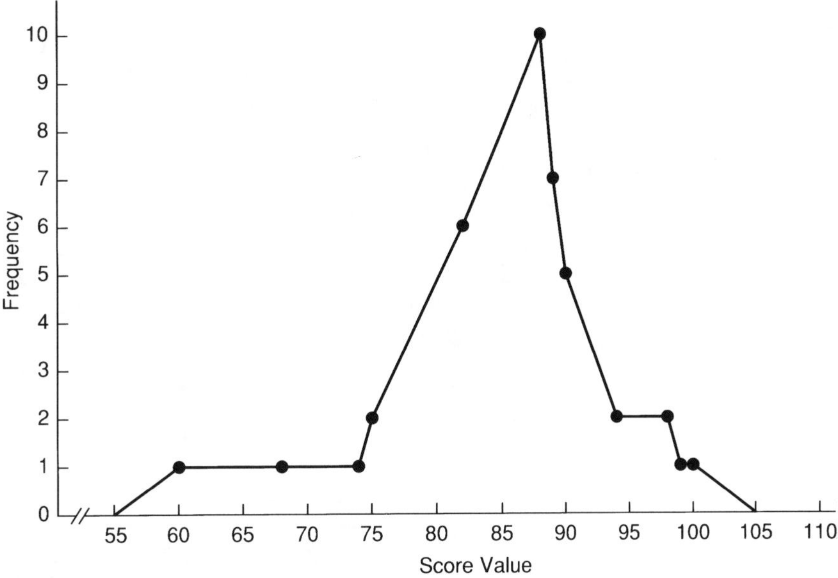

Figure 3.2 Frequency polygon for data set A.

> ***Apply Your Knowledge***
>
> What do you think it would mean to the teacher if the data of three sets of exams were distributed so that the mode always occurred at the high end of the scores? ______________________________
> ____

bimodal distribution A distribution that has two most frequently occurring scores.

multimodal distribution A distribution with three or more modes.

frequency polygon A graphic representation of how often each score occurs in a set of data.

Some sets of data have two modes or two most frequently occurring scores. This type of distribution of scores is known as a **bimodal distribution.** A distribution with three or more modes is called a **multimodal distribution.**

A clear representation of the distribution of a set of data can be illustrated graphically with a **frequency polygon.** A frequency polygon is a graph with test scores represented on the horizontal axis and the number of occurrences, or frequencies, represented on the vertical axis, as shown for data set A in Figure 3.2.

Check Your Understanding

Complete Activity 3.4.

> ***ACTIVITY 3.4***
>
> Rank order the data, complete a frequency count, and make a frequency polygon.

Data Set D

50, 52, 68, 67, 51, 89, 88, 76, 76, 88, 88, 68, 90, 91, 98, 69, 89, 88, 76, 76, 82, 85, 72, 85, 88, 76, 94, 82

Score	Tally	Frequency	Score	Tally	Frequency
____			____		
____			____		
____			____		
____			____		
____			____		
____			____		
____			____		
____			____		

Draw the frequency polygon here:

45 50 55 60 65 70 75 80 85 90 95 100

Apply Your Knowledge

What type of distribution did you plot using data set D? ____________

median The middlemost score in a set of data.

The data that have been rank ordered and for which a mode or modes have been determined give the teacher some idea of how the students performed as a group. Another method of determining how the group performed is to find the middlemost score, or the **median.** After the data have been rank ordered, the teacher can merely count halfway down the list of scores; however, each score must be listed each time it occurs. For example, here is a rank-ordered set of data for which the median has been determined:

100
97
89
85

85
78
78 median score
79
79
79
68
62
60

The median score has 50% of the data listed above it and 50% of the data listed below it. In this example, six of the scores are listed above 78 and six are listed below the median. Notice that although 78 is the median, it is not the mode for this set of data. In a normal distribution, which is distributed symmetrically, the median and the mode are represented by the same number.

In a set of data with an even number of scores, the median is the middlemost score even though the score may not actually exist in that set of data. For example,

100
96
95
90
85
83
82
80
78
77

The scores 85 and 83 occur in the middle of this distribution; therefore, the median is 84, even though 84 is not one of the scores.

Check Your Understanding

Complete Activity 3.5.

ACTIVITY 3.5

Find the median for the following sets of data.

Data Set E	Data Set F
100	88
99	88

Data Set E	Data Set F
96	88
88	86
84	80
83	76
82	75
79	74
76	70
75	68
70	
62	
60	
Median: _____	Median: _____

Apply Your Knowledge

Data set E has a higher median. Did the students represented by data set E perform significantly better than the students represented by data set F? Why or why not? Explain your answer. ____________

____

mean Arithmetic average of a set of data.

Although the mode and median indicate how a group performed, these measures of central tendency do not accurately describe the average, or typical, performance. One of the best measures of average performance is the arithmetic average, or **mean,** of the group of scores. The mean is calculated as a simple average: Add the scores and divide by the number of scores in the set of data. For example:

90
80
75
60
70
65
80
100
80
80

780 ÷ 10 = 78

The sum of the scores is 780. There are 10 scores in the set of data. Therefore, the sum, 780, is divided by the number of scores, 10. The average, or typical, score for this set of data is 78, which represents the arithmetic average.

Often teachers choose to use the mean score to represent the average score on a particular test or assignment. If this score seems to represent the typical performance on the specific test, the teacher may assign a letter grade of C to the numerical representation of the mean score. However, as discussed next, extremely high or low scores can render the mean misrepresentative of the average performance of the class.

Check Your Understanding

Complete Activity 3.6.

ACTIVITY 3.6

Find the mean, median, and mode for each set of data.

Data Set G

90, 86, 80, 87, 86, 82, 87, 92

Mean: _____ Median: _____ Mode: _____

Data Set H

41, 42, 45, 42, 46, 47, 48, 47, 41, 41

Mean: _____ Median: _____ Mode: _____

Apply Your Knowledge

Using the mean, median, and mode you obtained for data sets G and H, can you determine which group of students performed in a more similar manner as a group? Explain your answer. ____________

____

Using measures of central tendency is one way teachers can determine which score represents an average performance for a particular group on a particular measure. This aids the teacher in monitoring student progress and knowing when a student is performing well above or well below the norm or average of the group.

The mean can be affected by an extreme score, especially if the group is composed of only a few students. A very high score can raise the mean, whereas a very low score can lower the mean. For this reason, the teacher may wish to omit an extreme score before averaging the data. If scores seem to be widely dispersed, or scattered, using measures of central tendency may not be in the students' best interests. Moreover, such scatter may suggest that the teacher needs to qualitatively evaluate the students' performance and other factors such as teaching methods.

In research and test development, it is necessary to strive for and understand the normal distribution. Because of the symmetrical quality of the normal curve, the mean, median, and mode are all represented by the same number. For example, on tests measuring intelligence, the mean IQ is 100. One hundred is also the middlemost score (median) and the most frequently occurring score (mode). In fact, more than 68% of all of the IQ scores will cluster within one **standard deviation,** or one determined typical unit, above and below the score of 100. The statistic known as standard deviation is very important in special education assessment when the use of tests that compare an individual student with a norm-referenced group is necessary. Finding the standard deviation is one method of calculating difference in scores, or **variability** of scores, known as dispersion.

standard deviation A unit of measurement that represents the typical amount that a score can be expected to vary from the mean in a given set of data.

variability Describes how scores vary.

MEASURES OF DISPERSION

Because special educators must determine the degree or amount of difference exhibited by individuals in behaviors, skills, or traits, they must employ methods of calculating difference from the average or expected score. Just as measures of central tendency are used to see how sets of data cluster together around an average score, **measures of dispersion** are used to calculate how scores are spread from the mean.

The way that scores in a set of data are spread apart is known as the variability of the scores, or how much the scores vary from each other. When scores fall very close together and are not widely spread apart, the data are described as not having much variability, or **variance.**

measures of dispersion Statistical methods for observing how data spread from the mean.

variance Describes the total amount that a group of scores varies in a set of data.

Compare the following two sets of data:

Data Set I		**Data Set J**	
100	75	98	75
98	75	96	75
95	75	87	75
91	72	78	75
88	70	75	72
87	69	75	72
82	68	75	72
80	67	75	72
75	51	75	72
75	50	75	72

range The distance between the highest and lowest scores in a data set.

An easy way to get an idea about the spread is to find the **range** of scores. The range is calculated by subtracting the lowest score from the highest score.

Set I	**Set J**
100 − 50 = 50	98 − 72 = 26

The range for set J is about half that of set I. It appears that set I has more variability than set J. Look at the sets of data again. Both sets have the same median and the same mode, yet they are very different in terms of variability. When the means are calculated, it seems that the data are very similar. Set I has a mean of 77.15, and set J has a mean of 77.05. By using only measures of central tendency, the teacher may think that the students in both of these classes performed in a very similar manner on this test. Yet one set of data has approximately twice the spread, or variability of scores. In educational testing, it is necessary to determine the deviation from the mean in order to have a clearer picture of how students in groups such as these performed. By calculating the variance and the standard deviation, the teacher can find out the typical amount of difference from the mean. By knowing these typical or standard deviations from the mean, the teacher will be able to find out which scores are a significant distance from the average score.

To find the standard deviation of a set of scores, the variance must first be calculated. The variance can be described as the degree or amount of variability or dispersion in a set of scores. Looking at data sets I and J, one could probably assume that set I would have a larger variance than J.

Four steps are involved in calculating the variance:

Step 1 To calculate the amount of distance of each score from the mean, subtract the mean for the set of data from each score.

Step 2 Find the square of each of the difference scores found in step 1 (multiply each difference score by itself).

Step 3 Find the total of all of the squared score differences. This is called the sum of squares.

Step 4 Calculate the average of the sum of squares by dividing the total by the number of scores.

Data Set I

	Step 1: Difference	**Step 2: Multiply by Itself**		**Squared**
100 − 77.15 =	22.85	22.85 × 22.85	=	522.1225
98 − 77.15 =	20.85	20.85 × 20.85	=	434.7225
95 − 77.15 =	17.85	17.85 × 17.85	=	318.6225
91 − 77.15 =	13.85	13.85 × 13.85	=	191.8225

	Step 1: Difference	Step 2: Multiply by Itself	Squared
88 − 77.15 =	10.85	10.85 × 10.85 =	117.7225
87 − 77.15 =	9.85	9.85 × 9.85 =	97.0225
82 − 77.15 =	4.85	4.85 × 4.85 =	23.5225
80 − 77.15 =	2.85	2.85 × 2.85 =	8.1225
75 − 77.15 =	−2.15	−2.15 × −2.15 =	4.6225
75 − 77.15 =	−2.15	−2.15 × −2.15 =	4.6225
75 − 77.15 =	−2.15	−2.15 × −2.15 =	4.6225
75 − 77.15 =	−2.15	−2.15 × −2.15 =	4.6225
75 − 77.15 =	−2.15	−2.15 × −2.15 =	4.6225
72 − 77.15 =	−5.15	−5.15 × −5.15 =	26.5225
70 − 77.15 =	−7.15	−7.15 × −7.15 =	51.1225
69 − 77.15 =	−8.15	−8.15 × −8.15 =	66.4225
68 − 77.15 =	−9.15	−9.15 × −9.15 =	83.7225
67 − 77.15 =	−10.15	−10.15 × −10.15 =	103.0225
51 − 77.15 =	−26.15	−26.15 × −26.15 =	683.8225
50 − 77.15 =	−27.15	−27.15 × −27.15 =	737.1225

Step 3: Sum of Squares: 3,488.55

Step 4: Divide the Sum of Squares by the Number of Scores

$$3{,}488.55 \div 20 = 174.4275$$

Therefore, the variance for data set I = 174.4275.

Check Your Understanding

Complete Activity 3.7.

ACTIVITY 3.7

Calculate the variance for data set J and compare with data set I.

Data Set J

	Step 1: Difference	Step 2: Multiply by Itself	Squared
98 − 77.05 =			
96 − 77.05 =			
87 − 77.05 =			
78 − 77.05 =			
75 − 77.05 =			
75 − 77.05 =			
75 − 77.05 =			
75 − 77.05 =			
75 − 77.05 =			
75 − 77.05 =			
75 − 77.05 =			

	Step 1: Difference	Step 2: Multiply by Itself	Squared
75 − 77.05 =			
75 − 77.05 =			
75 − 77.05 =			
72 − 77.05 =			
72 − 77.05 =			
72 − 77.05 =			
72 − 77.05 =			
72 − 77.05 =			
72 − 77.05 =			____

Step 3: Sum of Squares:

Step 4: Divide the Sum of Squares by the Number of Scores

Which set of data, J or I, has the larger variance? ____

Apply Your Knowledge

Data sets I and J have means that are very similar. Why do you think there is such a large difference between the variance of I and the variance of J? ________________________________

____

STANDARD DEVIATION

Once the variance has been calculated, only one more step is needed to calculate the standard deviation. The standard deviation helps the teacher determine how much distance from the mean is typical and how much is considered significant.

The standard deviation of a set of data is the square root of the variance.

$$\text{Standard Deviation} = \sqrt{\text{Variance}}$$

Because the variance for data sets I and J has already been calculated, merely enter each number on a calculator and hit the square root button. If a calculator is not available, use the square root tables located in most introductory statistics textbooks.

The square root of the variance for data set I is 13.21. Therefore, any test score that is more than 1 standard deviation above or below the mean score, either 13.21 above the mean or 13.21 below the mean, is considered significant. Look at data set I. The test scores that are more than 1 standard deviation above the mean (77.15) are 100, 98, 95, and 91. The scores that are more than 1 standard deviation below the mean are 51 and 50. These scores represent the extremes for this distribution and may well receive the extreme grades for the class: A's and F's. Figure 3.3 illustrates the distribution of scores in data set I.

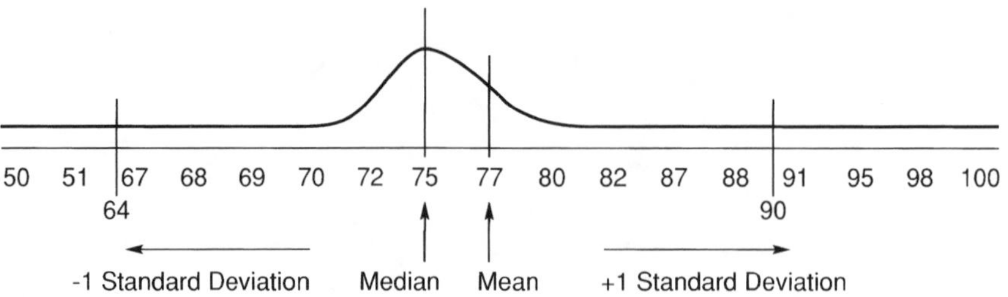

Figure 3.3 Distribution for data set I.

Look at data set J. To locate significantly different scores, find those that are 1 or more standard deviations away from the mean of 77.05. Which scores are considered to be a significant distance from the mean?

Check Your Understanding

Complete Activity 3.8.

ACTIVITY 3.8

Using the following sets of data, complete a frequency count and a frequency polygon; calculate the mean, median, and mode; calculate the range, variance, and standard deviation; and list the scores that are a significant distance from the mean.

Ms. Jones's Class Data

95, 82, 76, 75, 62, 100, 32, 15, 100, 98, 99, 86, 70, 26, 21, 26, 82

Frequency count:

Draw the frequency polygon here:

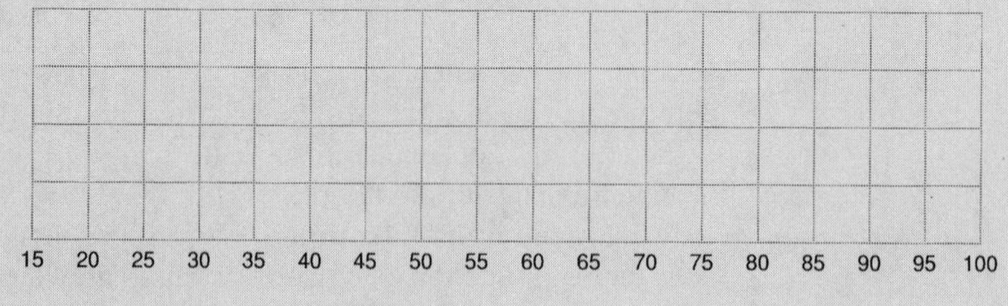

Mean: _____ Median: _____ Mode: _____

Range: _____ Variance: _____ Standard deviation: _____

Test scores that are a significant distance from the mean are

____

Mrs. Smith's Class Data

76, 75, 83, 92, 85, 69, 88, 87, 88, 88, 88, 88, 77, 78, 78, 95, 98
Frequency count:

Draw the frequency polygon here:

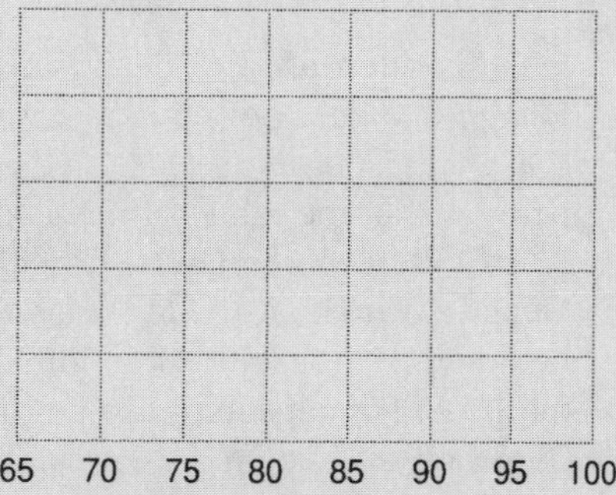

Mean: _____ Median: _____ Mode: _____
Range: _____ Variance: _____ Standard deviation: _____

Test scores that are a significant distance from the mean are

____

Apply Your Knowledge

Using the information you obtained through your calculations, what can you say about the performance of the students in Ms. Jones's class compared with the performance of the students in Mrs. Smith's class?

____

____

STANDARD DEVIATION AND THE NORMAL DISTRIBUTION

In a normal distribution, the standard deviations represent the percentages of scores shown on the bell curve in Figure 3.4. More than 68% of the scores fall within 1 standard deviation above or below the mean. A normal distribution is symmetrical and has the same number representing the mean, median, and mode. Notice that approximately 95% of the scores are found within 2 standard deviations above and below the mean (Figure 3.4). To clarify the significance of standard deviation, it is helpful to remember that one criterion for the diagnosis of mental retardation is an IQ score of more than 2 standard deviations below the mean. The criterion of 2 standard deviations above the

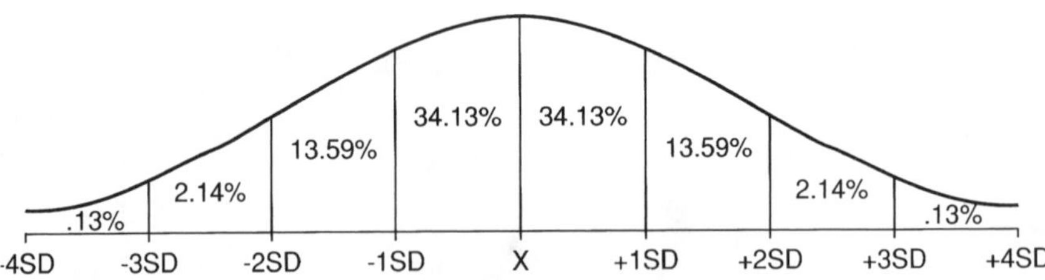

Figure 3.4 Percentages of population that fall within standard deviation units in a normal distribution.

mean is often used to determine that a student is within the gifted range. Using a standard deviation of 15 IQ points, an individual with an IQ of 70 or less and a subaverage adaptive behavior scale score might be classified as being within the range of mental retardation, whereas an individual with an IQ of 130 or more may be classified as gifted. The American Association on Mental Retardation (AAMR) classification system allows additional flexibility by adding 5 points to the minimum requirement; that is, the student within the 70–75 IQ range may also be found eligible for services under the category of mental retardation if there are additional supporting data.

Check Your Understanding

Complete Activity 3.9 using Figure 3.4.

ACTIVITY 3.9

1. Joan, a second-grade student, was referred for a comprehensive evaluation by the child study committee following unsuccessful interventions. After the assessment, the team met and reviewed the following information. Joan's overall academic scores and classroom performance measures were well below the level expected for her age and grade placement. Her IQ scores for overall IQ and verbal and nonverbal IQ were as follows: Full Scale IQ score 68, Verbal IQ 65, Performance IQ 67. Joan's parents and teachers provided information regarding her adaptive behavior, and it was determined that she was below age expectancy as well. According to her assessment results, what might the team consider about Joan's current functioning? ____________________
2. Alonzo, a first-grade student, was referred for an assessment by his teacher, Ms. Stewart, who felt that Alonzo was well ahead of his age peers. Ms. Stewart reported that Alonzo reads at the third-grade level and completes fifth-grade level math problems correctly. Assessment results indicate that Alonzo's Full Scale IQ score is 138 and his academic scores are above age and grade level expectations. Using Figure 3.4, how do Alonzo's scores compare with the general population? ____________________
____

MEAN DIFFERENCES

Test results such as those discussed in the preceding section should be interpreted with caution. Many tests that have been used historically to diagnose disabilities such as mental retardation have been shown to exhibit *mean differences.* A specific cultural or linguistic group may have a different mean or average score than that reported for most of the population; this is a mean difference. Accordingly, minority students should not be judged by an acceptable average for a different population. This issue is elaborated on in chapter 10, "Measures of Intelligence and Adaptive Behavior."

SKEWED DISTRIBUTIONS

skewed Describes a distribution that has either more positively distributed scores or more negatively distributed scores.

positively skewed Describes a distribution in which more of the scores fall below the mean.

negatively skewed Describes a distribution in which more of the scores fall above the mean.

When small samples of populations are tested or when a fairly restricted population is tested, the results may not be distributed in a normal curve. Distributions can be **skewed** in a positive or negative direction. When many of the scores are below the mean, the distribution is said to be **positively skewed** and will resemble the distribution in Figure 3.5. Notice that the most frequently occurring scores (mode) are located below the mean.

When a large number of the scores occur above the mean, the distribution is said to be **negatively skewed,** as shown in Figure 3.6. Notice that the mode and median scores are located above the mean.

Figures 3.5 and 3.6 illustrate different ways that groups of scores fall, cluster, and are dispersed. As already discussed, extreme scores can change the appearance of a set of scores. Often, when working with scores from teacher-made tests, one or two scores can be so extreme that they influence

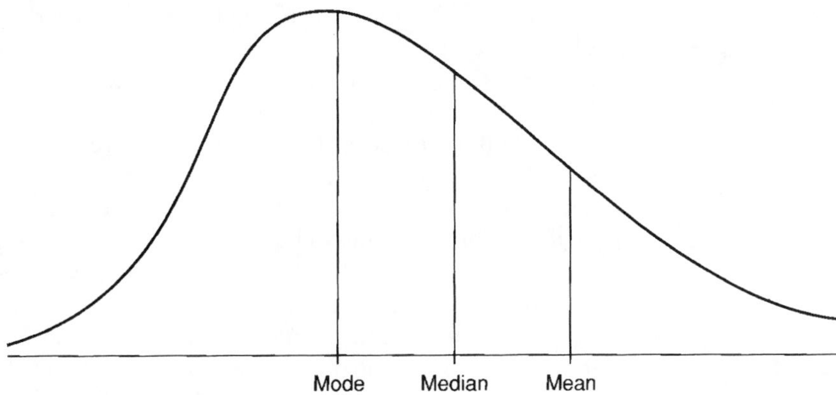

Figure 3.5 Positively skewed distribution.

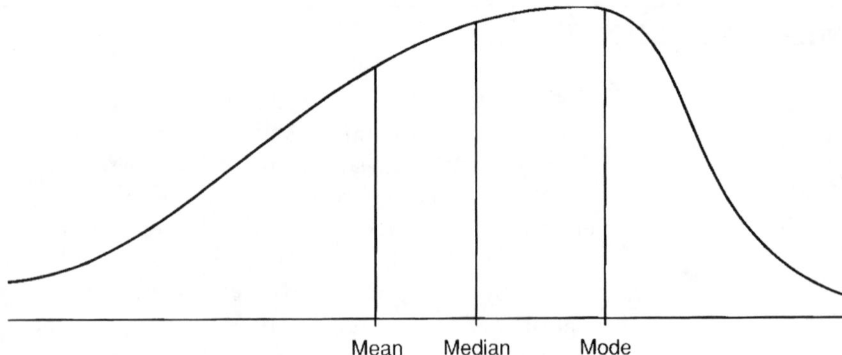

Figure 3.6 Negatively skewed distribution.

the way the data are described. That is, the scores may influence or pull the mean in one direction. Consider the following examples:

Ms. Brown	**Ms. Blue**
100	100
92	92
86	86
80	80
78	78
78	78
78	78
75	75
74	72
72	6
813 ÷ 10 = 81.3	745 ÷ 10 = 74.5

The sets of data are very similar except for the one extreme low score. The greater the number of scores in the class, the less influence an extreme score has on the set of data. In small classes like those often found in special education settings, the mean of the class performance is more likely to be influenced by an extreme score. If Ms. Brown and Ms. Blue each had a class objective stating that the class would pass the test with an average score of 80, Ms. Brown's class would have passed the objective, but Ms. Blue's class would not have. When the extreme score is omitted, the average for Ms. Blue's class is 82.1, which meets the class objective.

When selecting norm-referenced tests, special educators must take care to read the test manual and determine the size of the sample used in the norming process. Tests developed using larger samples are thought to result in scores that are more representative of the majority population.

PERCENTILE RANKS AND z SCORES

percentile ranks Scores that express the percentage of students who scored as well as or lower than a given student's score.

***z* scores** Derived scores that are expressed in standard deviation units.

Percentile ranks and ***z* scores** provide additional ways of looking at data. Using percentile ranks is a method of ranking each score on the continuum of the normal distribution. The extreme scores are ranked at the top and bottom, and very few people obtain scores at the extreme ends. Percentiles range from the 99.9th percentile to less than the 1st percentile. A person who scores at the extremely high end of a test may be ranked near the 99th percentile. This means that she scored as well as or better than 99% of the students the same age or grade who took the same test. A person who scores around the average, say 100 on an IQ test, would be ranked in the middle, or the 50th percentile. A person who scores in the top fourth would be above the 75th percentile; in other words, the student scored as well as or better than 75% of the students in that particular age group. The various percentile ranks and their location on a normal distribution are illustrated in Figure 3.7.

Some have argued that using a percentile rank may not convey information that is as meaningful as other types of scores, such as *z* scores (May and Nicewander, 1994, 1997). deGruijter (1997) argued that May and Nicewander were faulty in their reasoning regarding percentile ranks and stated that percentile ranks are not inferior indicators of ability.

Some tests use *T* scores to interpret test performance. *T* scores have an average or mean of 50 and standard deviation of 10. One standard deviation above the mean would be expressed as a *T* score of 60, and 40 would represent one standard deviation below the mean.

Another type of score used to describe the data in a normal distribution is called a *z* score. A *z* score indicates where a score is located in terms of standard deviation units. The mean is expressed as 0, 1 standard deviation above the mean is expressed as +1, 2 standard deviations above as +2, and so on, as illustrated in Figure 3.8. Standard deviation units below the

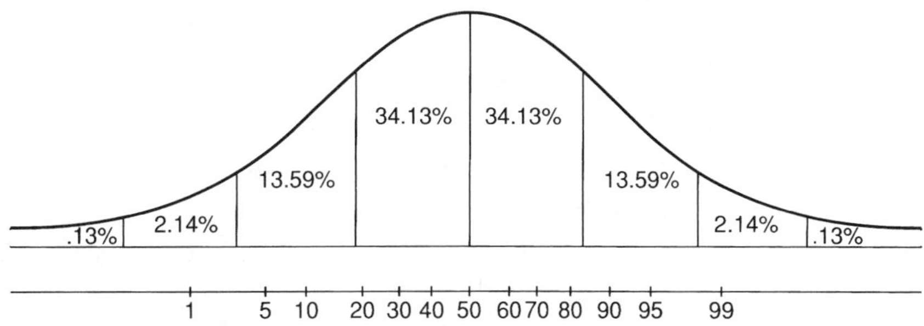

Figure 3.7 Relationship of percentiles and normal distribution. (*Source:* From *Assessing Special Students* (3rd ed., p. 63) by J. McLoughlin and R. Lewis, 1990, Upper Saddle River, NJ: Merrill/Prentice Hall. Copyright 1990 by Prentice Hall. Adapted with permission.)

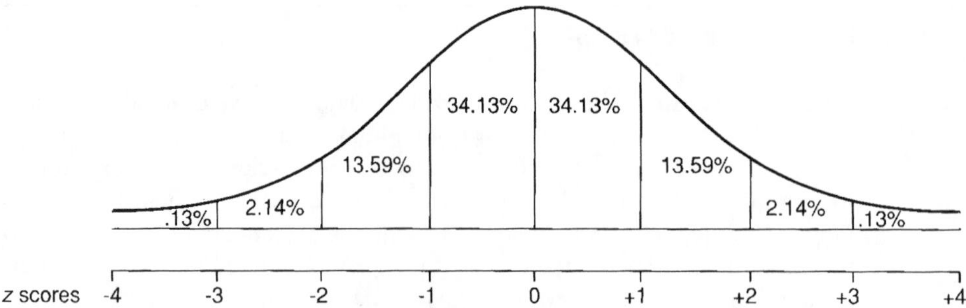

Figure 3.8 Relationship of *z* scores and the normal distribution. (*Source:* From *Assessing Special Students* (3rd ed,. p. 63) by J. McLoughlin and R. Lewis, 1990, Upper Saddle River, NJ: Merrill/Prentice Hall. Copyright 1990 by Prentice Hall. Adapted with permission.)

mean are expressed as negative numbers. For example, a score that is 1 standard deviation below the mean is expressed using *z* scores as −1, and a score that is 2 standard deviations below is expressed as −2. Conversely, +1 is 1 standard deviation above the mean, and +2 is 2 standard deviations above the mean.

THINK AHEAD

Now that you know how to compare students' scores with each other, you will read about how to compare tests. You will learn how to determine whether tests are reliable and valid. Do you think a test must be both reliable and valid to obtain information about a student's abilities?

EXERCISES

Part I

Match these terms with the statements that follow.

a. nominal scale
b. positively skewed
c. measures of central tendency
d. frequency distribution
e. bimodal distribution
f. ordinal scale
g. multimodal
h. frequency polygon
i. measures of dispersion
j. negatively skewed
k. standard deviation
l. ratio scale
m. interval scale
n. mode

o. range
p. rank order
q. median
r. descriptive statistics
s. mean
t. normal distribution

_____ 1. In this set of data, what measures of central tendency are represented by the number 77? 65, 66, 82, 95, 77

_____ 2. If the heights of all fifth-grade elementary students in one large city were measured, in what manner would the resulting data be displayed?

_____ 3. The following set of data is interesting because it is _____? 22, 47, 88, 62, 65, 22, 63, 89, 55, 74, 88, 99, 44, 65, 100

_____ 4. In a university, all students are given a new student identification number upon registration. These numbers are on what scale?

_____ 5. All fourth-grade students in a Little City School were asked to participate in a reading contest to see which students could read the most books in a 3-month period. At the end of the three months, the winners were determined. The 10 students who read the most books were awarded prizes. On the final day of the contest, the students anxiously looked at the list where the names were _____ from the highest number of books read to the fewest.

_____ 6. The mean, median, and mode make up _____.

_____ 7. A seventh-grade pre-algebra class completed the first test of the new school year. Here are the data resulting from the first test: 100, 99, 95, 90, 89, 85, 84, 82, 81, 80, 79, 78, 77, 76, 70, 68, 65, 62, 60, 59, 55. For this set of data, what does the number 45 represent?

_____ 8. The following set of data has what type of distribution?

88, 33, 78, 56, 44, 37, 90, 99, 76, 78, 77, 62, 90

_____ 9. A set of data has a symmetrical distribution of scores with the mean, median, and mode represented by the number 82. This set of data represents a _____.

_____ 10. When a set of data has a mean that is less than the most frequently occurring scores.

Part II

Rank order the following data; complete a frequency distribution and a frequency polygon; calculate the mean, median, and mode; and find the range, variance, and standard deviation. Identify scores that are significantly above or below the mean.

Data

85, 85, 99, 63, 60, 97, 96, 95, 58, 70, 72, 92, 89, 87, 74, 74, 74, 85, 84, 78, 84, 78, 84, 78, 86, 82, 79, 81, 80, 86

_____	_____
_____	_____
_____	_____
_____	_____
_____	_____
_____	_____
_____	_____
_____	_____
_____	_____
_____	_____
_____	_____
_____	_____
_____	_____
_____	_____
_____	_____
_____	_____

Mean: _____ Median: _____ Mode: _____
Range: _____ Variance: _____ Standard deviation: _____

Scores that are a significant distance from the mean are ____

Draw the frequency polygon here:

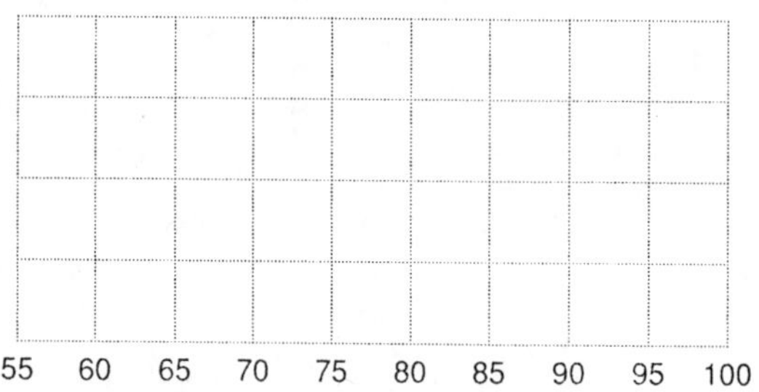

Use the normal distribution shown in Figure 3.9 to answer the following questions. You may need to use a ruler or straightedge, placed on the figure vertically, to identify the answers.

1. What percentage of the scores would fall between the z scores of -2.0 and $+2.0$? _______________
2. What percentile rank would be assigned to the z score of 0? _______________

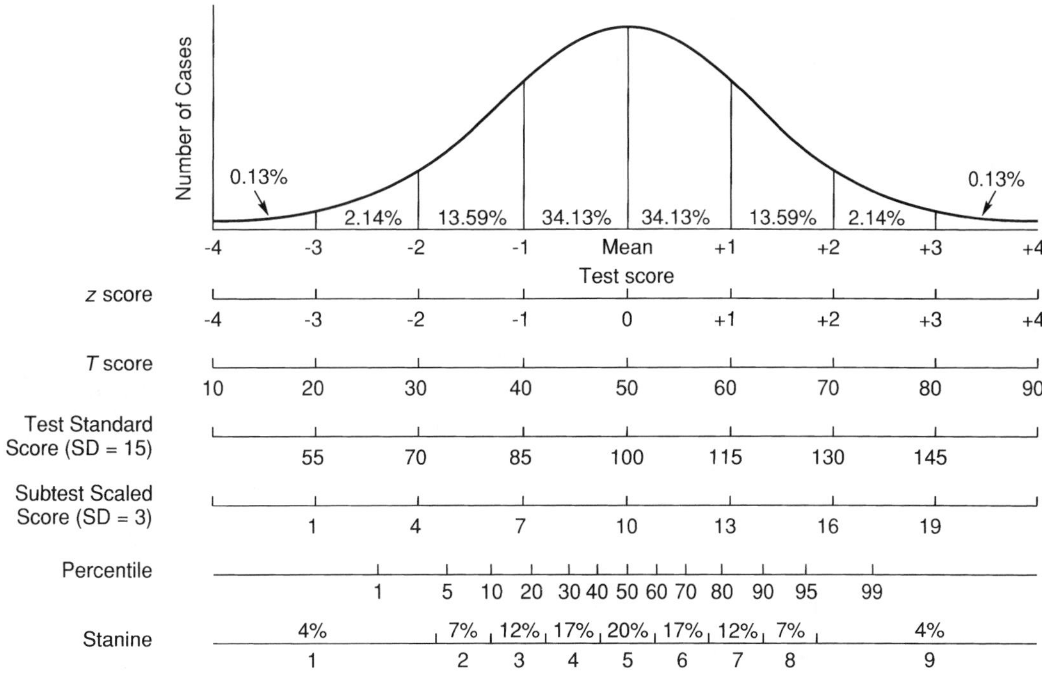

Figure 3.9 Relationships among different types of scores in a normal distribution. (*Source:* From *Assessing Special Students* (4th ed., p. 61) by J. McLoughlin and R. Lewis, 1994, Columbus, OH: Merrill. Copyright 1994 by Macmillan Publishing Company. Reprinted with permission.)

3. What percentile rank would represent a person who scored at the z score of +3.0? ______________
4. Approximately what percentile rank would be assigned for the IQ score of 70? ______________
5. Approximately how many people would be expected to fall in the IQ range represented by the z scores of +3.0 to +4.0? ______________

ANSWER KEY FOR CHECK YOUR UNDERSTANDING

Activity 3.1

1. interval
2. interval
3. ordinal
4. nominal
5. ratio

Apply Your Knowledge. The answer is ratio.

Activity 3.2

Score	Tally	Frequency
100	|	1
98	||	2
96	|	1
92	||	2
90	|	1
89	|	1
87	|	1
85	||	2
83	|	1
82	|	1
73	|	1
70	|||	3
66	|	1
62	|	1
61	|	1

Apply Your Knowledge. All but nominal scales.

Activity 3.3

Score	Tally	Frequency
96	|	1
94	|	1
92	|	1
88	|	1
81	||	2
78	|	1
77	|	1
75	||	2
74	|	1
63	|||	3
62	|	1
60	|	1
51	|	1
50	|	1
49	|	1
42	|	1

The mode is 63.

Apply Your Knowledge. When more students consistently perform at the high end of the distribution, it may mean that the tests are not challenging the students or that the material presented is too easy for the group of students who repeatedly score high.

Activity 3.4

Score	Tally	Frequency
98	|	1
94	|	1
91	|	1
90	|	1
89	||	2
88	~~||||~~	5
85	||	2
82	||	2
76	~~||||~~	5
72	|	1
69	|	1
68	||	2
67	|	1
52	|	1
51	|	1
50	|	1

Apply Your Knowledge. The distribution is bimodal. The frequency polygon is below.

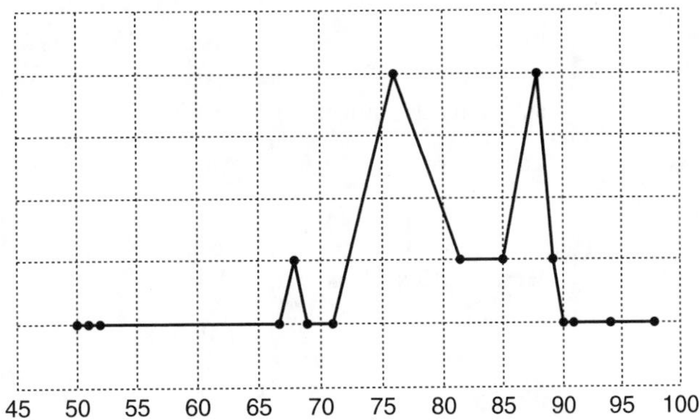

Activity 3.5

Data set E: median 82
Data set F: median 78

Apply Your Knowledge. The scores were more similar or closer together for data set F and more spread apart for data set E.

Activity 3.6

Data Set G		**Data Set H**	
mean	86.25	mean	44
median	86.50	median	43.5
mode	86.87	mode	41

Apply Your Knowledge. Although the mean, median, and mode are nearly the same for data set G, this set of data has a greater range of scores, with 12 points between the highest and lowest scores. The mean, median, and mode do not always provide the needed information when attempting to determine how far apart the data may be dispersed.

Activity 3.7

Data set I has the larger variance.

Apply Your Knowledge. The variance of data set I is larger because the numbers are more widely dispersed.

Activity 3.8

Ms. Jones's Class Data

mean	67.35
median	76
mode	26, 82, 100
range	100 − 15 = 85
variance	902.46
standard deviation	30.04

Test scores that are a significant distance from the mean (± 1 SD): 100, 99, 26, 26, 21

Mrs. Smith's Class Data

mean	84.294117
median	87
mode	88
range	98 − 69 = 29
variance	56.560588
standard deviation	7.520

Test scores that are a significant distance from the mean (± 1 SD): 98, 95, 92, 76, 75, 69

Apply Your Knowledge. Ms. Jones has students with more diverse abilities or more diverse levels of understanding of the concepts presented in class.

Activity 3.9

1. The team members may consider that Joan will need interventions for persons functioning within the range of mental retardation.
2. Alonzo's score is more than 2 standard deviations above the mean. Fewer than 3% of the population scored as well as or better than Alonzo.

REFERENCES

Algozzine, B., & Ysseldyke, J. (1981). Special education services for normal children: Better safe than sorry? *Exceptional Children, 48,* 238–243.

American Psychological Association (1985). *Standards for educational and psychological testing.* Washington, DC: Author.

Bennett, R., & Shepherd, M. (1982). Basic measurement proficiency of learning disability specialists. *Learning Disabilities Quarterly, 5,* 177–184.

Borg, W., Worthen, B., & Valcarce, R. (1986). Teachers' perceptions of the importance of educational measurement. *Journal of Experimental Education, 5,* 9–14.

Davis, W., & Shepard, L. (1983). Specialists' use of tests and clinical judgments in the diagnosis of learning disabilities. *Learning Disabilities Quarterly, 6,* 128–137.

deGruijter, D. N. M. (1997). On information of percentile ranks. *Journal of Educational Measurement, 34,* 177–178.

Eaves, R. (1985). Educational assessment in the United States [Monograph]. *Diagnostique, 10,* 5–39.

Huebner, E. S. (1988). Bias in teachers' special education decisions as a function of test score reporting format. *Journal of Educational Researcher, 21,* 217–220.

Huebner, E. S. (1989). Errors in decision making: A comparison of school psychologists' interpretations of grade equivalents, percentiles, and deviation IQs. *School Psychology Review, 18,* 51–55.

May, K., & Nicewander, W. A. (1994). Reliability and information functions for percentile ranks. *Journal of Educational Measurement, 31,* 313–325.

May, K. O., & Nicewander, W. A. (1997). Information and reliability for percentile ranks and other monotonic transformations of the number-correct score: Reply to De Gruijter. *Journal of Educational Measurement, 34,* 179–183.

McLoughlin, J. (1985). Training educational diagnosticians [Monograph]. *Diagnostique, 10,* 176–196.

McLoughlin, J., & Lewis, R. (1994). *Assessing special students* (4th ed.). Upper Saddle River, N.J.: Merrill/Prentice Hall.

Ysseldyke, J., Algozzine, B., Regan, R., & Potter, M. (1980). Technical adequacy of tests used by professionals in simulated decision making. *Psychology in the Schools, 17,* 202–209.

Ysseldyke, J., Algozzine, B., Richey, L., & Graden, J. (1982). Declaring students eligible for learning disability services: Why bother with the data? *Learning Disabilities Quarterly, 5,* 37–44.

CHAPTER 4

Reliability and Validity

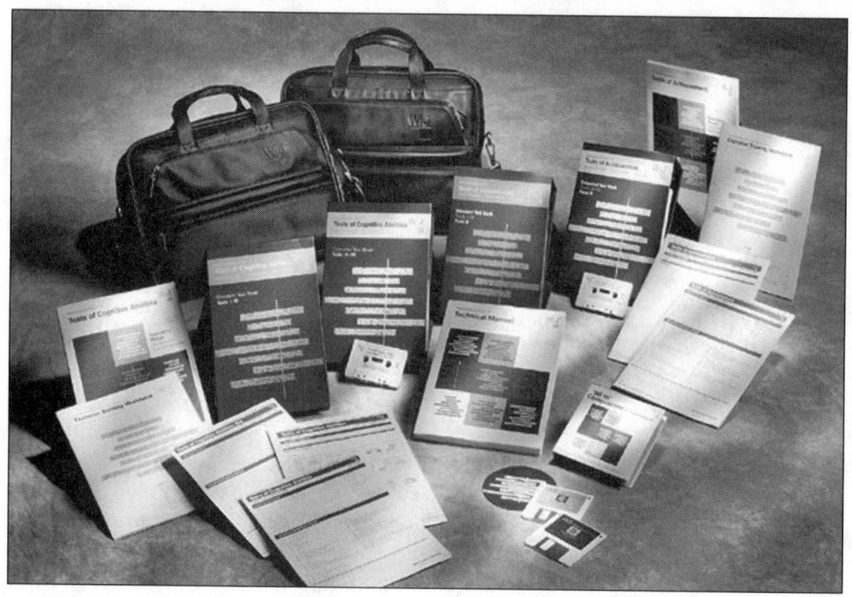

Key Terms

reliability
correlation
correlation coefficient
scattergram
Pearson's r
internal consistency
test-retest reliability
equivalent forms reliability
alternate forms reliability
split-half reliability
Kuder-Richardson (K-R) 20
coefficient alpha
interrater reliability
true score
standard error of measurement
obtained score
confidence interval
estimated true score
validity
criterion-related validity
concurrent validity
predictive validity
content validity
presentation format
response mode
construct validity
validity of test use

CHAPTER FOCUS

This chapter presents reliability and validity of test instruments. You will learn the various methods of researching reliability and validity and which methods are appropriate for specific types of tests.

RELIABILITY AND VALIDITY IN ASSESSMENT

It is important for educators to feel that the assessment methods used in teaching are providing accurate information. Usually, inferences are made from test data. In each school district, these inferences and subsequent interpretations of test results may change or set the educational future of hundreds of students each school year. An understanding of the concepts of reliability and validity aids the educator in determining test accuracy and dependability as well as how much faith can be placed in the use of instruments in the decision-making process.

reliability The dependability or consistency of an instrument across time or items.

Reliability in assessment refers to the confidence that can be placed in an instrument to yield the same score for the same student if the test were administered more than once and to the degree with which a skill or trait is measured consistently across items of a test. Teachers administering tests of any type, formal or informal, must be aware that error will be present to some degree during test administration. Statistical methods for estimating the probable amount of error and the degree of reliability allow professionals to select instruments with the lowest estimate of error and the greatest degree of reliability. Because educators use assessment as a basis for educational intervention and placement decisions, the most technically adequate instruments are preferred.

CORRELATION

correlation A statistical method of observing the degree of relationship between two sets of data or two variables.

One concept important to the understanding of reliability in assessment is **correlation.** Correlation is a method of determining the degree of relationship between two variables. Reliability is determined by the degree of relationship between the administration of an instrument and some other variable (including a repeated administration of the same instrument). The greater the degree of the relationship, the more reliable the instrument.

Correlation is a statistical procedure calculated to measure the relationship between two variables. The two variables might be two administrations of the same test, administration of equivalent forms of the same test, administration of one test and school achievement, or variables such as amount of time spent studying and final exam grades. In short, correlation is a method of determining whether two variables are associated with each other and, if so, how much.

correlation coefficient The expression of a relationship between two variables.

There are three types of correlations between variables: positive, negative, and no relationship. The degree of relationship between two variables is expressed by a **correlation coefficient** (r). The correlation coefficient will be a number between +1.00 and −1.00. A −1.00 or +1.00 indicates a perfect degree of correlation. In reality, perfect correlations are extremely rare. A correlation coefficient of 0 indicates no relationship.

The closer to ±1.00 the coefficient, the stronger the degree of the relationship. Hence, an r of .78 represents a stronger relationship than .65. When relationships are expressed by coefficients, the positive or negative sign does not indicate the strength of a relationship but indicates the direction of the relationship. Therefore, r values of −.78 and +.78 are of equal strength.

POSITIVE CORRELATION

Variables that have a positive relationship are those that move in the same direction. For example, this means that when test scores representing one variable in a set are high, scores representing the other variable also are high, and when the scores on one variable are low, scores on the other variable are low. Look at the following list of scores. Students who made high scores on a reading ability test (mean = 100) also had fairly high classroom reading grades at the end of the 6-week reporting period. Therefore, the data appear to show a positive relationship between the ability measured on the reading test (variable Y) and the student's performance in the reading curriculum in the classroom (variable X).

	Scores on the Reading Ability Test (Variable *Y*)	**Reading Grade at End of 6 Weeks (Variable *X*)**
John	109	B+
Ralph	120	A+
Sue	88	C−
Mary	95	B+
George	116	A−
Fred	78	D−
Kristy	140	A+
Jake	135	A
Jason	138	A
Betty	95	B−
Jamie	85	C+

scattergram Graphic representation of a correlation.

To better understand this positive relationship, the scores on these two variables can be plotted on a **scattergram** (Figure 4.1). Each student is represented by a single dot on the graph. The scattergram shows clearly that as the score on one variable increased, so did the score on the other variable.

When plotting correlations on a scattergram, the closer the dots approximate a straight line, the nearer to perfect the correlation. Hence, a strong relationship will appear more linear. Figure 4.2 illustrates a perfect positive correlation (straight line) for the small set of data shown here.

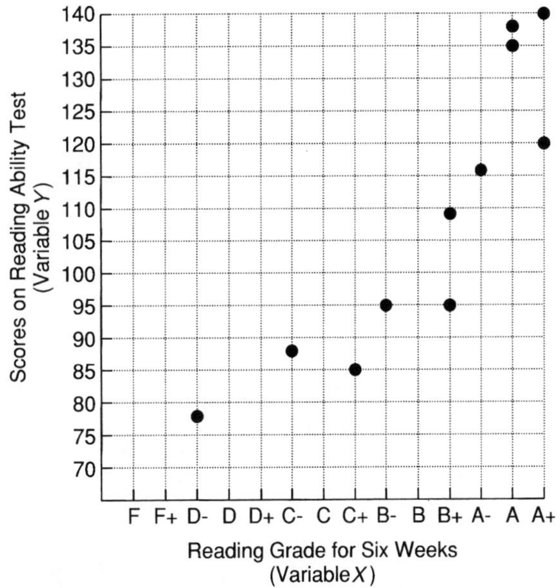

Figure 4.1 Graph showing relationship between scores on reading ability test and reading grade for 6 weeks.

	Test 1 (Variable *Y*)	**Test 2 (Variable *X*)**
George	100	100
Bill	95	95
Mary	87	87
Sue	76	76

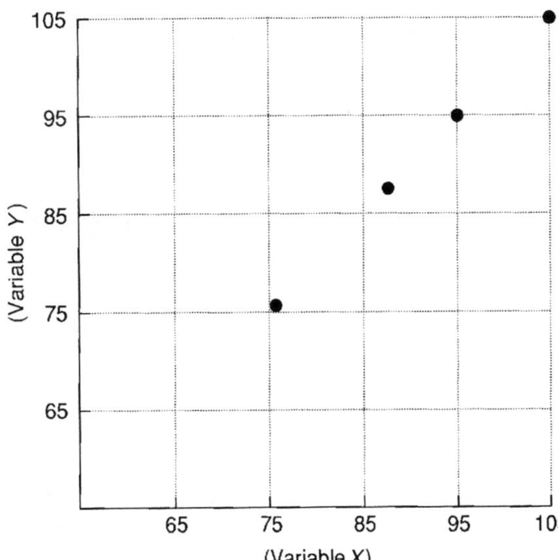

Figure 4.2 Scattergram showing a perfect positive correlation.

Check Your Understanding

Complete Activity 4.1.

ACTIVITY 4.1

The following sets of data are scores on a mathematics ability test and grade-level achievement in math for fifth graders. Plot the scores on the scattergram shown here.

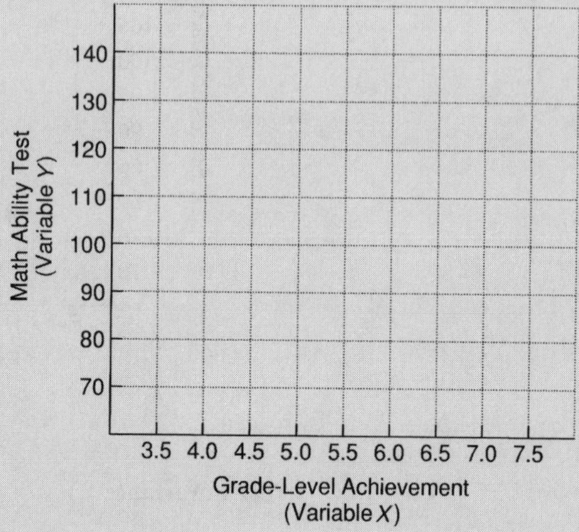

	Mathematics Ability Test Score (Variable *Y*)	**Grade-Level Achievement (Variable *X*)**
Wendy	115	6.5
Mary	102	5.5
Brad	141	7.4
Randy	92	4.7
Jamie	106	5.8
George	88	3.9

Apply Your Knowledge

Explain why this scattergram represents a positive correlation. ______

____

Examples of other variables that would be expected to have a positive relationship are number of days present in class and semester grade, number of chapters studied and final exam grade, and number of alcoholic drinks consumed and mistakes on a fine-motor test.

NEGATIVE CORRELATION

A negative correlation occurs when high scores on one variable are associated with low scores on the other variable. Examples of probable negative correlations are number of days absent and test grades, number of hours spent at parties and test grades, and number of hours missed from work and amount of hourly paycheck.

Check Your Understanding

Complete Activity 4.2.

ACTIVITY 4.2

Here is an example of a negative correlation between two variables. Plot the scores on the scattergram.

	Test 1 (Variable *Y*)	**Test 2 (Variable *X*)**
Heather	116	40
Ryan	118	38
Brent	130	20
William	125	21
Kellie	112	35
Stacy	122	19
Marsha	126	23
Lawrence	110	45
Allen	127	18
Aaron	100	55
Jeff	120	27
Sharon	122	25
Michael	112	43
James	105	50
Thomas	117	33

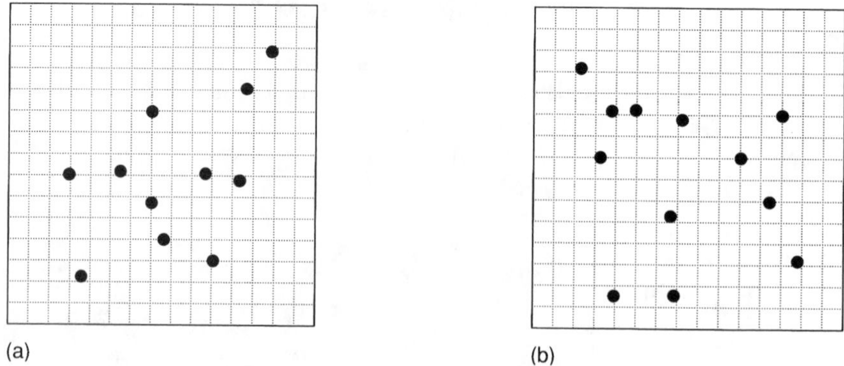

Figure 4.3 Scattergrams showing (a) weak positive and (b) weak negative relationships.

> ***Apply Your Knowledge***
> Explain the relationship that resulted in a negative correlation for this activity. ____
> ____

When the strength of a relationship is weak, the scattergram will not appear to have a distinct line. The less linear the scattergram, the weaker the correlation. Figure 4.3 illustrates scattergrams representing weak positive and weak negative relationships.

NO CORRELATION

When data from two variables are not associated or have no relationship, the $r = .00$. No correlation will be represented on a scattergram, with no linear direction either positive or negative. Figure 4.4 illustrates a scattergram of variables with no relationship.

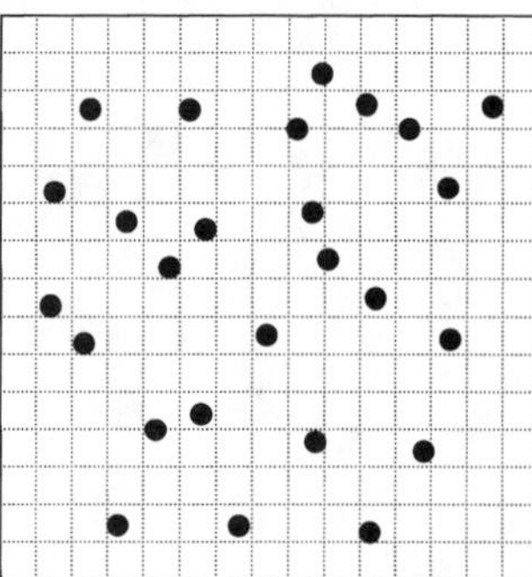

Figure 4.4 Scattergram showing no relationship.

Check Your Understanding

Complete Activity 4.3.

ACTIVITY 4.3

Complete the scattergrams using the following sets of data. Determine whether the scattergrams illustrate positive, negative, or no correlation.

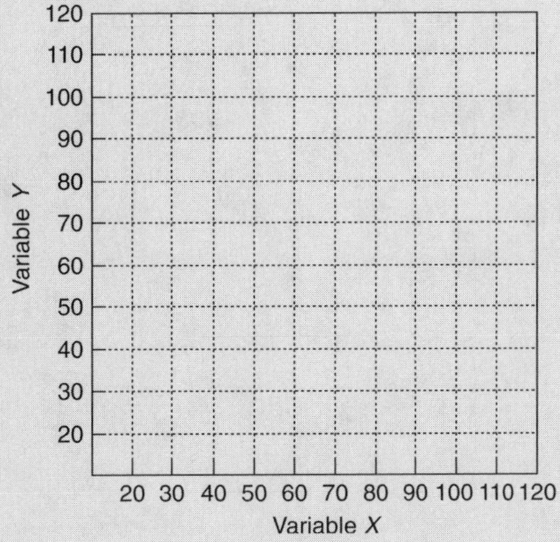

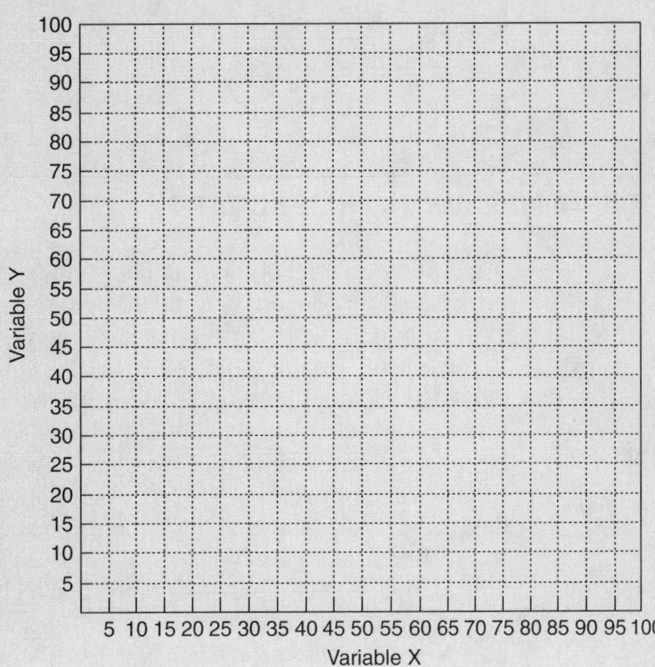

Variable *Y*	**Variable *X***
100	110
96	94
86	91
67	72
77	85

Correlation appears to be

____

Variable *Y*	**Variable *X***
6	87
56	98
4	80
10	85
40	84
30	20
20	40
50	20

Correlation appears to be

____

Apply Your Knowledge

Explain the concept of correlations: positive, negative, and no correlation. ____

____

METHODS OF MEASURING RELIABILITY

A teacher who administers a mathematics ability test to a student on a particular day and obtains a standard score of 110 (mean = 100) might feel quite confident that the student has ability in math above expectancy for her age level. Imagine that a teacher recommended a change in the student's educational placement based on the results of that particular math test and later discovered that the math test was not reliable. Educators must be able to have confidence that test instruments used will yield similar results when administered at different times. Professionals must know the degree with which they can rely on a specific instrument.

Different methods can be used to measure the reliability of test instruments. The reliability statistics are calculated using correlational methods. One correlational method used is the Pearson's Product Moment correlation, known as **Pearson's *r*.** Pearson's *r* is a commonly used formula for data on an interval or a ratio scale, although other methods are used as

Pearson's *r* A statistical formula for determining strength and direction of correlations.

well. The correlational studies of the reliability of tests involve checking the reliability of a test over time or the reliability of items within the test, known as **internal consistency.** For such studies, the procedures of test-retest, equivalent forms, split-half, and statistical methods called Kuder-Richardson formulas may be used.

internal consistency The consistency of the items on an instrument to measure a skill, trait, or domain.

TEST-RETEST RELIABILITY

One way to determine the reliability of a test is to measure the correlation of test scores obtained during one administration with the scores obtained on a repeated administration. The assumption of **test-retest reliability** is that the trait being measured is one that is stable over time. Therefore, if the trait being measured remained constant, the readministration of the instrument would result in scores very similar to the first scores, and thus the correlation between the two administrations would be positive.

test-retest reliability Study that employs the readministration of a single instrument to check for consistency across time.

Many of the traits measured in psychoeducational assessment are variable and respond to influencing factors or changes over time, such as instruction or student maturity. The readministration of an instrument for reliability studies should therefore be completed within a fairly short time period in an effort to control the influencing variables that occur naturally in the educational environment of children and youth. Typically, the longer the interval between test administrations, the more chance of variation in the obtained scores. Conversely, the shorter the interval between the two test administrations, the less likelihood that students will be influenced by time-related factors (experience, education, etc.). The difficulty with readministering the same instrument within a short period of time is that the student may remember items on the test. This *practice effect* most likely would cause the scores obtained on the second administration to be higher than the original scores, which would influence the correlation. The shorter the interval between administrations, the greater the possibility of practice effect; the longer the interval, the greater the influence of time variables.

The disadvantages of test-retest methods for checking test reliability have led to the use of other methods.

EQUIVALENT FORMS RELIABILITY

To control for the influence of time-related and practice-effect variables of test-retest methods, test developers may choose to use **equivalent forms reliability,** also called **alternate forms reliability.** In this method, two forms of the same instrument are used. The items are matched for difficulty on each test. For example, if three items for phonetic attack of consonant blends are included on one version of a reading test, three items of the same nature must be included at the same level on the alternate form of the test. During the reliability study, each student is administered both forms,

equivalent forms reliability Consistency of a test to measure some domain, trait, or skill using like forms of the same instrument.

alternate forms reliability Synonymous term for equivalent forms reliability.

and the scores obtained on one form of the test are then paired with the scores obtained on the equivalent form. The following are scores obtained on equivalent forms of a hypothetical reading test:

The Best-Ever Diagnostic Reading Test (x = 100)*

	Form 1	Form 2
John	82	85
Sue	76	78
Bill	89	87
Randy	54	56
Sally	106	112
Sara	115	109

*x = mean of sample.

This positive correlation indicates a fairly high reliability using equivalent forms reliability. In reality, an equivalent forms reliability study would involve a much larger sample of students. If this example had been an equivalent forms study using a large national sample, the educator could assume that both forms of the Best-Ever Reading Diagnostic Test are measuring the tested trait with some consistency.

If the test developer of the Best-Ever Reading Diagnostic Test also wanted the test to measure the stability of the trait over time, the manual would recommend that an interval of time pass between the administration of each form of the test. In using equivalent forms for measuring the stability over time, the reliability coefficient usually will not be as high as in the case of administering the same form of a test a second time. In the case of administering equivalent forms over a period of time, the influence of time-related variables will decrease the reliability coefficient as well as the practice effect that occurs in a test-retest reliability study of the same instrument.

Several published achievement and diagnostic tests that are used in special education consist of two equivalent forms. The advantage of this format is that it provides the educator with two tests of the same difficulty level that can be administered within a short time frame without the influence of practice effect. Often, local educational agencies practice a policy of administering one of the equivalent forms before writing short-term objectives for the year and administering the second form following educational interventions near the end of the school year. Educators administer the second form of the test to determine whether the educational objectives were achieved.

split-half reliability A method of checking the consistency across items by halving a test and administering two half-forms of same test.

INTERNAL CONSISTENCY MEASURES

Several methods allow a test developer to determine the reliability of the items on a single test using one administration of the test. These methods include **split-half reliability,** Kuder-Richardson (K-R) 20, and coefficient alpha.

Split-Half Reliability. Test developers rely often on the split-half method of determining reliability because of its ease of use. This method uses the items available on the instrument, splits the test in half, and correlates the two halves of the test. Because most tests have the items arranged sequentially, from the easiest items at the beginning of the test to the most difficult items at the end, the tests are typically split by pulling every other item, which in essence results in two equivalent half-forms of the test. Because this type of reliability study can be performed in a single administration of the instrument, split-half reliability studies are often completed even though other types of reliability studies are used in the test development. While this method establishes reliability of one half of the test with the other half, it does not establish the reliability of the entire test. Because reliability tends to increase with the number of items on the test, using split-half reliability may result in a lower reliability coefficient than that calculated by another method for the entire test (Mehrens & Lehmann, 1978). In this case, the reliability may be statistically adjusted to account for the variance in length (Mehrens & Lehmann, 1978).

Kuder-Richardson (K-R) 20 A formula used to check consistency across items of instrument with right/wrong responses.

coefficient alpha A formula used to check consistency across items of instrument with responses with varying credit.

Kuder-Richardson 20 and Coefficient Alpha. As the name implies, internal consistency reliability methods are used to determine how much alike items are to other items on a test. An advantage of this type of reliability study is that a single test administration is required. This reflects the unidimensionality in measuring a trait rather than the multidimensionality (Walsh & Betz, 1985).

Internal consistency is computed statistically by using either the K-R 20 formula for items scored only right or wrong or the coefficient alpha formula for items when more than 1 point is earned for a correct response (Mehrens & Lehmann, 1978).

When a high correlation coefficient is expressed by an internal consistency formula such as K-R 20 or coefficient alpha, the educator can be confident that the items on the instrument measure the trait or skill with some consistency. These methods measure the consistency of the items but not the consistency or dependability of the instrument across time, as do the test-retest method or using equivalent forms in separate test administrations.

INTERRATER RELIABILITY

Many of the educational and diagnostic tests used in special education are standardized with very specific administration, scoring, and interpretation instructions. Tests with a great deal of structure reduce the amount of influence that individual examiners may have on the results of the test. Some tests, specifically tests that allow the examiner to make judgments about student performance, have a greater possibility of influence by test examiners. In other words, there may be more of a chance that a score would vary from one examiner to another if the same student were tested by different examiners. On tests such as this, it is important to check the

interrater reliability The consistency of a test to measure a skill, trait, or domain across examiners.

interrater reliability, or interscorer reliability. This can be accomplished by administering the test and then having an objective scorer also score the test results. The results of the tests scored by the examiner are then correlated with the results obtained by the objective scorer to determine how much variability exists between the test scores. This information is especially important when tests with a great deal of subjectivity are used in making educational decisions.

WHICH TYPE OF RELIABILITY IS THE BEST?

Different types of reliability studies are used to measure consistency over time, consistency of the items on a test, and consistency of the test scored by different examiners. An educator selects assessment instruments for specific purposes according to the child's educational needs. The reliability studies and information in the test manual concerning reliability of the instrument are important considerations for the educator when determining which test is best for a particular student. An educator should select the instrument that has a high degree of reliability related to the purpose of assessment. An adequate reliability coefficient would be .60 or greater, and a high degree of reliability would be above .80. For example, if the examiner is interested in measuring a trait over time, the examiner should select an instrument in which the reliability or consistency over time had been studied. If the examiner is more concerned with the instrument's ability to determine student behavior using an instrument that allowed for a great degree of examiner judgment, the examiner should check the instrument's interrater reliability.

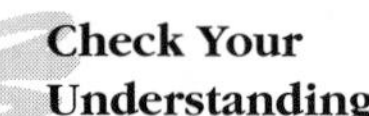
Check Your Understanding

Complete Activity 4.4.

ACTIVITY 4.4

Select the appropriate reliability study for the purposes described. (More than one answer may be correct.)

A. split-half reliability
B. equivalent forms, separate administration times
C. K-R 20
D. interrater reliability
E. test-retest
F. coefficient alpha
G. equivalent forms, same administration time

_______1. Educator is concerned with item reliability; items are scored as right or wrong.

_______2. Educator wants to administer same test twice to measure achievement of objectives.

_______3. Examiner is concerned with consistency of trait over time.

_______4. Educator is concerned with item consistency; items are scored with different point values for correct responses.

_______5. Examiner wants to administer a test that allows for examiner judgment.

Apply Your Knowledge

Explain the difference between internal reliability and the other types of reliability. ____

____

RELIABILITY FOR DIFFERENT GROUPS

The calculation of the reliability coefficient is a group statistic and can be influenced by the makeup of the group. The best test development and the manuals accompanying those tests will include information regarding the reliability of a test with different age or grade levels and even the reliability of a test with populations who differ on demographic variables such as cultural or linguistic backgrounds. The information in Table 4.1 illustrates how reliability may vary across different age groups.

Check Your Understanding

Complete Activity 4.5.

ACTIVITY 4.5

Refer to Table 4.1 to answer the following questions.

1. What type of reliability is reported in Table 4.1? _______________
2. Look at the reliability reported for age 7. Using fall statistics, compare the reliability coefficient obtained on the Numeration subtest with the reliability coefficient obtained for the Estimation subtest. On which subtest did 7-year-olds perform with more reliability? _______________
3. Compare the reliability coefficient obtained by 9-year-olds on the Estimation subtest with the reliability obtained by 7-year-olds on the same subtest using fall statistics. Which age group performed with more reliability? _______________

Apply Your Knowledge

Explain why the reliability of an instrument may vary across age groups. ____

____

Table 4.1 Split-half reliability coefficients, by age, for subtest, area, and total-test raw scores from the fall and spring standardization programs.

Subtest/Composite	Program (Fall/Spring)	Age 5	6	7	8	9	10
1. Numeration	F	.73	.82	.85	.90	.81	.85
	S	.51	.82	.89	.88	.89	.81
2. Rational Numbers	F	—	.24	.71	.68	.88	.89
	S	—	.27	.42	.86	.82	.86
3. Geometry	F	.63	.81	.79	.77	.82	.80
	S	.80	.81	.76	.77	.80	.75
4. Addition	F	.63	.65	.79	.84	.78	.40
	S	.58	.78	.84	.82	.84	.66
5. Subtraction	F	.25	.68	.64	.85	.89	.86
	S	.30	.70	.85	.90	.92	.85
6. Multiplication	F	.23	.41	.11	.76	.89	.90
	S	.07	.67	.68	.91	.93	.89
7. Division	F	.55	.49	.52	.51	.82	.86
	S	.18	.34	.53	.77	.80	.84
8. Mental Computation	F	—	.78	.68	.80	.85	.88
	S	—	.65	.67	.78	.78	.90
9. Measurement	F	.77	.89	.57	.77	.76	.77
	S	.92	.84	.85	.87	.84	.70
10. Time and Money	F	.50	.61	.73	.89	.87	.93
	S	.38	.70	.84	.89	.92	.86
11. Estimation	F	.44	.43	.50	.74	.86	.72
	S	.59	.50	.53	.85	.76	.84
12. Interpreting Data	F	.41	.86	.81	.80	.88	.85
	S	.32	.79	.83	.85	.88	.87
13. Problem Solving	F	.36	.60	.73	.71	.82	.86
	S	.55	.60	.77	.76	.87	.92
Basic Concepts Area[a]	F	.78	.87	.89	.91	.92	.93
	S	.82	.88	.87	.92	.92	.92
Operations Area[a]	F	.66	.86	.87	.93	.96	.96
	S	.73	.88	.92	.96	.96	.96
Applications Area[a]	F	.82	.91	.89	.94	.96	.96
	S	.88	.90	.93	.96	.96	.96
TOTAL TEST[a]	F	.90	.95	.95	.97	.98	.98
	S	.92	.95	.97	.98	.98	.98

[a] Reliability coefficients for the areas and the total test were computed by using Guilford's (1954, p. 393) formula for estimating the reliability of composite scores.
Source: From *KeyMath—Revised: A Diagnostic Inventory of Essential Mathematics, Manual. Forms A and B* (p. 67) by A. Connolly, 1988, Circle Pines, MN: American Guidance Service. Copyright 1988 by American Guidance Service. Reprinted by permission.

STANDARD ERROR OF MEASUREMENT

In all psychoeducational assessment, there is a basic underlying assumption: Error exists. Errors in testing may result from situational factors such as a poor testing environment or the health or emotions of the student, or errors may occur due to inaccuracies within the test instrument. Error should be considered when tests are administered, scored, and interpreted. Because tests are small samples of behavior observed at a given time, many variables can affect the assessment process and cause variance in test scores. This variance is called error because it influences test results. Professionals need to know that all tests contain error and that a single test score may not accurately reflect the student's **true score.** Salvia and Ysseldyke (1988a) stated, "A true score is a hypothetical value that represents a person's score when the entire domain of items is assessed at all possible times, by all appropriate testers" (p. 369). The following basic formula should be remembered when interpreting scores:

true score The student's actual score.

$$\text{Obtained score} = \text{True score} + \text{Error}$$

Conversely,

$$\text{Obtained score} - \text{True score} = \text{Error}$$

True score is never actually known; therefore, a range of possible scores is calculated. The error is called the **standard error of measurement,** and an instrument with a large standard error of measurement would be less desirable than an instrument with a small standard error of measurement.

standard error of measurement The amount of error determined to exist using a specific instrument, calculated using the instrument's standard deviation and reliability.

To estimate the amount of error present in an individual **obtained score,** the standard error of measurement must be obtained and applied to each score. The standard deviation and the reliability coefficient of the instrument are used to calculate the standard error of measurement. The following formula will enable the educator to determine the standard error of measurement when it has not been provided by the test developer in the test manual.

obtained score The observed score of a student on a particular test on a given day.

$$SEM = SD\sqrt{1 - r}$$

where: SEM = the standard error of measurement
SD = the standard deviation of the norm group of scores obtained during development of the instrument
r = the reliability coefficient

Figure 4.5 uses this formula to calculate the standard error of measurement for an instrument with a given standard deviation of 3 and a reliability coefficient of .78. The manual for this test would probably report the *SEM* as 1.4. Knowing the *SEM* allows the teacher to calculate a range of scores for a particular student, thus providing a better estimate of the student's true ability. Using the *SEM* of 1.4, the teacher adds and subtracts 1.4 to the

Figure 4.5 Calculating the standard error of measurement (*SEM*) for an instrument with a standard deviation of 3.

$$SEM = 3\sqrt{1 - .78}$$
$$SEM = 3\sqrt{.22}$$
$$SEM = 3 \times .4690415$$
$$SEM = 1.4071245$$

obtained score. If the obtained score is 9 (mean = 10), the teacher adds and subtracts the *SEM* to the obtained score of 9:

$$9 + 1.4 = 10.4$$
$$9 - 1.4 = 7.6$$

The range of possible true scores for this student is 7.6 to 10.4.

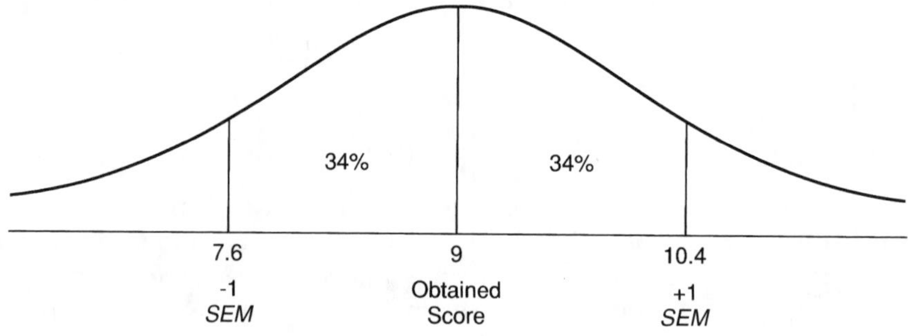

Thought to represent a range of deviations from an individual's obtained score, the standard error of measurement is based on the normal distribution theory. In other words, by using the standard error of measurement, one can determine the typical deviation for an individual's obtained score as if that person had been administered the same test an infinite number of times. When plotted, the scores form a bell curve, or a normal distribution, with the obtained score representing the mean, median, and mode. As with normal distributions, the range of ±1 standard error of measurement of the obtained score will occur approximately 68% of the times that the student takes the test. This is known as a **confidence interval** because the score obtained within that range can be thought to represent the true score with 68% accuracy. In the previous example, for instance, the student would score between 7.6 and 10.4 about 68% of the time.

confidence interval The range of scores for an obtained score determined by adding and subtracting standard error of measurement units.

If the teacher wanted 95% confidence that the true score was contained within a range, the band would be extended to ±2 standard errors of measurement of the obtained score. For the example, the extended range would be 6.2 to 11.8. The teacher can assume, with 95% confidence, that the student's true score is within this range.

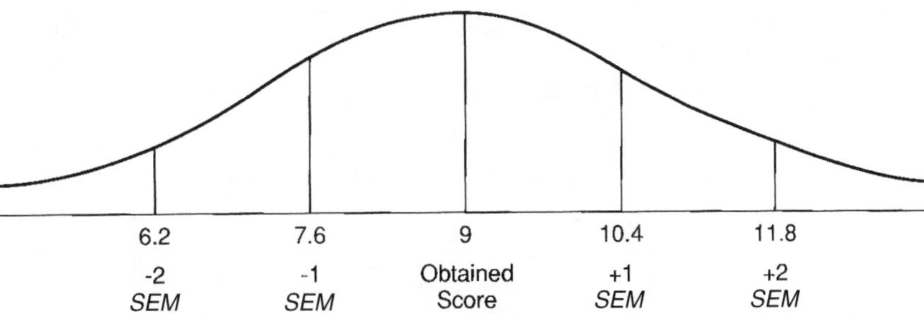

Check Your Understanding

Complete Activity 4.6.

ACTIVITY 4.6

Use the formula to determine the standard error of measurement with the given standard deviations and reliability coefficients.

$$SEM = SD\sqrt{1 - r}$$

1. $SD = 5$ $r = .67$ *SEM:* _____
2. $SD = 15$ $r = .82$ *SEM:* _____
3. $SD = 7$ $r = .73$ *SEM:* _____
4. $SD = 7$ $r = .98$ *SEM:* _____
5. $SD = 15$ $r = .98$ *SEM:* _____

Notice the influence of the standard deviation and the reliability coefficient on the standard error of measurement. Compare the *SEM*s in problems 3 and 4, which have the same standard deviation but different reliability coefficients. Now compare the *SEM*s in problems 4 and 5, which have the same reliability coefficient but different standard deviations.

6. What happens to the standard error of measurement as the reliability increases? ____
____
7. What happens to the standard error of measurement as the standard deviation increases? ____
____

Apply Your Knowledge

How might a test with a large *SEM* result in an inaccurate evaluation of a student's abilities? ____
____

As seen in Activity 4.6, a test with better reliability will have less error. The best tests for educational use are those with high reliability and a smaller standard error of measurement.

Check Your Understanding

Complete Activity 4.7.

ACTIVITY 4.7

All other factors being equal, which test would you select?

1. Test A: $SD = 4$, $r = .89$ Test B: $SD = 7$, $r = .88$
   Select test: _____
2. Test C: $SEM = 3.20$, $r = .76$ Test D: $SEM = 5.6$, $r = .62$
   Select test: _____

In each of the following problems, calculate the standard error of measurement. Use the calculated *SEM* to determine the range of scores for the obtained student score. Include the ranges for both the 68% confidence level and the 95% confidence level. Plot the range of scores on the distribution curves provided.

3. $SD = 8$, $r = .74$ Student's score = 85 ($x = 100$)
   $SEM =$ _____ Range for 68% confidence = _____
   Range for 95% confidence = _____

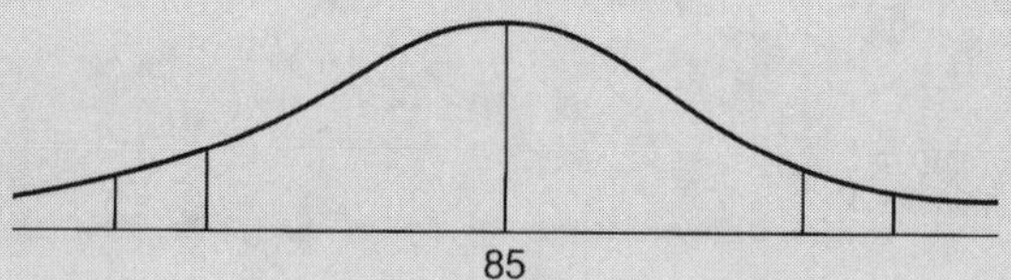

4. $SD = 7$, $r = .82$ Student's score = 82 ($x = 100$)
   $SEM =$ _____ Range for 68% confidence = _____
   Range for 95% confidence = _____

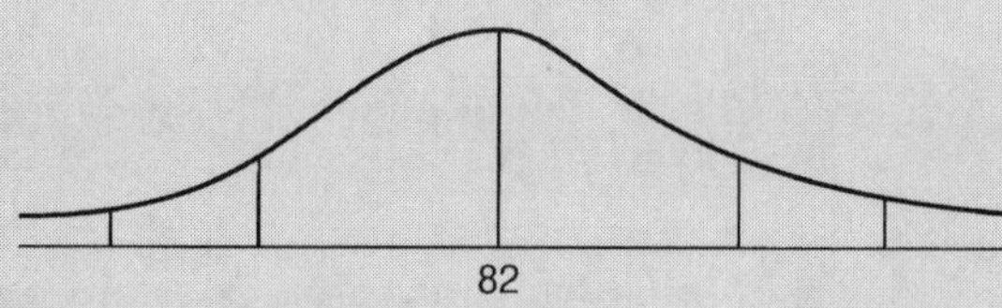

Apply Your Knowledge

Of the two obtained scores in this activity, which one would be more representative of a student's true score? Why? ____________________
____

APPLYING STANDARD ERROR OF MEASUREMENT

Williams and Zimmerman (1984) stated that whereas test validity remains the most important consideration in test selection, using the standard error of measurement to judge the test's quality is more important than reliability.

Williams and Zimmerman pointed out that reliability is a group statistic easily influenced by the variability of the group on whom it was calculated.

Sabers, Feldt, and Reschly (1988) observed that some, perhaps many, testing practitioners fail to consider possible test error when interpreting test results of a student being evaluated for special education services. The range of error and the range of a student's score may vary substantially, which may change the interpretation of the score for placement purposes.

In addition to knowing the standard error of measurement for an assessment instrument, it is important to know that the standard error of measurement will actually vary by age or grade level and by subtests. A test may contain less error for certain age or grade groupings than for other groupings. This information will be provided in the technical section of a good test manual.

Table 4.2 is from the *KeyMath—Revised* (Connolly, 1988) technical data section of the examiner's manual. The standard errors of measurement for the individual subtests are low and fairly consistent. There are some differences, however, in the standard errors of measurement on some subtests at different levels.

Consider the standard error of measurement for the Division subtest at ages 7 and 12 in the spring (S row). The standard error of measurement for age 7 is 2.0, but for age 12 it is 1.0. The larger standard error of measurement reported for age 7 is probably due to variation in the performance of students who may or may not have been introduced to division as part of the school curriculum. Most 12-year-olds, on the other hand, have probably practiced division in class for several years, and the sample of students tested may have performed with more consistency during the test development.

Given the two standard errors of measurement for the Division subtest at these ages, if a 7-year-old obtained a scaled score (a type of standard score) of 9 on this test ($x = 10$), the examiner could determine with 68% confidence that the true score lies between 7 and 11 and with 95% confidence that the true score lies between 5 and 13. The same scaled score obtained by a 12-year-old would range between 8 and 10 for a 68% confidence interval and between 7 and 11 for 95% confidence. This smaller range of scores is due to less error at this age on this particular subtest.

Check Your Understanding

Complete Activity 4.8.

ACTIVITY 4.8

Use Table 4.2 to locate the standard error of measurement for the following situations.

1. The standard error of measurement for a 7-year-old who was administered the Problem Solving subtest in the fall: _____
2. A 12-year-old's standard error of measurement for Problem Solving if the test was administered in the fall: _____

Table 4.2 Standard errors of measurement, by age, for scaled scores and standard scores from the fall and spring standardization programs.

Subtest/Composite	Program (Fall/Spring)	Age 5	6	7	8	9	10	11	12
1. Numeration	F	1.3	1.2	1.0	1.0	1.1	1.1	1.2	1.1
	S	1.7	1.1	1.0	1.0	1.0	1.2	1.1	1.0
2. Rational Numbers	F	—	—	—	—	1.2	1.0	1.0	1.0
	S	—	—	—	1.1	1.3	1.1	1.0	0.8
3. Geometry	F	1.5	1.3	1.4	1.4	1.2	1.2	1.3	1.1
	S	1.2	1.2	1.3	1.3	1.4	1.3	1.3	1.1
4. Addition	F	1.6	1.4	1.4	1.3	1.4	1.7	1.5	1.3
	S	1.8	1.4	1.3	1.4	1.4	1.5	1.3	1.3
5. Subtraction	F	—	1.6	1.5	1.3	1.1	1.1	1.5	1.3
	S	—	1.5	1.3	1.3	1.0	1.1	1.0	1.1
6. Multiplication	F	—	—	—	1.4	1.2	0.9	1.2	1.4
	S	—	—	—	1.0	1.1	1.2	1.1	1.1
7. Division	F	—	—	1.8	1.9	1.6	1.1	1.2	1.0
	S	—	—	2.0	1.6	1.4	1.2	1.1	1.0
8. Mental Computation	F	—	—	—	1.4	1.2	1.1	1.2	1.0
	S	—	—	1.7	1.3	1.2	1.1	1.1	0.9
9. Measurement	F	1.3	1.1	1.5	1.3	1.3	1.2	1.1	1.1
	S	1.2	1.1	1.2	1.1	1.1	1.3	1.1	0.9
10. Time and Money	F	—	1.6	1.3	1.1	1.0	1.0	1.0	1.0
	S	—	1.5	1.2	1.0	0.9	1.0	0.9	0.9
11. Estimation	F	—	1.7	1.8	1.4	1.3	1.3	1.2	1.0
	S	—	1.7	1.7	1.3	1.3	1.2	1.2	1.0
12. Interpreting Data	F	—	—	1.4	1.3	1.1	1.1	1.1	1.1
	S	—	—	1.3	1.2	1.1	1.1	1.1	1.0
13. Problem Solving	F	—	—	1.8	1.6	1.3	1.1	1.2	0.9
	S	—	—	1.6	1.4	1.2	1.1	1.1	0.9
Basic Concepts Area	F	5.8	5.3	4.8	4.7	4.0	3.7	3.9	3.3
	S	5.5	4.8	4.8	4.0	4.2	3.9	3.7	3.0
Operations Area	F	7.7	5.0	4.8	4.0	3.5	3.0	3.7	3.1
	S	7.1	5.0	4.3	3.5	3.2	3.3	2.9	2.7
Applications Area	F	5.8	4.1	4.3	3.6	3.1	2.8	3.0	2.6
	S	5.3	4.4	3.9	3.0	2.9	2.9	2.7	2.3
TOTAL TEST	F	4.1	3.0	2.9	2.5	2.2	1.9	2.2	1.8
	S	3.8	3.0	2.7	2.1	2.1	2.0	1.8	1.6

Source: From *KeyMath—Revised: A Diagnostic Inventory of Essential Mathematics, Manual. Forms A and B* (p. 72) by A. Connolly, 1988, Circle Pines, MN: American Guidance Service. Copyright 1988 by American Guidance Service. Reprinted by permission.

3. Using the standard errors of measurement found in problems 1 and 2, calculate the ranges for each age level if the obtained scores were both 7. Calculate the ranges for 68% and 95% confidence intervals.
   Range for 7-year-old for 68% confidence: _____
   Range for 7-year-old for 95% confidence: _____
   Range for 12-year-old for 68% confidence: _____
   Range for 12-year-old for 95% confidence: _____

Apply Your Knowledge

When comparing the concepts of a normal distribution and the *SEM*, the *SEM* units are distributed around the _____________ and the standard deviation units are evenly distributed around the _____________.

ESTIMATED TRUE SCORES

estimated true score A method of calculating the amount of error correlated with the distance of the score from the mean of the group.

Another method for approximating a student's true score is called the **estimated true score.** This calculation is founded in theory and research that the farther from a test mean a particular student's score is, the greater the chance for error within the obtained score. Chance errors are correlated with obtained scores (Salvia & Ysseldyke, 1988b). This means that as the score increases away from the mean, the chance for error increases. As scores regress toward the mean, the chance for error decreases. Therefore, if all the obtained scores are plotted on a distribution and all the values of error are plotted on a distribution, the comparison would appear like that in Figure 4.6. Note that the true scores are located closer to the mean with less spread, or variability. The formula for estimated true score (Nunnally, 1967, p. 220) is

$$\text{Estimated true score} = M + r(X - M)$$

where M = mean of group of which person is a member
r = reliability coefficient
X = obtained score

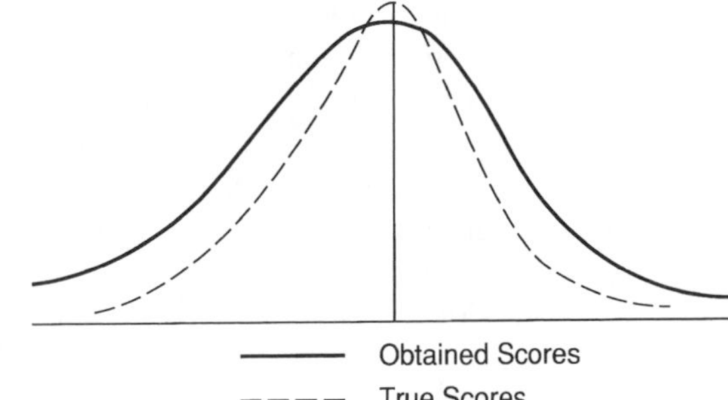

Figure 4.6
Comparison of obtained and true scores.

This formula enables the examiner to estimate a possible true score. Because of the correlation of error with obtained scores, the true score is always assumed to be nearer to the mean than the obtained score. Therefore, if the obtained score is 120 (mean = 100), the estimated true score will be less than 120. Conversely, if the obtained score is 65, the true score will be greater than 65.

Using the formula for estimated true score, the calculation for an obtained score of 115 with an r of .78 and a mean of 100 would be as follows:

$$\begin{aligned}\text{Estimated true score} &= 100 + .78\,(115 - 100)\\ &= 100 + .78(15)\\ &= 100 + 11.7\\ &= 111.7\end{aligned}$$

In this example, 111.7 is closer to the mean of 100 than 115.

Following is an example where the obtained score is less than the estimated true score:

Obtained score = 64, mean = 100, r = .74

$$\begin{aligned}\text{Estimated true score} &= 100 + .74(64 - 100)\\ &= 100 + .74(-36)\\ &= 100 - 26.64\\ &= 73.36\end{aligned}$$

The estimated true score can then be used to establish a range of scores by using the standard error of measurement for the estimated true score. Assume that the standard error of measurement for the estimated true score of 111.7 is 4.5. The range of scores ±1 standard error of measurement for 111.7 would be 107.2 to 116.2 for 68% confidence and 102.7 to 120.7 for 95% confidence.

The use of estimated true scores to calculate bands of confidence using standard error of measurement rather than using obtained scores has received some attention in the literature (Cahan, 1989; Feldt, Sabers, & Reschly, 1988; Sabers et al., 1988; Salvia & Ysseldyke, 1988a, 1988b). Whether using estimated true scores to calculate the range of possible scores or obtained scores to calculate the range of scores, several important points must be remembered. All test scores contain error. Error must be considered when interpreting test scores. The best practice, whether using estimated true scores or obtained scores, will employ the use of age- or grade-appropriate reliability coefficients and standard errors of measurement for the tests or subtests in question. When the norming process provides comparisons based on demographic variables, it is best to use the appropriate normative comparison.

TEST VALIDITY

To review, reliability refers to the dependability of the assessment instrument. The questions of concern for reliability are (a) Will students obtain similar scores if given the test a second time? (b) If the test is halved, will the administration of each half result in similar scores for the same student? (c) If different forms are available, will the administration of each form yield similar scores for the same student? (d) Will the administration of each item reliably measure the same trait or skill for the same student?

validity The quality of a test; the degree to which an instrument measures what it was designed to measure.

Validity is concerned not with repeated dependable results but rather with the degree of good results for the purpose the test is designed. In other words, does the test actually measure what it is supposed to measure? If the educator wants to assess multiplication skills, will the test provide the educator with a valid indication of the student's math ability? Several methods can be used to determine the degree to which the instrument measures what the test developers intended the test to measure. Some methods are better than others, and some of the methods are more easily understood. When selecting assessment instruments, the educator should carefully consider the validity information.

CRITERION-RELATED VALIDITY

criterion-related validity Statistical method of comparing an instrument's ability to measure a skill, trait, or domain with an existing instrument or other criterion.

Criterion-related validity is a method for determining the validity of an instrument by comparing its scores with other criteria known to be indicators of the same trait or skill that the test developer wishes to measure. The test is compared with another criterion. The two main types of criterion-related validity are differentiated by time factors.

concurrent validity A comparison of one instrument with another within a short period of time.

Concurrent Validity. **Concurrent validity** studies are conducted within a small time frame. The instrument in question is administered, and shortly thereafter an additional device is used, typically a similar test. Because the data are collected within a short time period, often the same day, this type of validity study is called concurrent validity. The data from both devices are correlated to see whether the instrument in question has significant concurrent criterion-related validity. The correlation coefficient obtained is called the *validity coefficient*. As with reliability coefficients, the nearer the coefficient is to ±1.00, the greater the strength of the relationship. Therefore, when the students in the sample obtain similar scores on both instruments, the instrument in question is said to be measuring the same trait or a degree or component of the same trait with some accuracy.

Suppose the newly developed Best in the World Math Test was administered to a sample of students, and shortly thereafter the Good Old Terrific Math Test was administered to the same sample. The validity coefficient obtained was .83. The educator selecting the Best in the World Math Test would have some confidence that it would measure, to some degree, the same traits or skills measured by the Good Old Terrific Math Test. Such studies are helpful in determining whether new tests and revised tests are measuring with some degree of accuracy the same skills as those measured by older, more researched instruments. Studies may compare other criteria as well, such as teacher ratings or motor performance of a like task. As expected, when comparing unlike instruments or criteria, these would probably not correlate highly. A test measuring creativity would probably not have a high validity coefficient with an advanced algebra test, but the algebra test would probably correlate better with a test measuring advanced trigonometry.

predictive validity A measure of how well an instrument can predict performance on some other variable.

Predictive Validity. **Predictive validity** is a measure of a specific instrument's ability to predict performance on some other measure or criterion at a later date.

Common examples of tests that predict a student's ability are a screening test to predict success in first grade, a Scholastic Aptitude Test (SAT) to predict success in college, a Graduate Record Exam (GRE) to predict success in graduate school, and an academic potential or academic aptitude test to predict success in school. Much of psychoeducational assessment conducted in schools concerns using test results to predict future success or failure in a particular educational setting. Therefore, when this type of testing is carried out, it is important that the educator selects an instrument with good predictive validity research. Using a test to predict which students should enroll in basic math and which should enroll in advanced algebra will not be in the students' best interests if the predictive validity of the instrument is poor.

CONTENT VALIDITY

content validity Occurs when the items contained within the test are representative of the content purported to be measured.

Professionals may assume that instruments reflecting a particular content in the name of the test or subtest have **content validity.** In many cases, this is not true. For example, on the Wide Range Achievement Test—Revision 3 (Wilkinson, 1993), the subtest Reading does not actually measure reading ability. It measures only one aspect of reading: word recognition. A teacher might use the score obtained on the subtest to place a student, believing that the student will be able to comprehend reading material at a particular level. In fact, the student may be able to recognize only a few words from that reading level. This subtest has inadequate content validity for measuring overall reading ability.

For a test to have good content validity, it must contain the content in a representative fashion. For example, a math achievement test that has only 10 addition and subtraction problems and no other math operations has not adequately represented the content of the domain of math. A good representation of content will include several items from each domain, level, and skill being measured.

Some of the variables of content validity may influence the manner in which results are obtained and can contribute to bias in testing. These variables may conflict with the nondiscriminatory test practice regulations of IDEA and the APA *Standards* (1985). These variables include **presentation format** and **response mode.**

presentation format The method by which items of an instrument are presented to a student.

response mode The method required for the examinee to answer items of an instrument.

1. *Presentation format.* Are the items presented in the best manner to assess the skill or trait? Requiring a student to silently read math problems and supply a verbal response could result in test bias if the student is unable to read at the level presented. The content being assessed may be math applications or reasoning, but the reading required to complete the task has reduced the instrument's ability to assess math skills for this particular student. Therefore, the content validity has been threatened, and the results obtained may unduly discriminate against the student.
2. *Response mode.* Like presentation format, the response mode may interfere with the test's ability to assess skills that are unrelated to the response mode. If the test was designed to assess reading ability but required the student to respond in writing, the test would discriminate against a student who had a motor impairment that made writing difficult or impossible. Unless the response mode is adapted, the targeted skill—reading ability—will not be fairly or adequately measured.

Content validity is a primary concern in the development of new instruments. The test developers may adjust, omit, or add items during the field-testing stage. These changes are incorporated into a developmental version of the test that is administered to samples of students.

CONSTRUCT VALIDITY

construct validity The ability of an instrument to measure psychological constructs.

Establishing **construct validity** for a new instrument may be more difficult than establishing content validity. *Construct,* in psychoeducational assessment, is a term used to describe a psychological trait, personality trait, psychological concept, attribute, or theoretical characteristic. To establish construct validity, the construct must be clearly defined. Constructs are usually abstract concepts, such as intelligence and creativity, that can be observed and measured by some type of instrument. Construct validity may be more difficult to measure than content because constructs are hypothetical and even seem invisible. Creativity is not seen, but the products of that trait may be observed, such as in writing or painting.

In establishing the construct validity of an instrument, the validity study may involve another measure that has been researched previously and has been shown to be a good indicator of the construct or of some degree or component of the construct. This is, of course, comparing the instrument to some other criterion, which is criterion-related validity. (Don't get confused!)

Often in test development, the validity studies may involve several types of criterion-related validity to establish different types of validity. Anastasi (1988) listed the following types of studies that are considered when establishing a test's construct validity:

> 1. *Developmental changes.* Instruments that measure traits that are expected to change with development should have these changes reflected in the scores if the changeable trait is being measured (such as academic achievement).
> 2. *Correlations with other tests.* New tests are compared with existing instruments that have been found valid for construct being measured.
> 3. *Factor analysis.* This statistical method determines how much particular test items cluster, which illustrates measurement of like constructs.
> 4. *Internal consistency.* Statistical methods can determine the degree with which individual items appear to be measuring the same constructs in the same manner or direction.
> 5. *Convergent and discriminant validation.* Tests should correlate highly with other instruments measuring the same construct but should not correlate with instruments measuring very different constructs.
> 6. *Experimental interventions.* Tests designed to measure traits, skills, or constructs that can be influenced by interventions (such as teaching) should have the intervention reflected by changes in pretest and posttest scores. (pp. 153–159)

Table 4.3 illustrates how construct validity is applied.

VALIDITY OF TESTS VERSUS VALIDITY OF TEST USE

validity of test use The appropriate use of a specific instrument.

Professionals in special education and in the judicial system have understood for quite some time that test validity and **validity of test use** for a particular instrument are two separate issues (Cole, 1981). Tests may be used inappropriately even though they are valid instruments (Cole, 1981). The results obtained in testing may also be used in an invalid manner by placing children inappropriately or inaccurately predicting educational futures (Heller, Holtzman, & Messick, 1982).

Some validity-related issues contribute to bias in the assessment process and subsequently to the invalid use of the test instruments. Content, even though it may validly represent the domain of skills or traits being assessed, may discriminate against different groups. *Item bias,* a term used when an item is answered incorrectly a disproportionate number of times by one group compared to another group, may exist even though the test appears to represent the content domain. An examiner who continues to use an instrument found to contain bias may be practicing discriminatory assessment, which is failure to comply with IDEA.

Predictive validity may contribute to test bias by predicting accurately for one group and not another. Educators should select and administer instruments only after careful study of the reliability and validity research contained in test manuals.

Table 4.3 The Gray Oral Reading Tests: Applying construct validity to a reading instrument.

Constructs Underlying the Gray Oral Reading Tests
1. Because reading ability is developmental in nature, performance on the GORT-4 should be strongly correlated to chronological age.
2. Because the GORT-4 subtests measure various aspects of oral reading ability, they should correlate with each other.
3. Because reading is a type of language, the GORT-4 should correlate significantly with spoken language abilities.
4. Because reading is the receptive form of written language, the GORT-4 should correlate with tests that measure expressive written language.
5. Because reading is a cognitive ability, the GORT-4 should correlate with measures of intelligence or aptitude.
6. Because the GORT-4 measures reading, it should correlate with measures of automatized naming.
7. Because the GORT-4 measures reading, the results should differentiate between groups of people known to be average and those known to be low average or below average in reading ability.
8. Because the GORT-4 measures reading, changes in scores should occur over time due to reading instruction.
9. Because the items of a particular subtest measure similar traits, the items of each subtest should be highly correlated with the total score of that subtest.

Source: From *Gray Oral Reading Tests-4: Examiner's Manual.* By J. L. Wiederholt & B. R. Bryant, 2001. Copyright: Pro-Ed., Austin, Texas. Reprinted with permission.

RELIABILITY VERSUS VALIDITY

A test may be reliable; that is, it may measure a trait with about the same degree of accuracy time after time. The reliability does not guarantee that the trait is measured in a valid or accurate manner. A test may be consistent and reliable but not valid. It is important that a test has had thorough research studies in both reliability and validity.

THINK AHEAD

The concepts presented in this chapter will be applied in the remaining chapters of the text. How do you think these concepts help professionals evaluate instruments?

EXERCISES

Part I

Match the following terms with the correct definitions.

a. reliability
b. validity
c. internal consistency
d. correlation coefficient
e. coefficient alpha
f. scattergram
g. estimated true score
h. Pearson's *r*
i. interrater reliability
j. test-retest reliability
k. equivalent forms reliability
l. true score
m. predictive validity
n. criterion-related validity
o. positive correlation
p. K-R 20
q. validity of test use
r. negative correlation
s. confidence interval
t. split-half reliability
u. standard error of measurement

_____ 1. A new academic achievement test assesses elementary-age students' math ability. The test developers found, however, that students in the research group who took the test two times had scores that were quite different upon the second test administration, which was conducted two weeks after the initial administration. It was determined that the test did not have acceptable _____.

_____ 2. A new test was designed to measure the self-concept of students at middle-school age. The test required students to use essay-type responses to answer three questions regarding their feelings about their own self-concept. Two assessment professionals were comparing the students' responses and how these responses were scored by the professionals. On this type of instrument, it is important that the _____ is acceptable.

_____ 3. In studying the relationship between the scores of the administration of one test administration with the second administration of the test, the number .89 represents the _____.

_____ 4. One would expect that the number of classes a college student attends in a specific course and the final exam grade in that course would have a _____.

_____ 5. In order to have a better understanding of a student's true abilities, the concept of _____ must be understood and applied to obtained scores.

_____ 6. The number of times a student moves during elementary school may likely have a _____ to the student's achievement scores in elementary school.

_____ 7. A test instrument may have good reliability; however, that does not guarantee that the test has _____.

_____ 8. On a teacher-made test of math, the following items were included: 2 single-digit addition problems, 1 single-digit subtraction problem, 4 problems of multiplication of fractions, and 1 problem of converting decimals to fractions. This test does not appear to have good _____.

_____ 9. A college student failed the first test of the new semester. The student hoped that the first test did not have strong _____ about performance on the final exam.

_____ 10. No matter how many times a student may be tested, the student's _____ may never be determined.

Part II

Complete the following sentences and solve the problem.

1. The score obtained during the assessment of a student may not be the score, because all testing situations are subject to chance __________.
2. A closer estimation of the student's best performance can be calculated by using the __________ score.
3. A range of possible scores can then be determined by using the __________ for the specific test.
4. The smaller the standard error of measurement, the more __________ the test.
5. When calculating the range of possible scores, it is best to use the appropriate standard error of measurement for the student's __________ provided in the test manual.
6. The larger the standard error of measurement, the less __________ the test.
7. Use the following set of data to determine the mean, median, mode, range, variance, standard deviation, standard error of measurement, and possible range for each score assuming 68% confidence. The reliability coefficient is .85.

   Data: 50, 75, 31, 77, 65, 81, 90, 92, 76, 76, 74, 88

   Mean: _____ Median: _____ Mode: _____

   Range: _____ Variance: _____ Standard deviation: _____

Standard error of measurement: _____

Obtained Score:	Range of True Scores:
a. 50	From _____ to _____
b. 75	From _____ to _____
c. 31	From _____ to _____
d. 77	From _____ to _____
e. 65	From _____ to _____
f. 81	From _____ to _____
g. 90	From _____ to _____
h. 92	From _____ to _____
i. 76	From _____ to _____
j. 71	From _____ to _____
k. 59	From _____ to _____
l. 88	From _____ to _____

ANSWER KEY TO CHECK YOUR UNDERSTANDING

Activity 4.1

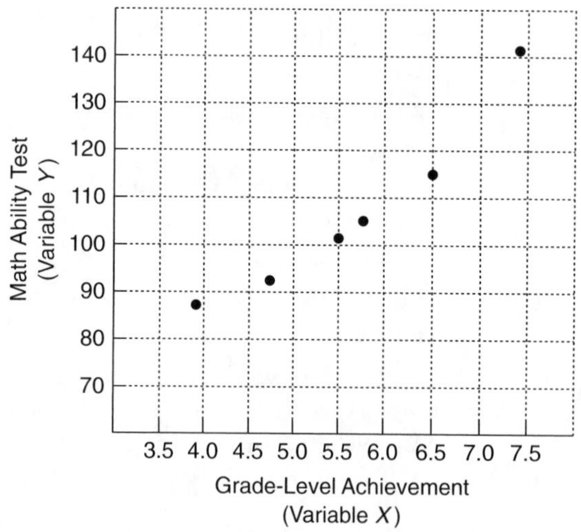

Apply Your Knowledge. Students who scored high on one measure also scored high on the second measure.

Activity 4.2

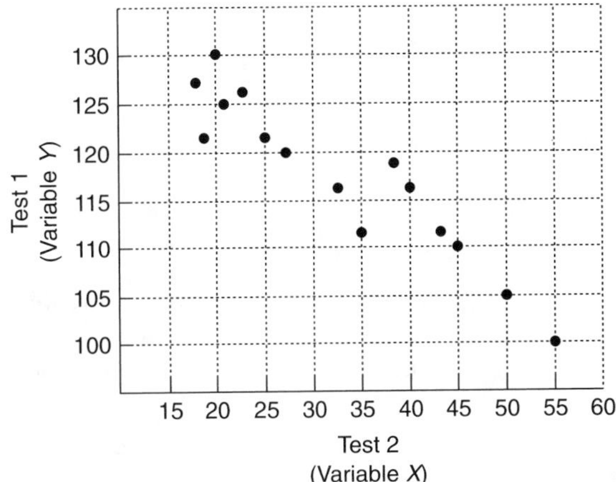

Apply Your Knowledge. Students who scored high on one measure tended to score low on the other measure.

Activity 4.3

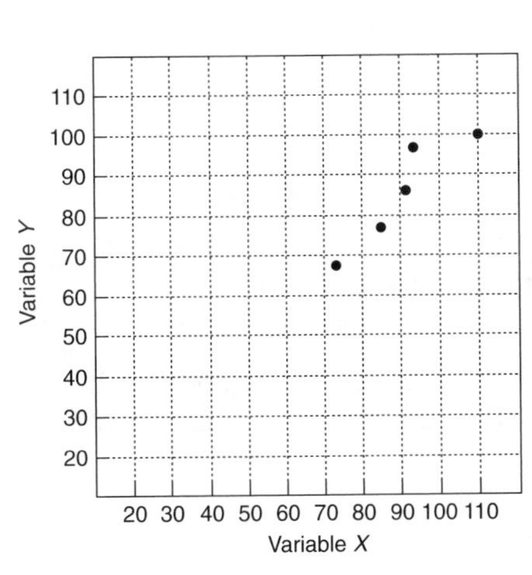

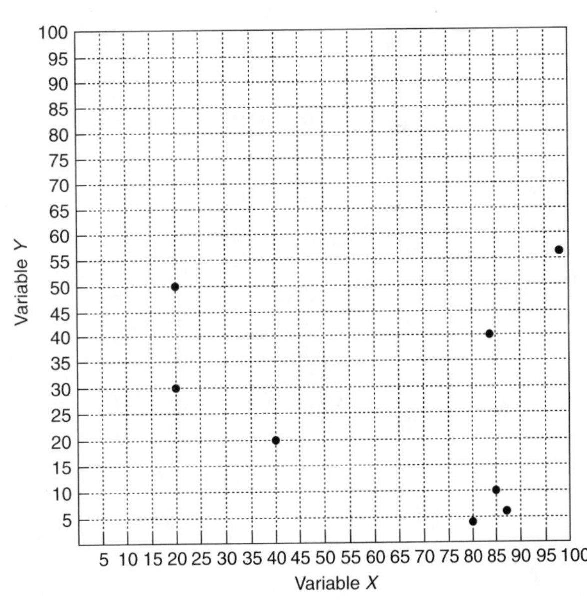

Apply Your Knowledge. Correlation attempts to look at the relationship between two variables. If the variables are related, students perform in a similar way. If the variables are not related, students may perform very differently or there may be no pattern in their performance across variables.

Activity 4.4

1. C
2. B, E
3. B, E
4. F
5. D

Apply Your Knowledge. Internal reliability attempts to measure the consistency among the items within a test. Other types of reliability studies attempt to measure the consistency of the test as a whole instrument.

Activity 4.5

1. Split-half reliability coefficients, by age, for subtest, area, and total test raw scores
2. numeration
3. 9-year-olds

Apply Your Knowledge. Children vary widely in development and acquisition of skills and knowledge. The curriculum and the life experiences of children vary as well. These contribute to the differences in reliability across ages.

Activity 4.6

1. 2.872281
2. 6.36396
3. 3.6373064
4. .9899491
5. 2.1213195
6. more reliability, standard error of measurement is smaller
7. greater standard deviation, standard error of measurement is greater

Apply Your Knowledge. A student's true ability or level of knowledge may not be fairly represented by a score obtained with an instrument that has a large standard error of measurement.

Activity 4.7

1. Test A
2. Test C
3. Standard error of measurement is 4.0792 or 4.079

range for 68% confidence is 81–89
range for 95% confidence is 77–93

4. Standard error of measurement is 2.969 or 2.97
   range for 68% confidence is 79–85
   range for 95% confidence is 76–88

Apply Your Knowledge. 82; smaller standard error of measurement.

Activity 4.8

1. 1.8
2. 0.9
3. 7-year-old 68% confidence is 5.2–8.8
   95% confidence is 3.4–10.6
   12-year-old 68% confidence is 6.1–7.9
   95% confidence is 5.2–8.8

Apply Your Knowledge. Obtained score; mean.

REFERENCES

American Psychological Association (1985). *Standards for educational and psychological testing*. Washington, DC: Author.

Anastasi, A. (1988). *Psychological testing* (pp. 153–159). New York: Macmillan.

Cahan, S. (1989). Don't throw the baby out with the bath water: The case for using estimated true scores in normative comparisons. *Journal of Special Education, 22,* 503–506.

Cole, N. (1981). Bias in testing. *American Psychologist, 36,* 1067–1075.

Connolly, A. (1988). *KeyMath—Revised: A diagnostic inventory of essential mathematics, manual. Forms A and B.* Circle Pines, MN: American Guidance Service.

Feldt, L., Sabers, D., & Reschly, D. (1988). Comments on the reply by Salvia and Ysseldyke. *Journal of Special Education, 22,* 374–377.

Flaugher, R. (1978). The many definitions of test bias. *American Psychologist, 33,* 671–678.

Heller, K., Holtzman, W., & Messick, S. (Eds.). (1982). *Placing children in special education: A strategy for equity.* Washington, DC: National Academy Press.

Mehrens, W., & Lehmann, I. (1978). *Standardized tests in education.* New York: Holt, Rinehart & Winston.

Nunnally, J. (1967). *Psychometric theory.* New York: McGraw-Hill.

Sabers, D., Feldt, L., & Reschly, D. (1988). Appropriate and inappropriate use of estimated true scores for normative comparisons. *Journal of Special Education, 22,* 358–366.

Salvia, J., & Ysseldyke, J. (1988a). *Assessment in remedial and special education* (4th ed.). Dallas: Houghton Mifflin.

Salvia, J., & Ysseldyke, J. (1988b). Using estimated true scores for normative comparisons. *Journal of Special Education, 22,* 367–373.

Walsh, B., & Betz, N. (1985). *Tests and assessment.* Upper Saddle River, NJ: Prentice-Hall.

Wiederholt, J. L., & Bryant, B. R. (2001). *Gray Oral Reading Tests, 4th Edition.* Austin, TX: Pro-Ed.

Wilkinson, G. S. (1993). *The Wide Range Achievement Test: Administration manual.* Wilmington, DE: Jastak, Wide Range.

Williams, R., & Zimmerman, D. (1984). On the virtues and vices of standard error of measurement. *Journal of Experimental Education, 52,* 231–233.

CHAPTER 5

An Introduction to Norm-Referenced Assessment

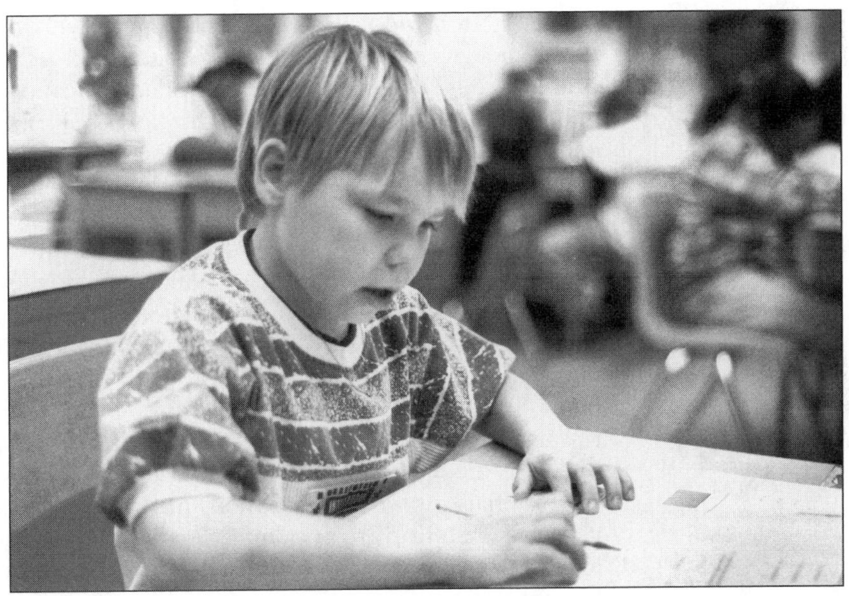

Key Terms

domain
item pool
developmental version
field test
norm-referenced test
sample
norm group
interpolation
chronological age
test manual
protocol
raw score
basal
ceiling
accommodations
assistive technology

CHAPTER FOCUS

This chapter presents the basic mechanics of test design and test administration that the examiner needs to know before administering norm-referenced tests. Following a description of test construction, various techniques for completing test protocols and administering instruments are explained. Both individual norm-reference testing and statewide high-stakes accountability assessment are discussed.

HOW NORM-REFERENCED TESTS ARE CONSTRUCTED

domain An area of cognitive development or ability thought to be evidenced by certain behaviors or skills.

item pool A large collection of test items thought to effectively represent a particular domain or content area.

developmental version The experimental edition of a test that is field-tested and revised before publication.

field test The procedure of trying out a test by administering it to a sample population.

norm-referenced test A test designed to yield average performance scores, which may be used for comparing individual student performances.

sample A small group of people thought to represent the population for whom the test was designed.

norm group A large number of people who are administered a test to establish comparative data of average performances.

Test developers who wish to develop an instrument to assess an educational **domain,** behavioral trait, cognitive ability, motor ability, or language ability, to name a few areas, will establish an item pool of test items. An **item pool** is a representation of items believed to thoroughly assess the given area. The items are gathered from several sources. For example, developers may use published educational materials, information from educational experts in the field, published curriculum guides, and information from educational research to collect items for the initial item pool for an educational domain. These items are carefully scrutinized for appropriateness, wording, content, mode of response required, and developmental level. The items are sequentially arranged according to difficulty. The developers consult with professionals with expertise in the test's content area and, after thorough analysis of the items, administer a **developmental version** to a small group as a **field test.** During the field-testing stage, the test is administered by professionals in the appropriate discipline (education, psychology, speech-language, etc.). The professionals involved in the study critique the test items, presentation format, response mode requirements, administration procedures, and the actual test materials. At this time, revisions may be made, and the developmental version is then ready to be administered to a large sample of the population for whom it was designed. The steps of test construction are illustrated in Figure 5.1.

A **norm-referenced test** is designed to provide the teacher with the capability of comparing the performance of one student with the average performance of other students in the country who are of the same age or grade level. Since it is not practical or possible to test every student of that same age or grade level, a **sample** of students is selected as the comparison group, or **norm group.** In the norming process, the test is administered to a representative sample of students from across the country. A good representation will include a large number of students, usually a few thousand students, who represent diverse groups. Ideally, samples of students from all cultures and linguistic backgrounds who represent the diverse

1. Domain, theoretical basis of test defined. This includes support for construct as well as defining what the domain is not.
2. Exploration of item pool. Experts in the field and other sources of possible items are used to begin collecting items.
3. Developmental version of test or subtests.
4. Field-based research using developmental version of test or subtests.
5. Research on developmental versions analyzed.
6. Changes made to developmental versions based on results of analyses.
7. Standardization version prepared.
8. Sampling procedures to establish how and where persons in sample will be recruited.
9. Testing coordinators located at relevant testing sites representing preferred norm sample.
10. Standardization research begins. Tests are administered at testing sites.
11. Data collected and returned to test developer.
12. Data analyzed for establishing norms, reliability, validity.
13. Test prepared for final version, packaging, protocols, manual.
14. Test available for purchase.

Figure 5.1 Steps in test development.

students for whom the test was developed will be included in the norming process. The norming process should also include students with various disabilities.

The development of a norm-referenced test and the establishment of comparison performances usually occur in the following manner. The items of the test, which are sequentially arranged in the order of difficulty, are administered to the sample population. The performance of each age group and each grade group is analyzed. The average performance of the 6-year-olds, 7-year-olds, 8-year-olds, and so on is determined. The test results are analyzed by grade groups as well, determining the average performance of first graders, second graders, and so on. The analysis of the test results might resemble Table 5.1.

The average number correct in Table 5.1 represents the arithmetic average number of items successfully answered by the age or grade group of students who made up the norming sample. Because these figures will later be used to compare other students' performances on the same instrument, it is imperative that the sample of students be representative of the

Table 5.1 Analysis of results from the Absolutely Wonderful Academic Achievement Test.

Grade	Average Number of Items Correct	Age	Average Number of Items Correct
K	11	5	9
1	14	6	13
2	20	7	21
3	28	8	27
4	38	9	40
5	51	10	49
6	65	11	65
7	78	12	79
8	87	13	88
9	98	14	97
10	112	15	111
11	129	16	130
12	135	17	137

students who will later be assessed. Comparing a student to a norm sample of students who are very different from the student will not be an objective or fair comparison. Factors such as socioeconomic, cultural, or linguistic background; existing disabilities; and emotional environment are variables that may influence a student's performance. The student should be compared with other students with similar backgrounds and of the same age or grade level.

The data displayed in Table 5.1 illustrate the mean performance of students in a particular age or grade group. Although the data represent an average score for each age or grade group, often test developers analyze the data further. For example, the average performance of typical students at various times throughout the school year may be determined. To provide this information, the most accurate norming process would include nine additional administrations of the test, one for each month of the school year. This is usually not practical or possible in most instances of test development. Therefore, to obtain an average expected score for each month of the school year, the test developer usually calculates the scores using data obtained in the original administration through a process known as **interpolation,** or further dividing the existing data (Anastasi & Urbina, 1998).

interpolation The process of dividing existing data into smaller units for establishing tables of developmental scores.

Suppose that the test developer of the Absolutely Wonderful Academic Achievement Test actually administered the test to the sample group during the middle of the school year. To determine the average performance of students throughout the school year, from the first month of the school year

Table 5.2 Interpolated grade equivalents for corresponding raw scores.

Number of Items Correct	Grade
17	2.0
17	2.1
18	2.2
18	2.3
19	2.4
20	2.5
20	2.6
21	2.7
22	2.8
23	2.9
24	3.0
25	3.1
26	3.2
27	3.3
27	3.4
28	3.5
29	3.6
30	3.7
31	3.8
32	3.9
33	4.0
34	4.1
35	4.2
36	4.3
37	4.4
38	4.5
39	4.6
40	4.7
42	4.8
43	4.9

through the last month, the test developer further divides the correct items of each group. In the data in Table 5.1, the average performance of second graders in the sample group is 20, the average performance of third graders is 28, and the average performance of fourth graders is 38. These scores might be further divided and listed in the test manual on a table similar to Table 5.2.

chronological age The numerical representation of a student's age, expressed in years, months, and days.

The obtained scores also might be further divided by age groups so that each month of a **chronological age** is represented. The scores for age 11 might be displayed in a table similar to Table 5.3.

Table 5.3 Interpolated age equivalents for corresponding raw scores.

Average Number of Items Correct	Age Equivalents
57	11-0
58	11-1
60	11-2
61	11-3
62	11-4
63	11-5
65	11-6
66	11-7
68	11-8
69	11-9
70	11-10
71	11-11
72	12-0

It is important to notice that age scores are written with a dash or hyphen, whereas grade scores are expressed with a decimal. This is because grade scores are based on a 10-month school year and can be expressed by using decimals, whereas age scores are based on a 12-month calendar year and therefore should not be expressed using decimals. For example, 11-4 represents an age of 11 years and 4 months, but 11.4 represents the grade score of the 4th month of the 11th grade. If the scores are expressed incorrectly, a difference of about 6 grades or 5 years could be incorrectly interpreted.

Check Your Understanding

Complete Activity 5.1.

ACTIVITY 5.1

Answer the following questions.

1. In Table 5.1, what was the average score of the sample group of students in grade 7? _____
2. According to Table 5.1, what was the average number of correct items of the sample group of students who were 16 years of age? _____
3. What was the average number of correct items of the sample group of students who were 6 years of age? _____

4. Why did students who were in first grade have an average number of 14 correct responses while students in grade 6 had an average of 65 correct responses? ______________________________

____
5. According to the information provided in Table 5.2, what was the average number of correct responses for students in the third month of grade 3? _____
6. Were students in the sample tested during the third month of the third grade? _____ By what means was the average for each month of the school year determined? ______________________________
7. According to the information provided in Table 5.3, what was the average number of correct responses for students of the chronological age 11-2? _____
8. Write the meaning of these expressions:
   4.1 means ______________________________
   4-1 means ______________________________
   3.3 means ______________________________
   6-7 means ______________________________
   10.8 means ______________________________

Apply Your Knowledge

Write an explanation for a parent that clarifies the difference between a grade-equivalent score and the grade level of academic functioning.

____

____

____

BASIC STEPS IN TEST ADMINISTRATION

test manual A manual that accompanies a test instrument and contains instructions for administration and norm tables.

When administering a norm-referenced standardized test, it is important to remember that the test developer specified the instructions for the examiner and the examinee. The **test manual** contains much information, which the examiner must read thoroughly and understand before administering the test. The examiner should practice administering all sections of the test many times before using the test with a student. The first few attempts of practice administration should be supervised by someone who has had experience with the instrument. Legally, according to IDEA, any individual test administration should be completed in the manner set forth by the test developer and should be administered by trained personnel. Both legal

Comprehensive Form

K-TEA

KAUFMAN TEST of EDUCATIONAL ACHIEVEMENT

by Alan S. Kaufman & Nadeen L. Kaufman

INDIVIDUAL TEST RECORD

Student's Name ______ Sex ______
Parent's Name ______
Home Address ______ Home Phone ______
Grade ______ Teacher ______
School ______ Examiner ______

	Year	Month	Day
Test Date			
Birth Date			
Chronological Age			

Figure 5.2 Kaufman Test of Educational Achievement, Comprehensive Form protocol. (*Source:* From *Kaufman Test of Educational Achievement*, K-TEA Comprehensive Form protocol, by A. Kaufman and N. Kaufman, 1985. Circle Pines, MN: American Guidance Service. Copyright 1985 by American Guidance Service. Reprinted by permission.)

regulations and standards and codes of ethics hold testing personnel responsible for accurate and fair assessment.

The examiner should carefully carry out the mechanics of test administration. The first few steps are simple, although careless errors can occur and may make a difference in the decisions made regarding a student's educational future. The **protocol** of a standardized test is the form used during the test administration and for scoring and interpreting test results. The first page of the protocol provides space for writing basic information about the student. Figure 5.2 shows the first page of the protocol of the *Kaufman Test of Educational Achievement* (Kaufman & Kaufman, 1985). The examiner must complete the top portion of the protocol before administering the test. The remainder of the protocol is completed during and after the administration of the test.

protocol The response sheet or record form used by the examiner to record the student's answers.

BEGINNING TESTING

The following suggestions will help you, the examiner, establish a positive testing environment and increase the probability that the student will feel comfortable and therefore perform better in the testing situation.

1. Establish familiarity with the student before the first day of testing. Several meetings in different situations with relaxed verbal exchange are recommended. You may wish to participate in an activity with the student and informally observe behavior and language skills.

2. When the student meets with you on test day, spend several minutes in friendly conversation before beginning the test. Do not begin testing until the student seems to feel at ease with you.
3. Explain why the testing has been suggested at the level of understanding that is appropriate for the student's age and developmental level. It is important that the student understand that the testing session is important, although the child should not feel threatened by the test. Examples of explanations include the following:
   - To see how you work (solve) math problems.
   - To see how we can help you achieve in school.
   - To help you make better progress in school.
   - [Or if the student has revealed specific weaknesses] To see how we can help you with your spelling [or English, or science, etc.] skills.
4. Give a brief introduction about the test, such as: "Today we will complete some activities that are like your other school work. There are some math problems and reading passages like you have in class," or, "This will help us learn how you think in school," or "This will show us the best ways for you to . . . (learn, read, work math problems)."
5. Begin testing in a calm manner. Be certain that all instructions are followed carefully.

During test administration, the student may ask questions or give answers that are very close to the correct response. On many tests, clear instructions are given that tell the examiner when to prompt for an answer or when to query for a response. Some items on certain tests may not be repeated. Some items are timed. The best guarantee for accurate assessment techniques is for the examiner to become very familiar with the test manual. General guidelines for test administration, suggested by McLoughlin and Lewis (2001), are presented in Figure 5.3.

As stated in professional ethics and IDEA, tests must be given in the manner set forth by the test developer, and adapting tests must be done by professionals with expertise in the specific area being assessed who are cognizant of the psychometric changes that will result.

CALCULATING CHRONOLOGICAL AGE

Many tests have protocols that provide space for calculating the student's chronological age on the day that the test is administered. It is imperative that this calculation is correct because the chronological age may be used to determine the correct norm tables used for interpreting the test results.

The chronological age is calculated by writing the test date first and then subtracting the date of birth. The dates are written in the order of year, month, and day. In performing the calculation, remember that each of the columns represents a different numerical system, and if the number that is

Test administration is a skill, and testers must learn how to react to typical student comments and questions. The following general guidelines apply to the majority of standardized tests.

STUDENT REQUESTS FOR REPETITION OF TEST ITEMS

Students often ask the tester to repeat a question. This is usually permissible as long as the item is repeated verbatim and in its entirety. However, repetition of memory items measuring the student's ability to recall information is not allowed.

ASKING STUDENTS TO REPEAT RESPONSES

Sometimes the tester must ask the student to repeat a response. Perhaps the tester did not hear what the student said, or the student's speech is difficult to understand. However, the tester should make every effort to see or hear the student's first answer. The student may refuse to repeat a response or, thinking that the request for repetition means the first response was unsatisfactory, answer differently.

STUDENT MODIFICATION OF RESPONSES

When students give one response, then change their minds and give a different one, the tester should accept the last response, even if the modification comes after the tester has moved to another item. However, some tests specify that only the first response may be accepted for scoring.

CONFIRMING AND CORRECTING STUDENT RESPONSES

The tester may not in any way—verbal or nonverbal—inform a student whether a response is correct. Correct responses may not be confirmed; wrong responses may not be corrected. This rule is critical for professionals who both teach and test, because their first inclination is to reinforce correct answers.

REINFORCING STUDENT WORK BEHAVIOR

Although testers cannot praise students for their performance on specific test items, good work behavior can and should be rewarded. Appropriate comments are "You're working hard" and "I like the way

Figure 5.3 General guidelines for test administration. (*Source:* From *Assessing Special Students* (5th ed., p. 87 by J. McLoughlin and R. Lewis, 2001, Upper Saddle River, NJ: Merrill/Prentice Hall. Copyright by Prentice Hall. Reprinted by permission.)

subtracted is larger than the number from which the difference is to be found, the numbers must be converted appropriately. This means that the years are based on 12 months, and the months are based on 30 days. An example is shown in Figure 5.4.

Notice in Figure 5.4 that when subtracting the days, the number 30 is added to 2 to find the difference. When subtraction of days requires borrowing, a whole month, or 30 days, must be used. When borrowing to subtract months, the number 12 is added, because a whole year must be borrowed.

When determining the chronological age for testing, the days are rounded to the nearest month. Days are rounded up if there are 15 or more days by adding a month. The days are rounded down by dropping the days you're trying to answer every question." Students should be praised between test items or subtests to ensure that reinforcement is not linked to specific responses.

ENCOURAGING STUDENTS TO RESPOND

When students fail to respond to a test item, the tester can encourage them to give an answer. Students sometimes say nothing when presented with a difficult item, or they may comment, "I don't know" or "I can't do that one." The tester should repeat the item and say, "Give it a try" or "You can take a guess." The aim is to encourage the student to attempt all test items.

QUESTIONING STUDENTS

Questioning is permitted on many tests. If in the judgment of the tester the response given by the student is neither correct nor incorrect, the tester repeats the student's answer in a questioning tone and says, "Tell me more about that." This prompts the student to explain so that the response can be scored. However, clearly wrong answers should not be questioned.

COACHING

Coaching differs from encouragement and questioning in that it helps a student arrive at an answer. The tester must *never* coach the student. Coaching invalidates the student's response; test norms are based on the assumption that students will respond without examiner assistance. Testers must be very careful to avoid coaching.

ADMINISTRATION OF TIMED ITEMS

Some tests include timed items; the student must reply within a certain period to receive credit. In general, the time period begins when the tester finishes presentation of the item. A watch or clock should be used to time student performance.

Figure 5.3 continued.

and using the month found through the subtraction process. Here are some examples:

	Years	Months	Days	
Chronological age:	7-	4-	17	rounded up to 7-5
Chronological age:	9-	10-	6	rounded down to 9-10
Chronological age:	11-	11-	15	rounded up to 12-0

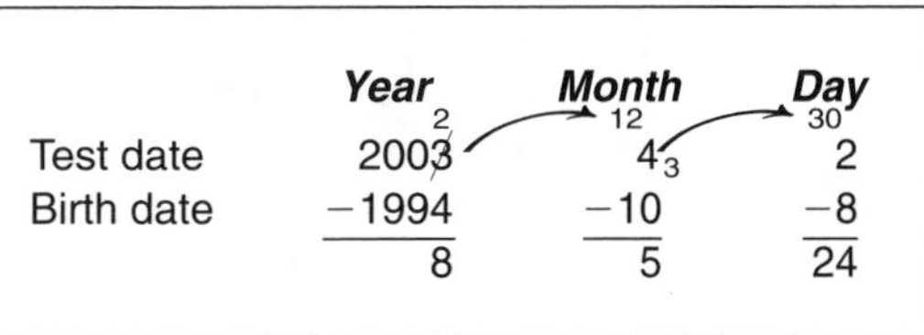

	Year	Month	Day
Test date	2003 (2)	4 (12, 3)	2 (30)
Birth date	−1994	−10	−8
	8	5	24

Figure 5.4 Calculation of chronological age for a student who is 8 years, 6 months old.

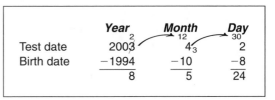

Check Your Understanding

Complete Activity 5.2.

ACTIVITY 5.2

Calculate the chronological ages using the following birth dates and test dates.

				Year	Month	Day
1. Birth date:	3-2-1991		Date of test:	____	____	____
Test date:	5-4-2001		Date of birth:	____	____	____
			Chronological age:	____	____	____
2. Birth date:	7-5-1996		Date of test:	____	____	____
Test date:	11-22-2004		Date of birth:	____	____	____
			Chronological age:	____	____	____
3. Birth date:	10-31-1997		Date of test:	____	____	____
Test date:	6-20-2000		Date of birth:	____	____	____
			Chronological age:	____	____	____

Round the following chronological ages to years and months.

	Years	Months	Days	Rounded to
4.	7-	10-	23	____
5.	11-	7-	14	____
6.	14-	11-	29	____

Apply Your Knowledge

Why do you think it is so important to have the exact chronological age of a student before you administer and score a test? ____________

____

CALCULATING RAW SCORES

raw score The first score obtained in test administration; usually the number of items counted as correct.

The first score obtained in the administration of a test is the **raw score.** On most educational instruments, the raw score is simply the number of items the student answers correctly. Figure 5.5 shows the calculation of a raw score for one student. The student's correct responses are marked with a 1, incorrect responses with a 0.

The number of items answered correctly on this test was 8, which is expressed as a raw score. The raw score will be entered into a table in the test manual to determine the derived scores, which are norm-referenced scores expressed in different ways. The administration of this test was stopped when the student missed 3 consecutive items because the test manual stated to stop testing when this occurred.

Figure 5.5
Calculation for student who began with item 1 and correctly answered 8 of 15 attempted items.

1.	1	**11.**	0
2.	1	**12.**	1
3.	1	**13.**	0
4.	1	**14.**	0
5.	0	**15.**	0
6.	0	**16.**	
7.	1	**17.**	
8.	1	**18.**	
9.	0	**19.**	
10.	1	**20.**	

Raw Score: 8

DETERMINING BASALS AND CEILINGS

The student whose scores are shown in Figure 5.5 began with item 1 and stopped after making 3 consecutive errors. The starting and stopping points of a test must be determined so that unnecessary items are not administered. Some tests contain hundreds of items, many of which may not be developmentally appropriate for all students.

Most educational tests contain starting rules in the manual, protocol, or actual test instrument. These rules are guides that can help the examiner begin testing with an item at the appropriate level. These guides may be given as age recommendations—for example, 6-year-olds begin with item 10—or as grade-level recommendations—for example, fourth-grade students begin with item 25. These starting points are meant to represent a level at which the student could answer all previous items correctly and are most accurate for students who are functioning close to age or grade expectancy.

basal Thought to represent the level of skills below which the student would correctly answer all test items.

Often, students referred for special education testing function below grade- and age-level expectancies. Therefore, the guides or starting points suggested by the test developers may be inappropriate. It is necessary to determine the **basal** level for the student, or the level at which the student could correctly answer all easier items, those items located at lower levels. Once the basal has been established, the examiner can proceed with testing the student. If the student fails to obtain a basal level, the test may be considered too difficult, and another instrument should be selected.

The rules for establishing a basal level are given in the test manuals, and many tests contain the information on the protocol. The basal rule may be the same as a ceiling rule, such as 3 consecutively correct responses and 3 consecutively incorrect responses. The basal rule may also be expressed as correctly completing an entire level. No matter what the rule, the objective is the same: to establish a level that is thought to represent a foundation and at which all easier items would be assumed correct.

Figure 5.6 Basal level established for test I for 3 consecutive correct responses; basal level for test II established when all items in one level (grade 1) are answered correctly.

TEST I		TEST II		
1.		Level K	1.	
2.			2.	
3.			3.	
4.			4.	
5.		Grade 1	5.	1
6.	1		6.	1
7.	1		7.	1
8.	1		8.	1
9.	0	Grade 2	9.	0
10.	1		10.	1
			11.	0
			12.	1

The examples shown in Figure 5.6 illustrate a basal rule of 3 consecutive correct responses on Test I and a basal of all items answered correctly on an entire level of the test on Test II.

It may be difficult to select the correct item to begin with when testing a special education student. The student's social ability may seem to be age appropriate but his academic ability may be significantly below expectancy for his age and grade placement. The examiner may begin with an item that is too easy or too difficult. Although it is not desirable to administer too many items that are beneath the student's academic level, it is better to begin the testing session with the positive reinforcement of answering items correctly than with the negative reinforcement of answering several items incorrectly and experiencing a sense of failure or frustration. The examiner should obtain a basal by selecting an item believed to be a little below the student's academic level.

Even when the examiner chooses a starting item believed to be easy for a student, sometimes the student will miss items before the basal is established. In this case, most test manuals contain instructions for determining the basal. Some manuals instruct the examiner to test backward in the same sequence until a basal can be established. After the basal is determined, the examiner proceeds from the point where the backward sequence was begun. Other test manuals instruct the examiner to drop back an entire grade level or to drop back the number of items required to establish a basal. For example, if 5 consecutive correct responses are required for a basal, the examiner is instructed to drop back 5 items and begin administration. If the examiner is not familiar with the student's ability in a certain area, the basal may be even more difficult to establish. The examiner in this case may have to drop back several times. For this reason, the examiner should circle the number of the first item administered. This information can be used later in the test interpretation.

Students may establish two or more basals; that is, using the 5-consecutive-correct rule, a student may answer 5 correct, miss an item, then answer 5 consecutive correct again. The test manual may address this specifically, or it may not be mentioned. Unless the test manual states that the examiner may use the second or highest basal, it is best to use the first basal established.

Check Your Understanding

Complete Activity 5.3.

ACTIVITY 5.3

Using the following basal rules, identify basals for these students.

Test I		**Test II**		
(Basal: 5 consecutive correct)		**(Basal: 7 consecutive correct)**		
1.	____	Grade 4	25.	____
2.	____		26.	____
3.	____		27.	____
4.	____		28.	____
5.	____		29.	____
6.	1		30.	____
7.	1	Grade 5	31.	1
8.	1		32.	1
9.	1		33.	1
10.	1		34.	1
11.	0		35.	1
12.	1	Grade 6	36.	1
13.	0		37.	1
14.	1		38.	0
			39.	1
			40.	0

Basal items are ____ Basal items are ____

The instructions given in the test manual state that if a student fails to establish a basal with 5 consecutive correct items, the examiner must drop back 5 items from the first attempted item and begin testing. Which item would the examiner begin with in the following examples?

Example 1		**Example 2**	
22.	____	116.	____
23.	____	117.	____
24.	____	118.	____
25.	____	119.	____
26.	____	120.	____
27.	____	(121.)	1
28.	____	122.	1

Example 1 cont.	**Example 2 cont.**
(29.) 1	123. 0
30. 0	124. ____
31. ____	125. ____
32. ____	126. ____
Drop to item: ____	Drop to item: ____

Apply Your Knowledge

What is the meaning of basal level, and how does it relate to a student's ability? ______________________________

____

____

When calculating the raw score, all items that appear before the established basal are counted as correct. This is because the basal is thought to represent the level at which all easier items would be passed. Therefore, when counting correct responses, count items below the basal as correct even though they were not administered.

ceiling Thought to represent the level of skills above which all test items would be answered incorrectly; the examiner discontinues testing at this level.

Just as the basal is thought to represent the level at which all easier items would be passed, the **ceiling** is thought to represent the level at which more difficult items would not be passed. The ceiling rule may be 3 consecutive incorrect or even 5 items out of 7 items answered incorrectly. Occasionally, an item is administered above the ceiling level by mistake, and the student may answer correctly. Because the ceiling level is thought to represent the level at which more difficult items would not be passed, these items usually are not counted. Unless the test manual states that the examiner is to count items above the ceiling, it is best not to do so.

USING INFORMATION ON PROTOCOLS

The protocol, or response form, for each test contains valuable information that can aid in test administration. Detailed instructions regarding the basal and ceiling rules for individual subtests of an educational test may be found on most protocols for educational tests.

Many tests have ceiling rules that are the same as the basal rules; for example, 5 consecutive incorrect responses are counted as the ceiling, and 5 consecutive correct responses establish the basal. Since some tests have different basal and ceiling rules, it is necessary to read instructions carefully. If the protocol does not provide the basal and ceiling rules, the examiner is wise to note this at the top of the pages of the protocol for the sections to be administered.

Check Your Understanding

Complete Activity 5.4.

ACTIVITY 5.4

Calculate the raw scores for the following protocol sections. Follow the given basal and ceiling rules.

Protocol 1 (Basal: 5 consecutive correct; Ceiling: 5 consecutive incorrect)		**Protocol 2 (Basal: 3 consecutive correct; Ceiling: 3 consecutive incorrect)**	
223.	___	10.	___
224.	___	11.	1
225.	___	12.	1
226.	___	13.	1
227.	1	14.	0
228.	1	15.	1
229.	1	16.	1
230.	1	17.	1
231.	1	18.	1
232.	0	19.	0
233.	1	20.	1
234.	1	21.	1
235.	0	22.	1
236.	0	23.	0
237.	0	24.	0
238.	0	25.	0
239.	0	26.	___
Raw score:	___	Raw score:	___

1. Which protocol had more than one basal? _____
2. What were the basal items on protocol 1? _____
3. What were the ceiling items on protocol 1? _____
4. What were the basal items on protocol 2? _____
5. What were the ceiling items on protocol 2? _____

Apply Your Knowledge

What is the meaning of ceiling level, and how does it relate to the student's ability? ____

____

The protocols for each test are arranged specifically for that test. Some forms contain several subtests that may be arranged in more than one order. On very lengthy tests, the manual may provide information about selecting only certain subtests rather than administering the entire test. Other tests have age- or grade-appropriate subtests, which must be selected according to the student's level. Some instruments use the raw score on the first subtest to determine the starting point on all other subtests. And finally, some subtests require the examiner to begin with item 1 regardless of the age or grade level of the student. Specific instructions for individual subtests may be provided on the protocol as well as in the test manual.

Educational tests often provide training exercises at the beginning of subtests. These training exercises help the examiner explain the task to the student and better ensure that the student understands the task before answering the first scored item. The student may be allowed to attempt the training tasks more than once, or the examiner may be instructed to correct wrong answers and explain the correct responses. These items are not scored, however, and a subtest may be skipped if the student does not understand the task. The use of training exercises varies.

ADMINISTERING TESTS: FOR BEST RESULTS

Students tend to respond more and perform better in testing situations with examiners who are familiar with them (Fuchs, Zern, & Fuchs, 1983). As suggested previously, the examiner should spend some time with the student before the actual evaluation. The student's regular classroom setting is a good place to begin. The examiner should talk with the student in a warm manner and repeat visits to the classroom before the evaluation. It may also be helpful for the student to visit the testing site to become familiar with the environment. The examiner may want to tell the student that they will work together later in the week or month. The testing session should not be the first time the examiner and student meet. Classroom observations and visits may aid the examiner in determining which tests to administer. Chances for successful testing sessions will increase if the student is not overtested. Although it is imperative that all areas of suspected disability be assessed, multiple tests that measure the same skill or ability are not necessary.

Check Your Understanding

Complete Activity 5.5.

ACTIVITY 5.5

Using the protocol and the responses in Figure 5.7, calculate the raw score for this subtest of the Peabody Individual Achievement Test—Revised (Markwardt, 1989). Determine the basal and ceiling items for this student.

1. How many trials are allowed for the training exercises on this subtest? _____
2. According to the responses shown, what items are included in the student's basal level? _____
3. What instructions are provided about establishing the basal? _____

____

SUBTEST 2
Reading Recognition

Training Exercises

	Trial 1	Trial 2	Trial 3
Exercise A.	(1) _____	(1) _____	(1) _____
Exercise B.	(3) _____	(3) _____	(3) _____
Exercise C.	(2) _____	(2) _____	(2) _____

Basal and Ceiling Rules

Basal: *highest* 5 consecutive correct responses

Ceiling: *lowest* 7 consecutive responses containing 5 errors

Starting Point

The item number that corresponds to the subject's raw score on General Information.

43. ledge ____ 1 ____
44. escape ____ 1 ____
45. northern ____ 1 ____
46. towel ____ 1 ____
47. kneel ____ 1 ____
48. height ____ 0 ____
49. exercise ____ 1 ____
50. observe ____ 1 ____
51. ruin ____ 0 ____
52. license ____ 1 ____
53. uniforms ____ 0 ____
54. pigeon ____ 1 ____
55. moisture ____ 0 ____
56. artificial ____ 1 ____
57. issues ____ 0 ____
58. quench ____ 0 ____
59. hustle ____ 0 ____
60. thigh ____ 0 ____

READING RECOGNITION

Ceiling Item _____

minus Errors _____

equals RAW SCORE _____

Figure 5.7 Basal and ceiling rules and response items for a subtest from the Peabody Individual Achievement Test—Revised. (*Source:* From *Peabody Individual Achievement Test—Revised,* subtest 2, Reading Recognition, by F. C. Markwardt, 1989, Circle Pines, MN: American Guidance Service. Copyright 1989 by American Guidance Service. Reprinted by permission.)

4. According to the responses shown, what items are included in the student's ceiling level? _____

Apply Your Knowledge

What information are you able to learn from this page of the protocol?

____

____

____

After the examiner and student are in the testing room, the examiner should attempt to make the student feel at ease. The examiner should convey the importance of the testing situation without making the student feel anxious. As suggested by McLoughlin and Lewis (2001), the examiner should encourage the student to work hard and should reinforce the student's attempts and efforts, not correct responses. Responses that reinforce the efforts of the student may include statements such as "You are working so hard today," or "You like math work," or "I will be sure to tell your teacher [or mother or father, etc.] how hard you worked." If the student asks about his performance on specific items ("Did I get that one right?"), the examiner should again try to reinforce effort.

Young students may enjoy a tangible reinforcer upon the completion of the testing session. The examiner may tell the student near the end of the session to work just a few more items for a treat or surprise. Reinforcement with tangibles is not recommended during the assessment, because the student may lose interest in the test or no longer pay attention.

During the administration of the test, the examiner must be sure to follow all instructions in the manual. As stated in professional standards and IDEA, tests must be given in the manner set forth by the test developer, and adapting tests must be done by professionals with expertise in the specific area being assessed who are cognizant of the psychometric changes that will result.

Cole, D'Alonzo, Gallegos, Giordano, and Stile (1992) suggested that examiners consider several additional factors to decrease bias in the assessment process. The following considerations, adapted from Cole et al. (1992), can help the examiner determine whether the test can be administered in a fair way:

1. Do sensory or communicative impairments make portions of the test inaccessible?
2. Do sensory or communicative impairments limit students from responding to questions?
3. Do test materials or method of responding limit students from responding?
4. Do background experiences limit the student's ability to respond?
5. Does the content of classroom instruction limit students from responding?

6. Is the examiner familiar to the student?
7. Are instructions explained in a familiar fashion?
8. Is the recording technique required of the student on the test familiar? (p. 219)

OBTAINING DERIVED SCORES

The raw scores obtained during the test administration are used to locate other derived scores from norm tables included in the examiner's manuals for the specific test. The derived scores may include percentile ranks, grade equivalents, standard scores with a mean of 100 or 50, and other standardized scores, such as *z* scores.

There are advantages and disadvantages to using the different types of derived scores. Of particular concern is the correct use and interpretation of grade equivalents and percentile ranks. These two types of derived scores are used frequently because the basic theoretical concepts are thought to be understood; however, these two types of scores are misunderstood and misinterpreted by professionals (Huebner, 1988, 1989; Wilson, 1987). The reasons for this misinterpretation are the lack of understanding of the numerical scale used and the method used in establishing grade-level equivalents.

Percentile ranks are used often because they can be easily explained to parents. The concept, for example, of 75% of the peer group scoring at the same level as or below a particular student is one that parents and professionals can understand. The difficulty in interpreting percentile ranks is that they do not represent a numerical scale with equal intervals. For example, the standard scores between the 50th and 60th percentiles are quite different from the standard scores between the 80th and 90th percentile ranks.

The development of grade equivalents needs to be considered when using these derived scores. Grade equivalents represent the average number of items answered correctly by the students in the standardization sample of a particular grade. These equivalents may not represent the actual skill level of particular items or of a particular student's performance on a test. Many of the skills tested on academic achievement tests are taught at various grade levels. The grade level of presentation of these skills depends on the curriculum used. The grade equivalents obtained therefore may not be representative of the skills necessary to pass that grade level in a specific curriculum.

TYPES OF SCORES

The concepts of standard scores, percentile ranks, age and grade equivalents have been introduced. Standard scores and percentile ranks are scores used to compare an individual student with the larger norm group to determine relative standing in the areas assessed, such as mathematics skills or IQ. Standard scores include those scores with an average or mean of 100 as well as other scores such as *T* scores that have an average of 50 or *z* scores, which convey the student's standing in terms of standard deviation units. Refer to Figure 3.9 to locate scores. For example, the student with a *z* score of −1.0 indicates that the student is one standard deviation below average and if this score is converted to a standard score with a mean of 100, the standard score of this student is 85. If the student's *z* score is converted to *T* scores, the student's *T* score is 40 (*T* score average is 50; *SD* of 10).

Other scores that may be used to compare the student's standing to the norm group are stanine scores. Stanine scores, like percentile ranks, are not equidistant. Stanines are based on a system of dividing the distribution into 9 segments with an average or mean of 5 and a standard deviation of 2. This means that the previously presented student score of 85 and a *z* score of −10 would have a stanine score of 3. The data or student scores within the stanine sections represent large segments of ability and therefore do not convey very precise indications of a student's performance or ability.

GROUP TESTING: HIGH-STAKES ASSESSMENT

The protocol examples, basal and ceiling exercises presented thus far in the chapter are typical of individualized norm-referenced instruments. Other instruments commonly used in schools are norm-referenced standardized group achievement tests. These instruments are administered to classroom-size groups to assess achievement levels. Group achievement tests are increasingly used to assess accountability of individual students and school systems. These instruments are also known as high-stakes tests because the results of such tests often have serious implications of accountability, accreditation, and funding for school systems. States and districts use such instruments to be certain that students are meeting expected academic standards for their grade placement. In addition, at least 26 states use the results of statewide assessment to determine if students are allowed to graduate, and 6 states use such assessment for grade promotion (U.S. Department of Education, 2000).

Principles to guide the assessment of students for accountability have been proposed by Elliott, Braden, and White (2001). These authors suggest that school systems keep in mind that assessment should be logical and serve the purpose for which it is intended. They state that systems should set their standards or goals first before developing assessments. In addition, they remind school personnel that high-stakes testing should measure educational achievement rather than try to create achievement. As with individual assessment, these authors state that no single instrument has the capability to answer all achievement questions and that multiple measures should be used. And finally, as with other educational

Group achievement testing for educational accountability.

instruments, high-stakes assessments should be reliable and valid for their specific purpose.

Brigham, Tochterman, and Brigham (2000) point out that in order for high-stakes assessment to be beneficial for students with special needs, such tests should provide useful information for planning. Such information would inform the teacher about what areas students have mastered, what areas are at the level of instruction, and the areas to which students have not been exposed. These authors further state that the information provided to teachers in high-stakes assessment is often not provided in a timely manner so that instructional interventions can occur. In addition, high-stakes assessment may not be completed annually but rather biannually, so that the results have little if any impact on the student's actual educational planning.

The 1997 IDEA Amendments require that students with disabilities be included in statewide and district-wide assessments. For some students, the assessments are completed with **accommodations** for their specific disabilities. The amendments require that students who are unable to complete these assessments should be administered alternate assessments. When the 1997 amendments required that students with disabilities be included in statewide accountability assessment, most states did not have such accountability systems in place for students eligible under IDEA (Thurlow, Elliott, & Ysseldyke, 1998). The amendments required educators to decide and include in the IEP process which students would take statewide assessments, which students would require accommodations for

accommodations Necessary changes in format, response mode, setting, or scheduling that will enable a student with disabilities to complete general curriculum or test.

the statewide assessments, and which students would require alternate assessment for accountability.

This decision-making process has proved to be complicated and should be reached by the IEP team. Educators must also address the issue of statewide assessment for students being served under Section 504, and the decisions should be included in the student's Section 504 plan (Office of Special Education and Rehabilitative Services, 2000). Thurlow et al. have proposed a decision-making form to assist educators in determining which students should be included in statewide assessment or require accommodations or alternate assessment. This form is presented in Figure 5.8.

For students with disabilities who require accommodations for participation in statewide assessment, the accommodations must not alter what the test is measuring. Accommodations include possible changes in the format of the assessment, the manner in which the student responds, the setting of the assessment, or in scheduling (Office of Special Education and Rehabilitative Services, 2000). The team members determine the accommodations needed in order for the student to participate in the assessment and include such modifications in the student's IEP.

Students from culturally and linguistically diverse backgrounds who are considered to be English-language learners (limited English proficiency) may require accommodations to ensure that academic skills and knowl-

1. Is the student working toward the same standards as other students in the classroom? ___ YES ___ NO

   (If answer to 1 is YES, student should participate in the regular assessment)

2. If NO, is the student working on a modified set of standards (many are the same, but some are modified slightly)? ___ YES ___ NO

   (If answer to 2 is YES, student should participate in the regular assessment)

3. If NO, is the student working on an alternate set of standards? ___ YES ___ NO

   (If answer to 3 is YES, student should participate in an alternate assessment)

4. If the student is working on an alternate set of standards, are there any areas of unique skills that could be assessed through the regular assessment? ___ YES ___ NO

   (If answer to 4 is YES, student should participate in both the regular and an alternate assessment)

Figure 5.8 Participation decision-making form.

edge are being assessed rather than English skills. As with assessment to determine eligibility, students must be assessed in specific areas of content or ability rather than for their English reading or communication skills. If required, accommodations may be included for the student's language differences (Office of Special Education and Rehabilitative Services, 2000).

The team determines to use an alternate assessment method when the student will not be able to participate, even with accommodations, in the statewide or district-wide assessments. Alternate assessments are to be designed that include the same areas or domains as the statewide assessments. The test content should reflect the appropriate knowledge and skills and should be considered a reliable and valid measure of the content.

Check Your Understanding

Complete Activity 5.6.

ACTIVITY 5.6

Match these terms to the statements that follow.

a. alternate assessment
b. statewide assessment
c. high-stakes assessment
d. accommodations

_____ 1. Juan is receiving special education support in the general classroom setting. Although he reads the same textbooks as other students, he must use a word processor to complete his writing assignments. His IEP team has determined that he will require _____ for his standardized statewide assessment.

_____ 2. When assessment determines promotion to the next grade in secondary school, the assessment is called _____.

_____ 3. Allowing students to complete assessment in a small group in a separate room is considered a type of _____.

_____ 4. The IEP team must include statements that address _____.

_____ 5. Lupitina has been receiving her education within a self-contained special education environment since she entered school. Her development is 5 years below the level of her peers. The IEP team must determine if Lupitina should have accommodations for her assessment, or if she will require _____.

ACCOMMODATIONS IN HIGH-STAKES TESTING

Students who participate in the general education curriculum with limited difficulty most likely will not require accommodations for high-stakes testing. Students who require accommodations in the general education or

assistive technology Necessary technology that enables the student to participate in a free appropriate public education.

special education setting—such as extended time for task completion, or use of **assistive technology** (speech synthesizer, electronic reader, communication board)—to participate in the general curriculum will most likely require accommodations to participate in high-stakes testing. The purpose of accommodations during the assessment is to prevent measuring the student's disability and to allow a more accurate assessment of the student's progress in the general curriculum.

The determination of need for accommodations should be made during the IEP process. The types of accommodations needed must be documented on the IEP. Following the statewide or district-wide assessment, teachers should rate the accommodations that proved to be helpful for each specific student (Elliott, Kratochwill, & Schulte, 1998). The following adapted list of accommodations has been suggested by these authors:

1. Motivation—Some students may work best with extrinsic motivators such as verbal praise.
2. Providing assistance prior to administering the test—To familiarize the student with test format, test-related behavior or procedures that will be required.
3. Scheduling—Extra time or testing over several days.
4. Setting—Includes location, lighting, acoustics, specialized equipment.
5. Providing assistance during the assessment—To assist a student with turning pages, recording response, or allowing the child's special education teacher to administer the test.
6. Using aids—Any specialized equipment or technology the child requires.
7. Changes in test format—Braille edition or audiotaped questions.

Source: From The assessment accommodations checklist by S. N. Elliott, T. R. Kratochwill, and A. G. Schulte, 1998, *Teaching Exceptional Children,* Nov./Dec. 1998.

ALTERNATE ASSESSMENT

Students who are not able to participate in the regular statewide assessment, or in the statewide assessment with accommodations, are required to complete an alternate assessment. The alternate assessment should be designed to reflect progress in the general education curriculum at the appropriate level. The intent of the alternate assessment is to measure the student's progress along the continuum of general education expectations.

States participating in statewide assessments determine individually how the state will provide alternate assessments for students who are not able to complete the assessments with accommodations. A state may use a statewide curriculum with set expectations for each grade level. These skills and expectations exist on a continuum, and this may be used as a basis for the alternate assessment. The skill level measured on the alternate assessment may actually be at a level below the expectations for students in school. For example, a young student with a significant cognitive disability may not be able to master the skills expected of a first- or second-grade student. The skills that may be measured for progress may be the preacademic skills necessary to progress toward the first- and second-grade skills.

The type and level of the assessment may be determined individually for each student requiring alternate assessments. Portfolio assessment, performance-based assessment, authentic assessment, and observations are methods used by states as alternate assessment for high-stakes testing. Many states are continuing to develop both acceptable accommodations and alternate tests (Elliott et al., 1998; Thurlow et al., 1998; Ysseldyke, Nelson, & House, 2000).

ISSUES IN HIGH-STAKES TESTING

It has been typical in the field of special education assessment that new concepts and regulations in the assessment of students with special needs have been met with questions and issues that must be considered. The mandate in the 1997 amendments to include all students in high-stakes assessment was added to the law as a measure of accountability. Student progress must be measured to determine if programs are effective.

As this mandate has been implemented in schools, there have been problems and concerns. Ysseldyke, Thurlow, Kozleski, and Reschly identified sixteen critical issues (1998). Some of these issues include concerns about the inconsistency of definitions, federal law requirements, variability among states and districts, differences in standards of expectations for students with disabilities, lack of participation of students with disabilities in test development and standardization of instruments, and lack of consistency regarding decisions for accommodations and alternate assessment.

Other issues involve the conceptual understanding of the purpose and nature of the assessment. Gronna, Jenkins, and Chin-Chance state that students with disabilities have typically been excluded from national norming procedures, yet these students are now to be compared with these national samples to determine how much progress they have made. These authors raise the question of how to compare students with disabilities with the national norms when the students with disabilities, by definition, are expected to differ from the established norms. This is an area of continued research and debate in the field of special education.

CHAPTER SUMMARY

This chapter provided information about norm-referenced instruments used in individual and group settings. Both types of instruments are used to measure academic achievement in schools.

THINK AHEAD

The most frequently used tests in education are achievement tests. In the next chapter, you will use portions of commonly used instruments to learn about achievement tests and how they are scored.

EXERCISES

Part I

Match the following terms with the correct definitions.

a. domain
b. norm-referenced tests
c. item pool
d. test manual
e. accommodations
f. ceiling
g. raw score
h. developmental version
i. grade equivalent
j. norm group
k. interpolation
l. chronological age
m. stanines
n. basal
o. field test
p. protocol

_____ 1. When a test is being developed, the test developer attempts to have this represent the population for whom the test is designed.

_____ 2. This step is completed using the developmental version to determine what changes are needed prior to the completion of the published test.

_____ 3. This represents the level of items that the student would most probably answer correctly, although they may not all be administered to the student.

_____ 4. When a teacher scores a classroom test including 10 items and determines that a student correctly answered 7, the number 7 represents a _____.

_____ 5. Information regarding how a test was developed is usually contained in the _____.

_____ 6. A student's standard score that compares him with his age peers is found by using the student's raw score and the student's _____ and the norm tables.

_____ 7. A teacher discovers that although only 2nd, 3rd, and 5th graders were included in the norm sample of a test, scores were presented for 4th grade. The 4th-grade scores were _____.

_____ 8. A student's actual skill level is not represented by the _____.

_____ 9. Both individual and group assessments may be _____ that compare students with age or grade expectations.

_____ 10. Students with disabilities who have IEPs and students who are served under Section 504 may need _____ for statewide assessments.

_____ 11. A student score that is reported to be exactly average with a score of 5 is reporting using _____ scores.

Part II

Select the type of accommodation and match with the following statements.

a. setting
b. scheduling
c. response mode
d. assessment format

_____ 1. Lorenzo, who participates in the general curriculum requires Braille for all reading material. He will require changes in _____.

_____ 2. Lorenzo also requires the use of a stylus for writing or answers questions orally. He will also require changes in _____.

_____ 3. When Susie is in the general classroom setting, she often is distracted and requires additional time to complete her assignments. On her Section 504 plan, the team members should include accommodations of _____.

_____ 4. George is a student with a specific reading disability. In his general education classroom, George's teacher and the classroom aide must read all instructions to him and often must read questions and multisyllabic words to him. On his IEP, the team has included a statement of accommodation of _____.

Part III

Discuss the issues and concerns of the statewide assessment of students with disabilities.

Part IV

Using the portions from the *KeyMath—Revised* (Connolly, 1988) protocol in Figure 5.9, determine the following:

1. Chronological age: _____
2. Domain scores: _____
3. Raw score: _____
4. Basal item: _____
5. Ceiling item: _____

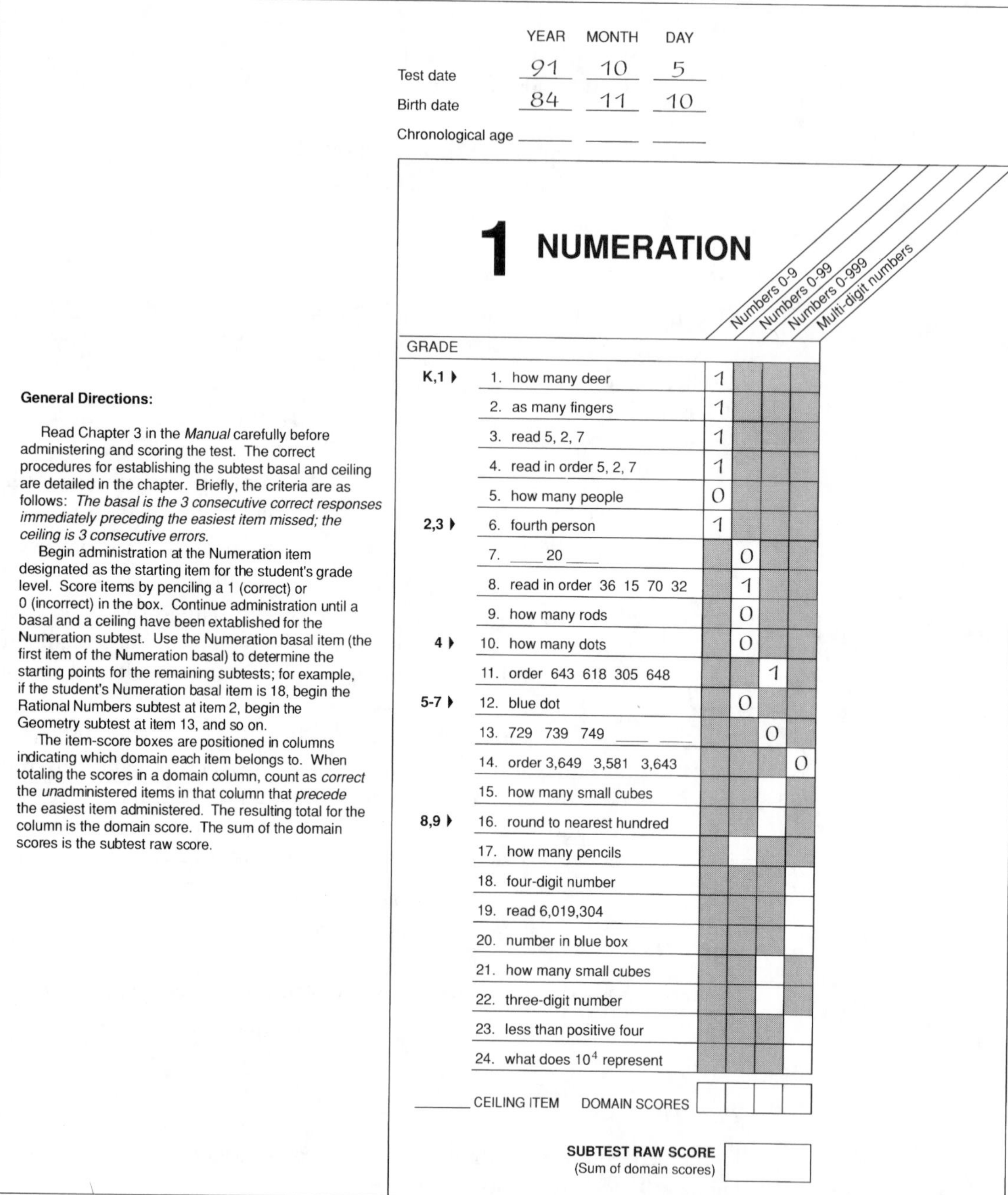

	YEAR	MONTH	DAY
Test date	91	10	5
Birth date	84	11	10
Chronological age	______	______	______

General Directions:

Read Chapter 3 in the *Manual* carefully before administering and scoring the test. The correct procedures for establishing the subtest basal and ceiling are detailed in the chapter. Briefly, the criteria are as follows: *The basal is the 3 consecutive correct responses immediately preceding the easiest item missed; the ceiling is 3 consecutive errors.*

Begin administration at the Numeration item designated as the starting item for the student's grade level. Score items by penciling a 1 (correct) or 0 (incorrect) in the box. Continue administration until a basal and a ceiling have been extablished for the Numeration subtest. Use the Numeration basal item (the first item of the Numeration basal) to determine the starting points for the remaining subtests; for example, if the student's Numeration basal item is 18, begin the Rational Numbers subtest at item 2, begin the Geometry subtest at item 13, and so on.

The item-score boxes are positioned in columns indicating which domain each item belongs to. When totaling the scores in a domain column, count as *correct* the *un*administered items in that column that *precede* the easiest item administered. The resulting total for the column is the domain score. The sum of the domain scores is the subtest raw score.

1 NUMERATION

GRADE	Item	Numbers 0-9	Numbers 0-99	Numbers 0-999	Multi-digit numbers
K,1 ▸	1. how many deer	1			
	2. as many fingers	1			
	3. read 5, 2, 7	1			
	4. read in order 5, 2, 7	1			
	5. how many people	0			
2,3 ▸	6. fourth person	1			
	7. ____ 20 ____		0		
	8. read in order 36 15 70 32		1		
	9. how many rods		0		
4 ▸	10. how many dots		0		
	11. order 643 618 305 648			1	
5-7 ▸	12. blue dot		0		
	13. 729 739 749 ____ ____			0	
	14. order 3,649 3,581 3,643				0
	15. how many small cubes				
8,9 ▸	16. round to nearest hundred				
	17. how many pencils				
	18. four-digit number				
	19. read 6,019,304				
	20. number in blue box				
	21. how many small cubes				
	22. three-digit number				
	23. less than positive four				
	24. what does 10^4 represent				

______ CEILING ITEM DOMAIN SCORES

SUBTEST RAW SCORE (Sum of domain scores)

Figure 5.9 Chronological age portion and Numeration subtest from the KeyMath—Revised protocol. (*Source:* From *Key Math—Revised,* protocol B, individual test record (pp. 1, 2) by A. J. Connolly, 1988, Circle Pines, MN: American Guidance Service. Copyright 1988 by American Guidance Service. Reprinted by permission.)

ANSWER KEY TO CHECK YOUR UNDERSTANDING

Activity 5.1

1. 78
2. 130
3. 13
4. As their age/grade increased, students were able to answer more of the sequentially arranged items correctly as a result of learning or academic achievement.
5. 27
6. no; interpolated scores were used
7. 60
8. 4th grade, 1st month
   4 years, 1 month
   3rd grade, 3rd month
   6 years, 7 months
   10th grade, 8th month

Apply Your Knowledge. A grade equivalent means that your child correctly answered as many items as a student in that grade. The level of academic functioning means that your child has actually mastered the skills expected of a student in that grade.

Activity 5.2

1. 10-2-2
2. 8-4-17
3. 2-7-19
4. 7-11
5. 11-7
6. 15-0

Apply Your Knowledge. The chronological age is often used to determine the starting point of a test for that student. The chronological age is also used when scoring the student's performance on a test.

Activity 5.3

Test I basal items: 6–10
Test II basal items: 31–37
Example 1: #24
Example 2: #116

Apply Your Knowledge. Basal level means that the student is able to complete all of the items that are easier than the first item missed. This indicates that the student's mastery ability level is represented at the basal level.

Activity 5.4

Protocol 1 raw score: 233

Protocol 2 raw score: 20

1. Protocol 2
2. 227–231
3. 235–239
4. 11–13
5. 23–25

Apply Your Knowledge. The ceiling level is that level above which the student will not be able to answer items correctly. This represents a level too difficult for the student.

Activity 5.5

1. three trials for each of three exercises
2. 43–47
3. use the highest 5 consecutive correct responses
4. 53–59

Apply Your Knowledge. The information presented on this protocol includes the number of training exercises, the number of trials per exercise, the rules for establishing the basal, the rules for establishing the ceiling, and starting points for this subtest.

Activity 5.6

1. d
2. c
3. d
4. b
5. a

REFERENCES

American Psychological Association. (1985). *Standards for Educational and Psychological Testing*. Washington, DC: Author.

Anastasi, A. & Urbina, S. (1998). *Psychological Testing* (7th ed.). Upper Saddle River, NJ: Prentice Hall.

Brigham, F. J., Tochterman, S., & Brigham, M. S. P. (2000). Students with emotional and behavioral disorders and their teachers in test-linked systems of accountability. *Assessment for Effective Intervention, 26,* 1, 19–27.

Cole, J., D'Alonzo, B., Gallegos, A., Giordano, G., & Stile, S. (1992). Test biases that hamper learners with disabilities. *Diagnostique, 17,* 209–225.

Connolly, A. J. (1988). *KeyMath–Revised.* Circle Pines, MN: American Guidance Service.

Elliott, S. N., Braden, J. P., & White, J. L. (2001). *Assessing one and all: Educational accountability for students with disabilities.* Arlington, VA: Council for Exceptional Children.

Elliott, S. N., Kratochwill, T. R., & Schulte, A. G. (1998). The assessment accommodation checklist. *Teaching Exceptional Children,* Nov./Dec., 10–14.

Fuchs, D., Zern, D., & Fuchs, L. (1983). A microanalysis of participant behavior in familiar and unfamiliar test conditions. *Exceptional Children, 50,* 75–77.

Gronna, S., Jenkins, A., & Chin-Chance, S. (1998). The performance of students with disabilities in a norm-referenced, statewide standardized testing program. *Journal of Learning Disabilities, 31*(5), 482–493.

Huebner, E. (1988). Bias in teachers' special education decisions as a further function of test score reporting format. *Journal of Educational Research, 21,* 217–220.

Huebner, E. (1989). Errors in decision-making: A comparison of school psychologists' interpretations of grade equivalents, percentiles, and deviation IQs. *School Psychology Review, 18,* 51–55.

Kaufman, A. S., & Kaufman, N. L. (1985). *Kaufman Test of Educational Achievement.* Circle Pines, MN: American Guidance Service.

Markwardt, F. C. (1989). *Peabody Individual Achievement Test—Revised.* Circle Pines, MN: American Guidance Service.

McLoughlin, J., & Lewis, R. (2001). *Assessing special students* (5th ed.). Upper Saddle River, NJ: Merrill/Prentice Hall.

Office of Special Education and Rehabilitative Services (2000). *Questions and answers about provisions in the Individuals with Disabilities Education Act Amendments of 1997 related to students with disabilities and state and district wide assessments.* Washington, DC: Author.

Thurlow, M. L., Elliott, J. L., & Ysseldyke, J. E. (1998). *Testing students with disabilities: Practical strategies for complying with district and state requirements.* Thousand Oaks, CA: Corwin Press, Inc.

U.S. Department of Education (2000). *The use of tests when making high-stakes decisions for students: A resource guide for educators and policymakers.* Washington, DC: Author.

Wilson, V. (1987). Percentile scores. In C. R. Reynolds & L. Mann (Eds.), *Encyclopedia of special education: A reference for the education of the handicapped and other exceptional children and adults* (p. 1656). New York: Wiley.

Ysseldyke, J. E., Nelson, J. R., & House, A. L. (2000). Statewide and district wide assessments: Current status and guidelines for student accommodations and alternate assessments. In C. F. Telzrow and M. Tankersley (Eds.), *IDEA Amendments of 1997: Practice guidelines for school-based teams.* Bethesda, MD: National Association of School Psychologists.

Ysseldyke, J. E., Thurlow, M. L., Kozleski, E., & Reschly, D. (1998). Accountability for the results of educating students with disabilities: Assessment conference report on the new assessment provisions of the 1997 Amendments to the Individuals with Disabilities Education Act (EC 306929), National Center on Educational Outcomes. (ERIC Document Reproduction Service No. ED 425 588)

PART 3

Assessing Students

Chapter 6 **Tests of Educational Achievement**
Chapter 7 **Standardized Diagnostic Testing**
Chapter 8 **Informal Assessment Techniques**
Chapter 9 **Assessment of Behavior**
Chapter 10 **Measures of Intelligence and Adaptive Behavior**
Chapter 11 **Special Considerations in Assessment**

CHAPTER 6

Tests of Educational Achievement

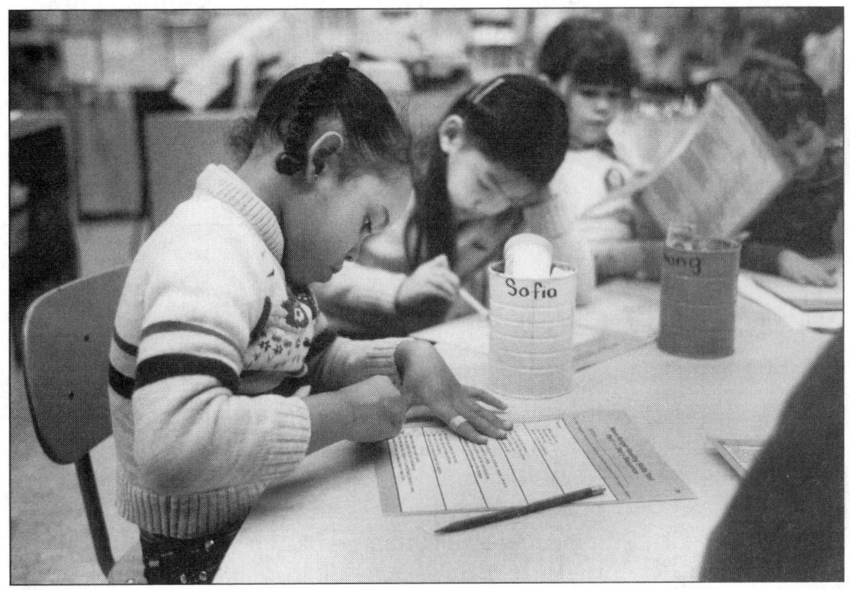

Key Terms

achievement tests
screening tests
aptitude tests
diagnostic tests
adaptive behavior scales
norm-referenced tests
curriculum-based assessment

CHAPTER FOCUS

This chapter includes several commonly used norm-referenced individual achievement tests. Information is presented that will enable you to understand how the basic methods of studying reliability and validity are applied to these instruments. You will learn some basic scoring methods that will allow you to generalize these skills to other instruments.

Professionals working with students who require special services are concerned with how students perform on educational measures. One way to measure educational performance is to use norm-referenced achievement tests. Of all standardized tests, individually administered achievement tests are the most numerous (Anastasi & Urbina, 1998). Other types of tests—such as group screening tests, diagnostic tests (chapter 7), aptitude tests, and adaptive behavior scales (chapter 10)—are used not only to measure educational performance but also to determine specific learning weaknesses and identify strengths. This chapter focuses on individually administered norm-referenced achievement tests.

ACHIEVEMENT TESTS

achievement tests Tests used to measure academic progress, what the student has retained in curriculum.

screening tests Brief tests that sample a few items across skills or domains.

aptitude tests Tests designed to measure strength, talent, or ability in a particular area or domain.

diagnostic tests Individually administered tests designed to determine specific academic problems or deficit areas.

adaptive behavior scales Instruments that assess a student's ability to adapt to the world in different situations.

Used in virtually every school, **achievement tests** are designed to measure what the student has learned. These tests may be developed to measure a specific area of the educational curriculum, such as written language, or to measure across several areas of the curriculum, such as math, reading, spelling, and science. Brief tests containing items that survey a range of skill levels, domains, or content areas are known as **screening tests.** Screening tests assess no one area in depth. Screening tests provide the educator with a method to determine weak areas that need additional assessment in order to determine specific skill mastery or weaknesses.

Aptitude tests contain items that measure what a student has retained but also are designed to indicate how much the student will learn in the future. Aptitude tests are thought to indicate current areas of strength as well as future potential. These tests are used in educational planning and include both group and individually administered tests. **Diagnostic tests** are those used to measure a specific ability, such as fine-motor ability. **Adaptive behavior scales** measure how well students adapt to different environments.

STANDARDIZED NORM-REFERENCED TESTS VERSUS CURRICULUM-BASED ASSESSMENT

The use of **norm-referenced tests** to measure academic achievement helps educators make both placement and eligibility decisions. When selected and administered carefully, these tests yield fairly reliable and valid

norm-referenced tests Tests designed to compare individual students with national averages, or norms of expectancy.

information. As discussed in the previous chapter, norm-referenced instruments are researched and constructed in a systematic way and provide educators with a method of comparing a student with a peer group evaluated during the standardization process of the test development. Comparing a student to a norm reference group allows the educator to determine whether the student is performing as expected for her age or grade. If the student appears to be significantly behind her peers developmentally, special services may be recommended.

curriculum-based assessment Using content from the currently used curriculum to assess student progress.

Curriculum-based assessment tests students on the very curriculum used for instruction. In this method of determining mastery of skills or specific curriculum, the student may be compared with his past performance on similar items or tasks. Curriculum-based testing, which is very useful and necessary in special education, is discussed further in chapter 8.

THE REVIEW OF ACHIEVEMENT TESTS

This text is designed to involve the student in the learning process and to help the student develop skills in administering and interpreting tests. Rather than include numerous tests, many of which the future teacher may not use, this chapter presents achievement tests selected because of their frequent use in schools or because of their technical adequacy. The following are individually administered screening achievement tests used frequently by educators:

1. *Woodcock-Johnson III.* This newly revised edition of the Woodcock-Johnson—Revised Psychoeducational Battery includes two forms, A and B. It contains cognitive and achievement tests, each of which includes standard and extended batteries. The same sample was assessed using all components of the battery to establish the normative data. Using the same sample enhances the diagnostic capability for determining domain-specific skills and their associated cognitive abilities as well as discrepancies between ability and achievement (McGrew & Woodcock, 2001).
2. *Peabody Individual Achievement Test—Revised.* This test was listed as one of the most frequently used by professionals in Child Service Demonstration Centers (Thurlow & Ysseldyke, 1979), by school psychologists (LaGrow & Prochnow-LaGrow, 1982), by special education teachers who listed this as one of the most useful tests (Connelly, 1985), and by teachers who are in both self-contained and resource classrooms for students with learning disabilities (German, Johnson, & Schneider, 1985).
3. *Kaufman Test of Educational Achievement (K-TEA).* This relatively new test has received favorable review (Worthington, 1987) and has had positive correlations with the Wide Range Achievement Test in

both spelling and math and moderate correlation with the reading subtests (Webster, Hewett, & Crumbacker, 1989).

4. *Wechsler Individual Achievement Test, Second Edition.* This revised instrument was designed to be used in conjunction with the Wechsler Intelligence Scales or other measures of cognitive ability and assesses the academic areas specified in special education regulations.
5. *Wide Range Achievement Test.* This test was listed as useful by teachers of students with emotional disabilities, learning disabilities, and mental retardation (Connelly, 1985); by teachers in self-contained and resource rooms for students with learning disabilities (German, Johnson, & Schneider, 1985); by school psychologists (LaGrow & Prochnow-LaGrow, 1982; Reschly, 1988); and by teachers in Child Service Demonstration Centers (Thurlow & Ysseldyke, 1979). This text describes the third edition of the Wide Range Achievement Test (Wilkinson, 1993).
6. *Mini-Battery of Achievement* (Woodcock, McGrew, & Werder, 1994) is included as a fairly new screening achievement battery. This test has a format similar to the Woodcock-Johnson Tests of Achievement—Revised. It is presented as an alternative to the WRAT3 and the K-TEA—Brief Form.

These tests, which represent several academic areas, are discussed in the following sections. Their reliability and validity are presented in an effort to encourage future teachers to be wise consumers of assessment devices.

WOODCOCK-JOHNSON III TESTS OF ACHIEVEMENT (WJ III)

This new edition of the Woodcock-Johnson (Woodcock, McGrew, & Mather, 2001), presented in an easel type of format, comprises two parallel achievement batteries that allow the examiner to retest the same student within a short amount of time with less practice effect. The battery of subtests allows the examiner to select the specific clusters of subtests needed for a particular student. This achievement battery has standard tests and extended tests. An Examiner Training Workbook is included that will assist examiners in learning how to administer the subtests, understand basal and ceiling rules, and learn how to complete the scoring included on the protocol (Wendling & Mather, 2001). A checklist is provided in the manual for each subtest of the WJ III Achievement Tests. Each of the checklists states the specific skills and steps the examiner must follow in order to complete standardized administration of the instrument.

Some features of the WJ III Tests of Achievement include the following:

1. Basal and ceiling levels are specified by individual subtests. For many of the subtests, when the student answers 6 consecutive

items correctly the basal is established, and when the student answers 6 consecutive items incorrectly the ceiling is established. Other subtests have basal levels of 4 consecutive correct and ceilings of 4 consecutive incorrect. Additional basal and ceiling rules include specific starting points and time limits for stopping the subtest administration. Examiners should study the basal and ceiling rules and refer to the protocol and the examiner's manual for specific rules.

2. Derived scores can be obtained for each individual subtest for age and grade equivalents estimations only. Other standard scores are available using the computer scoring program.
3. The norm group ranged in age from 2 to 90 years and older and included students at the college/university level through graduate school.
4. The use of extended age scores provides a more comprehensive analysis of children and adults who are not functioning at a school grade level.
5. The WJ III Tests of Achievement include subtests that require the student to use paper and pencil as well as subtests that are administered using a tape player. The protocol contains icons to denote when the test response booklet or the tape player is needed as well as which subtests are timed.
6. The examiner's manual includes suggested guidelines for using the WJ III with individuals who are English-language learners, individuals with reading and/or learning disabilities, individuals with attentional and behavioral difficulties, individuals with hearing or visual impairments, and individuals with physical impairments.
7. The computer scoring program includes an option for determining the individual's cognitive-academic language proficiency level.
8. A Test Session Observation Checklist is located on the front of the protocol for the examiner to note the individual student's behavior during the assessment sessions.
9. Transparent scoring templates are provided for reading and math fluency subtests.

Figure 6.1 illustrates the organization of the WJ III Tests of Achievement. Note that the subtests are grouped into broad clusters to aid in the interpretation of scores. The examiner may select the specific clusters needed to screen a student's achievement level and combine the administration of selected cognitive clusters to determine patterns of strengths and weaknesses.

Standard Battery. The following paragraphs describe the subtests in the Standard Battery.

	Tests of Achievement	Reading			Oral Language				Math			Written Lang.			Other Clusters					
		Broad Reading	Basic Reading Skills	Reading Comprehension	Oral Language–Standard	Oral Language–Extended	Listening Comprehension	Oral Expression	Broad Math	Math Calculation Skills	Math Reasoning	Broad Written Language	Basic Writing Skills	Written Expression	Academic Knowledge	Phoneme/Grapheme Knowledge	Academic Skills	Academic Fluency	Academic Applications	Total Achievement
Standard Battery	Test 1: Letter-Word Identification	■	■														■			■
	Test 2: Reading Fluency	■																■		■
	Test 3: Story Recall				■	■		■												
	Test 4: Understanding Directions				■	■	■													
	Test 5: Calculation								■	■							■			■
	Test 6: Math Fluency								■	■								■		■
	Test 7: Spelling											■	■				■			■
	Test 8: Writing Fluency											■		■				■		■
	Test 9: Passage Comprehension	■		■															■	■
	Test 10: Applied Problems								■		■								■	■
	Test 11: Writing Samples											■		■					■	■
	Test 12: Story Recall-Delayed																			
Extended Battery	Test 13: Word Attack		■													■				
	Test 14: Picture Vocabulary					■		■												
	Test 15: Oral Comprehension					■	■													
	Test 16: Editing												■							
	Test 17: Reading Vocabulary			■																
	Test 18: Quantitative Concepts										■									
	Test 19: Academic Knowledge														■					
	Test 20: Spelling of Sounds															■				
	Test 21: Sound Awareness																			
	Test 22: Punctuation & Capitalization																			

Figure 6.1 The Woodcock-Johnson, Third Edition Testing Table. (*Source: Woodcock-Johnson® III Tests of Achievement* used with permission of the publisher. Copyright © 2001 by The Riverside Publishing Company. All rights reserved. No part of the tests may be reproduced or transmitted in any form or by any means, electronic or mechanical, including photocopying and recording or by any information storage or retrieval system without the prior written permission of The Riverside Publishing Company unless such copying is expressly permitted by federal copyright law. Address inquiries to Contracts and Permission Department, The Riverside Publishing Company, 425 Spring Lake Drive, Itasca, Illinois 60143-2079.)

Letter-Word Identification. The student is presented with a picture, letter, or word and asked to identify it orally. The basal and ceiling levels are 6 lowest consecutive items correct and the 6 highest items incorrect, respectively.

Reading Fluency. This timed subtest presents statements for the student to read and determine if the statements are true or not true. It assesses how quickly the student reads the sentences, makes decisions about the statement validity, and circles the correct response. The time limit is 3 minutes.

Story Recall. All items are presented using the audio recording provided. The student listens to the short stories and then tells the story to the examiner. Instructions for continuing and stopping the administration of the subtest are provided in the protocol and are based on the number of points the student earns.

Understanding Directions. This subtest requires the stimulus pictures on the easel and oral instructions by the examiner. As the student looks at the pictures, the examiner provides instructions such as "First point to the dog then the bird if the dog is brown." Specific instructions are provided in the protocol regarding when the student discontinues the subtest based on the number of points earned.

Calculation. Math problems are presented in a paper-and-pencil format. The problems include number writing on the early items and range from addition to calculus operations on the more advanced items. The basal and ceiling levels are the 6 lowest consecutive items correct and the 6 highest consecutive items incorrect, respectively.

Math Fluency. This subtest is included in the student's response booklet. The student is required to complete problems of basic operations of addition, subtraction, multiplication, and division. This subtest is timed and the student solves as many problems as possible within 3 minutes.

Spelling. This subtest assesses the individual's ability to write words that are presented orally by the examiner. The early items include tracing lines and letters, and the more advanced items include multisyllabic words with unpredictable spellings. The basal and ceiling levels are 6 consecutive correct and incorrect items, respectively.

Writing Fluency. This paper-and-pencil subtest consists of pictures paired with three words. The examiner instructs the student to write sentences about each picture using the words. The student is allowed to write for 7 minutes. Correct responses are complete sentences that include the three words presented.

Passage Comprehension. The examiner shows the student a passage with a missing word, and the student must orally supply the word. The basal and ceiling levels are 6 lowest consecutive items correct and the 6 highest incorrect items, respectively.

Applied Problems. The examiner reads a story math problem, and the student must answer orally. Picture cues are provided at the lower levels. The basal and ceiling levels are determined in the same manner as for the Calculation subtest.

Writing Samples. This subtest requires the student to construct age-appropriate sentences meeting specific criteria (for syntax, content, etc.). The items are scored as 2, 1, or 0 based on the quality of the responses. The examiner's manual provides a comprehensive scoring guide.

Story Recall-Delayed. On this subtest, the student is asked to recall the stories presented in a previous subtest, Story Recall. The delayed subtest can be presented from 30 minutes to 8 days following the initial administration of Story Recall.

Extended Battery. The subtests included in the Extended Battery are described in the following paragraphs.

Word Attack. The student is asked to read nonsense words aloud. This subtest measures the student's ability to decode and pronounce new words. The basal is established when a student answers 6 consecutive items correctly, and the ceiling is 6 consecutive incorrect responses.

Picture Vocabulary. The items in this subtest require the student to express the names of objects presented in pictures on the easel. The basal and ceiling levels are 6 lowest consecutive correct and 6 highest incorrect items, respectively.

Oral Comprehension. These items are presented on the audiotape and require that the student complete the missing word in the presented items. The items range from simple associations to more complex sentences. The basal and ceiling levels are 6 lowest consecutive correct and 6 highest incorrect items, respectively.

Editing. This subtest requires the student to proofread sentences and passages and determine the errors of punctuation, capitalization, usage, or spelling. The student is asked to correct errors in written passages shown on the easel page. The basal and ceiling levels are 6 lowest consecutive correct and 6 highest incorrect items, respectively.

Reading Vocabulary. This subtest contains three sections: Part A, Synonyms; Part B, Antonyms; and Part C, Analogies. All three sections must be completed in order to obtain a score for the subtest. The student is asked to say a word that means the same as a given word in Part A and to say a word that has the opposite meaning of a word in Part B. In Part C, the student must complete analogies. Only one-word responses are acceptable for the subtest items. The examiner obtains a raw score by adding the number of items correct in the two subtests. The basal and ceiling levels are 4 lowest consecutive items correct and 4 highest incorrect responses, respectively.

Quantitative Concepts. This subtest includes two parts: Part A, Concepts; and Part B, Number Series. Both sections must be completed in order to obtain a score for the subtest. Items cover math vocabulary, concepts, and the completion of missing numbers presented in various types of series. The examiner's manual states that no mathematical decisions are made in response to these test items. Picture cues are given for some items in the lower levels. The basal and ceiling instructions are different for each part and are contained in the protocol.

Academic Knowledge. This subtest contains three parts: Part A, Science; Part B, Social Studies; and Part C, Humanities. For the science section, the examiner orally presents open-ended questions covering scientific content. The basal and ceiling levels are 3 lowest consecutive correct and highest incorrect items, respectively. Picture cues are given at the lower and upper levels. The Social Studies section orally presents open-ended questions covering topics about society and government. The basal and ceiling levels are the same as for the Science section. Picture cues are given at the lower level. The questions in the Humanities section cover topics the student may have learned from the cultural environment. The basal and ceiling levels are the same as for the Science and Social Studies sections.

Spelling of Sounds. The examiner presents the first few items of this subtest orally and the remaining items are presented using the audiotape. The individual is asked to write the spellings of nonsense words. This requires that the student be able to associate the sounds heard with the written letter. The basal and ceiling levels are the 4 lowest consecutive items correct and the highest 4 items incorrect, respectively.

Sound Awareness. This subtest contains four sections: Part A, Sound Awareness-Rhyming; Part B, Sound Awareness-Deletion; Part C, Sound Awareness-Substitution; and Part D, Sound Awareness-Reversal. The items for Part A require the student to determine and generate words that rhyme. Part B requires the student to say parts of the original stimulus provided on the audiotape. Part C requires that the individual change a specified part of the stimulus word. Part D requires the student to perform two tasks. First, the student is asked to reverse compound words. Then the student is required to reverse the sounds of letters to create new words. This subtest is arranged so that each part is more difficult than the previous part. Within each part, items are also sequenced from easier to more difficult items. The basal is one item correct for each of the sections, and the ceilings vary for each section.

Punctuation and Capitalization. This subtest includes items that require the student to write the correct punctuation for specific stimuli presented by the examiner and in the response booklet. For example, a sentence in the response booklet may need quotation marks or a capital letter. The individual writes the needed punctuation or capitalization in the response booklet. The basal and ceiling levels are 6 lowest consecutive correct and 6 highest incorrect items, respectively.

Check Your Understanding

Complete Activity 6.1.

ACTIVITY 6.1

Answer the following questions.

1. How many parallel forms are included in the third edition of the Woodcock-Johnson III Tests of Achievement? __________
   What is the advantage of having different forms of the same instrument? __________
2. What is the age range of the WJ III Tests of Achievement? __________
3. What populations were included in the norming process of the third edition? __________
4. What new school level is included in the third edition of the WJ? __________
5. According to the information provided in Figure 6.1, what subtests would be administered to measure broad mathematics? __________
6. What subtests would be administered to measure math reasoning? __________

Apply Your Knowledge

Look over the descriptions of the subtests of the Woodcock-Johnson III Tests of Achievement. Which subtests would not be appropriate for a student to complete in the standard fashion if the student had a severe fine-motor disability and could not use a pencil or keyboard? __________

What adaptations might be appropriate? __________

Explain the ethical considerations that should be addressed by making such adaptations. __________

Technical Data

Norming Process. For the standardization and norming process of the WJ III, the test developers included a sample of 8,818 subjects ranging in age from 2 to more than 90 years. The subjects represented a geographic variety of communities. Variables that were considered included sex, race, occupational status, occupation, Hispanic or non-Hispanic, level of education (including graduate college level), and community size. The examiner's manual includes information about studies with students from special populations, including students with learning disabilities and students with attention deficit disorder.

Reliability. The technical manual includes information regarding test-retest reliability, interrater reliability, alternate forms reliability, and internal consistency reliability. Most reliability coefficients for internal consistency are reported to be in the .90s.

Validity. The technical manual provides concurrent validity information for studies with the WJ III Total Achievement Cluster and the Kaufman Tests of Educational Achievement and the Wechsler Individual Achievement Test composite scores. The validity coefficients were .79 and .65, respectively. Additional studies and coefficients are provided comparing individual subtests. In addition to concurrent validity studies, the technical manual includes information regarding the support for content and construct validity.

PEABODY INDIVIDUAL ACHIEVEMENT TEST—REVISED (PIAT—R)

The PIAT—R (Markwardt, 1989) is contained in four easels, called Volumes I, II, III, and IV. For this revision, the number of items has been increased on the existing subtests. The subtests are General Information, Reading Recognition, Reading Comprehension, Mathematics, Spelling, and Written Expression.

Subtests

General Information. Questions in this subtest are presented in an open-ended format. The student gives oral responses to questions that range in topic from science to sports. The examiner records all responses. A key for acceptable responses is given throughout the examiner's pages of the subtest and provides suggestions for further questioning.

Reading Recognition. The items at the beginning level of this subtest are visual recognition and discrimination items that require the student to match a picture, letter, or word. The student must select the response from a choice of four items. The more difficult items require the student to pronounce a list of words that range from single-syllable consonant-vowel-consonant words to multisyllable words with unpredictable pronunciations.

Reading Comprehension. This subtest is administered to students who earn a raw score of 19 or better on the Reading Recognition subtest. The items are presented in a two-page format. The examiner asks the student to read a passage silently on the first page of each item. On the second page, the student must select from four choices the one picture that best illustrates the passage. The more difficult-to-read items also have pictures that are more difficult to discriminate.

Mathematics. Math questions are presented in a forced-choice format. The student is orally asked a question and must select the correct response from four choices. Questions range from numeral recognition to trigonometry.

Spelling. This subtest begins with visual discrimination tasks of pictures, symbols, and letters. The spelling items are presented in a forced-choice format. The student is asked to select the correct spelling of the word from four choices.

Written Expression. This subtest allows for written responses by the student; level I is presented to students who are functioning at the kindergarten or first-grade level, level II to students functioning in the 2nd- to 12th-grade levels. The basal and ceiling levels do not apply.

Scoring. The examiner uses the raw score on the first PIAT—R subtest, General Information, to determine a starting point on the following subtest, Reading Recognition. The raw score from the Reading Recognition subtest then provides a starting point for the Reading Comprehension subtest, and so on throughout the test. The basal and ceiling levels are consistent across subtests. A basal level is established when 5 consecutive items have been answered correctly. The ceiling level is determined when the student answers 5 of 7 items incorrectly. Because the Written Expression subtest requires written responses by the student, the basal and ceiling levels do not apply.

The PIAT—R yields standard scores, grade equivalents, age equivalents, and percentile ranks for individual subtests and for a Total Reading and a Total Test score. The manual provides for standard error of measurement for obtained and derived scores. The raw score from the Written Expression subtest can be used with the raw score from the Spelling subtest to obtain a written language composite. Scoring procedures are detailed in Appendix I of the PIAT—2 examiner's manual.

Check Your Understanding

Complete Activity 6.2.

ACTIVITY 6.2

Complete the following problems.

1. Using the information provided on the portion of the PIAT—R protocol in Figure 6.2, determine the Total Reading raw score. Add the Reading Recognition and the Reading Comprehension raw scores. To determine the Total Test raw score, add all subtest raw scores. Write the sums in the appropriate boxes in Figure 6.2.

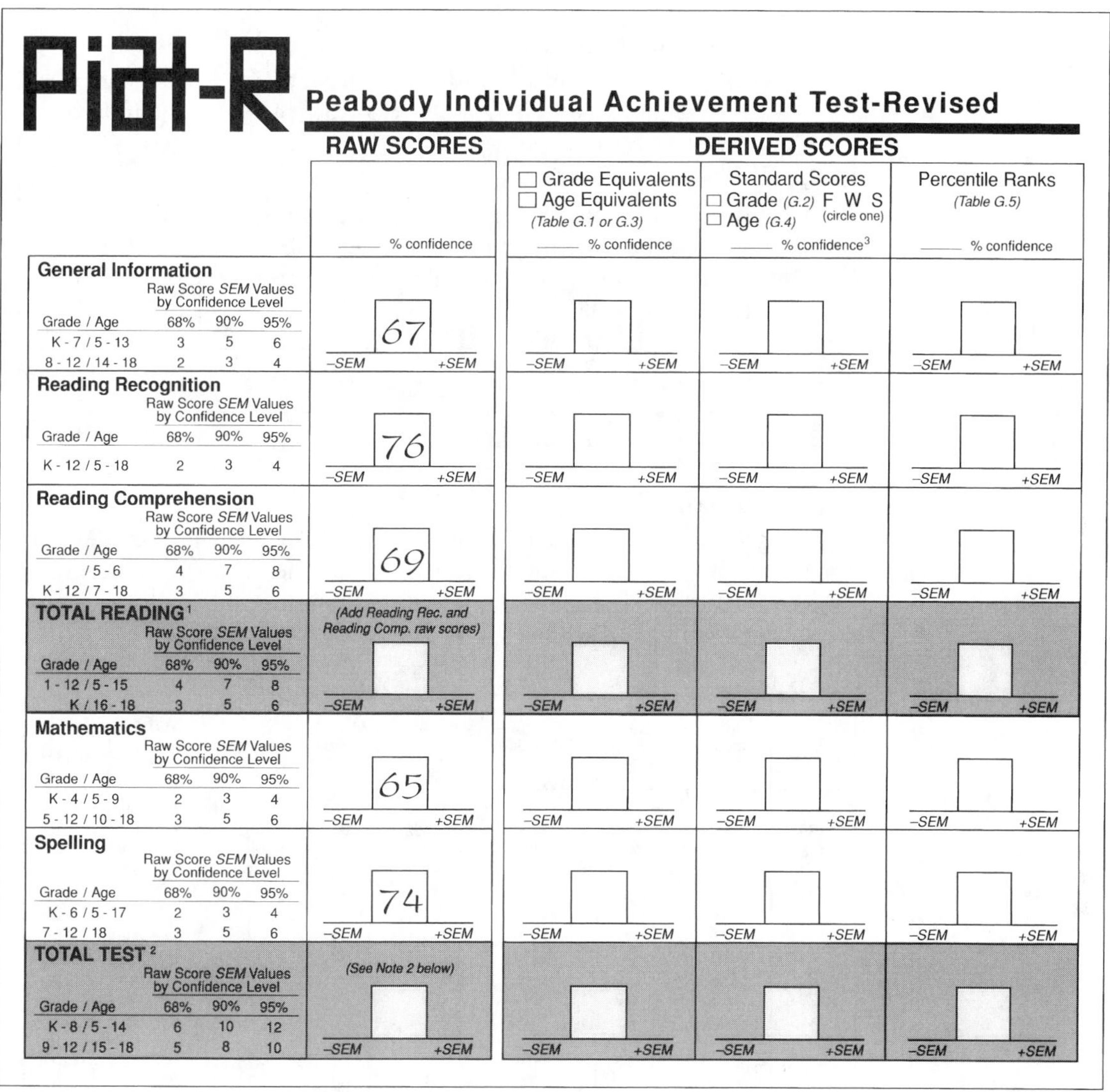

PIAT-R Peabody Individual Achievement Test-Revised

	RAW SCORES	DERIVED SCORES		
	____ % confidence	☐ Grade Equivalents ☐ Age Equivalents *(Table G.1 or G.3)* ____ % confidence	Standard Scores ☐ Grade *(G.2)* F W S ☐ Age *(G.4)* (circle one) ____ % confidence[3]	Percentile Ranks *(Table G.5)* ____ % confidence
General Information Raw Score *SEM* Values by Confidence Level Grade / Age — 68% 90% 95% K - 7 / 5 - 13 — 3 5 6 8 - 12 / 14 - 18 — 2 3 4	67 –SEM +SEM	–SEM +SEM	–SEM +SEM	–SEM +SEM
Reading Recognition Raw Score *SEM* Values by Confidence Level Grade / Age — 68% 90% 95% K - 12 / 5 - 18 — 2 3 4	76 –SEM +SEM	–SEM +SEM	–SEM +SEM	–SEM +SEM
Reading Comprehension Raw Score *SEM* Values by Confidence Level Grade / Age — 68% 90% 95% / 5 - 6 — 4 7 8 K - 12 / 7 - 18 — 3 5 6	69 –SEM +SEM	–SEM +SEM	–SEM +SEM	–SEM +SEM
TOTAL READING[1] Raw Score *SEM* Values by Confidence Level Grade / Age — 68% 90% 95% 1 - 12 / 5 - 15 — 4 7 8 K / 16 - 18 — 3 5 6	*(Add Reading Rec. and Reading Comp. raw scores)* –SEM +SEM	–SEM +SEM	–SEM +SEM	–SEM +SEM
Mathematics Raw Score *SEM* Values by Confidence Level Grade / Age — 68% 90% 95% K - 4 / 5 - 9 — 2 3 4 5 - 12 / 10 - 18 — 3 5 6	65 –SEM +SEM	–SEM +SEM	–SEM +SEM	–SEM +SEM
Spelling Raw Score *SEM* Values by Confidence Level Grade / Age — 68% 90% 95% K - 6 / 5 - 17 — 2 3 4 7 - 12 / 18 — 3 5 6	74 –SEM +SEM	–SEM +SEM	–SEM +SEM	–SEM +SEM
TOTAL TEST[2] Raw Score *SEM* Values by Confidence Level Grade / Age — 68% 90% 95% K - 8 / 5 - 14 — 6 10 12 9 - 12 / 15 - 18 — 5 8 10	*(See Note 2 below)* –SEM +SEM	–SEM +SEM	–SEM +SEM	–SEM +SEM

Figure 6.2 Portion of the protocol PIAT—R. (*Source:* From *Peabody Individual Achievement Test—Revised* (p. 10) by F. C. Markwardt, 1989, Circle Pines, MN: American Guidance Service. Copyright 1989 by American Guidance Service. Reprinted by permission.)

2. Using the raw score data determined in problem 1, locate the standard scores from the section of the table provided in Figure 6.3. Write the standard scores in the appropriate places in Figure 6.2.

Apply Your Knowledge

Make a general statement regarding this student's academic functioning based on the standard scores you determined on the PIAT—R. Does the student have any academic strengths or weaknesses according to these scores? If so, what are they? ______________________

____

____

____

Technical Data

Norming Process. The PIAT—R sample was selected with consideration for geographic region, socioeconomic status, and race or ethnic group (Markwardt, 1989). The manual gives no indication of the inclusion of students identified with disabilities.

Standard Score	General Information	Reading Recognition	Reading Comprehension	TOTAL READING	Mathematics	Spelling	TOTAL TEST	Standard Score
	Raw Score							
130	—	—	81	163	—	—	368-369	130
129	—	84	—	161-162	66	81	365-367	129
128	72	83	80	160	—	80	363-364	128
127	—	—	79	159	65	79	360-362	127
126	—	82	—	158	—	—	357-359	126
125	71	81	78	157	64	78	354-356	125
124	70	—	77	155-156	63	—	352-353	124
123	—	80	—	154	—	77	349-351	123
122	69	79	76	153	62	76	347-348	122
121	68	—	75	151-152	—	—	344-346	121
120	—	78	—	150	61	75	341-343	120
119	67	77	74	149	60	74	339-340	119
118	66	76	73	147-148	—	—	336-338	118
117	—	—	72	146	59	73	333-335	117
116	65	75	—	144-145	58	72	331-332	116
115	64	74	71	143	—	—	328-330	115
114	63	—	70	142	57	71	326-327	114
113	—	73	69	140-141	—	—	322-325	113
112	62	72	—	139	56	70	320-321	112
111	61	71	68	137-138	—	69	316-319	111

Figure 6.3 Standard scores corresponding to subtest and composite raw scores from the PIAT—R. (*Source:* From *Peabody Individual Achievement Test—Revised* (p. 117) by F. C. Markwardt, 1989, Circle Pines, MN: American Guidance Service. Copyright 1989 by American Guidance Service. Reprinted by permission.)

Reliability. Several reliability studies are presented in the examiner's manual, with coefficients ranging from the .80s to the high .90s. The studies included split-half, K-R 20, test-retest, and item response theory.

Validity. The manual reports on content validity and construct validity. The construct validity studies included correlation with other tests and factor analysis.

KAUFMAN TEST OF EDUCATIONAL ACHIEVEMENT (K-TEA)

The K-TEA (Kaufman & Kaufman, 1985a, 1985b) is an individually administered achievement test for school-aged students. It consists of two forms: the Comprehensive Form and the Brief Form. Both forms are presented in easel fashion with computation and spelling subtests using pencil-and-paper tasks. Starting points are suggested by grade-level functioning, and the ceiling level on both forms is determined when the student fails every item in one unit or section. The test authors have named this the "discontinue rule" (Kaufman & Kaufman, 1985a, 1985b).

Comprehensive Form. Although the two forms of the K-TEA are similar in format, the Comprehensive Form is much more detailed in scoring and provides better information for planning. The Comprehensive Form includes two more subtests than the Brief Form, and generally, each subtest contains more items.

Comprehensive Form subtests include Mathematics Applications, Reading Decoding, Spelling, Reading Comprehension, and Mathematics Computation. The subtest scores are combined into reading and mathematics composites as well as a total battery composite. The scores can be compared for intra-individual differences.

Mathematics Applications. This subtest presents story problems printed on the easel pages. The examiner reads the problems aloud to the student. The student may use pencil and paper to calculate the answers and may also use finger counting. Picture cues accompany some of the problems. The problems are presented orally and require an oral response.

Reading Decoding. This subtest presents words visually for the student to read aloud to the examiner. These are real words (not nonsense words as on the Woodcock-Johnson Word Attack subtest) and range from single letters and primer-level words to very difficult and unpredictable words.

Spelling. This subtest is presented as a typical spelling test. The examiner states a word, reads the given sentence containing the word, and states the word again. The student writes the word in a student answer booklet, which also contains the math computation problems. The examiner scans the student's protocol after each page to check for errors and to watch for the ceiling level to be reached.

Reading Comprehension. This subtest presents sentences and passages for the student to read and respond to. The lower level items are short sentences that require the student to respond by taking some action, such as "Open your mouth" (Kaufman & Kaufman, 1985b). The examiner prompts the student by saying, "Do what this says" (Kaufman & Kaufman, 1985b). The student may read silently or aloud and then responds by actions. The higher level items are short passages followed by questions. The student reads the passages and questions silently or aloud and then responds orally.

Mathematics Computation. This subtest includes 60 math problems presented in the student's answer booklet. The student may use a pencil and eraser, as well as finger counting, as needed to answer the problems. The examiner scans the answer booklet as the student works to determine when the discontinue rule has been reached and the student must stop working. The examiner then circles in blue the number of the problem that indicates the end of a unit or section. The problems range in difficulty from simple operations to algebra.

Scoring the Comprehensive Form. The examiner determines the raw score by counting the number of responses answered correctly. The advantage of using the K-TEA Comprehensive Form is that the protocol includes skill category information. This information helps the examiner to determine which skills are represented by items answered correctly and which unmastered skills can be identified by items answered incorrectly. The examiner can use the information obtained on the protocol to form IEP objectives. The information regarding the student's errors can be used to compare the number of errors the student made with the number of errors made by the norm group on those same skills. The inclusion of skill categories on this norm-referenced test means that the K-TEA is also considered a criterion-referenced test. These criteria can be used when determining whether a student has met specific criteria necessary to progress to a higher skill curriculum. For example, when a student has mastered all skills necessary for introduction to an algebra curriculum, the student will be considered ready to progress to that algebra curriculum. By the same token, if a student has not mastered basic operations, measurement, fractions, or decimals, beginning a curriculum of algebra would not be recommended.

Raw score information and errors made by skill categories are transferred to the error analysis summaries page by skill categories for all five subtests of the Comprehensive Form. This allows the examiner to compare the student with norm tables to determine whether the student's skill status is considered weak, average, or strong.

Check Your Understanding

Complete Activity 6.3.

ACTIVITY 6.3

Complete the following problems.

1. Look at the responses made by the third-grade student on the K-TEA Spelling subtest in Figure 6.4. Use the portion of the protocol to mark the errors and count the number of errors by skill category.
2. Transfer the number of items missed to the error analysis summaries page in Figure 6.5. Use the information from the norm table in Figure 6.6 to determine whether the number of spelling errors places the student in the average, weak, or strong category for a third-grade student. If the student made more errors than other third graders, the student is considered weak in the area or skill assessed. If the student made the same number of errors, the student is considered average. If the student made fewer errors, the student is considered strong in that area or skill. Circle the appropriate skill status in Figure 6.5 for each of the assessed skills.

Apply Your Knowledge

Using the information obtained from the errors by skill category, list the skills you would use to write lesson plans or objectives for this student. ____

____

____

____

The second part of scoring the K-TEA Comprehensive Form uses norm tables to determine standard scores, percentile ranks, bands of error, grade equivalents, and descriptive categories for student performance. The examiner transfers the raw scores to the front of the protocol and refers to norm tables to obtain scores. The norm tables are provided by age and grade and are listed by either fall or spring testing. The most accurate comparison of the student with the norm group will use the appropriate tables, which depend on the semester when the testing is completed. If the testing is completed in the fall, fall norm tables will be used.

The third step in scoring the K-TEA Comprehensive Form is to compare the student with his own performance. To determine *specific skill comparisons,* the examiner finds the difference between the Reading Decoding and Reading Comprehension standard scores and the difference between the Mathematics Applications and Mathematics Computation standard scores. To determine *global skill comparisons,* the examiner finds the difference between standard scores on the Reading Composite and Mathematics Composite, Reading Composite and Spelling subtest, and Mathematics Composite and

Spelling

Item	Stimulus	Score	Prefixes & Word Beginnings	Suffixes & Word Endings	Closed Syllable (Short) Vowels	Open Syllable (Long) & Final e Pattern Vowells	Vowel Digraphs & Diphthongs	r-Controlled Patterns	Consonant Clusters & Digraphs	Single & Double Consonants	Whole Word Error Type
			WORD PARTS								
26	praise	1				_e	ai		pr	s	
27	objection	1	ob	tion	e					j c	
28	education	1		tion	e	u a				d c	
29	celebrate	1		ate	e	e			br	c l	
30	accident	1	ac	ent		i				c d	
31	employed	1	em	ed			oy		pl		
32	loyalty	0		al ty			oy			l	
33	rumor	0		or		u				r m	
34	definition	0	de	tion	i	i				f n	
35	opposite	0	op	ite		o				p s	
36	initial	0		tial	i i					n	
37	schedule	0			e	u_e			ch	s d l	
38	anticipate	0	anti	ate		i				c p	
39	inferior	0	in	ior				er		f	
40	familar	0		iar	i	a				f m l	

Total Errors by Skill Category

	Prefixes & Word Beginnings	Suffixes & Word Endings	Closed Syllable (Short) Vowels	Open Syllable (Long) & Final e Pattern Vowells	Vowel Digraphs & Diphthongs	r-Controlled Patterns	Consonant Clusters & Digraphs	Single & Double Consonants	Whole Word Error Type
Ceiling Item ______ minus Errors ______ equals Raw Score ______									

Figure 6.4 Responses on the Spelling subtest protocol of the K-TEA. (*Source:* From *Kaufman Test of Educational Achievement, Comprehensive Form, Protocol* by A. S. Kaufman and N. L. Kaufman, 1985, Circle Pines, MN: American Guidance Service. Copyright 1985 by American Guidance Service. Reprinted by permission.)

Grade ________

Ceiling Item ________

Spelling	Average Number of Errors	Student's Number of Errors	**Skill Status**		
			Weak	Average	Strong
WORD PART	Table 20	Page 7			
Prefixes & Word Beginnings	________	________	W	A	S
Suffixes & Word Endings	________	________	W	A	S
Closed Syllable (Short) Vowels	________	________	W	A	S
Open Syllable (Long) & Final *e* Pattern Vowels	________	________	W	A	S
Vowel Digraphs & Diphthongs	________	________	W	A	S
r-Controlled Patterns	________	________	W	A	S
Consonant Clusters & Digraphs	________	________	W	A	S
Single & Double Consonants	________	________	W	A	S

Figure 6.5 Error comparison section of the K-TEA Comprehensive Form, Spelling subtest. (*Source:* From *Kaufman Test of Educational Achievement Comprehensive Form, Protocol* by A. S. Kaufman and N. L. Kaufman, 1985, Circle Pines, MN: American Guidance Service. Copyright 1985 by American Guidance Service. Reprinted by permission.)

Grade 3

Word Part	**Ceiling Item**									
	5	**10**	**15**	**20**	**25**	**30**	**35**	**40**	**45**	**50**
	Average Number of Errors									
Prefixes & Word Beginnings	—	—	—	—	0-1	1	1	1	1	1
Suffixes & Word Endings	—	—	—	—	0	0-1	2	3-5	3-5	4-6
Closed Syllable (Short) Vowels	0	0	0	0	0	0	0-1	1-2	2-3	1-2
Open Syllable (Long) & Final *e* Pattern Vowels	—	—	—	0	0	1-2	3-4	3-4	3-4	4-6
Vowel Digraphs & Diphthongs	—	—	0-1	1-3	1-2	1-2	1-2	0-1	0	1
r-Controlled Patterns	—	—	—	—	—	—	—	—	—	—
Consonant Clusters & Digraphs	—	0	0	0	0	0	0	0	0-1	0-1
Single & Double Consonants	0	0	0	0-1	0-1	1-3	2-4	2-4	3-5	3-5

Figure 6.6 Norm table of the Comprehensive Form of the K-TEA for average number of errors by category. (*Source:* From *Kaufman Test of Educational Achievement Comprehensive Form, Manual* (p. 536) by A. S. Kaufman and N. L. Kaufman, 1985, Circle Pines, MN: American Guidance Service. Copyright 1985 by American Guidance Service. Reprinted by permission.)

Spelling subtest. The examiner records the standard score differences in the standard score difference box and uses norm tables to determine whether the difference is significant. The determination of a significant difference between either specific or global skills may help the educator effectively plan strategies for the student.

Check Your Understanding

Complete Activity 6.4.

ACTIVITY 6.4

The following K-TEA standard scores are those obtained by a 9-year-old girl.

	Standard Score
Mathematics Applications	136
Reading Decoding	105
Spelling	100
Reading Comprehension	105
Mathematics Computation	141
Reading Composite	106
Mathematics Composite	141
Battery Composite	119

1. Write the scores in the appropriate spaces on the protocol in Figure 6.7.
2. Using the information provided on the norm table, Figures 6.8(a) and (b), determine whether the differences between both global and specific scores are significant. Circle the significance levels in the space provided on the protocol.

Apply Your Knowledge

Using the information you obtained by analyzing this student's strengths and weaknesses, write an explanation you would use to discuss the results with the student's parents. ____________________

____

____

____

Technical Data for the Comprehensive Form

Norming Process. The K-TEA examiner's manual contains information regarding the standardization and norming process. The test developers administered the Comprehensive Form during the fall and spring to establish norms for these two testing times of the school year. The fall sample included 1,067 students in the norm group, and the spring sample included 1,409 students in the norm group. The fall sample did not contain the desired number of at least 100 students per grade, but this number was reached during the spring testing.

Comprehensive Form

K-TEA

KAUFMAN TEST of EDUCATIONAL ACHIEVEMENT

by Alan S. Kaufman & Nadeen L. Kaufman

INDIVIDUAL TEST RECORD

Student's Name ____ Sex ____

Parent's Name ____

Home Address ____ Home Phone ____

Grade ____ Teacher ____

School ____ Examiner ____

	Year	Month	Day
Test Date			
Birth Date			
Chronological Age			

COMPREHENSIVE FORM SUBTESTS Mean = 100; SD = 15	RAW SCORES Reading Composite	Mathematics Composite	Battery Composite	Standard Score* Table___	Band of Error ___% Confidence Table 5 or 6	%ile Rank Table 7	Other Data	
Mathematics Applications					±			
Reading Decoding					±			
Spelling					±			
Reading Comprehension					±			
Mathematics Computation					±			
Sum of Subtest Raw Scores								

Transfer sums to Composite Scales, *Sum of Subtest Raw Scores* column.

***Standard Scores** Derived from (Circle the table used):*	AGE	GRADE
Fall Norms (August–January)	Table 1	Table 2
Spring Norms (February–July)	Table 3	Table 4

COMPREHENSIVE FORM COMPOSITE SCALES Mean = 100; *SD* = 15	Sum of Subtest Raw Scores	Standard Score* Table___	Band of Error ___% Confidence Table 5 or 6	%ile Rank Table 7	Descriptive Category	Other Data
Reading Composite			±			
Mathematics Composite			±			
Battery Composite			±			

		Indicate >, <, or ≈		Standard Score Difference	Circle the Significance Level
GLOBAL SKILL COMPARISONS	Reading Composite		Mathematics Composite		NS .05 .01
	Reading Composite		Spelling Subtest		NS .05 .01
	Mathematics Composite		Spelling Subtest		NS .05 .01
SPECIFIC SKILL COMPARISONS	Reading Decoding		Reading Comprehension		NS .05 .01
	Mathematics Applications		Mathematics Computation		NS .05 .01

AGS®

Figure 6.7 Portion of protocol from the K-TEA Comprehensive Form.

Age	Significance Level	Reading Composite versus Mathematics Composite	Reading Composite versus Spelling	Mathematics Composite versus Spelling
		Standard Score Difference Required for Significance		
8	.05	11	10	12
	.01	13	12	14
9	.05	9	9	10
	.01	11	11	13
10	.05	10	10	11
	.01	12	12	13

(a)

Age	Significance Level	Reading Decoding versus Reading Comprehension	Mathematics Applications versus Mathematics Computation
		Standard Score Difference Required for Significance	
8	.05	11	15
	.01	13	19
9	.05	10	12
	.01	12	15
10	.05	12	13
	.01	15	17

(b)

Figure 6.8 (a) K-TEA Comprehensive Form standard score differences when comparing global skills. (b) K-TEA Comprehensive Form standard score differences when comparing specific reading and mathematics skills. (*Source:* From *Kaufman Test of Educational Achievement, Comprehensive Form, Protocol* (p. 1) *and Manual* (pp. 500, 502) by A. S. Kaufman and N. L. Kaufman, 1985, Circle Pines MN: American Guidance Service. Copyright 1985 by American Guidance Service. Reprinted by permission.)

The ratio of male to female students was approximately equal for the standardization of this test. Other variables considered were geographic region, educational level of parents, and race or ethnic group.

Reliability. The test developers studied the reliability of the K-TEA Comprehensive Form using the methods of split-half reliability, test-retest, intercorrelations among subtests and composites, and a study comparing the two batteries, Brief and Comprehensive. Split-half reliability coefficients were high, ranging from .83 to .97 on individual subtests and from .93 to .99 on composite comparisons. Test-retest reliability coefficients ranged from .90 to .97 across all grade levels (Kaufman & Kaufman, 1985b).

Intercorrelations between subtests and composites ranged from .50 to .82. The reliability study (test-retest) on the Comprehensive and Brief forms yielded coefficients ranging from .66 to .97.

Validity. The examiner's manual presents information regarding the content validity of subtests. Concurrent validity studies for the K-TEA and several other tests are presented, including comparisons with the Wide Range Achievement Test, the PIAT, the Kaufman Assessment Battery for Children, and the Peabody Picture Vocabulary Test—Revised. The manual also gives information regarding concurrent validity between the K-TEA and group achievement tests. The validity coefficients are adequate, ranging from .24 to .92.

Brief Form. The major differences between the Brief and Comprehensive forms of the K-TEA are the test length and the data available from test results. The Brief Form contains fewer items per subtest and has only three subtests, compared with five on the Comprehensive Form. With less detailed scoring and no error analysis, the Brief Form provides the educator with only a screening tool for determining whether a student needed further diagnostic evaluation. The results allow for comparison between subtests but not between composites or global skills. The protocol contains the student response booklet, or answer sheet. The subtests are described in the following paragraphs.

Mathematics. This subtest presents some story problems with picture cues and some computation problems. The overall administration of the subtest combines the easel format and the student answer booklet. The first 25 problems are presented within the answer booklet, whereas problems 26 through 52 are presented on the easel. Students in the lower grades may not complete all the computation problems but may continue on to the orally presented story problems. The discontinue rule, which is used on the K-TEA Comprehensive Form, is applied on the Brief Form as well.

Reading. The examiner first presents single letters for the student to name aloud. The next several items are words for the student to read aloud. Items 24 through 52 are items that the student may read aloud or silently but require an oral or action response. Some items require the student to perform a gesture or action, whereas other items require oral responses to questions about short passages that the student has just read.

Spelling. The Spelling subtest is presented like a standard spelling test. The examiner reads a word, reads a sentence containing the word, and repeats the word. The student responds by writing the spelling word on the answer sheet. Since the discontinue rule is applied, the examiner should scan the student's work.

Scoring the Brief Form. The raw scores obtained on the individual subtests are transferred to the front page of the protocol. Norm tables are used to determine standard scores, percentile ranks, grade equivalents, and bands of error. The subtest scores can be compared by finding the difference between subtests and using a norm table to determine whether the difference is significant. The examiner should be sure to use the appropriate fall or spring norm tables according to the time when testing was completed.

Check Your Understanding

Complete Activity 6.5.

ACTIVITY 6.5

Complete the following problems and questions.

1. Record the following standard scores on the protocol in Figure 6.9. Using the 90% confidence level, determine the band of error (Figure 6.10) for the three subtests of the K-TEA Brief Form for a 10-year-old boy. Record the band of error information in Figure 6.9.

	Standard Score
Mathematics	110
Reading	85
Spelling	75

2. Write the range of possible standard scores that the student may obtain as true scores using the bands of confidence found in problem 1.

	Obtained Standard Score	**Range of Scores**
Mathematics	110	_____
Reading	85	_____
Spelling	75	_____

Apply Your Knowledge

How would the bands of error be used in test interpretation? ________

____

____

Based on this student's scores, what area(s) would you need to assess further to determine specific skill weaknesses? ________________

____

Technical Data for the Brief Form

Norming Process. The standardization of the Brief Form was carried out as part of the fall standardization of the Comprehensive Form. The variables of geographic region, educational level of parents, race or ethnic group, and male-to-female ratio are reflected. The total sample for the Brief Form was 589 students.

Brief Form					**Individual Test Record**
BRIEF FORM SUBTESTS Mean = 100 SD = 15	Raw Score	Standard Score*	Band of Error % Confidence Table 5 or 6	%ile Rank Table 7	Other Data
MATHEMATICS			±		
READING			±		
SPELLING			±		
BATTERY COMPOSITE Mean = 100 SD = 15			±		Descriptive Category

Figure 6.9 Portion of protocol of the K-TEA Brief Form. (*Source:* From *Kaufman Test of Educational Achievement, Brief Form* (p. 1) by A. S. Kaufman and N. L. Kaufman, 1985, Circle Pines, MN: American Guidance Service. Copyright 1985 by American Guidance Service. Reprinted by permission.)

Age	Confidence Level	Mathematics	Reading	Spelling	Battery Composite
		Band of Error			
8	99%	± 17	± 12	± 12	± 9
	95%	± 13	± 9	± 9	± 7
	90%	± 11	± 7	± 8	± 6
	85%	± 9	± 6	± 7	± 5
	68%	± 7	± 5	± 5	± 4
9	99%	± 11	± 7	± 8	± 6
	95%	± 9	± 5	± 6	± 5
	90%	± 7	± 4	± 5	± 4
	85%	± 6	± 4	± 4	± 3
	68%	± 4	± 3	± 3	± 2
10	99%	± 15	± 10	± 11	± 9
	95%	± 11	± 8	± 9	± 6
	90%	± 10	± 7	± 7	± 5
	85%	± 8	± 6	± 6	± 4
	68%	± 6	± 4	± 4	± 3
11	99%	± 12	± 11	± 12	± 8
	95%	± 9	± 8	± 9	± 6
	90%	± 8	± 7	± 7	± 5
	85%	± 7	± 6	± 6	± 4
	68%	± 5	± 4	± 5	± 3
12	99%	± 15	± 13	± 15	± 10
	95%	± 11	± 10	± 11	± 7
	90%	± 9	± 8	± 10	± 6
	85%	± 8	± 7	± 8	± 5
	68%	± 6	± 5	± 6	± 4

Figure 6.10 Bands of error (confidence intervals) for age standard scores, ages 8 through 12, from the K-TEA Brief Form. (*Source:* From *Kaufman Test of Educational Achievement, Brief Form* (p. 275) by A. S. Kaufman and N. L. Kaufman, 1985, Circle Pines, MN: American Guidance Service. Copyright 1985 by American Guidance Service. Reprinted by permission.)

Reliability. The examiner's manual includes information on split-half reliability, test-retest reliability, and the study between the Comprehensive and Brief forms discussed in the technical data section of the Comprehensive Form. The reliability coefficients ranged from .72 to .98 on the split-half reliability study and from .84 to .94 on the test-retest reliability study.

Validity. The examiner's manual provides information regarding concurrent validity studies with other tests. Tests compared with the K-TEA brief were the Wide Range Achievement Test, the Peabody Picture Vocabulary Test, the Kaufman Assessment Battery for Children, and the Peabody Picture Vocabulary Test—Revised. Correlations ranged from .25 to .92. Overall concurrent validity studies appear to be adequate for the K-TEA brief.

WECHSLER INDIVIDUAL ACHIEVEMENT TEST, SECOND EDITION (WIAT-II)

The WIAT-II (Psychological Corporation, 2001) is an individually administered achievement test made up of nine subtests. Students ages 4-0 to 19-11 or in grades PreK (age 5) through college may be administered this instrument. The administration of this instrument to college students and adults can be completed using the *WIAT-II Supplement for College Students and Adults.* This revised edition of the WIAT contains changes in individual items, subtests, and scoring. The revised edition expanded several subtests and added the new subtest, Pseudoword Decoding. The WIAT was designed to help educators in determining discrepancies between measured intellectual ability and academic achievement. The revised test format includes easels, paper-and-pencil tasks, and separate reading cards. Starting points and ceiling rules, which vary by subtests, are presented in the manual and on the protocol form. Some items are timed and cues are presented to the examiner in the test stimulus booklets and in the protocol. Examiners are also provided rules for reverse administration if the student does not establish a basal. These reverse rules are provided in the examiner's manual and on the protocol. A parent report form is included within the protocol.

The WIAT includes subtests in the areas of oral expression and listening comprehension. These areas are not typically included in other academic achievement tests and may offer the educator useful information for intervention. This test provides skill information on the protocol of the math subtests that can easily be adapted to write educational objectives. The protocol includes qualitative observation items that the examiner may simply check following the administration of each subtest. Additional information regarding each subtest follows.

Subtests

Word Reading. This subtest was called Basic Reading in the original version of the WIAT. This revised subtest has been expanded and includes items at the PreK level. The early items include visual memory and visual discrimination of letters. Items of letter recognition or letter naming are presented next, followed by items in which the student is asked to discriminate rhyming words. Students are then asked to generate rhyming words to specific stimuli. Students are then asked to require the student to determine two of three words that begin with the same sound followed by words with the same ending sounds. Students are then asked to discriminate the letters that make specific sounds; this includes isolated vowels, consonants, and consonant blends. On more difficult items, the student is presented with words on a card and asked to read the words aloud.

Numerical Operations. Items for PreK students include number recognition, number sequencing (1–10), dictation of specific numbers, and counting. Additional items require the student to respond in writing to solve calculation problems. More difficult items are problems that involve geometry, percent, decimals, and simple algebraic equations.

Reading Comprehension. In this subtest, the first-grade student is asked to point to the picture that matches the word. Simple sentence items follow with specific target words that are scored by the examiner. Beginning with second-grade items, the student reads written passages and then responds to questions asked by the examiner. In addition to passage items, sentences are also presented for oral reading accuracy. Beginning with the third-grade items, student reading speed is timed. Specific starting and stopping points are used rather than ceiling levels.

Spelling. The student responds in writing to letters, sounds, or words dictated by the examiner. Homonyms are presented in bold in the protocol.

Pseudoword Decoding. This subtest is presented on a reading card and is administered to students in grades 1 and above. The examiner should listen to the audiotape and become familiar with the correct pronunciation prior to the initial administration of the test. The student's responses are recorded exactly using correct pronunciation or phonetic symbols.

Math Reasoning. This subtest requires the student to solve math problems that require reasoning. The student is presented with items on the easel and may use pencil and paper if needed. The PreK items include counting pictures and distinguishing pictures with more objects. Other early level items include recognizing shapes and interpreting simple picture graphs. More difficult items include answering story-type problems and interpreting complex graphs.

Written Expression. This subtest contains the following five sections: alphabet writing, word fluency, sentences, paragraph, and essay. This subtest requires the student to respond in writing to various prompts. Written expression paragraphs and essays are scored for mechanics, organization, and vocabulary.

Listening Comprehension. This subtest was revised to include receptive vocabulary items, sentence comprehension, and expressive vocabulary. Following orally presented items, the student responds to questions asked by the examiner. The items include picture cues, and the lower levels require the student to point to the answer.

Oral Expression. This subtest was revised to include the following four sections: sentence repetition (for the early grades only), word fluency, visual passage retell, and giving directions. Sentence repetition requires the student to repeat sentences. The word fluency subtest is timed. Other items assess the student's ability to use words to describe picture cues, give directions, or provide explanations. The student responds orally. The examiner must write the student's responses or use a tape recorder to tape the responses.

Scoring. The scoring of the revised edition of the WIAT is more complex than the original version. Items on the Word Reading, Mathematics Reasoning, Spelling, Numerical Operations, Pseudoword Reading, and Listening Comprehension subtests receive 1 point when answered correctly and 0 when incorrect. Scoring for the Reading Comprehension and Written Expression subtests is slightly more complicated; the manual includes instructions. Practice exercises are provided for scoring this writing subtest. Raw scores are used to obtain derived scores that may be based on either grade- or age-normative data. Grade norm tables are presented for fall, winter, and spring. The correct table is determined by the date of testing according to the following guidelines: fall for August–November, winter for December–February, and spring for March–July. Standard scores—with a mean of 100, percentile ranks, age equivalents, and grade equivalents—are available for both subtests and composites. Supplemental scores, in quartiles and deciles, are available. Tables are provided to determine significance differences between individual subtest scores and composite scores. To assist in decisions regarding significant discrepancies between ability and achievement, tables are provided that display differences between scores on the WIAT II and the Wechsler Intelligence Scale for Children, Third Edition, between the WIAT II and the Wechsler Adult Intelligence Scale, Third Edition, and between the WIAT II and the Wechsler Preschool and Primary Scale of Intelligence. Tables are provided with levels of statistical significance for differences between predicted and actual subtest scores and composite scores for using the predicted-achievement method.

Technical Data

Norming Process. The standardization sample for grades PreK to 12 included 3,600 students. The age sample included 2,950 ranging in age from 4 to 19, in grades K through 12. Most age groups included from 100 to 200 students for each of two testing times, fall and spring. Genders were nearly equally represented and were approximately equal at all grade levels. Other variables considered in the sample were race/ethnicity, geographic region, and level of parents' education. The 1998 U.S. Census data provided the criteria for determining the representation of the sample.

Additional studies were completed with special populations and the mean standard scores, and standard deviations are provided in tabular form in the manual. The special groups included students classified as gifted, students with mental retardation, students with emotional disturbance, students with learning disabilities, students with attention deficit disorder, students with hearing impairments, and students with speech and/or language impairment.

Reliability. Reliability was studied using a split-half method, and correlations were corrected using the Spearman-Brown formula. Test-retest reliability and interscorer reliability studies were completed. All stability coefficients were acceptable and ranged from .81 to .99. Correlations were calculated for both individual subtests and composites. Reliability coefficients are reported by age and grade in the examiner's manual.

Validity. The manual presents information regarding the research studies of content validity, construct validity, and criterion-related validity. Instruments used in the criterion-related validity studies include the Wide Range Achievement Test—Revised, the Differential Ability Scales, and the Peabody Picture Vocabulary Test—Third Edition. Information is provided in the manual regarding criterion-related validity with group achievement instruments such as the Stanford Achievement Tests, Ninth Edition, and the Metropolitan Achievement Tests, Eighth Edition.

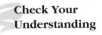

Check Your Understanding

Complete Activity 6.6.

ACTIVITY 6.6

Answer the following questions.

1. The student you are testing completed the spelling subtest of the WIAT-II. The student is 8 years and 2 months of age. Score the spelling subtest protocol shown in Figure 6.11.
2. Once you have determined the raw score of the spelling subtest, use the section of the age norm table shown in Figure 6.12 to look up the standard score. Enter the score in the correct place on the section of the protocol shown in Figure 6.13.

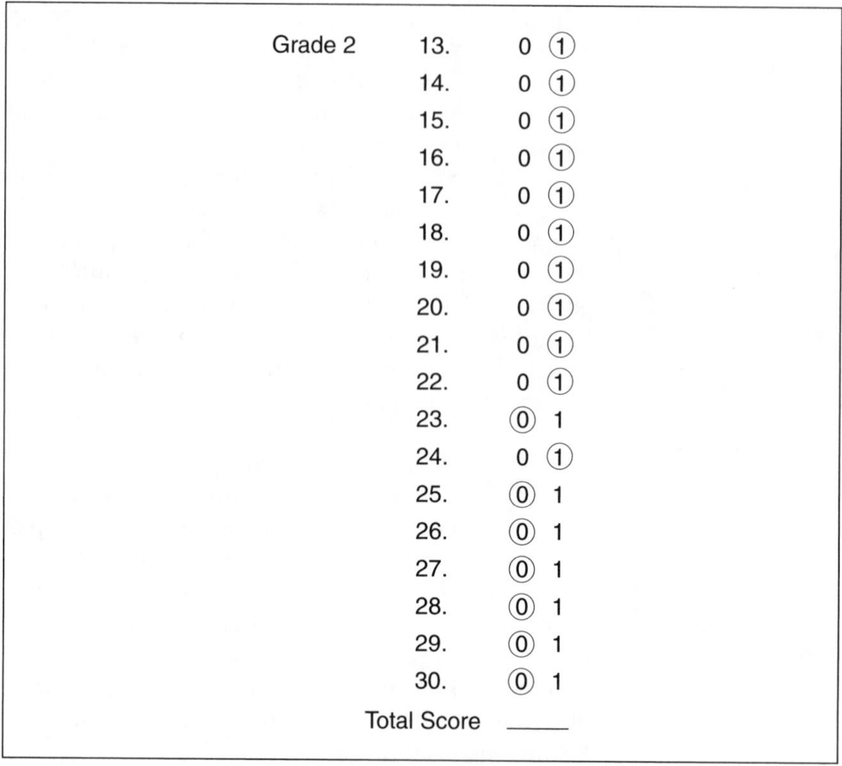

Grade 2	13.	0	(1)
	14.	0	(1)
	15.	0	(1)
	16.	0	(1)
	17.	0	(1)
	18.	0	(1)
	19.	0	(1)
	20.	0	(1)
	21.	0	(1)
	22.	0	(1)
	23.	(0)	1
	24.	0	(1)
	25.	(0)	1
	26.	(0)	1
	27.	(0)	1
	28.	(0)	1
	29.	(0)	1
	30.	(0)	1
	Total Score	____	

Figure 6.11 A student's performance on the WIAT-II spelling subtest. This student began at the starting point for second grade students, item 13.

3. Add the two subtest standard scores, spelling and written expression, and enter the sum in the correct space beneath the two scores on the protocol shown in Figure 6.13.
4. Use the norm table for composite scores shown in Figure 6.14 and determine the composite standard score. Write the composite standard score in the appropriate space on the protocol shown in Figure 6.13.

WIDE RANGE ACHIEVEMENT TEST—REVISION 3 (WRAT3)

The WRAT3 is a screening achievement test that was designed to "measure the codes which are needed to learn the basic skills of reading, spelling, and arithmetic" (Wilkinson, 1993, p. 10). This test is composed of three subtests that may be administered in any order and may be given to persons ages 5 through 75. Because it is a screening instrument, the WRAT3 should

Age-Based Subtest Standard Scores
Ages: 8 years, 0 months, 0 days—8 years, 3 months, 30 days (*continued*)

	Subtest Total Raw Scores				
Standard Score	Word Reading	Numerical Operations	Reading Comprehension	Spelling	Pseudoword Decoding
101	82		53		24
102	83		54		25
103	84		55	23	26
104	85	16	56		27
105	86–87		57	24	28
106	88		58		29
107	89		59		30
108	90		60	25	31
109	91	17	61		32
110	92		62	26	33
111	93		63		34
112	94		64		35
113	95	18	65	27	36
114	96		66		37
115	97		67	28	38

Figure 6.12 Wechsler Individual Achievement Test, Second Edition, Age-Based Subtest Standard Scores. (*Source:* From *WIAT-III Scoring and Normative Supplement for Grades PreK–12* (p. 230), 2001, San Antonio, TX: Psychological Corporation. Copyright 2001 by Psychological Corporation. Reprinted by permission.)

be used not to diagnose learning problems but rather to determine whether additional testing is necessary. This third revision, unlike the WRAT—R, may be given to any person within the age range of 5–75 and is no longer divided by age levels. The test includes alternate forms, the Blue Test and Tan Test, which may be administered alone or together for a combined score. Students who are not administered the items for ages 5–7 are given

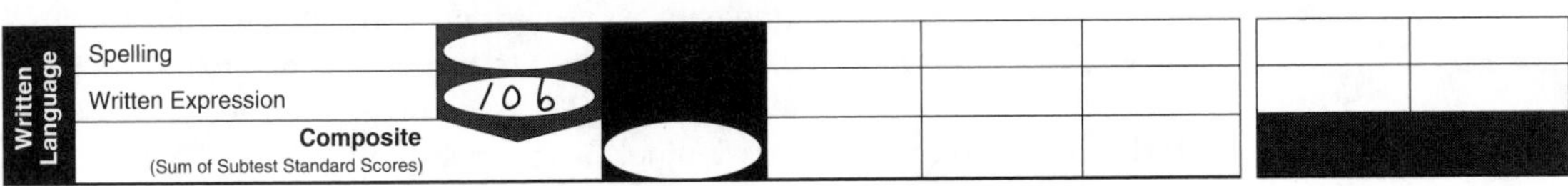

Figure 6.13 Written Language Section for the WIAT-II Protocol. (*Source:* From *Wechsler Individual Achievement Test, Second Edition* (p. 1), 2001, San Antonio, TX: Psychological Corporation. Copyright 2001 by Psychological Corporation. Reprinted by permission.)

Age-Based Composite Standard Scores (*continued*)

Standard Score	Composite Sums of Standard Scores		
	Reading	Mathematics	Written Language
101	310–312	204–205	204
102	313–314	206	205–206
103	315–316	207	207
104	317–318	208	208–209
105	319–320	209–210	210–211

Figure 6.14 Wechsler Individual Achievement Test, Second Edition, Age-Based Subtest Standard Scores. (*Source:* From *WIAT-III Scoring and Normative Supplement for Grades PreK–12* (p. 277), 2001, San Antonio, TX: Psychological Corporation. Copyright 2001 by Psychological Corporation. Reprinted by permission.)

credit for those items. The Spelling and Reading subtests use a 5/10 rule for the basal and ceiling. This means that individuals age 8 and above must be presented with the beginning items if they do not correctly answer the first 5 items presented, and that testing stops when students miss 10 consecutive items. The Arithmetic subtest uses a 5/15-minute criterion: Students age 8 and above must answer at least 5 items correctly or be given the beginning oral items, and testing stops at the 15-minute time limit.

Subtests

Reading. This subtest contains a plastic card with a small sample of letters and words that the student reads aloud to the examiner. The naming of letters is considered a prereading task. The student is allowed 10 seconds to recognize each word. The examiner scores the subtest by crossing out the first letter of incorrect words and by circling the item number for correct responses. Each correct item is worth 1 point. This subtest does not measure word attack or any form of reading comprehension.

Spelling. This subtest begins with name writing and letter writing for students ages 5 through 7. Students are asked to write their name and then to write letters spoken by the examiner. The student is then asked to spell words presented orally: The examiner pronounces a word, gives a sentence that includes the word, and then repeats the word; the student responds in writing on the protocol.

Arithmetic. This subtest contains a few counting items and oral response items, but the remainder of the subtest is a paper-and-pencil task of computation. Students may first solve a small sample of math problems presented on the protocol. Students ages 5 through 7 begin this subtest with the oral problems and progress to the calculation items. This subtest has a 15-minute time limit.

Scoring. The raw scores on the WRAT3 may be used to obtain standard scores, grade scores, and absolute scores. Absolute scores have a mean of 500 and were determined by using the Rasch analysis to determine item difficulty. The absolute scores allow for a person to be compared with the entire continuum of the domain or areas without using age or grade comparisons. Item analyses using the absolute scores are provided in the WRAT3 examiner's manual.

Check Your Understanding

Complete Activity 6.7.

ACTIVITY 6.7

Complete the problems and answer the questions that follow.

1. Figure 6.15 shows the responses of an 8-year-old student on the Spelling subtest of the WRAT3 Tan Test. Use this information to score the subtest. Remember to add the 15 points for the beginning items that were not administered.
2. What is the raw score for the Spelling subtest? Write your answer in the "Tan Test Scores" area on the protocol in Figure 6.16.
3. Use the raw score to obtain the absolute score, standard score, and grade score from the table in Figure 6.16 for the 8-year-old student. Write the scores in the "Tan Test Scores" area on the protocol in Figure 6.15. Leave the percentile column blank.
4. Plot the standard score for the Spelling subtest on the graph in Figure 6.17.

Apply Your Knowledge

According to the scores obtained on the WRAT3, in what areas does the student need additional assessment? ______________________

____

Technical Data

Norming Process. The norming sample for the WRAT3 included 4,433 persons from four geographic regions. Consideration was given for the following variables: male/female subjects; racial division of white, black, Hispanic, or other; and socioeconomic level. The sample included some students receiving special education services; only students who could not physically respond to items were excluded from the study.

WRAT3

WIDE RANGE ACHIEVEMENT TEST □ REVISION 3

NAME Jake GENDER: □M □F

DATE 11-5-94 BIRTH DATE 2-6-86 AGE 8

SCHOOL ________ GRADE 3

REFERRED BY ________ EXAMINER ________

TAN TEST SCORES

	Raw Score	Std. Score	%ile	Grade Score	Absolute Score
READING					
SPELLING					
ARITHMETIC					

Use only standard scores for comparisons

SPELLING/A MEASURE OF WRITTEN ENCODING by Gary S. Wilkinson

NAME ________ (1&2)

(3) (4) (5) (6) (7) (8) (9) (10) (11) (12) (13) (14) (15)

1. go	16. edct	31.
2. cat	17. purchus	32.
3. boy	18. instit	33.
4. run	19. sugeshion	34.
5. will	20.	35.
6. kut	21.	36.
7. arm	22.	37.
8. dres	23.	38.
9. train	24.	39.
10. showt	25.	40.
11. wach	26.	
12. gron	27.	
13. kichen	28.	
14. r salt	29.	
15. hevan	30.	

5/10 RULES

Name/Letter Writing	
Word Spelling +	
Total Spelling	

WR WIDE RANGE

15 Ashley Place, Suite 1A, Wilmington, DE 19804-1314

Figure 6.15 Portion of WRAT3 protocol with student responses for Spelling subtest. (*Source:* From *The Wide Range Achievement Test, Protocol* by G. S. Wilkinson, 1993, Wilmington, DE: Wide Range, Inc. Copyright 1993 by Jastak Associates. Reprinted by permission.)

SPELLING			
Raw Score	Absolute Score	Standard Score	Grade Score
0	407	—	—PRESCHOOL—
1	413	—	
2	424	—	
3	430	—	
4	434	—	
5	437	—	
6	440	—	
7	442	45	
8	444	48	
9	446	51	K
10	448	55	K
11	450	58	K
12	452	61	K
13	454	64	K
14	456	68	K
15	458	70	K
16	460	72	K
17	462	74	K
18	468	77	1
19	470	80	1
20	473	84	1
21	475	87	1
22	480	90	1
23	483	93	2
24	486	97	2
25	487	100	2
26	491	103	3
27	492	107	3
28	495	110	3
29	497	113	4
30	499	116	4

Figure 6.16 WRAT3 scoring table for Spelling subtest. (*Source:* From *The Wide Range Achievement Test: Administration Manual* by G. S. Wilkinson, 1993, Wilmington, DE: Wide Range, Inc. Copyright 1993 by Jastak Associates. Reprinted by permission.)

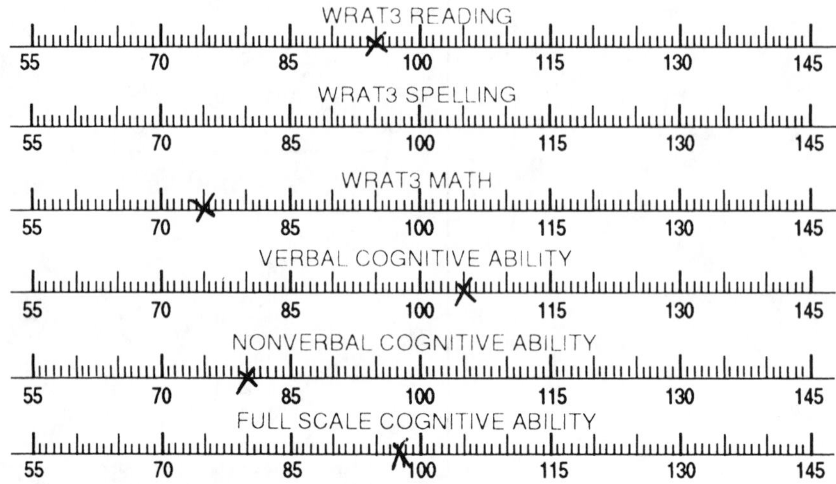

Figure 6.17 Profile of WRAT3 scores for student in Activity 6.7. (*Source:* From *The Wide Range Achievement Test: Administration Manual* by G. S. Wilkinson, 1993, Wilmington, DE: Wide Range, Inc. Copyright 1993 by Jastak Associates. Reprinted by permission.)

Reliability. Test-retest reliability is reported in the examiner's manual for both individual forms and combined scores. Internal consistency measured using coefficient alphas ranged from .85 to .91 (median for all ages). Alternate forms reliability coefficients ranged from .89 to .93 (median for all ages).

Validity. Validity measures discussed include content validity, construct validity, and criterion-related validity. Rationale are provided in the manual to establish a theoretical basis for content and construct validity. Criterion-related validity studies include correlations with the California Test of Basic Skills (CTBS), the California Achievement Test (CAT), and the Stanford Achievement Test (SAT). Coefficients ranged from .58 to .84 on the CTBS, from .41 to .77 on the CAT, and from .52 to .87 on the SAT.

WOODCOCK-MCGREW-WERDER MINI-BATTERY OF ACHIEVEMENT

This instrument is an individually administered easel test designed to screen academic achievement across several areas.

Subtests. The test is structured to include the following subtests.

Reading. Reading is assessed using three subtests: reading identification, reading vocabulary, and reading comprehension. The reading identification subtest includes a list of letters and words that the student reads aloud. The reading vocabulary subtest assesses a student's ability to provide antonyms for given words. The reading comprehension subtest includes short passages. Each passage has a word missing that the student must provide. The easier items present pictures and words. The student must find the picture that best represents the words.

Writing. A student's writing skills are screened by assessing writing mechanics such as spelling, punctuation, and grammar or usage. The subtests include dictation, which measures the student's ability to provide responses independently, and proofing, which requires the student to identify writing errors when presented with visual stimuli. This test does not include items that measure written expression but rather measures writing mechanics.

Mathematics. These skills are screened by assessing basic calculation using a pencil-and-paper format and by assessing math reasoning and concepts. The reasoning and concepts subtest includes visual stimuli in easel format as well as verbal cues.

Factual Knowledge. This is assessed through the use of questions presented orally. Information included on these items is information students learn through their environment and educational experiences.

Scoring. Items are scored as 1 or 0 for all subtests. Raw scores are entered into a computer scoring program that yields a one-page report that includes standard scores (mean of 100 and standard deviation of 15), percentile ranks, and age/grade equivalent for each subtest.

Technical Data

Norming. This test includes norms for persons ages 4 to 90. The standardization included 6,026 persons ranging in age from 4 to 95 years. The sample included adequate geographic and demographic representation across several variables.

Reliability. Test-retest and internal reliability were studied. Split-half reliability coefficients ranged from .70 to .98. Test-retest reliability coefficients ranged from .85 to .97. Internal consistency was variable and showed the most inconsistency for the younger ages (below 6 years of age).

Validity. Concurrent validity was researched comparing the Mini-Battery of Achievement (MBA) with the Woodcock-Johnson Tests of Achievement—Revised, the Wide Range Achievement Test—Revised, the Kaufman Test of Educational Achievement, and the Peabody Individual Achievement Test—Revised. Concurrent reliability coefficients were adequate and largely were in the mid .70s to upper .80s.

RESEARCH AND ISSUES

Research is emerging on the newly revised versions of the tests presented in this chapter but is scant on the newly developed instruments, such as the WIAT-II. Some of the existing research and reviews of the instruments are summarized here.

1. One study (Prewett & Giannuli, 1991a) found moderate correlations between scores on the reading subtests of the WJ—R, the K-TEA, and the PIAT—R and the Stanford-Binet IV Composite Score and the Wechsler Intelligence Scale for Children—Revised IQ score. This study used referred students for the sample.
2. The reading subtests of the WJ—R, K-TEA, WRAT—R, and the PIAT—R were highly intercorrelated in one study by Prewett and Giannuli (1991b), although scores varied when students were tested concurrently using these instruments. The scores obtained on the K-TEA and the WRAT—R reading subtests varied the most (11.1 points), indicating that caution should be applied when using these tests for educational decisions. Prewett, Bardos, and Fowler (1990) pointed out that when tests yield different scores from the same student, diagnosis may be influenced by the test instrument selected for assessment. The scores did not seem to vary as much on the WJ—R and the PIAT—R. Generally, the scores on the WRAT—R and the PIAT—R were lower than those on the WJ—R and the K-TEA reading subtests (Prewett & Giannuli, 1991b).
3. In a study comparing students with learning disabilities with students from the standardization sample without learning disabilities, it was found that the writing subtests of the WJ—R discriminated the students with learning disabilities (Mather, Vogel, Spodak, & McGrew, 1991). The lowest subtest scores for the students with learning disabilities were obtained on the Dictation subtest. This study also found high interrater reliabilities on the Writing Samples subtest. Merrell (1990) found that the WJ—R successfully discriminated between learning-disabled students and low-achieving students in elementary- and middle-school grades.
4. Hultquist and Metzke (1993) found that use of the WJ—R, the PIAT—R, and the K-TEA to measure survival reading words as well as to measure progress of general reading and spelling skills may result in lower scores because of curriculum bias. Use of the tests for these purposes may therefore enable fewer students to exit from special education services.
5. Daub and Colarusso (1996) found that there was a high positive correlation across reading subtests of the WJ—R, PIAT—R, and Diagnostic Achievement Battery. These subtests supported the diagnosis of learning disabilities in students who had been found eligible for services.

6. A study by Evans, Tannehill, and Martin (1995) found that a high positive correlation existed between forms A and B of the WJ—R on the reading decoding and phonetic subtests when presented in a traditional administration and a computerized administration. These researchers concluded that the items reliably assessed this domain when presented in both formats.
7. A study by Shull-Senn, Weatherly, Morgan, and Bradley-Johnson (1995) found that individual subtest and composites varied in test-retest reliability of the WJ—R and the K-TEA. These researchers reported that the correlations of the WJ—R were below .90 for the mathematics, reading, and written language subtests as well as the written language and math cluster scores. The WJ—R broad reading cluster was stable. The researchers also found that the K-TEA subtests and composite correlations were above .90 in all areas.
8. In a study comparing reading word lists of the PIAT, WRAT—R, K-TEA, Woodcock Reading Mastery Tests, and five basal reading series, grade-equivalent scores appeared to be more accurate in grades 1 and 2, with the variability of equivalents increasing with grade level (Shapiro & Derr, 1987).
9. Doll (1989) recommended caution in using the K-TEA with first-grade students. There do not appear to be enough lower level or floor items for students at the readiness level. Doll wrote, "For first graders, all subtests of both forms award standard scores higher than two standard deviations below the mean (i.e., within the normal range) to raw scores of 0" (p. 161).
10. A study that compared scores of students with learning disabilities on the K-TEA across a three-year interval found that the standard scores were, on the average, 3.3 points lower on the second administration (Hewett & Bolen, 1996). The researchers concluded that this instrument was adequate for the assessment of students with learning disabilities.
11. Prewett et al. (1991) found that the K-TEA Brief Form seemed to be more accurate as a screening instrument than the WRAT—R. In this study, the K-TEA Comprehensive Form was used to determine which screening instrument yielded scores most like the Comprehensive Form. The K-TEA Brief appeared to be a better predictor of the K-TEA Comprehensive scores, yielding scores with less difference than the WRAT—R, which yielded lower scores overall.
12. In another study, the WRAT—R and the K-TEA were administered to students with learning disabilities and referred students who were not placed (Prewett, Bardos, & Fowler, 1990). The administration of the WRAT—R resulted in lower scores for both groups of students than the K-TEA.

13. Prewett, Lillis, and Bardos (1991) found that administration of the K-TEA Brief and the WRAT—R level 2 to incarcerated youth yielded scores that were similar when the administration was in counter-balance order. This finding is in contrast to other studies cited.
14. Webster et al. (1989) found that scores obtained on the K-TEA were consistently higher than scores obtained on the WRAT—R. When these two measures were compared with student performance estimated by classroom teachers, neither instrument was significantly better in predicting actual classroom performance.
15. Students assessed on the K-TEA, WRAT—R, and PIAT reading subtests obtained scores that seem to vary as a function of their reading curriculum (Webster & Braswell, 1991). Some students scored significantly higher than current reading curriculum placement would suggest, whereas others scored significantly lower. The data obtained for the entire group were significantly higher than teacher estimates based on performance in reading curriculum.
16. A review of the PIAT—R (Allinder & Fuchs, 1992) cautioned that the format of the test instrument, including multiple choice on some subtests, may encourage guessing. These reviewers also cautioned that information obtained from multiple-choice items is diagnostically different from information obtained when a response must be produced independently by the student. They reminded consumers that this instrument was designed as a wide-range screening instrument and should therefore not be used in educational decision making involving placement, eligibility, or planning.
17. Kaufman and Kaufman (1996) found that the interrater agreement on the written expression subtest completed by adolescents and adults was comparable to the interrater reliability reported in the test manual. The ages included in this study ranged from 13 to 46 years. Luther (1992) reviewed the PIAT—R and stated that the scoring, reliability, and validity of the written expression subtest seriously limited its use. Another study found that changing the visual stimuli associated with the PIAT—R written expression subtest resulted in significantly higher scores for structure (Cole, Muenz, Ouchi, Kaufman, & Kaufman, 1997).
18. Weiss and Prifitera (1995) studied use of a regression line, as recommended in the WIAT manual, in assessing students with learning disabilities. These researchers found that female students performed better on the writing composite, reading composite, and math composite than would be predicted, indicating that the use of a common regression equation may underestimate the scores for some female students. This study also found that the scores of Hispanic students may overestimate the reading composite scores using this equation with the WIAT.

19. In a study of achievement assessment of students with emotional disturbances, Gentry, Sapp, and Daw (1995) found that performance on the WIAT was positively correlated with performance on the K-TEA. They also determined that the students in this study obtained significantly lower scores on the WIAT math reasoning subtest than on the K-TEA math application subtest.
20. Slate (1996) compared several measures frequently used in assessing students with learning disabilities. In this study, the WIAT, KeyMath—R, Woodcock-Reading Mastery—Revised, and the PIAT—R were compared. While many of the subtests were positively correlated, there remained significant variance and mean differences. Slate warned educators that such tests used in discrepancy formulas to determine learning disabilities are not interchangeable. In other words, although reading subtests may share common constructs and similar items, students may perform quite differently across such subtests of different achievement batteries. Therefore, what may be perceived as a true difference in abilities may really be the result of differences in the tests, not the student.
21. When the MBA was compared with the WRAT3 and the K-FAST, the MBA was found to have the broadest measure of reading and writing skills (Flanagan et al., 1997).
22. Ackerman (1998) stated that the WIAT seemed to be a quality measure but commented that the research summary of item bias by test developers did not include sufficient information, which leaves the test consumer suspect.
23. Michael (1998) reviewed the MBA and stated that the limited information provided in scoring may restrict the use of the MBA. The results provided by computer scoring may not include sufficient details for interpretation. The adequate validity of the instrument indicates that it is a good measure that has appeal because of its practicality.
24. In a review and comparison of screening achievement tests, Flanagan stated that the WRAT3 is improved over the previous version; however, there was no advantage to selecting it over the MBA or the WIAT Screener (1997).

SELECTING ACADEMIC ACHIEVEMENT TESTS

The tests reviewed in this chapter represent the more commonly used instruments in public school assessment. One instrument may be particularly better to use in one situation than in another. The strengths and weaknesses are presented in Table 6.1 to provide some guidance in selecting instruments.

Table 6.1 Summary of achievement tests.

Instrument	Strengths	Weaknesses
Woodcock-Johnson—III Tests of Achievement	Comprehensive academic achievement test Good technical quality Quick computer scoring	Requires fair amount of time to administer (45 min to 1½ hr for both batteries) Requires fair amount of time to score some subtests
Peabody Individual Achievement Test—Revised	Improved items Quick to administer Includes Writing Samples subtest Provides a total reading score and total test score Improved technical quality	Forced-choice Format for most subtests may inflate scores Screening test only
Kaufman Test of Educational Achievement—Comprehensive Form	Comprehensive academic test Provides error analysis and can assist in writing objectives Good technical quality Easy to score	Requires fair amount of time to administer (45 min to 1 hr) May yield some higher scores than Woodcock-Johnson
Kaufman Test of Educational Achievement—Brief Form	Quick to administer and score	Screening only Should not be used to make eligibility decisions No error analysis provided
Wechsler Individual Achievement Test—II	Designed for use with the Wechsler Intelligence Scales and provides for discrepancy analysis Includes measures in the areas of listening comprehension and oral expression not found on most achievement measures Skill information provided for math domains—can use in writing objectives	More complicated to give and score than some other well-established instruments
Wide Range Achievement Test—Revision 3	Quick to administer and score	Inadequate information obtained from administration of this test Should be used as rough screening only Should not be used for eligibility decisions
Woodcock-McGrew-Werder Mini-Battery of Achievement	Quick to administer and score; more comprehensive than the WRAT3	Should be used as rough screening only Should not be used for eligibility decisions

THINK AHEAD

As you progress through this text, you will learn other methods of assessing educational achievement that may be more sensitive to student growth in academics.

EXERCISES

Part I

Match the following terms with the correct definitions.

a. individual achievement tests
b. screening test
c. group achievement tests
d. diagnostic tests
e. composite scores
f. achievement tests
g. aptitude tests
h. assessment
i. adaptive behavior
j. norm-referenced tests
k. subtests
l. curriculum-based assessment

_____ 1. Instruments that assess a student's ability to adapt to the world in different situations.

_____ 2. Tests administered to a group of students to measure academic gains.

_____ 3. Using the content from the currently used curriculum to assess student progress.

_____ 4. Tests designed to compare individual students with national averages, or norms of expectancy.

_____ 5. Parts of a test that measure skills in specific areas or domains.

_____ 6. Tests used to measure academic progress.

_____ 7. Broad-based instrument that samples a few items across a curriculum.

_____ 8. Individually administered tests designed to determine specific academic problems or deficit areas.

_____ 9. An individually administered test that measures academic progress.

_____ 10. Designed to measure strength, talent, or ability in a particular area or domain.

Part II

Match the following test names with the correct descriptions.

a. Woodcock-Johnson III Tests of Achievement
b. Kaufman Test of Educational Achievement—Brief Form

c. Kaufman Test of Educational Achievement—Comprehensive Form
d. Peabody Individual Achievement Test—Revised
e. Wide Range Achievement Test—Revision 3
f. Wechsler Individual Achievement Test II
g. Woodcock-McGrew-Werder Mini-Battery of Achievement

_____ 1. This test provides an error analysis summary that is not provided in the shorter version.

_____ 2. This test, which includes a factual knowledge subtest, is a more comprehensive screening instrument than the WRAT3.

_____ 3. This test has standard and supplemental batteries.

_____ 4. This test provides cluster scores and individual subtest scores.

_____ 5. This test may be administered to persons ages 5–75.

_____ 6. This shorter test version should be used for screening purposes.

_____ 7. This achievement test includes a Language composite that measures both expressive and listening skills.

_____ 8. This test includes many multiple-choice items that may encourage guessing.

_____ 9. This test includes standard and extended batteries.

_____ 10. This test is the only one presented in this chapter that does not use an easel format.

Part III

Summarize the research findings presented in this chapter about the following tests.

Woodcock-Johnson Tests of Achievement III ______________________________
____

Peabody Individual Achievement Test—Revised ___________________________
____

Kaufman Test of Educational Achievement—Comprehensive Form ________
____

Wechsler Individual Achievement Test II ________________________________
____

Wide-Range Achievement Test—Revised _________________________________
____

Woodcock-McGrew-Werder Mini-Battery of Achievement ______________
____

What are the ethical and legal questions to consider when making a decision about when to use a screening instrument or a comprehensive instrument to test achievement? ____

____

____

ANSWER KEY TO CHECK YOUR UNDERSTANDING

Activity 6.1

1. Two. Allows examiner to test same student again with less practice effect.
2. 2–90 yrs of age
3. Persons ages 2–90 years, students in school from elementary through graduate school.
4. Graduate school ages/levels.
5. Calculation, math fluency, applied problems.
6. Applied problems, quantitative concepts.

Apply Your Knowledge. The student should not be administered the following subtests: understanding directions (pointing items), math calculation, spelling, writing fluency, math fluency, writing samples, spelling of sounds, punctuation and capitalization.

Answers may vary.

Activity 6.2

1. Total Reading Raw Score: 145
   Total Test Raw Score: 351
2. Standard Scores

General Information	119
Reading Recognition	118
Reading Comprehension	113
Total Reading	116
Mathematics	127
Spelling	119
Total Test	123

Apply Your Knowledge. This student performed at the high end of the average range on most subtests (average for standard score = 100). This student seems to have strength in the area of mathematics.

Activity 6.3

1. Errors by skill category

Prefix & Word Beginnings	Suffixes & Word Endings	Closed Syll. (Short) Vowels	Open Syll. (Long) & Final *e* Pat. Vowels	Vowel Dig. & Diph.	*r*-Cont. Pat.	Cons. Clusters & Dig.	Sing. & Dble Cons.	Whole Word Errors
—	4	1	3	1	—	—	—	—

2. You should have completed the error comparisons as follows:

Spelling Word Part	Avg. No. of Errors	Student No. of Errors	Skill Status
Pref. & Wd. Beg.	1	0	S
Suff. & Wd. End.	3–5	4	A
Closed Syll. (Short) Vowels	1–2	1	A
Open Syll. (Long) & Final *e* Vowels	3–4	3	A
V. Dig. & Diph.	0–1	1	A
r-Controlled Patterns	—	—	A
Cons. Clusters & Digraphs	0–1	0	A
Sing. & Double Cons.	2–4	0	S

Apply Your Knowledge. The two skill categories in which the student made the most errors were suffixes and word endings, and open syllables, long vowels, and final *e* patterns. These areas should be addressed in educational planning.

Activity 6.4

The scores should be placed in the appropriate spaces and the difference and significance levels should be analyzed as follows:

			Difference	Significance
106 Reading Composite	<	141 Math Composite	35	.01
106 Reading Composite	>	100 Spelling	6	NS
141 Math Composite	>	100 Spelling	41	.01
105 Reading Decoding	=	105 Reading Comprehension	0	NS

136 Math Application	<	141 Math Computation	5	NS

Apply Your Knowledge. This student performed in a manner expected for her current educational level in reading and spelling. She has significant strength in math computation and math application. She has significant strength in general math skills as indicated by her Math composite score.

Activity 6.5

1. Scores should be recorded on protocol in Figure 6.15.
2. Range of scores:

Mathematics	100–120
Reading	78–92
Spelling	68–82

Apply Your Knowledge. The bands of error provide a range of scores within which the student's true score is thought to be located (with 90% confidence). This means, for example, that the student's true score for mathematics is believed to be within the 100–120 (with 90% confidence) range.

This student may be having difficulty in the areas of reading and spelling and should have additional diagnostic assessment in these areas.

Activity 6.6

1. 23 is the total raw score
2. standard score is 103
3. 209 total for written language
4. standard score for written language composite is 104.

REFERENCES

Ackerman, T. (1998). Review of the Wechsler Individual Achievement Test. In J. C. Impara & B. S. Plake (Eds.), *The thirteenth mental measurements yearbook.* Lincoln: University of Nebraska Press.

Allinder, R. M., & Fuchs, L. S. (1992). Screening academic achievement: Review of the Peabody Individual Achievement Test—Revised. *Learning Disabilities Research & Practice, 7*(1), 45–47.

Anastasi, A., & Urbina, S. (1998). *Psychological testing,* (7th ed.). Upper Saddle River, NJ: Prentice Hall.

Cole, J. C., Muenz, T. A., Ouchi, B. Y., Kaufman, N. L., & Kaufman, A. S. (1997). The impact of pictorial stimulus on written expression output of adolescents and adults. *Psychology in the Schools, 34,* 1–9.

Connelly, J. (1985). Published tests: Which ones do special education teachers perceive as useful? *Journal of Special Education, 19,* 149–155.

Daub, D., & Colarusso, R. P. (1996). The validity of the WJ—R, PIAT—R, and DAB—2 reading subtests with students with learning disabilities. *Learning Disabilities Research & Practice, 11*(2), 90–95.

Doll, E. J. (1989). Review of the Kaufman Test of Educational Achievement. In J. C. Conoley, J. J. Kramer, & L. L. Murphey (Eds.), *The tenth mental measurements yearbook*. Lincoln: University of Nebraska Press.

Evans, L. D., Tannehill, R., & Martin, S. (1995). Children's reading skills: A comparison of traditional and computerized assessment. *Behavior Research Methods, Instruments, & Computers, 27,* 162–165.

Flanagan, D. P., McGrew, K. S., Abramowitz, E., Lehner, L., Untiedt, S., Berger, D., & Armstrong, H. (1997). Improvement in academic screening instruments? A concurrent validity investigation of the K-FAST, MBA, and WRAT3. *Journal of Psychoeducational Assessment, 15,* 99–112.

Flanagan, R. (1997). Mini-Battery of Achievement: The Wechsler Individual Achievement Test; Wide Range Achievement Test: Review and comparison. *Journal of Psychoeducational Assessment, 15,* 82–87.

Gentry, N., Sapp, G. L., & Daw, J. L. (1995). Scores on the Wechsler Individual Achievement Test and the Kaufman Test of Educational Achievement—Comprehensive Form for emotionally conflicted adolescents. *Psychological Reports, 76,* 607–610.

German, D., Johnson, B., & Schneider, M. (1985). Learning disability vs. reading disability: A survey of practitioners' diagnostic populations and test instruments. *Learning Disability Quarterly, 8,* 141–156.

Hewett, J. B., & Bolen, L. M. (1996). Performance changes on the K-TEA: Brief Form for learning disabled students. *Psychology in the Schools, 33,* 97–102.

Hultquist, A. M., & Metzke, L. K. (1993). Potential effects of curriculum bias in individual norm-referenced reading and spelling achievement tests. *Journal of Psychoeducational Assessment, 11,* 337–344.

Kaufman, A. S., & Kaufman, N. L. (1985a). *Kaufman Test of Educational Achievement, Brief Form.* Circle Pines, MN: American Guidance Service.

Kaufman, A. S., & Kaufman, N. L. (1985b). *Kaufman Test of Educational Achievement, Comprehensive Form.* Circle Pines, MN: American Guidance Service.

Kaufman, A. S. & Kaufman, N. L. (1996). Interrater reliability of the written expression subtest of the Peabody Individual Achievement Test—Revised: An adolescent and adult sample. *Psychological Reports, 79,* 1239–1247.

LaGrow, S., & Prochnow-LaGrow, J. (1982). Technical adequacy of the most popular tests selected by responding school psychologists in Illinois. *Psychology in the Schools, 19,* 186–189.

Luther, J. B. (1992). Review of the Peabody Individual Achievement Test—Revised. *Journal of School Psychology, 30,* 31–39.

Markwardt, F. C. (1989). *Peabody Individual Achievement Test—Revised.* Circle Pines, MN: American Guidance Service.

Mather, N., & Woodcock, R. W. (2001). *Examiner's Manual. Woodcock-Johnson III Tests of Achievement.* Itasca, IL: Riverside Publishing.

Mather, N., Vogel, S., Spodak, R. B., & McGrew, K. S. (1991). Use of the Woodcock-Johnson—Revised writing tests with students with learning disabilities. *Journal of Psychoeducational Assessment, 9,* 296–307.

McGrew, K. S., & Woodcock, R. W. (2001). *Technical Manual. Woodcock-Johnson III.* Itasca, IL: Riverside Publishing.

Merrell, K. W. (1990). Differentiating low achieving students and students with learning disabilities: An examination of performances on the Woodcock-Johnson Psychoeducational Battery. *Journal of Special Education, 24,* 296–304.

Michael, W. B. (1998). A review of the Woodcock-McGrew-Werder Mini-Battery of Achievement. In J. C. Impara and B. S. Plake (Eds.), *The thirteenth mental measurements yearbook.* Lincoln: University of Nebraska Press.

Prewett, P., Bardos, A. N., & Fowler, D. B. (1990). Use of the K-TEA and the WRAT—R with learning disabled and referred but not placed students. *Journal of Psychoeducational Assessment, 8,* 51–60.

Prewett, P. N., Bardos, A., & Fowler, D. B. (1991). Relationship between the K-TEA Brief and Comprehensive forms and the WRAT—R level 1 with referred elementary school students. *Educational and Psychological Measurement, 51,* 729–734.

Prewett, P. N., & Giannuli, M. M. (1991a). Correlations of the WISC—R, Stanford-Binet Intelligence Scale, fourth edition, and the reading subtests of three popular achievement tests. *Psychological Reports, 69,* 1232–1234.

Prewett, P. N., & Giannuli, M. M. (1991b). The relationship among reading subtests of the WJ—R, PIAT—R, K-TEA, and WRAT—R. *Journal of Psychoeducational Assessment, 9,* 166–174.

Prewett, P. N., Lillis, W. T., & Bardos, A. N. (1991). Relationship between the Kaufman Test of Educational Achievement Brief Form and the Wide Range Achievement Test—Revised level 2 with incarcerated juvenile delinquents. *Psychological Reports, 68,* 147–150.

Psychological Corporation. (2001). *Wechsler Individual Achievement Test, Second Edition.* San Antonio, TX: Author.

Reschly, D. (1988). Special education reform: School psychology revolution. *School Psychology Review, 17,* 459–475.

Shapiro, E., & Derr, T. (1987). An examination of overlap between curricula and standardized achievement tests. *Journal of Special Education, 21,* 59–67.

Shull-Senn, S., Weatherly, M., Morgan, S. K., & Bradley-Johnson, S. (1995). Stability reliability for elementary-age students on the Woodcock-Johnson Psychoeducational Battery—Revised (Achievement Section) and the Kaufman Test of Educational Achievement. *Psychology in the Schools, 32,* 86–92.

Slate, J. R. (1996). Interrelations of frequently administered achievement measures in the determination of specific learning disabilities. *Learning Disabilities Research & Practice, 11*(2), 86–89.

Thurlow, M., & Ysseldyke, J. (1979). Current assessment and decision-making practices in model programs. *Learning Disabilities Quarterly, 2,* 15–24.

Webster, R. E., & Braswell, L. A. (1991). Curriculum bias and reading achievement test performance. *Psychology in the Schools, 28,* 193–198.

Webster, R., Hewett, B., & Crumbacker, M. (1989). Criterion-related validity of the WRAT—R and the K-TEA with teacher estimates of actual classroom academic performance. *Psychology in the Schools, 26,* 243–248.

Weiss, L. G., & Prifitera, A. (1995). An evaluation of differential prediction of WIAT achievement scores from WISC—III FSIQ across ethnic and gender groups. *Journal of School Psychology, 33,* 297–304.

Wendling, B. J., & Mather, N. (2001). *Examiner Training Workbook Woodcock-Johnson III Tests of Achievement.* Itasca, IL: Riverside Publishing.

Wilkinson, G. S. (1993). *The Wide Range Achievement Test: Administration Manual.* Wilmington, DE: Jastak Associates.

Woodcock, R. W., McGrew, K. S., & Mather, N. (2001). *Woodcock-Johnson III Tests of Achievement.* Itasca, IL: Riverside Publishing.

Woodcock, R. W., McGrew, K. S., & Werder, J. K. (1994). Woodcock-McGrew-Werder Mini-Battery of Achievement. Itasca, IL: Riverside Publishing.

Worthington, C. (1987). Kaufman Test of Educational Achievement, Comprehensive and Brief. *Journal of Counseling and Development, 65,* 325–327.

CHAPTER 7

Standardized Diagnostic Testing

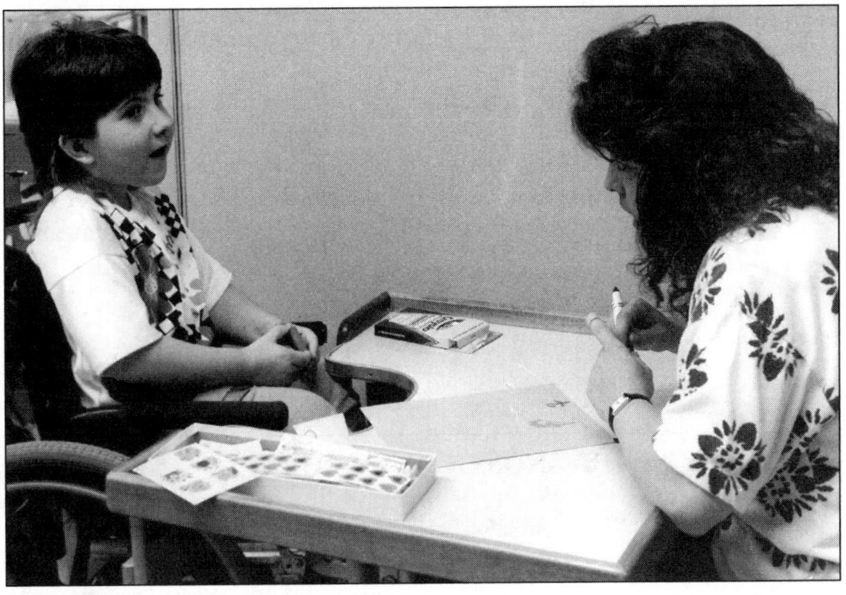

Key Terms

diagnostic instruments
instructional level
informal instruments
probes
direct measurement
domain
language assessment
receptive language
expressive language
written language

CHAPTER FOCUS

diagnostic instruments Individually administered tests designed to determine specific academic problems or deficit areas.

instructional level The determined level in the curriculum in which the student should receive instruction.

informal instruments Nonstandardized methods used to collect information about students.

probes Tests used for in-depth assessment of the mastery of a specific skill or subskill.

direct measurement Measuring progress by using the same instructional materials or tasks used in the classroom.

Diagnostic testing for specific skill deficits is necessary to write effective educational goals. This type of test will provide you with detailed information and, in some cases, error analyses, which may result in goals that are more sensitive to student progress.

The norm-referenced tests presented in chapter 6 assess achievement across a broad curriculum. Achievement tests are designed to provide the educator with a general view of the student so that he can determine areas of strengths and weaknesses. This information assists the educator in designing an evaluation plan to assess weaknesses diagnostically. The special educator assesses general areas of weakness in greater depth through the use of **diagnostic instruments.** These instruments aid the teacher in educational planning by revealing types of errors the student makes as well as strengths that may be used to determine the proper **instructional level** and possible teaching and learning strategies. The use of diagnostic instruments can also help the teacher in designing **informal instruments** and **probes** to assess student progress using **direct measurement** techniques. Informal assessment and direct measurement are presented in detail in chapter 8.

WHEN TO USE DIAGNOSTIC TESTING

Diagnostic tests may be used to measure mastery of specific skills, strengths, and weaknesses whenever the educator wishes to monitor student progress or change the educational program. These tests may be used as a part of assessment to determine eligibility, for reevaluation, for annual reviews, or for further diagnostic planning within the classroom. Because these instruments may be used more frequently than general achievement tests, the educator should select the tests or subtests carefully. The educator is encouraged to use equivalent forms of the same test, if available, when testing a student a second time.

The teacher of students with disabilities should select diagnostic academic tests based on the content area, the method of assessment (oral questions, oral reading, math paper-and-pencil items, silently read items, timed or untimed tests, etc.), and the method of response (written responses, oral responses, pointing, etc.) required of the student. The format for presentation and response should be considered when interpreting results and making educational intervention plans. Figure 7.1 illustrates appropriate uses of diagnostic tests.

Initial assessment process	To assess areas in which questions remain regarding a student's ability in an academic skill, such as reading; or subskill, such as phonological awareness
Reevaluation	To assess specific areas that the team determines necessary in order to make a decision regarding continued eligibility for services or interventions
Assessment of progress	Classroom teacher uses to measure progress toward objectives in specific academic area
Additional data for classroom interventions	Classroom teacher needs additional information to adjust interventions or planning or to obtain in-depth information about student's mastery of a specific skill

Figure 7.1 Appropriate uses of diagnostic tests.

THE REVIEW OF DIAGNOSTIC TESTS

The tests presented in this chapter represent those commonly used by teachers; they have also been selected because of existing research. The assessment of the basic skill areas of reading, mathematics, spelling, and written language are presented in this chapter.

KEYMATH—REVISED

The KeyMath—Revised (Connolly, 1988) is presented in an easel format and consists of two equivalent forms, A and B. Many of the items are presented orally by the examiner. The Operations items are presented as paper-and-pencil tasks. This test includes subtests that are grouped into three areas: Basic Concepts, Operations, and Applications. Table 7.1 presents the areas, **domains,** and strands of the revised KeyMath. Significant strengths and weaknesses may be determined by calculating the differences between standard scores for the various areas. The domain scores may be used to compare abilities and determine whether the student's performance is considered to be weak, average, or strong compared to the norm grade-level group.

domain Area of cognitive development or ability thought to be evidenced by certain behaviors or skills.

Subtests

Numeration. These items sample the student's ability to understand the number system and the functional application of that system. Items include tasks such as counting, identifying numbers, identifying missing numbers in

Table 7.1 Content specification of KeyMath—R: Areas, strands, and domains.

Areas	Basic Concepts	Operations	Applications
Strands and Domains	**Numeration** **1.** Numbers 0–9 **2.** Numbers 0–99 **3.** Numbers 0–999 **4.** Multidigit numbers and advanced numeration topics **Rational Numbers** **1.** Fractions **2.** Decimals **3.** Percents **Geometry** **1.** Spatial and attribute relations **2.** Two-dimensional shapes and their relations **3.** Coordinate and transformational geometry **4.** Three-dimensional shapes and their relations	**Addition** **1.** Models and basic facts **2.** Algorithms to add whole numbers **3.** Adding rational numbers **Subtraction** **1.** Models and basic facts **2.** Algorithms to subtract whole numbers **3.** Subtracting rational numbers **Multiplication** **1.** Models and basic facts **2.** Algorithms to multiply whole numbers **3.** Multiplying rational numbers **Division** **1.** Models and basic facts **2.** Algorithms to divide whole numbers **3.** Dividing rational numbers **Mental Computation** **1.** Computation chains **2.** Whole numbers **3.** Rational numbers	**Measurement** **1.** Comparisons **2.** Using nonstandard units **3.** Using standard units—length, area **4.** Using standard units—weight, capacity **Time and Money** **1.** Identifying passage of time **2.** Using clocks and clock units **3.** Monetary amounts to one dollar **4.** Monetary amounts to one hundred dollars and business transactions **Estimation** **1.** Whole and rational numbers **2.** Measurement **3.** Computation **Interpreting Data** **1.** Charts and tables **2.** Graphs **3.** Probability and statistics **Problem Solving** **1.** Solving routine problems **2.** Understanding nonroutine problems **3.** Solving nonroutine problems

Source: From *KeyMath—Revised: A Diagnostic Inventory of Essential Mathematics, Manual* (p. 6) by A. J. Connolly, 1988, Circle Pines, MN: American Guidance Service. Copyright 1988 by American Guidance Service. Reprinted by permission.

a sequence, understanding concepts of more and less, and reading multidigit numbers.

Rational Numbers. This subtest measures understanding of fractions, decimals, and percents. Lower level items include understanding of the two equal parts of an object, and higher level items include changing fractions into mixed numbers and percents.

Geometry. These items range from understanding spatial concepts and recognizing shapes to interpreting angles and three-dimensional figures.

Addition. This subtest assesses the student's ability to add objects and perform addition computation problems. Beginning items are orally presented, and later items are paper-and-pencil computations.

Subtraction. Presented in the same format as the addition subtest, this subtest measures the student's ability to perform subtraction computations. Items begin with simple subtraction of objects and progress to computations involving multidigit numbers, regrouping, and fractions and mixed numbers.

Multiplication. This subtest is presented in the same format as the addition and subtraction subtests and includes simple grouping problems (sets) and more difficult multiplication of mixed numbers and fractions.

Division. Like the Addition and other operations subtests, the Division subtest presents lower level items on the easel and more difficult items as paper-and-pencil computations. The items cover a range of difficulty levels and contain some multistep, or "long" division, computations.

Mental Computation. This orally administered subtest includes math operations problems and more difficult problems that require several steps and operations to complete.

Measurement. Items range from recognition and identification of units of measurement to problems that involve application and changing of the various units of measurement.

Time and Money. These items involve telling time, understanding concepts of time, recognizing times and money, and the understanding and application of money to solve problems of transaction.

Estimation. The student must estimate numbers for sums or amounts, estimate measurements, and estimate the answers in computations.

Interpreting Data. The student interprets charts, graphs, and tables that range from picture charts to tables involving numbers and statistical probabilities.

Problem Solving. These problems range from simple predictable problems to nonroutine problems.

Scoring. The basal and ceiling levels on the KeyMath—R are consistent throughout the test: 3 consecutive correct items constitute the basal, and 3 consecutive incorrect items determine the ceiling. The responses are recorded on the protocol within the appropriate domain boxes. The responses are recorded as 1 for correct and 0 for incorrect.

The examiner lists the domain scores separately and then sums the scores for the subtest raw score. The examiner uses the raw scores to locate scaled scores and percentile ranks for each subtest, and then sums the raw scores of the subtests for the area raw score. The area raw scores are used to determine area standard scores, percentile ranks, and age or grade equivalents.

In Activity 7.1, you will score the Basic Concepts area of the KeyMath—R.

Check Your Understanding

Complete Activity 7.1.

ACTIVITY 7.1

Complete the following problems.

1. One student's responses in the Geometry subtest are shown on the KeyMath—R protocol in Figure 7.2. Calculate the raw score and then write your answer on the protocol.
2. This student's other raw scores for the Basic Concepts subtests have been entered in Figure 7.3. Write the raw score calculated in problem 1 in the appropriate space in Figure 7.3. Add the subtest raw scores to determine the area raw score and then write this score on Figure 7.3.
3. The raw scores for Numeration, Rational Numbers, and Geometry were used to locate the following scaled scores:

	Scaled Scores
Numeration	8
Rational Numbers	1
Geometry	7

   Write these scaled scores in the appropriate spaces in Figure 7.3. Use the scaled scores to locate the percentile ranks from the table in Figure 7.4. Complete the "%ile Rank" column in Figure 7.3.
4. The area raw score was used to locate the standard score of 83. Write this in the appropriate space in Figure 7.3. Use the standard score to locate the percentile rank from Figure 7.4. Write this in the "%ile Rank" box in Figure 7.3.

3 GEOMETRY

NUMERATION BASAL	Item	Spatial/attribute relations	Two-dimensional shapes	Coordinates/transformations	Three-dimensional shapes
0-4 ▸	1. where is bird? flowers?				
	2. shapes alike				
	3. letters outside				
5-8 ▸	4. how alike? different?	1			
	5. circles		1		
	6. color next bead	1			
	7. triangles		1		
9-11 ▸	8. color/number pattern	1			
	9. same shape and size		1		
	10. same shape, different size		0		
12-16 ▸	11. angles same size			1	
	12. reflection of blocks		1		
17-20 ▸	13. third animal			0	
	14. cylinders				0
21,22 ▸	15. color of square				0
	16. shape of B-E-U-R				
23,24 ▸	17. parallel lines				
	18. diameter, radius				
	19. number of blocks				
	20. shape with square sides				
	21. view of blocks				
	22. degrees in angle				
	23. name solid figure				
	24. slide triangle				
______ CEILING ITEM	DOMAIN SCORES				

SUBTEST RAW SCORE
(Sum of domain scores)

Figure 7.2 Geometry section of protocol of the KeyMath—R. (*Source:* From *KeyMath—Revised: A Diagnostic Inventory of Essential Mathematics, Protocol* (p. 3) by A. J. Connolly, 1988, Circle Pines, MN: American Guidance Service. Copyright 1988 by American Guidance Service. Reprinted by permission.)

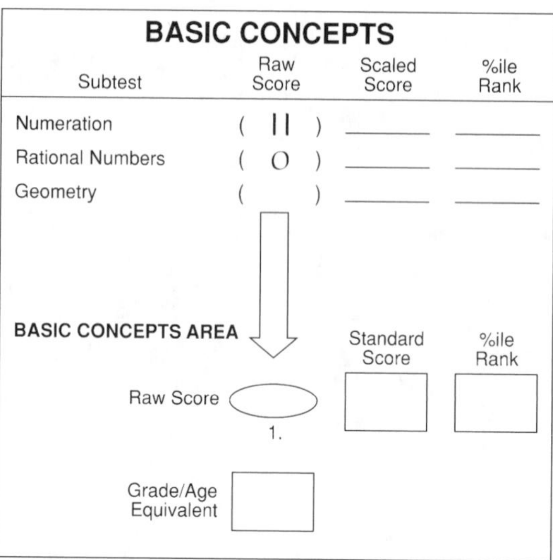

Subtest	Raw Score	Scaled Score	%ile Rank
Numeration	(11)	______	______
Rational Numbers	(0)	______	______
Geometry	( )	______	______

Figure 7.3
Summary of scores for the Basic Concepts area of the KeyMath—R. (*Source:* From *KeyMath—Revised: A Diagnostic Inventory of Essential Mathematics, Protocol* (p. 1) by A. J. Connolly, 1988, Circle Pines, MN: American Guidance Service. Copyright 1988 by American Guidance Service. Reprinted by permission.)

5. Use the area raw score to locate the grade equivalent in Figure 7.5. Write the answer in the appropriate space in Figure 7.3.

Apply Your Knowledge

How would you interpret this student's percentile ranks for his parents? Write your explanation. ______________________________
____

Comparing Area Standard Scores for Significance. The examiner compares the standard scores obtained on the three areas in the section of the protocol titled "Area Comparisons," shown in Figure 7.6. The examiner writes the standard scores in the appropriate spaces and writes >, <, or = on each of the lines between the boxes. The standard score differences are determined by subtracting the scores. To determine significance level, the examiner refers to a table in the manual that lists the differences that are considered significant. If the difference is listed as significant at the .05 level, this means that the chances are 95 out of 100 that a true difference exists, and there are only 5 chances out of 100 that the difference is by error or chance. The level of .01 means that the difference exists with only 1 possibility of 100 that the difference is by error or chance.

In Activity 7.2, you will determine whether a significant difference exists between the area standard scores.

Figure 7.4 Table from the revised KeyMath showing derived normative data for locating percentile ranks, stanines, and normal curve equivalents. (*Source:* From *KeyMath—Revised: A Diagnostic Inventory of Essential Mathematics, Manual* (p. 309) by A. J. Connolly, 1988, Circle Pines, MN: American Guidance Service. Copyright 1988 by American Guidance Service. Reprinted by permission.)

Scaled Score	Standard Score	Percentile Rank	Stanine	Normal Curve Equivalent
9	95	37		43
	94	34		42
	93	32	4	40
	92	30		39
8	91	27		37
	90	25		36
	89	23		35
	88	21		33
	87	19		32
	86	18		30
7	85	16	3	29
	84	14		28
	83	13		26
	82	12		25
	81	10		23
6	80	9		22
	79	8		21
	78	7		19
	77	6	2	18
	76	5		16
5	75	5		15
	74	4		13
	73	4		12
	72	3		11
	71	3		9
4	70	2		8
	69	2		6
	68	2		5
	67	1	1	4
	66	1		2
3	65	1		1
	64	1		Below 1
	63	1		
	62	1		
	61	Below 1		
2	60			
	59			
	58			
	57			
	56			
1	55			

Check Your Understanding

Complete Activity 7.2.

ACTIVITY 7.2

Complete the following problems.

1. A third-grade student obtained the KeyMath—R area standard scores shown at the bottom of Figure 7.6. Write the standard scores in the appropriate spaces. Indicate whether the comparisons are >, <, or = and determine the differences.
2. Using the information provided in Figure 7.7 for third-grade comparisons, determine whether the differences found in problem 1

Figure 7.5 Grade equivalents corresponding to area and total-test raw scores. (*Source:* From *KeyMath—Revised: A Diagnostic Inventory of Essential Mathematics, Manual* (p. 310) by A. J. Connolly, 1988, Circle Pines, MN: American Guidance Service. Copyright 1988 by American Guidance Service. Reprinted by permission.)

Grade Equivalent	Basic Concepts
	Raw Score
4.9	—
4.8	35
4.7	—
4.6	34
4.5	—
4.4	33
4.3	—
4.2	32
4.1	—
4.0	31
3.9	—
3.8	30
3.7	—
3.6	29
3.5	28
3.4	—
3.3	27
3.2	—
3.1	26
3.0	—
2.9	25
2.8	—
2.7	24
2.6	—
2.5	23
2.4	22
2.3	—
2.2	21
2.1	20
2.0	—

are significant. Mark the significance level—NS, .05, or .01—for each of the area comparisons in Figure 7.6.

Apply Your Knowledge

Identify this student's strengths and weaknesses according to the information obtained regarding significant differences. How would you explain this to the student's parents? Write your explanation. ________

____

____

Determining Domain Strengths and Weaknesses. A student's performance can be analyzed by domains by comparing the obtained domain scores with the average scores listed in the KeyMath—R manual (Figure 7.8). This information aids the educator in determining skill mastery or deficit in the various domains.

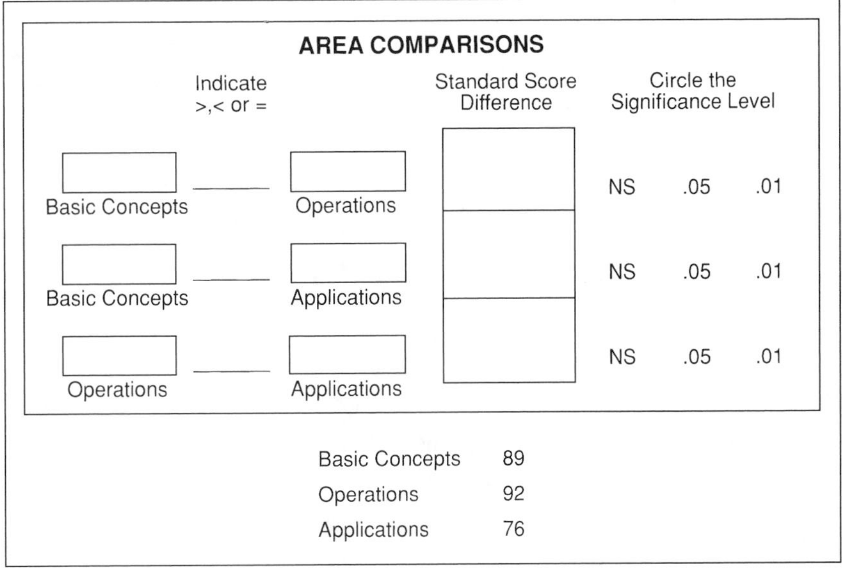
AREA COMPARISONS

	Indicate >,< or =		Standard Score Difference	Circle the Significance Level
Basic Concepts	____	Operations		NS .05 .01
Basic Concepts	____	Applications		NS .05 .01
Operations	____	Applications		NS .05 .01

Basic Concepts	89
Operations	92
Applications	76

Figure 7.6 Write scores for comparing three areas of KeyMath—R. (*Source:* From *KeyMath—Revised: A Diagnostic Inventory of Essential Mathematics, Protocol* (p. 12) by A. J. Connolly, 1988, Circle Pines, MN: American Guidance Service. Copyright 1988 by American Guidance Service. Reprinted by permission.)

In Activity 7.3, you will determine one student's weaknesses and strengths for each domain of the Numeration subtest.

Check Your Understanding

Complete Activity 7.3.

ACTIVITY 7.3

Complete the problems and answer the questions that follow.

1. A fourth-grade student obtained the following domain scores on the Numeration subtest. Write the scores in the appropriate spaces on the portion of the protocol in Figure 7.9. The ceiling item reached was 15.

Numeration Domain	**Score**
Numbers 0–9	6
Numbers 0–99	5
Numbers 0–999	0
Multidigit numbers and advanced numeration topics	0

2. Use the information provided in Figure 7.8 to determine whether the performance by this fourth-grade student is strong, average, or weak in each of the domains. Circle the correct domain statuses on Figure 7.9. The performance is considered weak if the raw score is less than the expected score, average if the raw score is the same

Grade	Significance Level	Basic Concepts Versus Operations	Basic Concepts Versus Applications	Operations Versus Applications
		Minimum Standard-Score Difference		
K	.05	23	19	22
	.01	28	23	27
1	.05	19	17	16
	.01	23	21	20
2	.05	19	17	17
	.01	23	21	21
3	.05	17	16	15
	.01	20	19	18
4	.05	14	13	13
	.01	18	16	16
5	.05	13	12	12
	.01	16	14	14
6	.05	14	12	12
	.01	17	15	15
7	.05	11	10	10
	.01	14	13	12
8	.05	11	11	10
	.01	14	13	13
9	.05	11	11	10
	.01	14	13	13

Figure 7.7 KeyMath—R minimum differences required for statistical significance in comparisons of area standard scores, grades K through 9. (*Source:* From *KeyMath—Revised: A Diagnostic Inventory of Essential Mathematics, Manual* (p. 312) by A. J. Connolly, 1988, Circle Pines, MN: American Guidance Service. Copyright 1988 by American Guidance Service. Reprinted by permission.)

as the expected score, and strong if the performance is better than the expected score.

3. Based on the student's strengths and weaknesses as determined in this activity, which skills should the teacher begin to teach and emphasize in planning the instructional program? ______________

____

____

____

Subtest and Domain	Ceiling Item															
	3	4	5	6	7	8	9	10	11	12	13	14	15	16	17	18
Numeration																
Numbers 0–9	3	4	5	6	6	6	6	6	6	6	6	6	6	6	6	6
Numbers 0–99	—	—	—	—	—	—	3	4	4	4–5	4–5	4–5	4–5	4–5	5–6	5–6
Numbers 0–999	—	—	—	—	—	—	—	—	—	—	—	—	2–3	2–3	2–3	2–3
Multidigit numbers and advanced numeration topics	—	—	—	—	—	—	—	—	—	—	—	—	—	—	—	—

Figure 7.8 KeyMath—R average domain scores, by ceiling item, grade 3, spring, to grade 4, fall. (*Source:* From *KeyMath—Revised: A Diagnostic Inventory of Essential Mathematics, Manual* (p. 324) by A. J. Connolly, 1988, Circle Pines, MN: American Guidance Service. Copyright 1988 by American Guidance Service. Reprinted by permission.)

> ***Apply Your Knowledge***
>
> Using the strengths and weaknesses identified in basic concepts, what skills should be addressed in educational objectives? ______________
>
> ____

Technical Data

Norming Process. The total number of students in the standardization and norming process for the KeyMath—R was 1,978. Test developers considered the variables of geographic region, grade, sex, socioeconomic status, race or ethnic group, and parental educational level. The sample included students from grades K through 9. The variables of parental educational level, geographic region, and race or ethnic group were representative of

BASIC CONCEPTS AREA

Subtest	Domain	Domain Score	Average Score (Table 16)	Domain Status		
Numeration: (24 items)	Numbers 0–9	______	______	W	A	S
	Numbers 0–99	______	______	W	A	S
Ceiling	Numbers 0–999	______	______	W	A	S
Item ________	Multidigit numbers and advanced numeration topics	______	______	W	A	S

Figure 7.9 Basic Concepts scoring area from KeyMath—R protocol. (*Source:* From *KeyMath—Revised: A Diagnostic Inventory of Essential Mathematics, Protocol* by A. J. Connolly, 1988, Circle Pines, MN: American Guidance Service. Copyright 1988 by American Guidance Service. Reprinted by permission.)

U.S. population data from the Bureau of Census. The census reports relied on 1985 data and projections through 2080 for the Hispanic population. The KeyMath—R offers both fall and spring testing norms, and the norming procedures are adequately detailed in the examiner's manual.

Reliability. Reliability studies included alternate forms reliability studies presented by age and grade from the fall testing sample and split-half reliability studies for both fall and spring testing. Data also are presented for an item response theory using the Rasch model (cited in Connolly, 1988). Total test reliability coefficients for the alternate forms study ranged from .91 for grade-based standard scores to .92 for total test age-based standard scores.

Validity. The examiner's manual presents information regarding the content validity based on the construction and model of the test, a construct validity study addressing both developmental change and internal consistency, and concurrent validity studies. The data from the concurrent validity studies included comparisons with the original KeyMath, the Comprehensive Test of Basic Skills, and the Iowa Test of Basic Skills. Data presented compare the instruments by subtests, areas, and total tests. Total test comparisons yielded validity coefficients that ranged from .66 comparing the Total Mathematics scores of the Comprehensive Test of Basic Skills to .93 comparing the performance of seventh-grade students on the original and revised versions of the KeyMath.

TEST OF MATHEMATICAL ABILITIES—2 (TOMA—2)

The TOMA (Brown, Cronin, & McEntire, 1994) was designed to assess some areas of math that may not be addressed by other instruments. This test, now in its second edition, was developed to be used with students who range in age from 8-0 to 18-11. The test authors present the following questions, not answered by other instruments, as their rationale for developing the TOMA:

1. What are the student's expressed attitudes toward mathematics?
2. What is the student's general vocabulary level when that vocabulary is used in a mathematical sense?
3. How knowledgeable is the student (or group of students) regarding the functional use of mathematics facts and concepts in our general culture?
4. How do a student's attitudes, vocabulary, and general math information compare with the basic skills shown in the areas of computation and story problems?
5. Do the student's attitudes, vocabulary, and level of general math information differ markedly from those of a group of age peers? (Brown, Cronin, & McEntire, 1994, p. 1)

This instrument was developed to help the teacher find the answers to these questions. The TOMA—2 consists of five subtests, with the fifth subtest, Attitude Toward Math, considered supplemental. The remaining subtests are Vocabulary, Computation, General Information, and Story Problems. The subtests yield standard scores with a mean of 10, a math quotient with a mean of 100, age equivalents, and percentile ranks. The manual gives precautions against misinterpretation of test scores and encourages further diagnostic assessment if a math disability is suspected.

The test authors list three diagnostic questions that the TOMA—2 may help educators answer:

1. Where should the student be placed in a curriculum?
2. What specific skills or content has the student mastered?
3. How does this student's overall performance compare with that of age or grade peers? (Brown, Cronin, & McEntire, 1994, p. 1)

Technical Data

Norming Process. The norming sample of the TOMA—2 consisted of 2,082 students in 26 states geographically spread across the United States. The variables of gender, race (black, white, and other), community (urban-suburban and rural), disability status (no disability, learning disabilities, other handicapping conditions), and region were considered and seemed to reflect the percentages from the 1990 census.

Reliability. Reliability was studied using coefficient alpha for internal consistency, and group coefficients ranged from .73 to .98. Test-retest coefficients appear to be adequate, .66 to .93.

Validity. Concurrent criterion-related validity was studied using the math tests of the PIAT, the KeyMath, WRAT, and the Scientific Research Associates (SRA) Achievement Series. Low to adequate correlations were found, with the Story Problems subtests of the TOMA—2 and the SRA having the highest coefficient of .72. Construct validity was supported in the presentation of developmental data and by comparing the TOMA to cognitive tests (the Wechsler and the Slosson intelligence tests), resulting in modest to adequate correlations.

WOODCOCK READING MASTERY TESTS—REVISED (WRMT—R)

The WRMT—R (Woodcock, 1987) consists of two forms that are not exactly equivalent. One form, G, contains two additional reading-readiness subtests and a supplementary Letter Checklist. For this reason, Form G is the version that should be used with younger or lower level readers. The other form, H, contains subtests equivalent to the four other subtests contained in Form G. A general screening of reading ability can be obtained by administering the Short Scale, which includes only the Word Identification and the Passage Comprehension subtests.

Subtests. For this revision of the WRMT, the subtests of Word Identification, Word Attack, and Passage Comprehension remained basically unchanged in presentation format. The Word Attack subtest contains an error analysis inventory, but the presentation format remains the same. Substantial changes have been made in some of the subtests, and these changes affect their presentation. A new subtest, Visual-Auditory Learning, has been added.

Visual-Auditory Learning. In this subtest, the examiner visually presents a picture or rebus type of symbol while orally presenting a word. After seeing four symbols and hearing their accompanying words, the student must use the newly learned symbols to "read" sentences presented on the subsequent easel page. The student then sees four new symbols and is asked to "read" sentences that include both the first symbols and the new symbols. This process continues throughout the subtest unless the student reaches a ceiling by making a specific number of errors. If the student reaches a ceiling, the cutoff score based on total errors is used to determine the raw score. If the student does not make the number of errors used to stop the testing but rather completes all of the stories on the subtest, the number of total errors is subtracted from the number 134 to determine the raw score. This subtest is found only on Form G of the WRMT—R.

Letter Identification and Supplementary Letter Checklist. These two subtests are contained only on Form G of the revised WRMT. The Letter Identification subtest does provide norm scores; however, the supplementary Letter Checklist is used for error analysis only. The examiner has the option of presenting the task to measure the student's ability to name the letters or the sounds of the letters.

Word Identification. This subtest measures the student's ability to orally read the visually presented words. The words at the easiest level represent sight words and other words selected from several basal reading series. The more difficult words were selected from various sources. This subtest attempts to measure identification of the word. The student must say the word aloud; comprehension of the word is not measured.

Word Attack. This subtest visually presents nonsense words, which the student must decode orally. This test measures the student's ability to use phonetic attack and structural analysis in reading new words aloud. An error analysis page included in the protocol assists the examiner in identifying specific phonetic errors that need educational remediation.

Word Comprehension. This subtest samples the student's ability to provide missing words for analogies, synonyms, and antonyms. This subtest actually comprises three smaller subtests, which can be analyzed by categories for understanding vocabulary. The examiner calculates three raw scores and locates the *W* score on the protocol rather than from norm tables.

Passage Comprehension. This subtest presents a sentence or passage with a missing word. The student orally provides the missing word after silently reading the passage. The lower level items contain picture cues, and most of the difficult items are fairly content specific. The most difficult items were taken from textbooks, newspaper articles, and the like.

Scoring. On most of the WRMT—R subtests, the student establishes the basal after answering 6 consecutive items correctly and the ceiling after answering 6 consecutive responses incorrectly. The Visual-Auditory Learning subtest, however, contains a cutoff score chart to determine when the student has reached a ceiling level.

In Activity 7.4, you will determine the student's score on the Visual-Auditory Learning subtest.

Check Your Understanding

Complete Activity 7.4.

ACTIVITY 7.4

Complete the following problems.

1. A student taking the WRMT—2 Visual-Auditory Learning subtest completed stories 1 through 4 and made 46 errors. In Figure 7.10, find the row that contains stories 1–4, because the student completed four stories. Locate the number 46, and then locate the total

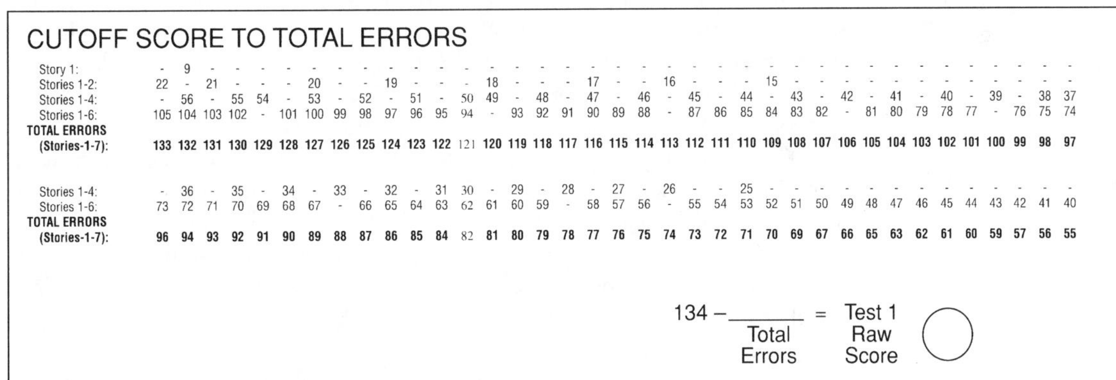

CUTOFF SCORE TO TOTAL ERRORS

Story 1:	-	9	-	-	-	-	-	-	-	-	-	-	-	-	-	-	-	-	-
Stories 1-2:	22	-	21	-	-	-	20	-	-	19	-	-	-	18	-	-	-	17	-
Stories 1-4:	-	56	-	55	54	-	53	-	52	-	51	-	50	49	-	48	-	47	-
Stories 1-6:	105	104	103	102	-	101	100	99	98	97	96	95	94	-	93	92	91	90	89
TOTAL ERRORS (Stories-1-7):	**133**	**132**	**131**	**130**	**129**	**128**	**127**	**126**	**125**	**124**	**123**	**122**	121	**120**	**119**	**118**	**117**	**116**	**115**

Story 1:	-	-	-	-	-	-	-	-	-	-	-	-	-	-	-	-	-	-
Stories 1-2:	-	16	-	-	-	15	-	-	-	-	-	-	-	-	-	-	-	-
Stories 1-4:	46	-	45	-	44	-	43	-	42	-	41	-	40	-	39	-	38	37
Stories 1-6:	88	-	87	86	85	84	83	82	-	81	80	79	78	77	-	76	75	74
TOTAL ERRORS (Stories-1-7):	**114**	**113**	**112**	**111**	**110**	**109**	**108**	**107**	**106**	**105**	**104**	**103**	**102**	**101**	**100**	**99**	**98**	**97**

Stories 1-4:	-	36	-	35	-	34	-	33	-	32	-	31	30	-	29	-	28	-	27
Stories 1-6:	73	72	71	70	69	68	67	-	66	65	64	63	62	61	60	59	-	58	57
TOTAL ERRORS (Stories-1-7):	**96**	**94**	**93**	**92**	**91**	**90**	**89**	**88**	**87**	**86**	**85**	**84**	82	**81**	**80**	**79**	**78**	**77**	**76**

Stories 1-4:	-	26	-	-	25	-	-	-	-	-	-	-	-	-	-	-	-	-
Stories 1-6:	56	-	55	54	53	52	51	50	49	48	47	46	45	44	43	42	41	40
TOTAL ERRORS (Stories-1-7):	**75**	**74**	**73**	**72**	**71**	**70**	**69**	**67**	**66**	**65**	**63**	**62**	**61**	**60**	**59**	**57**	**56**	**55**

134 – ______ = Test 1 Raw Score
Total Errors

Figure 7.10 Table to obtain total errors using cutoff score of the WRMT—R Visual-Auditory Learning subtest. (*Source:* From *Woodcock Reading Mastery Tests—Revised, Form G, Protocol* (p. 3) by R. W. Woodcock, 1987, Circle Pines, MN: American Guidance Service. Copyright 1976 by American Guidance Service. Reprinted from the *Woodcock-Johnson Psycho-Educational Battery,* copyright 1977, DLM Teaching Resources, Allen, TX 75002. Used under license.)

error estimate beneath in the total errors row (stories 1–7). Write the total error estimate in the appropriate space in Figure 7.10.

2. Subtract the total error estimate from 134 to obtain the raw score for this subtest. Write the score on Figure 7.10.

Apply Your Knowledge

What is the purpose of using the cutoff score table? ____________

____

____

Scoring the WRMT—R will result in comprehensive information about the student's individual reading ability. In addition to an error analysis for the Word Attack subtest and qualitative scoring of the supplementary Letter Checklist, this battery can provide the examiner with the following information:

1. Standard error of measurement is provided for each *W* score, and confidence bands may be calculated for each subtest.
2. Space on the protocol for error responses helps the examiner complete an error analysis of reading ability.
3. Several diagnostic profiles may be plotted according to the student's performance based on percentile ranks, grade equivalents, and relative performance index scores.

Once the examiner has mastered the scoring, he obtains a comprehensive evaluation of reading. The examiner uses raw scores to enter tables to obtain the derived scores of *W* scores, grade and age equivalents, and standard error of measurement for *W* scores. The examiner compares the student's obtained *W* scores with reference scores for age or grade-level comparisons.

The table that contains the reference scores also contains column numbers. The column numbers are used to find percentile ranks and standard scores on another table. Two column numbers are given for each reference score. When the examiner has made the comparison by subtracting the reference score from the obtained *W* score, he selects the correct column number and enters the relative performance index table, a portion of which is shown in Figure 7.11.

The examiner determines the correct column by the following criteria: If the difference between the *W* and the reference score is less than 100, the column number on the left is used to enter the table; if the difference is greater than 100, the column number on the right is used to enter the table. The column numbers may be different for the scores obtained in the standard error of measurement confidence bands. When the standard error of measurement is added to the difference score, the new score may be

Table G. Relative Performance Indexes, Percentile Ranks, and Standard Scores (mean = 100, *SD* = 15)

Column												
25		26		27		28		29		30		
PR	Std	PR	Std	PR	Std	PR	Std	PR	Std	PR	Std	DIFF
98	132	98	130	97	129	96	126	93	122	90	119	144
98	131	98	129	97	128	95	125	93	122	90	119	143
98	130	97	129	97	127	95	125	92	121	89	119	142
98	129	97	128	96	127	95	124	92	121	89	118	141
97	129	97	127	96	126	94	124	91	120	88	118	140
97	128	96	127	96	125	94	123	91	120	87	117	139
97	127	96	126	95	125	93	122	90	119	87	117	138
96	127	95	125	95	124	93	122	90	119	86	116	137
96	126	95	125	94	123	92	121	89	118	86	116	136
95	125	95	124	94	123	92	121	88	118	85	115	135
95	124	94	123	93	122	91	120	88	117	84	115	134
94	124	93	123	92	122	90	119	87	117	83	115	133
94	123	93	122	92	121	90	119	86	116	83	114	132
93	122	92	121	91	120	89	118	85	116	82	114	131
92	122	91	121	90	120	88	118	85	115	81	113	130
92	121	91	120	90	119	87	117	84	115	80	113	129
91	120	90	119	89	118	86	117	83	114	79	112	128
90	119	89	118	88	118	86	116	82	114	79	112	127
89	119	88	118	87	117	85	115	81	113	78	111	126
89	118	87	117	86	116	84	115	80	113	77	111	125
87	117	86	116	85	116	83	114	79	112	76	111	124
86	117	85	116	84	115	82	114	78	112	75	110	123
85	116	84	115	83	114	81	113	77	111	74	110	122
84	115	83	114	82	114	80	112	76	111	73	109	121
83	114	82	114	81	113	78	112	75	110	72	109	120
82	114	81	113	80	112	77	111	74	110	71	108	119
81	113	79	112	78	112	76	111	73	109	70	108	118
79	112	78	112	77	111	75	110	72	109	69	108	117
78	111	77	111	76	110	74	109	71	108	68	107	116
76	111	75	110	74	110	72	109	70	108	67	107	115

Figure 7.11 Table G all forms, columns 25 to 30, difference scores 115 to 144. (*Source:* From *Woodcock Reading Mastery Tests—Revised Examiner's Manual* (p. 172) by R. W. Woodcock, 1987. Circle Pines, MN: American Guidance Service. Copyright 1987 by American Guidance Service. Reprinted by permission.)

greater than 100 when the original difference score was less than 100. This means that the column number on the right would be used to determine the relative performance index and percentile rank for the confidence band scores. When the standard error of measurement is subtracted from the difference score, the new score may be less than 100 when the original score was not. Again, the new score found by using the standard error of measurement would require a different column number for the relative performance index table.

The WRMT—R presents cluster scores for reading as well as individual subtest scores. The clusters are Readiness (Form G only), Basic Skills, and Reading Comprehension. The Readiness cluster includes the Visual-Auditory and Letter Identification subtests. Word Identification and Word Attack subtests make up the Basic Skills cluster. The Reading Comprehension cluster is made up of the Word Comprehension and Passage Comprehension subtests. The cluster *W* scores are obtained by finding the average of the two subtest *W* scores in each cluster. A Total Reading cluster score is found by averaging the four subtests contained on both forms of the test: Word Identification, Word Attack, Word Comprehension, and Passage Comprehension.

Check Your Understanding

Complete Activity 7.5.

ACTIVITY 7.5

Complete the problems and answer the questions that follow.

1. Use the information in Figure 7.12 to determine the difference between the obtained *W* score and the reference score for the Word Identification subtest. Choose from the figure the column number that will be used to find the relative performance index and the percentile rank for the obtained *W* score.
2. Using the obtained difference score from problem 1, complete the confidence bands (Figure 7.12) by adding and subtracting the standard error of measurement given in the figure. Write the answers in the appropriate spaces on the portion of the protocol in Figure 7.12. Choose from the figure the column number that will be used to find the relative performance index and percentile ranks for the confidence band scores.
3. The relative performance index for this student is 99/90. Write 99 in the appropriate spaces in Figure 7.12. Use Figure 7.11 to find the standard score and percentile rank for the obtained difference score found in problem 1 for the Word Identification subtest. Write your answer in the appropriate spaces in Figure 7.12.
4. Use Figure 7.11 to obtain the standard scores and percentile ranks for the confidence bands. Write your answer in the appropriate spaces in Figure 7.12.

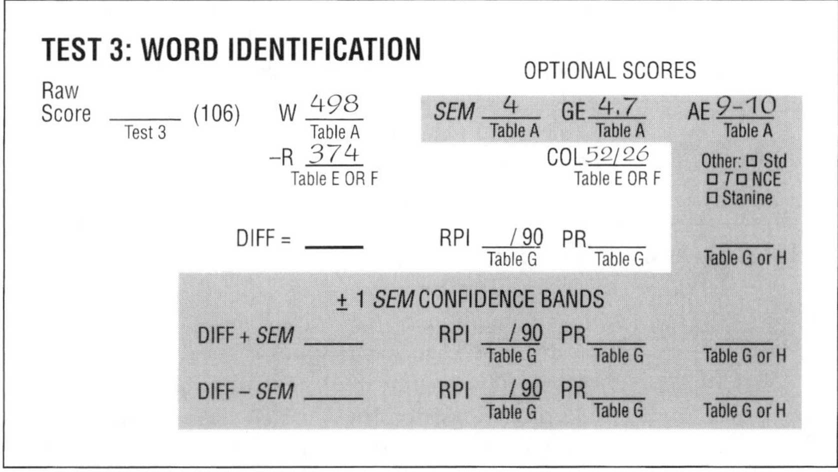

TEST 3: WORD IDENTIFICATION

OPTIONAL SCORES

Raw Score ______ (106) Test 3

W 498 Table A

–R 374 Table E OR F

DIFF = ____

SEM 4 Table A

GE 4.7 Table A

AE 9-10 Table A

COL 52/26 Table E OR F

Other: □ Std □ *T* □ NCE □ Stanine

RPI ___/90 Table G

PR____ Table G

____ Table G or H

± 1 *SEM* CONFIDENCE BANDS

DIFF + *SEM* ____ RPI ___/90 Table G PR____ Table G ____ Table G or H

DIFF – *SEM* ____ RPI ___/90 Table G PR____ Table G ____ Table G or H

Figure 7.12 Protocol section for WRMT—R Word Identification subtest. (*Source:* From *Woodcock Reading Mastery Tests—Revised, Protocol* (p. 12) by R. W. Woodcock, 1987, Circle Pines, MN: American Guidance Service. Copyright 1987 by American Guidance Service. Reprinted by permission.)

5. What do the confidence band scores represent? ____________________
____
____

Apply Your Knowledge

Why are the confidence bands necessary for accurate interpretation of the student's ability? ____
____

Technical Data

Norming Process. The standardization and norming process of the WRMT—R included a sample of 6,089 people, ranging from kindergarten to college/university and adult age levels. The test developers considered the variables of age, sex, community size, race, origin, and geographic regions for all subjects. The variables of occupation, adult occupation, and type of college (private, public, university, 2-year, or 4-year) were considered for the adult and college samples.

Reliability. The examiner's manual includes internal reliability studies. These split-half reliability coefficients for the equivalent forms (G and H) and cluster reliability coefficients were reported. Reliability coefficients for both Short Scale and Total Reading cluster scores were in the .90s.

Validity. The examiner's manual contains information on both content and concurrent validity. Correlations with the Woodcock-Johnson reading tests for selected groups were included in the manual. Total reading correlation coefficients ranged from .48 on the Short Scale to .91 on the Full Scale Total Reading scores.

OTHER DIAGNOSTIC TESTS

The remainder of this chapter summarizes several other tests frequently used in the classroom. Some of these tests will not require the lengthy test administration time required by tests presented in the first section of the chapter. Some of these tests may be administered, in part or in their entirety, to groups of students. These tests are included in this chapter because they provide useful information to the educator for diagnosing deficits in specific academic areas and aid in educational planning.

GRAY ORAL READING TESTS—FOURTH EDITION (GORT—4)

The GORT—4 provides the teacher with a method of analyzing oral reading skills. This instrument is a norm-referenced test that may be administered to students ages 7-0 through 18-11. The GORT—4 has equivalent forms so that students may be reassessed using the same instrument. This newest version of the GORT has an additional story for the lowest level on both forms of the instrument to allow for better exploration of the emerging reading skills of young students. On this instrument, the student reads stories aloud to the teacher, who scores rate, accuracy, fluency, comprehension, and overall reading ability. The comprehension score is derived from answers to questions asked by the teacher following each story. The oral reading miscues may be analyzed in the following areas: meaning similarity, function similarity, graphic/phonemic similarity, multiple sources (of errors), and self-correction. The authors state that the purposes of the GORT—4 are to identify students with problems, determine strengths and weaknesses, document progress, and to conduct research using the GORT—4 (Wiederholt & Bryant, 2001, pp. 4–5).

Technical Data

Norming Process. The manual reports that 1,677 persons in 28 states made up the sample group. Four geographic regions were included. Approximately 47% of the sample were males and 53% females. Race factors considered included the classifications of white, black, and other; and ethnicity included Native American, Hispanic, Asian, African American, European American, and other. Family income, educational status, and age were considered as well as the disability categories of learning disability, speech-language disorder, attention deficit disorder, other disability, and no disability.

Reliability. The content sampling included studies applying coefficient alpha, alternate forms reliability, time sampling, and interscorer reliability. Reliability coefficients ranged from .85 (comprehension scores on test-retest) to .99 on several reliability factors.

Validity. Content validity is addressed by the authors through presentation of information regarding construction of the stories, consideration of vocabulary levels and reading levels, and structure of the sentences. Readability levels were indexed using the Flesch-Kincaid Readability Formula. Differential item functioning analysis was used to explore possible bias for gender, race, and ethnicity. It was reported in the manual that there were no statistical differences of concern; the authors therefore concluded this was evidence of support for a nonbiased instrument. Criterion-related validity studies are included in the manual. There is evidence that the GORT—4 correlates best with other instruments that include oral reading subtests, and it does not correlate as highly with silent reading measures. Construct validity is presented with additional studies comparing the GORT—4 to other instruments with moderately adequate correlations. Evidence of discriminate validity comparing the subtest scores across eight subgroups is included.

TEST OF READING COMPREHENSION—THIRD EDITION (TORC—3)

The TORC—3 was designed to assess reading comprehension using eight subtests. The instrument includes four subtests in the reading comprehension core: general vocabulary, syntactic similarities, paragraph reading, and sentence sequencing. These skills are assessed using a variety of task formats, such as multiple-choice items for general vocabulary and discrimination of sentences for syntactic similarities. The diagnostic supplements include the following subtests: mathematics vocabulary, social skills vocabulary, science vocabulary, and reading the directions of schoolwork. The test manual includes suggestions for additional assessment methods.

Technical Data

Norming Process. The norming sample was composed of 1,962 persons with considerations for age, gender, race (white, black, other), geographic area, and ethnicity (Native American, Hispanic, Asian, African American, and other). The categories of disability included learning disability, speech-language disorder, other disability, and no disability.

Reliability. Reliability studies were presented for internal consistency, interscorer reliability, content sampling, and time sampling. Coefficients ranged from .79 to .98. Although coefficients were adequate to high, sample sizes were small for reliability research.

Validity. Information is provided regarding content validity, criterion-related validity, and construct validity. Additional information is provided regarding discriminate validity of various groups. The manual addresses using delta values to study possible bias due to gender or race.

TEST OF WRITTEN LANGUAGE—3 (TOWL—3)

The third edition of the TOWL includes two alternate forms test booklets (A and B) and is organized into three composites: Overall Written Language, Contrived Writing, and Spontaneous Writing (Hammill & Larsen, 1996). TOWL—3 contains eight subtests, of which three are calculated from the spontaneously written story. The student completes all test items in the student response booklet. This instrument may be administered in small groups, although for optimal monitoring of written responses, individual administration appears to be best. A description of each subtest follows:

1. Vocabulary—The student is provided a stimulus word and required to use the word in a sentence.
2. Spelling—The student is required to spell dictated words.
3. Style—The student writes dictated sentences and must punctuate sentences and capitalize properly.
4. Logical Sentences—The student is provided an illogical sentence and is required to edit it so that it is more logical.
5. Sentence Combining—The student is presented two or more sentences per item and must combine them into one meaningful and grammatically correct sentence.

For subtests 6, 7, and 8, the student is asked to write a story when shown a stimulus picture. The requirements for each subtest are:

6. Contextual Conventions—The student's story response is scored for punctuation, capitalization, spelling, and other conventional rules of writing.
7. Contextual Language—The student's story response is scored for sentence construction, quality of vocabulary, and grammar.
8. The student's story response is scored for the following: plot, prose, development of characters, interest, and additional aspects of composition (Hammill & Larsen, 1996).

Technical Data

Norming Process. The test developers standardized and normed the TOWL—3 on a sample of 2,217 students from 25 states. The following demographic variables were considered and appeared to reflect U.S. population information: gender, rural and urban communities, race (white, black, other), geographic area, and ethnicity (Native American, Hispanic, Asian, African American, other). The number of students for each age group (7 through 17) ranged from 105 to 350. Percentages of children with disabilities were fairly representative of percentages in the Statistical Abstract of the United States (1997). The disability categories included persons with learning disabilities, persons with speech-language impairments, persons in the range of mental retardation, and other disabilities.

Reliability. The manual provides information for the following reliability studies: interscorer correlation, internal consistency using coefficient alpha and split-half methods, and test-retest using alternate forms. All coefficients appear to be adequate to high on all reliability studies, with many falling in the .90s range.

Validity. The manual presents both concurrent criterion-related validity and construct validity information. Concurrent validity research was completed using the Comprehensive Scales of Student Abilities (Hammill & Hresko, 1994) and the Comprehensive Test of Nonverbal Intelligence (Hammill, Pearson, & Wiederholt, 1996). Correlations were variable; however, the tasks on these measures are quite different from the tasks on the TOWL—3. Therefore, the correlations would not be expected to be high. Construct validity was presented with the supporting data of age differentiation, interrelationships among subtests, group differentiation, grade differentiation, item validity, and relationship to both achievement and intelligence tests. Factor analysis supported a single-factor structure. The examiner's manual provides discussion of the attempt to decrease possible test bias.

TEST OF WRITTEN SPELLING—4 (TWS—4)

A standardized spelling test, the TWS—4 (Larsen, Hammill, & Moats, 1999) consists of two alternate forms that can be administered to individual students or to groups of students ages 6-0 to 18-11. Instructions for starting points and basal and ceiling levels are presented in the examiner's manual. During administration of this test, the student begins at the appropriate entry level and continues until the ceiling has been reached. The ceiling is established when the student misses 5 words consecutively. Once the ceiling has been reached, the examiner checks to see that the basal of 5 consecutive items answered correctly was obtained. For students who did not establish a basal, the examiner administers items in reverse order until 5 consecutive items are spelled correctly, or until the student reaches item 1. All items below the established basal are scored as correct. Raw scores are used to enter tables for standard scores with a mean of 100, percentile ranks, age equivalents, and grade equivalents.

This revision of the TWS includes more elaboration for examiners regarding the theoretical bases of the test and a discussion of the skills of spelling in English. The authors also provide a useful chapter on additional assessment methods of spelling and other related skills such as the assessment of phoneme awareness. These additional assessment methods offer the use of this instrument as part of a total evaluation effort in which teachers would use additional methods and may use an alternate form of the TWS for measuring gains following interventions.

Technical Data

Norming Process. The standardization sample included data from 3,805 students in the TWS—2 sample, plus an additional 855 new students from a total of 23 states. The total number of cases considered was 4,952. The variables of age, race, gender, ethnicity, and geographic region were considered. The sample appears to be representative of the national averages reported in the manual. No new cases were added in the 1999 version of the TWS—4. The test authors reported that the purpose of the revision was to change the test format, address issues of bias, and improve reliability and validity.

Reliability. Reliability studies included internal reliability and test-retest reliability studies. Internal reliability coefficients ranged from .93 to .99 for the three studies presented in the manual of content sampling, time sampling, and interscorer reliability. The coefficients are impressive; however, the sample sizes of the studies were fairly small.

Validity. Validity information presented in the manual includes content validity, criterion-related validity, and construct validity. Content validity is presented in terms of item selection, item analysis, differential item functioning analysis, and delta scores approach to investigate items for bias. These studies offer support for the validity of the TWS—4. Criterion-related validity studies compared the TWS with the Wide Range Achievement Test—Revised (WRAT—R) and local school system high-stakes achievement tests as well as the Metropolitan Achievement Tests. A discussion of construct validity focuses on developmental gains based on comparisons of mean scores by ages and the relationship of the TWS—4 to other types of tests.

ASSESSING OTHER LANGUAGE AREAS

language assessment Measuring verbal concepts and verbal understanding.

The ability to understand and express ideas using correct language is fundamental for school achievement. **Language assessment,** through tests that measure a student's understanding and use of language, is presented in this section. Tests administered by speech clinicians in an effort to diagnose and remediate speech disorders (articulation, voice, or fluency disorders) are beyond the scope of this text. Effective remediation of language disorders is considered a shared responsibility of the clinician, teacher, and parent, who each must be familiar with the tests to diagnose and monitor these skills. These tests assess a student's **receptive language** vocabulary, oral **expressive language,** and **written language** skills. In addition to actual test instruments, informal assessment of written language is conducted in the classroom as well and is presented in chapter 8.

receptive language Inner language concepts applied to what is heard.

expressive language Language skills used in speaking or writing.

written language Understanding language concepts and using them in writing.

PEABODY PICTURE VOCABULARY TEST—THIRD EDITION (PPVT—III)

The PPVT—III (Dunn & Dunn, 1997) measures the student's verbal comprehension skills by presenting a series of four visual stimuli and requesting the student to discriminate the stimulus that best represents the orally stated word. An example of this format is illustrated in Figure 7.13. Two equivalent forms of this individually administered language test, form IIIA and form IIIB, allow retesting to monitor progress. This test includes an easel test, examiner's manual, norms booklet, and protocol. Derived scores include standard scores, percentile ranks, normal curve equivalents, stanines, and age equivalents. Scoring is fairly easy, and the basal level is determined when the student correctly answers all of the items in a set or misses only one item in the set. The ceiling is determined when the student incorrectly answers at least 8 items in the set. The examiner's manual provides easy examples and cases to illustrate scoring and interpretation of raw scores.

Technical Data

Norming Process. The standardization sample included 2,725 persons ages 2 years, 6 months to 90 years and older. The sample was controlled for representation based on the U.S. Census data from March 1994. There were 240 test sites, which were balanced across the country to represent census data. The variables considered include gender, ethnicity, educational level of the person or parents, and age. The special education sample was representative of the U.S. data included in the *Seventeenth Annual Report to Congress on the Implementation of the Individuals with Disabilities Education Act* (U.S. Department of Education, 1995).

Reliability. Internal consistency studies included split-half reliability studies and alternative forms research. Reliability coefficients ranged from the mid-.80s to the upper .90s, with most coefficients in the mid to upper .90s. Test-retest reliability studies resulted in coefficients that were all in the .90s (using Guilford's formula [1954, p. 392] for correction; Dunn & Dunn, 1997).

Validity. Content validity is presented in the context of the validity of the construction of the original PPVT and subsequent revisions. Construct validity for the PPVT—III is presented as a discussion of the importance of

Figure 7.13 Example of visual stimuli presented to measure verbal comprehension skills in the PPVT—III. (*Source:* From *Peabody Picture Vocabulary Test—III* (training plate D) by L. M. Dunn and L. M. Dunn, 1997, Circle Pines, MN: American Guidance Service. Copyright 1981 by American Guidance Service. Reprinted by permission.)

the ability to define words, or having a hearing vocabulary, and how this relates to the constructs measured by intelligence tests. Item selection is presented, as well as criterion-related validity information. Concurrent validity studies included correlations with the Wechsler Intelligence Scale for Children, Third Edition (WISC—III), the Kaufman Adolescent and Adult Intelligence Test (KAIT), the Kaufman Brief Intelligence Test (KBIT), and Oral and Written Language Scales. Corrected coefficients for these studies ranged from .62 to .92.

TEST OF LANGUAGE DEVELOPMENT—PRIMARY: THIRD EDITION (TOLD—P:3)

The Primary edition of the TOLD—P:3 (Newcomer & Hammill, 1997) was designed for use with students ranging in age from 4-0 to 8-11. The theoretical structure is based on a two-dimensional language model, described in the manual. TOLD—P:3 contains the following subtests: Picture Vocabulary, Relational Vocabulary, Oral Vocabulary, Grammatic Understanding, Sentence Imitation, Grammatic Completion, Word Discrimination, Phonemic Analysis, and Word Articulation. The standard scores on these subtests may be used to obtain quotients for the following composites: spoken language, listening, organizing, speaking, semantics, and syntax. Derived scores include standard scores (mean = 10), quotients (mean = 100), and percentile ranks. Age equivalents are available. The format of response includes both forced-choice and open-ended responses. The student is also asked to repeat sentences on the Sentence Imitation subtest and fill in missing words for the Grammatic Completion subtest. In the Word Discrimination subtest, the student must discriminate between same and different items, which the examiner states orally. The student must name pictured items and correctly pronounce the names in the Word Articulation subtest. Table 7.2 lists the skills measured by the subtests; understanding the skills enables the teacher to interpret results and use the interpretations to develop educational plans.

Technical Data

Norming Process. The norming process for the TOLD—P:3 included 1,000 students ranging in age from 4-0 to 8-11. The variables considered were gender, community size, race (white, black, or other), ethnicity (Native American, Hispanic, Asian, African American, everyone else), geographic area, family income, and educational attainment of parents. The categories of disabilities included persons with learning disabilities, speech-language disorders, persons within the range of mental retardation, other disabilities, and no disabilities.

Reliability. Reliability studies included content sampling, internal consistency, time sampling, and interscorer reliability studies. All reliability coefficients ranged from .77 to .99.

Table 7.2 Content within subtests of the TOLD—P:3.

I. *Picture Vocabulary* measures the ability to understand the meaning of individual words when spoken.

II. *Relational Vocabulary* measures the ability to organize incoming language into categories that permit the perception of relationships.

III. *Oral Vocabulary* measures the ability to define individual stimulus words precisely.

IV. *Grammatic Understanding* measures the ability to comprehend sentences having differing syntactic structures.

V. *Sentence Imitation* measures the ability to repeat complex sentences accurately.

VI. *Grammatic Completion* measures the ability to complete a partially formed sentence by supplying a final word that has a proper morphological form.

VII. *Word Discrimination* measures the ability to discern subtle phonological differences between two words spoken in isolation.

VIII. *Phonemic Analysis* measures the ability to segment spoken words into smaller phonemic units by remembering and uttering the component of a word that remains after a portion is removed from the original stimulus word.

IX. *Word Articulation* measures the ability to say (i.e., articulate) a series of single words properly.

Source: Examiner's Manual for Test of Language Development—Primary: Third Edition (p. 44). Austin, TX: Pro-Ed. 1997.

Validity. The manual presents information regarding content validity, criterion-related validity, and construct validity. Criterion-related validity studies were conducted with the Bankson Language Test—Second Edition. Coefficients ranged from .52 to .97. The discussion of construct validity in the manual includes age differentiation, subtest interrelationships, factor analysis, and item validity. The authors present information regarding studying possible sources of bias in the instrument. The manual reports little or no bias found in the research of the instrument.

TEST OF LANGUAGE DEVELOPMENT—INTERMEDIATE: THIRD EDITION (TOLD—I:3)

The Intermediate edition of the TOLD—I:3 (Hammill & Newcomer, 1997) was constructed to aid in the diagnosis of students with language problems. The theoretical structure of the TOLD—I:3 is similar to the two-dimensional model of the TOLD—P:3. The following subtests are used to assess language skills for students aged 8-0 through 12-11: Sentence Combining, Picture Vocabulary, Word Ordering, Generals, Grammatic Comprehension, and Malapropisms. The examiner presents all subtests orally; items include forced-choice and open-ended questions. Derived scores of the TOLD—I:3 are standard scores (mean = 10), quotients (mean = 100), and percentile ranks by age norms. Age equivalents are available.

Technical Data

Norming Process. The norms for the TOLD—I:3 were based on the test scores of 779 children. A portion of the test results were from previous norming studies. Variables considered were age, sex, community size, race (white, black, or other), ethnicity (Native American, Hispanic, Asian, African American, everyone else), geographic area, and parental occupation.

Reliability. Reliability studies included content sampling, internal reliability studies using coefficient alpha and comparing demographic subgroups, and interscorer reliability. A summary table included in the manual presented coefficients ranging from .83 to .97.

Validity. In discussing content validity, the manual presents the rationales for item selection. Information regarding the differential item functioning analysis is included. Subgroup comparisons were analyzed applying delta values. Criterion-related validity was included by presenting coefficients between the TOLD—P:3 and the TOLD—I:3. Construct validity includes age differentiation, group differentiation, and interrelationships of subtests. Factor analysis and item validity are presented. The manual includes information on studying for possible test bias in items and indicates support for little or no bias in the groups studied.

TEST OF ADOLESCENT AND ADULT LANGUAGE—THIRD EDITION (TOAL—3)

The TOAL—3 (Hammill, Brown, Larsen, & Wiederholt, 1994) assesses students aged 12-0 to 24-11 for language problems. The test was constructed on the three-dimensional test model illustrated in Figure 7.14. The test composites include listening, speaking, reading, writing, spoken language, written language, vocabulary, grammar, receptive language, and expressive language. The third edition of the Test of Adolescent Language, the newly named Test of Adolescent and Adult Language, has an extended age range that allows it to be used in postsecondary settings. The administration procedures have also been improved in this revision.

The test authors caution the examiner to carefully interpret scores on the TOAL—3 because it is an ability test that assesses only specific areas of language (Hammill et al., 1994). The manual provides guidelines for interpreting significant composite differences and for testing the limits of student ability.

Figure 7.14 The three-dimensional TOAL—3 test model. (*Source:* From *Test of Adolescent and Adult Language, Third Edition* (p. 4) by D. D. Hammill, V. L. Brown, S. C. Larsen, and J. L. Wiederholt, 1994, Austin, TX: Pro-Ed. Copyright 1994 by Pro-Ed, Inc. Reprinted by permission.)

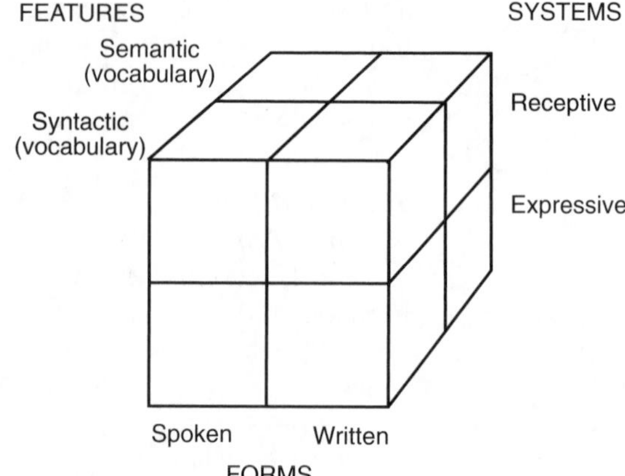

Technical Data

Norming Process. TOAL—3 developers used a normative sample of more than 3,000 persons in 22 states and 3 provinces in Canada. The sample representation was based on 1990 U.S. Census data.

Reliability. Internal consistency, test-retest, and interscorer reliability coefficients were reported to be above .80. Internal consistency reliability was studied using coefficient alpha, yielding coefficients from .80 to .96 on subtests and in the .90s on composite and overall scores. Interscorer reliability studies produced coefficients from .70 to .99 for three subtests.

Validity. Validity studies are reported for content, criterion-related, and construct validity. The manual discusses correlations between the TOAL—3 and other language tests (the TOLD—I:2, PPVT, Detroit Test of Learning Aptitude, Third Edition (DTLA—3), and Test of Written Language—2). The discussion of construct validity includes age differentiation, the relationship of the TOAL—3 to intelligence testing, and group differentiation. Content validity is covered briefly in the manual. Criterion-related validity studies included the PPVT, the DTLA Memory for Related Syllables, Reading and Language from the Comprehensive Test of Basic Skills, and total scores from the Test of Written Language. Coefficients ranged from not significant to .79. Additional research for studies of the TOAL and the TOLD—I yielded coefficients from not significant to .83. Discussion of construct validity focused on age differentiation, subtest interrelationships, relationship of the TOAL—2 to intelligence testing, and group differentiation. The manual includes a table containing mean standard scores for groups of learning-disabled students, students with mental retardation, students with emotional problems, judicated youth, poor readers, and non-disabled students.

SELECTING DIAGNOSTIC INSTRUMENTS

The instruments presented in this chapter are among those most used by educators to determine academic difficulties. Some instruments are recommended for specific academic areas or skills. Thus, an examiner may appropriately select one instrument because it contains subtests that will yield information necessary for academic planning and intervention. Table 7.3 summarizes some of the strengths and weaknesses of the tests presented in this chapter.

RESEARCH AND ISSUES

The following summaries represent some of the research and reviews on the diagnostic tests included in this chapter. Newly revised editions of tests may have little research to date.

1. Shriner and Salvia (1988) found little content validity when they compared items on the KeyMath with mathematics curriculum used in schools.
2. Greenstein and Strain (1977) determined that the KeyMath did successfully discriminate adolescent students with learning disabilities.
3. The KeyMath yielded fairly high correlation coefficients in a criterion-related study with the Cognitive Levels Test (Eaves, Darch, Mann, & Vance, 1989). Moderate correlations between the WRMT and the Cognitive Levels Test were also found.
4. In a concurrent validity study, Powell, Moore, and Callaway (1981) found that the Word Comprehension subtest on the WRMT appeared to measure word identification skills rather than a more general verbal factor.
5. In a review of the WRMT—R, Cooter (1989) found the revised edition to be a reliable instrument that should be considered useful for assessing different parts of reading tasks and skills.
6. In a review by Jaeger (1989), cautions were issued to examiners using the revised WRMT because the tests were not believed to be representative of "real" reading tasks. Jaeger stated that diagnosis and planning with the WRMT—R should be considered after more extensive testing or further observations of the students tested.
7. In a review of the revised TWS, Noyce (1989) stated that the TWS—2 seemed to measure the targeted types of spelling skills and pointed out the advantages of easy administration and good test construction.
8. Erickson's (1989) review of the TWS—2 described it as an excellent instrument for screening that does not, however, measure the many complex aspects involved in spelling.

Table 7.3 Summary of diagnostic tests in this chapter.

Instrument	Strengths	Weaknesses
KeyMath—Revised	• Equivalent forms available • Area comparisons for domains • Objectives given • Error analysis available • Good technical quality • Comprehensive math instrument • Good diagnostic capability	• Requires a substantial amount of time to administer and score
Test of Mathematical Abilities—2	• Addresses math attitude, conceptual understanding, and computational skills • May be given to groups of students	• Not comprehensive • Requires additional assessment for eligibility decisions
Woodcock Reading Mastery Tests—Revised	• Two versions available with some equivalent • Decoding words error analysis available • Reading readiness available on form G • Good technical quality • Good diagnostic capability	• Does not provide oral passage reading • Column scores confusing • Time-consuming to hand score
Gray Oral Reading Tests—4	• Equivalent forms available • Appears to be technically adequate with improved evidence of construct validity and indicators of nonbiased items • Additional stories at lowest level of both forms	• Examiner should practice scoring oral miscues prior to administration • Time-consuming to score • Scoring may be confusing for new examiners

THINK AHEAD

Academic achievement and diagnostic tests have been presented in the last two chapters. Now you will learn about other methods and techniques used to determine educational needs of students.

EXERCISES

Part I

Match the following terms with the correct definitions.

a. diagnostic tests
b. screening tests
c. ability tests
d. subtests

Instrument	Strengths	Weaknesses
Test of Reading Comprehension—3	• May be administered to small groups	• Small sample sizes in reliability and validity studies
Test of Written Language—3	• Nice format for written language assessment • May be administered to small groups	• Time-consuming to score • Somewhat subjective to score
Test of Written Spelling—4	• Improved presentation of underlying theoretical basis of instrument • Improved presentation and explanation of construct ability • Helpful information provided regarding additional assessment techniques • Alternate forms available	• No error analysis provided • No new norms were established with this revision
Peabody Picture Vocabulary Test—Third Edition	• Quick measure of verbal comprehension and receptive vocabulary • Adequate technical quality • Well-researched instrument	• Yields a single score rather than multiple language scores
Test of Language Development—Primary:3	• Several areas of language assessed • Variety of tasks for early ages	• Relatively small norm sample
Test of Language Development—Intermediate:3	• Several areas of language assessed	• Small norm sample
Test of Adolescent and Adult Language—3	• Extended age range allows for postsecondary administration	• Time-consuming to score • Some subjective scoring

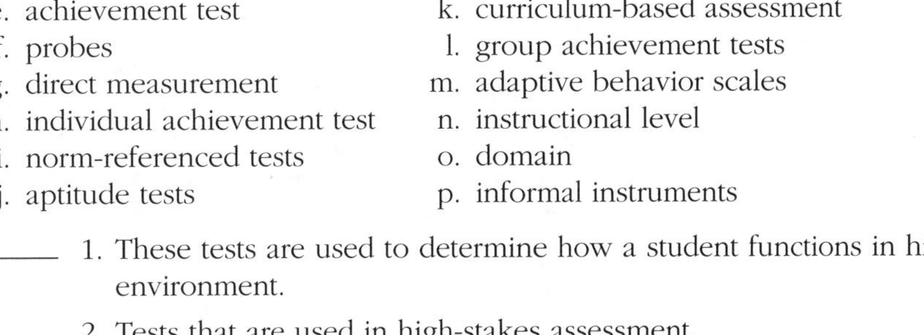

e. achievement test
f. probes
g. direct measurement
h. individual achievement test
i. norm-referenced tests
j. aptitude tests
k. curriculum-based assessment
l. group achievement tests
m. adaptive behavior scales
n. instructional level
o. domain
p. informal instruments

_____ 1. These tests are used to determine how a student functions in his environment.

_____ 2. Tests that are used in high-stakes assessment.

_____ 3. Items on an assessment instrument that are taken from the content of classroom instruction.

_____ 4. Tests designed to compare individual students with national averages, or norms of expectancy.

_____ 5. Rather than being used for high-stakes testing, these tests are often used to collect data for determining eligibility.

_____ 6. Tests that may be used for eligibility, reevaluation, or additional information for instructional decisions.

_____ 7. A part of a test that contains items to measure specific behaviors, content, or domains.

_____ 8. Broad-based tests that sample a few items across a curriculum.

_____ 9. General term used for tests that measure what a student has retained from school experiences.

_____ 10. This type of assessment includes a variety of instruments, including teacher-made tests.

_____ 11. When a teacher needs additional information about a subskill or task, the teacher may use this technique to pinpoint the exact difficulty.

_____ 12. Although this level may not represent mastery, tasks may be assigned at this level.

Part II

Match the following test names with the correct descriptions.

a. KeyMath—Revised
b. Woodcock Reading Mastery Tests—Revised
c. Tests of Written Spelling—4
d. Test of Mathematical Abilities—2
e. Test of Written Language—3
f. Gray Oral Reading Tests—Fourth Edition
g. Test of Reading Comprehension—Third Edition
h. Test of Adolescent and Adult Language

_____ 1. This test presents the items in domains.

_____ 2. This diagnostic test assesses accuracy, rate, and fluency.

_____ 3. This test includes a supplementary letter checklist.

_____ 4. This test might be used to determine more in-depth information about early reading skills.

_____ 5. This test would not be used to assess complex algebraic and calculus skills.

Part III

Answer the following questions.

1. Explain how fall and spring norm tables may provide a more accurate analysis of student performance. ______________________________
____
2. How does the analysis of individual domains on the KeyMath—R help in the planning for instructional intervention? ______________________
____
____
3. Explain the meaning of levels of significance for standard score differences. How does this analysis benefit the teacher in educational planning? ______________________________________
____

ANSWER KEY TO CHECK YOUR UNDERSTANDING

Activity 7.1

1. Raw score: 11
2.

	(11)
	(0)
	(11)
Basic Concepts Area	22

3.

	Percentile Ranks
Numeration	27
Rational Numbers	below 1
Geometry	16

4. Percentile Rank for Area 13
5. Grade Equivalent 2.4

Apply Your Knowledge. This student's percentile scores indicate significant weaknesses when compared with students in his same educational level. The student seems to have the greatest weakness in understanding rational numbers. His general math skills in basic concepts are weak.

Activity 7.2

1.			2.
89 Basic Concepts	<	92 Operations	NS
89 Basic Concepts	>	76 Applications	NS
92 Operations	>	76 Applications	.05

Apply Your Knowledge. This student has significant weakness in the applications area when compared with the operations area. This indicates that she seems to have difficulty when she is required to use math in an applied manner rather than when she is required to simply solve math problems such as math facts on a worksheet.

Activity 7.3

	Student's Domain Score	**Average Score**	**Domain Status**
Numbers 0–9	6	6	A
Numbers 0–99	5	4–5	A
Numbers 0–999	0	2–3	W
Multidigit numbers	0	—	—

Apply Your Knowledge. Based on this analysis, this student has weakness in the math area of basic concepts, specifically skills that involve understanding of the numbers 0–999. Since the skills up to 99 are within the average range, this student most likely has difficulty with the numbers between 99 and 999. The skills needed include the understanding of numerals greater than 99. The teacher should begin with 100.

Activity 7.4

This student made 46 errors in stories 1–4. This results in an estimated total error score of 114.

134 −	114	= Test 1	20
	Total	Raw	
	Errors	Score	

Apply Your Knowledge. Using a cutoff score allows you to discontinue testing when the student has missed too many items to continue. It allows you to estimate the number of errors the student would likely make if he continued through the entire subtest.

Activity 7.5

1. 124, column 26
2. 128
   120
3. Std. 116
   PR 86
4. PR 90 Std. 119
   PR 82 Std. 114
5. The range in which the student's true score would probably be found.

Apply Your Knowledge. The obtained score may not be an accurate estimate of the student's true score. Using the confidence bands, we can more accurately determine the student's true level of achievement. Instruction should begin within this range.

REFERENCES

Brown, V. L., Cronin, M. E., & McEntire, E. (1994). *Test of Mathematical Abilities* (2nd ed.). Austin, TX: Pro-Ed.

Brown, V. L., Hammill, D. D., & Wiederholt, J. L. (1995). *The Test of Reading Comprehension* (3rd ed.). Austin, TX: Pro-Ed.

Connolly, A. J. (1988). *KeyMath—Revised: A Diagnostic Inventory of Essential Mathematics.* Circle Pines, MN: American Guidance Service.

Cooter, R. (1989). Review of the Woodcock Reading Mastery Tests—Revised. In J. Conoley & J. Kramer (Eds.), *The tenth mental measurements yearbook* (pp. 910–913), Lincoln: University of Nebraska Press.

Dunn, L. M., & Dunn, L. M. (1997). *Peabody Picture Vocabulary Test—III.* Circle Pines, MN: American Guidance Service.

Eaves, R., Darch, C., Mann, L., & Vance, R. (1989). *The Cognitive Levels Test: Its relationship with reading and mathematics achievement.* Paper presented at the 67th Annual Council for Exceptional Children Convention, San Francisco.

Erickson, D. (1989). Review of the Test of Written Spelling—Revised Edition. In J. Conoley & J. Kramer (Eds.), *The tenth mental measurements yearbook* (pp. 860–861). Lincoln: The University of Nebraska Press.

Greenstein, J., & Strain, P. (1977). The utility of the KeyMath Diagnostic Arithmetic Test for adolescent learning disabled students. *Psychology in the Schools, 14,* 275–282.

Hammill, D. D., Brown, V. L., Larsen, S. C., & Wiederholt, J. L. (1994). *Test of Adolescent and Adult Language, Third Edition.* Austin, TX: Pro-Ed.

Hammill, D. D., & Hresko, W. P. (1994). *Comprehensive Scales of Student Abilities.* Austin, TX: Pro-Ed.

Hammill, D. D., & Larsen, S. C. (1996). *Test of Written Language.* Austin, TX: Pro-Ed.

Hammill, D. D., & Newcomer, P. L. (1997). *Test of Language Development—Intermediate: Third Edition.* Austin, TX: Pro-Ed.

Hammill, D. D., Pearson, N. A., & Wiederholt, J. L. (1996). *Comprehensive Test of Nonverbal Intelligence.* Austin, TX: Pro-Ed.

Hammill, D. D., & Larsen, S. C. (1999). *Test of Written Language, Third Edition.* Austin, TX: Pro-Ed.

Jaeger, R. (1989). Review of the Woodcock Reading Mastery Tests—Revised. In J. Conoley & J. Kramer (Eds.), *The tenth mental measurements yearbook* (pp. 913–916). Lincoln: University of Nebraska Press.

Larsen, S. C., Hammill, D. D., & Moats, L. C. (1999). *Test of Written Spelling—4.* Austin, TX: Pro-Ed.

Newcomer, P. L., & Hammill, D. D. (1997). *Test of Language Development—Primary: Third Edition.* Austin, TX: Pro-Ed.

Noyce, R. (1989). Review of the Test of Written Spelling—Revised Edition. In J. Conoley & J. Kramer (Eds.), *The tenth mental measurements yearbook* (pp. 860–861). Lincoln: The University of Nebraska Press.

Powell, G., Moore, D., & Callaway, B. (1981). A concurrent validity study of the Woodcock Word Comprehension Test. *Psychology in the Schools, 18,* 24–27.

Shriner, J., & Salvia, J. (1988). Chronic noncorrespondence between elementary math curricula and arithmetic tests. *Exceptional Children, 55,* 240–248.

Wiederholt, J. L., & Bryant, B. R. (2001). *Gray Oral Reading Tests* (4th ed.). Austin, TX: Pro-Ed.

Woodcock, R. W. (1987). *Woodcock Reading Mastery Tests—Revised.* Circle Pines, MN: American Guidance Service.

CHAPTER 8

Informal Assessment Techniques

Key Terms

informal assessment
criterion-referenced tests
probes
subskill
curriculum-based assessment
direct measurement
direct daily measurement
curriculum-based measurement
task analysis
subtask
error analysis
checklists
questionnaires
work samples
permanent products
performance assessment
authentic assessment
portfolio assessment

CHAPTER FOCUS

Teachers often need assessment methods that are more sensitive to the specific curriculum used in the classroom than standardized norm-referenced tests. Informal methods of assessment provide valuable information to assist with planning and effective interventions. The focus of this chapter is to present an overview of **informal assessment.**

informal assessment Nonstandardized methods of measuring student progress.

Norm-referenced assessment, the educational measurement method presented in the previous chapters, is the method that compares a student with the age or grade-level expectancies of a norm group. It is the standard method used in placement and classification decisions. The degree or amount of deviance from the expected norm is an important factor in determining whether a student meets the requirements of eligibility necessary to receive special education services (Shapiro, 1996).

Researchers have identified several problems in using norm-referenced assessment in the classroom. These weaknesses have influenced the development of other assessment techniques more suited to use in special education and regular education classrooms. These additional assessment methods are described as informal because they are not norm-referenced and, in most cases, not standardized. These methods assist the teacher and should be used with norm-referenced assessment in a multimethod approach to provide a complete assessment of the student's functioning levels (Bennett, 1982). This chapter presents methods other than norm-referenced assessment methods.

PROBLEMS OF NORM-REFERENCED ASSESSMENT

The weaknesses attributed to norm-referenced assessment include problems specific to the various instruments and problems with test administration and interpretation. Norm-referenced tests may not adequately represent material actually taught in a specific curriculum (Shapiro, 1996). In other words, items on norm-referenced tests may include content or skill areas not included in the student's curriculum. Salvia and Hughes (1990) wrote:

> The fundamental problem with using published tests is the test's content. If the content of the test—even content prepared by experts—does not match the content that is taught, the test is useless for evaluating what the student has learned from school instruction. (p. 8)

Good and Salvia (1988) studied the representation of reading curricula in norm-referenced tests and concluded that a deficient score on a norm-referenced reading test could actually represent the selection of a test with inadequate content validity for the current curriculum. Hultquist and Metzke (1993) determined that curriculum bias existed when using standardized achievement tests to measure the reading of survival words and reading and spelling skills in general. In addition, the frequent use of norm-referenced instruments may result in bias because limited numbers of alternate forms exist, creating the possibility of test wiseness among students (Fuchs, Tindal, & Deno, 1984; Shapiro, 1996).

Another study revealed that norm-referenced instruments are not as sensitive to academic growth as other instruments that are linked more directly to the actual classroom curriculum (Marston, Fuchs, & Deno, 1986). This means that norm-referenced tests may not measure small gains made in the classroom from week to week. According to Reynolds (1982), the psychometric assessment of students using traditional norm-referenced methods is fraught with many problems of bias, including cultural bias, which may result in test scores that reflect intimidation or communication problems rather than ability level. These difficulties in using norm-referenced testing for special education planning have led to the emergence of alternative methods of assessment.

CRITERION-REFERENCED ASSESSMENT

criterion-referenced tests Tests designed to accompany and measure a set of criteria or skill-mastery criteria.

Criterion-referenced tests compare the performance of a student to a given criterion. This criterion can be an established objective within the curriculum, an IEP criterion, or a criterion or standard of a published test instrument. The assessment that is designed to assess the student's ability to master the criterion is composed of many items across a very narrow band of skills. For example, a criterion-referenced test may be designed to assess a student's ability to read passages from the fifth-grade level reading series and answer comprehension questions with 85% accuracy. For this student, the criterion is an IEP objective. The assessment is designed with several passages and subsequent comprehension questions for each passage, all at the fifth-grade reading level. No other curriculum materials or content are included. The purpose of the assessment is to determine if the student can answer the comprehension questions with 85% accuracy. Criterion-related assessment that uses curriculum materials is only one type of curriculum-based assessment.

Although many criterion-referenced instruments are nonstandardized or perhaps designed by the teacher, a few criterion-referenced instruments are standardized. Some norm-referenced instruments yield criterion-related objectives or the possibility of adding criterion-related objectives with little difficulty. Examples of these instruments are the KeyMath—Revised (Connolly, 1988), K-TEA (Kaufman & Kaufman, 1985), and the WRMT—R (Woodcock, 1987).

Adapting standardized norm-referenced instruments to represent criterion-referenced testing is accomplished by writing educational objectives for the skills tested. To be certain that the skill or task has been adequately sampled,

Items missed	On the Word Attack subtest: the long a–e pattern in nonsense words—*gaked, straced;* the long i–e pattern in nonsense word—*quiles*
Deficit-skill	Decoding words with the long vowel-consonant-silent-*e* pattern
Probe	Decoding words orally to teacher: *cake, make, snake, rake, rate, lake, fake, like, bike, kite*
Criterion	Decode 10/10 words for mastery. Decode 8/10 words to 6/10 words for instructional level. Decode 5/10 words or fewer for failure level; assess prerequisite skill level: discrimination of long/short vowels (vowels: *a, i*).

Figure 8.1 Examples of criterion-referenced testing.

probes Tests used for in-depth assessment of the mastery of a specific skill or subskill.

however, the educator may need to prepare additional academic **probes** to measure the student's skills. Objectives written for skills tested or items on a norm-referenced instrument may represent long-term learning rather than short-term gains. This determination will be based on the amount of the material or the scope of the task tested by the norm-referenced test. Figure 8.1 illustrates how an item from the WRMT—R might be expanded to represent criterion-referenced testing.

In addition to adapting published norm-referenced instruments for criterion-related assessment, educators may use published criterion-referenced test batteries, such as the Brigance Inventories, that present specific criteria and objectives. Teachers may also create their own criterion-referenced tests.

THE BRIGANCE INVENTORIES

The Brigance (Brigance, 1977, 1981, 1991) is a standardized assessment system that provides criterion-referenced assessment at various skill levels. Each battery contains numerous subtests, and each item is referenced by objectives that may be used in developing IEPs. The Brigance system includes three criterion-referenced instruments for the various age groups served in special education. In each system, the educator should select only the areas and items of interest to identify specific strengths and weaknesses. The Brigance instruments should not be administered in their entirety.

Instruments. The *Brigance Diagnostic Inventory of Early Development—Revised* (Brigance, 1991) is an inventory within the system that was designed to assess the skills and development of children from birth to age 7. Many of

Figure 8.2 Areas tested by the Brigance Diagnostic Inventory of Basic Skills.

I. Readiness
II. Reading
- **A.** Word Recognition
- **B.** Reading
- **C.** Word Analysis
- **D.** Vocabulary

III. Language Arts
- **A.** Handwriting
- **B.** Grammar Mechanics
- **C.** Spelling
- **D.** Reference Skills

IV. Math
- **A.** Grade Level
- **B.** Numbers
- **C.** Operations
- **D.** Measurement

the subtests concern developmental areas of motor development. This test provides criterion-related measurement for self-help skills, prespeech and speech development, general knowledge, social and emotional development, reading readiness, manuscript writing, and beginning math.

The *Brigance Diagnostic Inventory of Basic Skills* (Brigance, 1977) was designed for use with elementary-school-aged students. This criterion-referenced inventory includes many areas and subtests within each area. Figure 8.2 lists the various areas and subtests for this level of the Brigance system.

subskill A small part of a skill, used in task analysis.

For each of the areas listed in Figure 8.2, several **subskill** areas are assessed. The subskill areas for Word Analysis are illustrated in Figure 8.3. For each of the items assessed within the subskill areas, objectives are included. When the student fails to show mastery of a particular subskill, the objective for that subskill will be used in educational planning. The objective for subskill C-10, "initial clusters visually," is shown in Figure 8.4.

The Brigance system comprises large, multiple-ring notebook binders that contain both student and examiner pages. The pages may be turned to resemble an easel format, or the pages to be administered may be removed from the binder. A warning included in the test cautions the examiner to select the necessary subtests and avoid overtesting.

The *Brigance Diagnostic Inventory of Essential Skills* (Brigance, 1981) is the part of the system designed for intermediate- and secondary-age students. This test contains subtest areas that allow criterion-referenced testing in the areas of academics, everyday survival skills, and vocational skills. The individual subskill areas for one subtest of the Brigance for secondary students are shown in Figure 8.5.

Figure 8.3 Subskill areas for Word Analysis tested by the Brigance Diagnostic Inventory of Basic Skills.

II. Reading
- C. Word Analysis
  - C-1, Auditory discrimination
  - C-2, Initial consonant sounds auditorily
  - C-3, Initial consonant sounds visually
  - C-4, Substitution of initial consonant sounds
  - C-5, Ending sounds auditorily
  - C-6, Vowels
  - C-7, Short vowel sounds
  - C-8, Long vowel sounds
  - C-9, Initial clusters auditorily
  - C-10, Initial clusters visually
  - C-11, Substitution of initial cluster sounds
  - C-12, Digraphs and diphthongs
  - C-13, Phonetic irregularities
  - C-14, Common endings of rhyming words
  - C-15, Suffixes
  - C-16, Prefixes
  - C-17, Meaning of prefixes
  - C-18, Number of syllables auditorily
  - C-19, Syllabication concepts

Technical Data. Because the Brigance tests are not norm-referenced, norming information is not provided. The tests were field tested and appear to have content validity. The manual includes suggested grade levels to provide teachers with an idea of where to place students in classroom curriculum materials. The suggested grade levels are not norm-referenced grade equivalents and should not be used as a basis for eligibility decisions.

TEACHER-MADE CRITERION-REFERENCED TESTS

curriculum-based assessment Using content from the currently used curriculum to assess student progress.

direct measurement Measuring progress by using the same instructional materials or tasks that are used in the classroom.

Instead of relying on published instruments, classroom teachers may develop their own criterion-referenced tests. This type of assessment allows the teacher to directly link the assessment to the currently used curriculum. By writing the criterion to be used as the basis for determining when the student has reached or passed the objective, the teacher has created a criterion-referenced test. When the test is linked directly to the curriculum, it also becomes a **curriculum-based assessment** device and may be referred to as **direct measurement.** For example, the teacher may use the

INITIAL CLUSTERS VISUALLY

SKILL: Can articulate correct sound when cluster is presented visually.

DIRECTIONS: Point to the first letters (sh).

Say: *Look at these letters. Tell me the sound they have when they are together at the beginning of a word.*

If the student does not understand, explain the first blend.

Say: *These letters have the sound of sh as in shock or shape.*

See NOTE #2 and the next page for alternate method of administration.

DISCONTINUE: After three consecutive errors.

TIME: 10 seconds per response.

ACCURACY: Give credit for each correct response.

NOTES:

1. You may wish to check the student's understanding of the voiced and unvoiced "th."

   Say: *Can you tell me the other sound "th" makes?, after the student has given one sound.*

2. An alternate method of assessing this skill is to present the initial clusters in combination with a vowel. The results of the alternate method may have more validity if the student has been taught by a method which always presents the clusters in combination with a vowel such as Duggins or *Words in Color.* See next page for alternate administration.

OBJECTIVE: When presented with a list of 33 blends and digraphs (clusters) listed in an order commonly taught, the student will indicate the sound ______ (quantity) the consonants have or make in the initial position.

Figure 8.4 Objective for "initial clusters visually," subskill C-10 of the Brigance Diagnostic Inventory of Basic Skills. (*Source:* From *Brigance Diagnostic Inventory of Basic Skills* (p. 56) by A. H. Brigance, 1977, N. Billerica, MA: Curriculum Associates. Copyright by Curriculum Associates. Reprinted by permission.)

Figure 8.5
Subskills of Travel and Transportation of the Brigance Diagnostic Inventory of Essential Skills.

X. Travel and Transportation
- X-1, Traffic signs
- X-2, Traffic symbols
- X-3, Car parts and vocabulary
- X-4, Identifies car parts
- X-5, Application for driver's instruction permit
- X-6, Auto safety rating scale
- X-7, Gas mileage and cost
- X-8, Mileage table
- X-9, Bus schedule and map of route
- X-10, Road maps

scope and sequence chart from the reading series or math text to write the objectives that will be used in the criterion-related assessment.

Research supports the use of criterion-referenced assessment in the classroom and other settings (Glaser, 1963; Hart & Scuitto, 1996; McCauley, 1996). The first questions regarding the use of criterion-referenced assessment were raised in the literature in 1963 by Glaser. The issues Glaser raised seemed to be current issues in the debate about better measurement techniques to accurately determine student progress. Glaser stated that the knowledge educators attempt to provide to students exists on a continuum ranging from no acquisition to mastery. He stated that the criterion can be established at any level where the teacher wishes to assess the student's mastery or acquisition. This type of measurement is used to determine the student's position along the continuum of acquisition or mastery.

Hart and Scuitto concluded that using criterion-referenced assessment is practical, has social validity, and may assist with educational accountability. This type of assessment can be adapted in other areas such as in assessing a child's speech and language development (McCauley, 1996). Criterion-referenced assessment has been shown to be useful in screening entering kindergarten and first-grade students for school readiness (Campbell, Schellinger, & Beer, 1991). This method of assessment has also been used to determine appropriate adaptations for vocational assessments to assist in planning realistic job accommodations (Lusting & Saura, 1996). In a review of criterion-referenced assessment during the past 30 years, Millman (1994) concludes that to represent a true understanding of the student's ability, this type of assessment requires "item density." He suggests that to accurately assess whether a student has mastered a domain or area, the assessments need to have many items per domain. Teachers who construct their own criterion-referenced assessments should be certain that enough items are required of the student to determine an accurate level of mastery of the domain.

One difficulty that teachers may have in constructing criterion-referenced tests is arriving at the exact criterion for determining whether the student has passed the objective or criterion. Shapiro (1989) suggested that one quantitative method of determining mastery would be to use a normative comparison of the performance, such as using a specific task that 80% of the peers in the class or grade have mastered. The teacher may wish to use a criterion that is associated with a standard set by the school grading policy. For example, answering 75% of the items correctly might indicate that the student needs improvement; 85% correct might be an average performance; and 95% correct might represent mastery. Or, the teacher might decide to use a criterion that the student can easily understand and chart. For example, getting 5 out of 7 items correct indicates the student could continue with the same objective or skill; getting 7 out of 7 items correct indicates the student is ready to move up to the next skill level. Often, the teacher sets the criterion using logical reasoning rather than a quantitative measurement (Shapiro, 1989).

Other considerations for establishing criteria for mastery have been suggested by Evans and Evans (1986):

> Does passing the test mean that the student is proficient and will maintain the skills?
>
> Is the student ready to progress to the next level in the curriculum?
>
> Will the student be able to generalize and apply the skills outside the classroom?
>
> Would the student pass the mastery test if it were given at a later date? (p. 10)

The teacher may wish to use the following indications for establishing criterion-referenced tests:

More than 95% = mastery of objective

90% to 95% = instructional level

76% to 89% = difficult level

Less than 76% = failure level

In Activity 8.1, you will determine whether the student responses illustrated indicate mastery of the subskill assessed by the Basic Skills test.

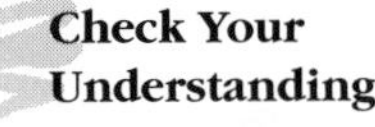
Check Your Understanding

Complete Activity 8.1.

ACTIVITY 8.1

Look at the student responses on the Brigance sample in Figure 8.6. Has the student mastered the objective?

Apply Your Knowledge

How is scoring this instrument different from scoring a norm-referenced instrument? ____

____

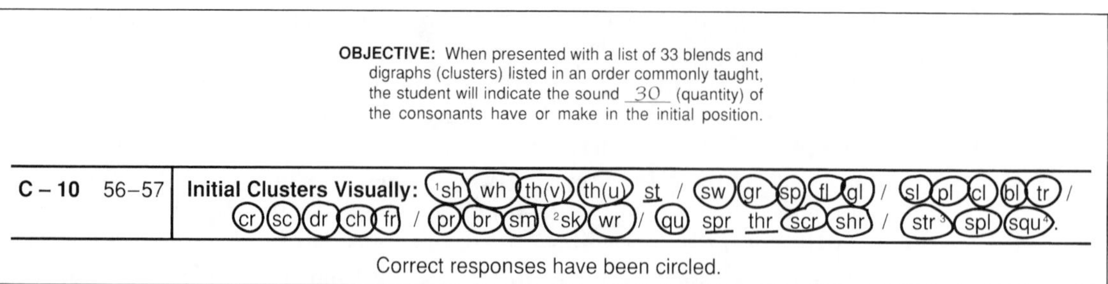

OBJECTIVE: When presented with a list of 33 blends and digraphs (clusters) listed in an order commonly taught, the student will indicate the sound 30 (quantity) of the consonants have or make in the initial position.

C – 10	56–57	**Initial Clusters Visually:** sh wh th(v) th(u) st / sw gr sp fl gl / sl pl cl bl tr / cr sc dr ch fr / pr br sm sk wr / qu spr thr scr shr / str spl squ.

Correct responses have been circled.

Figure 8.6 Sample student responses for Brigance subskill C-10. (*Source:* From *Brigance Diagnostic Inventory of Essential Skills* (p. v) by A. H. Brigance, 1981, N. Billerica, MA: Curriculum Associates. Copyright 1981 by Curriculum Associates. Reprinted by permission.)

Similar standards may be set by the individual teacher. The teacher may wish to adjust objectives when the student performs with 76% to 89% accuracy and when the student performs with more than 95% accuracy. It is important to remember that students with learning difficulties should experience a high ratio of success during instruction to increase the possibility of positive reinforcement during the learning process. Therefore, it may be better to design objectives that promote higher success rates.

Figure 8.7 illustrates a criterion-referenced test written by a teacher for addition facts with sums of 10 or less. The objective, or criterion, is included at the top of the test.

The skills included in Activity 8.2 resemble those that would be included in a beginning level of a reading series. In this activity, you will select the information from one skill to write an objective and construct a

OBJECTIVE

John will correctly answer 9 out of 10 addition problems with sums of 10 or less.

5	3	8	9	4	6	7	2	4	1
+2	+2	+2	+1	+5	+2	+3	+4	+3	+6

Performance: ________

Objective passed: ________ Continue on current objective: ________

Figure 8.7 Criterion-referenced test of addition facts.

short criterion-referenced test. The test should measure the student's mastery of the objective.

Using criterion-referenced assessment may provide better information about student achievement levels and mastery of academic objectives; however, the criterion-referenced test may not always adequately represent growth within a given curriculum. To more effectively measure student progress within a curriculum, teachers should rely on measures that use that curriculum, such as curriculum-based assessment and direct measurement.

CURRICULUM-BASED ASSESSMENT AND DIRECT MEASUREMENT

direct daily measurement The daily measurement of progress using instructional materials.

For the very best measure of how much a student has mastered in a curriculum, assessment items should be composed of material from the curriculum, or the items should be the actual curriculum tasks used daily in the instruction (**direct daily measurement**). The differences between these two types of assessment are minor but may be understood by this example: A second-grade math curriculum-based assessment will contain items from a second-grade math text used in the classroom instruction; a direct daily measurement of progress may be the assigned daily math problems from the text used in class or a sample of problems used in daily work. These daily measures may include teacher-made tests, classwork, independent work, homework, quizzes, and so on.

In designing curriculum-based measurement, the teacher must first determine what skills or concepts are to be developed from the instruction (Rosenfield & Kurait, 1990). These are the target behaviors that the teacher seeks to increase; and the measurement of these target skills, using the core curriculum, is curriculum-based measurement. The educator also must understand the scope of the curriculum and set educational goals for the student based on the curriculum. If there is an instructional mismatch, the educator should determine prerequisite competencies needed for the task and assess which competencies the student has mastered and which ones are weaknesses. Progress must be measured frequently throughout the instruction so that effective interventions can be implemented. According to Shinn, Nolet, and Knutson (1990), most curriculum-based measures should include the following tasks:

1. In reading, students read aloud from basal readers for 1 minute. The number of words read correctly per minute constitutes the basic decision-making metric.
2. In spelling, students write words that are dictated at specific intervals (either 5, 7, or 10 seconds) for 2 minutes. The number of correct letter sequences and words spelled correctly are counted.
3. In written expression, students write a story for 3 minutes after being given a story starter (e.g., "Pretend you are playing on the playground and

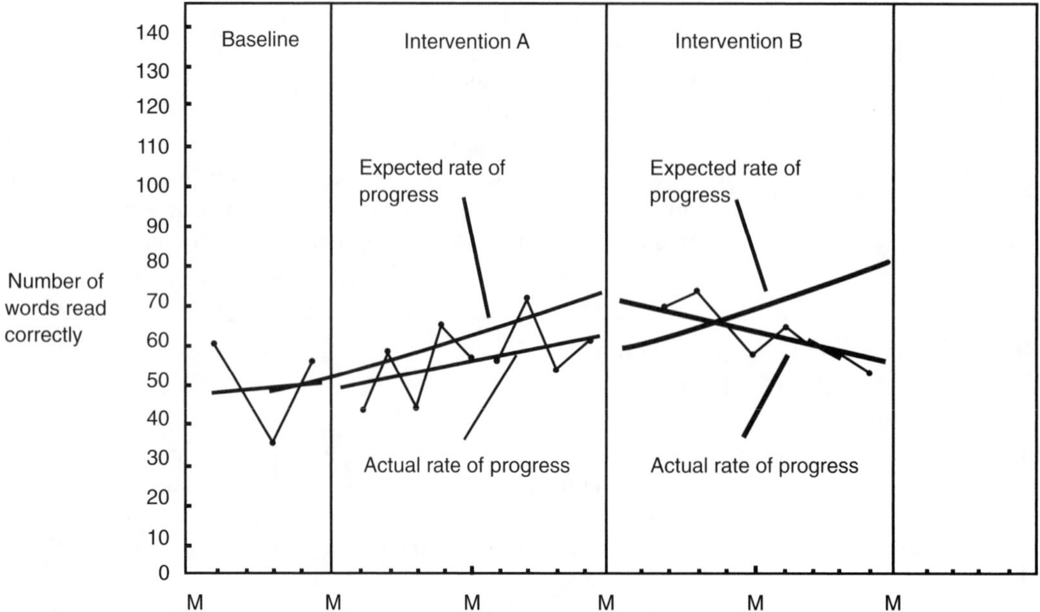

Figure 8.8 Curriculum-based measurement data for two interventions used with one student. (*Source:* From *Best Practices in School Psychology—II* (p. 301) by A. Thomas and J. Grimes, 1990, Silver Spring, MD: National Association of School Psychologists. Copyright 1990 by the National Association of School Psychologists. Reprinted by permission of the publisher.)

a spaceship lands. A little green person comes out and calls your name and . . . "). The number of words written, spelled correctly, and/or correct word sequences are counted.

4. In mathematics, students write answers to computational problems via 2-minute probes. The number of correctly written digits is counted. (p. 290)

Figure 8.8 presents an example of how curriculum-based measurement is used to determine when an instructional change is indicated. The student in Figure 8.8 failed to make the projected progress and therefore needs an educational change to progress within the curriculum.

Curriculum-based assessment and direct daily measurement of progress have been found to noticeably affect academic achievement when the results are used to modify instructional planning. A brief review of many years of research studies supports the use of curriculum-based measurement for several reasons.

When curriculum-based assessment was used for instructional programming, students were found to have somewhat greater gains than when it was used for testing purposes alone (Fuchs, Fuchs, & Hamlett, 1989). The more effective teachers were sensitive to the results of the assessment, they used them to adapt or modify instruction rather than merely using curriculum-based assessment as a measurement device, such as grading or establishing a working level for IEP objectives.

The use of curriculum-based assessment has been linked to better understanding by students of expectancies of academic performance (Fuchs, Butterworth, & Fuchs, 1989). Students in this study indicated that they received more feedback than students not receiving curriculum-based assessment. Research has also indicated that teachers using curriculum-based assessment tended to set goals with higher expectations than did teachers who were not using these methods (Fuchs et al., 1989). Use of curriculum-based assessment with instructional intervention strategies provided to general education teachers suggested promise in increasing the achievement of low-achieving students and students in general education classes with learning disabilities (Fuchs, Fuchs, Hamlett, Phillips, & Bentz, 1994). One study applied curriculum-based assessment in the general education classroom as part of a functional behavioral analysis (Roberts, Marshall, Nelson, & Albers, 2001). In this study, the use of curriculum-based assessment to determine appropriate instructional levels resulted in decreased off-task behaviors. When applied in this manner, the curriculum-based assessment enabled the instruction to be tailored and therefore may be viewed as a prereferral strategy.

Curriculum-based assessment has been studied as one method of determining special education eligibility (Marston, Mirkin, & Deno, 1984). Curriculum-based assessment was found to be an accurate screening measure for referral for special education and was less influenced by teacher variables (Marston et al., 1984). Its use appeared to result in less bias as evidenced by more equity in male-female ratio of referrals (Marston et al., 1984). Canter (1991) supported using curriculum-based assessment to determine eligibility for special education services by comparing the student's progress in the classroom curriculum with the expectations within the average range for the grade level. The student's actual progress may indicate the need for special education intervention.

CURRICULUM-BASED MEASUREMENT

curriculum-based measurement Frequent measurement comparing student's actual progress with expected rate of progress.

Curriculum-based measurement (CBM) has been studied as a possible method to identify students in special education placements who are ready to move back into the general education setting (Shinn, Habedank, Rodden-Nord, & Knutson, 1993). Using this method may help general education teachers smoothly integrate students from special education environments by providing data to assess progress and use in planning interventions. It also has been suggested that curriculum-based measures might be beneficial in measuring the effects of treatment by medication of students with attention disorders (Stoner, Carey, Ikeda, & Shinn, 1994). Curriculum-based measures for math and reading have been found useful for assessing medication effects when academic performance is of concern. Stoner and colleagues (1994) replicated an initial study, and evidence was found to suggest that CBM may be one measure of determining the effect of methylphenidate on academic performance. Additional research in this area may add insight in the emerging field of effective treatment of students with attention deficit disorder.

Another study found that when CBM was combined with peer tutoring, the students in a general classroom setting made significantly greater achievement gains (Phillips, Hamlett, Fuchs, & Fuchs, 1993). Meherns and Clarizio (1993) assert that CBM is helpful in determining when instruction should be adapted, but it does not necessarily provide information about what to change or how to provide the instruction. They advocate using CBM with other diagnostic assessment.

Baker and Good (1995) found that CBM used in assessing reading was as reliable and valid when used with bilingual students as when used with English-only students. They also found that using CBM was sensitive in measuring the reading progress made by bilingual students.

In their sample of fourth-grade students, Fuchs and Fuchs (1996) found that when curriculum-based measurement is combined with performance assessment, teachers have a more in-depth assessment, which results in better instructional decisions. Another study found that general education teachers who employed CBM designed better instructional programs and had students who experienced greater gains in achievement than did teachers who did not use CBM (Fuchs et al., 1994). Allinder (1995) found that teachers who used CBM and had high teacher efficacy set high student goals, and their students had significantly greater growth. In the Allinder study, special education teachers using CBM who had greater teaching efficacy set more goals for their students. Teachers who were asked to compare CBM with norm-referenced assessments rated CBM as a more acceptable method of assessment (Eckert, Shapiro, & Lutz, 1995). Another study suggested that students enjoy participating in CBM and that their active participation in this process may increase their feelings of responsibility for learning (Davis, Fuchs, Fuchs, & Whinnery, 1995).

Teachers can easily adapt curriculum-based assessment methods to include direct daily measurement. Although several methods of developing precise direct daily measurement have been described (Howell & Morehead, 1987; Shapiro, 1996), teachers may construct their own direct measurements from curriculum materials used in the classroom.

CAUTIONS

Several researchers issue statements of caution when employing curriculum-based measurement. Like other types of assessment, curriculum-based measurement may be more useful in some situations and less useful in others. Heshusius (1991) cautions that curriculum-based assessment may not allow for measurement of some important constructs in education, such as assessment of creativity, areas of interest, and original ideas. Hintze, Shapiro, and Lutz (1994) found that CBM was more sensitive in measuring progress when used to assess progress in traditional basal readers rather than literature samples, indicating that the materials contribute to difficulty in accurate measurement. Meherns and Clarizio (1993) suggest that CBM should be used as part of the comprehensive assessment with other measures because of continuing concerns about reliability and validity of CBM.

Check Your Understanding

Complete Activity 8.2.

ACTIVITY 8.2

Read the following list of skills necessary to complete level P1 of the Best in the Country Reading Series, adopted by all school systems in the world. Answer the questions that follow.

P1 Skills

- Associates pictures with story content.
- Follows sequence of story by turning pages at appropriate times.
- Associates the following letters with their sounds: b, d, c, g, h, j, k, l, m, n, p, q, r, s, t.
- Can match letters (from 3) to pictures of objects that begin with the same sounds.
- Can correctly sequence the following stories:
  "A School Day": Mary gets on the bus, goes to school. George brings a rabbit to class; the rabbit gets out of the cage. Mary helps George catch the rabbit.
  "The Field Trip": Ralph invites the class to visit his farm. Sue, John, Mary, and George go on the trip. The animals are (a) a chicken, (b) a goat, (c) a cow, and (d) a horse. The goat follows the class; the goat tries to eat Ralph's shirt.
- Can name all characters in preceding stories.
- Can summarize stories and answer short comprehension questions.

Answer the Following

1. Select one P1 skill and write a behaviorally stated objective that includes the criterion acceptable for passing the objective. ______
   ____
2. Design a short criterion-referenced test to measure the skill objective written in number 1 of P1-level reading series. ______
   ____

Apply Your Knowledge

Write a behaviorally stated objective for students reading this chapter.

____

____

TASK ANALYSIS AND ERROR ANALYSIS

task analysis Analyzing a task by breaking it down into the smallest steps or skills.

subtask Small units of a task used to complete a task analysis.

Teachers often use task and error analyses without realizing that an analysis of student progress has been completed. **Task analysis** involves breaking down a task into the smallest steps necessary to complete the task. The steps actually reflect subskills, or **subtasks,** which the student must complete before finishing a task. In academic work, many of these subskills and tasks form a hierarchy of skills that build throughout the school years. As students master skills and tasks, they face new, more advanced curricular tasks that depend on the earlier skills. In mathematics, for example, understanding of numerals and one-to-one correspondence must precede understanding of basic addition facts. A student must conquer addition and subtraction before tackling multiplication and division. Therefore, a thorough task analysis of skill deficits, followed by an informal assessment, may provide the teacher with information about what the student has or has not mastered.

Check Your Understanding

Complete Activity 8.3.

ACTIVITY 8.3

Answer the following questions.

1. Look at the following task analysis. Can you identify other smaller steps, or subskills, that should be included? Write the additional steps in the spaces provided.

   Skill: Adding numbers greater than 10
   Adds numbers 0–10 with sums greater than 10.
   Adds number facts 1–9 with sums greater than 10.
   Adds number facts 1–9 with sums less than 10.
   Adds number facts 1–8 with sums less than 10.
   Identifies numbers 1–10.
   Can count objects 1–10.

Additional subskills ______________________________

____

2. Write a task analysis for the following skills.

   Skill: Recognizes initial consonant sounds and their association with the consonant letters of the alphabet.

Necessary subskills ______________________________

____

Apply Your Knowledge

Select one of the subskills and write an idea for instruction. ________

____

error analysis Analyzing a student's learning problems by determining error patterns.

Error analysis is an assessment method that a teacher can use with formal, informal, and direct measures, such as classwork. This is a method of discovering patterns of errors. A teacher may notice that a student who understands difficult multiplication facts, such as those of 11s, 12s, and 13s, continues to miss computation problems of those facts. With a careful error analysis of responses on a teacher-made test, the teacher determines that the student has incorrectly lined up the multiplicands. The student understands the math fact but has made a mistake in the mechanics of the operation.

One way that teachers can perform error analyses is to become familiar with the scope and sequence of the classroom curriculum materials. The teacher guides that accompany classroom materials are a good starting place to develop a thorough understanding of the materials and how to perform an error analysis of the students' responses. For example, a basal reading series may provide a sequence chart of the sounds presented in a given book at a specific level. Using this sequence chart, the teacher can first determine which errors the student has made and then analyze the possible reason for the errors. Perhaps the student's errors are all errors in words with vowel combinations (such as *ea, ie, ee, oa*). The teacher can next perform a task analysis of the prerequisite skills the child needs to master those sounds and be able to decode words with those sounds.

Task analysis is a breaking down of the actual task or response expected to determine which prerequisite skills are lacking or have not been mastered. Error analysis often precedes task analysis because the teacher may need to look for a pattern of errors to determine exactly which task needs additional analysis.

Check Your Understanding

Complete Activities 8.4 and 8.5.

ACTIVITY 8.4

1. Look carefully at the student's responses in the following work sample from a language class. Analyze the errors the student made. Write your analysis in the space provided.

Items missed	On the Word Attack subtest: the long a–e pattern in nonsense words—*gaked, straced;* the long i–e patter in nonsense word—*quiles*
Deficit-skill	Decoding words with the long vowel-consonant-silent pattern
Probe	Decoding words orally to teacher: *cake, make, snake, rake, rate, lake, fake, like, bike, k*
Criterion	Decode 10/10 words for mastery. Decode 8/10 words to 6/10 words for instructional lev Decode 5/10 words or fewer for failure level; assess ı req isite skill level: discrimination of long/short vowel

2. What prerequisite skills may not have been mastered by this student? ______________________

Apply Your Knowledge

Use these prerequisite skills to write a behavioral objective for one of the errors you analyzed.

Error: __________ Behavioral objective: __________

Check Your Understanding

ACTIVITY 8.5

Use the terms discussed in the chapter to complete the following sentences.

1. Using material from the curriculum content in test items is called __________.
2. Using informal assessment composed of actual class-work curriculum materials is called __________.
3. A teacher who adds behavioral objectives following the analysis of test items on a standardized norm-referenced test has adapted the instrument to reflect __________ testing.
4. When a student has not mastered a specific skill, the teacher may wish to test the student more thoroughly on the one skill by developing a __________.
5. When a teacher assesses daily from the curriculum content, the assessment is called __________.
6. Assessing the subskills, or substeps, within a task is referred to as __________.
7. Analyzing the types of errors made on a test or on student work samples is called __________.
8. Teacher-made quizzes, curriculum-based assessment, criterion-referenced assessment, class assignments, and tests are all types of __________ assessment.

Apply Your Knowledge

Why would teachers prefer informal tests for measuring progress rather than standardized tests? ______________________

____.

TEACHER-MADE TESTS

Many of the types of informal assessment described in this chapter are measures that can be designed by teachers. A study by Marso and Pigge (1991) found that teachers made several types of errors in test construction and tended to test items only at the knowledge level. This study also found that the number of years of experience teaching did not make a significant difference in the number and type of errors made in test construction. The types of items developed by teachers in this study included short response, matching, completion, true-false, and multiple choice, with essay items used infrequently. In constructing tests, these teachers made the most errors in matching items, followed by completion, essay, and true-false. Teachers may write test items using different levels of learning, although many teachers use items at the knowledge level because they are easier to write. Such items require the student to merely recall, recognize, or match the material. Higher order thinking skills are needed to assess a student's ability to sequence, apply information, analyze, synthesize, infer, or deduct. These items may be more difficult and time-consuming to construct.

In addition to being aware of the level of difficulty of test items, teachers must be aware of types of errors made in constructing items, and how the items are associated on a test. Some of the most common types of errors made in Marso and Pigge's study are presented in Figure 8.9.

Check Your Understanding

Complete Activity 8.6.

ACTIVITY 8.6

Use the information presented in Figure 8.9 to determine the errors made in the following examples of teacher-made test items. Write a corrected item for each of the following items:

TRUE-FALSE ITEMS

T F 1. It is not true that curriculum-based assessment can be developed by the classroom teacher.

T F 2. Compared to norm-referenced assessment and other types of assessment used in general and special education to assess the classroom performance of students, curriculum-based assessment may be more sensitive to assessing the current classroom performance of students.

MULTIPLE-CHOICE ITEMS

1. In the assessment of students to determine the individual needs of learners, what types of assessment may be used?
   a. norm-referenced tests, curriculum-based assessment, teacher-made instruments

Matching Items

Columns not titled

"Once, more than once, or not at all" not used in directions to prevent elimination

Response column not ordered

Directions do not specify basis for match

Answering procedures not specified

Elimination due to equal numbers

Columns exceed 10 items

Multiple-Choice Items

Alternatives not in columns or rows

Incomplete stems

Negative words not emphasized or avoided

"All or none of above" not appropriately used

Needless repetitions of alternatives

Presence of specific determiners in alternatives

Verbal associations between alternative and stem

Essay Exercises

Response expectations unclear

Scoring points not realistically limited

Optional questions provided

Restricted question not provided

Ambiguous words used

Opinion or feelings requested

Problem Exercises

Items not sampling understanding of content

No range of easy to difficult problems

Degree of accuracy not requested

Nonindependent items

Use of objective items when calculation preferable

Figure 8.9 Most common test format construction errors. (*Source:* Adapted with permission from Ronald Marso and Fred Pigge, 1991, "An Analysis of Teacher-Made Tests: Item Types, Cognitive Demands, and Item Construction Errors," *Contemporary Educational Psychology, 16,* pp. 284–285. Copyright 1991 by Academic Press.)

Completion Items

Not complete interrogative sentence

Blanks in statement, "puzzle"

Textbook statements with words left out

More than a single idea or answer called for

Question allows more than a single answer

Requests trivia versus significant data

True-False Items

Required to write response, time waste

Statements contain more than a single idea

Negative statements used

Presence of a specific determiner

Statement is not question, give-away item

Needless phrases present, too lengthy

Interpretive Exercises

Objective response form not used

Can be answered without data present

Errors present in response items

Data presented unclear

Test Format

Absence of directions

Answering procedures unclear

Items not consecutively numbered

Inadequate margins

Answer space not provided

No space between items

Figure 8.9 continued.

b. norm-referenced instruments, curriculum-based assessment, teacher-made tests, classroom observations, probes
c. any of the above
d. only a and b
e. only a and d
f. none of the above

2. The results of assessment may assist the team in making an:
a. goal
b. IEP
c. objectives
d. decision

Apply Your Knowledge

Use the information in Figure 8.9 to write matching test items for the terms: curriculum-based assessment, direct assessment, and teacher-made tests.

____

____

OTHER INFORMAL METHODS OF ACADEMIC ASSESSMENT

checklists Lists of academic or behavioral skills that must be mastered by the student.

questionnaires Questions about a student's behavior or academic concerns that may be answered by the student or by the parent or teacher.

work samples Samples of a student's work; one type of permanent product.

permanent products Products made by the student that may be analyzed for academic or behavioral interventions.

Teachers employ many other informal assessment methods to monitor the academic progress of students. Some of these methods combine the techniques of error analysis, task analysis, direct measurement, curriculum-based assessment, probes, and criterion-related assessment. These methods include making **checklists** and **questionnaires** and evaluating student **work samples** and **permanent products.**

Teacher-made checklists may be constructed by following an error analysis, identifying the problem area, and completing a task analysis. For each subskill that is problematic for the student, the teacher may construct a probe, or more in-depth assessment instrument. Probes may appear to be short quizzes and may be timed to determine content mastery. For example, a teacher may give 10 subtraction facts for students to complete in 2 minutes. If the teacher uses items from the curriculum to develop the probe, the probe will be curriculum-based. The teacher may also establish a criterion for mastery of each probe or in-depth teacher-made test. This added dimension creates a criterion-referenced assessment device. The criterion may be 9 out of 10 problems added correctly. To effectively monitor the growth of the student, the teacher may set criteria for mastery each day as direct measurement techniques are employed. As the student meets the mastery criterion established for an objective, the teacher checks off the subskill on the checklist and progresses to the next more difficult item on the list of subskills.

Another informal method designed by teachers is an interview or questionnaire method. Figures 8.10 and 8.11 represent, respectively, a teacher-constructed interview form and a checklist that includes behavioral observations of the student (Wiener, 1986).

Teachers can also gather helpful information by informally reviewing students' work samples—actual samples of work completed by the student. Samples can include daily work, homework, tests, and quizzes. Work samples are one kind of permanent product. Other permanent products evaluated by the teacher include projects, posters, and art.

INFORMAL ASSESSMENT OF READING

Comprehension, decoding, and fluency are the broad areas of reading that teachers assess using informal methods. Comprehension is the ability to derive meaning from written language, whereas decoding is the ability to associate sounds and symbols. Fluency is the rate and ease with which a student reads orally.

Howell and Morehead (1987) presented several methods to informally assess comprehension:

1. Answering questions. After reading a passage, the student answers questions about the passage. These questions may focus on details, sequence of events in the story, or the main idea of the story. This method provides a general screening of which students are able to comprehend written material and which students are not. It may be difficult to obtain diagnostic information unless the questions are carefully constructed by the teacher.
2. Paraphrasing. The student restates the story in her own words.
3. Story retelling. This technique requires that the student read the story and then retell it using the same words that were used in the story.
4. Cloze. The student does not read the story in advance. The teacher selects a passage and rewrites it with selected words left out. The first and last sentences in the passage have all original words. The student must read the passage and supply the missing words.
5. Maze. As in the cloze method, sentences are written with missing words. In this method, however, the student selects the correct response from words provided beneath each blank. The level of difficulty may be increased by making the choices of words more similar; thus, the student must discriminate between words with like meanings.
6. Sentence verification. The teacher selects the sentences for the assessment and, for each sentence, writes three other sentences. The student must select the sentence that has the same meaning as the original sentence.
7. Vocabulary. Sentences are written with synonyms provided for specific words. The student selects the word, from three choices, with the same meaning.

Variations of this approach are shown in Figure 8.12.

Student Name: _______ Date: _______ Examiner: _______

The Task Environment

1. How did you select the topic/book? _______
2. Are you interested in it?
   very interested _______ somewhat interested _______ not at all interested _______
3. What did the teacher do when giving out the assignment? _______

	Yes	No	Notes
Probes: • give oral guidelines	_______	_______	
• give written guidelines	_______	_______	
• select the topic/book	_______	_______	
• provide structure	_______	_______	
• increase your interest	_______	_______	
• specify length	_______	_______	

4. Who are you expecting to read the essay? _______

Previous Knowledge

5. Have you previously been taught to write essays/projects/reports?
   Yes _______ No _______ What were you taught? _______
6. What did you know about the topic before you started? _______
7. What do you think are the expectations of your reader/teacher? _______

Planning

8. Did you have a plan for writing the essay/project/report: Yes _______ No _______
   What was it? _______
9. When did you begin thinking about the topic? _______
10. Did you do any research? Yes _______ No _______ What resources did you use? _______
11. How much time did you have for writing (i.e., between date assignment was given and assignment due)? ___ days. How did you use that time? _______
12. Did you make an outline? Yes _______ No _______ What kind of thinking did you do first? _______
    What was your organizational plan (outline)? _______

Translating/Reviewing

13. How many drafts did you write? 1 _______ 2 _______ 3 _______
14. How long did it take to write each one?
    1. _______ hrs/mins 2. _______ hrs/mins 3. _______ hrs/mins
15. Did you write your first draft with pencil? _______ pen? _______ typewriter? _______
    word processor? _______
16. Did you double space your first draft: Yes _______ No _______
17. Did you read your first draft over? Yes _______ No _______ What kind of changes did you make? _______
18. Did you ask a friend or family member to read the first draft and make suggestions? Yes ____ No ____
    What kind of suggestions did they have? _______
19. Did you proof read the final draft? Yes _______ No _______

Evaluating

20. How did you feel about the essay/project/report in the end? _______
21. What grade did you think you would get? _______ Why? _______
22. What was the teacher's evaluation? _______

Figure 8.10 Interview questions on essay/project/report writing. (*Source:* From "Interview Questions on Essay/Project/Report Writing." In "Alternatives in the Assessment of the Learning Disabled Adolescent: A Learning Strategies Approach" by J. Wiener, 1986, *Learning Disabilities Focus, 1,* p. 100. Copyright 1986 by Council for Exceptional Children. Reprinted by permission.)

Student Name: _______ Date: _______ Examiner: _______

Type of Test

Multiple-Choice _______ Short-Answer _______ Essay _______ Standardized _______

Class Test _______ % of Grade _______

Subject: _______

Test Preparation

Interview the student by asking the open-ended question first, followed by the probe question as required. Tell me how you study: _______

Probes

1. Do you usually study in a special place? Yes _______ No _______ Where? _______
2. Do you have a special time for study? Yes _______ No _______ When? _______
3. How long can you study before you take a break? _______ hours _______ minutes
4. When you know you have a test coming up a week away, when do you start studying for it? _______
5. Do you usually find yourself having to cram the night before? Yes _______ No _______ For how long can you cram before you can't concentrate any longer? _______ hours _______ minutes
6. Do you prefer to study in a quiet place, with music playing, or in front of the television set? _______ What do you normally do? _______
7. Do you sit at a desk, sit in an easy chair, or lie on the bed or the floor when you study? _______
8. Do you study from your notebook? _______ textbook? _______ both? _______ Which do you like best? _______
9. Tell me what goes through your head as you study. _______
10. When you study, do you try to figure out what information is most important? Yes _______ No _______ Do you try to predict what questions will be on the test? Yes _______ No _______ How do you do that? _______
11. Which subjects do you find the easiest to study? _______ Why? _______
12. Which subjects do you find hardest to study? _______ Why? _______

Test-Taking Behavior

Evaluate the student's performance in each area by marking a √ in the appropriate column:

	Excellent	Adequate	Inadequate	Notes
• Punctuality • Equipped (e.g., pen, pencil) • Motivation • Planning of time • Checking of work • Accuracy of prediction of grade				
	High	Moderate	Low	
• Anxiety Level				

Test Product

Analyze a recent examination or test by examining the areas listed below and questioning the student when clarification is needed. Evaluate the student's performance in each area by marking a √ in the appropriate column:

	Excellent	Adequate	Inadequate	Not Applicable	Notes
• Handwriting • Accuracy of Reading of Questions • Comprehension of Subtleties of Questions • Spelling • Grammar • Punctuation • Appropriateness of Vocabulary to Discipline • Sequencing & Organization of Thoughts • Relevance of Answers • Conceptualization of Answers • Elaboration of Answers					

Comments: _______

Figure 8.11 Checklist for assessing students' examinations. (*Source:* From "Checklist for Assessing Students' Examinations." In "Alternatives in the Assessment of the Learning Disabled Adolescent: A Learning Strategies Approach" by J. Wiener, 1986, *Learning Disabilities Focus, 1,* p. 101. Copyright 1986 by Council for Exceptional Children. Reprinted by permission.)

FORMAT A

Target word: *drill*

Synonyms: A. practice B. tool

Directions: "Match the synonym to the correct sentence."

1. Hand me the *drill.*
2. We need *drill* on our skills.

Answer(s): Sentence 1—synonym B. Sentence 2—synonym A.

FORMAT B

Target word: *drill*

Directions: "Select the words which make sentence 2 most like sentence 1."

Sentence 1. We need *drill* on our skills.
Sentence 2. If we want to get better at our skills, we should
. . . study them.
. . . put a hole in them.
. . . do them a lot.

FORMAT C

Target word: *drill*

Directions: "Write a synonym for the target word which can be used in each of the following sentences."

Sentence 1. Hand me the *drill.*
Sentence 2. We need *drill* on our skills.

Synonym 1: ______________________________
Synonym 2: ______________________________

FORMAT D

Target word: *drill*

Directions: "Read this sentence—"We need *drill* on our skills." In this sentence, does the *drill* mean to:

a. make a hole in something?
b. work on something over and over again?

Figure 8.12 Methods of informally assessing vocabulary. (*Source:* From *Curriculum-Based Evaluation for Special and Remedial Education* (p. 185) by K. W. Howell and M. K. Morehead, 1987, Columbus, OH: Merrill. Copyright 1987 by Macmillan Publishing Company. Reprinted by permission.)

A study by Fuchs and Fuchs (1992) found that the cloze and story retelling methods were not technically adequate and sensitive enough to measure the reading progress of students over time. The maze method, however, was determined to be useful for monitoring student growth. This seems to suggest that the story retelling and the cloze methods may be best used for diagnostic information or as instructional strategies rather than as a means to monitor progress within a curriculum.

Barnes (1986) suggested using an error analysis approach when listening to students read passages aloud. With this approach, the teacher notes the errors made as the student reads and analyzes the errors to determine whether they change the meaning of the passage. The teacher then notes whether the substituted words look or sound like the original words.

Decoding skills used in reading can also be assessed informally. The teacher may design tests to measure the student's ability to

Orally read isolated letters, blends, syllables, and real words.

Orally read nonsense words that contain various combinations of vowel sounds and patterns, consonant blends, and digraphs.

Orally read sentences that contain new words.

The teacher may sample the reader used by the student to develop a list of words to decode, if one has not been provided by the publisher. A sample may be obtained by selecting every 10th word, selecting every 25th word, or, for higher level readers, randomly selecting stories from which random words will be taken. Proper nouns and words already mastered by the student may be excluded (e.g., *a, the, me, I*).

Fluency is an area assessed to determine the reading rate and accuracy of a student using a particular reading selection. Reading fluency will be affected by the student's ability to decode new words and by the student's ability to read phrase by phrase rather than word by word. The teacher may assess oral reading fluency of new material and previously read material. Howell and Morehead (1987) suggested that the teacher listen to the student read a passage, mark the location reached at the end of 1 minute, and then ask the student to read again as quickly as possible. The teacher may note the difference between the two rates as well as errors.

Another assessment device used by teachers to measure reading skills is informal reading inventories, which assess a variety of reading skills. Inventories may be teacher-made instruments that use the actual curriculum used in instruction or commercially prepared devices. Commercially prepared instruments contain passages and word lists and diagnostic information that enables the teacher to analyze errors. One such instrument has been designed by Burns and Roe (1989).

Informal Reading Inventory—Third Edition. The Informal Reading Inventory—Third Edition (Burns & Roe, 1989) contains reading word-placement lists that enable the teacher to determine the level at which to begin passage testing. This instrument contains four equivalent forms of passages, which the student reads aloud. The teacher marks mistakes or miscues. The student is asked to answer comprehension questions as well. Comprehension is analyzed for main idea, detail, inference, vocabulary, sequence, and cause and effect. Figure 8.13 contains a summary of the errors analyzed in reading decoding skills on this instrument.

The Burns and Roe Informal Reading Inventory is contained in a spiral-bound book, allowing the teacher to reproduce necessary pages and to laminate the student reading passages. Teachers should study the directions for administration before using the instrument. The scoring system provides percentages of errors, types of miscues, and percentages of comprehension. Such information can be used in planning interventions but may need to be verified by the teacher using the classroom curriculum. Grade levels provided are suggestions of placement and are not to be considered as grade-level equivalents, as in norm-referenced testing.

Considerations When Using Informal Reading Inventories. The cautions about grade levels and curriculum verification stated in the previous section should be considered when using any commercially prepared informal reading inventory. Gillis and Olson (1987) advised teachers and diagnosticians to consider the following guidelines when selecting commercially prepared informal reading inventories:

1. If possible, select inventories that have mostly narrative selections and mostly expository selections for placing elementary students in basal materials.
2. If possible, select inventories in which most of the selections are well organized.
3. When a passage on the form you are using is poorly organized or not of the appropriate text type for your purpose, use a passage at the same level from an alternate form. If an appropriate passage is not available, rewrite a passage from the inventory or write an appropriate passage.
4. When a student's comprehension scores are erratic from level to level, examine the passages to see whether the variability could be due to shifts between types of text or between well- and poorly organized passages.
5. Finally, remember that the instructional level you find is just an estimate. Confirm it by observing the student's performance with classroom materials. Adjust placement if necessary. (pp. 36–44)

Check Your Understanding

Complete Activity 8.7.

ACTIVITY 8.7

Use the following passage to design brief informal assessment instruments in the spaces provided.

Elaine sat on the balcony overlooking the mountains. The mountains were very high and appeared blue in color. The trees swayed in

SUMMARY OF QUALITATIVE ANALYSIS

Miscue Analysis of Phonic and Structural Analysis Skills

(Tally total miscues on appropriate lines.)

Miscue	For Words in Isolation	For Words in Context		For Words in Isolation	For Words in Context
Single consonants	_____	_____	Word beginnings	_____	_____
Consonant blends	_____	_____	Word middles	_____	_____
Single vowels	_____	_____	Word endings	_____	_____
Vowel digraphs	_____	_____	Compound words	_____	_____
Consonant digraphs	_____	_____	Inflectional endings	_____	_____
Diphthongs	_____	_____	Syllabication	_____	_____
Prefixes	_____	_____	Accent	_____	_____
Suffixes	_____	_____			

Oral Reading Skills

(Place a [+] by areas that are strong and a [−] by areas that are weak.)

Reads in phrases (not word by word) _____
Uses expression _____
Attends to punctuation _____
Pronounces words correctly _____
Comments:

(Note: In order to fill out the analysis for words in context, it is helpful to make a list of expected reader responses and unexpected responses for easy comparison as to graphic similarity, syntactic acceptability, and semantic acceptability. See page 168 for a good way to record this information.)

Summary of Strengths and Weaknesses in Word Recognition (Include all of the important data that have been collected on word recognition skills):

Summary of Strengths and Weaknesses in Comprehension (Include all of the important data that have been collected about comprehension):

Figure 8.13 Analysis summary of the Burns and Roe Informal Reading Inventory. (*Source:* From *Informal Reading Inventory* (3rd ed., p. 166) by P. C. Burns and B. D. Roe, 1989, Boston: Houghton Mifflin Company.)

the breeze. The valley below was covered by a patch of fog. It was a cool, beautiful fall day.

1. Write an informal test using the cloze method. Remember to leave the first and last sentences intact. ______________________________
____
____

2. Write an informal test using the maze method. Remember to leave three word choices beneath each blank provided for the missing words. ______________________________
____

3. Select a sentence from the passage and write an informal test using the sentence verification method. Write three sentences, one of which has the same meaning as the original sentence.

Apply Your Knowledge

Which of these methods was easiest for you to write? Why? ________
____

INFORMAL ASSESSMENT OF MATHEMATICS

The teacher may use curriculum-based assessment to measure all areas of mathematics. The assessment should be combined with both task analysis and error analysis to determine specific problem areas. These problem areas should be further assessed by using probes to determine the specific difficulty. In addition to using these methods, Liedtke (1988) suggested using an interview technique to locate deficits in accuracy and strategies. Liedtke included such techniques as asking the student to create a word problem to illustrate a computation, redirecting the original computation to obtain additional math concept information (e.g., asking the student to compare two of his answers to see which is greater), and asking the student to solve a problem and explain the steps used in the process.

Howell and Morehead (1987) suggested several methods for assessing specific math skills. Their techniques provide assessment of accuracy and fluency of basic facts, recall, basic concepts, operations, problem-solving concepts, content knowledge, tool and unit knowledge, and skill integration. The procedure for checking the recall and handwriting necessary for a basic facts math test is illustrated in Figure 8.14.

INFORMAL ASSESSMENT OF SPELLING

A common type of informal spelling assessment is a spelling test of standard format. The teacher states the word, uses the word in a sentence, and repeats the word. Most elementary spelling texts provide this type of

Specific-Level Procedure 2: Checking Recall and Handwriting. We use a two-part procedure to determine if writing slowly or inadequate recall of facts is the cause of the rate failure on the basic facts survey-level test.

DIRECTIONS 2.1

1. Administer a basic facts test for each area of concern (+, −, ×, ÷). Have the student say the answers rather than write. (Flashcards or a fact sheet are appropriate stimuli.)
2. Say, "Tell me the answer to each problem."
3. Note corrects and errors. Compare the student's performance to your CAP* or the one we list in Appendix C. One hundred percent accuracy is an appropriate criterion for facts.

DIRECTIONS 2.2

1. Administer a writing-digits or a copying-digits test.
2. Say, "Write/copy numbers from 1 to 100 as quickly and carefully as you can. Please, begin."
3. Time the student for 60 seconds. Say, "Stop."
4. Score the sample and use the procedure for comparing basic movement cycle—writing digits to the skill of math facts.

Interpretation Guidelines

Question. Are the student's oral responses accurate?

If yes, answer the next question and use Teaching Recommendation 2.

If no, teach basic facts and use Teaching Recommendation 1, or employ Specific-Level Procedure 3.

Question. Can the student write fast enough to demonstrate math fact fluency?

If yes, teach fact fluency (Teaching Recommendation 2.2).

If no, teach the student to write digits (Teaching Recommendation 2.1).

Question. Is the student having trouble with both accuracy on facts and writing digits?

If yes, teach accuracy on facts (Recommendation 1) and writing digits (Recommendation 2.1). Also use Specific-Level Procedure 3.

*CAP = criterion for acceptable performance.

Figure 8.14 Procedure for checking recall and handwriting necessary for a basic facts math test. (*Source:* From *Curriculum-Based Evaluation for Special and Remedial Education* (p. 260) by K. W. Howell and M. K. Morehead, 1987, Columbus, OH: Merrill. Copyright 1987 by Macmillan Publishing Company. Reprinted by permission.)

direct curriculum-based assessment. The teacher may wish to assign different words or may be teaching at the secondary level, where typical spelling texts are not used. The teacher may also need to assess the spelling of content-related words in areas such as science or social studies. Or, the teacher may use written samples by the student to analyze spelling errors.

One method of analyzing spelling errors, proposed by Guerin and Maier (1983), is shown in Table 8.1.

INFORMAL ASSESSMENT OF WRITTEN LANGUAGE

A student's written language ability may be assessed informally by collecting and analyzing written work samples. Written samples may be analyzed for spelling, punctuation, correct grammar and usage, vocabulary, creative ability, story theme, sequence, and plot. If the objective of instruction is to promote creativity, actual spelling, punctuation, and other mechanical errors should not be scored against the student on the written sample. These errors, however, should be noted by the teacher and used in educational planning for English and spelling lessons.

One informal assessment technique for written language skills proposed by Shapiro (1996) includes the following steps:

1. A series of "story starters" should be constructed that can be used to give initial ideas for students to write about. These starters should contain items that most children will find of sufficient interest to generate a written story.
2. The evaluator should give the child a copy of the story starter and read the starter to him or her. The evaluator then tells the student that he will be asked to write a story using the starter as the first sentence. The student should be given a minute to think about a story before he or she is asked to begin writing.
3. After 1 minute, the evaluator should tell the child to begin writing, start the stopwatch, and time for 3 minutes. If the child stops writing before the 3 minutes are up, he or she should be encouraged to keep writing until time is up.
4. The evaluator should count the number of words that are correctly written. "Correct" means that a word can be recognized (even if it is misspelled). Capitalization and punctuation are ignored. The rate of the correct and incorrect words per 3 minutes is calculated. If the child stops writing before the 3 minutes are up, the number of words correct should be multiplied by 180 for the number of words correct per 3 minutes. (p. 125)

Shapiro also suggested creating local norms to compare students. The number of words correct may be used as a basis for writing short-term

Table 8.1 Analysis of spelling errors used in informal assessment.

	Definitions	Example	
		Heard	*Written*
Phonetic Ability			
PS	Substitutions: placing another sound or syllable in place of the sound in the word	match nation	mach nashun
PO	Omissions: leaving out a sound or syllable from the word	grateful temperature	graful tempature
PA	Additions: adding a sound or syllable to the original	purchase importance	purchasing importantance
PSe	Sequencing: putting sounds or syllables in the wrong order	animal elephant	aminal efelant
Visualization			
VS	Substitutions: substitution of a vowel or consonant for those in the given word	him chapel	hin chaple
VO	Omissions: leaving out a vowel, or consonant, or syllable from those in the given word	allow beginning	alow begining
Phonetic Ability			
VA	Additions: adding a vowel, consonant, or syllable to those in the given word	welcome fragrant	wellcome fragerant
VSe	Sequencing: putting letters or syllables in the wrong order	guardian pilot	guardain pliot
Linguistic Performance			
LS	Substitution: substitution of a word for another having somewhat the same meaning	ring house	bell home
	Substitution: substituting another word because of different language structure (teacher judgment)	came ate	come et
	Substitution: substitution of a completely different word	pear polish	pair collage
LO	Omissions: omitting word endings, prefixes, suffixes	pushed unhelpful	pusht helpful
LA	Additions: adding endings, prefixes, suffixes	cry forget	crys forgetting
LSe	Sequencing: reversing syllables	discussed disappoint	discusted dispapoint

Source: From *Informal Assessment in Education* (pp. 218–219) by G. R. Guerin and A. S. Maier, 1983, Palo Alto, CA: Mayfield Publishing. Copyright 1983 by Mayfield Publishing. Reprinted by permission.

Directions: Analysis of handwriting should be made on a sample of the student's written work, not from a carefully produced sample. Evaluate each task and mark in the appropriate column. Score each task "satisfactory" (1) or "unsatisfactory" (2).

I. Letter formation

A. Capitals (score each letter 1 or 2)

A	______	G	______	M	______	S	______	Y	______
B	______	H	______	N	______	T	______	Z	______
C	______	I	______	O	______	U	______		
D	______	J	______	P	______	V	______		
E	______	K	______	Q	______	W	______		
F	______	L	______	R	______	X	______		

Total ______

B. Lowercase (score by groups)	Score (1 or 2)
1. Round letters	
a. Counterclockwise	
a, c, d, g, o, q	______
b. Clockwise	
k, p	______
2. Looped letters	
a. Above line	
b, d, e, f, h, k, l	______
b. Below line	
f, g, j, p, q, y	______
3. Retraced letters	
i, u, t, w, y	______
4. Humped letters	
h, m, n, v, x, z	______
5. Others	
r, s, b	______

Figure 8.15 One method of handwriting analysis. (*Source:* From *Informal Assessment in Education* (p. 228) by G. R. Guerin and A. S. Maier, 1983, Palo Alto, CA: Mayfield Publishing. Copyright 1983 by Mayfield Publishing. Reprinted by permission.)

C. Numerals (score each number 1 or 2)

1	________	4	________	7	________	10–20	________
2	________	5	________	8	________	21–99	________
3	________	6	________	9	________	100–1,000	________
						Total	________

II. Spatial relationships

	Score (1 or 2)
A. Alignment (letters on line)	________
B. Uniform slant	________
C. Size of letters	
1. To each other	________
2. To available space	________
D. Space between letters	________
E. Space between words	________
F. Anticipation of end of line (hyphenates, moves to next line)	________
Total	________

III. Rate of writing (letters per minute)

	Score (1 or 2)
Grade 1:20	
2:30	
3:35	
4:45	
5:55	
6:65	
7 and above: 75	________

Scoring

	Satisfactory	*Questionable*	*Poor*
I. *Letter formation*			
A. Capitals	26	39	40+
B. Lowercase	7	10	11+
C. Numerals	12	18	19+
II. *Spatial relationships*	7	10	11+
III. *Rate of writing*	1	2	6

objectives. This informal method may be linked directly to classroom curricula and may be repeated frequently as a direct measure of student writing ability.

Writing samples may also be used to analyze handwriting. The teacher uses error analysis to evaluate the sample, write short-term objectives, and plan educational strategies. One such error analysis of handwriting skills is shown in Figure 8.15.

PERFORMANCE ASSESSMENT AND AUTHENTIC ASSESSMENT

performance assessment Assessment that requires the student to create an answer or product to demonstrate knowledge.

Performance testing is designed for the student to create a response from her existing knowledge base. The U.S. Office of Technology Assessment defines **performance assessment** as "testing methods that require students to create an answer product that demonstrates their knowledge or skills" (1992, p. 16). The teacher may use a variety of formats in performance assessment, including products that the student constructs. Harris and Graham (1994) state that performance assessment stresses the student's active construction in demonstrating knowledge.

The types of tasks that teachers may require a student to complete in performance assessment may include the student's explanation of process as well as the student's perception of the task and the material learned. This type of assessment may involve several levels of cognitive processing and reasoning and may allow educators to tap into areas not assessed by more traditional types of assessment. When considering performance assessment as an alternative for making educational placement decisions, Elliott and Fuchs (1997) caution that performance assessment should be used in conjunction with other types of assessment because of the lack of knowledge regarding psychometric evidence and the lack of professionals who are trained to use this type of assessment reliably. Glatthorn suggested criteria for educators to use in the evaluation of performance tasks (1998). These criteria are presented in Table 8.2.

authentic assessment Assessment that requires the student to apply knowledge in the real world.

Authentic assessment differs from performance assessment in that students must apply knowledge in a manner consistent with generalizing into a real-world setting, or students may complete the task in the real world. Archbald (1991) states that authentic assessment requires a disciplined production of knowledge using techniques that are within the field in which the student is being assessed. The student's tasks are instrumental and may require a substantial amount of time to complete. The student may be required to use a variety of materials and resources that may include working in collaboration with other students.

Table 8.2 Criteria for evaluating performance tasks.

Does the performance task

- Correspond closely and comprehensively with the standard and benchmarks it is designed to assess?
- Require the student to access prior knowledge in completing the task?
- Require the use of higher order thought processes including creative thinking?
- Seem real and purposeful, embedded in a meaningful context that seems authentic?
- Engage students' interest?
- Require the students to communicate to classmates and others in the processes they used and the results they obtained, using multiple response modes?
- Require sustained effort over a significant period of time?
- Provide the student with options?
- Seem feasible in the context of schools and classrooms, not requiring inordinate resources or creating undue controversy?
- Convey a sense of fairness to all, being free of bias?
- Challenge the students without frustrating them?
- Include criteria and rubrics for evaluating student performance?
- Provide both group and individual work, with appropriate accountability?

Source: Performance Assessment and Standards-Based Curricula: The Achievement Cycle by A. A. Glatthorn (1998). Copyright by Eye on Education. Larchmont, NY.

PORTFOLIO ASSESSMENT

portfolio assessment Evaluating student progress, strengths, and weaknesses using a collection of different measurements and work samples.

One method of assessing a student's current level of academic functioning is through **portfolio assessment.** A portfolio is a collection of student work that provides a holistic view of the student's strengths and weaknesses. The portfolio collection contains various work samples, permanent products, and test results from a variety of instruments and methods. For example, a portfolio of reading might include a student's test scores on teacher-made tests, including curriculum-based assessments, work samples from daily work and homework assignments, error analyses on work and test samples, and the results of an informal reading inventory with miscues noted and analyzed. The assessment of the student's progress would assess decoding skills, comprehension skills, fluency, and so on. These measures would be collected over a period of time. This type of assessment may be useful in describing the current progress of the student with his parents (Taylor, 1993).

The essential elements of effective portfolio assessment were listed by Shaklee, Barbour, Ambrose, and Hansford (1997), who included the following assessment elements:

> Assessment should
>
> be authentic and valid.
>
> encompass the whole child.
>
> involve repeated observations of various patterns of behavior.
>
> be continuous over time.
>
> use a variety of methods for gathering evidence of student performance.
>
> provide a means for systematic feedback to be used in the improvement of instruction and student performance.
>
> provide an opportunity for joint conversations and explanations between students and teachers, teachers and parents, and students and parents. (p. 10)

Ruddell (1995) provides the following list of possible products that could be included in a portfolio for assessing literacy in the middle grades:

> samples of student writing
>
> story maps
>
> reading log or dated list of books student has read
>
> vocabulary journal
>
> artwork, project papers, photographs, and other products of work completed
>
> group work, papers, projects, and products
>
> daily journal
>
> writing ideas
>
> reading response log, learning log, or double-entry journal or writing from assigned reading during the year
>
> letters to pen pals, letters exchanged with teacher
>
> out-of-school writing and artwork
>
> unit and lesson tests collected over the grading period or academic year (p. 191)

Paratore (1995) reports that establishing common standards for assessing literacy through the use of portfolio assessment provides a useful alternative in the evaluation of students' reading and writing skills. Hobbs (1993) found portfolio assessment useful in providing supplemental information for eligibility consideration that included samples of the quality of work that was not evident in standardized assessment.

Portfolio data was also found to result in providing information to teachers that was more informative and led to different decisions for instructional planning (Rueda & Garcia, 1997). This study found that the recommendations were more specific and that student strengths were more easily identifiable using this form of assessment.

THINK AHEAD

In addition to having academic difficulties, students may have behavioral or emotional problems that may impact their classroom performance. Teachers are asked to assist in the assessment of these problems through observation and other methods. Teachers must also interpret results of behavioral assessment and implement effective strategies to address these concerns. Chapter 9 presents an overview of the assessment of behavior.

EXERCISES

Part I

Match the terms with the correct definitions.

a. criterion-referenced assessment
b. curriculum-based measurement
c. task analysis
d. error analysis
e. informal assessment
f. questionnaire
g. direct measurement
h. direct daily measurement
i. probes
j. checklist
k. portfolio
l. subskill
m. authentic assessment
n. performance asessment

_____ 1. A teacher reviews the information provided in a student's norm-referenced achievement scores. She determines that the student has a weakness in the area of multiplication with regrouping, but she is not certain exactly how the student is completing the process. In order to determine this, the teacher decides to use _____.

_____ 2. A teacher who works with students in the range of mild mental retardation would like to assess the students' ability to return the correct amount of change when given a $10.00 bill to pay for an item that costs $2.85. How might the teacher decide to assess this skill?

_____ 3. To determine the specific skills applied in completing double-digit addition problems, the teacher can complete a _____.

_____ 4. In a daily living skills class, a teacher can assess the student's ability to make a complete meal by using _____.

_____ 5. A teacher assesses the students' knowledge of the science unit by each student's book report, test grade, written classroom assignments, lab experiences, and journal. This group of science products demonstrates one example of _____.

_____ 6. Error analysis, checklists, direct measurement, authentic assessment, portfolio assessment, probes, and curriculum-based assessment are examples of _____.

_____ 7. A teacher sets a standard of reaching 90% mastery on the test assessing basic reading decoding skills of second-grade level words. This test is an example of _____.

_____ 8. Asking the parent of a child about the specific behaviors observed during homework time is an example of using _____ as part of the assessment.

Part II

Use the terms in Part I to select a method of informal assessment for the following situations. Write the reason for your selection.

1. Standardized test results you received on a new student indicate that she is performing two grade levels below expectancy. You want to determine which reading book to place her in.
   Method of assessment _______________
   Reason _______________
2. A student who understands division problems when presented in class failed a teacher-made test. You want to determine the reason for the failure.
   Method of assessment _______________
   Reason _______________
3. Following a screening test of fifth-grade level spelling, you determine that a student performs inconsistently when spelling words with short vowel sounds:
   Method of assessment _______________
   Reason _______________
4. A student seems to be performing at a different level than indicated by norm-referenced math test data. You think you should meet with his parents and discuss actual progress in the classroom.
   Method of assessment _______________
   Reason _______________

ANSWER KEY TO CHECK YOUR UNDERSTANDING

Activity 8.1

1. Yes

Apply Your Knowledge. The student's performance is compared with a criterion rather than with the performance of other students in the same grade or students the same age.

Activity 8.2

1. You should have selected one of the skills and written an objective that can be measured, such as:
   The student will be able to match the letters b, d, and c with pictures of objects that begin with the sounds b, d, and c with 90% accuracy by the end of September.
2. You should have designed a short criterion-referenced test using the skill of associating specific pictures with a story. Answers will vary.

Apply Your Knowledge. Answers may vary.

Activity 8.3

1. Answers will vary.
2. Answers will vary.

Apply Your Knowledge. Answers may vary.

Activity 8.4

1. Failed to capitalize first word in sentences and "I"; left out *the* before *zoo;* used *him* for *he, an* for *and,* and *me* for *I,* left off period; used *to* when *too* was needed or transposed *to come* (come too).
2. Use of capital letters for beginning of sentence, proper nouns, usage of pronouns, mastery of sentence writing.

Apply Your Knowledge. Answers will vary.

Activity 8.5

1. curriculum-based assessment
2. direct measurement; curriculum-based measurement
3. criterion-referenced assessment
4. probe
5. direct daily measurement
6. task analysis
7. error analysis
8. informal

Apply Your Knowledge. Informal measures are more closely related to actual material presented in the classroom, more sensitive for assessing progress within curriculum.

Activity 8.6

True-False Items

1. Use of negative in item
2. Needless phrases, too lengthy

Multiple-Choice Items

1. "Any of the above," "none of the above," and "only . . . " used inappropriately
2. Presence of specific determiners

Apply Your Knowledge. Answers may vary.

Activity 8.7

Answers will vary for all items.

REFERENCES

Allinder, R. M. (1995). An examination of the relationship between teacher efficacy and curriculum-based measurement and student achievement. *Remedial and Special Education, 16,* 247–254.

Archbald, D. A. (1991). Authentic assessment: Principles, practices, and issues. *School Psychology Quarterly 6,* 279–293.

Baker, S. K., & Good, R. (1995). Curriculum-based measurement of English reading with bilingual Hispanic students: A validation study with second grade students. *School Psychology Review, 24,* 561–578.

Barnes, W. (1986). Informal assessment of reading. *Pointer, 30,* 42–46.

Bennett, R. (1982). Cautions for the use of informal measures in the educational assessment of exceptional children. *Journal of Learning Disabilities, 15,* 337–339.

Brigance, A. H. (1977). *Brigance Diagnostic Inventory of Basic Skills.* N. Billerica, MA: Curriculum Associates.

Brigance, A. H. (1981). *Brigance Diagnostic Inventory of Essential Skills.* N. Billerica, MA: Curriculum Associates.

Brigance, A. H. (1991). *Brigance Diagnostic Inventory of Early Development—Revised,* N. Billerica, MA: Curriculum Associates.

Burns, P. C., & Roe, B. D. (1989). *Informal Reading Inventory* (3rd ed.). Boston: Houghton Mifflin.

Campbell, E., Schellinger, T., & Beer, J. (1991). Relationship among the ready or not parental checklist for school readiness, the Brigance Kindergarten and first grade screen, and SRA scores. *Perceptual and Motor Skills, 73,* 859–862.

Canter, A. (1991). Effective psychological services for all students: A data based model of service delivery. In G. Stoner, M. R. Shinn, & H. M. Walker (Eds.), *Interventions for achievement and behavioral problems* (pp. 49–78). Silver Spring, MD: National Association of School Psychologists.

Connolly, A. J. (1988). *KeyMath—Revised: A Diagnostic Inventory of Essential Mathematics.* Circle Pines, MN: American Guidance Service.

Davis, L. B., Fuchs, L. S., Fuchs, D., & Whinnery, K. (1995). "Will CBM help me learn?" Students' perception of the benefits of curriculum-based measurement. *Education and Treatment of Children, 18,* 19–32.

Eckert, T. L., Shapiro, E. S., & Lutz, J. G. (1995). Teachers' ratings of the acceptability of curriculum-based assessment methods. *School Psychology Review, 24,* 497–511.

Elliott, S. N., & Fuchs, L. S. (1997). The utility of curriculum-based measurement and performance assessment as alternatives to traditional intelligence and achievement tests. *School Psychology Review, 26,* 224–233.

Evans, S., & Evans, W. (1986). A perspective on assessment for instruction. *Pointer, 30,* 9–12.

Fuchs, L., Butterworth, J., & Fuchs, D. (1989). Effects of ongoing curriculum-based measurement on student awareness of goals and progress. *Education and Treatment of Children, 12,* 41–47.

Fuchs, L., & Fuchs, D. (1992). Identifying a measure for monitoring student reading progress. *School Psychology Review, 21,* 45–58.

Fuchs, L. S., & Fuchs, D. (1996). Combining performance assessment and curriculum-based measurement to strengthen instructional planning. *Learning Disabilities Research & Practice, 11,* 183–192.

Fuchs, L., Fuchs, D., & Hamlett, C. (1989). Effects of instrumental use of curriculum-based measurement to enhance instructional programs. *Remedial and Special Education, 10,* 43–52.

Fuchs, L., Fuchs, D., Hamlett, C. L., Phillips, N. B., & Bentz, J. (1994). Classwide curriculum-based measurement: Helping general educators meet the challenge of student diversity. *Exceptional Children, 60,* 518–537.

Fuchs, L., Tindal, G., & Deno, S. (1984). Methodological issues in curriculum-based assessment. *Diagnostique, 9,* 191–207.

Gillis, M., & Olson, M. (1987). Elementary IRIs: Do they reflect what we know about text/type structure and comprehension? *Reading Research and Instruction, 27,* 36–44.

Glaser, R. (1963). Instructional technology and the measurement of learning outcomes: Some questions. *American Psychologist, 18*(2), 519–521.

Glatthorn, A. A. (1998). *Performance assessment and standards-based curricula: The achievement cycle.* Larchmont, NY: Eye on Education.

Good, R., & Salvia, J. (1988). Curriculum bias in published, norm-referenced reading tests: Demonstrable effects. *School Psychology Review, 17,* 51–60.

Guerin, G. R., & Maier, A. S. (1983). *Informal assessment in education.* Palo Alto, CA: Mayfield.

Harris, K., & Graham, S. (1994). Constructivism: Principles, paradigms, and integration. *Journal of Special Education, 28,* 233–247.

Hart, K. E., & Scuitto, M. J. (1996). Criterion-referenced measurement of instructional impact on cognitive outcomes. *Journal of Instructional Psychology, 23,* 26–34.

Heshusius, L. (1991). Curriculum-based assessment and direct instruction: Critical reflections on fundamental assumptions. *Exceptional Children, 57,* 315–328.

Hintze, J. M., Shapiro, E. S., & Lutz, J. G. (1994). The effects of curriculum on the sensitivity of curriculum-based measurement in reading. *Journal of Special Education, 28,* 188–202.

Hobbs, R. (1993). Portfolio use in a learning disabilities resource room. *Reading & Writing Quarterly: Overcoming Learning Difficulties, 9,* 249–261.

Howell, K. W., & Morehead, M. K. (1987). *Curriculum-based evaluation for special and remedial education.* Columbus, OH: Merrill.

Hultquist, A. M., & Metzke, L. K. (1993). Potential effects of curriculum bias in individual norm-referenced reading and spelling achievement tests. *Journal of Psychoeducational Assessment, 11,* 337–344.

Kaufman, A. S., & Kaufman, N. L. (1985). *Kaufman Test of Educational Achievement.* Circle Pines, MN: American Guidance Service.

Liedtke, W. (1988). Diagnosis in mathematics: The advantages of an interview. *Arithmetic Teacher, 36,* 26–29.

Lusting, D. D., & Saura, K. M. (1996, Spring). Use of criterion-based comparisons in determining the appropriateness of vocational evaluation test modifications for criterion-referenced tests. *Vocational Evaluation and Work Adjustment Bulletin.*

Marso, R. N., & Pigge, F. L. (1991). An analysis of teacher-made tests: Item types, cognitive demands, and item construction errors. *Contemporary Educational Psychology, 16,* 279–286.

Marston, D., Fuchs, L., & Deno, S. (1986). Measuring pupil progress: A comparison of standardized achievement tests and curriculum related measures. *Diagnostique, 11,* 77–90.

Marston, D., Mirkin, P. K., & Deno, S. L. (1984). Curriculum-based measurement: An alternative to traditional screening, referral, and identification. *Journal of Special Education, 18,* 109–118.

McCauley, R. J. (1996). Familiar strangers: Criterion-referenced measures in communication disorders. *Language, Speech, and Hearing Services in the Schools, 27,* 122–131.

McLoughlin, J. A., & Lewis, R. B. (1994). *Assessing special students* (4th ed.). Upper Saddle River, NJ: Merrill/Prentice Hall.

Meherns, W. A., & Clarizio, H. F. (1993). Curriculum-based measurement: Conceptual and psychometric considerations. *Psychology in the Schools, 30,* 241–254.

Millman, J. (1994). Criterion-referenced testing 30 years later: Promise broken, promise kept. *Educational Measurement: Issues and Practices, 13,* 19–20, 39.

Paratore, J. R. (1995). Assessing literacy: Establishing common standards in portfolio assessment. *Topics in Language Disorders, 16,* 67–82.

Phillips, N. B., Hamlett, C. L., Fuchs, L. S., & Fuchs, D. (1993). Combining classwide curriculum-based measurement and peer tutoring to help general educators provide adaptive education. *Learning Disabilities Research & Practice, 8,* 148–156.

Reynolds, C. R. (1982). The problem of bias in psychological assessment. In C. R. Reynolds & T. B. Gutkin (Eds.), *The handbook of school psychology,* (pp. 178–208). New York: Wiley.

Roberts, M. L., Marshall, J., Nelson, J. R., & Albers, C. A. (2001). Curriculum-based assessment procedures embedded within functional behavioral assessments: Identifying escape-motivated behaviors in a general education classroom. *School Psychology Review, 30*(2), 264–277.

Rosenfield, S., & Kurait, S. K. (1990). Best practices in curriculum-based assessment. In A. Thomas & J. Grimes (Eds.), *Best practices in school psychology—II,* pp. 275–286. Washington, DC: National Association of School Psychology.

Ruddell, M. R. (1995). Literacy assessment in middle level grades: Alternatives to traditional practices. *Reading & Writing Quarterly: Overcoming Learning Difficulties, 11,* 187–200.

Rueda, R., & Garcia, E. (1997). Do portfolios make a difference for diverse students? The influence of type of data on making instructional decisions. *Learning Disabilities Research & Practice, 12*(2), 114–122.

Salvia, J., & Hughes, C. (1990). *Curriculum-based assessment: Testing what is taught.* New York: Macmillan.

Shaklee, B. D., Barbour, N. E., Ambrose, R., & Hansford, S. J. (1997). *Designing and using portfolios.* Boston: Allyn & Bacon.

Shapiro, E. S. (1989). *Academic skills problems: Direct assessment and intervention.* New York: Guilford.

Shapiro, E. S. (1996). *Academic skills problems: Direct assessment and intervention* (2nd ed.). New York: Guilford.

Shinn, M. R., Habedank, L., Rodden-Nord, K., & Knutson, N. (1993). Using curriculum-based measurement to identify potential candidates for reintegration into general education. *Journal of Special Education, 27,* 202–221.

Shinn, M. R., Nolet, V., & Knutson, N. (1990). Best practices in curriculum-based measurement. In A. Thomas & J. Grimes (Eds.), *Best practices in school psychology.* Washington, DC: National Association of School Psychologists.

Stoner, G., Carey, S. P., Ikeda, M. J., & Shinn, M. R. (1994). The utility of curriculum-based measurement for evaluating the effects of methylphenidate on academic performance. *Journal of Applied Behavior Analysis, 27,* 101–113.

Taylor, R. L. (1993). *Assessment of exceptional students: Educational and psychological procedures* (3rd ed.). Boston: Allyn & Bacon.

Thomas, A. & Grimes, J. (1990). *Best practices in school psychology—II.* Silver Spring, MD: National Association of School Psychologists.

Tindal, G. (1991). Operationalizing learning portfolios: A good idea in search of a method. *Diagnostique, 2,* 127–133.

U.S. Office of Technology Assessment (1992, February). *Testing in American schools: Asking the right questions* (OTA-SET-519). Washington, DC: U.S. Government Printing Office.

Wesson, C., King, R., & Deno, S. (1984). Direct and frequent measurement of student performance: If it's so good for us, why don't we do it? *Learning Disabilities Quarterly, 7,* 45–48.

Wiener, J. (1986). Alternatives in the assessment of the learning disabled adolescent: A learning strategies approach. *Learning Disabilities Focus, 1,* 97–107.

Woodcock, R. W. (1987). *Woodcock Reading Mastery Tests—Revised.* Circle Pines, MN: American Guidance Service.

CHAPTER 9

Assessment of Behavior

Key Terms

academic engaged time
manifestation determination
behavioral intervention plan
functional behavioral assessment
replacement behaviors
functional behavioral analysis
direct observation
event recording
interval recording
anecdotal recording
duration recording
latency recording
interresponse time
functional assessment interviews
target behaviors
baseline
antecedent
setting events
establishing operations
frequency counting
time sampling
checklists
questionnaires
interviews
sociograms
ecological assessment
projective techniques
sentence completion tests
drawing tests
apperception tests

CHAPTER FOCUS

academic engaged time The time when the student is actively involved in the learning process.

This chapter addresses the assessment of behaviors that decrease **academic engaged time** and interfere with learning, such as externalizing (acting out) behaviors (including those attributed to attention deficit disorders), and the assessment of emotional and social difficulties of students. The 1997 IDEA Amendments include new mandates for the assessment of behaviors that may impede student academic success. The legal requirements of functional behavioral assessment and the requirements of manifestation determinations are presented first. Methods used for functional behavioral assessment are discussed, followed by published instruments used to measure behavioral and emotional difficulties. Computerized methods of assessing attention disorders are presented at the end of the chapter.

REQUIREMENTS OF THE 1997 IDEA AMENDMENTS

The behavioral assessment and behavioral planning mandates of the 1997 IDEA Amendments were included as a method of ensuring procedural safeguards for students with behaviors that interfere with educational success. Prior to the amendments, the application of discipline procedures for students with disabilities and students without disabilities was inconsistent (Yell, Drasgow, & Ford, 2000). Special education students who were repeatedly suspended from school for several days each time or who were expelled from school were no longer receiving a free appropriate education. In addition, these punitive types of disciplinary procedures often resulted in more harm to the student or in causing the negative behaviors to escalate (Kubick, Bard, & Perry, 2000).

Congress also sought to make schools safe for all learners and therefore provided educators with the means to discipline students fairly (Drasgow & Yell, 2001). To ensure that students requiring special education support were assisted with their behavioral needs rather than merely punished for behaviors, the 1997 IDEA Amendments required schools to determine if the behaviors were the result of or manifested by the student's existing disability. This is referred to as a **manifestation determination,** which is a procedure required before a student receiving special education services can be suspended for more than 10 school days.

manifestation determination A hearing to determine if a student's behavior is the result of the student's disability.

behavioral intervention plan A plan designed to increase positive behaviors and decrease negative behaviors before these become problematic.

The manifestation determination is required to be completed as quickly as possible and must meet federal regulations. Part of the requirements of manifestation determinations includes confirming that the student's IEP was appropriately written and followed. The IEP must include the present levels of educational performance and behavioral functioning, as well as goals and objectives based on those levels. In addition, the student exhibiting the behaviors should have a **behavioral intervention plan** in place that is based on a

functional behavioral assessment A multi-component assessment to determine the purpose of target behaviors.

replacement behaviors Appropriate behaviors that are incompatible with the negative behaviors they replace.

functional behavioral analysis An analysis of the exploration of behaviors that occur when variables such as antecedents or consequences are manipulated.

functional behavioral assessment. The student's present levels of behavioral functioning are to be based on information obtained in the functional behavioral assessment and should be written in clear understandable language (Drasgow, Yell, Bradley, & Shriner, 1999). The regulations required that the behavioral intervention plan include strategies for positive behavioral support and interventions that provide the student with acceptable **replacement behaviors** to be used by the student rather than the problematic behaviors.

Functional behavioral assessments are measures to determine the function or purpose of a child's behavior. Functional behavioral assessment does not aim to label or name the type of behavior or disorder, such as hitting or depression respectively, but rather seeks to answer the question of why. Why is the student using the behavior? Once this has been determined, interventions can be developed to promote positive acceptable replacement behaviors. A functional behavioral assessment should define the target behavior, determine when the behavior occurs and when it does not occur, and generate hypotheses about the possible function of the behavior. Once these have been determined, the hypotheses are tested or tried so that the exact function can be found (O'Neill, Horner, Albin, Sprague, Storey, & Newton, 1997). The testing out of hypotheses is also called **functional behavioral analysis.** Personnel who are responsible for this phase of the functional behavioral assessment should receive additional training in the procedures due to the possibility that manipulating the student's environment may result in more negative behaviors being exhibited (O'Neill et al., 1997). Drasgow and Yell summarized when functional behavioral assessments should be conducted and when they must be conducted. This information is presented in Figure 9.1.

When an FBA *Should* Be Conducted	When an FBA *Must* Be Conducted
• When a student's problem behavior impedes his or her learning or the learning of others.	• When suspensions or placements in an alternative setting exceed 10 consecutive days or amount to a change in placement.
• When a student's behavior presents a danger to himself or herself or others.	• When a student is placed in an interim alternative educational setting for 45 days when his or her misconduct involves weapons or drugs.
• When a student's suspension or placement in an interim alternative educational setting approaches 10 cumulative days.	• When a due process hearing officer places a student in an interim alternative educational setting for behavior that is dangerous to himself or herself or others.

Figure 9.1 IDEA '97 Requirements regarding FBAs. (*Source:* Functional behavioral assessments: Legal requirements and challenges by Erik Drasgow and Mitchell Yell. In *School Psychology Review, 30*(2), 239–251, p. 243. Copyright 2001 by the National Association of School Psychologists. Reprinted by permission of the publisher.)

Federal regulations require that both special education personnel and general education personnel participate in the functional behavioral assessment along with the student's parents (Conroy, Clark, Gable, & Fox, 1999). Initial efforts to apply functional behavioral assessments may have resulted in schools treating the requirements as merely a compliance issue (Gable, Hendrickson, & Smith, 1999). In other words, schools may not have completed extensive functional behavioral assessments but rather completed the minimal amount of paperwork needed to comply with the mandates. This resulted in numerous due process hearings brought by parents who believed that their children were not appropriately served or assessed prior to suspensions or other disciplinary actions (Drasgrow & Yell, 2001). Most of these hearings found in favor of the parents due to inadequate or nonexistent functional behavioral assessments. It is necessary to fully understand the functional behavioral assessment process in order to fully comply with the law.

FUNCTIONAL BEHAVIORAL ASSESSMENTS

direct observation Observations of student behaviors in the environment in which the behaviors occur.

event recording Recording the frequency of a target behavior; also called frequency counting.

interval recording Sampling a behavior intermittently for very brief periods of time; used to observe frequently occurring behaviors.

anecdotal recording Observations of behavior in which the teacher notes all behaviors and interactions that occur during a given period of time.

duration recording Observations that involve the length of time a behavior occurs.

The gathering of information to determine why a student displays a specific behavior can be obtained through three broad methods of assessment (O'Neill et al., 1997; Witt, Daly, & Noell, 2000). The first method of assessment is the indirect method of assessment. It includes techniques such as interviewing the classroom teacher and parents, reviewing data in the school records, completing behavioral rating scales, checklists, and so on. These methods are presented later in the chapter. Another method used in functional behavioral assessment is called the **direct observation** or descriptive observational method. This requires that the student is observed in the environment in which the behaviors are occurring. During this part of the assessment, several techniques may be employed such as **event recording, interval recording, anecdotal recording, duration recording, latency recording,** and **interresponse time.** These terms are presented in the following section of the chapter. Finally, the third broad method of assessment is the functional behavioral analysis method. During both the indirect assessment and the direct observation phases of the assessment, hypotheses are generated regarding the purpose or function of the behavior. In the functional behavioral analysis portion of the assessment, the variables believed to be triggering the behavior and the possible consequences following the behavior are manipulated. By this manipulation, it can be determined exactly why the student is using the behavior. For example, following the initial phases of the functional behavioral assessment, it is hypothesized that the reason a student is calling out in class is to receive peer attention. During the functional behavioral analysis, the hypothesis of peer attention is tested. Students in the class are instructed to ignore the calling-out behavior, and the calling out decreases.

latency recording Observations involving the amount of time that elapses from the presentation of a stimulus until the response occurs.

interresponse time The amount of time between target behaviors.

functional assessment interview The interview component of the functional behavioral assessment (FBA) that provides information about possible purposes of target behaviors.

When students react to the calling out behavior, such as by turning to look at the target student when calling out occurs, the calling out increases. Thus, the function of the calling out is to receive peer attention. Following the functional behavioral analysis and additional assessment, the students in the class are instructed to ignore all calling-out behavior and to reinforce appropriate hand raising by paying attention to the target student. This manipulation of the consequence (peer attention) resulted in decreasing the calling out and in an appropriate replacement behavior (raising hand).

Educational personnel may also need to use **functional assessment interviews** with teachers, parents, and the target student (Gresham, Watson, & Skinner, 2001). During these interviews, the goal is to obtain information that will assist in formulating a hypothesis about the function of the target behavior. These interviews will provide information concerning how the student functions in various environments. When interviewed, the student can share feelings and concerns about school and other areas of her life.

DIRECT OBSERVATION TECHNIQUES

target behaviors Specific behaviors that require intervention by the teacher to promote optimal academic or social learning.

baseline The frequency, duration, or latency of a behavior determined before behavioral intervention.

antecedent An event that occurs prior to the target behavior and increases or decreases the probability of the target behavior.

The first step in the intervention of behavioral problems is the identification of **target behaviors.** Once the exact behavior or behaviors have been identified, direct observations can begin. Direct observation enables the teacher to note how often a behavior occurs and to establish a **baseline,** which will be used to monitor the student's progress following intervention. Direct observation also enables the teacher to note the possible **antecedent** events that may trigger the target behavior or that may increase the likelihood that it will occur.

Behavioral observations can be completed by the teacher or by another objective professional or trained paraprofessional. Behaviors may be observed for frequency, duration, intensity, or for the length of time between responses or interresponse time (Gresham et al., 2001). The observer should remember two important guidelines for effective behavioral observation: Be objective and specific. The observer should be fair and nonjudgmental and should precisely pinpoint or identify problem behaviors. The identified behaviors should be stated exactly so that two observers would be able to agree about whether the behavior is or is not occurring.

ANTECEDENTS

setting event A specific event that occurs before the target behavior but is removed from the actual environment in which the behavior occurs.

Antecedents may be actual events that increase the probability of target behaviors occurring. Antecedents may also be events that occur in another setting prior to the actual target behavior. These are called **setting events.** For example, a setting event may be that a student has an argument at home with his older sibling before coming to school. This antecedent may increase the probability that the student will exhibit externalizing target behaviors within the school environment. Other events that may increase the probability of a target behavior may be the events that make a consequence more attractive. For example, a student may be more anxious to receive an edible reward as a consequence when the student is hungry. This may increase the probability that a student will behave in a specific way, such as stealing another student's lunch. This type of an event is known as an **establishing operation** or EO (Michael, 2000).

establishing operation Events occurring before the target behavior that alter the receptivity of the consequence and increase or decrease the probability of occurrence of the target behavior.

ANECDOTAL RECORDING

Behavioral intervention strategies are based on a clear understanding of why a behavior occurs. Behavioristic principle is founded in the theory that behaviors are maintained or increased by the reinforcing events that follow the event or behavior. Events that happen prior to the target behavior may increase the likelihood that the behavior will be exhibited. These conditions occurring prior to the exhibited behavior are known as antecedents. The teacher may recognize when a behavior occurs but not be able to identify the reinforcing event or the antecedent event. One behavioral observation technique that will enable the teacher to hypothesize about the exact antecedent event, and reinforcing event, or consequence, is called anecdotal recording.

In the anecdotal recording method, the teacher observes the student and writes down everything that occurs in the situation. The teacher or other educational or behavioral professional observes the student for a specific time period, usually when the behavior seems to occur most frequently. The teacher may wish to observe during a particular academic subject time, such as math class, or during a nonacademic time when the behavior occurs, such as lunch or recess.

An anecdotal recording might look like this:

Name Mary

Observation Time

9:30 a.m. Language Arts—Mary enters the classroom and walks around the room twice, then sits in her chair. Mary looks out of the window.

9:32 a.m. Mary speaks out: Teacher, can I go to the office?

Response: Mary, get your workbook out and turn to page 56.

9:33 a.m. Mary gets workbook out and begins to look at the pictures on several of the pages. Continues for quite some time.

9:45 a.m. Mary speaks out: What page, teacher?

Teacher responds: Page 56.

9:47 a.m. Mary speaks out: Teacher, can I use a pencil?

Response: Here is a pencil, Mary.

Using the anecdotal format for observation provides a basis for analyzing the antecedent, behavior, and consequence. The antecedent is the event preceding the behavior, and the consequence is the event following the behavior. The antecedent may actually trigger the behavior, whereas the consequence is thought to maintain or reinforce the behavior. In the preceding example, the antecedent, behavior, and consequence analysis, or A-B-C, might look like this:

A	B	C
Mary enters room sits in chair and	walks around	allowed to walk freely
looks at the teacher	talks out	teacher responds
looks at pages in workbook, then looks at teacher	talks out	teacher responds
looks at the teacher	talks out	teacher responds

This analysis provides information that will help the teacher plan a behavioral intervention strategy. It appears that the reinforcing event for Mary's talking out is the teacher responding to Mary. It also seems that the teacher has not provided an organizational intervention plan that will convey to Mary the behaviors expected of her when beginning academic work or instruction. Through this observation, two behaviors have been targeted for intervention: organizational behavior (ready for work) and talking out. The organizational behaviors expected can be broken down into specific behaviors for intervention: student in chair, pencils ready, books out, paper ready.

Check Your Understanding

Complete Activity 9.1.

ACTIVITY 9.1

Read the following anecdotal recording, which covers 2 days of class, and then answer the questions.

Name: John

Monday

John enters classroom.

Teacher (T): Let's get ready for math class.
John (J): Can we go on the field trip Thursday?
T: Yes, John. We will go on Thursday.
J: I can't find my math book.
T: Look in your desk, John. Now, let's work problems 1 to 10 on page 284.
J: [Throws pencil on the floor. Picks pencil up.]

T: John, let's get to work.
J: [Crumbles paper up, throws on floor. Throws book on floor.]
T: That's it, John! Go to the office.
J: [Smiles. Leaves the room.]

Tuesday

John enters classroom.

T: Now class, let's get our math books out.
J: [Out of seat. Goes to pencil sharpener.]
T: John, when do we sharpen our pencils?
J: [No response.]
T: Pencil time is after lunch. Now, get your math book out. Turn to page 286. Let's check our homework.
J: [Slams book on desk. Groans.]
T: Today we will continue the division problems. John, get your book open—
J: [Throws book on floor.]
T: Okay! To the office!
J: [Smiles, leaves the room.]

Analyze the observations of John's behavior for antecedent, behavior, and consequence.

A	B	C
______________	______________	______________
______________	______________	______________
______________	______________	______________
______________	______________	______________
______________	______________	______________
______________	______________	______________

Functional Assessment Interview

During the functional assessment interview, John describes how he feels about his behavior. He reports that he is not happy in class and that the tasks have become too difficult. He states that he has not been able to keep up with the assignments the teacher gives each day for homework. Additional questioning about his homework routine reveals that John's parents work different shifts and that he often is responsible for younger siblings in the evenings until his father returns. He adds that due to child care difficulties, his mother wakes the children at 4:30 a.m. each day so that they may be at an aunt's house by 5:00, where he then sleeps for another hour before getting ready to come to school. He believes that he is too tired on some days to concentrate on his schoolwork. When asked if he has discussed these issues with his teachers, he states that it is too hard for him to talk about these concerns with other students in the classroom.

What additional important information was obtained in the functional interview? ______________________________

____

____

____

Apply Your Knowledge

Based on your analysis of the antecedents, behaviors, and consequences, what purpose is the behavior serving for John? What would you recommend for an intervention plan? ______________________________

____

____

____

EVENT RECORDING

Event recording assesses the frequency with which behaviors occur. The teacher marks or tallies the number of times specific behaviors occur. This information, the initial recording of data, creates a baseline for the teacher to use as a comparison following intervention. This type of recording is useful for observing easily detectable behaviors for short periods of time. Examples of this type of behavior include time on task, talking out, and hitting. One illustration of **frequency counting,** another name for event recording, is shown in Figure 9.2.

frequency counting Counting the occurrence of a specific behavior; same as event recording.

Observations using event recording are typically completed for an entire class period or continuously for a specified time period. Other meth-

Name Joe

Target behavior: Out of seat

	Mon.	Tues.	Wed.
9:00 – 10:00	𝍸 𝍸	𝍸 𝍸 𝍷𝍷	𝍸 𝍸 𝍷
10:00 – 11:00	𝍷𝍷	𝍷	𝍷𝍷𝍷
11:00 – 12:00	𝍷	𝍷𝍷𝍷	𝍷𝍷

Figure 9.2 An example of event recording (frequency counting).

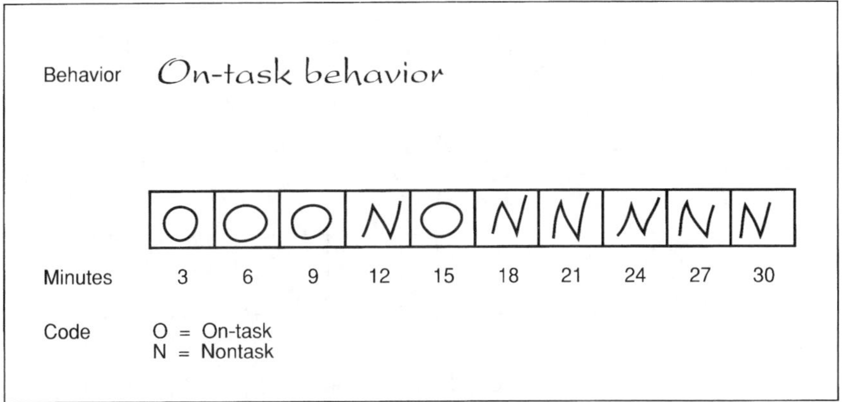

Figure 9.3 Sample chart for time sampling of on-task and nontask behaviors. (*Source:* From *Teaching Strategies for Children in Conflict* (2nd ed., p. 84) by H. L. Swanson and H. R. Reinert, 1984, New York: Times Mirror/Mosby College Publishing. Copyright 1984 by Times Mirror/Mosby College Publishing. Reprinted by permission.)

ods for observing behaviors intermittently or for short periods of time are **time sampling** and interval recording.

time sampling When the behavioral observation samples behavior through the day or class period.

TIME SAMPLING

Time sampling uses frequency counting or event recording techniques for various times throughout the day or class period. The teacher identifies the target behaviors and records student activity for a time period, such as 2 or 5 minutes, throughout the period or day. The teacher is sampling the behavior to get an idea of how often the behavior occurs, without observing continuously. This enables the teacher to observe more than one student or more than one behavior throughout the day. An example of a time-sampling observation is shown in Figure 9.3.

INTERVAL RECORDING

Interval recording is used when the teacher wants to observe several students or behaviors at one time, record intermittently throughout the day or class period, and record behaviors that occur too frequently to record each event, such as stereotypical behaviors (Kerr & Nelson, 2002). During interval recording, the teacher notes whether the behavior is occurring or not occurring. The time intervals may be very short throughout the day. The observation might be for a very brief period of time, such as 2 minutes, during which the teacher notes every 30 seconds whether or not the behavior is occurring. An example of interval recording is shown in Figure 9.4.

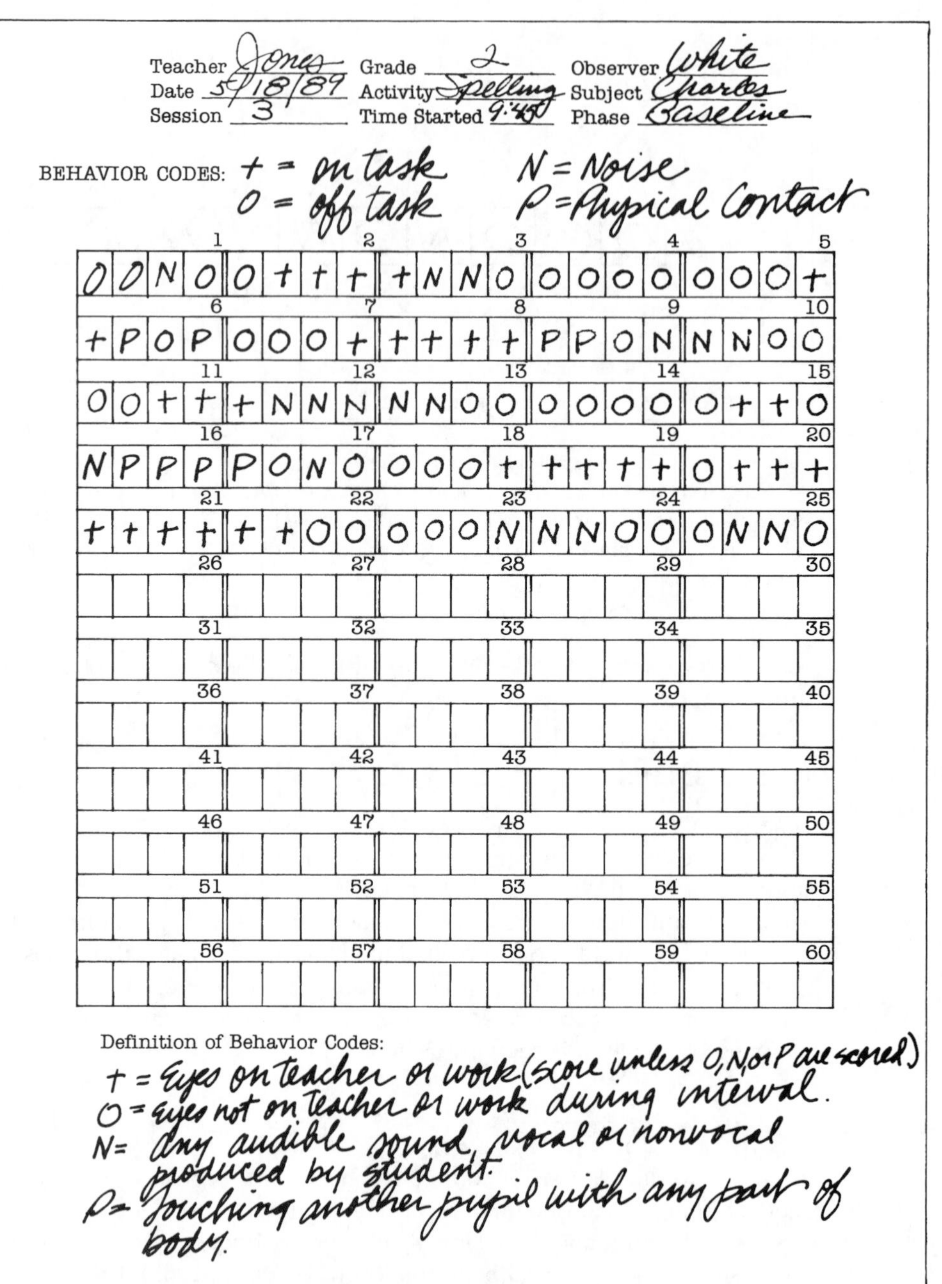

Teacher Jones Grade 2 Observer White
Date 5/18/89 Activity Spelling Subject Charles
Session 3 Time Started 9:45 Phase Baseline

BEHAVIOR CODES: + = on task N = Noise
O = off task P = Physical Contact

1	2	3	4	5
O O N O	O + + +	+ N N O	O O O O	O O O +
6	**7**	**8**	**9**	**10**
+ P O P	O O O +	+ + + +	P P O N	N N O O
11	**12**	**13**	**14**	**15**
O O + +	+ N N N	N N O O	O O O O	O + + O
16	**17**	**18**	**19**	**20**
N P P P	P O N O	O O O +	+ + + +	O + + +
21	**22**	**23**	**24**	**25**
+ + + +	+ + O O	O O O N	N N O O	O N N O
26	**27**	**28**	**29**	**30**
31	**32**	**33**	**34**	**35**
36	**37**	**38**	**39**	**40**
41	**42**	**43**	**44**	**45**
46	**47**	**48**	**49**	**50**
51	**52**	**53**	**54**	**55**
56	**57**	**58**	**59**	**60**

Definition of Behavior Codes:
+ = Eyes on teacher or work (score unless O, N, or P are scored)
O = eyes not on teacher or work during interval.
N = Any audible sound, vocal or nonvocal produced by student.
P = Touching another pupil with any part of body.

Figure 9.4 Sample interval recording form. (*Source:* From *Strategies for Addressing Behavior Problems in the Classroom* (4th ed., p. 97) by M. M. Kerr and C. M. Nelson, 1989. Upper Saddle River, NJ: Merrill/Prentice Hall. Copyright 2002 by Prentice Hall. Reprinted by permission.)

DURATION RECORDING

The duration recording technique is used when the length of the behavior is the target variable of the behavior. For example, a student may need to increase the amount of time spent on task. The teacher will record how long the student remains on task following the directive to do so. The duration recording might look like this:

Name *Ralph*
Task *writing assignment*

On Task	Off Task
2 min	60 s
60 s	2 min
60 s	60 s

On-task/off-task ratio is 4:8 min = 50% on task

This brief duration recording revealed that Ralph is on task only 50% of the expected time. Following intervention by the teacher, such as a prompting signal or behavioral contract or other strategy, it is hoped that the student's on-task time would increase, while off-task time would decrease. Reinforcement for on-task time would increase the probability that Ralph would remain on task longer. A duration recording of on-task time during the intervention or treatment should be compared with the baseline data of 50% to note the effectiveness of the intervention strategies.

LATENCY RECORDING

The latency recording method of observation also involves the element of time. This is an observation in which the time is recorded from the moment a stimulus (such as a command) is given until the response occurs. The element of elapsed time is recorded. For example, the time is recorded from the moment the teacher gives spelling instructions until the student begins the assignment. If the student must be prompted several times during the completion of the task, the latency is recorded each time the student is prompted (Evans, Evans, & Schmid, 1989).

INTERRESPONSE TIME

Latency recording measures the amount of time elapsed between the specific stimulus and the actual response. Interresponse time assesses the length of time between the behaviors or responses (Gresham et al., 2001). For example, a student may be distracted or off task every 2 minutes between the observation period of 2:00 to 3:00 p.m., but become distracted only every 20 minutes during the observation period of 10:00 to 11:00 a.m.

This assessment would then pose additional questions—such as, is the subject matter more interesting or easier in the morning observation, are there more hands-on activities, is the student tired in the afternoons, or has the student been prescribed a medication for distractibility that is administered only in the morning?

Check Your Understanding

Complete Activity 9.2.

ACTIVITY 9.2

Use the following information to analyze the behavior of a fifth-grade student named Amber.

Day 1

Anecdotal recording:

Amber was presented with her arithmetic worksheet following the direct instruction lesson with her group. After several minutes, she began to work on the first problem. During the time period of receiving the work and beginning the work, she was observed looking through her desk to find the necessary materials. When she located her pencil and paper, she dropped the assignment page on the floor. She picked the paper up and placed it on her desk. She sharpened her pencil and began to work. During the period that she was seated at her desk working, approximately 10 minutes, she was observed looking around the room and watching other students. When a sound occurred outside the room, she would look in the hallway or out the window. When papers were collected, she had completed the first 2 of 15 problems. One problem was correct, but the second problem was not calculated correctly because of a careless error.

Day 2

Latency recording: Time elapsed from assignment to working behavior: 5 minutes.

Interval recording: Observations during work time:

+ = On task 0 = Off task

	0	0	0	0	0	+	+	0	0	+
Minutes	1	2	3	4	5	6	7	8	9	10

1. Analyze the anecdotal recording. What are the antecedents, behaviors, and consequences?

A	B	C
____________	____________	____________
____________	____________	____________

2. Analyze the latency recording information. ____________________

____

3. Analyze the interval recording data. How often is the student on task? ____________________

Apply Your Knowledge

Based on the information provided, why do you think Amber is having difficulty with this task? What recommendations would you suggest for Amber? ____________________

____

STRUCTURED CLASSROOM OBSERVATIONS

Observation methods discussed so far in this chapter may be teacher-made, informal instruments that can be used for prereferral, assessment, and intervention of behavioral problems. A structured classroom observation form called the Direct Observation Form (Achenbach, 1986) is one part of the Child Behavior Checklist (CBCL) system, a multiaxial system for assessment of behavioral and emotional problems. Other forms in this system are described throughout the chapter in the appropriate topical sections.

CHILD BEHAVIOR CHECKLIST: DIRECT OBSERVATION FORM, REVISED EDITION

The Direct Observation Form (Achenbach, 1986) is four pages in length, including general instructions and guidelines. The first page consists of the student's identifying information (name, date of birth, observation settings, and so on) and the general administration instructions. The inside pages of the form comprise three parts: an observation rating scale on which to mark observed behaviors and rate their intensity or severity, a space for anecdotal recording of all events during the observation period, and an interval recording form. The observer makes several observations of the target student across several different settings. The observer compares the target student with two grade and gender peers. When comparing the target student, the observer ascertains whether the student is significantly different from the two control students in on-task behavior. This method is often used to assess behavioral disorders such as attention deficit disorder. Often, the criterion for indicating possible attention problems is that the target student's off-task behavior score is 1.5 or 2 standard deviations above the control students' scores. The observer marks the items on the rating scale if the target child exhibits the behaviors during the observation. Figure 9.5 illustrates the types of items represented on the Direct Observation

	Yes	No
1. Student is prepared for work each period.	______	______
2. Student begins assignment on request.	______	______
3. Student stays on task with no distractions.	______	______
4. Student completes tasks.	______	______
5. Student stays on task but is sometimes distracted.	______	______
6. Student complies with teacher requests.	______	______
7. Student raises hand to speak.	______	______
8. Student talks out inappropriately.	______	______
9. Student completes homework.	______	______
10. Student is aggressive toward peers.	______	______
11. Student is disruptive during class.	______	______
12. Student talks out of turn.	______	______
13. Student is verbally aggressive.	______	______
14. Student has damaged property belonging to others.	______	______

Figure 9.5 Behavioral checklist.

Form. These items are then scored, as are the other rating scales and interviews of the multiaxial CBCL system, for significant behavior problems. The behaviors are defined on two broad bands: (1) externalizing (acting out); and (2) internalizing (turning inward), which includes problems such as anxiety or withdrawal. In addition, the system notes the occurrence of several clinical behavioral syndromes, such as social problems, somatic complaints, aggressive behavior, and attention problems. The other components of the CBCL are scored along the same broad and narrow bands of behavior and emotional functioning.

OTHER TECHNIQUES FOR ASSESSING BEHAVIOR

checklists Lists of academic or behavioral skills that must be mastered by the student.

questionnaires Questions about a student's behavior or academic concerns that may be answered by the student or by the parent or teacher; also called interviews.

Some techniques for assessing behavior do not involve direct observation of behavior. These techniques include **checklists, questionnaires, interviews, sociograms,** and **ecological assessment.** These methods rely on input from others, such as parents, teachers, or peers, rather than on direct observation of behavior. When these indirect methods are used with direct observation, the teacher can plan effective behavioral intervention strategies.

CHECKLISTS AND RATING SCALES

A checklist is a list of questions that the respondent completes by checking the appropriate responses. The respondent may answer yes or no, or they may check off the statements that apply to the student. The teacher, the

interviews Formal or informal questions asked orally by the examiner.

sociograms Graphic representation of the social dynamics within a group.

ecological assessment Analysis of the student's total learning environment.

parents, or both may complete the checklist. An example of a behavioral checklist was given earlier, in Figure 9.5.

A rating questionnaire may be similar in content to a checklist, although the respondent rates the answer. For example, the format of the checklist in Figure 9.5 would change so that the respondent would rate student behaviors as never, almost never, sometimes, somewhat often, frequently, or almost always. This format allows for interpretation of the extremes. The student behavior might be rated as almost never completing assignments, but frequently being verbally aggressive and sometimes damaging property. This information helps the teacher pinpoint areas that need observation and further evaluation.

Elliot, Busse, and Gresham (1993) suggested that the following issues be considered when using rating scales:

1. Ratings are summaries of observations of the relative frequency of specific behaviors.
2. Ratings of social behavior are judgments affected by one's environment and rater's standards for behavior.
3. The social validity of the behaviors one assesses and eventually treats should be understood.
4. Multiple assessors of the same child's behavior may agree only moderately.
5. Many characteristics of a student may influence social behavior; however, the student's sex is a particularly salient variable.

Several rating forms are commonly used in the assessment of behavior problems. Many of these include forms for teachers and parents. Common examples include the Teacher Report Form (Achenbach, 1991b) and the Child Behavior Checklist (Achenbach, 1991a), the Behavior Rating Profile-2 (Brown & Hammill, 1990), and the Conners Teacher Rating Scales and Conners Parent Rating Scales (1997). These forms and scoring systems ask a variety of questions about the student, and the parent or teacher rates the student on each item.

Child Behavior Checklist: Parent, Teacher, and Youth Report Forms. The CBCL system is built upon the Child Behavior Checklist (Achenbach, 1991a), which is the parent report form, and companion forms such as the Teacher Report Form (Achenbach, 1991b) and the Youth Self-Report (Achenbach, 1991c). (The system's Direct Observation Form and interview form are discussed in other sections of this chapter.)

The Achenbach system allows for the student to be rated on both positive, or adaptive, behaviors and behavioral syndromes. In 1991, the author revised the system to allow the profiles to be scored consistently across the parent, teacher, and youth scales (McConaughy & Achenbach, 1993). The

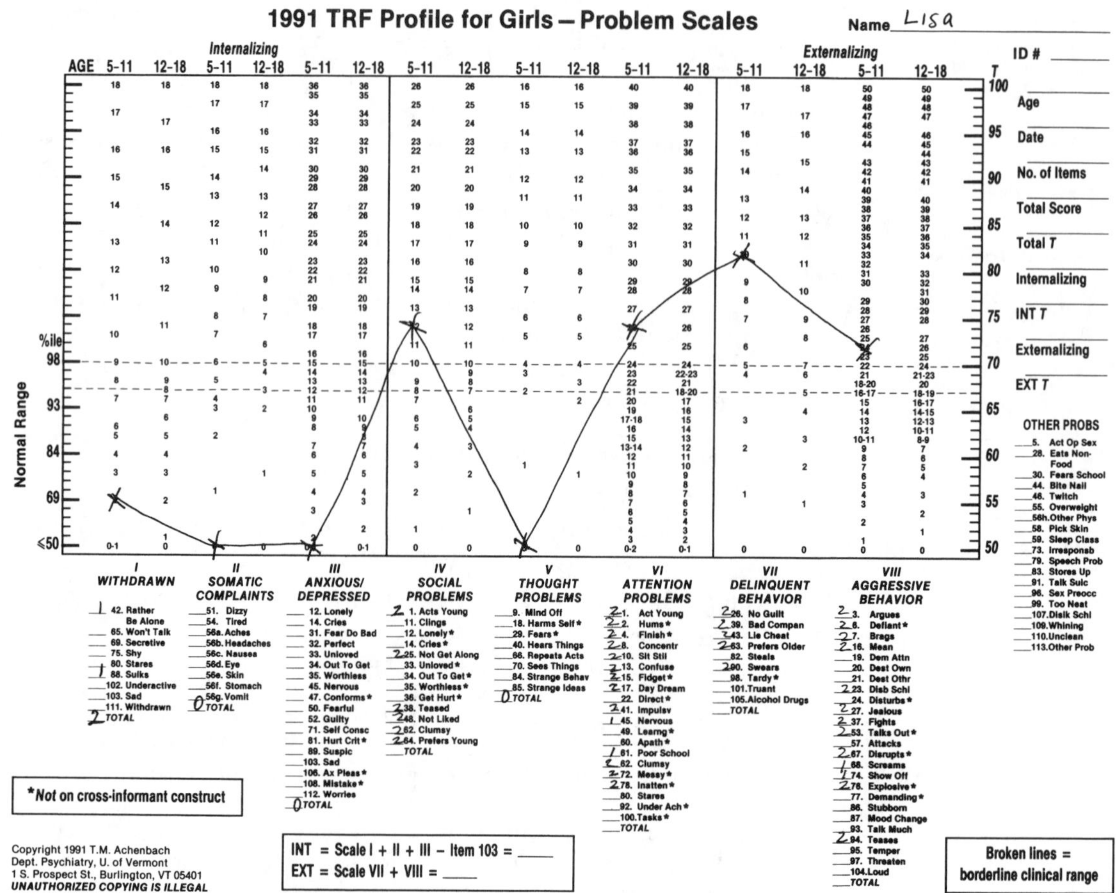

Figure 9.6 CBCL Teacher Report Form showing sample profile for female student. (*Source:* From *Manual for the Teacher Report Form and 1991 Profile* by T. M. Achenbach, 1991, Burlington: University of Vermont Department of Psychiatry. Copyright 1991 by T. M. Achenbach. Reprinted by permission.)

parent form includes, in addition to the rating scales, some open-ended questions, such as "What concerns you most about your child?"

Two CBCL forms are available for parents: one for children aged 2–3 years and another for students aged 4–18 years. The Teacher Report Form is for students aged 5–18. Items on these instruments are closely related so that both parents and teachers are rating the student on similar dimensions. An example of a Teacher Report Form profile is shown in Figure 9.6.

In addition to the teacher and parent forms, a self-rating form is available for students aged 11–18. The Youth Self-Report (Achenbach, 1991c) covers many of the same topics as the teacher and parent forms. This instrument can be evaluated qualitatively to determine the student's perceptions of himself. The student also answers items concerning current academic achievement and rates himself on social dimensions such as getting along with family members.

Examiner manuals address the issues of validity and reliability for each of the individual parts of the multiaxial CBCL system by Achenbach (1991a, 1991b, 1991c). The examiner is provided with detailed information about content and criterion-related validity and the discriminant validity of using cutoff scores to identify students with specific behavioral problems. Test-retest, testing across time, and reliability of raters are presented, and technical quality of the systems appears to be adequate or above on all measures.

Behavior Assessment System for Children (BASC). This assessment system includes rating scales for parents to complete, rating scales for teachers to complete, a developmental history form for parents, and self-reports for students ages 8–18. This system includes an observation form for recording observations within the classroom environment. The BASC system was developed to be used with students ages 2½ to 18 years of age. The system provides a method for distinguishing students with attention deficit disorder, depression, and social maladjustments. Scores indicate students who are within a clinical range of significance; at risk for having difficulties; and average, low, and very low. The BASC also indicates how well students are adapting in a positive manner. Scores on the adaptive scales are noted to be very high, high, average, at risk, and clinically significant. The BASC includes an audiotape provided for students who have difficulty reading the self-report form in English but who understand spoken English. The student self-report form is presented in a true-false format. The hand scoring of the BASC is a multistep process, and it is more complex than other rating scales. It provides a means of comparing the student with both the norm sample and clinical samples. This may be more helpful in determining the severity of behavioral difficulties.

The examiner's manual provides information regarding the standardization and norm samples for all components of the BASC. The total number of students and parents for the norm samples was 2,401 for the Teacher Rating Scale; 3,483 for the Parent Rating Scale; and 9,861 for the Self-Report of Personality. The samples were representative geographically, and gender and race/ethnicity were also considered and approximated U.S. population estimates.

The manual presents reliability and validity information for all scales. Ample technical data for internal consistency, test-retest reliability, interrater reliability, standard error of measurement, factor structure of scales, and concurrent validity data are presented.

Behavior Rating Profile—2. The Behavior Rating Profile—2 (Brown & Hammill, 1990) includes forms for the student, parent, and teacher. The student completes the rating by marking that items are true or false about herself. The teacher and parents rate the student by marking that the items are very much like the student, not like the student, like the student, or not at all like the student. This system allows the examiner to compare how the student, teacher, and parent perceive the student. It also categorizes the student's perceptions into the various environments of the student's life: school, home, and peer relationships. This enables the examiner to determine whether the student has more positive feelings about school, relationships with peers, or relationships with parents. The instrument is scored using a standard score with a mean of 10 and a standard deviation of 3. The examiner can plot a profile that presents a view of how the student, parent, and teacher perceive the student.

The manual provides reliability and validity information that includes studies conducted with relatively small samples. The internal consistency and test-retest coefficients seem to be adequate, with many reported to be in the .80s. Validity studies include criterion-related research, with reported coefficients ranging from below acceptable levels to adequate. The authors provide discussion of content and construct validity.

Conners Rating Scales—Revised. The Conners system (Conners, 1997) includes the following scales:

Conners Parent Rating Scale—Revised: Long Version
Conners Parent Rating Scale—Revised: Short Version
Conners Teacher Rating Scale—Revised: Long Version
Conners Teacher Rating Scale—Revised: Short Version
Conners-Wells' Adolescent Self-Report Scale: Long Version
Conners-Wells' Adolescent Self-Report Scale: Short Version
Auxiliary Scales
Conners Global Index—Parent
Conners Global Index—Teacher
Conners ADHD/DSM-IV Scales—Parent
Conners ADHD/DSM-IV Scales—Adolescent

The revised version of this instrument includes several substantial changes. The author states that the revised version provides multidimensional scales that assess ADHD and other disorders that may exist with the attention disorders. The new version includes additional methods for assisting mental health professionals in making *DSM-IV* (*Diagnostic and Statistical Manual*, 4th Edition) of the American Psychiatric Association (1994). The former edition of the Conners included a Hyperactivity Index, which is now called the Conners' Global Index.

The Conners Rating Scales—Revised was developed with a large standardization sample (more than 8,000) with representative samples in the United States and Canada. In addition to representative norms, several studies are included in the manual that compare ethnic differences in samples of the following groups: African American/Black, Asian, Caucasian, Hispanic, Native American, and Other. These studies are presented in adequate detail in the manual, with main effect differences by ethnic group provided for each scale. Consumers of this instrument are encouraged to read this section of the manual carefully when using the instrument for diagnostic purposes with the mentioned ethnic groups.

The dimensions of the Conners Rating Scales include oppositional, cognitive problems/inattention, hyperactivity, anxious-shy, perfectionism, social problems, and psychosomatic. The special "Quick Score" paper included with the rating scales enables the teacher or other member of the multidisciplinary team to score the short form in minutes. The long versions of the various rating scales involve much more effort to score, and hand scoring using the profile sheets is difficult because of the large number of columns included on the page. Computer scoring is available.

Reliability studies included internal reliability. Internal consistency for the various scales ranged from .72 to .95. Some variability exists on some scales with different age groups. For example, teacher ratings were more consistent for the younger and older age groups than for other age groups.

Validity studies in the Conners examiner's manual address factorial validity, convergent validity, divergent validity, discriminant validity, and concurrent validity. Information concerning this research is much more extensive than the previous edition and seems to range from below acceptable levels to adequate. Many of the studies included small samples. The author states that research in this area is continuing.

QUESTIONNAIRES AND INTERVIEWS

The questions found on questionnaires are similar to the items on checklists, but the respondent is encouraged to describe the behaviors or situations where the behavior occurs. The respondent answers with narrative statements. For example, the questions might appear as follows:

1. How is the student prepared for class each day?
2. Describe how the student begins assignments during class.

Figure 9.7
Interview questions adapted for both parent and student.

Parent Interview	***Student Interview***
1. How do you think your child feels about school this year?	**1.** Tell me how you feel about school this year.
2. Tell me how your child completes homework assignments.	**2.** Describe how you go about finishing your homework.
3. Describe the responsibilities your child has at home.	**3.** What type of things are you expected to do at home? Do you think you complete those things most of the time?

3. How does the student perform during distractions?
4. How often does the student complete homework assignments?
5. How does the student respond during class discussions?

The respondent should be encouraged to provide objective responses that describe as many variables of the behavior as possible. Interviews are completed using questions similar to those used on questionnaires. The evaluator verbally asks the respondent the questions and encourages objective, detailed information. The interview format may also be used with the student to obtain information about the student's feelings and perceptions about the target behaviors. Figure 9.7 illustrates how an interview could be adapted so that both parents and the student could provide answers.

Child Behavior Checklist: Semistructured Clinical Interview. Interviews may be conducted by different members of the multidisciplinary team. Often, these interviews are unstructured and informal. Achenbach and McConaughy (1989, 1990) developed a semistructured interview and observation form to be used with students aged 5–11. This interview assesses the student's feelings about school, family, and peers as well as affect or emotional functioning. The examiner is provided with, in addition to the interview, an observation form to rate behaviors of and comments by the student observed during the interview. The student is asked open-ended questions and guided through the interview process. This interview can be useful in determining the current social and emotional issues concerning the student.

SOCIOGRAMS

The sociogram method enables the teacher to obtain information about the group dynamics and structure within the classroom. This information can be interpreted to determine which students are well liked by their peers, which students are considered to be the leaders in the group, and which students are believed to be successful in school.

A sociogram is constructed by designing questions that all members of the class will be asked to answer. The questions might include, "Whom would you select to be in your group for the science project?" or "Whom would you invite to the movies?" The answers are then collected and interpreted by the teacher. The diagram in Figure 9.8a illustrates a sociogram; Figure 9.8b lists questions asked of a class of fourth-grade students.

The data are analyzed to determine who the class members perceive as being the class stars, the social isolates, and so on. The teacher also can determine where mutual choices exist (where two students share the same feelings about each other) and can identify cliques and persons who are neglected. The teacher can then use this information to intervene and structure social and academic situations that would promote fair social skills development. Role plays, class projects, and school social activities could be used to increase the interpersonal interaction opportunities for social isolates and neglectees.

Check Your Understanding

Complete Activity 9.3.

ACTIVITY 9.3

Use Figure 9.8a to analyze the social dynamics of this classroom.

1. Which students have made mutual choices?
   ____
2. Which students seem to be isolated from their peers? __________
   ____
3. Which students appear to be in cliques or groups? __________
   ____
4. Which students seem to be the most socially popular?
   ____
5. Who are the academic stars? __________
   ____

Apply Your Knowledge

List other questions that you may find useful in a sociogram:
____

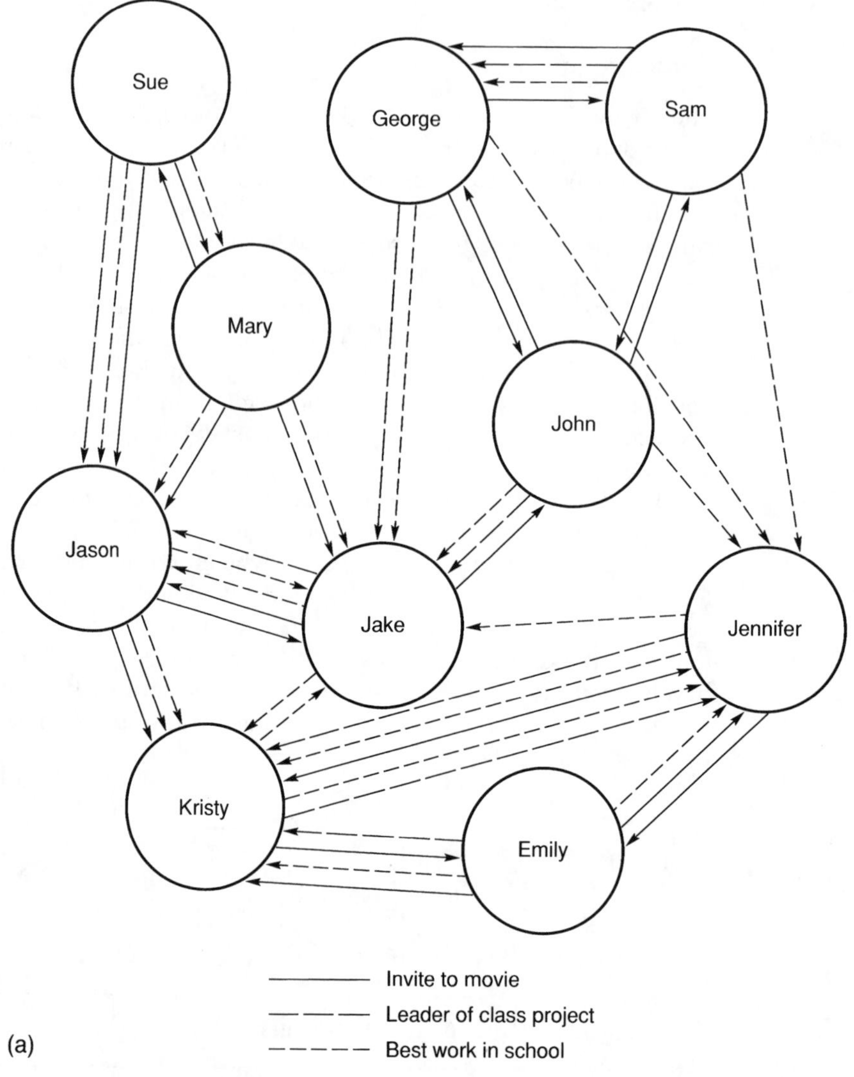

> ***Sociogram questions.***
>
> **1.** Name two students in our class whom you would most like to invite to a movie (or other activity).
>
> **a.** ______________
>
> **b.** ______________
>
> **2.** In our class, whom would you like to be the leader of our class project? ______________
>
> **3.** Name two students in our class who do the best work in school.
>
> **a.** ______________
>
> **b.** ______________

(b)

Figure 9.8 Sociogram (a) and sociogram questions (b).

ECOLOGICAL ASSESSMENT

Ecological assessment analyzes the student's total learning environment. This analysis includes the student's interactions with others (peers, teachers, paraprofessionals, parents, and other persons who are directly involved with the student's learning process); the teacher's interactions with other students in the classroom; the methods of presentation of materials; materials used in the classroom; the physical environment; and the student's interactions with others in different settings, such as the playground or lunchroom. All of the informal behavioral assessment methods presented thus far may be used as a part of ecological assessment.

The teacher variable is one area that can be assessed by direct observation and other techniques, such as questionnaires and self-assessment. One method of observing the teacher interaction variable, suggested by Guerin and Maier (1983), is a survey form to evaluate teaching competency (Figure 9.9). This type of survey can be completed by the teacher or by an objective observer. This information can also be obtained by using student evaluations that ask similar questions. The student's educational materials should be evaluated for their appropriateness for the individual student. The level of difficulty, format, and mode of presentation and response are important considerations. The following variables should be evaluated when assessing materials:

Analyzing Instructional Materials

1. Are the objectives of the materials appropriate for the student?
2. Do the ability/readability levels match the current instructional level of the student?
3. Is the interest level appropriate for the student?
4. Does the method of presentation match the student's strength for learning?
5. Are prerequisite steps needed before the student can attempt the task?
6. Does the format of the material contain extraneous stimuli that can confuse or distract the student?
7. Does the material contain information not necessary for task completion?
8. Are too many tasks contained on one page?
9. Is the student capable of completing the task in the amount of time allowed?
10. Does the task need to be broken down into smaller tasks?
11. Is the student capable of responding with relative ease in the manner required by the materials?
12. Can the criterion level for success be reduced?
13. Does the material allow the student to self-check or self-correct?
14. Does the material allow the student to observe progress? (Overton 1987, pp. 111–115)

Competencies	Evaluation: Excellent	Average	Improvement Comments
1. Classroom organization			
a. Instructional strategies are varied.	________	________	________
b. All materials are ready when lesson begins.	________	________	________
c. Lessons are planned in accordance with curriculum goals.	________	________	________
2. Instructional objectives			
a. Instructional objectives are identified.	________	________	________
b. Objectives are age- and ability-appropriate.	________	________	________
c. Objectives are in measurable terms.	________	________	________
3. Instruction			
a. Direct instruction is maximized.	________	________	________
b. Assignments are geared so that they meet needs of different abilities.	________	________	________
c. Individualized instruction is well monitored.	________	________	________
d. Instruction involves different student learning modalities.	________	________	________
e. Aides effectively managed.	________	________	________
4. Skill development			
a. Ideas are sequentially developed from simple to complex.	________	________	________
b. Steps in growth are monitored.	________	________	________
c. Teacher's language is clear and appropriate.	________	________	________
d. Questions and activities are appropriate.	________	________	________
5. Assessment and evaluation			
a. Group tests used to monitor program effectiveness.	________	________	________
b. Individual assessment used to measure pupil growth.	________	________	________
c. Informal assessment of program and pupil movement.	________	________	________
d. Group and individual records maintained in understandable form.	________	________	________
6. Reporting			
a. Parent conferences are preplanned and well organized.	________	________	________
b. Relationship with parents is supportive, cooperative, and informative.	________	________	________

Figure 9.9 Survey to evaluate teaching competency. (*Source:* From *Informal Assessment in Education* (pp. 341–344) by G. R. Guerin and A. S. Maier, 1983, Palo Alto, CA: Mayfield Publishing. Copyright 1983 by Mayfield Publishing. Reprinted by permission.)

Competencies	Evaluation: Excellent	Average	Improvement Comments
7. Materials			
a. Audiovisual material is used effectively.	______	______	______
b. Aides are used to assist students understand concepts and develop skills	______	______	______
c. Seat work is appropriate and can be successfully completed.	______	______	______
d. Blackboard is used to present material, illustrate lessons, organize activities, etc.	______	______	______
8. Interaction			
a. Communicates clearly and respectfully with students.	______	______	______
b. Maintains classroom order and discipline.	______	______	______
c. Listens to students and attempts to understand what they say.	______	______	______
d. Is positive and supportive of student accomplishments.	______	______	______

Figure 9.9 continued.

PROJECTIVE ASSESSMENT TECHNIQUES

projective techniques Techniques used to analyze a student's feelings by what the student projects into the story card or other stimulus.

The measures presented in this section are measures that are scored more subjectively; they are often referred to as **projective techniques.** These measures include sentence completion tests, drawing tests, and apperception tests, which require the student to tell a story about some stimulus, such as picture cards. These instruments are most likely administered by the school psychologist, school counselor, or other professional, such as a clinical psychologist, who has the training and experience required to administer such instruments. Teachers and other members of the multidisciplinary team may be required to make eligibility and planning decisions based on the results of these instruments. It is beneficial to teachers, therefore, to understand the nature of the instruments and how they might be used in the assessment process.

SENTENCE COMPLETION TESTS

sentence completion tests Stems of sentences that the student completes; analyzed for themes.

Sentence completion tests provide stems or beginnings of sentences that the student is required to finish. The stems have been selected to elicit comments from the student on such topics as relationships with parents

1. Sometimes I wish ______________________.
2. I wish my mother would ______________________.
3. I feel sad when ______________________.
4. My friends always ______________________.
5. My father ______________________.

Figure 9.10 Sample items from a sentence completion test.

and friends and feelings about oneself. The examiner analyzes the comments written by the student for themes rather than analyzing each sentence independently. The Rotter Incomplete Sentence Blank (Rotter & Rafferty, 1950) is an example of this type of instrument. Figure 9.10 presents stems similar to those on sentence completion tests.

DRAWING TESTS

drawing tests Tests in which student draws figures, houses, trees, or families; scored developmentally and projectively.

Drawing tests attempt to screen the student's feelings about self, home, and family. Each of these instruments follows a simple format. The student is presented with a form or a piece of plain paper and is asked to draw a picture of himself; of a house, a tree, and a person; or of his family doing something together. These tests are commonly known as the Draw-a-Person, Human-Figure Drawing, House-Tree-Person, and Kinetic Family Drawings. The drawings may be scored subjectively by an examiner who has had training and experience in this type of assessment. More empirically based scoring systems are also available: the Kinetic Family Drawing System for Family and School (Knoff & Prout, 1985), the Draw-a-Person: Screening Procedure for Emotional Disturbance (Naglieri, McNeish, & Bardos, 1991), and the Human Figure Drawing Test (Koppitz, 1968). The Draw-a-Person can be scored developmentally using a system like that by Naglieri (1988) or Harris (1963).

The newer versions of scoring systems include standardization information and developmental information. The Kinetic Family Drawing System for Family and School includes questions that the examiner asks the student about the drawings. For example, one question is "What does this person need most?" (Knoff & Prout, 1985, p. 5). The scoring booklet provides various characteristics that the student may have included in the drawings. The examiner checks to see whether a characteristic, such as the omission of body parts, is present in the student's drawing. Guidelines for interpreting these characteristics are provided in the manual through a listing of relevant research on drawing analysis. The examiner analyzes themes that exist within the drawing on such dimensions as figure characteristics and actions between figures. Several case studies are provided for the examiner to use as guidelines for learning how to interpret the drawings.

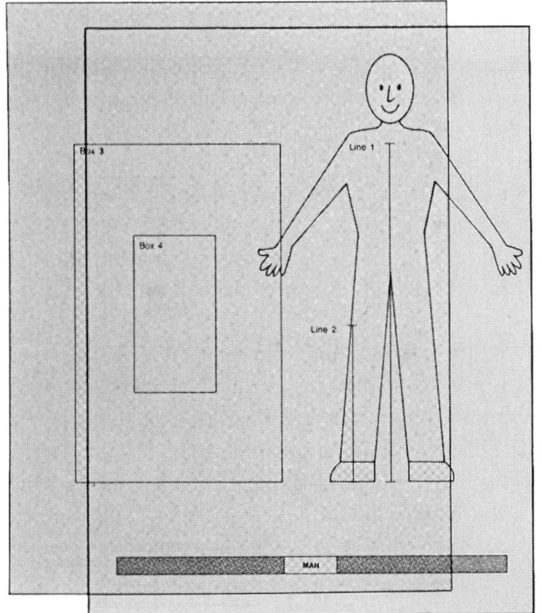

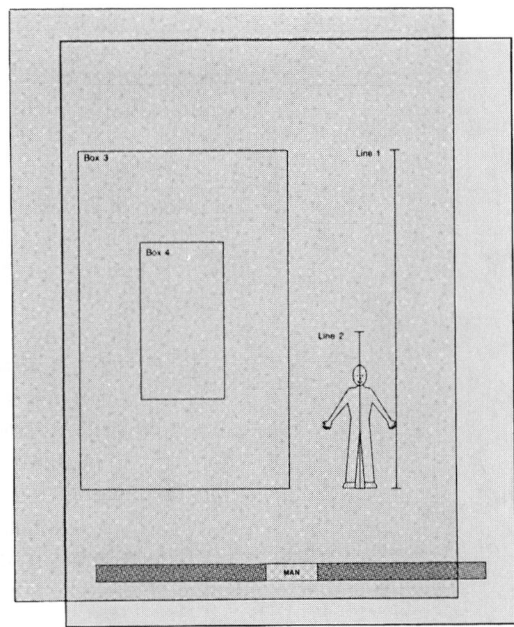

Figure 9.11 Example of the Naglieri et al. template scoring system for the Draw-a-Person test. (*Source:* From *Draw a Person: Screening Procedure for Emotional Disturbance, Examiner's Manual* (p. 23) by J. A. Naglieri, T. J. McNeish, and A. N. Bardos, 1991, Austin, TX: Pro-Ed. Copyright 1991 by Pro-Ed, Inc. Reprinted by permission.)

The scoring system of the Draw-a-Person: Screening Procedure for Emotional Disturbance uses scoring templates and a norm-referenced method of scoring the drawings. The instrument is to be used as a screening device to determine whether the student needs further emotional or behavioral assessment. The manual provides examples of using the templates and scoring exercises using case studies for learning the system. Derived scores include *T* scores with a mean of 50 and a standard deviation of 10 and percentile ranks. The scores are interpreted as follows (Naglieri et al., 1991):

Less than 55	Further evaluation is not indicated
55 to 64	Further evaluation is indicated
65 and above	Further evaluation is strongly indicated (p. 63)

An example of the template scoring system from the manual is presented in Figure 9.11.

The standardization information and technical data provided in the Naglieri et al. (1991) manual is fairly extensive and impressive for a projective drawing instrument. The sample included 2,260 students, ages 6 to 17 years. Approximately 200 students were represented in each age group. Consideration was given for age, sex, geographic region, population of community, ethnicity, race, parent occupation, and socioeconomic status. Internal consistency was researched using the coefficient alpha, and coefficients were adequate, ranging from .67 to .78. The standard error of measurement is approximately 5 for all ages. The test-retest information gives a coefficient of .67, although the sample for this study was fairly small (n = 67). Both intrarater and interrater agreement was studied and resulted in coefficients of .83 and .84, respectively. This study was also small, using 54 cases and 2 raters.

Descriptive statistics are included for validity studies that used the scoring system to compare students who had been clinically diagnosed with emotional or behavioral problems to students without such problems. The scoring system did discriminate between the groups, at least at the .05 significance level. Construct validity is supported by discriminant validity studies of intelligence testing and the Naglieri et al. Draw-a-Person scoring system. The research presented indicates that two separate areas are assessed by the Draw-a-Person and intelligence tests.

APPERCEPTION TESTS

apperception tests Student's feelings about what she perceives to be happening in a picture or other stimulus; influenced by personal experiences.

Apperception tests consist of a set of picture or story cards that have been designed to elicit responses about emotional issues. These instruments may be administered and interpreted only by professionals with the training and experience required by the test developers. Most of these projective techniques require that the examiner possess advanced graduate-level training in psychological assessment. Because apperception tests may contribute information used by the multidisciplinary team to determine educational and behavioral interventions, teachers should understand what these instruments attempt to measure and how they are interpreted. Two commonly used instruments are the Children's Apperception Test (Bellak & Bellak, 1949, 1952; Bellak & Hurvich, 1965) and the Roberts Apperception Test for Children (Roberts, 1982).

Children's Apperception Test (CAT). The CAT comprises two tests and a supplement for special situations (Bellak & Bellak, 1949, 1952; Bellak & Hurvich, 1965). The original test (animal figures) consists of 10 picture cards that depict animals engaged in human situations. The authors developed the instrument as an apperception method, which they define as "a method of investigating personality by studying the dynamic meaningfulness of the individual differences in perception of standard stimuli" (Bellak & Bellak, 1949, p. 1). The examiner evaluates a student's verbal responses to the picture cards in an effort to better understand how the student feels about herself and her relationships with family members.

Figure 9.12 Picture card 8 of the Children's Apperception Test. (*Source:* From *Children's Apperception Test (Animal Figures)* by L. Bellak and S. S. Bellak, 1949, Larchmont, NY: C.P.S. Copyright 1991 by C.P.S., Inc. Reprinted by permission of C.P.S., Inc., Box 83, Larchmont, NY 10538.)

The authors originally believed that younger children would identify more readily with animal figures and that these figures were more cultural and gender free. They later developed the CAT human figures as an answer to research studies that indicated the value of human-figure picture cards (Bellak & Hurvich, 1965). These picture-story cards maintain many of the same story themes and emotionally charged situations as in the animal figures; but the figures are now human, with some remaining fairly gender neutral.

The supplement to the CAT (Bellak & Bellak, 1952) contains various pictures depicting unusual situations using animal figures. Examples include a picture of a pregnant "mother" type of animal, an animal in a doctor's office, and an animal walking with crutches. Any of these specific cards may be selected by the examiner and used with the animal or human figures.

The CAT is scored subjectively along psychoanalytic themes such as regression, fear, anxiety, and denial; the manuals provide guidelines for scoring the instrument. Technical data provided in the manuals do not meet the standards set forth by many test developers in terms of reliability and validity. Figure 9.12 presents a picture-story card from the animal figures of the CAT.

Roberts Apperception Test for Children. The Roberts Apperception Test for Children (McArthur & Roberts, 1982) presents story picture cards of human figures engaged in situations with family members and peers. The test was developed for use with students aged 6 through 15 years. Of 27 stimulus cards, the student responds to 11 cards that are specific to the student's gender, as well as to 5 gender-neutral cards. The cards were designed to elicit comments about the student's feelings about fear, parental relationships, dependency, peer and racial interaction, and so on. The examiner instructs the student to tell a story about what happened before, during, and after each scene pictured and to tell what the characters are doing, saying, and thinking. The examiner scores responses according to guidelines set forth in the manual, which gives information on adaptive indicators, clinical problems such as aggression or anxiety, and supplemental measures such as ego functioning. An interpersonal matrix allows the examiner to compute the child's responses about specific individuals, such as siblings, mother, father, and school personnel.

The manual includes information about the standardization of the instrument as well as studies comparing students within the normal range of emotional functioning with several different clinical samples. Reliability information includes interrater reliability and split-half reliability studies. Coefficients ranged from .44 to .86 on split-half measures. The validity information included in the manual presents several studies of the factors measured as well as the instrument's ability to discriminate clinical from nonclinical groups. Generally, the information presented appears to be adequate for this type of projective instrument.

COMPUTERIZED ASSESSMENT OF ATTENTION DISORDERS

Instruments have been developed for the assessment of sustained focused attention and impulsive responding patterns. Difficulty with these behaviors is believed to be characteristic of students with attention deficit disorders. This type of difficulty may be manifested as distractibility, impulsivity, and overactivity in classroom situations. These instruments should not be used as a single measure of attention problems, but rather should be used in combination with other measures, particularly classroom observations. Two such computerized systems currently used in clinical practice and research are the Continuous Performance Test (Gordon, 1983) and the Conners Continuous Performance Test (Conners, 1993). All tests of this general type are known as CPTs.

CONTINUOUS PERFORMANCE TEST

In Gordon's (1983) Continuous Performance Test, the student must discriminate between visual stimuli presented for a period of 9 minutes. The stimuli are numbers that appear at the rate of 1 per second. Scores are computed for the number of correct responses, omissions, and commissions. This instrument has been widely researched, and the author reports reliability coefficients ranging from .66 to .80.

CONNERS CONTINUOUS PERFORMANCE TEST

The Conners Continuous Performance Test is presented in much the same manner as Gordon's version (Conners, 1993; Conners, 1997). This CPT, however, lasts for 14 minutes, and the visual stimuli—letters—appear at varying rates throughout the administration. The student must maintain focused sustained attention, and the number of targets hit is calculated to determine impulsivity and loss of attention. Interpretive, computer-generated reports give derived scores for hit rate, reaction time, pattern for standard error or variability, omissions, commissions, attentiveness, and response tendencies such as risk taking. Data included in the manual and from computer reports compare the student with age and gender peers in a clinical group of students with attention deficit disorders.

RESEARCH AND ISSUES

The assessment of emotional and behavioral problems is by nature more ambiguous than other types of assessment, such as assessment of intellectual or academic achievement ability. The techniques range from systematic observations and computer assessment to projective techniques, such as telling stories about picture cards. The research on each of these methods has existed in volumes in the literature for many years. The research summarized in the following list represents some of the recent studies using the instruments often employed in settings that serve children and youth. Other measures, such as the Rorschach inkblot test (Rorschach, 1921, 1942), are more often used in clinical settings and therefore were not included in this text.

1. In a review of literature about functional behavioral assessment, it was found that FBA has been largely studied high-rate behaviors in students with low-incidence disabilities, such as self-injurious behaviors in children with mental retardation (Ervin, Radford, Bertsch, Piper, Ehrhardt, and Poling, 2001). Additional research is needed on low-rate behaviors (such as aggressive acts) in students with high-incidence disabilities, such as learning disabilities.
2. Northup and Gulley reviewed research that applied functional behavioral assessment in samples of students with attention deficit hyperactivity disorder and found that it is a useful technique to use in determining the interaction and effectiveness of medication with various environmental stimuli (2001).

3. Curriculum-based assessment used as part of a functional behavioral assessment was found to be an effective strategy in identifying escape-motivated behaviors of students within a general education classroom (Roberts, Marshall, Nelson, & Albers, 2001).
4. Information gained from functional behavioral assessments in preschool students at risk for attention deficit hyperactivity disorder was found to be an effective method of identifying specific strategies that decreased the problematic behaviors (Boyajian, DuPaul, Handler, Eckert, & McGoey, 2001).
5. In a review of the Behavior Rating Profile, Second Edition, the instrument's strengths include high criterion-related, concurrent, and construct validity, a sociogram, and the ability for assessment of behavioral, social, emotional, and interpersonal areas (Javorsky, 1998–1999). The weaknesses cited included the lack of students with behavioral/emotional difficulties in the norming group, lack of interrater reliability, lack of the ability to discriminate between different diagnostic categories of behavioral/emotional problems, limited use with younger age students, and no information regarding intervention strategies.
6. In a study using school-referred males comparing the Teacher Report Form and the Child Behavior Checklist to the Youth Self-Report, it was found that the youth and the teacher and parent forms did not have high agreement, especially when the students rated themselves on externalizing behaviors (Lee, Elliott, & Barbour, 1994). The study found a somewhat higher agreement between parents and teachers in rating students. These findings seem to suggest that youth tend to underrate themselves on problem behaviors, which emphasizes the need for multimethod and multiinformant assessment.
7. An extensive review of the use of rating scales in different cultures resulted in noticeable differences related to culture (Reid, 1995). Because of the reliance of subjective interpretation by the rater, Reid suggests that use of rating scales in other cultures may not be appropriate for use in diagnosing attention deficit disorder. He cautions that some symptoms may be influenced with variables related to culture, such as low socioeconomic status (SES) or other stressors.
8. In a study by Weine, Phillips, and Achenbach (1995) comparing results of the Child Behavior Checklist, differences were found in Chinese and American children. The Chinese children were found to be rated higher by their teachers for delinquent behavior, for being anxious/depressed, and on the internalizing scale. American children were rated higher on the Child Behavior Checklist on aggressive behavior. American children were rated higher by their teachers in attention problems.

9. A study comparing teacher responses on a teacher rating scale for Caucasian and African American students found that teachers rated African American students higher on all symptoms (Reid, DuPaul, Power, Anastopoulos, Rogers-Adkinson, Nell, & Ricco, 1998). Reid et al. caution that measures should be used for diagnosis of attention deficit disorder for African Americans other than just relying on teacher rating scales.
10. In a review by Walker of the Behavior Assessment System for Children, the BASC was stated to be fairly easy to administer and score, and it also had good evidence of interrater reliability (1998–1999). Walker stated that the weaknesses of the BASC were that no definitions were provided in the test manual; and students with disabilities were underrepresented in the normative sample, as well as students who are culturally, linguistically, and ethnically diverse. Walker noted that the instrument should be used only for screening purposes.
11. Oesterheld and Haber (1997) found that the items on the Conners test and the Child Behavior Checklist were difficult for Native American parents to understand. The Native Americans often did not have similar words or concepts in their language or feared that their responses would be misinterpreted by the dominant culture.
12. Stanford and Hynd (1994) studied the difference in students with attention deficit disorder with and without hyperactivity and students with learning disabilities. Parents and teachers of students with hyperactivity endorsed more externalizing types of items on the Child Behavior Checklist. Parents and teachers of students who had attention deficit disorder without hyperactivity and students with learning disabilities endorsed fewer externalizing items.
13. The Child Behavior Checklist, Teacher Report Form, and Semistructured Clinical Interview for Children were found to have discriminant validity when comparing children with behavior disorders and nonreferred children (McConaughy & Achenbach, 1996). The discriminant validity was not as high when comparing children with behavior disorders and children with learning disabilities.
14. A study in a public school setting focused on interrater reliability among teachers using the Conners Teacher Rating Scale. Both certified teachers of students with emotional problems and their teacher aides were consistent in their ratings (Mattison, Bagnato, Mayes, & Felix, 1990). The strongest interrater correlations were on the scale's hyperactivity and conduct disorders factors. This seems to suggest that the Conners Teacher Rating Scale has adequate interrater reliability and may be an appropriate instrument in conjunction with other assessment techniques for screening for acting out or externalizing behaviors.

15. Research of family drawings by students with divorced parents and those without divorced parents indicated differences around themes of interpersonal relationships (Spigelman, Spigelman, & Englesson, 1992). Students from homes with divorce seemed to have more omissions of family members and indications of conflict within relationships with siblings.
16. A study of human figure drawings with 5-year-old students resulted in finding no significant differences between the drawings of aggressive and nonaggressive students (Norford & Barakat, 1990). It appears that this type of technique is not developmentally appropriate for use with students younger than 6.
17. Research using chronically ill children found that the Roberts Apperception Test for Children was able to differentiate children with adaptive coping styles from children with maladaptive coping styles (Palomares, Crowley, Worchel, Olson, & Rae, 1991).
18. Kroon, Goudena, and Rispens (1998) reviewed the Roberts Apperception Test for Children and stated that the psychometrics of the instrument appeared adequate, although the research presented in the manual is quite limited.
19. A study of students with and without attention deficit disorder identified both false positives and false negatives during use of a Continuous Performance Test (Trommer, Hoeppner, Lorber, & Armstrong, 1988). In addition, differences in these groups on other measures suggest that CPTs may involve some higher level cognitive tasks rather than pure attentive ability. Thus, CPTs should be interpreted with caution and always should be analyzed with data from multiple sources.
20. Research comparing CPT performance of students with learning disabilities and a matched control group indicated that students with learning disabilities made more omission errors but did not differ on the number of commission errors (Eliason & Richman, 1987). The authors suggest that the constructs of attention and memory are highly interrelated and may result in students with learning disabilities making more omission errors on this type of measure.
21. Research using a CPT determined favorable decreases in the number of errors made in a sample of students with attention deficit disorder following treatment with methylphenidate—Ritalin (Forness, Swanson, Cantwell, Guthrie, & Sena, 1992). This suggests that CPTs may be sensitive to measurement of the treatment of students with stimulant medication.
22. In a review of research, Loiser, McGrath, and Klein (1996) found that children with ADHD made a higher number of omission and

commission errors than did non-ADHD children. It was also found that children treated with methylphenidate were found to make significantly fewer errors on the CPT than those who were not treated.

23. On a CPT, students with attention deficit disorder with hyperactivity made almost twice the number of errors of commission as did students with attention deficit disorder without hyperactivity (Barkley, DuPaul, & McMurray, 1990). In this same study, it was determined that students with attention deficit disorder and hyperactivity scored significantly worse on the CBCL aggressive and delinquent scales than did students with attention deficit disorder without hyperactivity, students with learning disabilities, and the control sample of students.
24. Although the Children's Apperception Test has been revised, it continues to receive criticism by professional reviewers due to the lack of adequate psychometric quality (Knoff, 1998; Reinehr, 1998).
25. Mueller, Brozovich, and Johnson reviewed the Conners Rating Scales—Revised (1998–1999). These reviewers noted the difficulty in scoring the Conners; they also noted that the readability level for the parent form was ninth grade. These reviewers questioned whether the readability level might be too high for some parents.

It is evident from the small sample of research reviewed in this chapter that many factors are to be considered in the assessment of students exhibiting behavioral and emotional problems. It is important that multiple measures and multiple informants be used and that the individual student's environment be assessed as well (Clarizio & Higgins, 1989). In a review of relevant research on assessment of attention and behavioral disorders, Schaughency and Rothlind (1991) stressed the need for the use of a variety of methods such as interviews, teacher ratings, observations, and peer nominations. These techniques may aid in the assessment of the student to determine whether the difficulties are reactions to the environment or reactions to current stress within the student's world. As with all assessment, a holistic view of the complete student and his environment is necessary.

THINK AHEAD

Cognitive abilities and the assessment of intelligence remain a part of the assessment process in determining the need for special education intervention. Chapter 10 presents the most commonly used measures of intelligence and adaptive behavior.

EXERCISES

Part I

Match the following terms with the statements.

a. checklist
b. direct observation
c. permanent product recording
d. setting event
e. anecdotal recording
f. interresponse time
g. functional behavior assessment
h. time sampling
i. projective techniques
j. target behavior
k. an apperception test
l. work samples
m. CPT
n. establishing operation
o. event recording
p. latency
q. interval recording
r. drawing tests
s. baseline

_____ 1. A teacher wants to determine the exact number of times a student inappropriately leaves his seat. The teacher needs this information before an intervention begins. This initial data collection technique about the student's behavior is referred to as the _____.

_____ 2. Although information can be obtained by questioning persons who work with a specific student, in order to determine what behavior occurs in a specific environment, the method of _____ will need to be used over multiple sessions.

_____ 3. By writing down information about a student's behavior that can later be analyzed for antecedent, behavior, and consequence, the teacher has used _____ as part of the functional behavioral assessment.

_____ 4. A teacher notices that one specific student has not been able to complete class work in the amount of time allotted. He notices that all other students in the class usually finish within the time frame expected. This specific student seems to take some time getting prepared to begin assignments. To establish a baseline about this specific behavior, the teacher will need to record the _____ time between the time the assignment is presented and the time the student begins to work.

_____ 5. A teacher and additional objective educational personnel have observed a student's off-task behavior in several settings. During the assessment process, the school psychologist may administer a _____ to measure distractibility and sustained focused attention on a computerized assessment.

_____ 6. A test that requires the psychologist to analyze story responses a student gives when shown specific picture cards is called _____.

_____ 7. Although much information can be obtained from norm-referenced standardized assessments, in order to analyze a student's progress and productivity in a curriculum, _____ should be collected and evaluated.

_____ 8. The evaluation of the information collected in question 7 is called _____.

_____ 9. An elementary teacher questions a third-grade student following a fight on the playground. The student is quite upset and relays to the teacher that his parents were fighting that morning before school and he witnessed his father shoving his mother. This incident may be referred to as the _____ of the child's behavior on the playground.

_____ 10. Assessment techniques such as completing sentence stems and drawing pictures of a house or person are called _____.

_____ 11. An assessment reveals that a child's continued calling out during class time is a method used by the child to gain the teacher's attention. This assessment, that identifies the reason for the student's calling out, is known as _____.

_____ 12. Students display many varieties of behaviors during a school day. When specific behaviors are identified as problematic behaviors that require interventions, they are referred to as _____.

Part II

Read the following scenario. Complete an analysis of the scenario and identify the highlighted phrases or words behaviorally.

A middle-school student has begun **arguing** and **getting into fights** during **unstructured times** during the school day. You observe that nobody seems to provoke the student, but rather the student becomes argumentative **whenever another student jokingly touches** or **comes near** the target student. The result of the student's problematic behaviors is that the student who was jokingly touching or coming near the target student **backs away** and **leaves the target student alone.** The target student seems to be happier during structured times during adult supervision. Upon questioning the target student, you learn that his older brother **has been hitting the target** student when **the parents are not at home.**

Provide your analysis below: ______________________________

____

____

ANSWER KEY FOR CHECK YOUR UNDERSTANDING

Activity 9.1

A	B	C
John enters class; teacher comments on math class	John responds with irrelevant questions	Teacher responds; may be distracted momentarily
John looks for math book	John comments to teacher	Teacher responds
Demands of teacher Get work is implied by her response	John throws a pencil on the floor	Teacher responds
Work in math expected	John crumbles paper; throws it on the floor; throws book on floor	Teacher responds
John sent out of math class	John smiles and leaves	

Almost the identical sequence is repeated on Tuesday.

Additional information from interview: Conditions within John's home environment affect his school performance and achievement.

Apply Your Knowledge. John's difficulties at home and his lack of mastery in the math curriculum are resulting in his motivation to escape math class. Interventions should include strategies to assist with acquisition of skills in the math curriculum. Recommend other outreach intervention and contact with John's parents to offer assistance and resources if possible.

Activity 9.2

	A	B	C
1.	presented with worksheet	looked for supplies	delayed starting work
	located supplies	sharpened pencil	delayed starting work
	noise	looked up	distracted from work

2. During the time period between getting the assignment and beginning work, Amber delayed working for 5 minutes. The information from the anecdotal recording during the 5 minutes indicates that Amber was disorganized and had difficulty finding needed materials.
3. The interval recording information indicates that when Amber began working, she was on task about 40% of the time she was observed.

Apply Your Knowledge. Based on the information in the anecdotal recording and the interval recording, Amber appears to have some indications of difficulty remaining on task. Additional observation and assessment may be required to determine the significance of the distractibility. Amber may also have difficulty with mathematics, and this should be further evaluated.

Behavioral objectives may vary but should include some indication of increasing on task time, decreasing latency, and increasing the number of math problems Amber correctly solves during class.

Activity 9.3

1. Jennifer & Emily, Kristy & Emily, Kristy & Jennifer, Jake & Jason, Mary & Sue, George & Sam, John & Sam, John & George.
2. While all of the students were selected for at least one activity, Mary and Sue seem to be pretty isolated.
3. Looking at the bottom of the diagram, it seems that Jason, Jake, Kristy, Emily, and Jennifer may be in cliques.
4. Jennifer, Kristy, Jason, and Jake.
5. Jennifer, Kristy, Jake, and Jason.

Apply Your Knowledge. Answers may vary.

REFERENCES

Achenbach, T. M. (1986). *Child Behavior Checklist: Direct Observation Form, Revised Edition*. Burlington: University of Vermont Center for Children, Youth, and Families.

Achenbach, T. M. (1991a). *Manual for the Child Behavior Checklist/4–18 and 1991 Profile*. Burlington: University of Vermont Department of Psychiatry.

Achenbach, T. M. (1991b). *Manual for the Teacher Report Form and 1991 Profile*. Burlington: University of Vermont Department of Psychiatry.

Achenbach, T. M. (1991c). *Manual for the Youth Self-Report and 1991 Profile*. Burlington: University of Vermont Department of Psychiatry.

Achenbach, T. M. (1992). *Manual for the Child Behavior Checklist/2–3 and the 1992 Profile*. Burlington: University of Vermont Department of Psychiatry.

Achenbach, T. M., & McConaughy, S. H. (1989, 1990). *Semistructured Clinical Interview: Observation Form*. Burlington: University of Vermont Center for Children, Youth, and Families.

American Psychiatric Association (1994). *Diagnostic and Statistical Manual of Mental Disorders* (4th ed.). Washington, DC: Author.

Barkley, R. A., DuPaul, G. J., & McMurray, M. B. (1990). Comprehensive evaluation of attention deficit disorder with and without hyperactivity as defined by research criteria. *Journal of Consulting and Clinical Psychology, 58,* 775–789.

Bellak, L., & Bellak, S. S. (1949). *Children's Apperception Test (animal figures)*. Larchmont, NY: C.P.S.

Bellak, L., & Bellak, S. S. (1952). *Manual for the supplement for the Children's Apperception Test*. Larchmont, NY: C.P.S.

Bellak, L., & Hurvich, M. S. (1965). *Children's Apperception Test (human figures) Manual*. Larchmont, NY: C.P.S.

Boyajian, A. E., DuPaul, G. J., Handler, M. W., Eckert, T., & McGoey, K. E. (2001). The use of classroom-based brief functional analyses with preschoolers at-risk for attention deficit hyperactivity disorder. *School Psychology Review, 30*(2), 278–293.

Brown, L., & Hammill, D. (1990). *Behavior Rating Profile* (2nd ed.). Austin, TX: Pro-Ed.

Clarizio, H. F., & Higgins, M. M. (1989). Assessment of severe emotional impairment: Practices and problems. *Psychology in the Schools, 26,* 154–162.

Conners, C. K. (1993). *Conners' Continuous Performance Test.* North Tonawanda, NY: Multi-Health Systems.

Conners, C. K. (1997). *Conners Rating Scales—Revised: Technical Manual.* North Tonawanda, NY: Multi-Health Systems.

Conroy, M. A., Clark, D., Gable, R. A., & Fox, J. (1999). Building competence in the use of functional behavioral assessment. *Preventing School Failure, 43*(4), 140–144.

Drasgow, E. & Yell, M. (2001). Functional behavioral assessments: Legal requirements and challenges. *School Psychology Review, 30*(2), 239–251.

Drasgow, E., Yell, M. L., Bradley, R., Shriner, J. G. (1999). The IDEA Amendments of 1997: A school-wide model for conducting functional behavioral assessments and developing behavioral intervention plans. *Education and Treatment of Children, 22*(3), 244–266.

Eliason, M. J., & Richman, L. C. (1987). The Continuous Performance Test in learning disabled and nondisabled children. *Journal of Learning Disabilities, 20,* 614–619.

Elliot, S. N., Busse, R. T., & Gresham, F. M. (1993). Behavior rating scales: Issues of use and development. *School Psychology Review, 22,* 313–321.

Ervin, R. A., Radford, P. M., Bertsch, K., Piper, A. L., Ehrhardt, K. E., & Poling, A. (2001). A descriptive analysis and critique of the empirical literature on school-based functional assessment. 193–210.

Evans, W. H., Evans, S. S., & Schmid, R. E. (1989). *Behavioral and instructional management: An ecological approach*. Boston: Allyn & Bacon.

Forness, S. R., Swanson, J. M., Cantwell, D. P., Guthrie, D., & Sena, R. (1992). Responses to stimulant medication across six measures of school related performance in children with ADHD and disruptive behavior. *Behavioral Disorders, 18,* 42–53.

Gable, R. A., Hendrickson, J. M., & Smith, C. (1999). Changing discipline policies and practices: Finding a place for functional behavioral assessments in schools. *Preventing School Failure, 43*(4), 167–170.

Gordon, M. (1983). *Gordon Diagnostic System.* DeWitt, NY: Gordon Diagnostic Systems.

Gresham, F. M., Watson, T. S., & Skinner, C. H. (2001). Functional behavioral assessment: Principles, procedures, and future directions. *School Psychology Review, 30*(2), 156–172.

Guerin, G. R., & Maier, A. S. (1983). *Informal assessment in education*. Palo Alto, CA: Mayfield.

Harris, D. B. (1963). *Goodenough-Harris Drawing Test.* New York: Harcourt Brace Jovanovich.

Javorsky, J. (1998–1999). Behavior-Rating Profile, Second Edition. *Monograph: Assessment for the New Decade, Diagnostic, 24*(1–4), 33–40.

Kerr, M. M., & Nelson, C. M. (2002). *Strategies for addressing behavioral problems in the classroom* (4th ed.). Upper Saddle River, NJ: Merrill/Prentice Hall.

Knoff, H. M. (1998). Review of the Children's Apperception Test (1991 Revision). In J. C. Impara and B. S. Plake (Eds.), *The thirteenth mental measurements yearbook* (pp. 231–233). Lincoln: University of Nebraska Press.

Knoff, H. M., & Prout, H. T. (1985). *Kinetic Family Drawing System for Family and School: A Handbook.* Los Angeles: Western Psychological Services.

Koppitz, E. (1968). *Human Figure Drawing Test.* New York: Grune & Stratton.

Kroon, N., Goudena, P. P., Rispens, J. (1998). Thematic apperception tests for child and adolescent assessment: A practitioner's consumer guide. *Journal of Psychoeducational Assessment, 16,* 99–117.

Kubick, R. J., Bard, E. M., & Perry, J. D. (2000). Manifestation determinations: Discipline guidelines for children with disabilities. In Telzrow, C. F., & Tankersley, M. (Eds.), *IDEA: Amendments of 1997: Practice Guidelines for school-based teams* (pp. 1–28). Bethesda, MD: National Association of School Psychologists.

Lee, S. W., Elliott, J., & Barbour, J. D. (1994). A comparison of cross-informant behavior ratings in school-based diagnosis. *Behavioral Disorders, 192,* 87–97.

Loiser, B. J., McGrath, P. J., & Klein, R. M. (1996). Error patterns on the continuous performance test in nonmedicated and medicated samples of children with and without ADHD: A meta-analytic review. *Journal of Child Psychology and Psychiatry, 37,* 971–987.

Mattison, R. E., Bagnato, S. J., Mayes, S. D., & Felix, B. C. (1990). Reliability and validity of teacher diagnostic ratings for children with behavioral and emotional disorders. *Journal of Psychoeducational Assessment, 8,* 509–517.

McArthur, D. S., & Roberts, G. E. (1982). *Roberts Apperception Test for Children: Manual.* Los Angeles: Western Psychological Services.

McConaughy, S. H., & Achenbach, T. M. (1993). Advances in empirically based assessment of children's behavioral and emotional problems. *School Psychology Review, 22,* 285–307.

McConaughy, S. H., & Achenbach, T. M. (1996). Contributions of a child interview to multimethod assessment of children with EBD and LD. *School Psychology Review, 25,* 24–39.

Michael, J. (2000). Implications and refinements of the establishing operation concept. *Journal of Applied Behavior Analysis, 33,* 401–410.

Mueller, F., Brozovich, R., & Johnson, C. B. (1998–1999). Conners' Rating Scales—Revised (CRS—R). *Monograph: Assessment for the New Decade, Diagnostic, 24* (1–4), 83–97.

Naglieri, J. A. (1988). *Draw-a-Person: A quantitative scoring system.* New York: Psychological Corporation.

Naglieri, J. A., McNeish, T. J., & Bardos, A. N. (1991). *Draw-a-Person: Screening Procedure for Emotional Disturbance.* Austin, TX: Pro-Ed.

Norford, B. C., & Barakat, L. P. (1990). The relationship of human figure drawings to aggressive behavior in preschool children. *Psychology in the Schools, 27,* 318–325.

Northup, J., & Gulley, V. (2001). Some contributions of functional analysis to the assessment of behaviors associated with attention deficit hyperactivity disorder and the effects of stimulant medication. *School Psychology Review, 30*(2), 227–238.

Oesterheld, J. R., & Haber, J. (1997). Acceptability of the Conners parent rating scale and child behavior checklist to Dakotan/Lakotan parents. *Journal of the American Academy of Child and Adolescent Psychiatry, 36,* 55–64.

O'Neill, R. E., Horner, R. H., Albin, R. W., Sprague, J. R., Storey, K., & Newton, J. S. (1997). *Functional assessment and program development for problem behavior.* Pacific Grove, CA: Brooks/Cole Publishing Company.

Overton, T. (1987). Analyzing instructional material as a prerequisite for teacher effectiveness. *Techniques: A Journal for Remedial Education and Counseling, 3,* 111–115.

Palomares, R. S., Crowley, S. L., Worchel, F. F., Olson, T. K., & Rae, W. A. (1991). The factor analytic structure of the Roberts Apperception Test for Children: A comparison of the standardization sample with a sample of chronically ill children. *Journal of Personality Assessment, 53,* 414–425.

Reid, R. (1995). Assessment of ADHD with culturally different groups: The use of behavioral rating scales. *School Psychology Review, 24,* 537–560.

Reid, R., DuPaul, G. J., Power, T. J., Anastopoulos, A. D., Rogers-Adkinson, D., Nell, M., & Ricco, C. (1998). Assessing culturally different students for attention deficit hyperactivity disorder using behavior rating scales. *Journal of Abnormal Child Psychology, 26,* 187–198.

Reinehr, R. C. (1998). Review of the Children's Apperception Test (1991 Revision). In J. C. Impara and B. S. Plake (Eds.), *The thirteenth mental measurements yearbook.* Lincoln: University of Nebraska Press, pp. 233–234.

Reynolds, C. R., & Kamphaus, R. W. (1998). *Behavior assessment system for children.* Circle Pines, MN: American Guidance Service.

Roberts, G. E. (1982). *Roberts Apperception Test for Children: Test pictures.* Los Angeles: Western Psychological Services.

Roberts, M. L., Marshall, J., Nelson, J. R., & Albers, C. A. (2001). Curriculum-based assessment procedures embedded within functional behavioral assessments: Identifying escape-motivated behaviors in a general education classroom. *School Psychology Review, 30*(2), 264–277.

Rorschach, H. (1921, 1942). *Psycho-Diagnostics: A diagnostic test based on perception* (P. Lemkau & B. Kroenburg, Trans.). Berne: Heber. (First German Edition, 1921. Distributed in the United States by Grune & Stratton.)

Rotter, J., & Rafferty, J. (1950). *The Rotter Incomplete Sentence Test.* New York: Psychological Corporation.

Schaughency, E. A., & Rothlind, J. (1991). Assessment and classification of attention deficit hyperactive disorders. *School Psychology Review, 20,* 187–202.

Spigelman, G., Spigelman, A., & Englesson, I. L. (1992). Analysis of family drawings: A comparison between children from divorce and nondivorce families. *Journal of Divorce & Remarriage, 18,* 31–51.

Stanford, L. D., & Hynd, G. W. (1994). Congruence of behavioral symptomology in children with ADD/H, ADD/WO, and learning disabilities. *Journal of Learning Disabilities, 27,* 243–253.

Trommer, B. L., Hoeppner, J. B., Lorber, R., & Armstrong, K. (1988). Pitfalls in the use of a Continuous Performance Test as a diagnostic tool deficit disorder. *Developmental and Behavioral Pediatrics, 9,* 339–345.

Walker, D. (1998–1999). Behavior assessment system for children (BASC). *Monograph: Assessment for the New Decade, Diagnostic, 24*(1–4), 17–31.

Watson, T. S., Gresham, F. M., & Skinner, C. H. (2001). Introduction to the mini-series: Issues and procedures for implementing functional behavior assessments in schools. *School Psychology Review, 30*(2), 153–155.

Weine, A. M., Phillips, J. S., & Achenbach, T. M. (1995). Behavioral and emotional problems among Chinese and American Children: Parent and teacher reports for ages 6 to 13. *Journal of Abnormal Child Psychology, 23,* 619–639.

Witt, J. C., Daly, E., & Noell, G. H. (2000). *Functional assessments: A step-by-step guide to solving academic and behavior problems.* Longmont, CO: Sopris West.

Yell, M. L., Drasgow, E., & Ford, L. (2000). The individuals with disabilities education act amendments of 1997: Implications for school-based teams. In C. F. Telzrow & M. Tankersley (Eds.), *IDEA: Amendments of 1997: Practice Guidelines for school-based teams* (pp. 1–28). Bethesda, MD: National Association of School Psychologists.

CHAPTER 10

Measures of Intelligence and Adaptive Behavior

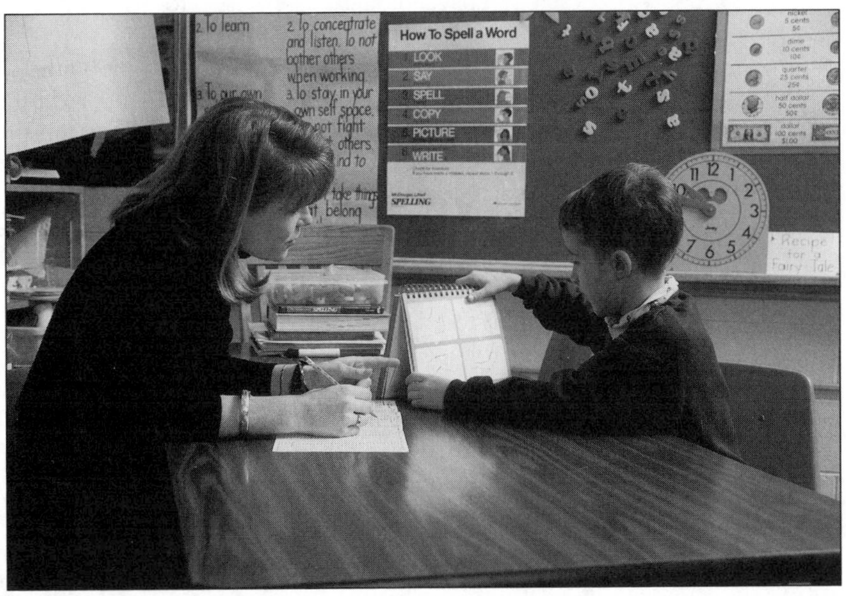

Key Terms

intelligence
adaptive behavior
IQ
innate potential
environmental influence
acculturation
Verbal tests
Performance tests
scaled scores
factor analysis
bidialectal

CHAPTER FOCUS

Chapter 10 presents common assessment measures of cognitive ability and adaptive behavior. Teachers may be required to complete adaptive behavior measures and should also have an understanding of the use of intelligence tests.

MEASURING INTELLIGENCE

intelligence A general concept of an individual's ability to function effectively within various settings; usually assessed by intelligence tests.

adaptive behavior One's ability to function in various environments.

The measurement of **intelligence** has been a controversial issue in educational and psychological assessment for the past several years. Even though professionals in the field disagree to some extent about the definition of intelligence and about the fairness and importance of intelligence testing, the assessment of intellectual ability is mandated by IDEA for the diagnosis of many disabilities. This federal law also requires the assessment of **adaptive behavior,** or how a student functions within her environment, for the diagnosis of mental retardation.

This chapter presents a review of individual measures of intelligence and adaptive behavior that commonly are used in schools to diagnose students with learning or emotional disabilities. Group intelligence tests may be administered in school systems to students in the regular education curriculum; for special education diagnostic purposes, however, group IQ tests are not appropriate. Tests constructed to be administered in an individual setting are commonly used to measure cognitive abilities. Although teachers in most cases will not be responsible for administering intelligence tests, special education teachers should possess an understanding of the interpretation of intelligence test results and their possible implications for educational planning. A general discussion of intelligence testing and the court cases that have influenced current practice are presented before the review of intelligence tests.

THE MEANING OF INTELLIGENCE TESTING

IQ Intelligence quotient; expressed as a standard score, usually with a mean of 100.

The results of intelligence tests are usually reported in the form of a standardized **IQ** (intelligence quotient) score. The IQ score is a quotient that is derived in the following manner:

$$IQ = MA \div CA \times 100.$$

In this calculation, MA means the mental age of the student and CA is the chronological age of the student. Using this formula, a child with a mental age of 9 and a chronological age of 11 would have an IQ of around 82. A student with a mental age of 14 and a chronological age of 10 would have an IQ of 140. It is important for the special education professional to understand what an IQ score is and is not. To possess a basic understanding of IQ scores, the professional educator should consider what is measured by IQ tests, that is, the content and presentation of the items on an IQ test and what the items represent. It is a commonly held myth that IQ scores are measurements of potential that is innate in a person. The following statements illustrate some current views about intelligence and intelligence testing expressed in the literature:

> The IQ does not reflect a global summation of the brain's capabilities and is certainly not an index of genetic potential, but it does predict school achievement effectively. (Kaufman, 1979, p. 9)
>
> Ultimately, intelligence is not a kind of ability at all, certainly not in the same sense that reasoning, memory, verbal fluency, etc., are so regarded. Rather it is something that is inferred from the way these abilities are manifested under different conditions and circumstances. (Wechsler, 1974, p. 5)
>
> Intelligence—unlike height and weight, but like all psychological constructs—must be measured indirectly; it must be inferred from intelligent behavior, past and present. (Hopkins, Stanley, & Hopkins, 1990, p. 374)
>
> Measurement of current intellectual performance has become confused with measurement of innate potential. Intelligence tests do not assess potential; they sample behaviors already learned in an attempt to predict future learning. (McLoughlin & Lewis, 1990, p. 187)
>
> Child-standardized intelligence performance provides a quantitative index of developmental status, but does not provide information on those functions that have not developed nor on the route by which the child arrived at his or her current developmental state. (Swanson & Watson, 1989, p. 93)
>
> Historically, intelligence has been an enigmatic concept. It is a much valued construct or quality that is extremely difficult to define. Is intelligence the same as verbal ability? Analytical thinking? Academic aptitude? Strategic thinking? The ability to cope? Different theorists might argue for each, or a combination of these abilities. Similarly, they might ask whether intelligence is, or should be, defined in the same way for individuals of different cultural, ethnic, or social backgrounds. (Taylor, 1989, pp. 185–186)

Even more controversial than the meaning of intelligence is the apparent bias that may occur by using individual IQ tests to classify and place students in special education (Reschly, 1981). Taylor (1989) questioned using the same definition of intelligence for individuals of all cultures, which reflects the concern that minority students are overrepresented in special education classrooms (Heller, Holtzman, & Messick, 1982). Specifically, African American students have been overrepresented in classrooms for students with mental retardation (Heller et al., 1982; Tucker, 1980), and Hispanic students have been increasingly found in classrooms for the learning disabled (Mick, 1985; Tucker, 1980).

Salvia and Ysseldyke (1988) underscored the importance that culture and background have on intellectual assessment:

> Acculturation is the single most important characteristic in evaluating a child's performance on intelligence tests. . . . The culture in which a child lives and the length of time that the child has lived in that culture effectively determine the psychological demands a test item presents. (p. 149)

Taylor and Richards (1991) noted that persons obtaining similar scores on IQ tests manifest differences in their pattern of responding. These authors found that while white students scored higher on the Wechsler Scales than black and Hispanic students, different patterns were evident, with black students showing verbal strength and Hispanic students showing strength in perceptual ability.

innate potential Thought to be one's ability from birth.

environmental influence The impact of the environment on the student's learning ability.

acculturation The influence of one culture on another culture.

The issues of **innate potential,** learned behaviors, **environmental influence,** and **acculturation,** and their influence on intelligence testing, have fueled the fire of many professional debates (Herrnstein & Murray, 1994). Intelligence testing, however, like all testing in education, is simply the way that a student responds to a set of stimuli at a specific point in time. Reynolds (1982) reviewed and summarized the general problems with bias in assessment; these are presented, as adapted, in Figure 10.1. Some of the problems of intelligence testing stem from content validity, construct validity, predictive validity (Messick, 1980), and the mean differences obtained by groups of different cultural or ethnic backgrounds (Reschly, 1981), as well as problems that affect all types of standardized testing, such as examiner familiarity (Fuchs & Fuchs, 1989).

ALTERNATIVE VIEWS OF INTELLECTUAL ASSESSMENT

The use of traditional intelligence tests in schools has been criticized for resulting in different results for different groups (Canter, 1997). The movement toward change in special education assessment, accountability, and educational reform in schools has also had an influence on the use of traditional assessment methods. Due to these trends, it is likely that assessment personnel along with researchers will seek alternative types of assessment models and methods of determining intellectual ability. Canter stated that "intelligence testing as we practice it today seems increasingly out-of-step with the needs of tomorrow's schools" (1997, p. 256). Dissatisfaction with the traditional psychometric approach has stimulated research and theoretical exploration of additional definitions and techniques used to assess intellectual ability. For example, Gardner (1993) presents a model with seven intelligences:

> But there is an alternative vision that I would like to present—one based on a radically different view of the mind and one that yields a very different view of the school. It is a pluralistic view of mind, recognizing many different and dis-

1. *Inappropriate content.* Black or other minority children have not been exposed to the material involved in the test questions or other stimulus materials. The tests are geared primarily toward white middle-class homes and values.
2. *Inappropriate standardization samples.* Ethnic minorities are underrepresented in the collection of normative reference group data.
3. *Examiner language bias.* Since most psychologists are white and speak primarily only standard English, they intimidate black and other ethnic minorities. They are also unable to accurately communicate with minority children. Lower test scores for minorities then are said to reflect only this intimidation and difficulty in the communication process and not lowered ability levels.
4. *Inequitable social consequences.* As a result of bias in educational and psychological tests, minority group members, who are already at a disadvantage in the educational and vocational markets because of past discrimination, are disproportionately relegated to dead-end educational tracts and are thought unable to learn. Labelling effects also fall under this category.
5. *Measurement of different constructs.* Related to (1) above, this position asserts that the tests are measuring significantly different attributes when used with children from other than the white middle-class culture.
6. *Differential predictive validity.* While tests may accurately predict a variety of outcomes for white middle-class children, they fail to predict at an acceptable level any relevant criteria for minority group members. Corollary to this objection is a variety of competing positions regarding the selection of an appropriate, common criterion against which to validate tests across cultural groupings. Scholastic or academic attainment levels are considered by a variety of black psychologists to be biased as criteria.
7. *Qualitatively distinct minority and majority aptitude and personality.* The idea here is that majority and minority cultures are so different that they result in substantial influences on personality and aptitude development. Due to these influences, different tests are required to accurately measure personality and aptitude.

Figure 10.1 Indicators of possible bias in assessment. (*Source:* Adapted from "The Problem of Bias in Psychological Assessment" by C. R. Reynolds, P. A. Lowe, & A. L. Saenz; in C. R. Reynolds and T. B. Gutkin (Eds.), *The Handbook of School Psychology,* 3rd ed., 1999 (pp. 556–557), New York: John Wiley & Sons. Copyright 1999 by John Wiley & Sons. Adapted by permission.)

> crete facets of cognition, acknowledging that people have different cognitive strengths and contrasting cognitive styles . . . One such approach I have called my "theory of multiple intelligences." (1993, pp. 6–7)

The seven types of intellectual ability proposed by Gardner include linguistic intelligence, logical-mathematical intelligence, spatial intelligence, musical intelligence, bodily-kinesthetic intelligence, interpersonal intelligence, and intrapersonal intelligence. Gardner stresses the need for fair intellectual assessment that would assess all areas rather than only the linguistic and logical-mathematical assessment included in traditional intellectual assessment instruments.

The concept of dynamic assessment is another area of current research in the quest for alternate assessment models. This model uses the assessment experience to measure the precise task of learning. The tasks used in dynamic assessment are those in which the learner is presented with interventions to determine how the learner responds to those strategies or interventions. The learner begins a task and is assisted by the examiner rather than merely observed by the examiner. Lidz (1997) points out the differences between traditional and dynamic assessment:

> Most of our (traditional) procedures provide information only about the learner's independent level of performance and infer future from previous functioning. . . . Dynamic assessment begins where traditional psychometric assessment ends. Instead of terminating the procedure with the establishment of a ceiling, the dynamic assessor views the ceiling as an area of functioning that warrants assessment. (1997, pp. 281–282)

Even though IQ testing has received much criticism, MacMillan and Forness remind assessment personnel that traditional IQ scores derived from traditional methods serve a function in schools today (1998). As these authors point out,

> What IQ tells us is that if nothing is done and the child remains in general education with no adjustment to instructional strategies, the child with a low score is likely to experience failure—the lower the score, the greater the probability and the greater the degree of failure that the child will encounter. (1998, p. 251)

Others caution against the rapid adoption of alternative measures of intelligence without scientific basis for the changes (Lopez, 1997). Brown, Reynolds, and Whitaker (1999) state that although many alternate assessment measures of IQ have been proposed, professionals should rely on research-based methods, including traditional standardized assessment instruments. Therefore, in most states, traditional IQ tests continue to be used as a part of the assessment process. Based on the individual student's measured performance on tasks on the IQ tests, the team members infer the student's intellectual ability (Turnbull, Turnbull, Shank, Smith, & Leal, 2002).

LITIGATION AND INTELLIGENCE TESTING

The issues of intelligence testing and the overrepresentation of minorities in special education classrooms led to litigation that has affected current practice in the field, including the decreased use of intelligence tests by some

Larry P. v. Riles (1984). This case resulted in the court's finding that schools could no longer use standardized but unvalidated IQ tests for the purpose of identifying and placing black children into segregated special education classes for children designated as educable mentally retarded (EMR) (Turnbull, 1990, p. 92).

PASE v. Hannon (1980). Although PASE (Parents in Action on Special Education) found that some of the items in the tests were discriminatory, the court upheld that the tests were generally nondiscriminatory. More important, it found that the tests were not the sole basis for classification and that the school district therefore was complying with the Education of the Handicapped Act, EHA, which requires multifaceted testing (Turnbull, 1990, p. 95).

Diana v. State Board of Education (1970). In this case, the state board of education of California agreed to test students in their native language, to omit unfair test items of a verbal nature, to construct tests that would reflect the culture of Mexican American students, and to provide tests that would be standardized for Mexican Americans (Ysseldyke & Algozzine, 1982).

Lora v. New York City Board of Education (1984). This case required that the school system use objective and improved referral and assessment methods and multidisciplinary evaluations to reach decisions for diagnosis of students with emotional disturbance. The court found that the method previously in use was racially discriminatory and ruled that the school system could no longer consider school monetary problems or availability of services as reasons to place or not to place students in special education (Wood, Johnson, & Jenkins, 1990).

Figure 10.2 Summary of court cases involving IQ assessment.

state and local education agencies for the diagnosis of disabling conditions (Bersoff, 1981). Major court cases that have involved the assessment of intellectual ability are *Larry P. v. Riles* (1984) and *PASE v. Hannon* (1980). Other cases have involved assessment and placement procedures: *Diana v. State Board of Education* and *Lora v. New York City Board of Education*. These cases are summarized in Figure 10.2.

Due to the recent litigation involving the testing of intelligence as well as the information included in the assessment sections of IDEA, a movement toward more objective testing practices is currently under way in the assessment field. In addition, professionals are reminded to follow the *Code of Fair Testing Practices in Education* (see appendix) by the Joint Committee on Testing Practices and the standards set forth by the APA (1985).

Check Your Understanding

Complete Activity 10.1.

ACTIVITY 10.1

Match the following terms to the descriptions.

A. *PASE v. Hannon*
B. *Diana v. State Board of Education*
C. inappropriate content
D. inequitable social consequences
E. inappropriate standardization sample
F. differential predictive validity
G. *Lora v. New York City Board of Education*
H. *Larry P. v. Riles*
I. examiner language bias
J. measurement of different constructs
K. IQ score
L. intelligence testing

_____ 1. Case involving administering tests in a language other than the child's native language.

_____ 2. Case concerning students who were placed in a school for students with emotional disturbance without the benefit of nondiscriminatory assessment.

_____ 3. Standardized norm-referenced assessment of cognitive abilities; the indirect measurement of the construct of intelligence.

_____ 4. When, as the result of discriminatory assessment, minority students are placed in dead-end educational or vocational tracts.

_____ 5. When a test measures different constructs for people of different groups.

_____ 6. A test may accurately predict for one group of students but not as accurately for another group, which results in this.

_____ 7. A numerical representation of intellectual ability.

_____ 8. When the examiner does not possess skill in communicating in the student's native language, it may result in this.

_____ 9. Case finding that the use of IQ tests to place black students in classes for persons with mental retardation was discriminatory practice.

_____ 10. Case finding the same IQ tests to be nondiscriminatory even though a few items were found to be biased.

Apply Your Knowledge

Summarize how court cases have influenced the use of intelligence tests. ____

____

USE OF INTELLIGENCE TESTS

The use of intelligence tests remains controversial in part because of inappropriate use in the past. Revised instruments, alternative testing practices, and understanding of the ethnic or cultural differences that may occur are promising improvements in the assessment of intelligence. Intelligence testing is likely to remain a substantial part of the assessment process because of the known correlation between performance on IQ tests and school achievement (Reschly & Grimes, 1995). Kaufman (1994) states that intelligence tests should be used "as a helping agent rather than an instrument for placement, labeling, or other types of academic oppression" (p. 1). Kaufman has long advocated for the intelligent use of intelligence tests. McGrew and Flanagan (1998) state that to have a complete picture of a person's true intellectual ability, a cross battery or multiple measures of intelligence tests should be used. Given that IQ tests will continue to be used, educators must promote fair and appropriate use of intelligence measures. Reschly and Grimes (1995) set forth the following guidelines for appropriate use of IQ tests.

1. Appropriate use requires a context that emphasizes prevention and early intervention rather than eligibility determination as the initial phase in services to students with learning and behavior problems.
2. Intellectual assessment should be used when the results are directly relevant to well-defined referral questions and other available information does not address those questions.
3. Mandatory use of intellectual measures for all referrals, multifactored evaluations, or reevaluations is not consistent with best practices.
4. Intellectual assessment must be part of a multifactored approach, individualized to a child's characteristics and the referral problems.
5. Intellectual assessment procedures must be carefully matched to characteristics of children and youth.
6. Score reporting and interpretation must reflect known limitations of tests, including technical adequacy, inherent error in measurement, and general categories of performance.
7. Interpretation of performance and decisions concerning classification must reflect consideration of overall strengths and weaknesses in intellectual performance, performance on other relevant dimensions of behavior, age, family characteristics, and cultural background.
8. Users should implement assertive procedures to protect students from misconceptions and misuses of intellectual test results. (pp. 436–437)

Special education professionals can obtain meaningful information from IQ test results if they understand the types of behavior that are assessed by individual subtests and items. Readers should take notice of the possible areas of testing bias as well as previous court decisions as they study the tests reviewed in this chapter.

REVIEW OF INTELLIGENCE TESTS

This chapter reviews some of the tests most commonly used by schools to measure cognitive ability or intelligence.

Perhaps the best-known intelligence measures are the Wechsler Scales, three separate tests designed to assess intellectual functioning at different age levels. The Wechsler Preschool and Primary Scale of Intelligence—Revised (WPPSI—R) was developed for use with children aged 4 to 6½; it is reviewed in chapter 12, "Early Childhood Assessment." The Wechsler Adult Intelligence Scale—Third Edition (WAIS—III); (discussed later) is used with youth 16 years of age through adulthood. The Wechsler Intelligence Scale for Children—Third Edition assesses school-aged children ranging in age from 6 through 16-11. Called "the most popular and widely used individual intelligence test" (Taylor, 1989, p. 189), this particular test of the Wechsler Scales is covered in depth in the following subsection.

Other measures of intelligence are commonly used with school-aged children. The following are reviewed briefly in this chapter: the Woodcock-Johnson—Revised Tests of Cognitive Ability, Stanford-Binet Intelligence Scale—Fourth Edition, Kaufman Assessment Battery for Children, Detroit Tests of Learning Aptitude—4, Kaufman Adolescent and Adult Intelligence Test, and Kaufman Brief Intelligence Test. As with the Wechsler Scales, these tests may not be administered by the teacher; however, test results provided by the psychologist or diagnostician may be useful to the teacher.

WECHSLER INTELLIGENCE SCALE FOR CHILDREN—THIRD EDITION (WISC—III)

Verbal tests A group of subtests on the Wechsler scales thought to measure verbal conceptual ability.

Performance tests A group of subtests on the Wechsler Scales thought to measure nonverbal ability.

scaled scores Derived scores on the Wechsler Scales for subtests; each has a mean of 10.

The WISC—III (Wechsler, 1991) is composed of two separate tests, the **Verbal tests** and **Performance tests,** which yield three IQ scores; Verbal IQ, Performance IQ, and Full Scale IQ. These scores, along with additional information provided by a multidisciplinary team evaluation, may be useful in determining a diagnosis. This edition of the WISC also provides scores, called indexes, that are based on the factor structure of the test. These scores are Verbal Comprehension Index, Perceptual Organization Index, Freedom from Distractibility Index, and a Processing Speed Index. Even more useful to the teacher may be information provided by individual subtest **scaled scores** when the influences on test performance and behaviors assessed are known.

Verbal Subtests. The Verbal subtests are presented in the following paragraphs along with factors that may influence individual student performance.

Information. Questions in this subtest, presented to the student orally, assess general information and knowledge believed to be common to most school-aged youngsters. This subtest is designed to survey the knowledge of everyday events that the student gains from the world around her. A student's performance is highly influenced by school-related learning (Kaufman, 1993b).

Similarities. The examiner orally presents pairs of words, and the student must say how the two things (such as a wheel and a ball) are alike (Wechsler, 1991). This type of subtest is believed to measure verbal comprehension and conceptualization, cognition, degree of abstract thinking, distinguishing essential from nonessential details, verbal reasoning, and verbal expression; a student's performance can be influenced by interests or outside reading (Kaufman, 1979, p. 103).

Arithmetic. This subtest is basically composed of questions that the examiner presents orally, with some questions presented in written form at the higher end of the test. The questions are math story problems that the student must answer within a time limit. In addition to measuring some math abilities and familiarity with math processes, this type of subtest is believed to measure freedom from distractibility, verbal comprehension, sequencing, acquired knowledge, cognition, memory, facility with numbers, mental alertness, long-term memory, computational skill, and reasoning. A student's performance on this subtest is thought to be influenced by attention span, anxiety, concentration, distractibility, or working under time pressure (Kaufman, 1979, pp. 103–104) and general school-related learning (Kaufman, 1993b).

Vocabulary. The student is asked to define words presented orally. This type of subtest is thought to measure verbal comprehension and conceptualization, acquired knowledge, cognition, degree of abstract thinking, fund of information, learning ability, long-term memory, verbal concept formation, and verbal expression. A student's performance can be influenced by cultural opportunities at home, interests, outside reading, richness of early environment, or school-related learning (Kaufman, 1979, p. 104).

Comprehension. This subtest contains questions of a general nature that the examiner asks orally. This type of subtest assesses verbal comprehension and conceptualization, evaluation, common sense of cause-effect relationships, verbal reasoning, social judgment, verbal expression, demonstration of practical information, and evaluation and use of past experience. A student's ability to perform on this subtest can be influenced by cultural opportunities in the home and development of conscience or moral sense (Kaufman, 1979, pp. 104–105). This subtest is heavily weighted by cultural factors (Kaufman, 1993b).

Digit Span. This supplementary Verbal subtest, which may be chosen in place of another subtest, may help the psychologist document specific types of memory or attentional deficits when used with other information obtained during assessment. The items consist of series of numbers that the examiner orally presents, and the student must repeat them in the given order first and in reverse order on the second part of the test. This type of subtest is believed to assess freedom from distractibility, sequencing, memory, facility with numbers, mental alertness, and auditory short-term memory; performance can be influenced by attention span, distractibility, or anxiety (Kaufman, 1979, p. 105).

Performance Subtests. The Performance subtests of the WISC—III contain many timed manipulative tasks. The subtests and the variables that could influence a student's performance are described in the following paragraphs.

Picture Completion. This subtest is visually presented to the student, who is asked to tell the examiner what important part of the picture stimulus is missing. This type of subtest is thought to assess perceptual organization, verbal comprehension, spatial ability, cognition, evaluation, distinguishing essential from nonessential details, holistic processing, visual organization without essential motor activity, visual perception of meaningful stimuli, visual alertness, and visual recognition and identification. A student's performance on this subtest can be influenced by ability to respond when uncertain, cognitive style, concentration, or working under time pressure (Kaufman, 1979, pp. 105–106).

Coding. This test requires that the student copy symbols to match those presented as they are paired with other symbols, such as numbers, within a specific time period. This type of subtest assesses freedom from distractibility, sequencing, convergent production, evaluation, facility with numbers (on Coding B), integrated brain functioning, learning ability, paper-and-pencil skill, reproduction of models, visual-motor coordination, visual perception of abstract stimuli, ability to follow directions, clerical speed and accuracy, psychomotor speed, and visual short-term memory. Anxiety, distractibility, or working under time pressure can influence a student's performance (Kaufman, 1979, p. 108).

Picture Arrangement. The student must sequence sets of pictures in the correct order to complete a story sequence. This type of subtest is thought to measure perceptual organization, verbal comprehension, sequencing ability, convergent production, evaluation, common sense of cause-effect relationships, distinguishing essential from nonessential details, integrated brain functioning, planning ability, reasoning, social judgment, synthesis, visual perception of meaningful stimuli, visual organization without essential motor activity, anticipation of consequences, and temporal sequencing of time events. Creativity, cultural opportunities in the home, exposure to comic strips, or working under time pressure can influence a student's performance (Kaufman, 1979, p. 106).

Block Design. The student arranges three-dimensional blocks with red and white color patterns to match a specific pattern within a given period of time. The initial patterns require two blocks for young students and four blocks for older students, and the most difficult items require nine blocks. This type of subtest measures perceptual organization, spatial ability, cognition, evaluation, integrated brain functioning, reproduction of models, synthesis, visual-motor coordination, visual perception of abstract stimuli, analysis of whole into component parts, nonverbal concept formation, and spatial visualization. A student's ability to perform on this subtest can be influenced by cognitive style or working under time pressure (Kaufman, 1979, pp. 106–107).

Object Assembly. This subtest is also known as the puzzle subtest. The student is presented with sets of puzzle pieces, which must be correctly put together within a given period of time. The amount of time allowed increases for the more difficult items. This type of subtest assesses perceptual organization, spatial ability, cognition, evaluation, holistic processing, synthesis, visual-motor coordination, visual perception of meaningful stimuli, ability to benefit from sensory-motor feedback, anticipation of relationships among parts, and flexibility. A student's ability to perform on this subtest can be influenced by the ability to respond when uncertain, cognitive style, experience with puzzles, or working under time pressure (Kaufman, 1979, p. 107).

Symbol Search. This is a new fine-motor subtest. Presented with a series of pairs of symbols in a test booklet, the student must scan quickly and discriminate whether the symbol exists in a given row of symbols. The student then marks a yes or no response. This is a timed subtest and is optional.

Mazes. This supplementary Performance subtest consists of several mazes that the student must solve within a specific time period. This type of subtest is believed to measure perceptual organization, spatial ability, cognition, integrated brain function, paper-and-pencil skill, planning ability, reasoning, visual-motor coordination, following a visual pattern, and foresight. The student's ability to respond when uncertain, experience in solving mazes, or working under time pressure can influence performance on this subtest (Kaufman, 1979, pp. 108–109).

Technical Data

Norming Process. The standardization sample of the WISC—III reflected the total U.S. population statistics as obtained from 1988 census data. The following variables were addressed: gender, age, geographic region, parent(s) occupation, community size, and race/ethnicity.

Reliability. The reliability studies employed included split-half coefficients and test-retest reliability. Stability coefficients appear adequate for most subtests at most ages; however, the WISC—III seems to have somewhat lower stability on individual subtests when compared with the WISC—R (Kaufman, 1993b).

Validity. The examiner's manual provides extended information on validity studies and factor structure of the WISC—III. Information is presented for several studies with special populations, including students with giftedness, learning disabilities, mental retardation, attention deficit disorders, severe conduct disorders, epilepsy, hearing impairments, and speech or language delay. A table in the manual gives means and standard deviations for IQ and index scores for persons with learning disabilities, reading disorders, and attention deficit hyperactivity disorder.

Interpreting Scores of the WISC—III. The mean score for subtest scaled scores is 10 with a standard deviation of 3. The average IQ score for the Wechsler Scales is 100 with a standard deviation of 15. The classifications given in the manual are as follows (Wechsler, 1991, p. 32):

IQ	Intelligence Classification	Percent Included in Theoretical Normal Curve
130 and above	Very superior	2.2
120–129	Superior	6.7
110–119	High average	16.1
90–109	Average	50.0
80–89	Low average	16.1
70–79	Borderline	6.7
69 and below	Intellectually deficient	2.2

Much information can be gained by carefully studying the results a teacher might receive about a student's performance on the WISC—III. Each of the subtests on the WISC—III measures many behaviors and skills, and many factors can influence a student's performance. It is quite common for average students with no disabilities to perform inconsistently on the various subtests on the WISC—III. Because the standard deviation on the scaled scores is 3, students' scores may differ greatly between several subtests.

Students who perform with severe discrepancies between subtests and the three IQ scores may do so because of processing or learning difficulties. Psychologists often use this information, along with other test results, classroom observations, informal data, permanent products, and diagnostic academic tests to document the existence of a learning disability or deficiency. Typically, discrepancies between the three IQ scores must be significantly different and should be interpreted with caution because of other factors that might influence these differences (Kaufman, 1979).

The protocol for the WISC—III is shown in Figure 10.3. This protocol allows the examiner to calculate raw scores for the factors or indexes and then obtain the derived standard scores from the manual. This model, based on **factor analysis** research of the Wechsler, allows the examiner to compare the student's own strengths and weaknesses in addition to comparing the student with the norm group.

factor analysis A statistical method of reducing the variables of a test to lower the number of factors thought to influence test performance.

The individual discrepancies between subtest scores and the three obtained IQ scores are often used to diagnose specific learning disabilities. A student who exhibits academic problems, scores within the average IQ range, and exhibits significant discrepancies between factors or between performance and verbal abilities may be diagnosed as learning disabled. For example, a student may have significant difficulties according to the obtained scores on the WISC—III in verbal comprehension, have significant deficits on measures of academic achievement, and be average in intellectual ability. This student may very likely be diagnosed as having a learning disability.

WECHSLER ADULT INTELLIGENCE SCALE—THIRD EDITION

The Wechsler Adult Intelligence Scale—Third Edition (WAIS—III) was published in 1997. Many of the same subtests of the children's version are included on the scales for adults.

Subtests. In addition, the following subtests are included on the adult version.

Letter Number Sequencing. This additional verbal subtest presents a mixed series of numbers and letters that the examinee must repeat back to the examiner, with the numbers in ascending order and the letters in alphabetical order. This subtest assesses short-term auditory memory as well as the ability to mentally manipulate stimuli according to specific parameters and to respond orally. This subtest is optional and is not required to determine IQ scores.

Matrix Reasoning. This additional performance subtest presents visual stimuli that the examinee must evaluate to determine which of the stimuli will complete the visual pattern. This subtest assesses visual analytical and abstract reasoning.

WISC-III®

Wechsler Intelligence Scale for Children®–Third Edition

Name ______________________ Sex ______

School ______________________ Grade ______

Examiner ______________________ Handedness ______

Subtests	Raw Scores	Scaled Scores					
Picture Completion							
Information							
Coding							
Similarities							
Picture Arrangement							
Arithmetic							
Block Design							
Vocabulary							
Object Assembly							
Comprehension							
(Symbol Search)			( )				
(Digit Span)		( )					
(Mazes)			( )				
Sum of Scaled Scores		Verbal	Perfor.	VC	PO	FD	PS
		Full Scale Score		OPTIONAL			

	Year	Month	Day
Date Tested			
Date of Birth			
Age			

	Score	IQ/ Index	%ile	___% Confidence Interval
Verbal				–
Performance				–
Full Scale				–
VC				–
PO				–
FD				–
PS				–

Subtest Scores

	Verbal						Performance						
	Inf	Sim	Ari	Voc	Com	DS	PC	Cd	PA	BD	OA	SS	Mz
19													
18													
17													
16													
15													
14													
13													
12													
11													
10													
9													
8													
7													
6													
5													
4													
3													
2													
1													

	IQ Scores			Index Scores (Optional)			
	VIQ	PIQ	FSIQ	VCI	POI	FDI	PSI
160							
150							
140							
130							
120							
110							
100							
90							
80							
70							
60							
50							
40							

THE PSYCHOLOGICAL CORPORATION®
HARCOURT BRACE JOVANOVICH, INC.

9 10 11 12 A B C D E

09–980004

Figure 10.3 First page of the WISC—III protocol. (*Source:* From *Wechsler Intelligence Scale for Children—Third Edition: Manual* by D. Wechsler, 1991, San Antonio, TX: The Psychological Corporation. Copyright © 1991 by the Psychological Corporation. Reproduced by permission. All rights reserved.)

The third edition provides additional items on the lower end and additional practice items on some of the subtests. This instrument is clinically more user friendly for examinees who are functioning significantly below the average. These additional items may allow examinees at the lower end to respond to more items before reaching a ceiling, providing the clinician with a better picture of an examinee's ability.

This edition eliminated several items of the WAIS—R that proved to be biased or outdated (Wechsler, 1997). The third edition moved Object Assembly to the optional status rather than keep it as a mandatory subtest. In general, the materials are more attractive, sturdier, and easier to handle. The sequence of administration is also improved and is easier to administer.

Technical Data. The Wechsler Adult Intelligence Scale—Third Edition was developed and normed in conjunction with the Wechsler Memory Scale—Third Edition (Psychological Corporation, 1997). The following information is provided in the technical manual.

Norming Process. The standardization sample comprised adults 16 to 89 years of age. This sample was representative of the 1995 U.S. Census and considered the following variables: age, race/ethnicity, educational level, and geographic region. To provide sufficient numbers for the items scores to assess item bias, an additional 200 African American and Hispanic individuals were included. The sample included 2,450 adults in the standardization.

In addition to the general representative sample, special group studies were included. Data presented in the technical manual provide information about five clinical samples:

> Various Neurological Disorders (Alzheimer's disease, Huntington's disease, Parkinson's disease, traumatic brain injury, multiple sclerosis, and temporal lobe epilepsy)
>
> Alcohol-Related Disorders (chronic alcohol abuse and Korsakoff's syndrome)
>
> Neuropsychiatric Disorders (schizophrenia)
>
> Psychoeducational and Developmental Disorders (mental retardation, learning disabilities in reading and math)
>
> Deaf and Hearing Impaired (Psychological Corporation, 1997, p. 144)

Reliability. Reliability was studied using test-retest methods that resulted in correlations ranging from .69 to .96. The test-retest reliability correlations for the IQ scores ranged from .91 to .96. Interscorer agreement was reported to range from .91 to .95 for the subtests requiring examiner judgment.

Validity. Content validity, criterion-related validity, and construct validity are addressed. The WAIS—III was compared with the WAIS—R with coefficients ranging from .50 to .94. The IQ scores maintained the highest criterion-related validity coefficients. Additional studies compared the WAIS—III with the WISC—III, the Standard Progressive Matrices, the Stanford-Binet Intelligence Scale—Fourth Edition, and the WIAT. The correlation coefficients of the WAIS—III IQ scores and the Stanford-Binet IV Composite score ranged from .78 to .89.

Check Your Understanding

Complete Activity 10.2.

ACTIVITY 10.2

Match the following terms with the correct descriptions.

A. WAIS—III	K. Block Design
B. WPPSI—R	L. Picture Arrangement
C. WISC—III	M. Picture Completion
D. Verbal tests	N. Vocabulary
E. Performance tests	O. Mazes
F. Full-scale IQ	P. Processing Speed Index
G. Digit Span	Q. Comprehension
H. Coding	R. Information
I. Object Assembly	S. Arithmetic
J. Similarities	T. Matrices

_____ 1. The Wechsler Intelligence Scale for Children—Third Edition.

_____ 2. This Wechsler test is designed to be used through adulthood.

_____ 3. This subtest presents math story problems, and performance can be influenced by attention span and concentration.

_____ 4. Performance on this subtest can be influenced by interests and outside reading; the examiner asks the student how two things are alike.

_____ 5. Performance on this Verbal subtest can be influenced by early environment, cultural opportunities in the home, or school learning; the examiner presents words for the student to define.

_____ 6. Students are presented with visual stimuli to determine what important part is missing. Performance on this subtest can be influenced by working under time pressure or cognitive style.

_____ 7. Performance on these puzzles can be influenced by the ability to respond when uncertain, cognitive style, or previous puzzle experiences.

_____ 8. Many of the subtests on this portion of the WISC—III are timed, and thus the student's performance can be influenced by the ability to work under time pressure.

_____ 9. This subtest contains red and white cubes and measures perceptual organization, spatial ability, synthesis, and reproduction of models.

_____ 10. The items of these tests are presented, for the most part, orally, and the student responds orally.

_____ 11. This subtest is included on the adult version of the Wechsler Scales but not the children's version.

_____ 12. Performance on this Verbal subtest can be influenced by the student's conscience or moral sense.

_____ 13. This subtest is divided into two parts, forward and backward, and measures auditory short-term memory and freedom from distractibility.

_____ 14. Performance on this subtest can be influenced by the student's previous experience with comic strips.

_____ 15. This paper-and-pencil performance subtest measures visual-motor coordination, psychomotor speed, and visual short-term memory.

_____ 16. Performance on this supplementary subtest can be influenced by the student's previous experience with mazes.

_____ 17. This IQ score reflects the performance of the student on both Verbal and Performance subtests.

_____ 18. This Wechsler test was designed to be used with children from the ages of 4 to 6½.

Apply Your Knowledge

Which of the subtests described for the Wechsler Scales can be influenced by weakness in the visual-motor areas? ____________________

____

____

WOODCOCK-JOHNSON III TESTS OF COGNITIVE ABILITIES

The Woodcock-Johnson III Tests of Cognitive Abilities was designed to be used with the Woodcock-Johnson III Tests of Achievement. This instrument provides for the measurement of cognitive clusters, cognitive factors, clinical clusters, intra-cognitive discrepancies, and predicted achievement. This allows for the assessment team to compare the cognitive and academic achievement measures and to compare the level of predictive achievement with actual achievement scores. Figure 10.4 presents the measures obtained from both the cognitive and achievement measures.

Measures Obtained From the WJ III Tests of Cognitive Abilities	**Measures Obtained From the WJ III Tests of Achievement**
• General Intellectual Ability (*g*) Cognitive Performance Clusters Verbal Ability Thinking Ability Cognitive Efficiency • Cognitive Factors Comprehension-Knowledge (*Gc*) Long-Term Retrieval (*Glr*) Visual-Spatial Thinking (*Gv*) Auditory Processing (*Ga*) Fluid Reasoning (*Gf*) Processing Speed (*Gs*) Short-Term Memory (*Gsm*) • Clinical Clusters Phonemic Awareness Working Memory Broad Attention Cognitive Fluency Executive Processes • Intra-Cognitive Discrepancies • Predicted Achievement	• Total Achievement • Oral Language Oral Language Oral Expression Listening Comprehension • Reading Broad Reading Basic Reading Skills Reading Comprehension • Mathematics Broad Math Math Calculation Skills Math Reasoning • Written Language Broad Written Language Basic Writing Skills Written Expression • Other Clusters Academic Knowledge Phoneme/Grapheme Knowledge Academic Skills Academic Fluency Academic Applications • Intra-Achievement Discrepancies • Oral-Language Ability/Achievement Discrepancies

Figure 10.4 Interpretation Capabilities of the WJ III Cob and WJ III Ach. (*Source:* Woodcock, R. W., McGrew, K. S., & Mather, N. (2001). *Woodcock-Johnson Third Edition Technical Manual.* (p. 3) Itasca, IL: Riverside Publishing.)

The cognitive tests, like the achievement measures, are divided into the standard battery and the extended battery. The subtests included on the standard battery are verbal comprehension, visual-auditory learning, spatial relations, sound blending, concept formation, visual matching, numbers reversed, incomplete words, auditory working memory, and visual-auditory learning-delayed.

The WJ III Tests of Cognitive Abilities, like the achievement tests, are computer scored. The scoring program is easy to use, and comparative data for age and grade norms, confidence intervals, standard scores, and percentile ranks are available.

Technical Data. The technical manual of the WJ III presents comprehensive information regarding the norm sampling procedures, standardization procedures, and reliability and validity information.

Norming Procedures. The WJ III tests, both cognitive and achievement, were completed during the same research phases spanning a 3-year period. The data for the norming process were completed with 8,818 subjects from over 100 geographically diverse communities in the United States. The following sampling variables were addressed: geographic region, community size, sex, race (white, black, American Indian, Asian Pacific Islander), designation of Hispanic/non-Hispanic, parents' educational levels. For the college sample, the additional variables of public or private college and 2- or 4-year college were addressed. For the adult sample, the additional variables relating to type of occupation, occupational status, and educational level—including graduation from college or graduate school—were included.

Reliability. The technical manual includes information regarding test-retest reliability, interrater reliability, alternate forms reliability, and internal consistency reliability. Most reliability coefficients for internal consistency are reported to be in the .90s.

Validity. The technical manual provides concurrent validity information for studies with the WJ III Tests of Cognitive Abilities with other measures of intelligence such as the Stanford-Binet IV, the Wechsler Preschool and Primary Scale of Intelligence—Revised, as well as measures of attention and behavior. On like measures, the coefficients ranged from moderate to adequate. Additional studies and coefficients are provided comparing individual subtests. In addition to concurrent validity studies, the technical manual presents ample information about the factor structure and evidence to support content and construct validity.

STANFORD-BINET INTELLIGENCE SCALE—FOURTH EDITION (STANFORD-BINET IV)

The Stanford-Binet IV (Thorndike, Hagen, & Sattler, 1986) was significantly revised in 1986, and the revisions made the test much more like the Wechsler Scales in number of scores. The earlier versions of this test yielded a single IQ score heavily weighted on verbal ability. The newer version contains 15 subtests grouped into four areas. The test manual describes a three-level hierarchical model, shown in Figure 10.5, that underlies this instrument. The three levels are defined by Thorndike et al. (1986) in the following manner:

1. *First level.* Measures general ability, or *g*. The term *g* is defined as "what an individual uses when faced with a problem that he or she has not been taught to solve."

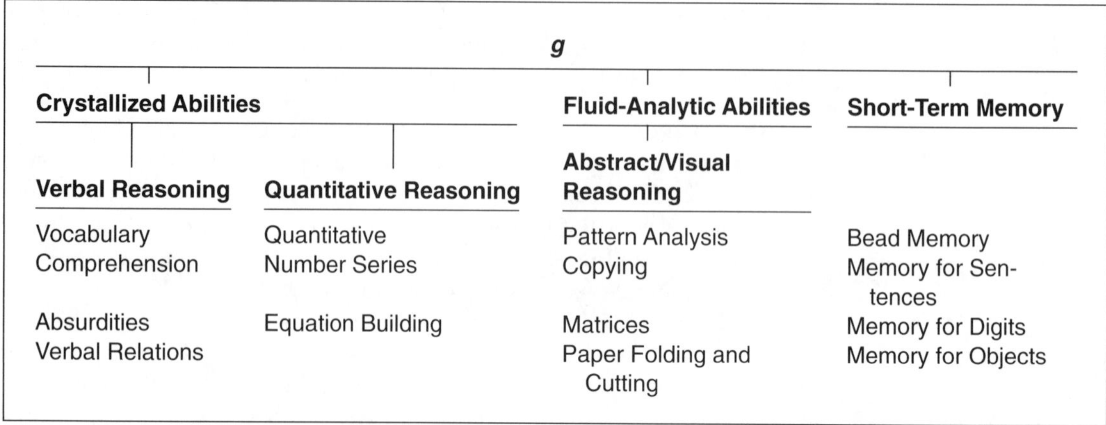

Figure 10.5 Cognitive abilities factors appraised in the Stanford-Binet IV. (*Source:* From *Guide for Administering and Scoring, Fourth Edition* (p. 4), by R. L. Thorndike, E. P. Hagen, and J. M. Sattler, 1986, Chicago: Riverside. Copyright 1986 by The Riverside Publishing Company. Reproduced with permission of The Riverside Company, Chicago, Illinois.)

2. *Second level.* Composed of three factors (Figure 10.5): crystallized abilities, fluid-analytic abilities, and short-term memory. Crystallized abilities include the cognitive skills needed to learn and use information about verbal and quantitative concepts to solve problems. Fluid-analytic abilities include the skills needed to solve problems of figural or other nonverbal stimuli. Short-term memory includes the skills needed to retain new information for a short period of time until it is processed into long-term memory and the ability needed to hold information from long-term memory as it is used to solve problems.
3. *Third level.* Includes content-specific areas such as verbal reasoning, quantitative reasoning, and abstract/visual reasoning. This level is thought to be useful for diagnosticians and educators as they plan interventions for students. (p. 3)

Because subtest and area scores can now be determined, examiners will find that comparing individual abilities is easier with the Stanford-Binet IV than it was with earlier versions of this test. Area and total test scores have a mean of 100 with a standard deviation of 16. The age-normed standardized subtest scores are presented with a mean of 50 and a standard deviation of 8.

The Stanford-Binet IV was designed for use with students ages 2 to 23. This instrument seems to provide an adequate alternative measure for students of preschool age.

Check Your Understanding

Complete Activity 10.3.

ACTIVITY 10.3

Answer the following questions.

1. According to the information in the Wechsler classification system, what percentage of the population should be classified as gifted? ______________
2. According to the information in the Wechsler classification system, what percentage of the population would have an IQ score of 69 or below? ______________
3. The WJ III Tests of Cognitive Ability were designed to be used for persons between the ages of ______________ and ______________.
4. Unlike the Wechsler Scales and the Stanford-Binet IV, the WJ III Tests of Cognitive Ability are a(n) ______________ test rather than a test kit with manipulatives.
5. The older Stanford-Binet test yielded a single IQ score; however, test results for the Stanford-Binet IV include ______________ scores and ______________ scores.
6. What are the three levels of the Stanford-Binet IV? ______________

____

____

____

Apply Your Knowledge

Explain how a student from an educationally deprived environment might score lower on these tests than a student from an educationally abundant environment. ______________________________

____

Technical Data

Norming Process. The Stanford-Binet IV was standardized using more than 5,000 persons from 47 states and the District of Columbia (Thorndike et al., 1986). The variables considered were geographic region, sex, community size, occupational and educational levels, and race/ethnic group. The standardization sample was representative of the 1980 census data.

Reliability. Reliability information provided includes test-retest reliability and internal reliability using the split-half method.

Validity. Concurrent validity studies were conducted using the 1973 Stanford-Binet, the WISC—R, WPPSI, WAIS—R, and Kaufman Assessment

Battery for Children. The coefficients ranged from .73 to .91. Factor analysis information is provided in the technical manual.

KAUFMAN ASSESSMENT BATTERY FOR CHILDREN (K-ABC)

The K-ABC contains both achievement and intelligence measures for children from the ages of 2½ to 12½ (Kaufman & Kaufman, 1983a). This instrument was designed with heavy emphasis on neuropsychological and cognitive theory and is organized to reflect this theoretical basis. This test will not be administered by special education teachers but is administered by psychologists or educational diagnosticians. The test authors list the following goals for the K-ABC:

1. Measure intelligence from a strong theoretical and research base.
2. Separate acquired factual knowledge from the ability to solve unfamiliar problems.
3. Yield scores that translate to educational intervention.
4. Include novel tasks.
5. Be easy to administer and objective to score.
6. Be sensitive to the diverse needs of preschool, minority group, and exceptional children. (Kaufman & Kaufman, 1983b)

The K-ABC is organized to yield four global scores: Sequential Processing, Simultaneous Processing, Mental Processing Composite (a combination of both the Simultaneous and Sequential areas), and Achievement. The scores are reported as standard scores with a mean of 100 and a standard deviation of 15. The protocol, shown in Figure 10.6, illustrates the various scores that can be obtained from this instrument.

Because it contains both mental and achievement measures, the K-ABC may aid in the diagnosis of learning disabilities when using a discrepancy criterion. The test also contains supplementary sociocultural norms that can be applied when testing students from culturally different backgrounds (Kaufman & Kaufman, 1983b).

The test kit includes three easels, additional manipulative materials, protocols, and two manuals: one for test administration and scoring and one for test interpretation. The administration manual contains Spanish instructions and correct responses for the Mental Processing and Achievement portions of the test. The Spanish instructions are for use with students who understand some English. Spanish-speaking students who do not know English should be administered the complete Spanish version of the K-ABC. Some of the subtests of the K-ABC are grouped in a Nonverbal Scale and can also be used for students with receptive language problems.

K·ABC Kaufman Assessment Battery for Children

by Alan S. Kaufman and Nadeen L. Kaufman

INDIVIDUAL TEST RECORD

Name ______________________ Sex ________

Parent's names ______________________

Home address ______________________

Home phone ______________________

Grade ________ School ______________________

Examiner ______________________

SOCIOCULTURAL INFORMATION (IF PERTINENT)

Race ______________________

Socioeconomic background ______________________

	YEAR	MONTH	DAY
Test date			
Birth date			
Chronological age			

Mental Processing Subtests $\bar{X}$ = 10; *SD* = 3	Scaled Score: Sequen-tial	Simul-taneous	Non-verbal	Nat's. %ile rank Table 4	S or W Table 11	Other data
1. Magic Window						
2. Face Recognition						
3. Hand Movements						
4. Gestalt Closure						
5. Number Recall						
6. Triangles						
7. Word Order						
8. Matrix Analogies						
9. Spatial Memory						
10. Photo Series						
Sum of subtest scores						

Transfer sums to Global Scales, Sum of subtest scores column.

Achievement Subtests $\bar{X}$ = 100; *SD* = 15	Standard score ± band or error ___% confidence	Nat's. %ile rank Table 4	Socio-cultural %ile rank Table 5	S or W Table 11	Other data
11. Expressive Vocabulary	±				
12. Faces & Places	±				
13. Arithmetic	±				
14. Riddles	±				
15. Reading/ Decoding	±				
16. Reading/ Understanding	±				
Sum of subtest scores					

Transfer sums to Global Scales, Sum of subtest scores column.

Global Scales $\bar{X}$ = 100; *SD* = 15	Sum of subtest scores	Standard score ±band or error ___% confidence Table 2	Nat's. %ile rank Table 4	Socio-cultural %ile rank Table 5	Other data
Sequential Processing					
Simultaneous Processing					
Mental Processing Composite					
Achievement					
Nonverbal					

Global Scale Comparisons

	Indicate >, <, or ≈		Circle the significance level		
Sequential	______	Simultaneous (Table 10)	NS	.05	.01
Sequential	______	Achievement (Table 10)	NS	.05	.01
Simultaneous	______	Achievement (Table 10)	NS	.05	.01
M P C	______	Achievement (Table 10)	NS	.05	.01

AGS®

Figure 10.6 The protocol of the K-ABC provides a format for scoring mental processing, achievement, and other global scales. (*Source:* From *Kaufman Assessment Battery for Children: Protocol* (p. 1) by A. S. Kaufman and N. L. Kaufman, 1983, Circle Pines, MN: American Guidance Service. Copyright 1983 by American Guidance Service. Reprinted by permission.)

Technical Data

Norming Process. The standardization of the K-ABC involved 2,000 students from various geographic regions in the United States. Demographic information reflects the national demographic information of the 1980 census, with the following variables considered: race or ethnic group, sex, geographic region, parental education, community size, and educational placement of students. The category of educational placement included students who were currently served in regular education, special education, and talented and gifted programs.

Reliability. The test interpretation manual provides in-depth information on reliability studies, including split-half reliability, test-retest, alternate levels reliability, and standard error of measurement. These reliability studies yield a psychometrically "tight" instrument (Wiebe, 1986), with reliability coefficients ranging from .71 to .97 for total group reliability.

Validity. The information provided on validity includes construct validity, predictive validity research, and concurrent criterion-related validity. The test interpretation manual also contains supportive validity information concerning factor analysis research founded in neuropsychological and cognitive theory.

DETROIT TESTS OF LEARNING APTITUDE—4 (DTLA—4)

The DTLA—4 contains 10 subtests, which are grouped into a variety of composites. These composites include the General Mental Ability Composite, the Optimal Composite, the Domain Composites, and the Theoretical Composites. The General Mental Ability Composite is made up of the scores of all 10 of the subtests. The Optimal Composite is found by using the four highest scores obtained on the individual subtests in an effort to find the "best estimate of a person's overall 'potential'" (Hammill, 1998, p. 20). The Domain Composites include the following four domains: Linguistic Domain, Cognitive Domain, Attentional Domain, and Motoric Domain. The Theoretical Composites comprise a variety of combinations of subtests that the author believes represent assessment of abilities according to theoretical models such as those set forth by Cattell and Horn, Das, Jensen, and Wechsler.

The author presents additional research in this 4th edition of the DTLA in an effort to support the validity of test constructs and theoretical foundation. The research presented is an improvement over previous editions, although the studies do not appear to have been carried out with the same rigor expected of other well-known tests that measure intelligence and abilities.

As suggested by the subtest and composite titles, some of the subtests are verbal, some are presented visually and require fine-motor responses such as reproducing line drawings, and still others require short-term auditory memory and the ability to follow oral directions. This instrument may be used, along with other measures, to document the possibility of distractibility or visual-motor difficulties. This instrument may provide insight into a student's abilities in some areas, although it seems to lack adequate research to stand alone as a measure of intelligence for the purposes of placement and intervention decisions.

Technical Data

Norming Process. The DTLA—4 was standardized using a sample of 1,350 students in 37 states (Hammill, 1998). The description of the method of sample selection and of the actual persons included in the norming of the DTLA—4 is somewhat confusing as presented in the manual. Data from the DTLA—3 were combined with the DTLA—4 data. Data obtained on clinical samples were obtained from existing data submitted by "users of DTLA—3" (Hammill, 1998, p. 104). This raises the question of standardized training of these test consumers from whom the data were drawn.

Demographic data appear to represent those of the nation as presented in the manual. Demographic variables considered were gender, rural or urban community, race (white, black, other), ethnicity (African American, Hispanic, Native American, or other), and geographic region. Family income, educational attainment of parents, disability status, and age (6 years to 17 years of age) were also considered.

Reliability. Internal consistency coefficients were calculated using coefficient alpha and ranged from .71 to .97. Test-retest reliability yielded coefficients ranging from .71 to .99 when compared across the various age groups.

Validity. Content validity, criterion-related validity, and construct validity information are presented in the manual. Content validity is discussed theoretically and in terms of the tasks required by each subtest. A discussion of item analysis is presented as a form of content validity. The criterion-related studies include correlational information with the K-ABC, the Woodcock-Johnson Psycho-Educational Battery—Revised, and various achievement tests. The coefficients are reported as not significant (NS) for many subtests and range from NS to modestly adequate for others.

Check Your Understanding

Complete Activity 10.4.

ACTIVITY 10.4

Answer the following questions.

1. The K-ABC is administered to children aged ______________ to ______________.
2. The K-ABC has a strong ______________ base, which applies the ______________ - ______________ model of processing.

3. The K-ABC has the advantage of containing both ______________ and ______________ measures, which is useful in calculating discrepancies.
4. The K-ABC has a complete ______________ version, which is used for Spanish-speaking children who do not know English.
5. The DTLA—4 has four domains, which include ______________ ______________

Apply Your Knowledge

Which of the measures of cognitive ability are probably used most often in schools for elementary ages when determining eligibility? ______________

KAUFMAN ADOLESCENT AND ADULT INTELLIGENCE TEST (KAIT)

The KAIT (Kaufman & Kaufman, 1993) was designed to measure the general intellectual ability of persons aged 11 to 85+. The theoretical construction includes measurement of fluid and crystallized scales. The manual states that the crystallized scales are thought to measure acquired concepts that may be influenced by one's previous educational and cultural experiences. The fluid scales are thought to measure the abilities one needs to solve new problems. The test may be administered as a whole battery or may be administered as a core battery comprising six subtests. The standard scores are based on only the six core subtests: Definitions, Rebus Learning, Logical Steps, Auditory Comprehension, Mystery Codes, and Double Meanings.

Available scores include subtest percentile ranks, scaled scores for crystallized and fluid scales, crystallized IQ, fluid IQ, and standard IQ score (composite intelligence scale) derived from the core battery. The KAIT manual includes research that is relevant for professionals working with special adult populations, such as persons with clinical depression and persons with Alzheimer's type of dementia.

Technical Data

Norming Process. The standardization of the KAIT included a sample of more than 2,600 persons aged 11 to 94 years. Twenty-seven states participated in the standardization process. The 1988 U.S. census data served as the framework for addressing the diversity of the sample. Geographic region, age, parental education, and race and ethnicity (white, black, Hispanic, or other) were considered in the selection of the sample.

Reliability. The reliability studies include split-half internal reliability and test-retest reliability studies. The average split-half reliability coefficients ranged from .71 to .97. Total sample average test-retest coefficients ranged from .63 to .95.

Validity. Research presented in the KAIT manual includes construct validity, criterion-related validity, and factor analysis. Data from concurrent validity studies vary by age, with the most acceptable correlations occurring with the WAIS for persons in the 16–19 age range. Correlations with the K-ABC ranged from not acceptable to modestly adequate for students ages 11–12. Concurrent validity research with the Stanford-Binet IV yielded coefficients that are modestly adequate.

KAUFMAN BRIEF INTELLIGENCE TEST (KBIT)

Designed to be used as a screening instrument, the KBIT (Kaufman & Kaufman, 1990) should not be used as part of a comprehensive evaluation to determine eligibility or placement. According to the manual, the test serves to screen students who may be at risk for developing educational problems and who then should receive a comprehensive evaluation. The test takes about 15–30 minutes to administer and consists of two subtests: Vocabulary and Matrices. The Vocabulary subtest has two parts: Expressive and Definitions. These two subtests are designed to measure crystallized intelligence (Vocabulary) and fluid intelligence (Matrices).

Technical Data

Norming Process. The standardization sample of the KBIT included 2,022 persons ranging in age from 4 to 90 years. Consideration was given to gender, educational level of parents, geographic region, and race and ethnicity. The sample selection was based on U.S. census data for 1985.

Reliability. Reliability information presented in the manual consists of split-half reliability and test-retest reliability. The split-half reliability coefficients are acceptable, with most reported to be in the .80s and .90s. Test-retest coefficients are all reported to be within the .80s and .90s.

Validity. The manual reports on item validity, construct validity, and criterion-related validity. Criterion-related validity studies were conducted with the WISC—R, K-ABC, and the WAIS—R. The criterion-related validity coefficients were modestly adequate for the K-ABC achievement scores and for the full-scale IQ scores of the Wechsler Scales.

SPECIAL CONSIDERATIONS FOR STUDENTS FROM CULTURALLY AND LINGUISTICALLY DIVERSE ENVIRONMENTS

bidialectal Persons who speak English using two different dialects.

Students who are from culturally and linguistically diverse environments include students whose dominant language is not English; students who have some knowledge of two languages, however, neither language is particularly strong; and students from **bidialectal** environments (Turnbull et al., 2002). A student from a bidialectal language environment is one who uses two variations of English, one being a nontraditional form of English and one being standard English. As noted previously, many traditional tests of intelligence include a large number of items that are verbally based (Gardner, 1993).

The debate about the appropriateness of using traditional IQ tests with students from culturally and linguistically diverse populations continues. This debate has stimulated research and exploration of possible alternative types of assessment to determine intellectual ability. These methods, such as dynamic assessment, to date lack the empirical data to support their use instead of traditional psychometric standardized assessments. Therefore, research continues.

Some have proposed the use of traditional assessment measures in what is believed to be a more culturally fair context (GoPaul-McNicol & Thomas-Presswood, 1998). For example, these authors propose a multitiered assessment model that incorporates the use of psychometric assessment in the traditional standardized manner to establish the traditional measured IQ score. Following this administration of the test instrument, the test is used again for psychometric potential assessment. In this second step, the instrument is used a different way by suspending time requirements, presenting vocabulary within a context rather than isolated words to be defined, allowing for the use of paper and pencil on items used for mental processing and calculation, and allowing missed items to be presented in a test-teach-retest format. Although these techniques appear to be more fair to students from various cultures and linguistic backgrounds, the obtained scores will be estimates of potential due to the nonstandardized administration techniques.

Others advocate that best practice procedures should include the administration of all standardized tests in both English and the child's other language if it is determined that the child is dominant in the other language (Alvarado, 2001). This method may be problematic for assessment of students who have equally low language scores in both languages, specifically in the determination of learning disabilities. This is due in part to the heavy language emphasis in both academic achievement testing and assessment of intelligence.

Several years ago, Figueroa raised several issues that require additional research to determine best practice in the assessment of students who are considered to be linguistically in the minority (1989). These issues include how to assess and rule out the effects of environmental, cultural, linguistic, and economic disadvantage in the assessment of students with linguistic differences; how poverty and language differences affect intelligence; how to weigh missed educational opportunity; and how to define and determine specific learning disabilities in students with linguistic differences. It is clear that these same issues exist today and will continue to concern educational professionals for many years.

NONVERBAL MEASURES OF INTELLECTUAL ABILITY

Because IQ tests include many items that rely on verbal comprehension and vocabulary, there are times when using a nonverbal intelligence test may be the fairest method to obtain an estimate of a student's intellectual ability. For example, in cases where the student appears to lack language dominance in either of two languages, or has a severe language disability, or has significant hearing impairments, a nonverbal measure may assist educators in collecting data to make educational decisions. Two commonly used measures—the Comprehensive Test of Nonverbal Intelligence and the Test of Nonverbal Intelligence, Third Edition—are reviewed to provide examples of this type of assessment.

COMPREHENSIVE TEST OF NONVERBAL INTELLIGENCE (CTONI)

This instrument includes six subtests that may be used with persons ages 6-0 to 89-11 years of age (Hammill, Pearson, & Wiederholt, 1997). The six subtests include: pictorial analogies, geometric analogies, pictorial categories, geometric categories, pictorial sequences, and geometric sequences. An example of the pictorial and geometric categories are shown in Figure 10.7. The administration of all subtests will yield a nonverbal intelligence composite. The administration of the pictorial subtests will provide a pictorial nonverbal composite, and administration of the geometric subtests will provide a geometric nonverbal intelligence component.

The CTONI has three principal uses according to the authors. The CTONI can be used with persons for whom other instruments assessing intelligence would be inappropriate or biased; to make comparisons between verbal measures and nonverbal intelligence; and to use in research. The authors report that the instrument was developed using multiple theoretical bases rather than a single theory.

This test may be administered by using oral instructions or by presenting the instructions through pantomime. The instrument should be administered through pantomime for all persons who are hearing impaired and for persons who speak a language other than English.

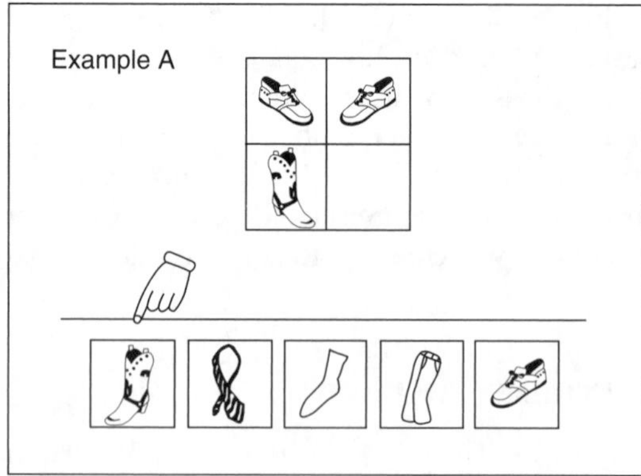

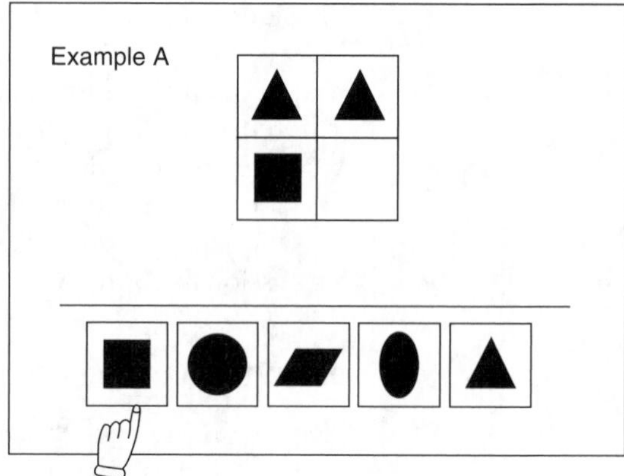

Figure 10.7 Examples of pictorial categories and geometric categories. (*Source:* From *Comprehensive Test of Nonverbal Intelligence, Examiner's Manual,* p. 11. *Examiner's Manual for the Comprehensive Test of Nonverbal Intelligence,* by D. D. Hammill, N. A. Pearson, & J. L. Wiederholt (1997). Austin, TX: Pro-ED. Reprinted by permission.)

Technical Data. The examiner's manual includes sufficient data regarding the technical quality of the instrument. The following information is provided:

Norming Process. The norm sample of the CTONI included 2,901 persons in 30 states. The characteristics of geographic area, gender, race (white, black, other) urban/rural residence, ethnicity (Native American, Hispanic, Asian, African American, other), family income, and parents' educational level were considered in the norm sample. The percentages of each of these characteristics were representative of the general population of the United States based on the 1997 Census (U.S. Bureau of the Census, 1997).

Reliability. Reliability information was provided for internal consistency, standard error of measurement, test-retest reliability, and interrater reliability. A summary of reliability data is included for quick reference. All coefficients were within the adequate to high range.

Validity. The examiner's manual included the validity information for content validity including analyses of the content validity of other measures of nonverbal intelligence, relationship to theories of intelligence, item analysis, and differential item functioning analysis. Evidence of criterion-related validity was presented comparing the CTONI with the WISC—III, the Test of Nonverbal Intelligence, Second Edition (TONI—2), the PPVT—R, and the

TONI—3 (see next section). Evidence of the instrument's ability to discriminate between groups was also included.

TEST OF NOVERBAL INTELLIGENCE—THIRD EDITION (TONI—3)

This instrument was designed to assess a single cognitive process of solving novel abstract problems (Brown, Sherbenou, & Johnsen, 1997). The authors state that the TONI—3 is a language- and motor-reduced instrument that also reduces cultural influence. It may be used with students ages 6-0 to 89-11. This test includes two equivalent forms, A and B. The instructions are presented to the examinee using pantomime. The authors state that the administration time is approximately 45 minutes.

Technical Data. The technical data provided in the examiner's manual includes norm sample information, reliability, and validity information.

Norming Process. A total of 3,451 persons representing 28 states were included in the norming sample. The demographic considerations in the norming process were based on the 1997 Statistical Abstracts of the United States (U.S. Bureau of the Census, 1997). These factors included geographic region, gender, race (white, black, other), residence (urban/rural), ethnicity (Native American, Hispanic, Asian, African American, and other), disability status (no disability, learning disability, speech-language disorder, mental retardation, other disability). In addition, the family income of parents, educational level of parents, and educational level of adult subjects were considered.

Reliability. Evidence of reliability includes internal consistency measures using coefficient alpha and standard error of measurement, alternate forms reliability, test-retest reliability, and interrater reliability. All reliability coefficients presented in the manual were within the .90s.

Validity. The examiner's manual provides evidence of content validity, criterion-related validity comparing the TONI—3 with instruments such as the CTONI, the WISC—III, and the WAIS—R, the Clinical Evaluation of Language Fundamentals—Revised (CELF—R), K-ABC, and the TOLD. Criterion-related validity coefficients were adequate for comparisons with nonverbal measures and low for verbal measures providing some evidence of discriminate construct validity. Additional measures of construct validity include the correlations with school achievement and age, group differentiation, factor structure, and item validity.

RESEARCH ON INTELLIGENCE MEASURES

Many of the most popular intelligence measures have recently been reviewed, and research continues to emerge in the literature. Some current research studies and test reviews are summarized here.

1. In a review of the WJ—R Tests of Cognitive Ability, Schrank (1993) stated that this instrument measures eight factors of cognitive functioning as defined in the theoretical construct of crystallized intelligence. Schrank further suggested that this allows the evaluator to describe the individual student's pattern of cognitive strengths and weaknesses. McGrew and Murphy (1995) found that the factors were inconsistent across ages.
2. Prewett (1992) found that the KBIT's correlation with the WISC—III supports its use as a screening instrument. Prewett and McCaffery (1993) found that the KBIT should be interpreted as only a rough estimate of the IQ that can be obtained on the Stanford-Binet. Kaufman and Wang (1992) found that the differences in means obtained by blacks, Hispanics, and whites on the KBIT are in agreement with mean differences found on the WISC—R. Canivez (1996) found high levels of agreement between the KBIT and the WISC—III in the identification of students with learning disabilities using discrepancies between these measures and the WJ—R.
3. For students 11 to 12½ years of age, the KAIT was found to be a more accurate measure of general intelligence than the K-ABC (Kaufman, 1993a). This may be partly the result of the ages specified for each test: the KAIT for ages 11–85 and the K-ABC for ages 2½ to 12½.
4. Statistically significant differences were found between the performance of women and men on the fluid and crystallized intelligence subtests on the KAIT (Kaufman & Horn, 1996). This research also found an interaction effect between gender and age for two of the subtests studied.
5. Analysis of data from the standardization sample indicated significant differences in scores obtained by blacks, whites, and Hispanics (Kaufman, McLean, & Kaufman, 1995). This research found that whites had higher scores than blacks and Hispanics and that the Hispanics performed higher on the fluid tasks than the crystallized tasks. This study also found that the results were consistent even when the level of educational attainment was covaried.
6. Differences in scores were found between Asian and white children on the K-ABC (Mardell-Czudnowski, 1995). In this study, the Asian children scored higher on the sequential processing scale

but showed no differences on the mental processing scales. The achievement scale scores were higher for children who had previously lived in the United States for at least 4 years.

7. Valencia, Rankin, and Livingston (1995) found evidence of content bias in the items of the K-ABC. In this study, 14% of the items on the Mental Processing scale and 63% of the items on the Achievement scale were determined to be biased against the Mexican American children who participated in the research. These authors suggest that the opportunity to learn specific test content may be the contributing reason for the bias of these items.
8. An analysis of data from the standardization sample indicated that the construct validity was similar for both African American and white children (Fan, Wilson, & Reynolds, 1995). This research included four statistical analyses of existing data. An analysis of the data by Keith et al. (1995) determined a similar conclusion.
9. In a study of Sioux children residing on a reservation, the scores obtained on Simultaneous Processing were significantly higher than the scores for Sequential Processing and Achievement on the K-ABC (Cummings & Merrell, 1993).
10. Several researchers have questioned the factor structure of the WISC—III indicating that there is evidence for the first two factors of verbal comprehension and performance; however, the freedom from distractibility and processing speed factors appear to be weak and perhaps misnamed (Carroll, 1997; Keith & Witta, 1997; Kranzler, 1997; Kush, 1996; Ricco, Cohen, Hall, & Ross, 1997).
11. Konold, Kush, and Canivez (1997) found that the WISC—III does support a four-factor theory when 12 subtests rather than 13 are used in the analysis. This analysis employed the scores of students who were receiving special education services.
12. Researchers warn that using individual subtest scatter on the WISC—III to make decisions about eligibility or classification may not be accurate and recommend interpreting individual scores with extreme caution (Daley & Nagle, 1996; Dumont & Willis, 1995; Keith, 1997; Maccow & Laurent, 1996).
13. Lukens and Hurrell (1996) assessed students within the range of mild mental deficiency with both the WISC—III and the Stanford-Binet IV. They concluded that most of these students scored higher on the Binet Test Composite than the WISC—III Full Scale IQ score. Lavin (1996) compared the WISC—III and the Binet on a nonreferred sample and found no significant differences between the mean scores obtained on the instruments.

14. Maller (1996) researched the verbal subtest score results of the WISC of students with hearing impairments. She found that verbal scores should not be used to determine delays in verbal skills in students with hearing impairments.
15. Hishinuma (1995) reviewed possible accommodations that could be implemented in administering the WISC—III to students with disabilities in order to test the limits. He called for guidelines for accommodations to be developed in accordance with standards and psychometric theory.
16. Plante and Sykora (1994) found that the performance of children in a clinical sample who suffered stress and difficulty coping as a result of factors such as abuse was significantly affected on the Freedom from Distractibility Index.
17. In one study using the Stanford-Binet IV, students in a general education classroom were found to have more variability in their scores than students already receiving special education services. This may be due in part to the greater degree of homogeneity of the group of students receiving services. Gridley and McIntosh (1991) found that the scores of children aged 2 to 6 years and 7 to 11 years did not support the factor theory purported by the test authors.
18. In a concurrent validity study, Canivez (1995) found similarities in the WISC—III and KBIT scores. However, he suggested that the KBIT be used only for screening, and more comprehensive measures should be used for detailed interpretations of ability. Other researchers have found that the KBIT may be suitable for screening but it is not suitable for determining other comprehensive information (Parker, 1993; Prewett & McCaffery, 1993).
19. Vig and Jedrysek (1996) researched the performance of children with language impairments on the Stanford-Binet and found that the Stanford-Binet IV may be inappropriate for use with 4- and 5-year-olds because of the minimal expectations of this age group on the Binet.
20. Prewett and Matavich (1994) compared the performance of referred students from low economic status on the WISC—III and the Binet and found that the WISC—III Full Scale IQ scores were, on the average, 9 points lower than the Binet Test Composite. WISC—III Verbal IQ scores were 13 points lower than the Stanford-Binet IV Verbal Reasoning Area scores.
21. Law and Faison (1996) compared the WISC—III and the KAIT scores of a sample of adolescent delinquent males. In this study, the scores for the KAIT were found to be significantly higher than the WISC—III scores for this sample.

22. In a review of the CTONI, Nicholson warned examiners to use additional assessment instruments when using the CTONI (1998–1999). Nicholson noted that the CTONI does not provide a comprehensive measure of intelligence or nonverbal intelligence.
23. Smith reviewed the K-BIT and noted that use of the instrument with persons of different cultural backgrounds may be measuring acculturation rather than ability, especially on the vocabulary subtest (1998–1999). The review also pointed out the strong psychometric characteristics of this screening instrument.

ASSESSING ADAPTIVE BEHAVIOR

Adaptive behavior is a term used to describe how well a student adapts to her environment. The importance of this concept was underscored by the passage of PL 94-142, which contained the requirement of nondiscriminatory assessment—specifically, the mandate to use more than one instrument yielding a single IQ score for diagnosis (*Federal Register*, 1977). The measurement of adaptive behavior must be considered before a person meets the criteria for mental retardation. A student who functions within the subaverage range of intelligence as measured on an IQ test but who exhibits age-appropriate behaviors outside the classroom should not be placed in a setting designed for students with mental retardation.

Adaptive behavior measurement is also emphasized as one possible method of promoting nonbiased assessment of culturally different students (Mercer, 1979; Reschly, 1982). Use of adaptive behavior scales in the assessment of students with learning problems can add another perspective that may be useful in planning educational interventions (Bruininks, Thurlow, & Gilman, 1987; Horn & Fuchs, 1987). Other researchers have found the assessment of adaptive behavior useful in educational interventions for learning-disabled students (Bender & Golden, 1988; Weller, Strawser, & Buchanan, 1985). Adaptive behavior scales are instruments that usually are designed to be answered by a parent or teacher or some other person familiar with the student's functioning in the everyday world. The questions are constructed to obtain information about the student's independent functioning level in and out of school. Many of the items measure self-reliance and daily living skills at home and in the community.

Reschly (1982) reviewed literature of adaptive behavior and determined that several common features were presented. The measuring of adaptive behavior had the common concepts of (a) developmental appropriateness, (b) cultural context, (c) situational or generalized behaviors, and (d) domains. Reschly found that definitions of adaptive behavior and the measurement of that behavior were based on expectations of a particular age, within the person's culture, in given or general situations, and that the behaviors measured were classified into domains.

Harrison (1987) reviewed research on adaptive behavior and drew the following conclusions:

1. There is a moderate relationship between adaptive behavior and intelligence.
2. Correlational studies indicate that adaptive behavior has a low relationship with school achievement, but the effect of adaptive behavior on achievement may be greater than the correlations indicate and adaptive behavior in school may have a greater relationship with achievement than adaptive behavior outside school.
3. There is typically a moderate to a moderately high relationship between different measures of adaptive behavior.
4. Adaptive behavior is predictive of certain aspects of future vocational performance.
5. There is a possibility that the use of adaptive behavior scales could result in the declassification of mentally retarded individuals, but no evidence was located to indicate that this is actually happening.
6. There are few race and ethnic group differences on adaptive behavior scales.
7. There are differences between parents' and teachers' ratings on adaptive behavior scales.
8. Adaptive behavior scales differentiate among different classification groups such as normal, mentally retarded, slow learner, learning disabled, and emotionally disturbed.
9. Adaptive behavior scales differentiate among mentally retarded people in different residential and vocational settings.
10. Adaptive behavior is multidimensional.
11. Adaptive behavior can be increased through placement in settings which focus on training adaptive behavior skills.
12. Adaptive behavior scales exhibit adequate stability and interrater reliability.

Source: From "Research with Adaptive Behavior Scales" by P. Harrison, 1987, *The Journal of Special Education,* 21, pp. 60–61. Copyright 1987 by PRO-ED, Inc. Reprinted by permission.

Although earlier research found that there were differences between parent and teacher ratings on adaptive behavior, Foster-Gaitskell and Pratt (1989) found that when the method of administration and familiarity with the adaptive behavior instrument were controlled, differences between parent and teacher ratings were not significant.

The formal measurement of adaptive behavior began with the development of the Vineland Social Maturity Scale (Doll, 1935). The assessment of adaptive behavior as a common practice in the diagnosis of students, however, did not occur until litigation found fault with school systems for the placement of minority students based only on IQ results (Witt & Martens, 1984). Some researchers feel that the assessment of adaptive behavior in students being evaluated for special education eligibility should not be mandated until further research on adaptive behavior instruments has occurred (Kamphaus, 1987; Witt & Martens, 1984). After reviewing several of the newer adaptive behavior scales, Evans and Bradley-Johnson (1988) cautioned examiners to select instruments carefully because of the low reliability and validity of the instruments. These authors issued the following considerations for professionals using adaptive behavior instruments:

(a) Scales must be selected that were standardized using the type of informant to be employed in the assessment (e.g., ABI [Adaptive Behavior Inventory] with teachers and Vineland Survey Form or SIB [Scales of Independent Behavior] with caregivers).

(b) If valid information is to be obtained, the response format of the scale must be readily understood by the informant, i.e., not be confusing.

(c) In some cases it will be helpful to select a scale with both normative data on both a nonretarded and a retarded group.

(d) If information on maladaptive behavior is desired, only ABS:SE [Adaptive Behavior Scale, School Edition], the SIB, and the Vineland Survey Form address this area.

(e) The number of items on subtests of interest should be considered in interpretation to insure that an adequate sample of behavior has been obtained.

(f) For eligibility decisions, total test results, rather than subtest scores, should be used. Total test results are based upon a larger sample of behavior and are much more reliable and valid.

(g) If different scales are used for the same student, quite different results may be obtained due to many factors, including different response formats, content, and technical adequacy.

(h) Different informant (teacher vs. parent) may perceive a student's performance differently due to personal biases and the different demands of the settings.

(i) Validity of results must be evaluated in each case based upon problems inherent to rating scales (e.g., informant bias, avoidance of extreme choices).

Source: From "A Review of Recently Developed Measures of Adaptive Behavior" by L. Evans and S. Bradley-Johnson, 1988, *Psychology in the Schools,* 25, p. 286. Copyright 1988 by Psychology in the Schools. Reprinted by permission.

The examiner should remember these considerations when selecting an adaptive behavior scale and choose the instrument that best suits the needs of the student.

Check Your Understanding

Complete Activity 10.5.

ACTIVITY 10.5

Complete the sentences and answer the question that follows.

1. Adaptive behavior is the ability one has to ______________________________

2. Assessments of adaptive behavior may be used to ______________________________

3. According to Reschly (1982), what are the four common concepts in the assessment of adaptive behavior? ______________________________

Apply Your Knowledge

What are some of the findings summarized by Harrison (1987) about research of adaptive behavior? ______________________________

REVIEW OF ADAPTIVE BEHAVIOR SCALES

The adaptive behavior scales reviewed in this chapter are the Vineland Adaptive Behavior Scales (Survey Form, Expanded Form, and Classroom Edition), the AAMR Adaptive Behavior Scale—School, Second Edition, the Adaptive Behavior Inventory (ABI and ABI Short Form), and the Adaptive Behavior Inventory for Children. As stated previously, examiners should be cautious in selecting the scale appropriate for the student's needs. Some scales have been normed using special populations only, some scales have been normed using both special and normal populations, and some scales contain items for assessing maladaptive behavior as well as adaptive behavior. The size of the samples used during standardization and the reliability and validity information should be considered.

VINELAND ADAPTIVE BEHAVIOR SCALES

A revision of the original Vineland Social Maturity Scale (Doll, 1935), the Vineland Adaptive Behavior Scales (Sparrow, Balla, & Cicchetti, 1984) con-

Table 10.1 Number of items in each version of the Vineland by domain and subdomain.

Domain and Subdomain	Survey Form	Expanded Form	Classroom Edition
Communication	67	133	66
Receptive	13	23	10
Expressive	31	76	29
Written	23	34	24
Daily Living Skills	92	201	99
Personal	39	90	36
Domestic	21	45	21
Community	32	66	42
Socialization	66	134	53
Interpersonal Relationships	28	50	17
Play and Leisure Time	20	48	18
Coping Skills	18	36	18
Motor Skills	36	72	29
Gross	20	42	16
Fine	16	31	13
ADAPTIVE BEHAVIOR COMPOSITE	261	541	244
Maladaptive Behavior	36	36	0

Source: From *Vineland Adaptive Behavior Scales* (p. 3) by S. S. Sparrow, D. A. Balla, and D. V. Cicchetti, 1984, Circle Pines, MN: American Guidance Service. Copyright 1984 by American Guidance Service. Reprinted by permission.

tain revisions so extreme that the battery can be considered new. The scales have three forms: Interview Edition, Survey Form; Interview Edition, Expanded Form; and Classroom Edition. The differences between the three instruments are number of items, method of administration, and areas assessed (the Classroom Edition does not contain items to assess maladaptive behavior). Table 10.1 illustrates the number of items for each version of the scale. Materials used for each of the three scales are different.

Interview Edition Survey Form. The Interview Edition Survey Form (Sparrow, Balla, & Cicchetti, 1984) was designed to replace the original Vineland Social Maturity Scale. The 297 items, administered in an interview fashion to a parent or caregiver, are used to assess the adaptive behavior of individuals from birth through 18-11 years of age. The areas assessed include communication, daily living skills, socialization, motor skills, and maladaptive behavior. The maladaptive portion is an optional section that may be administered if worrisome behavior is of concern for a particular student. The scores that may be obtained include standard scores (mean, 100; standard deviation, 15), percentile ranks, stanines, adaptive levels, and age equivalents. The "Score Summary" portion of the protocol is shown in Figure 10.8. The Survey Form includes supplementary norms that enable the examiner to compare students with disabilities to other students with the same disabling conditions. The supplementary norms include students with mental retardation, emotional disturbance, visual impairments, and hearing impairments.

Technical Data for the Survey Form

Norming Process. The standardization sample for the Vineland included 3,000 persons ranging in age from birth to 18-11 years. Variables considered in the sample were sex, geographic region, parental educational level, race or ethnic group, community size, and age. Variables considered for the supplementary norm group were disabling condition, ambulatory and non-ambulatory persons with mental retardation, and age. The Vineland was administered to 723 persons from six states in a national tryout before the actual norming and standardization process. This tryout enabled the authors to refine items and scoring procedures in the developmental version of the interview format.

Reliability. Three types of reliability studies are included in the manual: split-half, test-retest, and interrater reliability. The split-half reliability coefficients ranged from .83 to .94 for median coefficients reported for domains and adaptive behavior composites. Test-retest coefficients ranged from the low .80s to the high .90s for a sample of 484 persons. The interrater reliability coefficients ranged from .62 to .78.

Validity. Validity information included construct validity, content validity, and criterion-related validity studies. Construct validity was based on developmental progression and factor analysis of domains and subdomains. Content validity is presented as a discussion of item development and the national tryout of items in a developmental version of the Interview Edition. In criterion-related validity studies, the new version was compared with the original Vineland, the K-ABC, and the Peabody Picture Vocabulary Test—Revised. The domain of communication had the highest correlation with the K-ABC achievement scale and the Peabody Picture Vocabulary Test—Revised. As would be expected when comparing an adaptive behavior scale with academic or intellectual measures, other areas compared yielded low correlations. This is due to the different domains or constructs measured by these different types of instruments.

Interview Edition Expanded Form. Like the Survey Form, this scale is administered in an interview format. The Expanded Form contains 577 items and can be used to design IEP objectives for adaptive behavior

Vineland Adaptive Behavior Scales: INTERVIEW EDITION Survey Form

Individual's name ______ Chronological age ______

Date of interview ______ Supplementary norm group (if applicable) ______

SCORE SUMMARY

Before beginning the score summary, read Chapter 5 in the manual.

SUBDOMAIN		Raw Score	Standard Score $\bar{X}$ = 100, SD = 15 Tables B.1 and B.2	Band of Error ___% Confidence Tables B.3	National %ile Rank Tables B.4	Stanine Tables B.4	Supplementary Norm Group %ile Rank Tables B.5	Adaptive Level TableB.6 and B.8	Supplementary Norm Group Adaptive Level TableB.7 and B.9	Age Equivalent TableB.10 and B.11
	Receptive									
	Expressive									
	Written									
COMMUNICATION DOMAIN	SUM			±						
	Personal									
	Domestic									
	Community									
DAILY LIVING SKILLS DOMAIN	SUM			±						
	Interpersonal Relationships									
	Play and Leisure Time									
	Coping Skills									
SOCIALIZATION DOMAIN	SUM			±						
(For ages to 5-11-30)	Gross									
	Fine									
MOTOR SKILLS DOMAIN	SUM			±						
	SUM OF DOMAIN STANDARD SCORES									
ADAPTIVE BEHAVIOR COMPOSITE				±						

SCORE PROFILE

(See Chapter 5 in the manual to graph scores.)

	Standard Score ± Band of Error	20 30 40 50 60 70 80 90 100 110 120 130 140 150 160
COMMUNICATION DOMAIN	±	
DAILY LIVING SKILLS DOMAIN	±	
SOCIALIZATION DOMAIN	±	
MOTOR SKILLS DOMAIN	±	
ADAPTIVE BEHAVIOR COMPOSITE	±	percentile rank: 1 2 5 9 16 25 37 50 63 75 84 91 95 98 99

−5SD −4SD −3SD −2SD −1SD MEAN +1SD +2SD +3SD +4SD

OPTIONAL MALADAPTIVE BEHAVIOR DOMAIN (Administer for ages 5-0-0 and older)		Raw Score	Maladaptive Level: Table B.12	Supplementary Norm Group Maladaptive Level: Table b.13
	Part 1			
	Parts 1 and 2			

Additional interpretive information (see Chapters 5 and 6 in the manual) ______

Recommendations ______

AGS®

Figure 10.8 Score summary portion of the protocol for the Vineland Adaptive Behavior Scales. (*Source:* From *Vineland Adaptive Behavior Scales, Protocol* by S. S. Sparrow, D. A. Balla, and D. V. Cicchetti, 1984, Circle Pines, MN: American Guidance Service. Copyright 1984 by American Guidance Service. Reprinted by permission.)

(Sparrow, Balla, & Cicchetti, 1984). Of the 577 items, 297 are contained in the Survey Form. Adaptive behavior for persons ranging in age from birth through 18-11 may be assessed using the Expanded Form. This form requires from 60 to 90 minutes to administer and provides a detailed assessment of adaptive behavior functioning of the student. It also includes normative data for both nondisabled and disabled populations. Figure 10.9 illustrates the Expanded Form program planning report.

Technical Data for the Expanded Form

Norming Process. The standardization and norming process was the same for both the Expanded and Survey Forms of the Interview Edition.

Reliability. The manual reports on reliability studies using split-half, test-retest, and interrater reliability measures. Split-half reliability coefficients were in the .80s for the standardization sample and in the .80s and .90s for supplementary norms. Information for the test-retest and interrater reliability is based on the Survey Form information. The manual also gives information regarding intercorrelations and standard error of measurement.

Validity. Information given includes construct validity, content validity, and criterion-related validity. Studies were based on the Survey Form, and discussion of estimating coefficients for the Expanded Form is included.

Classroom Edition. The Classroom Edition of the Vineland contains 244 items designed to assess the adaptive behavior functioning of students in the classroom (Sparrow et al., 1984). Students from the age of 3 to 12-11 may be assessed using this version. Figure 10.10 illustrates the type of items and the format used on the Classroom Edition. The areas assessed include communication, daily living skills, socialization, and motor skills.

Technical Data for the Classroom Edition

Norming Process. Although the norming process was representative of the U.S. population for the other editions of this instrument, the Classroom Edition sample was underrepresented by students from rural areas, and other differences in norming have been noted (McLoughlin & Lewis, 1990).

Reliability. Test developers studied internal consistency using coefficient alpha, with coefficients for specific domains ranging from .77 to .96 and .96 to .98 for composites.

Validity. Validity studies included construct, content, and criterion-related studies. The manual presents construct validity through a discussion of developmental progression and factor analysis. Selection and development of test items are given as evidence of content validity. The Classroom Edition was compared with the K-ABC, the Peabody Picture Vocabulary Test—Revised,

COMMUNICATION DOMAIN

GENERAL OBJECTIVES: **Improvement will be exhibited in the following areas of *Receptive* communication (check all that apply):**

____ A. Beginning to understand
____ B. Beginning to listen
____ C. Pointing to body parts
____ D. Following instructions
____ E. Listening and attending

Short-term Objective	Program Beginning Date	Method of Implementation	Method of Evaluation	Mastery Criterion	Program Ending Date

GENERAL OBJECTIVES: **Improvement will be exhibited in the following areas of *Expressive* communication (check all that apply):**

____ A. Beginning affective expression
____ B. Pre-speech sounds
____ C. Pre-speech nonverbal expression
____ D. Beginning to talk
____ E. Vocabulary
____ F. Talking in sentences
____ G. Using names
____ H. Asking questions
____ I. Using abstract concepts
____ J. Relating experiences
____ K. Using prepositions
____ L. Using function words
____ M. Articulating
____ N. Reciting
____ O. Using plural nouns and verb tense
____ P. Giving information about self
____ Q. Expressing complex ideas

Short-term Objective	Program Beginning Date	Method of Implementation	Method of Evaluation	Mastery Criterion	Program Ending Date

Figure 10.9 Expanded Form program planning report of the Vineland Adaptive Behavior Scales. (*Source:* From *Vineland Adaptive Behavior Scales, Program Planning Report* (p. 2) by S. S. Sparrow, D. A. Balla, and D. V. Cicchetti, 1984, Circle Pines, MN: American Guidance Service. Copyright 1984 by American Guidance Service. Reprinted by permission.)

	Observed Performance			Estimated Performance		
40. Demonstrates understanding of $\frac{1}{2}$, $\frac{1}{3}$, and $\frac{1}{4}$. (If the child demonstrates understanding of only one or two of the symbols, score 1.)	2	1	0	2	1	0
41. Demonstrates understanding of the following symbols: $, =, %, and [decimal point]. (If the child demonstrates understanding of only two or three of the symbols, score 1.)	2	1	0	2	1	0
42. Demonstrates knowledge of the multiplication tables through 9. (If the child demonstrates knowledge of the multiplication tables through some number between 1 and 9, score 1.)	2	1	0	2	1	0

FOR PERSON SCORING AND INTERPRETING ONLY:

Sum of 2s, 1s, 0s

COMMUNITY RAW SCORE (Total observed and estimated sums)

COMMENTS AND OBSERVATIONS

ITEM SCORES
2—Yes, usually
1—Sometimes or partially
0—No, never

SOCIALIZATION DOMAIN
INTERPERSONAL RELATIONSHIPS SUBDOMAIN

	Observed Performance			Estimated Performance		
1. Shows desire to please parent or caregiver or other familiar person (for example, gives a gift or performs a helpful task).	2	1	0	2	1	0
2. Labels happiness, sadness, fear, and anger in self (for example, says, "I'm sad").	2	1	0	2	1	0
3. Imitates simple adult movements, such as clapping hands or waving good-bye, in response to a model.	2	1	0	2	1	0
4. Imitates a relatively complex task several hours after it was performed by another. (For example, the child imitates sweeping, hammering nails, or drying dishes. Any object required to do the actual task need not be present.)	2	1	0	2	1	0
5. Imitates adult phrases heard on previous occasions. (For example, the child has one doll call to another, "Honey, I'm home.")	2	1	0	2	1	0
6. Addresses at least two familiar people by name (for example, "Mommy," "Daddy," a first name, or a nickname).	2	1	0	2	1	0
7. Identifies people by characteristics other than name, when asked (for example, says, "That's Tony's sister").	2	1	0	2	1	0
8. Laughs or smiles appropriately in response to positive statements. (The child must understand what is being said, not simply respond to the tone of voice, to score 2.)	2	1	0	2	1	0
9. Responds verbally and positively to good fortune of others. (For example, the child congratulates a friend who receives an award.)	2	1	0	2	1	0
10. Initiates conversations on topics of particular interest to others. (If the child does so only when the topic is also of interest to the child, score 0.)	2	1	0	2	1	0

The next item is on the following page. Before going on, please determine that you recorded a score for every item on this page.

Figure 10.10 A portion of the protocol for the classroom edition of the Vineland Adaptive Behavior Scales, showing the type of items and the format. (*Source:* From *Vineland Adaptive Behavior Scales, Classroom Edition, Protocol* (p. 11) by S. S. Sparrow, D. A. Balla, and D. V. Cicchetti, 1984, Circle Pines, MN: American Guidance Service. Reprinted by permission.)

Part I: Independent Living Domains	***Part II: Social Behavior Domains***
Independent Functioning	Social Behavior
Physical Development	Conformity
Economic Activity	Trustworthiness
Language Development	Stereotyped and Hyperactive Behavior
Numbers and Time	Self-Abusive Behavior
Prevocational/Vocational Activity	Social Engagement
Self-Direction	Disturbing Interpersonal Behavior
Responsibility	
Socialization	

Figure 10.11 Areas assessed by the AAMR Adaptive Behavior Scale—School, Second Edition.

and the WISC—R. Additional studies compared the Classroom Edition with the Stanford-Binet and the Woodcock-Johnson Preschool Scale. Correlation coefficients ranged from low (.20s) to fair (.50s to .60s).

AAMR ADAPTIVE BEHAVIOR SCALE—SCHOOL, SECOND EDITION (ABS—S2)

Test developers constructed the ABS—S2 (Lambert, Nihira, & Leland, 1993) as one method to determine whether persons meet the criteria for the diagnosis of mental retardation. The ABS—S2 is divided into two parts based on (a) independent living skills and (b) social behavior. The domains assessed in each are listed in Figure 10.11.

The person most familiar with the student may administer the scale by completing the items, or a professional who is familiar with the child may complete the items. The information is plotted on a profile sheet to represent the student's adaptive behavior functioning. Standard scores, percentile ranks, and age equivalents are provided in the manual.

Technical Data

Norming Process. The ABS—S2 was normed on a sample of 2,074 persons with mental retardation and 1,254 persons who were nondisabled. The variables of race, gender, ethnicity, urban and rural residence, geographic region, and age (3–18) were considered in the sample.

Reliability. Information on interrater reliability, internal consistency, and test-retest reliability is presented in the manual. All coefficients presented range from adequate to high.

Validity. The examiner's manual addresses construct and item validity for students with and without mental retardation.

ADAPTIVE BEHAVIOR INVENTORY (ABI)

The ABI (Brown & Leigh, 1986) was constructed for use with students with mental retardation and students with developmental delay ranging in age from 6-0 to 18-11; it can also be used for nondisabled students aged 5-0 to 18-11. The ABI contains five scales: Self-Care, Communication, Social Skills, Academic Skills, and Occupational Skills. Each of the scales contains approximately 30 items that are rated by a teacher or professional who is familiar with the student.

Also available is the ABI Short Form, an abbreviated form of the ABI that can be used as a screening or research instrument. Items were selected from all five scales to make up this 50-item instrument.

The scoring of both the ABI and the ABI Short Form is the same. This instrument uses a basal level of 5 consecutive items scored perfectly (3-point response) and a ceiling level of 5 consecutive failures (scored as 0 points: Student does not perform skill). The scoring system is located on the protocol as well as explained in the manual. The derived scores available include scaled scores (mean, 10; standard deviation, 3), Adaptive Behavior Quotient (mean, 100; standard deviation, 15), and percentile ranks. The protocol for the full ABI is shown in Figure 10.12.

Technical Data

Norming Process. The ABI has two norm-reference groups: 1,296 students aged 5-0 to 18-11 in the nondisabled sample population and 1,076 students aged 6-0 to 18-11 in the sample population with mental retardation. The variables considered in the nondisabled population were sex, age, race, ethnicity, language spoken in the home, geographic region, community size, parental occupation, and parental educational level. In the sample of persons with mental retardation, the variables were sex, measured intelligence, etiology of retardation, instructional arrangement, presence of other disabling conditions, the parental variables of educational and occupational level, community size, and geographic region. The manual also contains the following information regarding the teachers who responded in the norming process: sex, years of experience, and highest degree completed. In most cases, variables appeared to represent total U.S. population percentages reported in the manual.

Reliability. Internal consistency reliability using the coefficient alpha method was studied for sample populations with and without mental retardation. Coefficients were in the .80s and .90s for both groups for both the full scale and the ABI Short Form. Test-retest reliability studies on both sample populations and for the full scale and the Short Form yielded coefficients in the .90s.

ABI

Adaptive Behavior Inventory

ABI Profile
Response Sheet

Linda Brown & James E. Leigh

Student's Name ______
Address ______

School ______ Grade ______
Examiner's Name ______
Examiner's Title ______
Date of ABI Rating ______ year ______ year
Student's Date of Birth ______ year ______ year
Student's Age ______ year ______ year

SECTION I. ABI PROFILE

ABI SCALES STANDARD SCORES						ABQ-FS	OTHER MEASURES OF INTELLIGENCE, ACHIEVEMENT, OR ADAPTIVE BEHAVIOR					
M = 10 SD = 3	Self-Care	Communication	Social	Academic	Occupational	M = 100 SD = 15	Test Used	Test Used	Test Used	Test Used	Test Used	Test Used
	•	•	•	•	•	160	•	•	•	•	•	•
	•	•	•	•	•	155	•	•	•	•	•	•
20	•	•	•	•	•	150	•	•	•	•	•	•
19	•	•	•	•	•	145	•	•	•	•	•	•
18	•	•	•	•	•	140	•	•	•	•	•	•
17	•	•	•	•	•	135	•	•	•	•	•	•
16	•	•	•	•	•	130	•	•	•	•	•	•
15	•	•	•	•	•	125	•	•	•	•	•	•
14	•	•	•	•	•	120	•	•	•	•	•	•
13	•	•	•	•	•	115	•	•	•	•	•	•
12	•	•	•	•	•	110	•	•	•	•	•	•
11	•	•	•	•	•	105	•	•	•	•	•	•
10	-•-	-•-	-•-	-•-	-•-	100	-•-	-•-	-•-	-•-	-•-	-•-
9	•	•	•	•	•	95	•	•	•	•	•	•
8	•	•	•	•	•	90	•	•	•	•	•	•
7	•	•	•	•	•	85	•	•	•	•	•	•
6	•	•	•	•	•	80	•	•	•	•	•	•
5	•	•	•	•	•	75	•	•	•	•	•	•
4	•	•	•	•	•	70	•	•	•	•	•	•
3	•	•	•	•	•	65	•	•	•	•	•	•
2	•	•	•	•	•	60	•	•	•	•	•	•
1	•	•	•	•	•	55	•	•	•	•	•	•
	•	•	•	•	•	50	•	•	•	•	•	•
	•	•	•	•	•	45	•	•	•	•	•	•
	•	•	•	•	•	40	•	•	•	•	•	•

X = Normal Intelligence Sample **O = MR Sample**

SECTION II. SCORE SUMMARY

ABI SCALES

		Self-Care Skills	Communication Skills	Social Skills	Academic Skills	Occupational Skills
Raw Score	=	____	____	____	____	____

Performance Based on the Normal Intelligence Normative Sample

Standard Score (SS) (Table A)	=	____	____	____	____	____
Standard Error of Measurement (SEM) (Tables 8 & 9)	=	____	____	____	____	____
Percentile Rank (PR) (Table A)	=	____	____	____	____	____
Performance Descriptor (Table 1)	=	____	____	____	____	____

Performance Based on the Mentally Retarded Normative Sample

Standard Score (SS) (Table B)	=	____	____	____	____	____
Standard Error of Measurement (SEM) (Tables 8 & 9)	=	____	____	____	____	____
Percentile Rank (PR) (Table B)	=	____	____	____	____	____
Performance Descriptor (Table 1)	=	____	____	____	____	____

ABI COMPOSITE QUOTIENT

		Performance Based on the Normal Sample	MR Sample
Sum of 4 or 5 Standard Scores (SS)	=	____	____
ABQ-FS (Table C)	=	____	____
Standard Error of Measurement (SEM) (Tables 8 & 9)	=	____	____
Percentile Rank (PR) (Table C)	=	____	____
Performance Descriptor (Table 1)	=	____	____

SECTION III. ADMINISTRATION CONDITIONS

How long has the examiner known the subject being rated?

If the examiner employed information that was obtained from secondary sources (subjects themselves, parents, other professionals), please specify the source(s), the items to which the source(s) contributed, and the degree of reliability which the examiner attributes to the information:

Source	Items	Reliability + Avg. -

How often has the examiner used the ABI?

______ less than 5 times ______ 5 times or more

SECTION IV. INTERPRETATION/RECOMMENDATIONS

______
______
______
______
______
______

Figure 10.12 Protocol for the Adaptive Behavior Inventory. (*Source:* From *Adaptive Behavior Inventory* (p. 1) by L. Brown and J. E. Leigh, 1986, Austin, TX: Pro-Ed. Copyright © 1986 by Linda Brown and James E. Leigh. Reprinted by permission.)

Validity. The manual includes information on content and criterion-related validity. Item discrimination coefficients are briefly discussed and reported as high. Criterion-related validity studies for both the full scale and the Short Form were conducted with the Vineland Social Maturity Scale, the Vineland Adaptive Behavior Scales, and the AAMD Adaptive Behavior Scales (a previous edition of the ABS—S2). Coefficients ranged from .35 on Part II of the AAMD scales (maladaptive behavior) to .89 on the AAMD scales' Cognitive domain. Construct validity studies included developmental progression and correlation with measures of intellectual ability, including the WISC—R, Cognitive Abilities Test, Stanford-Binet, Slosson Intelligence Test, Otis-Lennon School Ability Test, the K-ABC, Peabody Picture Vocabulary Test—Revised, and the Arthur Adaptation of the Leiter International Performance Scale. Most coefficients were in the .30s to .60s range, with the highest coefficient of .86 for the Slosson and the Cognitive Abilities Test.

Reliability. The technical manual includes information on reliability coefficients and standard error of measurement of the scaled scores by age and ethnic group. Coefficients ranged from the .70s to the high .90s.

Validity. The technical manual discusses predictive validity but provides little statistical information to support the ABIC's ability to predict performance.

INTELLIGENCE AND ADAPTIVE BEHAVIOR: CONCLUDING REMARKS

Intelligence tests for diagnosis of learning problems should be applied with caution. Tables 10.2 and 10.3 summarize the strengths and weaknesses of the intelligence and adaptive behavior scales presented in this chapter. In addition to the many problems and issues surrounding the use of intelligence tests, the interpretation of test results is largely dependent on the training of the individual examiner. Some professionals believe that appropriate classification can occur only after numerous formal and informal assessments and observations. Others rely on only quantitative test data. Some professionals may use a factor analysis approach to determine learning disabilities, while others use informal and curriculum-based achievement measures.

The determination of the classification of mild mental retardation or educational disability is complicated by many social and legal issues. In a review of the problems and practices in the field for the past 20 years, Reschly (1988) advocated the need for a change of focus in the diagnosis and classification of students with mental retardation.

> The classification system reforms advocated would place more emphasis on three dimensions: (1) severe, chronic achievement deficits; (2) significantly

Table 10.2 Summary of intelligence measures.

Instrument	Strengths	Weaknesses
Wechsler Scales	Available for various ages Good technical quality Yield several scaled scores to be used for intra-individual interpretation Computer-assisted scoring available	Time-consuming to administer and score Have been found to be biased culturally Have mean differences for minority populations
Woodcock-Johnson III Tests of Cognitive Ability	Can be compared with achievement tests (WJ III Tests of Achievement) for determining discrepancies Good technical quality Computer-assisted scoring available Yield several scores for intra-individual interpretation	Time-consuming to administer and score
Stanford-Binet Intelligence Scale—Fourth Edition	Yields subtest and area scores Can be used for intra-individual interpretation Adequate technical quality	Some researchers reported difficulty with initial norm tables and scoring procedures Requires significant amount of training to administer and interpret Time-consuming to administer and score
Kaufman Assessment Battery for Children	Strong theoretical base Yields information for achievement and cognitive fucntioning Good technical quality Allows for cultural differences in interpretation	Yields nontraditional scores as a result of theoretical basis but may be difficult to use for traditional interpretation Time-consuming to administer and score Limited age range
Detroit Test of Learning Aptitude—4	Yield scores for support in diagnosis of motor-enhanced and attention-enhanced skills Fair technical quality	To be used with other cognitive measures: not to be used alone for eligibility decisions Time-consuming to administer and score
Comprehensive Test of Nonverbal Intelligence	Provides alternate method of assessment of intelligence Includes different types of tasks May be more cutlure free	Should use additional assessment measures for more complete assessment of IQ
TONI—3	Quick to administer and score	Best used for screening only, presents a single task

deficient achievement across most if not all achievement areas; and (3) learning problems largely resistant to regular interventions. The students meeting these criteria will be virtually the same as the current population with MMR; however, their classification will not carry the stigma of comprehensive incompetence based on biological anomaly that is permanent. (p. 298)

Table 10.3 Summary of adaptive behavior measures.

Instrument	Strengths	Weaknesses
Vineland Adaptive Behavior Scales	Three versions available Interview Edition contains a measure of maladaptive behavior Classroom Edition was designed for use by educational professionals Contain norms for students with mental retardation, visual and hearing disabilities, and emotional disturbance Good technical quality	Time-consuming to administer
AAMR Adaptive Behavior Scale—School, Second Edition	To be used with students who have mental retardation Coincides with AAMR criteria for adaptive behavior	Does not have as many items in areas as other scales
Adaptive Behavior Inventory (full scale; Short Form)	Has norms for both nondisabled and mentally retarded populations Adequate technical quality Short Form may be used for screening	Designed for use with student mental retardation or developmentally delayed students Short Form to be used not for diagnosis but for screening only

THINK AHEAD

This text has been concerned primarily with the assessment of students within school age, typically from about age 6 to 18. Students who require the assistance of special education services as part of their educational intervention often require services during preschool years and have additional needs for postsecondary years. The assessment of students in the years of early childhood and in the years requiring special considerations for transition to adulthood are presented in chapter 12.

EXERCISES

Part I

Select the terms to complete the statements that follows.

a. intelligence
b. adaptive behavior
c. IQ
d. achievement
e. bidialectal
f. traditional measures of IQ
g. nonverbal
h. acculturation
i. multiple intelligences
j. environmental influence
k. dynamic assessment

_____ 1. Because many of the instruments used to assess intelligence and achievement include numerous items of a verbal nature, the assessment of students whose primary language is not English should be given a _____ measure in addition to other measures.

_____ 2. IDEA includes statements of determining eligibility that require the team to exclude _____ as the primary reason for a disability before determining a student as eligible for special education services.

_____ 3. Minority students who may appear to be within the range of mental retardation on measures developed for use with students from the majority culture may not be within the range of mental retardation on _____ measures.

_____ 4. Students who have a dominant language other than English are often referred to as being bilingual, and students whose primary language is English and nonstandard English are referred to as _____.

_____ 5. Bilingual students may have difficulty with both the language items on standardized assessments and the level of _____ required to perform well on the items.

_____ 6. Once the standardized assessment has been completed, an examiner may use the method of _____, incorporating teaching, to determine the student's potential to learn the failed items.

_____ 7. The measure of this is actually a ratio comparing a student's mental age and chronological age.

ANSWER KEY TO CHECK YOUR UNDERSTANDING

Activity 10.1

1. B
2. G
3. L
4. D
5. J
6. F
7. K
8. I
9. H
10. A

Apply Your Knowledge. Answers may vary but should include recognition of possible bias within the test instruments, bias of the examiner or situation, and the possible inequitable consequences that can result from using IQ test results for educational placement of some persons.

Activity 10.2

1. C
2. A
3. S
4. J
5. N
6. M
7. I
8. E
9. K
10. D
11. T
12. Q
13. G
14. L
15. H
16. O
17. F
18. B

Apply Your Knowledge. Subtests that require the student to use her hands and organizational or fine-motor skills such as block design, picture arrangement, coding, mazes, and object assembly.

Activity 10.3

1. 2.2% of the student population should be classified in this category.
2. 2.2% of the student population should be classified in this category.
3. 2 years, 90 years
4. easel
5. subtest, area
6. (1) general ability; (2) crystallized abilities, fluid-analytic abilities, short-term memory; (3) verbal reasoning, quantitative reasoning, abstract/visual reasoning.

Apply Your Knowledge. Students who have many opportunities and educational experiences available to them in their everyday environment are more likely to develop a fund of knowledge to use as they respond to items.

Activity 10.4

1. 2½ years, 12½ years
2. theoretical, simultaneous-sequential
3. mental, achievement

4. Spanish
5. linguistic, cognitive, attentional, motoric

Apply Your Knowledge. The Wechsler Intelligence Scales for Children—III, the Stanford-Binet IV, the K-ABC, and the Woodcock-Johnson Tests of Cognitive Ability—Revised

Activity 10.5

1. function in various environments.
2. determine if a student meets the criteria for services for persons with mental retardation.
3. developmental appropriateness, cultural context, situational or generalized behaviors, domains.

Apply Your Knowledge. Answers may vary but should include findings summarized by Harrison.

REFERENCES

Alvarado, C. G. (2001). *Best practices in the special education assessment of culturally and linguistically diverse (CLD) students.* Available e-mail: cris.alvarado@juno.com.

American Psychological Association (1985). *Standards for educational and psychological testing.* Washington, DC: Author.

Anastasi, A. (1988). *Psychological testing* (6th ed.). New York: Macmillan.

Bender, W., & Golden, L. (1988). Adaptive behavior of learning disabled and nonlearning disabled children. *Learning Disability Quarterly, 11,* 55–61.

Bersoff, D. N. (1981). Testing and the law. *American Psychologist, 36,* 1047–1056.

Brown, L., & Leigh, J. E. (1986). *Adaptive Behavior Inventory.* Austin, TX: Pro-Ed.

Brown, L., Sherbenou, R. J., & Johnsen, S. K. (1997). *Test of nonverbal intelligence,* 3rd Edition. Austin, TX: Pro-Ed.

Brown, T., Reynolds, C. R., & Whitaker, J. S. (1999). Bias in mental testing since Bias in Mental Testing. *School Psychology Quarterly, 14*(3), 208–238.

Bruininks, R., Thurlow, M., & Gilman, C. (1987). Adaptive behavior and mental retardation. *Journal of Special Education, 21,* 69–88.

Canivez, G. L. (1995). Validity of the Kaufman Brief Intelligence Test: Comparisons with the Wechsler Intelligence Scale for Children—Third Edition. *Psychological Assessment Resources, Inc. 2*(2), 101–111.

Canivez, G. L. (1996). Validity and diagnostic efficiency of the Kaufman Brief Intelligence Test in reevaluating students with learning disability. *Journal of Psychoeducational Assessment, 14,* 4–19.

Canter, A. S. (1997). The future of intelligence testing in the schools. *School Psychology Review, 26*(2), 255–261.

Carroll, J. B. (1997). Commentary on Keith and Witta's hierarchical and cross-age confirmatory factor analysis of the WISC—III. *School Psychology Quarterly, 12*(2), 108–109.

Clark, G., & Patton, J. R. (1997). Transition Planning Inventory. Austin, TX: Pro-Ed.

Code of Fair Testing Practices in Education. (1988). Washington, DC: Joint Committee on Testing Practices.

Cummings, M. A., & Merrell, K. W. (1993). K-ABC score patterns of Sioux children: Mental processing styles, effects of school attendance, and relationship between raw scores and age. *Journal of Psychoeducational Assessment, 11,* 38–45.

Daley, C. E., & Nagle, R. J. (1996). Relevance of WISC—III indicators for assessment of learning disabilities. *Journal of Psychoeducational Assessment, 14,* 320–333.

Diana v. State Board of Education, Civil Act. No. C-70-37 (N.D. Cal, 1970, further order, 1973).

Doll, E. A. (1935). A genetic scale of social maturity. *American Journal of Orthopsychiatry, 5,* 180–188.

Dumont, R., & Willis, J. O. (1995). Intrasubtest scatter on the WISC—III for various clinical samples vs. the standardization sample: An examination of WISC folklore. *Journal of Psychoeducational Assessment, 13,* 271–285.

Elliot, R. (1987). *Litigating intelligence: IQ tests, special education, and social science in the courtroom.* Dover, DE: Auburn House.

Evans, L., & Bradley-Johnson, S. (1988). A review of recently developed measures of adaptive behavior. *Psychology in the Schools, 25,* 276–287.

Fan, X., Wilson, V. L., & Reynolds, C. R. (1995). Assessing the similarity of the factor structure of the K-ABC for African American and white children. *Journal of Psychoeducational Assessment, 13,* 120–131.

Federal Register. (1977, August 23). Washington, DC: U.S. Government Printing Office.

Figueroa, R. A. (1989). Psychological testing of linguistic-minority students: Knowledge gaps and regulations. *Exceptional Children, 56*(2), 145–152.

Foster-Gaitskell, D., & Pratt, C. (1989). Comparison of parent and teacher ratings of adaptive behavior of children with mental retardation. *American Journal of Mental Retardation, 94,* 177–181.

Fuchs, D., & Fuchs, L. (1989). Effects of examiner familiarity on Black, Caucasian, and Hispanic children: A meta-analysis. *Exceptional Children, 55,* 303–308.

Gardner, H. (1993). *Multiple intelligences: The theory in practice.* New York: Basic Books.

Gopaul-McNicol, S., & Thomas-Presswood, T. (1998). *Working with linguistically and culturally different children: Innovative clinical and educational approaches.* Boston: Allyn & Bacon.

Gridley, B. E., & McIntosh, D. E. (1991). Confirmatory factor analysis of the Stanford-Binet: Fourth Edition for a normal sample. *Journal of School Psychology, 29,* 237–248.

Grossman, H. J. (Ed.). (1983). *Classification in mental retardation.* Washington, DC: American Association on Mental Deficiency.

Hammill, D. D. (1998). *Detroit Tests of Learning Aptitude—4.* Austin, TX: Pro-Ed.

Hammill, D. D., Pearson, N. A., & Wiederholt, J. L. (1997). *Comprehensive test of nonverbal intelligence.* Austin, TX: Pro-Ed.

Harrison, P. (1987). Research with adaptive behavior scales. *Journal of Special Education, 21,* 37–61.

Harrison, P. L., & Robinson, B. (1995). Best practices in the assessment of adaptive behavior. In A. Thomas & J. Grimes (Eds.), *Best practices in school psychology* (3rd ed.). Washington, DC: National Association of School Psychologists.

Heller, K., Holtzman, W., & Messick, S. (Eds.). (1982). *Placing children in special education: A strategy for equity.* Washington, DC: National Academy Press.

Herrnstein, R. J., & Murray, C. (1994). *The bell curve: Intelligence and class structure in American life.* New York: The Free Press.

Hishinuma, E. S. (1995). WISC—III accommodations: The need for practitioner guidelines. *Journal of Learning Disabilities, 28,* 130–135.

Hopkins, K. D., Stanley, J. C., & Hopkins, B. R. (1990). *Educational and psychological measurement and evaluation* (7th ed.). Englewood Cliffs, NJ: Prentice-Hall.

Horn, E., & Fuchs, D. (1987). Using adaptive behavior in assessment and intervention. *Journal of Special Education, 21,* 11–26.

Jensen, A. R. (1998). *The g factor: The science of mental ability.* Westport, CT: Praeger.

Kamphaus, R. (1987). Conceptual and psychometric issues in the assessment of adaptive behavior. *Journal of Special Education, 21,* 27–35.

Kaufman, A. S. (1979). *Intelligent testing with the WISC—R.* New York: Wiley.

Kaufman, A. S. (1993a). Joint exploratory factor analysis of the Kaufman Assessment Battery for Children and the Kaufman Adolescent and Adult Intelligence Test for 11 and 12 year olds. *Journal of Clinical Child Psychology, 22,* 355–364.

Kaufman, A. S. (1993b). King WISC the third assumes the throne. *Journal of School Psychology, 31,* 345–354.

Kaufman, A. S. (1994). *Intelligent Testing with the WISC—III.* New York: Wiley.

Kaufman, A. S., & Horn, J. L. (1996). Age changes on tests of fluid and crystallized ability for women and men on the Kaufman Adolescent and Adult Intelligence Test (KAIT) at ages 17–94 years. *Archives of Clinical Neuropsychology, 11,* 97–121.

Kaufman, A. S., & Kaufman, N. L. (1983a). *Kaufman Assessment Battery for Children: Administration and scoring manual.* Circle Pines, MN: American Guidance Service.

Kaufman, A. S., & Kaufman, N. L. (1983b). *Kaufman Assessment Battery for Children: Interpretive manual.* Circle Pines, MN: American Guidance Service.

Kaufman, A. S., & Kaufman, N. L. (1990). *Kaufman Brief Intelligence Test.* Circle Pines, MN: American Guidance Service.

Kaufman, A. S., & Kaufman, N. L. (1993). *Kaufman Adolescent and Adult Intelligence Test.* Circle Pines, MN: American Guidance Service.

Kaufman, A. S., McLean, J. E., & Kaufman, J. C. (1995). The fluid and crystallized abilities of White, Black, and Hispanic adolescents and adults, both with and without an education covariate. *Journal of Clinical Psychology, 51,* 636–647.

Kaufman, A. S., & Wang, J. (1992). Gender, race, and education differences on the K-BIT at ages 4 to 90 years. *Journal of Psychoeducational Assessment, 10,* 219–229.

Keith, T. Z. (1997). What does the WISC—III measure? A reply to Carroll and Kranzler. *School Psychology Quarterly, 12*(2), 117–118.

Keith, T. Z., Fugate, M. H., DeGraff, M., Diamond, C. M., Shadrach, E. A., & Stevens, M. L. (1995). Using multi-sample confirmatory factor analysis to test for construct bias: An example using the K-ABC. *Journal of Psychoeducational Assessment, 13,* 347–364.

Keith, T. Z., & Witta, E. L. (1997). Hierarchical and cross-age confirmatory factor analysis of the WISC—III: What does it measure? *School Psychology Quarterly, 12*(2), 89–107.

Konold, T. R., Kush, J. C., & Canivez, G. L. (1997). Factor replication of the WISC—III in three independent samples of children receiving special education. *Journal of Psychoeducational Assessment, 15,* 123–137.

Kranzler, J. H. (1997). What does the WISC—III measure? Comments on the relationship between intelligence, working memory capacity, and information processing speed and efficiency. *School Psychology Quarterly, 12*(2), 110–116.

Kush, J. C. (1996). Factor structure of the WISC—III for students with learning disabilities. *Journal of Psychoeducational Assessment, 14,* 32–40.

Lambert, N., Nihira, K., & Leland, H. (1993). *AAMR Adaptive Behavior Scale-School, Second Edition.* Austin, TX: Pro-Ed.

Larry P. v. Riles, 343 F. Supp. 1306, aff'd., 502 F.2d 963, further proceedings, 495 F. Supp. 926, aff'd., 502 F.2d 693 (9th Cir. 1984).

Lavin, C. (1996). The Wechsler Intelligence Scale for Children—Third Edition and the Stanford-Binet Intelligence Scale: Fourth Edition: A preliminary study of validity. *Psychological Reports, 78,* 491–496.

Law, J. G., & Faison, L. (1996). WISC—III and KAIT results in adolescent delinquent males. *Journal of Clinical Psychology, 52,* 699–703.

Lidz, C. S. (1997). Dynamic assessment approaches. In D. P. Flanagan, J. L. Genshaft, & P. L. Harrison (Eds.), *Contemporary intellectual assessment: Theories, tests, and issues* (pp. 281–296). New York: Guilford Press.

Lopez, R. (1997). The practical impact of current research and issues in intelligence test interpretation and use for multicultural populations. *School Psychology Review, 26*(2), 249–254.

Lora v. New York City Board of Education, 1984: Final order, August 2, 1984, 587F. Supp. 1572 (E.D.N.Y. 1984).

Lukens, J., & Hurrell, R. M. (1996). A comparison of the Stanford-Binet IV and the WISC—III with mildly mentally retarded children. *Psychology in the Schools, 33,* 34–37.

Maccow, G., & Laurent, J. (1996). Analyzing WISC—III profiles: A comparison of two approaches. *Journal of Psychoeducational Assessment, 14,* 20–31.

MacMillan, D. L., & Forness, S. R. (1998). The role of IQ in special education placement decisions. *Remedial and Special Education, 19*(4), 239–253.

Maller, S. J. (1996). WISC—III verbal item invariance across samples of deaf and hearing children of similar measured ability. *Journal of Psychoeducational Assessment, 14,* 152–165.

Mardell-Czudnowski, C. (1995). Performance of Asian and White children on the K-ABC: Understanding information processing differences. *Psychological Assessment Resources, Inc., 2*(1), 19–29.

McGrew, K. S., & Flanagan, D. P. (1998). *The intelligence test desk reference (ITDR): Gf-Gc cross-battery assessment.* Boston: Allyn & Bacon.

McGrew, K., & Murphy, S. (1995). Uniqueness and general factor characteristics of the Woodcock-Johnson Tests of Cognitive Ability—Revised. *Journal of School Psychology, 33,* 235–245.

McGrew, K. S., & Woodcock, R. W. (2001). *Technical manual, Woodcock-Johnson III.* Itasca, IL: Riverside Publishing.

McLoughlin, J. A., & Lewis, R. B. (1990). *Assessing special students* (3rd ed.). Upper Saddle River, NJ: Merrill/Prentice Hall.

Messick, S. (1980). Test validity and the ethics of assessment. *American Psychologist, 35,* 1012–1027.

Mick, L. (1985). Assessment procedures as related to enrollment patterns of Hispanic students in special education. *Educational Research Quarterly, 9,* 27–35.

Nicholson, C. L. (1998–1999). Comprehensive test of nonverbal intelligence (CTONI). *Monograph: Assessment for the New Decade, Diagnostic, 24,*(1–4), 57–68.

Nihira, K., Foster, R., Shellhaas, M., & Leland, H. (1974). *AAMD Adaptive Behavior Scale*. Washington, DC: American Association on Mental Deficiency.

Overton, T., & Mardoyan-Apperson, J. (1988). *The relationship between the CLT and the PPVT—R in a college freshman sample: Part 2. CLT Technical Reports*. Norristown, PA: Arete.

Parker, L. D. (1993). The Kaufman Brief Intelligence Test: An introduction and review. *Measurement and Evaluation in Counseling and Development, 26,* 152–156.

PASE (Parents in Action in Special Education) v. Hannon, 506 F. Supp. 831 (N.D. Ill. 1980).

Plante, T. G., & Sykora, C. (1994). Are stress and coping associated with WISC—III performance among children? *Journal of Clinical Psychology, 50,* 759–762.

Prewett, P. N. (1992). The relationship between the Kaufman Brief Intelligence Test (K-BIT) and the WISC—R with referred students. *Psychology in the Schools, 29,* 25–27.

Prewett, P. N., & Matavich, M. A. (1994). A comparison of referred students' performance on the WISC—III and the Stanford-Binet Intelligence Scale: Fourth Edition. *Journal of Psychoeducational Assessment, 12,* 42–48.

Prewett, P. N., & McCaffery, L. K. (1993). A comparison of the Kaufman Brief Intelligence Test (K-BIT) with the Stanford-Binet, a two-subtest short form, and the Kaufman Test of Educational Achievement (K-TEA) Brief Form. *Psychology in the Schools, 30,* 299–304.

Psychological Corporation. (1997). *WAIS—III WMS—III Technical Manual*. San Antonio: Author.

Reschly, D. (1981). Psychological testing in educational classification and placement. *American Psychologist, 36,* 1094–1102.

Reschly, D. (1982). Assessing mild mental retardation: The influence of adaptive behavior, sociocultural status, and prospects for nonbiased assessment. In C. R. Reynolds & T. B. Gutkin (Eds.), *The handbook of school psychology* (pp. 209–242). New York: Wiley.

Reschly, D. (1988). Assessment issues, placement litigation, and the future of mild mental retardation classification and programming. *Education and Training in Mental Retardation, 23,* 285–301.

Reschly, D. J., & Grimes, J. P. (1995). Best practices in intellectual assessment. In A. Thomas & J. Grimes (Eds.), *Best practices in school psychology—II*. Washington, DC: National Association of School Psychologists.

Reynolds, C. R. (1982). The problem of bias in psychological assessment. In C. R. Reynolds & T. B. Gutkin (Eds.), *The handbook of school psychology* (pp. 178–208). New York: Wiley.

Ricco, C. A., Cohen, M. J., Hall, J., & Ross, C. M. (1997). The third and fourth factors of the WISC—III: What they don't measure. *Journal of Psychoeducational Assessment, 15,* 27–39.

Salvia, J., & Ysseldyke, J. E. (1988). *Assessment in special and remedial education* (4th ed.). Boston: Houghton Mifflin.

Schrank, F. A. (1993). Unique contributions of the Woodcock-Johnson Psychoeducational Battery—Revised to psychoeducational assessment. *Journal of Psychoeducational Assessment Monograph Series: Advances in Psychoeducational Assessment: Woodcock-Johnson Psychoeducational Battery—Revised,* 71–79.

Smith, D. K. (1998–1999). Kaufman brief intelligence test (K-BIT). *Monograph: Assessment for the New Decade, Diagnostic, 24*(1–4), 125–134.

Sparrow, S. S., Balla, D. A., & Cicchetti, D. V. (1984). *Vineland Adaptive Behavior Scales.* Circle Pines, MN: American Guidance Service.

Swanson, H. L., & Watson, B. L. (1989). *Educational and psychological assessment of exceptional children* (2nd ed.). Columbus, OH: Merrill.

Taylor, R. T. (1989). *Assessment of exceptional students: Educational and psychological procedures* (2nd ed.). Upper Saddle River, NJ: Prentice Hall.

Taylor, R. L., & Richards, S. B. (1991). Patterns of intellectual differences of black, Hispanic, and white children. *Psychology in the Schools, 28,* 5–9.

Thorndike, R. L., Hagen, E. P., & Sattler, J. M. (1986). *Technical manual, Stanford-Binet Intelligence Scale, Fourth Edition.* Chicago: Riverside.

Tucker, J. (1980). Ethnic proportions in classes for the learning disabled: Issues in nonbiased assessment. *Journal of Special Education, 14,* 93–105.

Turnbull, H. R. (1990). *Free and appropriate public education: The law and children with disabilities* (3rd ed.). Denver: Love.

Turnbull, R., Turnbull, A., Shank, A., Smith, S., & Leal, D. (2002). *Exceptional lives: Special education in today's schools.* Upper Saddle River, NJ: Merrill/Prentice Hall.

U.S. Bureau of the Census. (1997). *Statistical abstract of the United States: 1997* (117th ed.). Washington, DC: Author.

Valencia, R. R., Rankin, R. J., & Livingston, R. (1995). K-ABC content bias: Comparisons between Mexican American and White children. *Psychology in the Schools, 32,* 153–169.

Vig, S., & Jedrysek, E. (1996). Stanford-Binet Fourth Edition: Useful for young children with language impairment? *Psychology in the Schools, 33,* 124–131.

Wechsler, D. (1974). *Manual for the Wechsler Intelligence Scale for Children—Revised.* San Antonio: Psychological Corporation.

Wechsler, D. (1991). *Wechsler Intelligence Scale for Children—Third Edition: Manual.* San Antonio: Psychological Corporation.

Wechsler, D. (1997). *Wechsler Adult Intelligence Scale, Third Edition: Administration and Scoring Manual.* San Antonio: Psychological Corporation.

Weller, C., Strawser, S., & Buchanan, M. (1985). Adaptive behavior: Designator of a continuum of severity of learning disabled individuals. *Journal of Learning Disabilities, 18,* 200–203.

Wiebe, M. J. (1986). Test review: The Kaufman Assessment Battery for Children. *Education and Training for the Mentally Retarded, 21,* 76–79.

Witt, J. C., Elliot, S. N., Gresham, F. M., & Kramer, J. J. (1988). *Assessment of special children: Tests and the problem-solving process.* Glenview, IL: Scott, Foresman.

Witt, J., & Martens, B. (1984). Adaptive behavior: Tests and assessment issues. *School Psychology Review, 13,* 478–484.

Wood, F., Johnson, J., & Jenkins, J. (1990). The Lora case: Nonbiased referral, assessment, and placement procedures. *Exceptional Children, 52,* 323–331.

Woodcock, R. W., & Mather, N. (1989). *Woodcock-Johnson Tests of Cognitive Ability: Standard and Supplemental Batteries manual.* Allen, TX: DLM Teaching Resources.

Woodcock, R. W., McGrew, K. S., & Mather, N. (2001). *Woodcock-Johnson III tests of cognitive abilities.* Itasca, IL: Riverside Publishing.

Ysseldyke, J., & Algozzine, B. (1982). *Critical issues in special and remedial education.* Boston: Houghton Mifflin.

CHAPTER 11

Special Considerations in Assessment

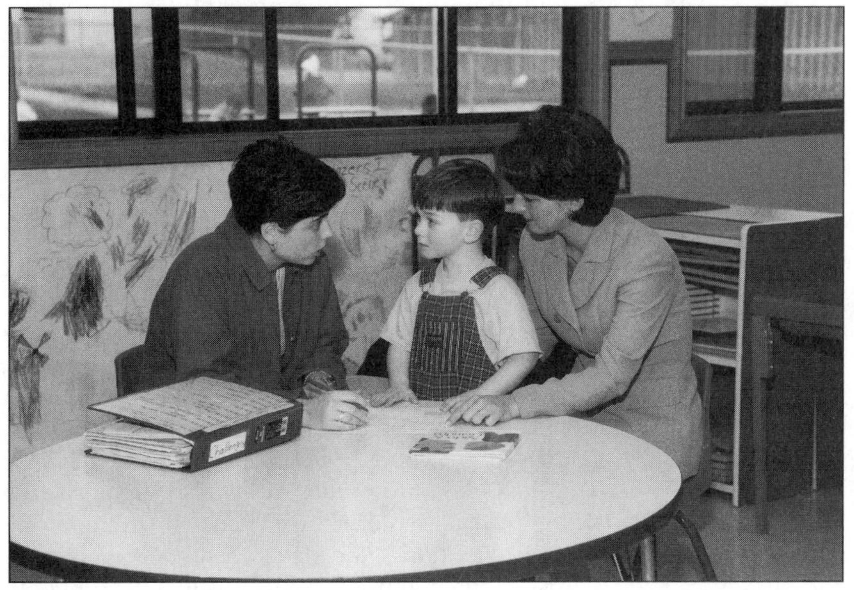

Key Terms

Public Law 99-457
developmental delay
at risk for developmental delay
biological risk factors
environmental risk factors
Individual Family Service Plan
family-centered program
family-focused program
play evaluations
arena assessment
interactive strategies
observations
situational questionnaires
ecobehavioral interviews
phonemic awareness
phonemic synthesis
phonemic analysis
transition planning
supported employment

CHAPTER FOCUS

The assessment process included thus far in the text concerns primarily the assessment of students of school age. This chapter includes the issues and procedures needed to assess very young children and older students with transition needs. The assessment of infants and young children involves different procedures and methods from assessment of school-aged children. Federal regulations require that much of the assessment process include extensive interviews with parents and that the family needs be considered. Federal regulations also require additional procedures to assist students and parents with the transition from school to adulthood. These methods and issues are presented in this chapter.

LEGAL GUIDELINES OF EARLY CHILDHOOD EDUCATION

Public Law 99-457 IDEA amendments that extend services for special needs children through infancy and preschool years; mandates services for children ages 3–5 with disabilities.

Public Law 99-457 is the law that set forth many of the guidelines and provisions of serving infants and toddlers. Many of the guidelines were incorporated into the 1997 amendments. The assessment of infants and young children presents several issues and concerns not found in the assessment of school-age children. Many of these issues are related to the young age of the child. For example, these young children present unique challenges in assessment because they must be evaluated in domains and areas that are not based on school-related competencies such as academic achievement. These children are evaluated in other areas such as physical challenges, developmental motor skills, functional communication skills, behaviors in specific situations, and developmental competence. The assessment of young children and infants also includes the unique component of family needs and a family plan for appropriate intervention.

IDEA provides for educational intervention for children beginning at age 3. Part C of the IDEA Amendments of 1997 authorizes funding for states for intervention for special-needs children for infants and toddlers. The aspects of IDEA that pertain to the assessment of infants, toddlers, and preschool children are presented in the following section.

INFANTS, TODDLERS, AND YOUNG CHILDREN

Federal regulations define the population of children eligible to be served, define the methods of assessment, provide procedural safeguards, and outline procedures to be used for intervention based on the family's needs.

ELIGIBILITY

developmental delay When an infant or child experience delay in physical, cognitive, communicative, social, emotional, or adaptive development.

Infants and toddlers from birth to age 2 who are experiencing **developmental delays** in one or more of the following areas are eligible for services: cognitive development, physical development (includes vision and hearing), communication development, social or emotional development, and adaptive development. Infants and toddlers may also be eligible for services if they have a diagnosed physical or mental condition that is likely to result in developmental delay. The law gives the individual states discretion to determine the lead agency that would provide services for infants and toddlers with special needs. The states also have the option to provide services for children 3 years of age and younger considered to be **at risk for developmental delay** unless the child has appropriate interventions.

at risk for developmental delay When a child is believed to be at risk for delay in one or more areas if interventions are not provided.

Children eligible for early childhood services are those with the same disabilities defined for school-aged children: autism, deaf-blindness, deafness, hearing impairment, mental retardation, multiple disabilities, orthopedic impairment, other health impairment, serious emotional disturbance, specific learning disability, speech or language impairment, traumatic brain injury, and visual impairment. Infants and toddlers who have a diagnosed physical or mental condition that is known to have a high probability of resulting in developmental delay are also eligible (IDEA Amendments, 1997).

Although not all states choose to serve infants and toddlers who are at risk for developmental delays, many states have responded to this category of infants and toddlers and provide intervention services. Katz (1989) lists as **biological risk factors** "prematurity associated with low birth weight, evidence of central nervous system involvement (intraventricular hemorrhage, neonatal seizures), prolonged respiratory difficulties, prenatal maternal substance use or abuse" (p. 100). These risk factors may not always result in an early diagnosed physical condition but may prove problematic as the child develops.

biological risk factors Health factors, such as birth trauma, that place a child at risk for developmental disabilities.

In addition to biological risk factors, **environmental risk factors** often exist. The most often cited environmental risk factors found by Graham and Scott (1988) are poor infant/child interaction patterns, low maternal educational level, young maternal age, disorganization or dysfunction of the family, and few family support networks. Suggestions for assessing infants at risk are given later in this chapter.

environmental risk factors Environmental influences, such as the mother's young age, that place a child at risk for developmental disabilities.

EVALUATION AND ASSESSMENT PROCEDURES

The 1997 IDEA Amendments define evaluation as the ongoing procedures used by qualified personnel to determine the child's eligibility and continued eligibility while the child is served under this law. The amendments state that

> § 636
> (a) . . . the state shall provide, at a minimum for each infant or toddler with a disability, and the infant's or toddler's family, to receive—

(1) a multidisciplinary assessment of the unique strengths and needs of the infant or toddler and the identification of services appropriate to meet such needs;

(2) a family-directed assessment of the resources, priorities, and concerns of the family and the identification of the supports and services necessary to enhance the family's capacity to meet the developmental needs of the infant or toddler. (IDEA Amendments of 1997, p. 62)

Individual Family Service Plan (IFSP) Plan required by PL 99-457 that includes the related needs of the family of the child with disabilities.

The regulations require that an IFSP, or **Individual Family Service Plan,** be developed for each infant or toddler and its family. This family service plan shall include

(1) a statement of the infant's or toddler's present levels of physical development, cognitive development, communication development, social or emotional development, and adaptive development, based on objective criteria;

(2) a statement of the family's resources, priorities, and concerns relating to enhancing the development of the family's infant or toddler with a disability;

(3) a statement of the major outcomes expected to be achieved for the infant or toddler and the family, and the criteria, procedures, and timelines used to determine the degree to which progress toward achieving the outcomes is being made and whether modifications or revisions of the outcomes or services are necessary;

(4) a statement of specific early intervention services necessary to meet the unique needs of the infant or toddler and the family, including the frequency, intensity, and method of delivering services. (IDEA Amendments of 1997, pp. 62–63)

In addition, this plan must include a statement detailing how the services will be provided within the child's natural environment and to what extent any services will *not* be provided in the child's natural environment. The plan must also include the anticipated dates for the services to begin and a statement about the expected duration of the services. The coordinator of the services must be named, and the steps that will be taken to transition the child to preschool or other services must be outlined (IDEA Amendments, 1997).

The amendments require that the IFSP be reviewed every 6 months (or more frequently as appropriate) and the family given the review of the plan. The IFSP must be evaluated at least once a year.

The assessment of infants and young children must also follow IDEA's regulations concerning nondiscriminatory assessment, parental consent, confidentiality, and due process procedural safeguards. The law requires annual evaluation of progress but notes that because of the rapid development during this period of a child's life, some evaluation procedures may need to be repeated before the annual review.

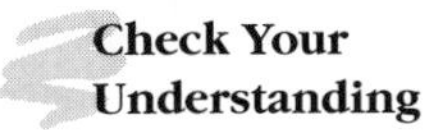
Check Your Understanding

Complete Activity 11.1.

ACTIVITY 11.1

Complete the sentences using the following terms.

developmental delay
at risk for developmental delay
family's
6 months
IFSP

1. Family assessment includes determining the ______________ priorities and concerns related to enhancing the development of the child.
2. A child with ______________ may be measured by the appropriate instruments and found in one or more of the following areas: cognitive development, physical development, communication development, social or emotional development, adaptive development.
3. ______________ must incorporate the family's description of its resources, priorities, and concerns related to the development of the child.
4. The time set for a review of the IFSP of infants and young children is ______________.

Apply Your Knowledge

Explain why the family involvement is emphasized in both the assessment stage and the development and implementation of the IFSP. _____
____

ISSUES AND QUESTIONS ABOUT SERVING INFANTS AND TODDLERS

A goal of PL 99-457 was to incorporate family members as partners in the assessment of and planning for the infant or child with developmental disabilities. Since the law's passage in 1986, many concerns have been raised by clinical practitioners working with these regulations. Of chief concern is the role of the parents in the assessment and planning process (Dunst, Johanson, Trivette, & Hamby, 1991; Goodman & Hover, 1992; Katz, 1989; Minke & Scott, 1993).

The issues raised by Goodman and Hover include confusion with the interpretation and implementation of the family assessment component. The regulations may be misunderstood as requiring mandatory assessment of family members rather than voluntary participation by the parents. The family's strengths and needs as they relate to the child, not the parents themselves, are the objects of the assessment. Furthermore, these authors contended that a relationship based on equal standing between parents and professionals may not result in a greater degree of cooperation and respect than the traditional client-professional relationship. When the parents and professionals are viewed as equal partners, the professional surrenders the role of expert. Goodman and Hover suggested that the relationship be viewed as reciprocal rather than egalitarian. An assessment process directed by the parents may not be in the child's best interest, because the parents retain the right to restrict professional inquiry.

Katz (1989) observed that the family's view of the child's most important needs takes precedence over the priorities perceived by the professional team members. In some instances, parents and professionals must negotiate to agree on the goals for the child. The family will be more motivated to achieve the goals that they believe are important.

The law clearly states that the IFSP be developed with parent participation. This is true whether or not the family participates in the assessment process. In practice, parent participation varies, according to a study of the development of IFSPs in three early-childhood intervention programs (Minke & Scott, 1993). This study found that parents do not always participate in goal setting for their children, play a listening role without soliciting input from professionals, appear to need better explanations by professionals, and may become better child advocates with early participation. These issues are similar to issues associated with parent participation during eligibility meetings for school-aged children (refer to chapter 2).

Differences in the implementation of PL 99-457 may be the result of state-determined policies and procedures. One area of difference seems to be in the interpretation of how families should be involved in the early intervention process. Dunst et al. (1991) described the **family-centered program** and the **family-focused program** as paradigms representing two such interpretations. In the family-centered program paradigm, family concerns and needs drive the assessment, anything written on the IFSP must have the family's permission, and the family's needs determine the actual roles played by case managers. The family-focused program paradigm restricts assessment to the family's needs only as they relate to the child's development, the goals are agreed on mutually by professionals and parents, and the case manager's role is to encourage and promote the family's use of professional services. It seems clear that the interpretation and implementation of PL 99-457 differ from state to state and may yet be problematic.

family-centered program Program in which the assessment and goals are driven by the family's needs and priorities.

family-focused program Program in which the family's needs are considered but goals and plans are reached through mutual agreement between the family and education professionals.

Another type of assessment of young children and their families, called Intervention-Based Multifactored Evaluation, has been proposed (Barnett, Bell, Gilkey, Lentz, Graden, Stone, Smith, & Macmann, 1999). These authors suggest that the assessment and eligibility process should be directly linked to the level of interventions required for instruction. Further, these authors believe that a child should be found eligible for services only when there are notable discrepancies between the child's ability and the peers within the environment. For example, the target child may have discrepancies between the level of assistance required and the rate of learning, the level of caregiver monitoring, or the adaptations of the curriculum, when compared to age peers. When these differences require more time or adaptation than can be accomplished within the general educational environment, special education support services are required. These authors propose a data collection method across tasks and behaviors, similar to the assessment methods used in curriculum-based measurement and in functional behavioral assessments. This method of assessment would be within the spirit of the federal regulations, which require that assessment results be linked directly to interventions.

An issue in the implementation of services for infants and toddlers is the identification of young children. A study by Snyder, Bailey, and Auer (1994) found that when children were identified, they may be identified differently than school-aged children. Snyder et al. found that 72% of the states used determination systems that included combinations or noncategorical systems.

Check Your Understanding

Complete Activity 11.2.

ACTIVITY 11.2

Answer the questions and complete the sentences.

1. What five areas of child development must the IFSP address? ____
2. The IFSP must include the expected ______________ of the interventions and the degree to which ______________ toward achieving them is being made.
3. In which of the program paradigms does the parent play a more active role in the assessment and planning process? ____
4. According to Minke and Scott (1993), parents may need better ______________ from professionals.
5. Katz (1989) stated that in some instances, parents and professionals must ______________ on goals for the child.
6. According to Goodman and Hover (1992), when assessment is directed by the parents, what problems may occur? ______________

Apply Your Knowledge

Discuss how the IFSP must balance the parents' and child's needs.

____

____

METHODS OF EARLY CHILDHOOD ASSESSMENT

As previously noted, many states serve children who are considered at risk for developmental disabilities. The discussion of assessment methods presented in this text applies to children with existing developmental disabilities as well as to those who may be at risk for developmental disabilities if they do not receive early childhood intervention.

Regulations require that qualified personnel assess children in many developmental areas; for example, assessments of vision, hearing, speech, and medical status are part of a multifactored evaluation. Detailed assessment in these areas is beyond the scope of this text. Measures presented include behavior questionnaires, observations, interviews, checklists, and measures of cognitive and language functioning. Techniques used in the assessment process are also presented.

ASSESSMENT OF INFANTS

Documenting developmental milestones and health history is primarily the responsibility of health professionals. Infants may be suspected of having developmental delays or of being at risk for developmental delays if there are clinical indications for concern. Mayes (1991) cited the following indications as need for an infant assessment:

1. Regulatory disturbances—Sleep disturbances, excessive crying or irritability, eating difficulties, low frustration tolerance, self-stimulatory or unusual movements.
2. Social/environmental disturbances—Failure to discriminate mother, apathetic, withdrawn, no expression of affect or interest in social interaction, excessive negativism, no interest in objects or play, abuse, neglect, or multiple placements, repeated or prolonged separations.
3. Psychophysiological disturbances—Nonorganic failure to thrive, recurrent vomiting or chronic diarrhea, recurrent dermatitis, recurrent wheezing.
4. Developmental delays—Specific delays (gross motor, speech delays). General delays or arrested development. (p. 445)

The prenatal, birth, and early neonatal health history is an important component of the evaluation of infants and is required by PL 99-457. Following the careful history taking of the infant's health factors, Greenspan (1992) organizes the infant/toddler/young child assessment using the following factors:

1. Prenatal and perinatal variables.
2. Parent, family, and environmental variables.

3. Primary caregiver and caregiver/infant-child relationship.
4. Infant variables: Physical, neurologic, physiologic, and cognitive.
5. Infant variables: Formation and elaboration of emotional patterns and human relationships. (pp. 316–317)

Of particular concern in assessing the infant are regulatory patterns, or how the infant reacts to stimuli in the environment and processes sensory information (Greenspan, 1992; Mayes, 1991). This includes how the infant interacts with and reacts to caregivers, the infant's sleeping habits, level of irritability, and so on. This type of assessment relies on observations using checklists and parent interviews or questionnaires. One commonly used observation assessment instrument for newborn infants is the Neonatal Behavioral Assessment Scale (Brazelton, 1984), which includes both reflex items and behavioral observation items. Use of this scale to determine control states (such as sleeping, alert) underscores the importance of this aspect of infant behavior to more complex functions, such as attention (Mayes, 1991). This scale can be used with infants up to 1 month of age.

The Uzgiris-Hunt Ordinal Scales of Psychological Development (Uzgiris & Hunt, 1975) present a Piagetian developmental perspective for assessment during the first 2 years of the infant's life. These six scales include assessment for such skills as visual pursuit, object permanence, manipulation of and interaction with factors in the environment, development of vocal and gestural imitation, and development of schemes for relating to the environment. This instrument requires the use of several objects and solicitation of reactions and responses of the infant. This system presents a comprehensive assessment based on the Piagetian model, although it has been criticized for being developed using primarily infants from middle-class families (Mayes, 1991).

Another instrument used to assess young children and toddlers (ages 1–42 months) is the Bayley Scales of Infant Development—II (Bayley, 1993). This recently revised formal instrument now includes improved statistical research regarding reliability and validity in the manual. Like most infant/toddler instruments, the Bayley requires the examiner to manipulate objects and observe the reactions and behavior of the infant. The scale assesses mental functions such as memory, problem solving, and verbal ability and motor functions such as coordination and control; it also includes a behavioral rating scale. In addition to the standardization sample, clinical samples were included in the development of this revision. The clinical samples included infants and young children who were premature, HIV positive, exposed prenatally to drugs, or asphyxiated at birth; and those who had Down syndrome, autism, developmental delays, or otitis media.

Check Your Understanding

Complete Activity 11.3.

ACTIVITY 11.3

Match the following terms with the correct descriptions.

A. Uzgiris-Hunt Ordinal Scales of Psychological Development
B. Bayley Scales of Infant Development—II
C. Neonatal Behavioral Assessment Scale
D. regulatory disturbances
E. infant variables
F. developmental delays

_____ 1. This measure of infant assessment is used to determine the possible risk of developmental disabilities of infants from birth to 1 month of age.

_____ 2. These include physical, neurological, and emotional factors that influence the child's development.

_____ 3. This instrument is based on Piagetian developmental theory and is used for infants through 2 years of age.

_____ 4. These include sleep disturbances, irritability, and unusual movements.

_____ 5. This revised instrument includes research on several clinical samples and is used for children aged 1 to 42 months.

Apply Your Knowledge

How do you think regulatory disturbances might influence a child's ability to learn? ____

____

ASSESSMENT OF TODDLERS AND YOUNG CHILDREN

Many of the instruments discussed in earlier chapters contain basal-level items for toddlers and young children; they include the K-ABC, WJ III Tests of Achievement, Vineland Adaptive Behavior Scales, Achenbach's Child Behavior Checklist, and Stanford-Binet IV. Following is a brief survey of some of the most commonly used and newest instruments that are specifically designed to assess the development and behavior of young children.

MULLEN SCALES OF EARLY LEARNING: AGS EDITION

This instrument assesses the cognitive functioning of children ages birth through 68 months (Mullen, 1995). It was developed to be used by assessment personnel with experience in the evaluation of infants and young children. The test author estimates the test administration time to range from 15 minutes to 60 minutes depending on the age of the child. The instrument uses many common manipulative objects to assess the child's gross motor, visual, fine motor, and receptive and expressive language abilities.

The theoretical basis of the test design is included in the manual and is presented in developmental stages. The expectations of a given developmental stage are listed, followed by the tasks used to assess each of the expected developmental indicators. For example, at stage 2–4 months 0 days to 6 months 30 days—a child's vision is refined and visual reception is assessed using the following items: stares at hand; localizes on objects and people; looks for an object in response to a visual stimulus followed by an auditory stimulus.

Technical Data

Norming Process. The manual provides information regarding the standardization process that included 1,849 children. The standardization process was completed over an 8-year time span and was conducted within the south, northeast, west, north and south central regions. The variables of gender, ethnicity, race, age, and community size were considered in construction of the sample.

Reliability. The reliability studies contained in the manual were split-half reliability for internal consistency, test-retest reliability, and interscorer reliability. The reliability coefficients ranged from adequate and low/adequate to high. This may in part reflect the instability of developmental scores at the very early ages. Several of the sample sizes used in the reliability studies for some ages were small (38 for test-retest of the gross motor scale for ages 1 to 24 months).

Validity. Evidence of construct validity, concurrent validity, and exploratory factor analyses is presented in the examiner's manual. The research regarding developmental progression to support the constructs being measured suggests validity of the scales as developmental indicators.

WECHSLER PRESCHOOL AND PRIMARY SCALE OF INTELLIGENCE—REVISED (WPPSI—R)

The WPPSI—R (Wechsler, 1989), like the Wechsler Intelligence Scale for Children, is composed of several subtests. Assessment of a young child using these subtests is believed to reflect the different aspects of intelligence (Wechsler, 1989) and provide standardized scores to indicate intellectual functioning. The WPPSI—R was normed for use with children ranging in age from 3-0 to 7-3 years. It is designed primarily to assess the cognitive functioning of young children.

Subtests

Object Assembly. Like the Object Assembly subtests on the other Wechsler Scales, this subtest comprises puzzles that the child assembles. Unlike the other subtests, this subtest on the WPPSI—R is presented in full color.

Information. This subtest presents items that concern environmental objects or events. Initial lower level items are presented as questions with visual stimuli. Upper level items are presented verbally.

Geometric Designs. This subtest assesses two different skills: visual matching of geometric shapes and the visual-motor task of copying geometric shapes.

Comprehension. The examiner asks the child to answer questions concerning concepts learned in everyday environmental and educational experiences. Items are presented orally.

Block Design. The blocks included in this scale are flat, two-colored blocks. The child must use the blocks to reproduce patterns in the stimulus booklet. These items must be completed within specified time limits.

Arithmetic. Lower level items present counting tasks to measure early concepts of math, and higher level items include simple mental operations. These items range in presentation format from concrete blocks and pictures for counting to verbal items for mental math.

Mazes. This subtest presents increasingly difficult mazes that the child must solve using a pencil and the maze booklet.

Vocabulary. This subtest is now composed of two parts. The easier level of the subtest includes pictures that the child must name. The higher level items are orally presented items in which the child is asked to explain the meaning of common words.

Picture Completion. In this subtest, the child must determine the missing parts of the pictures.

Similarities. Three separate tasks assess the child's ability to determine how things are similar. In the first task, the child views visual stimuli and indicates which of the objects pictured are similar to the group presented. In the second task, the child completes sentences that contain analogies. The third task requires the child to explain how two objects or events are similar.

Animal Pegs. The child places pegs of the correct color beneath a series of animal pictures. The colors must match the test stimuli of animals and colored pegs at the top of the pegboard. The score is based on both speed and accuracy of response. This subtest is optional.

Sentences. Designed to measure short-term auditory memory, this optional subtest presents verbal stimuli in the form of sentences that the child must repeat verbatim.

Technical Data

Norming Process. The manual includes much information about the revision of the WPPSI, discussing the developmental versions and national trials and reviewing old and new items. The standardization version of the WPPSI—R was administered to more than 2,100 children. Of this number, 1,700 were included in the standardization sample and 400 were minority children who were given the instrument to assess item bias. Variables considered in the representativeness of the standardization sample were age, gender, geographic location, ethnicity, educational level of parents, and parental occupation.

Reliability. The manual presents information on internal reliability, interrater reliability, and test-retest reliability. Reliability coefficients are adequate on most subtests, especially when the instability of the age group is considered. The reliability coefficients are most stable for the Verbal, Performance, and Full-Scale IQs—higher than individual subtest reliability coefficients.

Validity. Research on validity included concurrent criterion-related validity research with well-known cognitive measures for young children and predictive validity studies. Most coefficients presented are adequate, although some are below acceptable levels when compared to like measures. This is not surprising considering the greater variability of skills and abilities at such young ages.

AGS EARLY SCREENING PROFILES

The AGS Early Screening Profiles (Harrison et al., 1990) present a comprehensive screening for children aged 2 to 6-11 years. The battery contains items that are administered directly to the child and surveys that are completed by parents, teachers, or both. The components, shown in Figure 11.1, are described in the following paragraphs.

Components

Cognitive/Language Profile. The child demonstrates verbal abilities by pointing to objects named or described by the examiner, discriminates pictures and selects those that are the same as the stimulus, solves visual analogies by pointing to the correct picture, and demonstrates basic school skills such as number and quantity concepts and the recognition of numbers, letters, and words. Items are presented in an easel format, and sample items are included to teach the tasks.

PROFILES

Cognitive/Language Profile

Source: direct testing of child
Time: 5 to 15 minutes

Cognitive Subscale
- Visual Discrimination Subtest (14 items)
- Logical Relations Subtest (14 items)

Language Subscale
- Verbal Concepts Subtest (25 items)
- Basic School Skills Subtest (25 items)

Motor Profile

Source: direct testing of child
Time: 5 to 15 minutes

- Gross-Motor Subtest (5 items)
- Fine-Motor Subtest (3 items)

Self-Help/Social Profile

Source: parent, teacher questionnaires
Time: 5 to 10 minutes

- Communication Domain (15 items)
- Daily Living Skills Domain (15 items)
- Socialization Domain (15 items)
- Motor Skills Domain (15 items)

SURVEYS

Articulation Survey

Source: direct testing of child
Time: 2 to 3 minutes

- Articulation of Single Words (20 items)
- Intelligibility During Continuous Speech (1 rating)

Home Survey

Source: parent questionnaire
Time: 5 minutes

(12 items)

Health History Survey

Source: parent questionnaire
Time: 5 minutes

(12 items)

Behavior Survey

Source: examiner questionnaire
Time: 2 to 3 minutes

- Cognitive/Language Observations (9 items)
- Motor Observations (13 items)

Figure 11.1 Components of the AGS Early Screening Profiles. (*Source:* From *Early Screening Profiles* by Patti Harrison, Alan Kaufman, Nadeen Kaufman, Robert Bruininks, John Rynders, Steven Ilmer, Sara Sparrow, & Domenic Cicchetti. © 1990 American Guidance Service, Inc., 4201 Woodland Road, Circle Pines, MN 55014-1796. Reproduced with permission of the Publisher. All rights reserved.)

Motor Profile. These items assess both gross-motor and fine-motor developmental skills. Gross-motor skills measured include imitating movements, walking on a line, standing on one foot, walking heel-to-toe, and performing a standing broad jump. Fine-motor tasks include stringing beads, drawing lines and shapes, and completing mazes.

Self-Help/Social Profile. Questionnaires completed by teachers and parents measure the child's understanding of oral and written language, daily self-care skills such as dressing and eating, ability to do chores, and community skills such as telephone manners. Social skills that assess how well the child gets along with others and questions measuring the child's fine- and gross-motor skills are included in this section of the instrument.

Articulation Survey. In this easel-format task, the examiner asks the child to say words that sample the child's ability to articulate sounds in the initial, medial, and final position.

Home Survey and Health History Survey. These questionnaires completed by the parents assess parent-child interactions; types of play; frequency of parent reading to the child; health problems of the mother's pregnancy, labor, and delivery; and health history of the child, such as immunization schedule.

Behavior Survey. An observation form is used to rate the child's behavior in several categories such as attention, independence, activity level, and cooperativeness.

Technical Data

Norming Process. The test manual provides detailed descriptions of the development of test items and questions included on parent and teacher questionnaires. The following variables, representative of the 1986 U.S. Census data, were considered in the national standardization sample: age, gender, geographic region, parental educational level, and race or ethnic group.

Reliability. Reliability research presented in the manual includes coefficient alpha for internal consistency and immediate test-retest and delayed test-retest research. Coefficients are adequate to moderately high for all measures.

Validity. Validity studies presented in the manual include content validity, construct validity, part-total correlations, and concurrent validity research with cognitive measures used with early childhood students. Many of the validity coefficients are low to adequate.

KAUFMAN SURVEY OF EARLY ACADEMIC AND LANGUAGE SKILLS (K-SEALS)

The K-SEALS (Kaufman & Kaufman, 1993) was developed as an expanded version of the language measure of the AGS Early Screening Profiles. Normed for children aged 3-0 to 6-11, the instrument includes three subtests: Vocabulary; Numbers, Letters, and Words; and Articulation Survey. Scores for expressive and receptive language skills may be obtained from the administration of the Vocabulary and Numbers, Letters, and Words subtests. Scores for early academic skills, such as number skills and letter and word skills, may be computed for children aged 5-0 to 6-11. Items are presented in an easel format with visual and verbal stimuli and are similar to the items on the AGS Early Screening Profiles. Half of the items from the Vocabulary and Numbers, Letters, and Words subtests are identical to those on the AGS Early Screening Profiles. The Articulation Survey from the AGS test is repeated in its entirety on the K-SEALS, but the error analysis is expanded on the K-SEALS.

Scoring. The manual includes norm tables for converting raw scores into percentile ranks and cutoff scores for the categories of "potential delay" or "OK."

Technical Data. The K-SEALS was standardized as part of the standardization of the AGS Early Screening Profiles. The same variables were considered to promote representativeness in the sample. Reliability and validity information for the K-SEALS includes split-half reliability, test-retest reliability, intercorrelations, construct validity, content validity, concurrent validity, and predictive validity. Individual subtest coefficients for reliability and validity studies ranged from low to adequate, but total test coefficients appear adequate for most studies cited.

BRIGANCE SCREENS

The Brigance Screens (Brigance, 1997, 1998a, 1998b; Glascoe, 1998) are a system of assessment instruments designed to screen for both development risk and potential advanced development. The screens are designed for the ages of 1 year, 9 months, to 7 years, 6 months. These screens are arranged in easel format for administration. Parent and teacher ratings are included.

The domains assessed in the Brigance Screens include visual/fine/and graphmotor, gross motor, quantitative concepts, personal information, receptive vocabulary, prereading/reading skills, expressive vocabulary, and articulation/verbal fluency/syntax. These domains are assessed using the criterion-referenced approach. The instrument was designed to be administered in approximately 15 minutes.

Scoring. Norm tables are provided for age-equivalent scores for motor development, communication development, and cognitive development. Percentile ranks are presented for total scores.

Technical Data. The standardization sample for the 1995 restandardization included a total of 408 students. Demographic information is provided in the technical manual, which includes tables for the following characteristics: geographic sites, educational level of child, gender, racial and ethnic background, educational level of parents, family income (participation in free lunch program), parents' marital status, and ages. The technical manual also presents information regarding the performance of the sample by demographic characteristics (such as performance of participants in free lunch program).

Reliability. The technical manual presents information for internal consistency, test-retest reliability, and interrater reliability. Total internal reliability coefficients are in the .90s for 2-year-olds to first graders. The end-of-first-grade reliability coefficient was .52. Test-retest reliability coefficients ranged from the mid .50s to the upper .90s. Interrater reliability coefficients were reported to be in the mid- to upper .90s.

Validity. The technical manual reports information on content validity, construct validity, concurrent validity, predictive validity, and discriminant validity. Coefficients ranged widely from low to adequate.

DEVELOPMENTAL INDICATORS FOR THE ASSESSMENT OF LEARNING—THIRD EDITION (DIAL—3)

This instrument was developed in an effort to screen young children who may be at risk for future learning difficulties (Mardell-Czudnowski & Goldenberg, 1998). The test authors state that the purpose of this instrument is to "identify young children in need of further diagnostic assessment" (Mardell-Czudnowski & Goldenberg, 1998, p. 1). The test may be used to assess children ages 3 years through 6 years, 11 months. The test assesses the areas mandated by IDEA 1997, including motor skills, concepts, language, self-help, and social skills. The motor, concepts, and language skills are assessed through performance items presented to the child. The self-help or adaptive skills and social skills areas are assessed through parent questionnaires. Instructions are also presented for the examiner to assess social adjustment through observations obtained during the assessment session. A fairly detailed theoretical basis for the development of the test and research pertaining to specific areas assessed are presented in the manual.

The DIAL—3 has been developed in both English and Spanish, although there are no separate Spanish norms. Using item response theory (Rasch one-parameter model), the Spanish and English versions were equated so that the performance of the Spanish-speaking children could be compared with the performance of the English-speaking children (Mardell-Czudnowski & Goldenberg, 1998, p. 75). The test includes several concrete manipulative items, including three dials to be used as stimuli for items in the concepts, motor, and language areas. Pictures, blocks, and a color chart are among the other items included.

Components

Motor. This component of the DIAL—3 includes both fine- and gross-motor tasks. The child is requested to complete such items as jumping, cutting, and writing his name (as appropriate).

Concepts. This component assesses the child's ability to identify colors and parts of the body as well as concepts such as biggest, cold, and longest. The child is also assessed in counting skills and ability to sort by shape, and name shapes.

Language. This component assesses the child's ability to provide some personal information, such as name and age, identify pictures of objects, and name letters. In addition, the child's articulation is assessed for developmental risk.

Parent Questionnaire. Composed of several parts, this questionnaire is used to assess developmental history and self-help skills on a 15-item rating scale. It includes a social skills rating scale, a rating scale for areas of parental concern, and a section for rating the screening program using the DIAL—3.

Technical Data. The standardization sample included 1,560 children who ranged in age from 3 years to 6 years, 11 months. The sample matched the 1994 census data. The following variables were considered in selecting the sample: age, gender, geographic region, race/ethnicity, and parent educational level. Information was also provided in the manual regarding the children in the sample who were receiving special services.

Reliability. Internal reliability was researched using coefficient alpha. The coefficients ranged from .66 to .87 (for median coefficients). The total DIAL—3 test-retest reliability coefficients for two age groups were .88 and .84.

Validity. Extensive information is provided in the manual of the development of the items in both the English and the Spanish versions. Information is presented concerning the reviews of items for content and potential bias as well as rationale for selection of specific items. Concurrent validity studies were conducted with the DIAL—R, the Early Screening Profiles, the Battell, the Bracken Screening Test, the Brigance Preschool Screen, the PPVT—III, and the Social Skills Rating System. Corrected coefficients were scattered considerably, from extremely low to adequate.

Check Your Understanding

Complete Activity 11.4.

ACTIVITY 11.4

Answer the following questions about the assessment instruments used with young children.

1. Which instrument for younger ages includes many of the same subtests as the WISC—III? ____________
2. Which instrument was standardized at the same time as the AGS Early Screening Profiles? ____________
3. What instrument provides scores for expressive and receptive language skills as well as early academic skills for children aged 5 and 6 years? ____________
4. Which instrument includes an articulation survey but does not have the expanded error analysis included in the K-SEALS? ____________
5. Which instrument includes both direct assessment and questionnaires/ratings to be completed by caretakers? ____________

Apply Your Knowledge

Language development is consistently evaluated in preschool evaluations. What other areas of development does language development influence? ____________

____

TECHNIQUES AND TRENDS IN INFANT AND EARLY CHILDHOOD ASSESSMENT

The assessment methods presented in this chapter are formal methods of assessment. Current literature suggests that alternative methods of assessment be used with or in place of traditional assessment of infants and young children (Cohen & Spenciner, 1994; Fewell, 1991; Paget, 1990; Sinclair, Del'Homme, & Gonzalez, 1993). Among the alternative methods suggested

Table 11.1 Characteristics of play.

Characteristic	Description
Intrinsic motivation	Play is not motivated by biological drives (e.g., hunger) but comes from within the child and not from the stimulus properties of the play objects.
Spontaneous and voluntary	Play involves free choice; children engage in play because they want to, not because someone assigns it to them.
Self-generated	Play involves the child actively generating the activities.
Active engagement	Play involves active attention to the activities of play.
Positive affect	Play involves pleasurable or enjoyable activities or results in pleasurable or enjoyable consequences.
Nonliterality	Play involves activities that are carried out in a pretend or "as-if" nature—less serious or real.
Flexibility	Play involves variability in form or context and can be done in a variety of ways or situations.
Means more than ends	Play involves emphasis on the activity itself rather than on the goal of the activity.

Source: From *Assessing Infants and Preschoolers with Handicaps* (p. 432) by D. B. Bailey and M. Wolery, 1989, Upper Saddle River, NJ: Merrill/Prentice Hall. Reprinted by permission.

by various studies are play evaluations, arena assessment, interactive strategies, observations, situational questionnaires, and ecobehavioral interviews.

play evaluations Observational informal assessment in a natural play environment.

Play evaluations can yield useful information about how the child interacts with people and objects and can be completed in a naturalistic environment. They can be useful in determining the child's activity level, reaction to novel stimuli, and affect. The characteristics of play listed by Bailey and Wolery (1989) are presented in Table 11.1. Using these characteristics as guidelines, the examiner can assess many behaviors of the child in a naturalistic environment. These behaviors can be analyzed for developmental progress in social skills, activity level, motor skills, frustration tolerance, communication skills with the examiner or caretaker while playing, and so on.

arena assessment Technique that places the child and facilitator in center of the multidisciplinary team members during the evaluation.

Arena assessment can be arranged for any method of assessment defined in this chapter, except perhaps for formal cognitive assessment on standardized instruments. Arena assessment is a technique in which all members of the multidisciplinary team surround the child and examiner or facilitator and observe as they interact in multiple situations. Play evaluations, formal play or preacademic tasks, communication items, and so on may all be presented in this format. All members of the team record the child's responses throughout the evaluation session. This might be a more effective method of assessment of infants and young children because it may reduce the number of assessment sessions (Cohen & Spenciner, 1994). Figure 11.2 illustrates the arena assessment model.

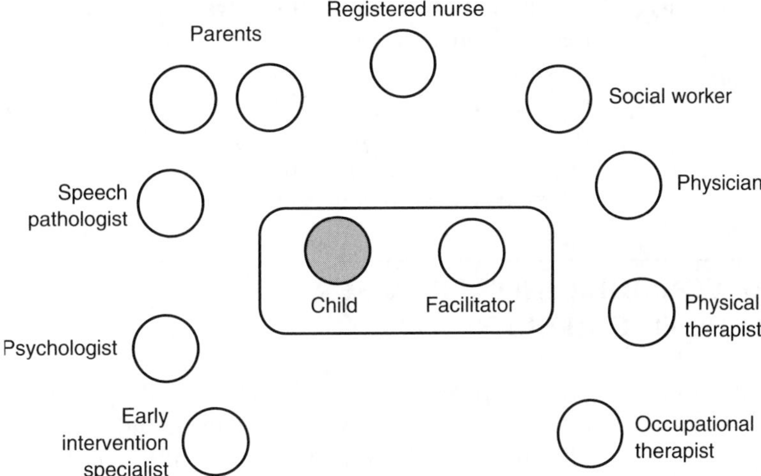

Figure 11.2 Team members conducting an arena assessment. (*Source:* From *Assessment of Young Children* by Libby G. Cohen and Loraine Spenciner. Copyright © 1992 by Longman Publishers. Reprinted with permission.)

interactive strategies Strategies used by the examiner that encourage the child to use communication to solve problems.

Interactive strategies can be useful in the assessment of young children. These strategies assess the child's abilities to solve problems through interpersonal interactions with the examiner (Paget, 1990). The examiner may alter the problems presented to observe the child's responses to frustration, humor, or different types or objects of play. The strategies are aimed at encouraging the child to communicate with the examiner to solve the problem.

observations An informal assessment method of activities, language, and interactions in various settings.

Observations can be used in a variety of settings and across a variety of tasks. The child may be observed in the home or preschool classroom environment with peers, siblings, and caretakers. All areas of assessment in early childhood can be enhanced through observations. The child's behavior, social skills, communication skills, cognitive level, speech, motor skills, motor planning, adaptive behaviors, activity level, frustration tolerance level, attention span, and self-help skills can be assessed through multiple observations. When observations are combined with information from parent questionnaires and more formal assessment measures, the examiner can gain a holistic view of the child's developmental progress.

situational questionnaires Questionnaires that assess the child's behavior in various situations.

Situational questionnaires are useful when comparing the child's behavior in specific situations. Examples of these are the Home Situations Questionnaire and the School Situations Questionnaire (Barkley, 1990). The parents and teachers rate the child's behavior, activity level, and attention span in a variety of situations, such as when the parents talk on the telephone, when visitors are in the home, and when the child is interacting with peers. These questionnaires allow for more direct analysis and intervention for problematic behaviors.

ecobehavioral interviews Interviews of parents and teachers that assess behavior in different settings and routines.

In **ecobehavioral interviews,** parents and teachers describe a child's behaviors in everyday situations, such as during daily routines, bedtimes, class activities, and transitions from one activity to the next (Barnett, Macmann, & Carey, 1992). These responses are analyzed to determine problem behaviors that occur across settings or situations. Behavioral interventions are then targeted to remediate the behaviors in the situations described by the parents and teachers.

OTHER CONSIDERATIONS IN ASSESSING VERY YOUNG CHILDREN

The best practice of assessment across all ages of children involves multiple measures, multiple examiners, and multiple situations or environments. This is especially important for infants, toddlers, and young children because of the influence that temperament, physical health, and current physical state (alertness or sleepiness) may have during an evaluation period. A holistic view of the child's developmental level can be gained by observing the child in many different settings, using both formal and informal assessment, and analyzing the observed behaviors.

Because of the very rapid pace of development of young children, assessment and monitoring of progress should be ongoing, as stated in PL 99-457 (*Federal Register,* 1993). This rapid progress contributes to the instability of scores obtained at very young ages. The variability of the educational and home environments can also contribute to the instability of scores.

Analysis of formal early childhood assessment instruments indicates that the reliability and validity of the subtests are moderately adequate to below acceptable levels. The coefficients tend to be more acceptable for total test or total instrument scores. Barnett et al. (1992) cautioned against using profile analysis of individual subtests at young ages and suggested that only global scores be used. Katz (1989) warned of the dangers that could occur when very young children are falsely identified through assessment. That is, the child's scores might indicate developmental difficulties, but in reality, the child is not disabled. This false identification may result in changes in parent-child interactions and diminished expectations held for the child.

At the other end of the identification process are the children who need services but remain unidentified. In a study by Sinclair et al. (1993), students who were previously undiagnosed were referred for assessment of behavioral disorders. This study involved a three-stage, multiple-gating system that was used to screen preschool children for behavioral disorders. In this study, 5% of the sample who had not previously been identified as having behavioral difficulties were referred for a comprehensive evaluation.

Table 11.2 Summary of instruments for early childhood assessment.

Instrument	Strengths	Weaknesses
Neonatal Behavioral Assessment Scale	Useful for infants through 1 month of age Assesses behavior and reflex actions	Not typically used in educational setting Requires specific training for use
Uzgiris-Hunt Ordinal Scales of Psychological Development	For children up to 2 years of age Good theoretical basis	Lengthy administration time Norm sample not representative
Bayley Scales of Infant Development—II	Manual has improved statistical data Standardization included clinical samples Assess many areas of development	Lengthy administration time Specific training necessary
Mullen Scales of Early Learning: AGS Edition	Integration of developmental concepts and theoretical foundations included in manual Includes ages birth–68 months	Small sample sizes for reliability, validity data
Wechsler Preschool and Primary Scales of Intelligence	Subtests are like those in other Wechsler Scales Appropriate for ages 3-0 to 7-3	Lengthy administration time Have lower reliability and validity coefficients than other Wechsler Scales
AGS Early Screening Profiles	Include both direct and indirect assessment across multiple situations and skills	Low to adequate reliability and validity coefficients
Kaufman Survey of Early Academic and Language Skills	Expands the language sections of the AGS Early Screening Profiles Offers expanded analysis of articulation errors	Subtest coefficients low to adequate
Brigance Screens	Assesses across various ages; criterion-referenced; provides parent and teacher rating system	Norms could be expanded
Developmental Indicators for the Assessment of Learning	Spanish and English versions; parent questionnaire included; fairly comprehensive	Does not provide age-equivalent scores

Review of the literature on the assessment of infants and young children indicates that new trends are emerging. It is hoped that these trends will remedy some of the difficulties of assessing children at very young ages.

Table 11.2 summarizes the strengths and weaknesses of the instruments presented in this chapter.

PHONEMIC AWARENESS

Legal regulations require that the child's level of functioning in the areas of physical development, cognitive development, communication development, social or emotional development, and adaptive development be addressed during the assessment process. Assessment in these areas provides information for educational personnel about how to implement interventions necessary for childhood development and future educational success. One skill area that may assist assessment personnel in understanding the preschool child's readiness for academic tasks is the area of **phonemic awareness.** A child with this skill is able to determine the separate sounds in spoken words. This awareness is a conscious awareness that words are made up of phonemes or sounds (Snider, 1995).

phonemic awareness Comprehension of individual sounds that make up words.

The skills involved in being able to distinguish the sounds of words are important in learning to read (Turnbull, Turnbull, Shank, Smith, & Leal, 2002). A comprehensive review of the literature regarding the effects of instruction in phonemic awareness on reading skills indicated that both word reading skills and reading comprehension improved with phonemic awareness (Ehri, Nunes, Willows, Schuster, Yaghoub-Zadeh, & Shanahan, 2001). Research also suggests that early interventions that promote phonemic awareness may reduce the number of young students referred for special education services (Lennon & Slesinski, 1999).

Phonemic awareness is composed of subskills and tasks that can be assessed by informal methods. For example, the skills of **phonemic synthesis** or blending of sounds, **phonemic analysis** or breaking the words into sounds, rhyming, and substitution, are some of the phonemic awareness skills that may be evaluated by educators (Snider, 1995). Specific tasks used to assess phonemic awareness listed by Ehri et al. (2001) include

phonemic synthesis The blending of isolated sounds into a whole word.

phonemic analysis The breaking up of a word into isolated sounds.

1. Phonemic isolation, which requires recognizing individual sounds in words; for example, "Tell me the first sound in paste." (/p/)
2. Phoneme identity, which requires recognizing the common sound in different words; for example, "Tell me the sound that is the same in bike, boy, and bell." (/b/)
3. Phoneme categorization, which requires recognizing the word with the odd sound in a sequence of three or four words, for example, "Which word does not belong? bus, bun, rug." (rug)
4. Phoneme blending, which requires listening to a sequence of separately spoken sounds and combining them to form a recognizable word; for example, "What word is /s//k//u//l/?" (school)
5. Phoneme segmentation, which requires breaking the word into its sounds by tapping out or counting the sounds or by pronouncing and positioning a marker for each sound; for example, "How many phonemes in ship?" (3:/s//i//p/)
6. Phoneme deletion, which requires recognizing what word remains when a specified phoneme is removed; for example, "What is smile without /s/?" (mile) (Ehri et al., 2001, p. 252)

An informal assessment instrument for assessing phonemic awareness was constructed by Snider (1997). This instrument, along with other published instruments to assess emerging reading skills, may be used to assess

Phoneme Segmentation

Model: Today we're going to play a word game. I'm going to say a word and I want you to break the word apart. You are going to tell me each sound in order. For example, if I say cat, you say /c/ /a/ /t/. Let's try a few more words.

Directions: Say the sounds in_____.

Practice Items: to, dog

Test Items:

1. she
2. red
3. lay

Strip Initial Consonant

Model: Listen to the word task. If I take away the sound /t/, ask is left. What word is left? Let's try some more.

Directions: Listen to the word _____. If you take away the // sound, what word is left?

Practice items: ball, pink

Test Items:

1. told
2. hill
3. nice

Figure 11.3 Sample items from Test of Phonemic Awareness. (*Source:* From "The relationship between phonemic awareness and later reading achievement, Test of Phonemic Awareness," by Vicki Snider. In *Journal of Educational Research* (Mar/Apr/97) *90*(4), pp. 203–212.) Reprinted with permission of the Helen Dwight Reid Educational Foundation. Published by Heldref Publications, 1319 Eighteenth St., NW, Washington, DC 20036-1802. Copyright 1997.

phonemic awareness in kindergarten students. Figure 11.3 presents sample items for the Test of Phonemic Awareness.

In addition to using informal assessment instruments designed by teachers, preacademic reading skills, such as identifying the sounds of letters or rhyming, may be assessed using many of the instruments previously presented in this text, such as the Woodcock Reading Mastery Test—Revised and instruments designed for use with preschool children, such as the Developmental Indicators for the Assessment of Learning, 3rd ed. (DIAL—3), and the Kaufman Brief Survey of Early Academic and Language Skills. The Woodcock-Johnson III Tests of Achievement include the subtest called Sound Awareness that contains rhyming, deletion, and substitution

Lesson	New Letter Sound	Review	Rhyming [onset][rime]	Blending/ Segmenting
1	/a/		[s,f,m,r] {at} [z,l,r,sh] {ip}	am, an, if, at
2	/m/	a,m	[f,m,r,v] {an} [f,m,n,s] {eat}	am, me, up, mat
3	/t/	a,m,t	[s,v,m,n] {et} [l,r,s] {ock}	mat, miss, at, Sam, mit
4	/s/	a,m,t	[s,l,th,k] {ick} [l,r,s,p] {ay}	sat, fat, fit, sit, am, mad
5		a,m,t,s	[m,s,b,t] {ee} [f,n,g,s] {ame}	it, am, mat, fit, Sam, Sid
6	/i/	a,m,t,s	[f,c,v,p] {an} [b,f,r,h] {ed}	at, sit, if, fit, sad, mat
7		a,m,t s,i	[b,n,s,r] {ag} [k,l,p,th] {ick}	sat, it, am, fat, fit, miss
8	/f/	a,m,t s,i	[b,c,f,t] {all} [b,s,f,sh] {ell}	mad, Sid, fit, rat, dad, at
9		a,m,t s,i,f	[d,f,m,sh] {ine} [b,j,qu,t] {ack}	rad, fit, sad, add, rat, mit
10		a,m,t s,i,f	[b,h,l,s] {and} [b,d,j,l] {ump}	rag, sad, did, fit, at, mad

Figure 11.4 Sample words for teaching letter sounds and phonemic awareness (*Source:* From "A Primer on Phonemic Awareness," by Vicki Snider, 1995, *School Psychology Review, 24*(3), p. 450.) Copyright 1995 by the National Association of School Psychologists. Reprinted by permission of the publisher.

sections. The Wechsler Individual Achievement Test II includes items that assess rhyming and ability to determine words with the same initial and ending sounds. These instruments may assist with determining how a student compares to a norm sample population as well as determining the specific skills mastered.

In the following activity, you will construct a teacher-made instrument to measure phonemic awareness. Use the information presented in Figure 11.4 to develop your items.

Check Your Understanding

Complete Activity 11.5.

ACTIVITY 11.5

Construction of a Teacher-Made Test of Phonemic Awareness

Look at the letter sounds and tasks presented in Figure 11.3 and Figure 11.4. Use these to construct a teacher-made test on phonemic awareness. For example, the first sound to assess is /a/. In order to make a rhyming item, provide an example of a rhyming word that uses the sounds /a//t/ or at. The words that may be formed using at and the other consonants provided are: sat, fat, mat, and rat.

Model: Listen to this word "at." I know some words that rhyme with at: "mat and fat."

Next sound to be assessed is /i/.

Directions: Now listen to this word: zip. Tell me a word that rhymes with zip. (Acceptable responses might be lip, rip, ship).

Continue with the construction of the test for the following items:

Blending/segmenting of am, an, if, at. To blend, you ask the student to say sounds together that you first say in isolation. When the sounds are said together, they form a word (/a//m/ together is am). To make segmenting items, you provide an example of how a word sounds, then how it sounds when each sound is pronounced (am then /a//m/).

1. Model (blending): ______________________________
____
____

2. Directions: ______________________________
____
____

3. Model (segmenting): ______________________________
____
____

4. Directions: ______________________________
____

Substitution Items. These items make new words when one sound is replaced with another sound. (fat/rat). Use any of the words presented in Figure 11.4 for the items.

5. Model (substitution): ______________________________
____
____

6. Directions: ____
____
____

Apply Your Knowledge

Use the information provided in Figure 11.3 and Figure 11.4 to complete an additional phonemic awareness item. This time, construct an item (model and directions) for the task of phoneme categorization. For this task, the student must tell you which word does not belong to a list of words.

Model: ____
____

Directions: ____
____

TRANSITION AND POSTSECONDARY CONSIDERATIONS

transition planning Planning for meeting students' needs following high school.

The legal requirements stated in the IDEA 1997 Amendments were presented in chapter 2. The important components for educators include the inclusion within the IEP of the transitional needs of students from the beginning age of 14. The statement addressing these needs in the IEP must be updated each year and include the specific **transition services** needed, as well as the areas of study required to meet those needs. By the time the student reaches 16, or sooner if determined necessary for the transition goals set out by the IEP team, the IEP must include information regarding other agencies and the responsibilities of stated agencies.

The other component that educators must remember is that one year before the student reaches the age of majority expressed in state law, the student must be informed of his or her rights that will be transferred to the student as the student reaches the age of majority. This is to be acknowledged in a statement of the IEP.

The emphasis on transitional services that assist students in their movement from school to adult life is a reflection of the data indicating negative outcomes for students with disabilities (Levinson, 1995; U.S. Department of Education, 1999; U.S. Department of Education, 2000). Students with disabilities graduate at a much lower rate than students without disabilities, with only 25.5% receiving a high school diploma (U.S. Department of Education, 2000). This represents 61.2% of all students with disabilities exiting high school. The remaining 38.8% of students with disabilities who leave high school receive a certificate of completion, reach the maximum age for services, or simply drop out of

Disability	Number	Percentage[a]
Specific learning disabilities	99,640	30.5
Speech or language impairments	4,099	35.0
Mental retardation	15,268	13.8
Emotional disturbance	13,861	22.3
Multiple disabilities	2,061	10.3
Hearing impairments	2,761	29.0
Orthopedic impairments	2,037	25.8
Other health impairments	5,052	29.6
Visual impairments	1,157	30.6
Autism	384	8.4
Deaf-blindness	132	39.2
Traumatic brain injury	671	27.7
All disabilities	147,123	25.5

[a] The percentages in this table were calculated by dividing (1) the number of students age 17 and older in each disability category who graduated with a diploma by (2) the total number of students with disabilities age 17 and older in each disability category.

Figure 11.5 Number and percentage of students ages 17 and older graduating with a standard diploma: 1997–98. (*Source: Twenty-Second Annual Report to Congress on the Implementation of the Individuals with Disabilities Education Act,* pp. IV–17. U.S. Department of Education, 2000).

school. Students with disabilities who are least likely to receive a high school diploma are students with mental retardation, students with multiple disabilities, and students with autism. The graduate rates by disability are presented in Figure 11.5.

One factor that may influence the number of students with disabilities who graduate from high school is the requirement by some states of exit examinations as criteria for graduation. Research indicates that students with disabilities are less likely to graduate if they are required to pass a high school exit examination. This finding was consistent regardless of the disability category; however, it proved to be most significant for students with mental retardation and speech and language impairments (Thurlow, Ysseldyke, & Anderson, 1995). This may continue to have an impact on the numbers of students with disabilities who are able to graduate due to the assessment requirements of the IDEA 1997 Amendments. Recall that the 1997 Amendments mandate that the assessments for students with disabilities be consistent with the assessment of students without disabilities.

Individuals with disabilities who leave the school environment are less likely to be employed than persons without disabilities, and those who are employed are more likely to earn less than persons without disabilities

(Kaye, 1998; Levinson, 1995). Persons with disabilities are likely to live at home with their parents or have other non-independent arrangements (Levinson, 1995; U.S. Department of Education, 1995). Persons with disabilities who are able to live in the community are more likely to live alone with little social participation (Kaye, 1998). As Levinson states,

> There is little doubt that, given the high unemployment and underemployment rates among persons with disabilities, the high percentage who continue to live at home following the completion of high school, and the elevated dropout rate among students with disabilities, efforts in the area of special education have not resulted in their successful integration into society. (Levinson, 1995, p. 910)

The research findings and requirements of the federal regulations result in additional assessment responsibilities of educational personnel to meet students' needs as they exit the educational system. The assessment process should begin before the student reaches age 14 and needs to continue until the student has exited from the educational system.

ASSESSMENT OF TRANSITION NEEDS

The focus of the assessment process of students nearing their teen years should change to reflect postsecondary school needs. The student's functioning and needs should be determined in the areas of educational or instructional needs, vocational training or employment needs such as **supported employment,** community experiences, and adult daily living skills. The goals and objectives must include consideration of future plans to enter the adult world as independently as possible.

supported employment Employing a person with a disability with persons without disabilities. Arrangement is for at least minimum wage and may include a job coach or other supports.

Research regarding best practice for transition assessment and planning has shown that the most successful transition plans with more successful outcomes result from involvement of both students and parents in the assessment and planning process (Brotherson, & Berdine, 1993; Thoma, Rogan, & Baker, 2001). Student participation includes teaching students how to advocate for their needs or use the skills of self-determination (Lindsey, Whemeyer, Guy, & Martin, 2001). Self-determination has been defined as "a combination of skills, knowledge, and beliefs that enable a person to engage in goal directed, self-regulated, autonomous behavior" (Field, Martin, Miller, Ward, & Wehmeyer, 1998, p. 2). In order to assist students with their transition needs, educators must assess the student's ability to advocate for their own needs.

Assessment for transition planning incorporates both standardized assessment methods to determine educational achievement, cognitive functioning, behavioral functioning, and other areas as needed. For example, assessment measures such as the Wechsler Intelligence Scales for Children, Third Edition; the Wechsler Intelligence Scales for Adults, Third Edition, the Stanford-Binet IV, the Woodcock-Johnson III Tests of Achievement and Tests of Cognitive Abilities, and the Wechsler Individual Achievement

Tests II may be used throughout the school and transitional periods to assess intelligence and achievement.

Assessment for transition also includes assessing the career and vocational interests, skills, life skills, and social and leisure skills. Clark offered several suggestions for assessment to plan for transition (Clark, 1996, pp. 89–90). The following list is adapted from Clark:

1. Select assessment instruments and procedures on the basis of how to answer key questions in a student's individual transition planning: Who am I? What do I want in life, now and in the future? What are some of life's demands that I can meet now?
2. Make assessment ongoing starting as early as possible, but no later than age 14, and continuing through life.
3. Use multiple types and levels of assessment.
4. Make 3-year reevaluations for all secondary students—useful for their next placement or environment.
5. Assessment procedures should be efficient and effective.
6. Organize assessment data for easy access for IEP planning and instructional planning.
7. Arrange for one person to be responsible for coordinating the assessment process.
8. Develop a transition assessment approach that is not only cultural/ language fair, but also culture/language enhanced—questions should be posed in culturally appropriate ways rather than reflecting only majority culture/language values.

Methods of determining the transitional needs of students include conducting a needs interview or using a commercially published instrument to determine such transition needs. One such instrument is the Transition Planning Inventory (Clark & Patton, 1997).

TRANSITION PLANNING INVENTORY (TPI)

This inventory contains four inventory forms: Student Form, Home Form, School Form, and Further Assessment Recommendations Form (Clark & Patton, 1997). The forms contain items on which the student, parent, and educational personnel rate the student's current functioning. The items survey the domains of employment, further education and training, daily living, leisure activities, community participation, health, self-determination, communication, and interpersonal relationships. The student form also includes questions of career awareness, future plans for living and working, community participation, and leisure and hobby interests. The forms are easy to administer. This instrument allows for multiple informants to participate in assessing transition needs for the student. The authors state that this instrument may be used to determine the future transition needs of any student. Additional information is provided in the manual regarding collecting a transitional planning portfolio; however, many of the forms and rating scales are not reproducible without copyright permission from the original authors. These forms may be useful in developing local portfolio forms and ideas for assessing transitional needs of students.

An example of a profile for a student whose needs were assessed using the TPI is presented in Figure 11.6.

Check Your Understanding

Complete Activity 11.6.

ACTIVITY 11.6

Use the student profile from the Transition Planning Inventory to determine the transition needs for Jimmy.

List possible needs below:

1. Employment needs: ____________________
2. Further education/training: ____________________
3. Daily living: ____________________
4. Leisure activities: ____________________
5. Community participation: ____________________
6. Health: ____________________
7. Self-determination: ____________________
8. Communication: ____________________
9. Interpersonal relationships: ____________________

Apply Your Knowledge

Use the information obtained from the TPI to write a behavioral objective for Jimmy's self-determination needs. ____________________

Technical Data

Instrument Construction. Because the TPI is not a norm-referenced instrument, the information included in the test manual focuses on test development and on the reliability and validity of the inventory. The authors indicate that the 46 transition planning statements reflect the domains used across various states. The instrument may be administered in alternative ways for students with special needs. An explanation of the expected student behaviors for each item is included in the manual. For example, for an education/training item of "Knows how to gain entry to an appropriate post-school community employment training program," the explanation provided is: "Students know the basic steps of locating, selecting and getting into job training programs that match their interests and abilities" (Clark & Patton, 1997, p. 12).

Reliability. The internal reliability was studied using coefficient alpha, and the reliability coefficients ranged between .70 and .95. Test-retest reliability coefficients ranged from .70 to .98.

Validity. Information for evidence of content and criterion-related validity was included in the manual. Evidence suggests that the TPI was viewed as including necessary content for transition planning.

ASSESSING FUNCTIONAL ACADEMICS

As previously stated, the standardized assessment instruments as well as informal methods may be used to assess the current level of academic functioning of students with transition needs. The informal methods presented in chapter 8 are very appropriate for determining the level of academic functioning as it applies to everyday living situations.

In addition to previously mentioned methods and tests, the Kaufman Functional Academic Skills Test (K-FAST) may be used (Kaufman & Kaufman, 1994). It is presented in the following section.

KAUFMAN FUNCTIONAL ASSESSMENT SKILLS TEST (K-FAST)

The K-FAST was designed to be administered individually to adolescent and adult students (Kaufman & Kaufman, 1994). This instrument assessed the skills needed for the math and reading skills needed in everyday life situations. The authors state that this test was not designed to replace other existing achievement batteries, but rather to add information regarding a student's competency for functioning outside the school environment. The instrument presents the items in an easel format with oral instructions by the examiner. The math items include such content as the value of money, telling time, reading graphs, and more difficult items covering percentages and calculating the area of a room. The reading items include reading signs, symbols, recipes, and want ads. The test may be administered to persons ranging from age 15 to age 75 and older. The scores provided include standard scores, percentile ranks, and descriptive categories.

Section V. Profile

Planning Areas	School Rating (Strongly Disagree … Strongly Agree)	Home Rating (Strongly Disagree … Strongly Agree)	Student Rating (Strongly Disagree … Strongly Agree)	Knowledge/Skills Goals	Linkage Goals
EMPLOYMENT					
1. knows job requirements and demands	NA 0 1 2 (3) 4 5 DK	NA 0 1 2 (3) 4 5 DK	NA (0) 1 2 3 4 5 DK	✓	✓
2. makes informed choices	NA 0 1 2 (3) 4 5 DK	NA 0 1 2 (3) 4 5 DK	NA 0 1 (2) 3 4 5 DK		
3. knows how to get a job	NA 0 1 (2) 3 4 5 DK	NA 0 1 2 (3) 4 5 DK	NA 0 1 2 (3) 4 5 DK		
4. demonstrates general job skills and work attitude	NA 0 1 (2) 3 4 5 DK	NA 0 1 (2) 3 4 5 DK	NA 0 1 2 (3) 4 5 DK		
5. has specific job skills	NA 0 1 (2) 3 4 5 DK	NA 0 1 (2) 3 4 5 DK	NA 0 1 (2) 3 4 5 DK		✓
FURTHER EDUCATION/TRAINING					
6. knows how to gain entry into community employment training	NA (0) 1 2 3 4 5 DK	NA (0) 1 2 3 4 5 DK	NA 0 (1) 2 3 4 5 DK	✓	✓
7. knows how to gain entry into GED program	NA (0) 1 2 3 4 5 DK	NA 0 (1) 2 3 4 5 DK	NA 0 (1) 2 3 4 5 DK		
8. knows how to gain entry into vocational/technical school	NA (0) 1 2 3 4 5 DK	NA 0 (1) 2 3 4 5 DK	NA 0 (1) 2 3 4 5 DK		
9. knows how to gain entry into college or university	NA (0) 1 2 3 4 5 DK	NA (0) 1 2 3 4 5 DK	NA (0) 1 2 3 4 5 DK		
10. can succeed in a postsecondary program	NA 0 1 (2) 3 4 5 DK	NA 0 (1) 2 3 4 5 DK	NA 0 1 2 3 (4) 5 DK		
DAILY LIVING					
11. maintains personal grooming and hygiene	NA 0 1 (2) 3 4 5 DK	NA 0 1 (2) 3 4 5 DK	NA 0 1 2 3 (4) 5 DK		
12. knows how to locate place to live	NA 0 (1) 2 3 4 5 DK	NA 0 (1) 2 3 4 5 DK	NA 0 1 2 3 (4) 5 DK	✓	
13. knows how to set up living arrangement	NA (0) 1 2 3 4 5 DK	NA 0 (1) 2 3 4 5 DK	NA 0 1 2 3 (4) 5 DK	✓	
14. performs everyday household tasks	NA 0 (1) 2 3 4 5 DK	NA 0 (1) 2 3 4 5 DK	NA 0 1 2 3 (4) 5 DK	✓	
15. manages own money	NA 0 (1) 2 3 4 5 DK	NA 0 (1) 2 3 4 5 DK	NA 0 1 2 3 (4) 5 DK		
16. uses local transportation systems	NA 0 (1) 2 3 4 5 DK	NA 0 (1) 2 3 4 5 DK	NA 0 1 2 3 (4) 5 DK	✓	
LEISURE ACTIVITIES					
17. performs indoor activities	NA 0 1 2 (3) 4 5 DK	NA 0 1 2 3 (4) 5 DK	NA 0 1 2 3 (4) 5 DK		
18. performs outdoor activities	NA 0 1 2 3 (4) 5 DK	NA 0 1 2 3 (4) 5 DK	NA 0 1 2 3 (4) 5 DK		
19. uses settings that offer entertainment	NA 0 1 2 3 (4) 5 DK	NA 0 1 2 3 (4) 5 DK	NA 0 1 2 3 (4) 5 DK		
COMMUNITY PARTICIPATION					
20. knows basic legal rights	NA (0) 1 2 3 4 5 DK	NA 0 (1) 2 3 4 5 DK	NA 0 1 2 (3) 4 5 DK	✓	✓
21. participates as an active citizen	NA 0 (1) 2 3 4 5 DK	NA 0 (1) 2 3 4 5 DK	NA 0 1 2 3 (4) 5 DK	✓	
22. makes legal decisions	NA (0) 1 2 3 4 5 DK	NA 0 (1) 2 3 4 5 DK	NA 0 1 2 3 (4) 5 DK		
23. locates community services and resources	NA 0 (1) 2 3 4 5 DK	NA 0 (1) 2 3 4 5 DK	NA 0 1 2 3 (4) 5 DK	✓	✓
24. uses services and resources successfully	NA (0) 1 2 3 4 5 DK	NA 0 (1) 2 3 4 5 DK	NA 0 1 2 3 (4) 5 DK	✓	
25. knows how to obtain financial assistance	NA 0 (1) 2 3 4 5 DK	NA 0 (1) 2 3 4 5 DK	NA 0 1 2 3 (4) 5 DK		

Item	Rating 1	Rating 2	Rating 3		
HEALTH					
26. maintains good physical health	NA 0 (1) 2 3 4 5 DK	NA 0 1 (2) 3 4 5 DK	NA 0 1 2 3 4 (5) DK	✓	
27. addresses physical problems	NA 0 (1) 2 3 4 5 DK	NA 0 (1) 2 3 4 5 DK	NA 0 1 2 3 4 (5) DK	✓	
28. maintains good mental health	NA 0 (1) 2 3 4 5 DK	NA 0 (1) 2 3 4 5 DK	NA 0 1 2 3 4 (5) DK	✓	
29. addresses mental health problems	NA 0 (1) 2 3 4 5 DK	NA 0 (1) 2 3 4 5 DK	NA 0 1 2 3 4 (5) DK	✓	✓
30. knows about reproduction	NA (0) 1 2 3 4 5 DK	NA (0) 1 2 3 4 5 DK	NA 0 1 2 3 4 (5) DK	✓	
31. makes informed choices regarding sexual behavior	NA (0) 1 2 3 4 5 DK	NA (0) 1 2 3 4 5 DK	NA 0 1 2 3 4 (5) DK	✓	
SELF-DETERMINATION					
32. recognizes and accepts own strengths and limitations	NA 0 (1) 2 3 4 5 DK	NA 0 1 (2) 3 4 5 DK	NA 0 1 2 3 4 (5) DK	✓	
33. expresses feelings and ideas appropriately	NA 0 (1) 2 3 4 5 DK	NA 0 (1) 2 3 4 5 DK	NA 0 1 (2) 3 4 5 DK	✓	
34. expresses feelings and ideas confidently	NA (0) 1 2 3 4 5 DK	NA (0) 1 2 3 4 5 DK	NA 0 (1) 2 3 4 5 DK	✓	
35. sets personal goals	NA 0 (1) 2 3 4 5 DK	NA 0 (1) 2 3 4 5 DK	NA 0 1 (2) 3 4 5 DK	✓	
36. makes personal decisions	NA (0) 1 2 3 4 5 DK	NA 0 (1) 2 3 4 5 DK	NA 0 1 (2) 3 4 5 DK	✓	
COMMUNICATION					
37. has needed speaking skills	NA 0 (1) 2 3 4 5 DK	NA 0 1 (2) 3 4 5 DK	NA 0 1 2 3 4 (5) DK	✓	
38. has needed listening skills	NA (0) 1 2 3 4 5 DK	NA 0 (1) 2 3 4 5 DK	NA 0 1 2 3 4 (5) DK	✓	
39. has needed reading skills	NA (0) 1 2 3 4 5 DK	NA (0) 1 2 3 4 5 DK	NA 0 1 2 3 (4) 5 DK	✓	
40. has needed writing skills	NA (0) 1 2 3 4 5 DK	NA (0) 1 2 3 4 5 DK	NA 0 1 2 3 4 (5) DK	✓	
INTERPERSONAL RELATIONSHIPS					
41. gets along well with family members	NA 0 1 (2) 3 4 5 DK	NA 0 1 (2) 3 4 5 DK	NA 0 1 2 3 (4) 5 DK		
42. demonstrates knowledge and skills of parenting	NA 0 (1) 2 3 4 5 DK	NA 0 (1) 2 3 4 5 DK	NA 0 1 2 (3) 4 5 DK		
43. establishes and maintains friendships	NA 0 1 (2) 3 4 5 DK	NA 0 1 (2) 3 4 5 DK	NA 0 1 2 3 (4) 5 DK	✓	
44. displays appropriate social behavior in variety of settings	NA 0 1 (2) 3 4 5 DK	NA 0 1 (2) 3 4 5 DK	NA 0 1 2 (3) 4 5 DK	✓	
45. demonstrates skills for getting along with coworkers	NA 0 1 (2) 3 4 5 DK	NA 0 (1) 2 3 4 5 DK	NA 0 1 2 (3) 4 5 DK		
46. demonstrates skills for getting along with supervisor	NA 0 1 (2) 3 4 5 DK	NA 0 1 (2) 3 4 5 DK	NA 0 1 2 3 (4) 5 DK		
ADDITIONAL PLANNING AREAS					
____________	0 1 2 3 4 5	0 1 2 3 4 5	0 1 2 3 4 5		
____________	0 1 2 3 4 5	0 1 2 3 4 5	0 1 2 3 4 5		
____________	0 1 2 3 4 5	0 1 2 3 4 5	0 1 2 3 4 5		

Figure 11.6 Case Study 1—Jimmy P. (*Source:* From *Transition Planning Inventory,* by Gary Clark & James R. Patton, 1997, pp. 44–45. Copyright 1997 by Pro-Ed. Austin, TX: Pro-Ed. Reprinted by permission.)

Technical Data

Norming Process. The development of the K-FAST included developmental versions and tryout exams. The total representative standardization sample included 1,424 people from 27 states. The variables were age, gender, geographic region, socioeconomic status of parents or of examinees, and race/ethnic groups. The sample reflected the U.S. population in terms of characteristics and distribution of abilities when compared with the theoretical normal distribution.

Reliability. Two measures of reliability were obtained for the K-FAST, including split-half reliability for internal consistency and test-retest reliability for consistency across time. Internal reliability coefficients ranged from .83 to .97. The test-retest coefficients ranged from .84 to .91.

Validity. The validity was studied using factor analytic studies for construct validity, developmental changes as support for construct validity, and concurrent criterion-related validity with general intellectual measures. The validity coefficients varied on the comparisons with tests of general intelligence; however, validity appears to range from adequate to high.

RESEARCH AND ISSUES RELATED TO TRANSITION PLANNING AND ASSESSMENT

The outcomes for students with disabilities continue to be problematic. Research indicates, for example, that young women with learning disabilities tend to be at risk for early age pregnancy and for single motherhood (Levine & Nourse, 1998).

Although self-determination has been cited as best practice for the development of effective transition planning, research indicates that students are not participating in a manner reflecting self-determination in the transition/IEP process (Thoma et al., 2001). These researchers found that students with cognitive disabilities attended meetings but were not active during the meetings. Moreover, teachers and parents tended to discuss issues about the students rather than engaging the students in the discussion.

Postsecondary research assessing the admission process and accommodations for students continuing their education in 2- and 4-year schools indicates that accommodations are applied inconsistently (Vogel, Leonard, Scales, Hayeslip, Hermansen, & Donnells, 1998). Differences were found in where and how services were delivered to students with disabilities.

Even though students are to be told their rights in the education process that will transfer to them upon reaching the age of majority, individuals with cognitive disabilities are often assumed to lack the competence to assert their opinions about their own education (Lindsey et al., 2001). This appears to be the case even though most students have not legally been declared as incompetent under state law.

THINK AHEAD

Once the student has been administered a battery of tests, the teacher must be able to interpret the results and make educational recommendations. The next chapter includes the steps for test interpretation.

EXERCISES

Part I

Match the correct terms with the statements that follow.

a. PL 99-457
b. developmental delays
c. phonemic synthesis
d. biological risk factors
e. environmental risk factors
f. IFSP
g. family-centered program
h. family-focused program
i. arena assessment
j. phoneme awareness
k. situational questionnaire
l. ecobehavioral interview
m. play evaluations
n. phonemic analysis

_____ 1. This technique used in the assessment of infants and toddlers may decrease the time spent in assessment.

_____ 2. Once the family's needs and the young child's needs are determined, the information is used to complete _____.

_____ 3. When a child is asked to sound out each isolated sound in a whole word, the teacher is requiring the child to use _____.

_____ 4. Among the possible reasons for _____ are physical development behind that of age peers and cognitive functioning below the levels expected.

_____ 5. While the transition needs of students age 14 years and older are required to be included in a student's IEP by the 1997 Amendments of IDEA, _____ mandates services for children aged 3 to 5 with disabilities.

_____ 6. When a child appears to behave and function differently in specific situations, a _____ may be used to assess these behaviors or abilities.

_____ 7. When a child is able to hear and say isolated sounds, recognize that sounds make up words, discriminate between sounds, provide rhyming words to target words, substitute sounds upon request, and identify words with specific sounds, the child is demonstrating evidence of _____.

Part II

Answer the following questions.

1. What are some criticisms and issues of family involvement as specified in early childhood assessment? ____________________
____
____
2. What are the clinical indications that an infant may need a full evaluation according to Mayes (1991)?____________________
____
3. What areas are assessed when infants are evaluated? Describe these areas in your answer.____________________
____
4. What are some general considerations and problems of assessing infants, toddlers, and young children?____________________
____

Part III

List and discuss some of the issues related to transition assessment and planning.

1. ____________________
____
2. ____________________
____
3. ____________________
____
4. ____________________
____

ANSWER KEY TO CHECK YOUR UNDERSTANDING

Activity 11.1

1. family's
2. developmental delay
3. IFSP
4. 6 months

Apply Your Knowledge. The family will be very involved in the child's intervention and will be the primary persons responsible for the interventions. To carry out the interventions the child requires, the family's needs and resources must be considered. Parents are also providers of the treatment and often are educated and assisted with implementation of therapeutic and educational interventions.

Activity 11.2

1. physical development, cognitive development, communication development, social/emotional development, and adaptive development
2. outcomes, progress
3. family-centered
4. explanations
5. negotiate
6. Such assessment may not result in greater cooperation and may possibly result in confusion.

Apply Your Knowledge. The parents' needs and resources must be balanced with the child's needs because the parents are primarily responsible for the implementation of the family-focused/family-centered IFSP. The family's time and budget constraints must be considered when designing the goals of the IFSP. For example, if the plan includes that the child will be treated within the home for occupational therapy goals three times per week, the parents' schedules and availability must be considered for the plan to be implemented.

Activity 11.3

1. C
2. E
3. A
4. D
5. B

Apply Your Knowledge. Regulatory disturbances can have an impact on relationships with family and peers because of the various demands made on caretakers and others due to these disturbances. In addition, regulatory disturbances can have an impact on educational and therapeutic interventions.

Activity 11.4

1. WPPSI—R
2. K-SEALS
3. K-SEALS
4. AGS Early Screening Profiles
5. AGS Early Screening Profiles, Brigance Screens

Apply Your Knowledge. Language has an influence on social and emotional development and may be a confounding disorder in a child with specific learning disabilities.

Activity 11.5

Phoneme Awareness Teacher-Made Test

1. Model (Blending): "Listen to these sounds /a//m/. When I say them together, they make the word am."
2. Directions: "Now you tell me this word: /a//n/" (student's response an)
3. Model (Segmenting): "Now listen to this word if. It has these sounds: /i//f/."
4. Directions: "Now you tell me the sounds in the word at." (student's response /a//t/)
5. Modeling (Substitution): "Listen to this word kick. Now I will make a new word with the sound /p/ pick."
6. Directions: "Listen to this word game. Tell me a new word with the sound /s/." (student's response same)

Apply Your Knowledge. Answers may vary but should include simple modeling and direction components using the sounds presented in Figure 11.4.

Activity 11.6

Transition Needs for Jimmy

1. Employment needs: Needs to learn about job requirements and how to make informed choices. Needs help in learning skills needed to get a job and job skills.
2. Further education/training: Needs to learn about community resources for job training, GED requirements, entrance requirements and procedures for vocational/technical school. May need assistance in understanding his abilities in regard to postsecondary education.
3. Daily living: Jimmy seems to have more confidence in his own personal and daily skills than do his parents and teachers. Needs assistance in learning actual requirements of daily living and personal skills (such as grooming). Additional assessment may be needed here to determine accuracy of ratings of parents, teachers, and student.
4. Leisure activities: Appears to be an area of strength for Jimmy. Should continue with this area of development.
5. Community participation: Here again Jimmy's perceptions are inconsistent with those of his parents and teachers. Additional assessment in this area may be needed to determine accuracy of his self-rating. Jimmy may overestimate his understanding of such concepts as legal rights and making legal decisions.
6. Health: An additional area of inconsistency in Jimmy's rating of his own ability compared with ratings by his teachers and parents. Additional assessment needed here.
7. Self-determination: Jimmy has rated himself highly in the understanding of his own strengths and limitations; however, as seen on this instrument, he may not have an accurate understanding of them. In addition,

he seems to need additional training in how to communicate his needs and in setting goals for himself. He feels somewhat unsure of his ability to make decisions.

8. Communication: Here is another area of inconsistency between his self-rating and the rating by adults. Additional assessment and instruction needed here.
9. Interpersonal relationships: It seems that Jimmy will need additional instruction and support in the areas of learning best possible interaction skills and maintaining interpersonal relationships.

Apply Your Knowledge. Answers may vary but should include a short-term objective in the area of self-determination.

REFERENCES

Bailey, D. B., & Wolery, M. (1989). *Assessing infants and preschoolers with handicaps*. Upper Saddle River, NJ: Merrill/Prentice Hall.

Barkley, R. A. (1990). *Attention deficit hyperactivity disorder: A handbook for diagnosis and treatment*. New York: Guilford.

Barnett, D. W., Bell, S. H., Gilkey, C. M., Lentz, F. E., Graden, J. L., Stone, C. M., Smith, J. J., & Macmann, G. M. (1999). The promise of meaningful eligibility determination: Functional intervention-based multifactored preschool evaluation. *Journal of Special Education, 33*(2), 112–124.

Barnett, D. W., Macmann, G. M., & Carey, K. T. (1992). Early intervention and the assessment of developmental skills: Challenges and directions. *Topics in Early Childhood Special Education, 12*(1), 21–43.

Bayley, N. (1993). *Bayley Scales of Infant Development—II*. San Antonio: Psychological Corporation.

Bowe, F. (1995). Population estimates: Birth-to-5 children with disabilities. *Journal of Special Education, 28,* 461–471.

Brazelton, T. (1984). *Neonatal Behavioral Assessment Scale—Second Edition*. Philadelphia: Lippincott.

Brigance, A. H. (1997). *K & 1 Screen*. North Billerica, MA: Curriculum Associates.

Brigance, A. H. (1998a). *Early Preschool Screen*. North Billerica, MA: Curriculum Associates.

Brigance, A. H. (1998b). *Preschool Screen*. North Billerica, MA: Curriculum Associates.

Brotherson, M. J., & Berdine, W. H. (1993). Transition to adult services: Support for ongoing parent participation. *Remedial & Special Education, 14*(4), 44–52.

Clark, G. M. (1996). Transition planning assessment for secondary-level students with learning disabilities. *Journal of Learning Disabilities, 29*(1), 79–93.

Clark, G., & Patton, J. (1997). Transition planning inventory. Austin, TX: Pro-Ed.

Cohen, L. G., & Spenciner, L. J. (1994). *Assessment of young children*. New York: Longman.

Dunst, C. J., Johanson, C., Trivette, C. M., & Hamby, D. (1991). Family-oriented early intervention policies and practices: Family-centered or not? *Exceptional Children, 58,* 115–126.

Ehri, L. C., Nunes, S. R., Willows, D. M., Schuster, B. V., Yaghoub-Zadeh, Z., & Shanahan, T. (2001). Phonemic awareness 1instruction helps children learn to read: Evidence from the national reading panel's meta-analysis. *Reading Research Quarterly, 36*(3), 250–287.

Federal Register (1993, July 30). Washington, DC: U.S. Government Printing Office.

Felton, R. H., & Pepper, P. P. (1995). Early identification and intervention of phonological deficits in kindergarten and early elementary children at risk for reading disability. *School Psychology Review, 24*(3), 405–414.

Fewell, R. R. (1991). Trends in the assessment of infants and toddlers with disabilities. *Exceptional Children, 58,* 166–173.

Field, S. Martin, J., Miller, R., Ward, M., & Wehmeyer, M. (1998). *A practical guide to teaching self-determination.* Reston, VA: Council for Exceptional Children.

Glascoe, F. P. (1998). *Technical Report for the Brigance Screens.* North Billerica, MA: Curriculum Associates.

Goodman, J. F., & Hover, S. A. (1992). The Individual Family Service Plan: Unresolved problems. *Psychology in the Schools, 29,* 140–151.

Graham, M., & Scott, K. (1988). The impact of definitions of high risk on services of infants and toddlers. *Topics in Early Childhood Special Education, 8*(3), 23–28.

Greenspan, S. I. (1992). *Infancy and early childhood: The practice of clinical assessment and intervention with emotional and developmental challenges.* Madison, CT: International University Press.

Harrison, P. L., Kaufman, A. S., Kaufman, N. L., Bruininks, R. H., Rynders, J., Ilmer, S., Sparrow, S. S., & Cicchetti, D. V. (1990). *AGS Early Screening Profiles.* Circle Pines, MN: American Guidance Service.

Individuals with Disabilities Education Act Amendments of 1997, Pub. L. 105-17, 105th Congress.

Katz, K. S. (1989). Strategies for infant assessment: Implications of P.L. 99-457. *Topics in Early Childhood Special Education, 9*(3), 99–109.

Kaufman, A. S., & Kaufman, N. L. (1993). *K-SEALS: Kaufman Survey of Early Academic and Language Skills.* Circle Pines, MN: American Guidance Service.

Kaufman, A. S., & Kaufman, N. L. (1994). *Kaufman functional academic skills test.* Circle Pines, MN: American Guidance Service, Inc.

Kaye, H. S. (1998). Is the status of people with disabilities improving? *Abstract 21: Disability Statistics Center.* San Francisco: University of California.

Lennon, J. E., & Slesinski, C. (1999). Early intervention in reading: Results of a screening and intervention program for kindergarten students. *School Psychology Review, 28,* 353–365.

Levine, P., & Nourse, S. W. (1998). What follow-up studies say about postschool life for young men and women with learning disabilities: A critical look at the literature. *Journal of Learning Disabilities, 31*(3), 212–233.

Levinson, E. M. (1995). Best practices in transition services. In A. Thomas & J. Grimes (Eds.), *Best practices in school psychology—III* (pp. 909–915). Washington, DC: The National Association of School Psychologists.

Lindsey, P., Wehmeyer, M. L., Guy, B., & Martin, J. (2001). Age of majority and mental retardation: A position statement of the division on mental retardation and developmental disabilities. *Education and Training in Mental Retardation and Developmental Disabilities, 36*(1), 3–15.

Mardell-Czudnowski, C., & Goldenberg, D. (1998). *Developmental indicators for the assessment of learning* (3rd ed.). Circle Pines, MN: American Guidance Service.

Mayes, L. C. (1991). Infant assessment. In M. Lewis (Ed.), *Child and adolescent psychiatry: A comprehensive textbook* (pp. 437–447). Baltimore: Williams & Wilkins.

Minke, K. M., & Scott, M. M. (1993). The development of Individualized Family Service Plans: Roles for parents and staff. *Journal of Special Education, 27,* 82–106.

Mullen, E. M. (1995). *Mullen scales of early learning: AGS edition.* Circle Pines, MN: American Guidance Service, Inc.

Paget, K. D. (1990). Best practices in the assessment of competence in preschool-age children. In A. Thomas & J. Grimes (Eds.), *Best practices in school psychology—II* (pp. 107–119). Washington, DC: National Association of School Psychologists.

Sinclair, E., Del'Homme, & M. Gonzalez. (1993). Systematic screening for preschool assessment of behavioral disorders. *Behavioral Disorders, 18,* 177–188.

Snider, V. E. (1995). A primer on phonemic awareness: What it is, why it is important, and how to teach it. *School Psychology Review, 24,*(3), 443–455.

Snider, V. E. (1997). The relationship between phonemic awareness and later reading achievement. *Journal of Educational Research, 90*(4), 203–212.

Snyder, P., Bailey, D., & Auer, C. (1994). Preschool eligibility determination for children with known or suspected learning disabilities under IDEA. *Journal of Early Intervention, 18,* 380–390.

Thoma, C. A., Rogan, P., & Baker, S. R. (2001). Student involvement in transition planning: Unheard voices. *Education and Training in Mental Retardation and Developmental Disabilities, 36*(1), 16–29.

Thurlow, M. L., Ysseldyke, J. E., & Anderson, C. L. (1995). *High school graduation requirements: What's happening for students with disabilities?* Minneapolis: National Center on Educational Outcomes.

Turnbull, R., Turnbull, A., Shank, M., Smith, S., & Leal, D. (2002). *Exceptional lives: Special education in today's schools* (3rd ed.). Upper Saddle River, NJ: Merrill/Prentice Hall.

U.S. Department of Education (1995). *The seventeenth annual report to Congress on the implementation of the Individuals with Disabilities Education Act.* Washington, DC: Author.

U.S. Department of Education (1999). *Twenty-first annual report to Congress on the implementation of the Individuals with Disabilities Education Act.* Washington, DC: Author.

U.S. Department of Education (2000). *Twenty-second annual report to Congress on the implementation of the Individuals with Disabilities Education Act.* Washington, DC: Author.

Vogel, S. A., Leonard, F., Scales, W., Hayeslip, P., Hermansen, J., & Donnells, L. (1998). The national learning disabilities postsecondary data bank: An overview. *Journal of Learning Disabilities, 31*(3), 234–247.

Uzgiris, I. C., & Hunt, J. McV. (1975). *Assessment in infancy: Ordinal Scales of Psychological Development.* Urbana: University of Illinois Press.

Wechsler, D. (1989). *Wechsler Preschool and Primary Scale of Intelligence—Revised.* San Antonio: Psychological Corporation.

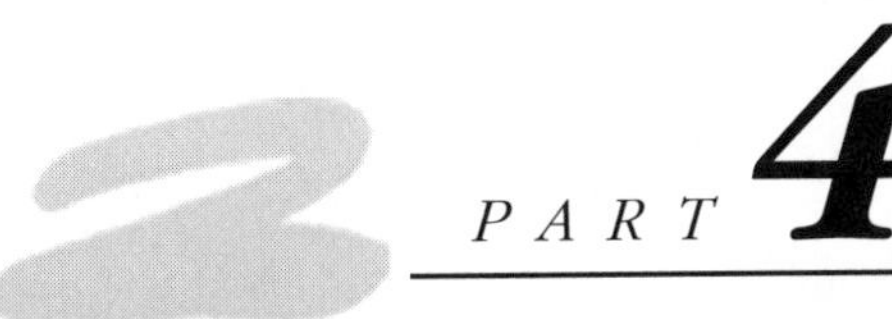

Interpreting Assessment for Educational Intervention

Chapter 12 **Interpreting Assessment for Educational Intervention**

Chapter 13 **Case Studies**

CHAPTER 12

Interpreting Assessment for Educational Intervention

Key Terms

educational planning
eligibility decisions
behaviorally stated short-term objectives
benchmarks
long-term goals
interindividual interpretation
intra-individual interpretation

CHAPTER FOCUS

This chapter provides suggestions for interpreting test results and designing educational goals for appropriate interventions. You will be presented with a complete case that includes test scores, interpretations, goals, and objectives. Test results help educators make decisions about educational interventions, planning, and possible eligibility for special education services. After the professional interprets a student's test results from norm-referenced tests, classroom observations, informal assessment, and parental input, the team members use the results as part of the data to make a decision concerning eligibility, interventions, and if age appropriate, long-term transition plans. The teacher then uses curriculum-based assessment, teacher-made tests, and direct measurement techniques to monitor progress and adapt instruction.

Test results are most useful when interpreted and presented in a clear format with specific information relating to educational and behavioral strategies. The regulations of the 1997 Amendments to IDEA require that assessment data be interpreted and used to develop educational and behavioral interventions that will be of benefit to the student. Hoy and Retish (1984) determined that test reports generally lacked the characteristics necessary for ease of **educational planning.** In this chapter, a model of interpreting test results to assist with **eligibility decisions** and plan program interventions is presented. The second part of the chapter illustrates how to use test results to write effective **behaviorally stated short-term objectives, benchmarks,** and **long-term goals** and how to continue to monitor student progress through direct assessment.

educational planning Interventions and strategies used to promote educational success.

eligibility decisions The determination of whether a student will receive special education services.

behaviorally stated short-term objectives Observable and measurable objectives that provide evidence of a student's progress toward annual goals.

benchmarks The major markers that provide evidence of a student's progress toward annual goals.

long-term goals Statements of anticipated progress that a student will make in one year upon which the short-term objectives and benchmarks are based.

When interpreting the results of standardized tests, classroom observations, student interviews, parent interviews, questionnaires, surveys, and other methods of assessment, it is important to remember the holistic view of the child or adolescent as well as the environment from which the child comes. Tharinger and Lambert (1990) offered the following guidelines for the assessment and interpretive process:

1. A child is dependent on the environment to fulfill basic physiological and psychological needs.
2. A child's family is the most active shaper of her or his environment.
3. A child is also an active participant in shaping her or his environment.
4. A child's functioning is multiply and transactionally determined.
5. A child strives to adapt to her or his environment regardless of the health of the environment.
6. A child's motivations for her or his behavior may not be conscious.
7. A child's attachment, separations, and losses are very significant factors in her or his psychological development.

8. A child's current functioning must be evaluated in light of her or his past functioning.
9. A child's behavior can only be understood in relation to current context and the influence of past contexts.
10. As a child develops, conflicts, tensions, and problems are inevitable and necessary. The important factor for assessment is how the child and significant others respond to these conflicts.
11. If the child's thoughts, behaviors, or feelings appear atypical, it is important to consider where, under what circumstances, and at what developmental level this thought pattern, behavior, or emotional expression would make sense.
12. Both the child and her significant environments (i.e., school and home) need to be assessed. (p. 95)

Source: From D. J. Tharinger, & N. M. Lambert (1990). The contributions of developmental psychology to school psychology; in T. Gutkin & C. R. Reynolds (Eds.), *The handbook of school psychology* (2nd ed.). New York: Wiley, pp. 74–103. (© John Wiley & Sons, Inc. Reprinted by permission of the publisher.)

INTERPRETING TEST RESULTS FOR EDUCATIONAL DECISIONS

One purpose of the assessment process is to consider test results to determine if a student requires interventions provided through special education services. Eligibility is determined by using set criteria stated in IDEA. These criteria may vary from state to state for the different types of disabilities but must remain within the IDEA guidelines. This means that the definitions and criteria may be written by the state; however, students who would be found eligible according to the federal law must not be excluded by the state criteria. The scope of this text focuses primarily on mild to moderate disabilities. The most common types of mild to moderate disabilities are learning disabilities, mental retardation, speech/language impairment, and emotional or behavioral disturbances. Students with attention disorders are also often served by educators who teach students with mild to moderate disabilities. These students may be served in the general education environment under the provisions of Section 504 of the Rehabilitation Act of 1973 (refer to chapter 2) or under the IDEA category of "other health impaired" if the attention problem does not coexist with another disability, such as a learning disability.

The criteria for the qualification of a specific category and eligibility for special education services as stated in IDEA are used as a basis for interpreting test results. Table 12.1 lists the criteria for mild to moderate disabilities as well as the common characteristics of students with attention deficit disorders.

Table 12.1 Key diagnostic criteria of IDEA for attention disorders and mild/moderate disabilities.

Disability	Key Criteria	Assessment Devices
Mental retardation	Subaverage intellectual, academic, and adaptive behavior (2 or more standard deviations below expectancy for age and according to generally accepted guidelines).	Standardized IQ tests, academic achievement and diagnostic tests, adaptive behavior scales, parent interviews, classroom observations.
Learning disability	Average or above in intelligence; specific deficits in academics, cognitive language, or perceptual processing (1 to 2 or more standard deviations between ability and academic performance and according to generally accepted guidelines).	Standardized IQ test, academic achievement and diagnostic tests, classroom observations, permanent products, informal measures, parent interviews, perceptual-motor tests.
Emotional disturbance	Behavioral or emotional difficulties that interfere with academic or developmental progress: unexplained physical problems, pervasive unhappiness, withdrawal, and so on.	Standardized IQ tests, academic achievement and diagnostic tests, clinical interviews, parent interviews, classroom observations, projective tests, personality or behavioral inventories.
Speech/language impairment	Communication difficulty that interferes with academic progress, ability to speak, or normal developmental progress.	Speech or language diagnostic tests, classroom observations, parent interviews, academic achievement tests.
Attention deficit disorders		
1. With hyperactivity	Externalizing behaviors, talking out, talking too much, impulsive actions, activity level beyond developmental expectations, poor schoolwork, incomplete or missing assignments.	DSM—IV evaluation, behavioral ratings by different persons and in different environments, Continuous Performance Tests, cognitive and achievement tests, multiple direct classroom observations.
2. Inattentive type	Poor schoolwork, incomplete or missing assignments, confusion, excessive daydreaming, self-distracting behavior, difficulty following directions and following through.	Same as for hyperactive type.
3. Combined (hyperactivity and inattention)	Combination of characteristics found in hyperactive and inattentive ADD.	Same as for hyperactive type.

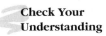

Check Your Understanding

Complete Activity 12.1.

ACTIVITY 12.1

Answer the following questions.

1. What are the general criteria used to determine if a student is functioning within the range of mental retardation? ____________________
2. Which term listed in Table 12.1 is used when the student has communication problems affecting developmental progress? __________
3. Which term listed in Table 12.1 indicates that a student has discrepancies between ability and academic performance? __________
4. In determining __________, behavioral observations, clinical interviews, information from multiple informants, and projective tests may be used.
5. Which tests are typically administered to assess for the possibility of learning disabilities? ____________________
6. For what categories of disabilities are classroom observations recommended as part of the assessment process? ____________________

Apply Your Knowledge

How are the characteristics of students with attention disorders with hyperactivity and the characteristics of students with attention disorders, inattentive type, similar? How are they different? ____________________

THE ART OF INTERPRETING TEST RESULTS

interindividual interpretation Comparing a student to a peer norm group.

intra-individual interpretation Comparing a student with his or her own performance.

Most of this text has focused on quantitative measurement, informal data collection, and information from multiple informants about student abilities. A teacher or diagnostician may know how to effectively administer test items, score tests, and collect data; however, the art of interpreting meaning from all of the data and information must also be mastered. Accurate interpretation involves both **interindividual** and **intra-individual interpretation** of test results. Interindividual interpretation involves comparing the student with other students in the norm group to determine how different the student is from that group. Intra-individual interpretation may be even more important than interindividual interpretation. For intra-individual interpretation, the teacher uses the test results and other data collected to compare the student's own performances in determining strengths and weaknesses. These strengths and weaknesses are then used in effective educational and behavioral planning.

Generally, all possible areas of suspected disability are assessed according to the recommended tests and evaluation measures given in Table 12.1. The following procedures are suggested for evaluating the student and interpreting test results.

1. ***Parental permission.*** The professional must secure parental permission before conducting an individual assessment or making a referral.
2. ***Screening for sensory impairments or physical problems.*** Before a psychoeducational evaluation is recommended, the student's vision, hearing, and general physical health should be screened. When these areas are found to be normal or corrections for vision/hearing impairments are made, the evaluation procedure can continue.
3. ***Parent interview.*** The professional should question the parent regarding the student's progress, development, developmental history, family structure, relationships with family and peers, and independent adaptive behavior functioning.
4. ***Intellectual and academic assessment.*** The team members should administer an intelligence measure and academic achievement or diagnostic instrument, conduct classroom observations, and complete an informal evaluation.
5. ***Behavioral assessment.*** If the assessment and the information from the parents and teacher indicate behavioral, emotional, or attention problems, the student should also be assessed by a school or clinical psychologist to obtain behavioral, emotional, and personality information.
6. ***Test interpretation.*** Several members of the evaluation team may interpret test results. The team members may write separate or combined reports. In interpreting results, the assessment team should accomplish the following:
   a. Rule out any sensory acuity problems and refer or consult with medical personnel if physical problems are suspected.
   b. Determine whether any home conflicts are present and refer to school psychologist or school counselor if they are suspected or indicated.
   c. If appropriate, consideration of previous educational experiences and how these experiences may have influenced student's achievement (such as frequent moves, migrant student experiences, period of time student has lived in the United States, parents' educational experiences and views on the education process, and frequent absences).

d. If appropriate, consideration and assessment of any language factors (assessment to determine primary language should be completed during the referral/assessment process, interviews to determine language spoken in the home, and for bilingual students, determination of proficiency level in both languages).
e. Determine whether learning or school problems are exhibited in a particular school environment (unstructured play or lunchroom) or are associated with one subject area or a particular teacher, peer, or adult.
f. Compare ability on intellectual, academic, or adaptive behavior measures. Are there apparent discrepancies in functioning? Do perceptual or motor deficits appear to influence ability in specific academic areas? Is the student functioning higher in one area than in others? Is the student functioning significantly below expectancy in one or more areas? How do the formal test results compare with classroom assessments?
g. Determine whether emotional/behavioral problems exist. Does the student appear to be progressing slowly because of behavioral or emotional difficulties? Does the student adapt well in various situations? Does the student have good relationships with peers and adults? Is attention or activity level interfering with academic and social progress? Does a functional behavioral assessment need to be completed?
h. Determine whether speech/language problems are present. Is the student having difficulty understanding language or following oral lectures or directions? Does the student make articulation errors that are not age appropriate?

As these questions are answered, the diagnostician or special education teacher begins to form a picture of how the student processes information and how the strengths and weaknesses noted during test performance and observations may affect learning and behavior. From these interpretations, the teacher can make recommendations that will provide educational intervention and support to benefit the student and promote academic progress. The psychoeducational report or reports are then written to facilitate appropriate intervention strategies.

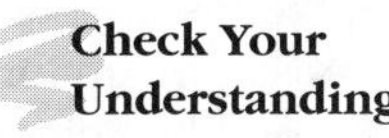

Complete Activity 12.2.

ACTIVITY 12.2

Complete the following sentences.

1. Before a decision is made that involves educational or intellectual ability, screening for ______________ should be completed.

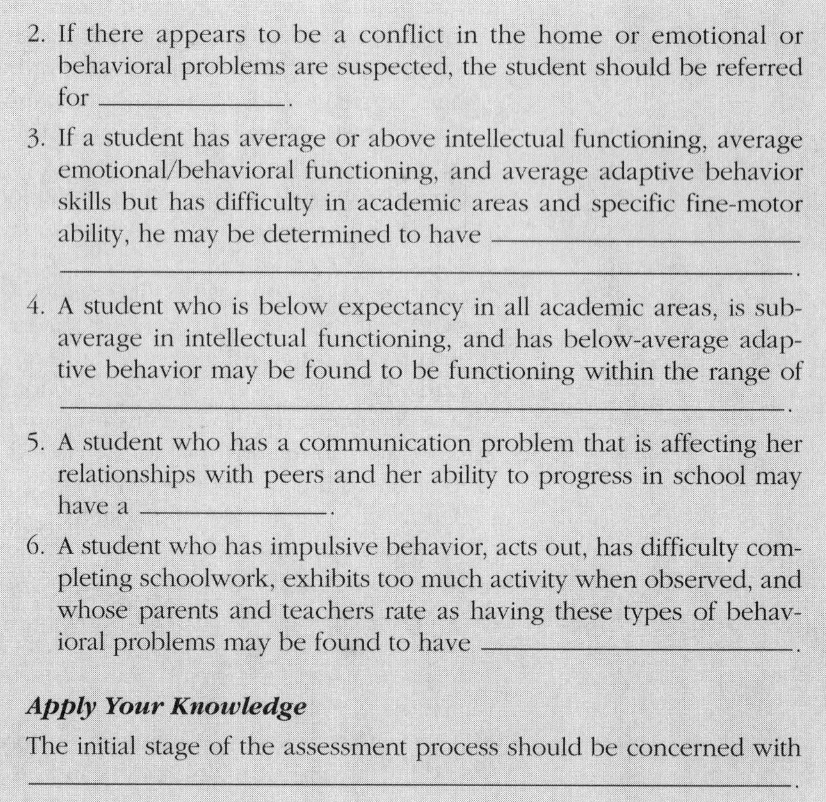

2. If there appears to be a conflict in the home or emotional or behavioral problems are suspected, the student should be referred for ________________.
3. If a student has average or above intellectual functioning, average emotional/behavioral functioning, and average adaptive behavior skills but has difficulty in academic areas and specific fine-motor ability, he may be determined to have ________________________________.
4. A student who is below expectancy in all academic areas, is subaverage in intellectual functioning, and has below-average adaptive behavior may be found to be functioning within the range of ________________________________.
5. A student who has a communication problem that is affecting her relationships with peers and her ability to progress in school may have a ________________.
6. A student who has impulsive behavior, acts out, has difficulty completing schoolwork, exhibits too much activity when observed, and whose parents and teachers rate as having these types of behavioral problems may be found to have ________________.

Apply Your Knowledge

The initial stage of the assessment process should be concerned with ________________________________.

INTELLIGENCE AND ADAPTIVE BEHAVIOR TEST RESULTS

Cognitive or intellectual measures are generally administered by school psychologists, clinical psychologists, or educational diagnosticians. The results from these tests should be interpreted and used to plan educational interventions. Interindividual interpretations may indicate that the student is within the range of mental retardation, has a specific learning disability, has emotional disturbance, developmental immaturity, or average or above-average intellectual functioning. Intra-individual interpretations should be provided by the person who administered the tests. These interpretations may pinpoint specific demonstrated strengths as well as problems with distractibility, attention deficits, auditory short-term memory, visual retention, verbal comprehension, abstract visual reasoning, visual memory difficulties, and so on. Interpretation of the cognitive measures may refer to patterns of functioning noticed. Patterns of functioning may be explained as significant differences between verbal areas of functioning and visual-motor abilities, spatial reasoning or functioning, or perceptual-organization abilities. These patterns may be indicated by significant weaknesses in particular areas or by more global scores, such as significant differences between verbal and performance IQ scores (e.g., a verbal IQ of 108 and a performance IQ of 71). These weaknesses or discrepancies may be linked to particular learning difficulties. The examiner's descriptions of the student's performance may help the team plan effective educational strategies.

EDUCATIONAL ACHIEVEMENT AND DIAGNOSTIC TEST RESULTS

The educator may be responsible for administering norm-referenced educational achievement and other diagnostic tests. Scoring these instruments may be somewhat mechanical, although great care should be taken when scoring tests and interpreting the results. The first method of interpretation involves interindividual interpretation: Compare the student with age/grade expectations. Data provided on norm tables will enable the examiner to determine how a student compares with age/grade peers. Is the student significantly above expectations (in the 90th percentile, for example)? Is the student average (in the 50th percentile range) on some measures but significantly below peers (below the 10th percentile) on other measures? The examiner must plot a profile of how the student performs when compared to these expectations.

Intra-individual interpretation means that the examiner will identify specific strengths and weaknesses in academic achievement, other abilities, and behavioral areas. Because the areas of strength and weakness should be defined as specifically as possible, tests that provide error analysis are most helpful. This analysis can be broken down further by task and used to develop teacher-made tests or informal probes if more information is needed.

WRITING TEST RESULTS

Interpreting and writing test results so that meaningful information is available for the persons responsible for the delivery of educational service is the most important concern when preparing reports. Bagnato (1980) suggested the following guidelines for making psychoeducational reports easy to use in the development of IEPs.

1. Be organized by multiple developmental or functional domains rather than only by tests given.
2. Describe specific areas of strength and skill deficits in clear behavioral terms.
3. Emphasize process variables and qualitative features regarding the child's learning strategies.
4. Highlight lists of developmental ceilings, functional levels, skill sequences, and instructional needs upon which assessment/curriculum linkages can be constructed to form the IEP.
5. Detail efficient suggestions regarding behavioral and instructional management strategies. (p. 555)

Although psychoeducational reports may differ in format, they include the same general content. Typically, the identifying information is presented first: student name, date of birth, parents' names, address, grade placement, date(s) of evaluation, methods of evaluation, and the name of the examiner. Presented next is the background and referral information, which may include sociological information such as the size of family, student's relationship with family members, other schools attended, and any previous academic, behavioral, developmental, or health problems.

Following the preliminary information are the test results. An interpretation is presented, and recommendations for interventions, further evaluations, or changes in placement are then suggested. The following is an outline of a psychoeducational report.

I. Identifying Data
II. Background and Referral Information
   A. Background
   B. Referral
   C. Classroom Observation
   D. Parent Information
III. Test Results
IV. Test Interpretations
V. Summary and Conclusions
   A. Summary
   B. Recommendations for Educational Interventions
   C. Recommendations for Further Assessment

Writing style is also important in writing test results. Words should be selected carefully to convey an objective assessment. Goff (2002) suggested specific guidelines for educators to follow in report preparation when normative tests are used. These guidelines, presented in Table 12.2, include samples of educators' reports and suggested improvements.

The following case study presents test results and interpretations. Read the results and notice interpretations and notice how they are implemented in the educational recommendations. For instructional purposes, the reasons for the recommendations are given with each recommendation.

CASE STUDY

Name: Sue Smith
Date of Birth: 6-8-94
Dates of Evaluation: 11-20-04, 11-28-04
Age: 10-6
Current Grade Placement: 3.3
Examiner: Hazel Competent
Instruments: Wechsler Intelligence Scale for Children—Third Edition

Woodcock-Johnson III Tests of Achievement: Standard and Extended Battery
Test of Auditory Perceptual Skills
Teacher Report Form (Achenbach)
Work sample analysis
Classroom observations
Conference with parents

BACKGROUND INFORMATION AND REFERRAL

Sue was referred for testing by her parents for the possible consideration of special education services. Sociological information reported normal developmental progress and a warm, caring home environment. Sue's parents reported that they felt education was important and wanted Sue's progress to improve. Sue appears to have good relationships with both parents and her two older brothers.

Sue repeated kindergarten and received low grades during her first- and second-grade years. Sue is currently enrolled in third grade, and the teacher reported that Sue has difficulty with phonics and reading words that "she should know." Sue attended a special summer program in an attempt to improve her reading skills.

Sue has normal vision and hearing and no apparent physical problems. Peer relationships are as expected for her age.

PARENT CONFERENCE

Sue's parents reported that Sue is a well-adjusted child who enjoys playing outside, listening to music, and playing on the computer. Her parents believe that Sue's academic difficulties began to surface over a year ago. They stated that they thought Sue would be able to catch up with her peers in reading; however, she still doesn't seem to "get it." Her parents have hired a tutor in the neighborhood to help Sue with her homework. They said that Sue seems to enjoy working with this high school student because she enjoys having another girl to talk to rather than her brothers. Her parents said Sue doesn't appear to get as frustrated as when she works with her parents.

CLASSROOM OBSERVATIONS

Sue was observed on three separate occasions before the testing sessions. She seemed to stay on task and attempted all assigned work. Her teacher reported that more than half of Sue's assignments were incomplete. It appeared that the pace of the class might be too rapid, especially in reading and language arts. Sue did not exhibit many inappropriate behaviors for her age and seemed to have friends within the classroom. Sue's teacher used peer tutors for some of the reading and language arts assignments, which she reports helped Sue to finish some of her work.

Table 12.2 Guidelines for writing objective reports.

Background Information

- Make sure that all statements are attributed. The statement *Jack's mother is very supportive, which contributes to his academic success* is not attributed. Jack's father may strongly disagree if there is a custody battle. This statement could easily be rewritten to attribute the comment to its source: *Ms. Jones, Jack's teacher, reported that Jack's mother has been very supportive and that this support has contributed to Jack's academic success.*
- Do not ask the reader to make assumptions. The statement *Her teacher reports a noticeable difference in Jill's attention span when she does not take her medication* requires the reader to make an assumption. Some students will perform better when not on medication because they become more diligent in monitoring their own behavior to prove they do not need it.

Classroom Observations and Test Observations

- Make sure that you provide observations, not interpretations of behavior. The statement *James really liked the lesson* is an interpretation. This could be rewritten as *James stated, "I really like this work."* NOTE: This is not an interpretation because you are directly quoting Jack. The statement *The work he was given was too hard for James* is also an interpretation and could be rewritten as *James did not complete the more difficult items successfully.*

Test Results

- Make a standard comment about mean and standard deviation of the test used. For example: *The standard scores for the WJ-III have a mean of 100 and a standard deviation of 15.*
- Report standard scores, percentile ranks, and standard errors of measure. Report both subtest scores and composite or broad area scores. A table in the body of the report or at the end is usually the clearest way to communicate this information.

Test Interpretation

- Discuss clear strengths and weaknesses in performance only if variation in scores reaches statistical significance (usually to the .05 level). Otherwise, the variation should be considered to be normal variability.

Summary and Conclusions

- Tie a review of the Background Information, Observations, Test Results, and Test Interpretation together in summary form. Your summary should pull everything together.
- Your strongest conclusions will be based on concerns supported by Background Information, Observations, and Test Interpretation.

  Observations and evaluation data support the parents' and teacher's concern that Billy has a reading deficit. In addition, he scored well below average on assessments of written language. This supports a recommendation of remediation services in language arts.
- If a student does better in one part of a domain than another, note this difference. *Tonya performed at an average level on a subtest that assesses reading comprehension, but scored well below average on a subtest that assesses word identification skills.* This supports a recommendation that, while remediating word attack skills, the student could continue to be presented with age appropriate content.

- If the testing data do not support a claim of weakness, look first to differences in task demands of the testing situation and the classroom when hypothesizing a reason for the difference.

  Although weaknesses in mathematics were noted as a concern by his teacher, Billy scored in the average range on assessments of mathematics skills. These tests required Billy to perform calculations and to solve word problems that were read aloud to him. It was noted that he often paused for ten seconds or more before starting pencil and paper tasks in mathematics.

  This supports a recommendation that the teacher attempt to redirect him to task frequently and to avoid the assumption that a long pause means that Billy is unable to solve a problem.

- If the testing data indicate a weakness that was not identified as a concern, give first priority to explaining the discrepancy to the limitations with the testing.

  Billy's teacher stated that he does well in spelling. However, he scored well below average on a subtest of spelling skills. Billy appeared to be bored while taking the spelling test so a lack of vigilance in his effort may have depressed his score. Also, the spelling tests he takes in school use words he has been practicing for a week. The lower score on the Spelling subtest of this assessment may indicate that he is maintaining the correct spelling of words in long-term memory.

- Do not use definitive statements of the "real" child when reporting assessment results. A forty-five minute test does not give you definitive knowledge of the student. The statement *The results of this screening show that Jack has strength in language arts and is weak in mathematics* could be rewritten as *Based on the results of this screening, Jack's language arts skills were assessed to be an area of strength while his mathematics skills were assessed to be an area of weakness.*

Recommendations

- Be careful of using "should" in your recommendations. It means that you are directing another professional on how to do his or her job even though that other professional may have a much more comprehensive knowledge of the child than you.
- Do not make placement recommendations based solely on the results of an achievement test. Make academic recommendations only if your full assessment provides adequate information to make these recommendations with confidence. Remember, specific recommendations can only be made by someone with thorough knowledge of the curriculum and the domain being assessed.

TEST RESULTS

Wechsler Intelligence Scale for Children—III

Verbal Subtests		*Performance Subtests*	
Information	2	Picture Completion	10
Similarities	7	Coding	9
Arithmetic	5	Picture Arrangement	9
Vocabulary	7	Block Design	7
Comprehension	7	Object Assembly	7
Digit Span	4		

Verbal IQ Score	73
Performance IQ Score	88
Full-Scale IQ Score	79

Woodcock-Johnson III Tests of Achievement: Standard and Extended Batteries

Cluster/Test	*PR*	*SS*	*(90% BAND)*	*GE*
Oral Language (Ext)	5	76	(69–82)	2.0
Oral Expression	12	83	(74–92)	2.1
Listening Comprehension	9	80	(73–86)	1.9
Total Achievement	.3	59	(56–62)	1.9
Broad Reading	.2	57	(54–60)	1.5
Broad Math	23	89	(85–93)	3.5
Broad Written Language	0.4	60	(54–66)	1.6
Basic Reading Skills	0.3	59	(55–63)	1.3
Reading Comprehension	1	67	(62–72)	1.7
Math Calculation Skills	39	96	(90–101)	4.4
Math Reasoning	30	92	(87–97)	3.8
Basic Writing Skills	2	68	(63–73)	1.7
Written Expression	4	74	(66–81)	2.3
Academic Skills	1	66	(63–69)	1.7
Academic Fluency	3	72	(69–76)	2.2
Academic Applications	4	75	(70–79)	1.9
Academic Knowledge	35	94	(87–101)	4.3
Phoneme/Grapheme Knowledge	0.2	56	(49–63)	1.0

The following achievement tests of Form A were administered:

Letter-Word Identification	<0.1	48	(43–52)	1.1
Reading Fluency	5	76	(72–79)	2.2
Story Recall	2	68	(50–86)	K.3
Understanding Directions	<0.1	50	(43–57)	K.0
Calculation	76	110	(101–120)	6.2
Math Fluency	1	62	(56–67)	1.5
Spelling	<0.1	52	(45–60)	K.9
Writing Fluency	5	75	(66–83)	2.5
Passage Comprehension	2	68	(61–74)	1.5
Applied Problems	12	82	(76–89)	2.6
Writing Samples	8	79	(68–90)	1.9
Word Attack	5	75	(68–82)	1.6
Picture Vocabulary	29	92	(84–100)	3.1
Oral Comprehension	47	99	(91–107)	4.5
Editing	14	84	(77–91)	2.9
Reading Vocabulary	7	78	(73–83)	1.9
Quantitative Concepts	70	108	(98–117)	5.9
Academic Knowledge	35	94	(87–101)	4.3
Spelling of Sounds	<0.1	26	(11–41)	<K.0
Sound Awareness	11	82	(76–88)	1.9

Punctuation & Capitals	<0.1	49	(35–62)	K.9
Handwriting	38	96	(85–106)	3.9

Test of Auditory-Perceptual Skills

		Scaled Score	***Percentile Rank***
Auditory Number Memory			
Forward		6	9
Reversed		5	5
Auditory Sentence Memory		8	25
Auditory Word Memory		5	5
Auditory Interpretation of Directions			
Total Correct Sentences		7	16
Auditory Word Discrimination		3	1
Auditory Processing (thinking and reasoning)		7	16
Auditory Quotient	70		

TEST INTERPRETATIONS

On measures of intellectual ability, Sue performed in the low-average range. This indicates that Sue is considered to have average general abilities; however, she is in the low-average range expected for her age. A discrepancy exists between her verbal and performance IQ scores and individual subtest scores. Overall, Sue's test performance was better on items measuring nonverbal or performance skills. Significant strength was noted in the area of visual memory, or remembering what she sees, and nonverbal ability, or items that do not require much skill in verbal reasoning. On this test, Sue did not perform as well on items that required verbal skills. She had the most difficulty on items measuring auditory memory, or remembering what she hears, and items that require more attention or concentration.

On overall achievement measures of the Woodcock-Johnson III Tests of Achievement, Sue performed as expected for her age on items of math calculation and math reasoning. Sue's general academic knowledge was in the range expected for her age when she completed tasks of science, social studies, and humanities. Sue also demonstrated age-appropriate skills in the ability to comprehend orally and in handwriting ability. She performed within the low average to slightly below the average range in areas of oral expression, oral language, and listening comprehension.

Sue's difficulties in academics were demonstrated through formal assessment in the areas of written language, including reading, spelling, sound awareness, and phoneme/grapheme knowledge. The weaknesses result in the inability to decode new words, spell sounds, and comprehend content that is read. An error analysis of word attack skills revealed weaknesses in decoding single consonants, digraphs, consonant blends, vowels, and multisyllabic words.

Sue demonstrated weakness in most areas assessed by the Test of Auditory-Perceptual Skills. She seems to have relative weaknesses on subtests that measure memory for isolated words and numbers. She appears to have slightly higher ability to remember meaningful auditory stimuli, such as sentences or directions. However, she had difficulty on similar items of the WJ III, indicating inconsistent skill mastery or inconsistent abilities.

On items requiring oral language responses, Sue was somewhat shy and tended to limit her responses to one-word answers. This may have affected some of her scores on tests assessing the language areas. These scores may underestimate her true ability.

Responses provided by Sue's teacher on the Teacher Report Form of the Child Behavior Checklist indicated that Sue is unable to complete most of her schoolwork as expected of students her age. The teacher endorsed items that indicate Sue may be having some emerging problems with anxiety. Items were also endorsed that are consistent with difficulties with concentration and attention. These may be related to her current performance in school. None of the scores were within a clinical range for behavior problems.

Work sample analysis indicated that Sue has a relative strength in the ability to compute simple math operations, and to understand math concepts and math reasoning. Her samples for spelling, writing, and reading comprehension were within the failure range. The work samples indicated difficulty with her ability to associate written letters with sounds consistently, which is consistent with her performance on standardized achievement measures.

Three separate classroom observations indicated that Sue was cooperative and remained quiet during all of the observation periods. She attempted to begin her work when instructed to do so but was unable to complete language arts assignments as instructed. She also appeared to increase the amount of time that she was off task during language-arts classes compared with her ability to concentrate during math class.

SUMMARY AND CONCLUSIONS

Sue is currently functioning in the low-average range of intellectual ability, with significant weaknesses in phoneme/grapheme awareness and short-term auditory memory. These weaknesses influence Sue's ability to decode words, spell, and comprehend new material. The weakness may also decrease the efficiency with which Sue can obtain new information through a standard teaching (lecture) format. Sue's performance on standardized and informal assessment instruments resulted in a profile consistent with that of a student with specific learning disabilities in the areas of reading and written language skills. This may be the result of her difficulties with processing information presented auditorily and an inability to form sound-symbol relationships.

RECOMMENDATIONS

1. Sue may benefit from additional educational support in the areas of reading and language arts. (Reasons: Student has difficulty with sound awareness, phoneme/grapheme awareness, auditory memory, verbal skills, and attention; this would support the decision that she may benefit from additional educational interventions.)
2. New material should be presented through both visual and auditory formats. (Reasons: Weakness appears to be auditory memory; pairing all auditory material with visual cues may help student to focus attention.)
3. Sue will benefit from direct instruction techniques that require her to actively respond to new material. (Reasons: Student may increase academic engaged time; active responding may help student to focus attention and receive positive feedback from teacher.)
4. Sue may benefit from phonemic awareness training activities. (Assessment results are consistently low in these areas; additional instruction may decrease her difficulties with reading).
5. Sue may benefit from advanced organizers in content areas, introduction of new vocabulary terms before reading them in new chapters, outlines of class lectures or presentations, and note-taking training. (Reasons: Student may increase ability to focus on relevant material, increase attention to task.)

Hazel Competent
Hazel Competent, M.Ed.
Educational Diagnostician

Check Your Understanding

Complete Activity 12.3.

ACTIVITY 12.3

Answer the following questions about the case study.

1. Why was Sue referred for testing? ______________________________
____
2. How is Sue functioning intellectually? ______________________________
____
3. What are the discrepancies in Sue's functioning according to the test results? ______________________________
____
____

4. What are Sue's strengths as indicated through the assessment process? ______________________________

____

5. What are Sue's weaknesses, and how do these weaknesses appear to influence Sue's academic functioning? ______________________________

____

____

6. What additional assessment was recommended for Sue? ______________________________

____

7. According to these results, what are Sue's specific academic skill deficits? ______________________________

____

8. What types of educational interventions and strategies were recommended? ______________________________

____

Apply Your Knowledge

Write any additional concerns you may have about Sue after reading this report. ______________________________

____

WRITING EDUCATIONAL OBJECTIVES

At the eligibility meeting, team members discuss the results and recommendations of the psychoeducational reports with the parents. If the student is eligible for special education services, the team writes the specific educational objectives that the student's IEP will comprise. If the student does not meet eligibility criteria, the student may be considered to need accommodations under Section 504. The team may also decide that the student does not need additional services under 504 or IDEA but additional referrals, programs, or interventions may be suggested within the general curriculum. Let's continue with the example of Sue Smith to see how the team would use its results to write Sue's educational objectives.

IEP TEAM MEETING RESULTS

The following results were presented in the IEP team meeting along with additional information from Sue's parents, school psychologist, and classroom teachers. At that time, the team agreed that Sue would receive reading and language-arts instruction in a resource room setting. This decision was made so that Sue could receive intensive training in phonemic awareness, reading decoding, reading comprehension, reading fluency, and spelling in a one-on-one and small-group environment. Additional assessments would be completed to further pinpoint the specific weaknesses in phoneme/grapheme awareness and other areas of language arts. The resource room teacher plans to use curriculum-based measurement to monitor progress.

SUE'S IEP

During the IEP meeting, the IEP was developed. Portions of the IEP are presented here.

Student's Present Level of Educational Performance

Cognitive Abilities. Current assessment data indicate that Sue is functioning in the low-average range of intelligence. Sue's strengths are in the areas of performance or nonverbal skills.

Reading

- *Basic Reading Skills.* Formal assessment, curriculum-based assessments, and informal measures indicate that Sue is performing below the range expected for her age on tasks of reading decoding, specifically word attack and phoneme/grapheme awareness. Her performance in curriculum-based measures are at the first- to second-grade level.
- *Comprehension.* Comprehension skills were at the first- to second-grade level on all measures.
- *Fluency.* Reading fluency was assessed to be at the first- to second-grade level.

Spelling. Sue's spelling skills were measured to be at the first-grade level. Sue has difficulty with the spelling of basic cvc (consonant-vowel-consonant) words.

Written Language. Sue's written language skills were measured to be at the first- to second-grade level on both formal and informal classroom measures.

Mathematics. Sue is performing at the level expected for her age in areas of math calculation and math reasoning.

Science. Sue's standardized achievement scores and classroom measures indicate that Sue is comprehending science at the level expected for her age.

Social Studies. Sue's standardized achievement scores and classroom measures indicate that Sue is performing at the level expected for her age.

Listening. Assessment results of Sue's listening comprehension were inconsistent with comprehension measured to be within the low-average range, consistent with her measured cognitive abilities. Other areas were assessed to be below the level expected for her age. Auditory discrimination and memory were below the level expected for her age.

Sample IEP Annual Goal for Basic Reading Skills. Sue will master the decoding skills required in the reading series, Spinners, at the mid-second-grade level by the end of the school year.

Sample IEP Short-term Objective. When given a list of 20 random words from the highest level first-grade reader (1.E Level) from the series Spinners, Sue will be able to decode the list with 85% accuracy at the end of the six-week reporting period.

Methods and Evaluation

Methods/Material Used	**Method of Monitoring/Assessment**
Spinners Reader Level 1.E	Curriculum-based measurement

Following is the general format for writing an educational behaviorally stated short-term objective:

When presented with ____________________, Sue will be able to ______________ with ______________% accuracy by ______________.

Check Your Understanding

Complete Activity 12.4.

ACTIVITY 12.4

Additional classroom assessment indicated that Sue has difficulty with the following sound/letter associations when asked to decode words. She also had difficulty with spelling of first-grade-level words. Using the following information, write behaviorally stated short-term objectives for these skills.

Reading Decoding Errors; Letter/Sound Association Errors: /cr/, /pl/, /dr/, /st/, /sh/, /ch/

Spelling Errors: tree, church, play, drop, drip, drank, drink, meat, meet, hand, sand, band, milk, silk, some, come, home

1. When presented with _____, Sue will be able to _____ with _____ % accuracy by ______________.
2. ____
3. ____
4. ____

Apply Your Knowledge

Using the information provided for this case, write a long-term annual goal for written expression. ______________________________
____

REEVALUATIONS

The 1997 IDEA Amendments changed the focus of the reevaluation process. In the past, students were assessed in the same areas they were assessed in for their initial evaluations (cognitive, academic, speech/language, adaptive functioning, and so on). The regulations now state that data is collected only in the areas that the team members feel they need additional information in order to make a decision regarding continued eligibility and interventions. For example, a student with a specific learning disability in math may need only additional data and/or assessment in the area of math. Rather than requiring total comprehensive evaluations every three years, reevaluations now consist of only the additional assessment determined to be needed in order to thoroughly review the case.

THINK AHEAD

The next chapter presents cases for you to analyze. The cases range from initial comprehensive evaluations to brief reevaluations. Use the suggestions presented in this chapter and previous chapters to interpret the test scores and write objectives.

EXERCISES

Part I

Match the following terms with the correct definitions.

a. educational planning
b. eligibility decisions
c. behaviorally stated objectives
d. Section 504
e. benchmarks
f. interindividual interpretation
g. intra-individual interpretation
h. projective tests
i. reevaluations

_____ 1. This level of test interpretation compares the student with the age or grade expectations according to the norm group statistics.

_____ 2. These are required by IDEA and must include how the evidence of progress will be collected and when it will be collected.

_____ 3. These are based on specific criteria included in state and federal regulations.

_____ 4. Interventions and strategies used to promote educational success.

_____ 5. This is a method of comparing a student's own strengths and weaknesses to determine a pattern of functioning that may be influencing a student's educational performance.

_____ 6. The 1997 IDEA Amendments changed this process so that less testing may be necessary for some students.

Part II

Identify the correctly written behavioral objectives by writing a plus sign (+) in front of the objective.

_____ 1. When given four addition problems, Mary will be able to find the sums with 100% accuracy by Friday.

_____ 2. To correctly solve multiplication facts by next year.

_____ 3. To read a passage with 90% accuracy and within a 2-minute time limit.

_____ 4. When presented with 10 cvc words, Joan will be able to spell the words with 90% accuracy by February 15.

_____ 5. To identify the 50 states with 100% accuracy on a map by November.

ANSWER KEY TO CHECK YOUR UNDERSTANDING

Activity 12.1

1. Overall functioning is 2 or more standard deviations below average in cognitive and adaptive functioning. In other words, the student must be subaverage in all general areas of functioning.
2. speech/language impairment
3. learning disability
4. emotional disturbance
5. standardized IQ tests, educational measures, parent interviews, classroom observations, perceptual measures
6. all disabilities

Apply Your Knowledge. The similar characteristics for these types of students are those dealing with schoolwork or productivity. Both types of attention disorder have an impact on a student's ability to complete schoolwork. Attention deficit disorder with hyperactivity may result in the student displaying more acting out types of behaviors and a high activity level.

Activity 12.2

1. sensory impairment
2. emotional/behavioral assessment

3. specific learning disability and possible visual-motor difficulties
4. mental deficiency or mental retardation
5. speech/language impairment
6. attention deficit disorder with hyperactivity

Apply Your Knowledge. The initial stage of assessment should be concerned with ruling out other possible causes for the learning or behavioral difficulties, including sensory impairments as well as difficulties with other areas of functioning, such as home or family factors.

Activity 12.3

1. Sue was experiencing learning difficulties.
2. Sue is in the low-average range of intellectual ability.
3. Sue has difficulty with auditory memory, reading decoding, comprehension, and written language skills when compared to other skills.
4. Sue seems to have relative strengths in math calculation, math reasoning, and the general knowledge areas of science, social studies, and humanities.
5. Sue's weaknesses in phonemic awareness and auditory memory appear to have caused difficulty in her ability to learn phonics, sound/symbol associations, and other skills that rely on auditory input.
6. Individualized instruction, teaching using multiple modalities and direct instruction, and advanced organizers.
7. Phoneme/grapheme awareness and short-term auditory memory and academic skills in reading and spelling.
8. Answers may vary but should include suggestions for direct instruction focusing on reading.

Apply Your Knowledge. Answers may vary.

Activity 12.4

Answers may vary but should include the elements specified in number 1.

Apply Your Knowledge. Answers may vary but should address weaknesses in written language area.

REFERENCES

Bagnato, S. (1980). The efficacy of diagnostic reports as individualized guides to prescriptive goal planning. *Exceptional Children, 46,* 554–557.

Goff, W. H. (2002). Guidelines for writing objective reports. Unpublished manuscript.

Hoy, M., & Retish, P. (1984). A comparison of two types of assessment reports. *Exceptional Children, 51,* 225–229.

Tharinger, D. J., & Lambert, N. M. (1990). The contributions of developmental psychology to school psychology. In T. Gutkin & C. R. Reynolds (Eds.), *The handbook of school psychology* (2nd ed.), pp. 74–103. New York: Wiley.

CHAPTER 13

Case Studies

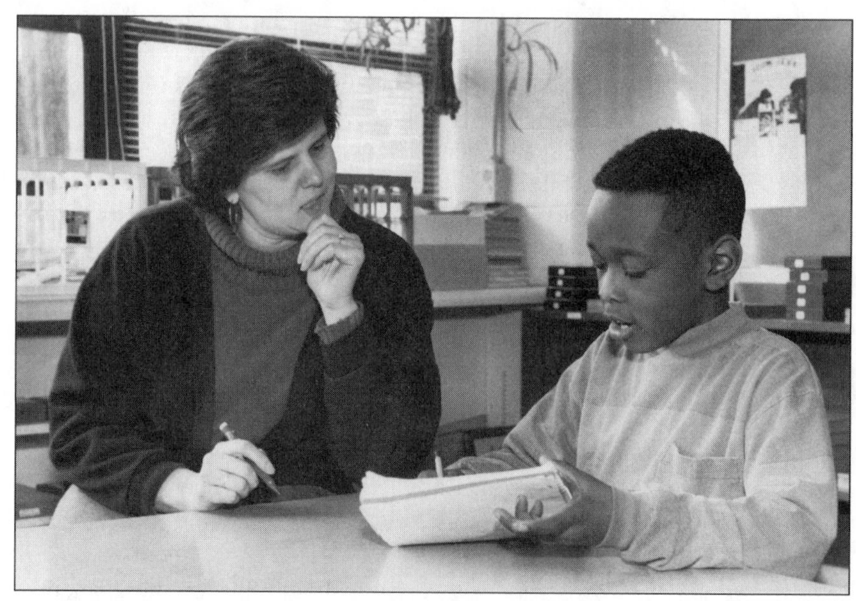

CHAPTER FOCUS

Using the skills you learned throughout this text, analyze each case presented in this chapter. These cases will prepare you to analyze and write reports for your students. This chapter contains partially completed case studies. Each case is different and requires different input to complete. Use information provided in chapter 12 to interpret the case study test results and to write short-term behaviorally stated objectives. Two cases include test results and partial interpretations. One reevaluation case includes transition issues, and one case includes a functional behavioral assessment. You will have one case that illustrates the complexities of determining eligibility for a student from a culturally and linguistically diverse background. You will be asked to interpret the educational test results, make recommendations, and write behaviorally stated short-term objectives. You may use the results of the cases to practice IEP meetings with your class in a role-play setting.

CASE 1: SHARON

Name: Sharon Williams
Date of Birth: 6-5-92
Date of Evaluation: 10-6-00
Age: 8-4
Current Grade Placement: 1.2
Examiner: Ruby Bright
Instruments: Wechsler Intelligence Scale for Children—III
Kaufman Test of Educational Achievement, Comprehensive Form
Informal curriculum-based measurement
Vineland Adaptive Behavior Scales: Interview Edition (Expanded Form)
Peabody Picture Vocabulary Test—Third Edition
Classroom observation
Parent conference

BACKGROUND AND REFERRAL INFORMATION

Sharon was referred for psychoeducational assessment by her teacher. Sharon repeated kindergarten and is currently in her second year in the first grade. Previous consideration for assessment was delayed at the parents' request. Sharon's parents felt that Sharon was developing slower than her siblings and requested that she be allowed to repeat kindergarten and, subsequently, first grade. Sharon's parents provide a warm home environment for Sharon and her five older siblings. Sharon's father works an evening shift and is consequently away from the home when Sharon attempts to complete her homework. Both parents completed the eighth grade in school.

CLASSROOM OBSERVATION AND TEACHER INTERVIEW

Although this is Sharon's second year in the first grade, Sharon was placed with a different teacher this year. Sharon's teacher reported that Sharon has difficulty with all schoolwork, although spelling short three- and four-letter words seems to be less difficult for her. Her teacher reported that Sharon does not interact much with her peers and has had some difficulty adjusting to the classroom environment. Sharon was observed on four different occasions. She was observed in the classroom setting on two occasions and one time each in the lunchroom and on the playground. When observed in the classroom, Sharon remained in her seat the entire period and did not attempt to participate in a classroom discussion. When asked questions by her teacher, she responded, "I don't know" or gave inappropriate answers (e.g., Question: "What do policemen do for us?" Answer: "My daddy and I seen one"). Sharon did not initiate interactions with her peers spontaneously, but she did respond when a peer asked her a question in the lunchroom. On the playground, Sharon tended to stay off to the side during activities rather than engaging with her peers. Her teacher reported that Sharon usually remains apart from the group or stays near the teacher while on the playground.

TEST RESULTS

Wechsler Intelligence Scale for Children—III

Verbal Subtests		***Performance Subtests***	
Information	5	Picture Completion	5
Similarities	4	Picture Arrangement	4
Arithmetic	3	Block Design	5
Vocabulary	4	Object Assembly	3
Comprehension	5	Coding	4
Digit Span	5		

Verbal IQ	65
Performance IQ	63
Full-Scale IQ	60

Kaufman Test of Educational Achievement

	Grade Equivalent	*Standard Score*	*Percentile Rank*
Subtest			
Math Applications	1.0	66	1
Reading Decoding	1.0	65	1
Spelling	1.0	73	4
Reading Comprehension	1.0	74	4
Math Computation	1.0	68	2
Composite			
Reading Composite	1.0	67	1
Math Composite	1.0	64	1
Battery Composite	1.0	65	1

Vineland Adaptive Behavior Scales:
Interview Edition (Expanded Form)

Communication	
Receptive	Adequate
Expressive	Moderately low
Written	Moderately low
Daily Living Skills	
Personal	Moderately low
Domestic	Moderately low
Community	Low
Socialization	
Interpersonal Relationships	Low
Play and Leisure Time	Moderately low
Coping Skills	Low

Peabody Picture Vocabulary Test—Third Edition

Standard score 65

Informal Curriculum-Based Assessment

On measures derived from the first-grade basal reader series, Sharon was not able to complete more than 50% of the items correctly for a set of three randomly selected reading stories. The items included both written and oral questions and both written and oral responses. Sharon recognized fewer than 30% of the words in an oral reading passage at the first-grade level. Sharon's teacher completed an assessment of phoneme awareness including tasks of phonemic analysis, synthesis, substitutions, deletions, and rhyming. Sharon was able to successfully answer 25% of the items. Sharon's teacher has adapted a parallel math series at the kindergarten level for Sharon. In the adapted math curriculum, Sharon is currently functioning with approximately 65% to 70% accuracy. Sharon was more successful on the early kindergarten level items that used concrete objects and manipulatives to solve the problems. She was able to complete 60% of those items correctly. No content area curriculum-based measurement results were obtained for science or social studies because Sharon continues with her reading, spelling, and math work during science and social studies class time.

TEST INTERPRETATIONS

Sharon's general intellectual ability was assessed using the Wechsler Intelligence Scale for Children. On this instrument, Sharon was assessed to be functioning significantly below the level expected for her age range. Her performance on the WISC was within the subaverage range of general cognitive ability. Her performance was consistent across all subtests.

The K-TEA was used as a measure of Sharon's academic ability. On this subtest, Sharon completed items in reading, spelling, and mathematics. On this instrument, Sharon was found to be significantly below the level expected for her age. Sharon answered about as many items correctly as a student at the beginning of the first grade. Informal classroom assessment measures indicate that Sharon is consistently performing at the kindergarten to first-grade level in all areas. She was able to work math problems more successfully with manipulative items.

Sharon's overall adaptive behavior is similar to that of a much younger child in most areas assessed. Her adaptive behavior in the area of receptive communication was adequate, and her adaptive behavior in all other areas ranged between moderately low to low.

Sharon's receptive vocabulary was assessed using the PPVT—III. On this instrument, she performed consistent with her measured level of cognitive ability.

SUMMARY

Sharon is functioning significantly below the level expected for her age in areas of cognitive ability, academic achievement, adaptive behavior, and receptive language. Sharon's social skills appear to be consistent with other areas assessed.

RECOMMENDATIONS

1. Sharon may benefit from receiving educational support through special education to meet her academic and social-behavioral needs.
2. Additional assessment should be completed in all areas of academics to determine the exact skills that Sharon has mastered so that the curriculum can be tailored to meet her needs.

For Case 1, add recommendations and discuss appropriate interventions in class, including determining eligibility based on data provided. Following the discussion, write annual goals and behaviorally stated short-term objectives.

Additional recommendations:

1. ____
____
2. ____
____

TEAM MEETING

Write the team's discussion and deliberations in the following space. What are the decisions for Sharon? What types of services are needed? Where will these services take place? Who will provide services? Include statements about Sharon's inclusion in the general education curriculum/environment. Include a statement about Sharon's participation in statewide assessments.

____
____
____
____
____
____
____
____
____
____

Write the present levels of performance for Sharon:

____
____
____
____
____
____

Write the annual goals for Sharon:

____
____
____
____
____
____
____
____
____

Write the short-term objectives for Sharon:

____
____
____
____
____
____
____
____
____
____
____
____

CASE 2: STEVE

Name: Steve Jones
Date of Birth: 10-6-90
Date of Evaluation: 11-15-00
Age: 11-1
Current Grade Placement: 5.3
Examiner: Tom Knowall
Instruments: Wechsler Intelligence Scale for Children—III
Woodcock Reading Mastery Tests—Revised, Form G
KeyMath—Revised, Form B
Watkins Bender-Gestalt Scoring System
Conners' Continuous Performance Test
Achenbach's Teacher Report Form, Direct Observation Form, Child Behavior Checklist (parent)
Parent conferece
Classroom work samples

BACKGROUND AND REFERRAL INFORMATION

Steve was referred for evaluation by his parents, who were concerned about Steve's academic progress. Steve was reported as always having difficulty in school, especially with reading and math. Steve appears to get along well with his peers and has not had behavioral problems in school or at home. Steve's family is supportive of taking whatever steps are necessary to improve Steve's academic performance. Steve's father reported that he too had difficulty learning to read and did not make good grades in school. Both parents completed a high school education, and the mother completed practical nurse's training. Steve's younger brother is not experiencing any learning difficulties, according to the parents.

CLASSROOM OBSERVATION AND TEACHER RATINGS

Steve's teacher reported that Steve often has difficulty decoding new words and copying material correctly from the board. Steve has been able to construct simple sentences and seems to be more able to write during independent seatwork than when copying from the board. Steve's teacher reported that Steve has been unable to keep up with the class during oral math lessons but responds better to one-to-one instruction using concrete objects or pictorial representations. Responses provided by the teacher on Achenbach's Teacher Report Form were within the clinical range for attention problems and slightly elevated for social problems.

During a classroom observation of his math period, Steve looked out the window for long periods of time and did not always seem to be attending to class or to be on task. Recordings taken on the Direct Observation Form indicated that when Steve was compared with his peers across multiple settings and times, he was off task 65% of the time—nearly 2 standard deviations more than his peers. Steve displayed the following behaviors during his off-task periods: talked to peers, looked out the window, looked through his book, looked around the room, tapped pencil repeatedly.

PARENT CONFERENCE

Steve's parents discussed Steve's current academic difficulties with the classroom teacher. His parents report that Steve sometimes gets the sequence of letters mixed up and may occasionally write a *d* as a *b* and a *p* as a *q*. They also reported that he does not like mathematics and has difficulty with writing the problems down correctly. They said that he sometimes writes the numbers down incorrectly, adds when he should subtract, and his numbers do not always end up in the correct columns. His parents added that Steve has trouble paying attention during homework time and that he tries to find other things to do rather than completing his homework.

Steve's parents stated that Steve is well liked by his peers. Steve is active in sports, although his parents said that Steve is not quite as coordinated or athletically talented as his younger brother. His parents also said that Steve has a great relationship with his family members and enjoys spending time with his younger brother and younger cousins. He is also active in community activities and in his church.

TEST RESULTS

Wechsler Intelligence Scale for Children—III

Verbal Subtests		***Performance Subtests***	
Information	10	Picture Completion	9
Similarities	9	Picture Arrangement	7
Arithmetic	7	Block Design	6
Vocabulary	9	Object Assembly	7
Comprehension	10	Coding	6
Digit Span	6		

Verbal IQ	94
Performance IQ	80
Full-Scale IQ	85

Woodcock Reading Mastery Tests—Revised, Form G

	Grade Equivalent	***Standard Score***	***Percentile Rank***
Subtest			
Visual Auditory Learning	16.4	110	80
Letter Identification	3.5	73	4
Word Identification	4.1	88	22
Word Attack	2.9	89	23
Word Comprehension	4.8	96	40
Passage Comprehension	3.5	88	22
Cluster			
Readiness Cluster	3.7	85	15
Basic Skills Cluster	3.9	88	21
Reading Comprehension	4.1	92	30
Total Reading Cluster	3.8	89	23

	Standard Score	***Percentile Rank***
Subtest		
Predictable Words	90	26
Unpredictable Words	86	17
Total Test	90	26

KeyMath—Revised, Form B

	Percentile Rank	***Standard Score***
Subtest		
Numeration	9	6
Rational Numbers	5	5
Geometry	37	9
Addition	2	4
Subtraction	5	5
Multiplication	16	7
Division	2	4
Mental Computation	9	6
Measurement	25	8
Time and Money	16	7
Estimation	50	10
Interpreting Data	37	9
Problem Solving	16	7

	Grade Equivalent	***Percentile Rank***	***Standard Score***
Area			
Basic Concepts	3.3	80	9
Operations	3.4	68	2
Applications	4.1	87	19
Total Test	3.7	78	7

Watkins Bender-Gestalt Scoring System

Steve's scores indicate that he has a moderate to severe visual-perceptual weakness. Errors included rotations, overlapping, shape of design lost, and disproportion of shapes.

Conners Continuous Performance Test

Measure	*Percentile Rank*	*Range of Performance*
Number of Hits	89.91	Mildly atypical
Number of Omissions	89.91	Mildly atypical
Number of Commissions	91.00	Mildly atypical
Hit Rate	11.41	A little slow
Hit Rate Standard Error	99.00	Markedly atypical
Variability of SEs	99.00	Markedly atypical
Attentiveness	94.48	Markedly atypical
Risk Taking	77.00	Within average
Hit Rate Block Change	93.46	Markedly atypical
Hit SE Block Change	98.36	Markedly atypical
Hit Rate ISI Change	86.35	Mildly atypical
Hit SE ISI Change	98.75	Markedly atypical

Steve's omission and commission errors were within the clinical range when compared to the sample of same-age males with attention disorders. Steve had difficulty sustaining his attention when the stimuli changed. He was within the clinical range on several measures of this instrument. The rate of hits was like that of the clinical sample. Sustained attention decreased across time.

Classroom Work Sample Analyses

Steve's work samples were collected for math class work, math homework, spelling tests, writing assignments, and reading chapter tests. All work samples used the fifth-grade level curriculum that is aligned with the state curriculum standards. Analyses indicate that Steve's math class work and homework assignments included numerous errors in aligning numerals correctly, with 60% of the incorrect answers stemming from this basic error. Steve's understanding of mathematics concepts was found to be more advanced and accurate than his ability to carry out the basic mathematics calculations and operations using pencil-and-paper format.

Steve's spelling tests, which were administered using the fifth-grade level spelling series, contained inconsistent errors indicating some emerging understanding of spelling rules and some inconsistent errors that point to a lack of mastery of basic spelling rules. His spelling included sequencing errors and some letter reversals. Steve does not have mastery of spelling words with unpredictable spellings.

The writing assignments that were analyzed included independent sentence-writing assignments. Steve has an age-appropriate command of written language, structuring simple and complex sentences that conveyed meaning and included some simple modifying words. His handwriting contained several errors and was judged to be similar to the handwriting of a much younger student. His writing assignments included numerous spelling errors.

SUMMARY

Write your summary in the space provided.

____
____
____
____
____
____
____

RECOMMENDATIONS

For Case 2, write recommendations and discuss appropriate interventions in class, including determining eligibility based on data provided.

Recommendations:

1. ____
____
2. ____
____
3. ____
____
4. ____
____

TEAM MEETING

Write the team's discussion and deliberations in the space provided. What are the decisions for Steve? What types of services are needed? Where will these services take place? Who will provide services? Include statements about Steve's inclusion in the general education curriculum/environment. Include a statement about Steve's participation in statewide assessments.

____
____
____
____
____
____
____
____
____

Write the present levels of performance for Steve:

____
____
____
____
____

Write the annual goals for Steve:

____
____
____
____
____
____
____
____

Write the short-term objectives for Steve:

____
____
____
____
____
____
____
____
____
____
____

CASE 3: ALICIA

Name: Alicia Young
Date of Birth: 2-7-98
Date of Evaluation: 4-7-01
Age: 3-2
Current Grade Placement: None
Examiner: Beth Child
Stanford-Binet IV
Vineland Adaptive Behavior Scales
Evaluation Methods: AGS Early Screening Profiles
Play evaluation
Home visit
Parent interview

BACKGROUND AND REFERRAL INFORMATION

Alicia was referred by her maternal grandmother, who is her legal guardian. Sociological information indicates that Alicia's grandmother does not know her daughter's residence at this time. Health information provided by the grandmother on the Health History Survey indicates that Alicia was born prematurely and that Alicia's mother has a long history of substance abuse. At the time of Alicia's birth, Alicia's mother was 17 years of age. Alicia has one older sibling, a 6-year-old brother who is currently receiving special education support services. Alicia's grandmother believes that Alicia is not developing at the expected pace and requested a screening evaluation to determine whether Alicia might be considered for the early childhood at-risk program.

TEST RESULTS

Stanford-Binet IV

	Standard Score
Verbal Reasoning SAS	66
Quantitative Reasoning SAS	60
Abstract/Visual Reasoning SAS	60
Short-Term Memory	62
Total Test	61

Vineland Adaptive Behavior Scales: Interview Edition (Expanded Form)

Communication	
Receptive	Moderately low
Expressive	Low
Written	Low
Daily Living Skills	
Personal	Moderately low
Domestic	Low
Community	Low
Socialization	
Interpersonal Relationships	Low
Play and Leisure Time	Moderately low
Coping Skills	Low

AGS Early Screening Profile

	Standard Score	***Percentile Rank***	***Age Equivalent***
Cognitive/Language	60	1	2-0
Motor	75	5	2-1
Self-Help/Parent	68	2	2-0

Survey Scores

Articulation	Below average/poor
Home Behavior	Average
Cognitive/Language	Below average
Motor	Below average

Play Evaluation and Home Visit

Alicia sat quietly on the carpet during the play evaluation. Alicia's grandmother was present during the first part of the evaluation. When her grandmother left the room to complete a survey, Alicia sat motionless and did not exhibit any change in her behavior following the separation. Alicia did not initiate any spontaneous use of language or communication, such as gesturing. She did not interact with the examiner when encouraged to do so and played with only one object, a stuffed toy. Her play can be best described as mechanistic and without any noticeable motive or affect exhibited. Alicia did not react to her grandmother when she returned, but joined her grandmother on the sofa when requested.

A home visit was made 2 days following the evaluation. The home environment was clean, and several educational toys and materials were available. All interactions between the grandmother and Alicia were initiated by the grandmother. Alicia displayed very flat affect during both the home visit and the evaluation. Alicia's grandmother stated that the only reaction she sees from Alicia is when it is time to eat. She described Alicia's appetite as fair because Alicia likes only a few types of food. When she is given something new to taste, she usually spits it out after she tries it.

Parent Interview

When Alicia's grandmother was asked to list her priorities and concerns for Alicia, she expressed the need for some support to help her toilet train Alicia, improve Alicia's speech development, and improve Alicia's self-help skills, such as dressing and washing her face. Alicia's grandmother believes that Alicia's motor skills are different from her grandson's. She believes that Alicia is somewhat clumsy and too dependent on her for routine activities that other 3-year-olds are learning to do, such as self-feed with a spoon.

Alicia's grandmother reported that she has been able to access monetary assistance using public resources including Medicaid for Alicia's medical needs and transportation to and from the community agencies for Alicia's care. She reported that Alicia's needs are primarily being met within the home environment, but expressed desire for additional assistance in training Alicia within the home environment and in managing her behavior.

SUMMARY

Write your summary for Alicia's assessment data in the space provided.

____

____

____

____

____

____

____

RECOMMENDATIONS

For Case 3, write recommendations, discussing appropriate interventions including interventions within the home and between the home and school environment. For this case, you must first determine how children of Alicia's age are served in your state and local community. Following the discussion, complete the "Team Meeting" section with members in your class.

Recommendations:

1. ____
   ____
2. ____
   ____
3. ____
   ____
4. ____
   ____

TEAM MEETING

Write the team's discussion and deliberations in the space provided. What are the decisions for Alicia? What types of services are needed? Where will these services take place? Who will provide services? Include statements about Alicia's inclusion activites with children who do not have disabilities. After discussing the results with members in your class, complete the IEP.

IEP

Write the present levels of development for Alicia in the following areas: physical development, cognitive development, social/emotional development, and adaptive development.

Write annual goals for Alicia:

Write the short-term objectives or benchmarks for Alicia:

CASE 4: TRAVIS

Name: Travis Shores
Date of Birth: 8-9-84
Date of Evaluation: 10-28-02
Age: 18-2
Examiner: Mark House
Instruments: Wechsler Adult Intelligence Scale—Third Edition
Conners' Continuous Performance Test
Woodcock Language Proficiency Battery—Revised
Clinical interview

BACKGROUND AND REFERRAL INFORMATION

Travis is currently enrolled as a freshman in Anywhere Community College and reported having difficulty with study habits, time management, spelling skills, writing skills, reading comprehension, and grammar. He also expressed concern about his ability to master a foreign language at the college level. Travis said that he has difficulty with attention span, finishing tasks, test taking, and listening in class. He reported that he gets distracted easily in lecture classes.

Travis reported that he has no history of testing for learning or attention difficulties. He stated that he had a difficult time in high school during his sophomore year but then felt that things were better for him during his junior and senior years. Travis attempted to take Spanish this semester and decided to drop the course because of his inability to make the progress he expected. He is taking economics and believes he is doing well in that class.

TEST RESULTS

Wechsler Adult Intelligence Scale—Third Edition

Verbal Tests		*Performance Tests*	
Vocabulary	9	Picture Completion	12
Similarities	11	Digit Symbol-Coding	10
Arithmetic	8	Block Design	14
Digit Span	8	Matrix Reasoning	13
Information	8	Picture Arrangement	9
Comprehension	12		

Verbal IQ	95
Performance IQ	110
Full-Scale IQ	96

Conners Continuous Performance Test

Measure	***Percentile***	***Range of Performance***
Number of Hits	99.59	Markedly atypical
Number of Omissions	94.86	Markedly atypical
Number of Commissions	50.90	Within average range
Hit Rate	21.46	Within average range
Hit Rate Standard Error	93.44	Markedly atypical
Variability of SES	77.87	Within average range
Attentiveness	84.42	Mildly atypical
Risk Taking	99.00	Markedly atypical
Hit RT Block Change	95.96	Markedly atypical
Hit SE Block Change	82.60	Within average range
Hit RT ISI Change	80.90	Within average range
Hit SE ISI Change	76.78	Within average range

Travis performed with some inconsistency on the Conners Continuous Performance Test. He performed like students his age with attention problems on several indices. He was within the average range on other indices. His performance indicates that he may have difficulty sustaining attention on some tasks but not others. His performance showed some evidence of an impulsive responding pattern.

Woodcock Language Proficiency Battery—Revised

	Standard Score	***Percentile Rank***	***Grade Equivalent***
Subtest			
Memory for Sentences	95	38	10.2
Picture Vocabulary	85	15	9.3
Oral Vocabulary	86	17	9.6
Listening Comprehension	103	57	14.2
Verbal Analogies	81	10	6.2
Letter-Word Identification	96	39	11.9
Passage Comprehension	90	25	10.0
Word Attack	103	57	14.4
Dictation	90	25	9.8
Writing Samples	136	99	16.9
Proofing	70	2	5.0
Writing Fluency	88	22	9.5
Punctuation	71	3	5.7
Spelling	92	29	10.5
Usage	86	18	8.8

Cluster Scores			
Oral Language	88	22	9.6
Broad Reading	93	31	10.9
Basic Reading Skills	99	47	12.5
Broad Written Language	107	67	16.0
Basic Writing Skills	77	6	7.2
Written Expression	110	74	16.1

Travis is currently functioning within the average range of intellectual ability. A significant discrepancy exists between his verbal IQ score of 95 and his performance IQ score of 110. This indicates that Travis is able to use nonverbal strategies rather than verbal strategies for most problem solving. This discrepancy also indicates that Travis's full-scale IQ score may not be representative of his true ability. Travis's performance IQ score may better represent his true cognitive potential. Analysis of individual subtests and factors also indicates strengths and weaknesses in processing. Travis demonstrated significant strength in the ability to comprehend common verbal concepts. He also demonstrated significant strength in visual perceptual organization of nonverbal stimuli. His performance on this instrument indicates relative weakness in short-term auditory memory and in the ability to remain free from distraction. Travis appears to have relative weakness in long-term retention of factual information.

Travis was administered the Conners Continuous Performance Test to determine whether he has significant difficulty maintaining sustained focused attention. On this instrument, the more measures found to be within the atypical range, the greater the likelihood that attention problems exist. On this test, Travis gave slower responses at the end than at the beginning of the test, indicating an ability to sustain attention. He made a larger number of omission errors, indicating poor attention to the task. He was highly inconsistent in responding, indicating inattentiveness as measured by standard error. Numerous indices strongly suggest that Travis has attention problems according to his performance on this test.

SUMMARY

Write your summary for the assessment data in the space provided.

____

____

____

____

____

____

RECOMMENDATIONS

For Case 4, write recommendations, discuss appropriate interventions in class and for studying outside of class. Include accommodations for the college environment based on data provided. Should Travis be referred for additional services in any other agencies or with other professionals? What considerations should be discussed with Travis regarding his future plans and course of study at the college level? What issues regarding his functioning as an adult should be considered?

Recommendations:

1. ____
2. ____
3. ____
4. ____

CASE 5: ERIC

Name: Eric Parks
Date of Birth: 1-15-1987
Date of Evaluation: 10-22-2004
Age: 17-9
Current Grade Placement: 11.3
Examiner: James Perfection
Instruments: Wechsler Adult Intelligence Scale—III
Kaufman Functional Academic Skills Test
Transition Planning Inventory
Student interview
Parent interview

BACKGROUND AND REFERRAL INFORMATION

Eric has been served with the assistance of special education services since he was a third-grade student. He has received services for educational support designed to assist students within the mild range of mental retardation. Eric was served in a special education self-contained classroom in grades 3 through 6. His placement was subsequently changed to the general classroom setting for all subject areas except reading, which he received in the resource room setting. He received his instruction in mathematics in the basic remedial mathematics program until he was in the eighth grade. During his eighth-grade year he began receiving his mathematics instruction in the resource room as well. His educational program has remained fairly consistent with the addition of vocational awareness training and vocational classes during the previous 2 years of school.

Eric is now scheduled for his triennial reevaluation. The team members, including Eric's parents, met to determine what data would be needed for the reevaluation. At that time, Eric's parents expressed the desire to have Eric's intellectual ability reevaluated using the adult form of the Wechsler Intelligence Scales. They felt that having the results on the adult measure may be useful because Eric plans to leave the school environment. His parents also expressed concerns about Eric's ability to function independently. The team members agreed that the traditional standardized norm-referenced testing was not needed at this time. They also felt that repeating a traditional adaptive behavior inventory was not needed but would rather get more information about Eric's ability to make a successful transition.

The team members decided to gather information that would be useful for transition planning and to provide documentation of Eric's skills and abilities that he may find useful in later years. The assessment sessions, including interview sessions with Eric and his parents, were scheduled. His parents agreed that Eric would also benefit from the standard assessment provided by the vocational center to determine Eric's skills in the mechanics program in which he is enrolled. That documentation will be included in Eric's file for future reference.

The data collected during this evaluation consists of Eric's cognitive assessment, the results of the TPI indicating his readiness for transition, subsequent planning that will take place as a result of this assessment, and the results of his functional academic abilities testing using the K-FAST.

TEST RESULTS

Wechsler Adult Intelligence Scale—Third Edition

Verbal Tests		*Performance Tests*	
Vocabulary	5	Picture Completion	7
Similarities	5	Digit Symbol-Coding	6
Arithmetic	4	Block Design	6
Digit Span	4	Matrix Reasoning	5
Information	4	Picture Arrangement	6
Comprehension	5		

Verbal IQ	59
Performance IQ	63
Full-Scale IQ	61

Kaufman Functional Academic Skills Test

	Standard Score	*Percentile Rank*
Subtest		
Arithmetic	74 (67–84)	4
Reading	69 (62–80)	2
Functional Academic Skills Composite	71 (66–78)	3

Transitional Planning Inventory

Areas of Need Indicated by Student (Completed with assistance of teacher)

Employment
How to get a job
General job skills and work attitude

Further Education and Training
How to gain entry into a community employment training program

Daily Living
How to locate a place to live
How to set up living arrangements
How to manage money

Community Participation
Understanding basic legal rights
How to make legal decisions
How to locate community resources
How to use community resources
How to obtain financial assistance

Eric's parents agreed with the areas of need identified by Eric and added the following concerns:

Self-Determination
How to recognize and accept his own strengths and limitations
How to express his ideas and feelings appropriately
How to set personal goals

Interpersonal Relationships
How to get along with supervisor

Parent Interview

Eric's parents met with his teacher and the school counselor for a conference about Eric's future plans. His parents reported that Eric gets along very well with all family members and with the other children in the neighborhood. They stated that they are allowing Eric to participate in the driver's education course at school. They have not decided if Eric will be able to take his driver's test and stated they are waiting to hear from the instructor regarding Eric's ability to drive. Eric's father said that he has taken Eric out for some practice runs in a neighborhood parking lot on Sundays when there is no traffic in the area.

Eric's parents expressed concern about Eric's independence and were especially eager to learn ways to assist Eric in learning independent living skills. His mother reported that she has made attempts to engage Eric in learning how to cook but that he is not really interested. She said that he would live on pizza if the choice were left to him.

Eric's parents said that they envision Eric living in his own apartment someday and marrying. They hope that he will be able to have a steady job and be able to support a family. They also stated that Eric currently has a crush on a neighborhood girl who lives on their block, but that she is not very interested in Eric. This has been a little difficult for Eric to understand, but his father reported that Eric seems to be feeling better about this issue.

Mr. and Mrs. Parks are interested in Eric continuing with vocational training program as long as possible. They also reported that they will assist Eric financially if needed, to complete enough training so that he can maintain a job. They were interested in learning of outside community agencies where they could go for assistance after Eric leaves the public school setting.

Interview with Eric

Eric was excited to come into the office for his interview. He said that his parents had told him about their interview the day before and now it was his turn to talk about getting a job and an apartment someday.

Eric said that his favorite part of school is when he goes to the vocational training center in the afternoons. He likes learning about the mechanical aspects of cars. He also reported that the last activity of the day is his drivers education class. He hopes to be able to pass his driving test by the end of the school year but remarked that he may not be able to do that until next year.

Eric stated that he wants to get an apartment someday when he is older, "like when I am about 40." He said that he enjoys living with his parents and he enjoys living in his neighborhood. He stated that even if he moved into an apartment, he wanted to remain in the area where he currently lives. He said that he knows his way around and wants to live close to his friends.

Eric reported that he wants to learn more about how to get a job so that when his training is completed, he can start to work right away. He said he would like to save his money to buy a car. He said that he is not really anxious to live by himself and that he doesn't know much about buying groceries or doing laundry. He said his mother usually helps him with these chores.

SUMMARY

Write your summary for the assessment of Eric in the space provided.

RECOMMENDATIONS

For Case 5, write recommendations, discussing appropriate interventions for educational planning and transition planning. For this case, it would be helpful for you to identify postsecondary training programs in your area as well as the types of agencies that might be useful for Eric.

Recommendations:

1.
2.
3.
4.

TEAM MEETING

Write the team's discussion and deliberations for Eric's transition. What types of services are needed? Where will these services take place? Who will provide services? After discussing the results with members in your class, complete the transition plan as part of the IEP.

IEP

Write the present levels of performance identified in this reevaluation.

____

Write the annual goals for Eric:

____

Write the short-term objectives for Eric:

____

CASE 6: BURT

Name: Burt Down
Date of Birth: 5-10-1989
Date of Evaluation: 11-27-2003
Age: 14-7
Current Grade Placement: 9.3
Examiner: Phil Mood
Instruments: Selected subtests of the Woodcock-Johnson III
Math Work Samples
Behavior Assessment System for Children: Self-Report (ages 12–18)
Behavioral Observation Data
Functional Behavioral Assessment

BACKGROUND AND REFERRAL INFORMATION

Burt was referred for a reevaluation due to recent behavioral difficulties. Burt has been receiving special education support for specific learning disabilities since he was in the fourth grade. He receives his English instruction in the resource room setting. He has previously been found to have attention deficit hyperactivity disorder and has been prescribed medication as part of his treatment for this disorder. His parents and teachers agree that his behavior improves when he complies with his medication treatment. His parents also acknowledge that things have been rough at home lately. They told the team that they have not been able to manage Burt's behavior within the home and attribute this to "just his age." They report that Burt has been staying out later than he is supposed to, and that he argues with them about school and homework. They said that Burt tells them he is old enough to make up his own mind about curfews and selecting his friends. Mr. and Mrs. Down said they do not approve of Burt's friends.

Burt was assessed last year for his regular triennial evaluation. His cognitive ability has been assessed to be within the average range (Full-Scale IQ 108, Verbal IQ 98, Performance IQ 110). Due to recent difficulties in mathematics and his behavioral difficulties, another reevaluation was requested. The team members, including Burt's parents, met to discuss possible data needed to analyze the current areas of difficulty. All members agreed that a behavioral analysis and other measures of behavior would be collected. In addition, selected subtests of the WJ III and math work samples would be analyzed.

TEST RESULTS

Woodcock-Johnson III Tests of Achievement

Clusters	***PR***	***SS (90% BAND)***	***GE***
Broad Math	6	77 (73–81)	4.7
Math Calculation Skills	7	78 (72–84)	5.2
Math Reasoning	16	85 (80–90)	5.3
Subtest			
Calculation	15	84 (76–93)	5.7
Math Fluency	3	71 (67–75)	4.2
Applied Problems	8	79 (74–84)	4.1
Quantitative Concepts	40	96 (89–104)	7.5

Math Work Samples

An analysis of Burt's math class work indicates that he attempted to answer 80% of the problems he was assigned in class; however, he successfully completed 35% of the problems he was given to complete in class. His errors included miscalculations, errors of alignment, errors of wrong applications in story problems (adding when he should subtract), and skipping steps needed in multiple-step problems. Eric was not able to complete an entire math assignment, working only about 75% to 85% of the problems before he either quit or ran out of time.

Burt's homework assignments did not show much evidence of his understanding the tasks presented. He turned in only 6 of 15 assignments since the beginning of the school year, and he successfully completed 38% of the problems assigned. His errors on homework assignments were consistent with the errors made on his class work assignments.

Behavioral Assessments

Behavioral Assessment System for Children: Self-Report (ages 12–18)

Rank*	***T-Score****	***Percentile***
Clinical Profile		
Attitude to School	68	95
Attitude to Teachers	68	94
Sensation Seeking	67	95
School Maladjustment Composite	72	99
Atypicality	52	65
Locus of Control	74	98
Somatization	50	62
Social Stress	64	94
Anxiety	49	51
Clinical Maladjustment Composite	60	81
Depression	85	99
Sense of Inadequacy	83	99

(*On the clinical scales, a *T*-score greater than 70 is considered to be the area of caution for the student's current behaviors. For percentile ranks on clinical scales, the higher the score, the more significant. A percentile rank of 50 is average.)

Rank*	***T-Score****	***Percentile***
Adaptive Profile		
Relations with Parents	12	1
Interpersonal Relations	43	18
Self-Esteem	26	4
Self-Reliance	39	15
Personal Adjustment Composite	23	2

(*High scores on the adaptive scales indicate high levels of adaptive skills.)

On the BASC, Burt endorsed critical items indicating that he feels he has trouble controlling his behavior, he feels he does not do anything right, he

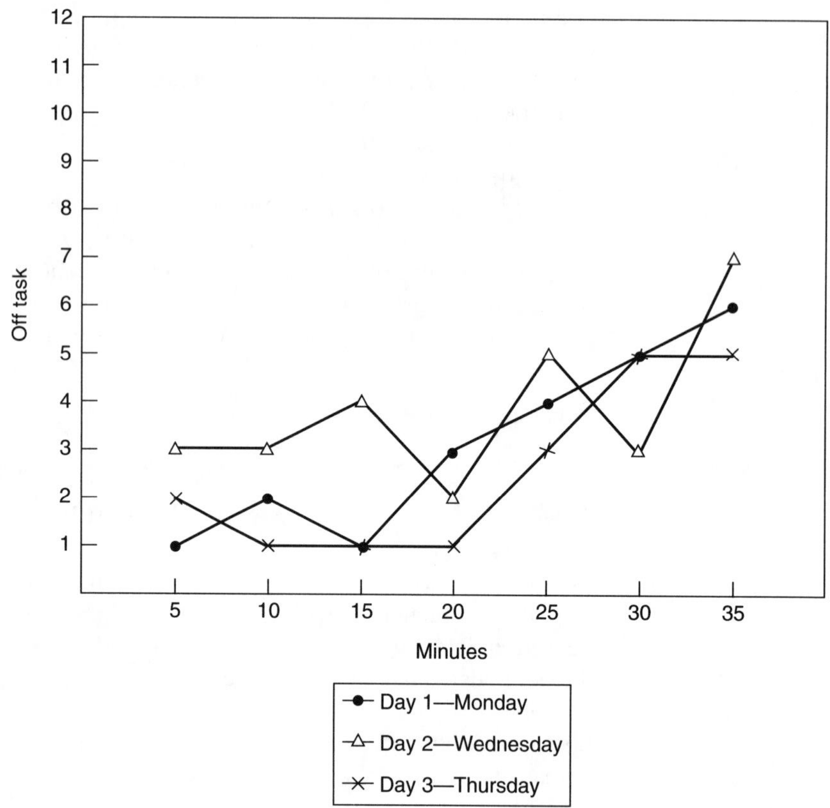

Figure 13.1 Frequency of off-task behavior in Math class (Burt).

thinks no one understands him, he doesn't care anymore, he feels that nothing goes his way and that no one listens to him.

Figure 13.1 illustrates the behavioral observations for Burt during math class for "off-task" behavior across three observation periods.

To compare Burt's behavior in additional settings, he was observed in his resource room, where he receives English instruction (Figure 13.2), and in his Art class (Figure 13.3).

Functional Behavioral Interview

Following the observations sessions, Burt was interviewed by the school psychologist to determine Burt's perspective on his recent behavioral difficulties and to determine the function of these behaviors. Burt told the psychologist he knows that he is not doing well in math and that he just can't seem to keep up. He stated that he was able to do math last year and felt

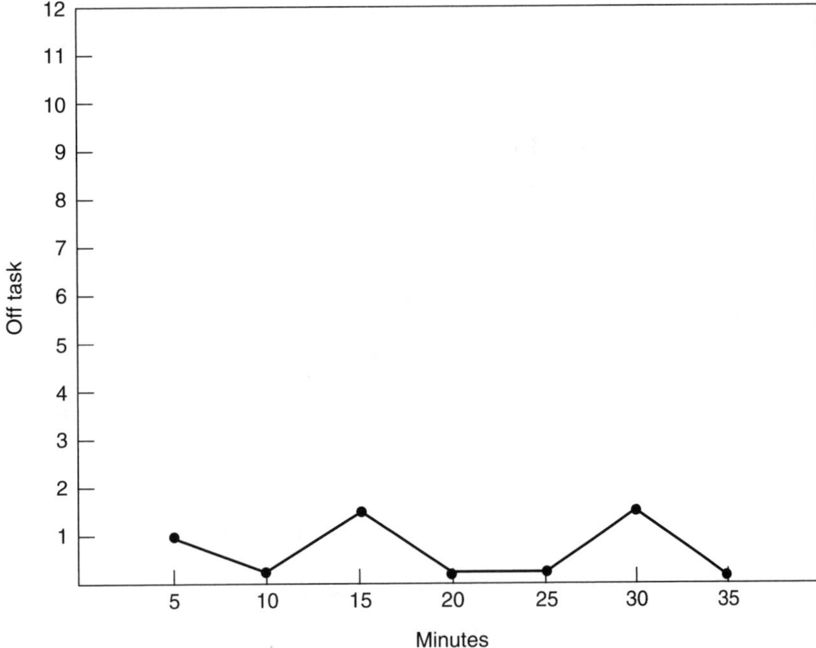

Figure 13.2 Frequency of off-task behavior in English class (Burt).

his teacher was "nicer to me." He stated that his teacher last year offered to stay after school and help him so he could complete his homework assignments. Burt reported that he feels lost in math so he gets bored and wants to do something else. He figures there is no use in trying to do the work, because "I just get Fs anyway."

When Burt is in his other classes, he says he can get along just fine. He says he has lots of friends in his other classes who help him with things he doesn't understand.

Burt reported that his parents have been yelling at him about his grades in math. He said his parents try to help him, but he still doesn't get it and so they get even more upset. He stated that he has been avoiding going home, because "I know they will yell at me some more."

When asked about his medication, Burt said that he hasn't been taking it as prescribed. He said he doesn't like the way he feels when he takes it even though he agreed that he can pay attention better in school when he takes his medicine. He reported that some of his friends found out that he has to take medicine and that they began calling him names like "hyper" and "dummy." He said that he doesn't feel as good about himself or his relationships with his peers as he did last year.

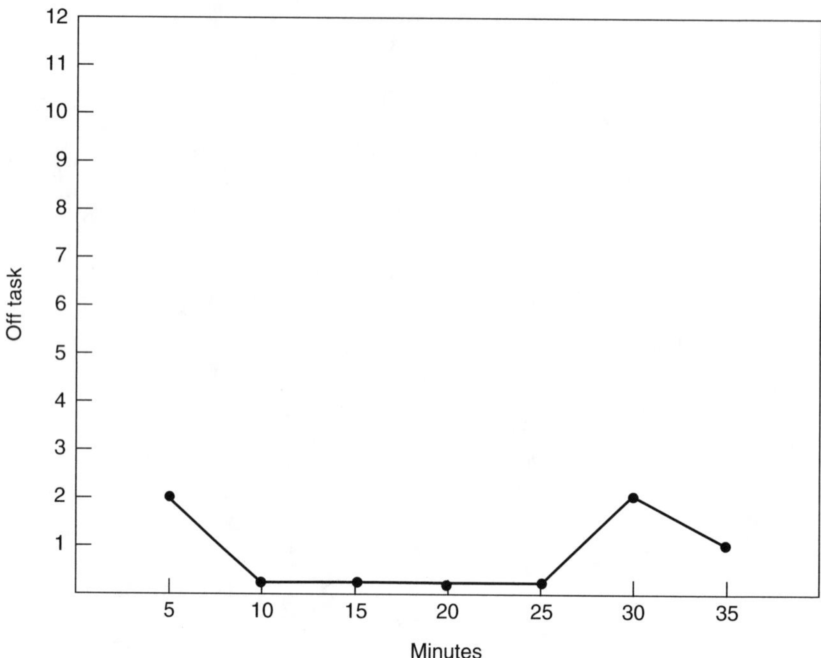

Figure 13.3 Frequency of off-task behavior in Art class (Burt).

SUMMARY

Write your summary in the space provided.

____
____
____
____
____
____
____
____
____

RECOMMENDATIONS

For Case 6, write recommendations, discussing appropriate interventions in class including determining any changes in setting or any needed additional assessment information based on data provided.

Recommendations:

1. ____
   ____
2. ____
   ____
3. ____
   ____
4. ____
   ____

TEAM MEETING

Write the team's discussion and deliberations in the space provided. What are the decisions for Burt? What types of services are needed? Where will these services take place? Who will provide services?

____
____
____
____
____
____
____
____
____
____

Write the present levels of performance for Burt:

____
____
____
____
____

Write behavioral objectives for Burt that will be the basis of the behavioral intervention plan for Burt:

____
____
____
____
____
____
____

Write the short-term objectives for Burt relating to the areas assessed in the reevaluation:

____
____
____
____
____
____
____
____

CASE 7: LUPITA

Name: Lupita Garcia
Date of Birth: 2-1-1996
Date of Evaluation: 4-6-2004
Age: 8-2
Grade Placement: 2.8

BACKGROUND AND REFERRAL INFORMATION

Lupita is currently enrolled in the second grade at Wonderful Elementary School. She has been attending this school since October of the current school year. There was a delay in receiving her school records from another state and therefore, it was not known for several months that Lupita had been in the referral process at her previous school. School records from her previous school indicate that she has attended three schools since she entered kindergarten about 3 years ago.

Lupita lives with her mother and father, who until recently were migrant farm workers. Her parents now have full-time employment in the city and plan to make this community their home. Lupita has two older sisters.

Information provided through a home study reveals that all family members speak both English and Spanish. Lupita's mother, who was born in the United States, reported that she learned English while growing up because in school she was not allowed to speak Spanish as her parents did at home. Lupita's father was raised in Mexico, where he attended school until he was 12 years of age. At that time, he stopped going to school in order to work the field with his parents. Mr. Garcia reported that his English is not as good as his wife's, and therefore she helps Lupita with all of her homework assignments.

Mrs. Garcia said that she has taught her children to speak English first because she knew that would be important for school. Although she has emphasized English in the home, Mr. Garcia usually speaks to the children in Spanish. Mr. Garcia is very proud of his daughter's ability to use English so well because he often must rely on his daughters to translate for him when they are in the community.

Lupita's reason for referral is due to academic difficulties in learning to read. The child study team met four times to plan and implement strategies for intervention in an attempt to assist Lupita. Lupita has been receiving additional assistance from the school system's bilingual program. As part of the referral process, Mrs. Garcia completed a home language assessment. The results of that assessment indicate that while both languages are spoken in the home, English is the primary language and is used in approximately 75% of communication within the home. Despite these findings, the team members were not certain about Lupita's mastery of English, particularly at the level required for academic learning and especially in the area of reading.

Following the last meeting of the team, the members agreed, at the urging of Mrs. Garcia, to complete a comprehensive evaluation.

TEST RESULTS

Wechsler Intelligence Scale for Children—III

Verbal Subtests		*Performance Subtests*	
Information	9	Picture Completion	9
Similarities	7	Picture Arrangement	10
Arithmetic	8	Block Design	9
Vocabulary	6	Object Assembly	10
Comprehension	6	Coding	11
Digit Span	8		

Verbal IQ	80
Performance IQ	95
Full-Scale IQ	88

Kaufman Assessment Battery for Children

Mental Processing Subtests	*Standard Score*	*Percentile Rank*
Face Recognition	100	50
Hand Movements	101	53
Gestalt Closure	101	53
Number Recall	95	37
Triangles	105	63
Word Order	90	25
Matrix Analogies	100	50
Spatial Memory	98	45
Photo Series	106	66
Mental Processing Composite	100	50

Batteria Woodcock-Munoz-Revisada

Pruebas de aprovechamiento-Revisada	***Standard Score***	***Percentile Rank***	***Grade Equivalent***
Identificacion de letras y palabras (Letter-Word Identification)	68	2	1.0
Comprension de textos (Passage Comprehension)	67	1	1.0
Calculo (Calculation)	70	2	1.2
Problemas aplicados (Applied Problems)	71	3	1.1
Dictado (Dictation)	61	.5	K.2
Muestras de redaccion (Writing Samples)	70	2	1.2
Amplia lectura (Broad Reading)	60	.4	K.1
Amplias matematicas (Broad Math)	70	2	1.2
Amplio lenguaje escrito (Broad Written Language)	68	2	1.0

Woodcock-Johnson Tests of Achievement—III

Cluster	***PR***	***SS (90% BAND)***	***GE***
Verbal Ability	16	85 (76–94)	1.5
Oral Language (Ext)	36	95 (88–101)	2.0
Oral Expression	68	107 (98–117)	3.6
Listening Comprehension	21	88 (82–94)	1.3
Total Achievement	1	65 (61–68)	1.2
Broad Reading	0.1	54 (50–58)	<K.8
Broad Math	64	105 (99–112)	3.0
Broad Written Lang	1	65 (58–72)	1.0
Basic Reading Skills	1	67 (64–71)	1.1
Reading Comp	3	71 (66–76)	1.1
Math Calculating Skills	93	122 (115–129)	4.3
Math Reasoning	5	75 (70–80)	1.0
Basic Writing Skills	2	70 (64–75)	<1.2
Written Expression	22	88 (79–98)	2.0
Academic Skills	1	67 (63–71)	1.0
Academic Fluency	10	81 (76–86)	1.7
Academic Applications	7	78 (74–83)	1.2
Academic Knowledge	47	99 (92–106)	2.8
Phoneme/Grapheme Knowledge	8	79 (74–84)	1.3

Subtest			
Verbal Comprehension	16	85 (76–94)	1.5
Visual-Auditory Learning	<0.1	44 (21–66)	<K.0
Letter-Word Identification	<0.1	52 (48–57)	K.4
Reading Fluency	5	75 (69–81)	1.3
Story Recall	19	87 (69–104)	1.0
Understanding Directions	7	78 (72–84)	<K.0
Calculation	99	133 (124–143)	5.7
Math Fluency	20	87 (81–94)	1.9
Spelling	<0.1	53 (45–61)	K.2
Writing Fluency	29	92 (82–101)	2.3
Passage Comprehension	1	63 (56–70)	K.7
Applied Problems	26	90 (84–97)	1.8
Writing Samples	24	90 (77–102)	1.7
Word Attack	25	90 (84–95)	1.8
Picture Vocabulary	84	115 (105–125)	4.9
Oral Comprehension	51	100 (92–109)	2.6
Editing	35	94 (87–101)	2.4
Reading Vocabulary	5	75 (60–81)	1.3
Quantitative Concepts	0.3	87 (81–94)	1.9
Academic Knowledge	47	99 (92–106)	2.8
Spelling of Sounds	0.4	60 (50–71)	K.1
Sound Awareness	0.4	60 (52–67)	<K.0
Punctuation & Capitals	<0.1	33 (19–47)	<K.0

Due to the difference between the WISC—III scores and the K-ABC, the items that Lupita missed on the WISC—III were administered using a cognitive potential strategy including suspending time on timed items, presenting vocabulary items in context, and allowing paper and pencil for the arithmetic subtest. The results of estimated potential IQ scores in a nonstandardized administration format are presented next.

Wechsler Intelligence Scale for Children—III (Nonstandardized Administration)

Verbal Subtests		***Performance Subtests***	
Information	10	Picture Completion	11
Similarities	9	Picture Arrangement	11
Arithmetic	11	Block Design	9
Vocabulary	10	Object Assembly	10
Comprehension	8		

Verbal IQ	99 (estimated potential)
Performance IQ	102 (estimated potential)
Full-Scale IQ	100 (estimated potential)

Lupita's general intellectual ability was found to be within the average range on both the K-ABC and the WISC—III nonstandardized administration. When assessed using the WISC—III in the standard administration format, Lupita's scores were in the average to low-average range with lower scores on language-related items. When allowing for the difference in language mastery for items on the WISC—III by using a nonstandardized format, Lupita's scores were consistently in the average range with no discrepancies in abilities noted.

On measures assessing language proficiency, Lupita scored significantly better on the English version of subtests assessing oral language and verbal ability than she did on the Spanish version (Batteria Woodcock de Proficiencia en el Idioma). This provides evidence of higher level skills in the English language than she has in Spanish.

On measures of academic achievement, Lupita was found to be achieving better than expected for her age on math calculations and picture vocabulary. She performed within the range expected for her age in oral language, oral expression, broad math, academic knowledge, oral comprehension, editing, applied mathematics, writing samples, and reading vocabulary. Lupita's areas of weakness are primarily in the areas of reading, spelling, and sound awareness.

Continue to write additional interpretations of Lupita's academic achievement performance on achievement testing here:

____
____
____
____
____
____
____
____

SUMMARY

Write your summary in the space provided.

____
____
____
____
____
____
____
____

RECOMMENDATIONS

For Case 7, write recommendations, discussing appropriate interventions in class including determining eligibility based on data provided. To reach the best solutions, you will need to review information regarding the assessment of students from culturally and linguistically diverse backgrounds. You will also need to know any specific state regulations regarding the determination of learning disabilities in students from linguistically diverse backgrounds.

Recommendations:

1. ______________________________
____
2. ______________________________
____
3. ______________________________
____
4. ______________________________
____

TEAM MEETING

Write the team's discussion and deliberations in the space provided. What are the decisions for Lupita? What types of services are needed? Where will these services take place? Who will provide services? Include statements about Lupita's inclusion in the general education curriculum/environment. Include a statement about Lupita's participation in statewide assessments.

____
____
____
____
____
____
____
____
____
____

Write the present levels of performance for Lupita:

____
____
____
____

Write the annual goals for Lupita:

____

Write the short-term objectives for Lupita:

____

THINK AHEAD

As you continue with your professional goals, think about the most effective methods for assessing your students' needs and providing appropriate instruction. Remember that effective teaching includes keeping informed of new methods of assessment and teaching.

AUTHOR INDEX

Abramowitz, E., 239
Achenbach, T. M., 347, 349, 351, 354, 366, 367
Ackerman, T., 239
Albers, C. A., 301, 366
Albin, R. W., 336, 337
Alff, M., 21, 21*n*
Algozzine, B., 11, 27, 98, 383
Allinder, R. M., 238, 302
Alvarado, C. G., 406
Ambrose, R., 326
American Psychiatric Association, 353
American Psychological Association, 23, 79
Anastasi, A., 154, 166, 200
Anastopoulos, A. D., 367
Anderson, C. L., 465
Anderson, M. G., 30
Andrews, T. J., 11
Angelopoulos, J., 5
Anselmo, M., 5
Archbald, D. A., 324
Armstrong, H., 239
Armstrong, K., 368
Auer, C., 443

Bagley, R., 11–12
Bagnato, S. J., 367, 491
Bailey, D. B., 443, 456
Baker, S. R., 302, 466, 472
Balla, D. A., 416, 417, 419, 420, 421, 422
Barakat, L. P., 368
Barbour, J. D., 366
Barbour, N. E., 326
Bard, E. M., 335
Bardos, A. N., 236, 237, 238, 360, 361–362
Barkley, R. A., 369, 457
Barnes, W., 315
Barnett, D. W., 70, 442, 458
Barringer, K., 74
Bayley, D. B., 445
Beebe, M. F., 76
Beer, J., 296
Bell, S. H., 442
Bellak, L., 362, 363
Bellak, S. S., 362, 363
Bender, W., 413
Bennett, R., 74, 99, 290
Bennett, T., 78
Benowitz, S., 74
Bentz, J., 301, 302
Berdine, W., 466
Berger, D., 239
Bersoff, D. N., 383
Bertsch, K., 365
Betz, N., 139
Bocian, K. M., 76
Bolen, L. M., 237
Bonstrom, O., 17
Borg, W., 99
Bos, C., 70
Boyajian, A. E., 366
Boyer-Stephens, A., 21, 21*n*
Braden, J. P., 184
Bradley, R., 336
Bradley-Johnson, S., 237, 415
Brantlinger, E., 70
Braswell, L. A., 238
Brazelton, T., 445
Brigance, A. H., 292, 293, 452
Brigham, F. J., 185
Brigham, M. S. P., 185
Brotherson, M. J., 466
Brown, L., 349, 352, 382, 425
Brown, V. L., 262, 279
Brozovich, R., 369
Bruininks, R. H., 413, 449, 450
Bryant, B. R., 155, 270
Buchanan, M., 413
Budoff, M., 79
Burger, D. L., 74
Burger, S. E., 74
Burnett, J., 31
Burns, P. C., 315–316, 317
Busse, R. T., 349
Butterworth, J., 301

Cahan, S., 150
Calhoun, M., 26, 27
Callaway, B., 281
Campbell, E., 296
Canivez, G. L., 411, 412
Canter, A. S., 301, 380
Cantwell, D. P., 368
Carey, K. T., 458
Carey, S. P., 301–302
Carroll, J. B., 411
Carter, J., 9
Casey, A., 14, 17
Cattell, 402
Chalfant, J. C., 17
Chin-Chance, S., 189
Chissom, B., 74
Christenson, S., 11, 14
Cicchetti, D. V., 416, 417, 419, 420, 421, 422, 449
Clarizio, H. F., 12, 302, 303, 369
Clark, D., 337
Clark, G. M., 467, 469, 471
Clark, H. T., 76
Cohen, L. G., 455, 456, 457
Cohen, M. J., 411

Cohen, P., 78
Colarusso, R. P., 236
Cole, J. C., 182–183, 238
Cole, N., 154
Connelly, J., 201, 202
Conners, C. K., 364, 365, 369
Connolly, A. J., 147, 251, 252, 255, 256, 259, 260, 261, 262, 291
Connors, C. K., 352
Conroy, M. A., 337
Cornell, D. G., 31
Cowan, P. J., 70, 71*n*
Cronin, M. E., 262
Crowley, S. L., 368
Crumbacker, M., 202, 238
Cummings, M. A., 411
Curry, L., 70

Daley, C. E., 411
D'Alonzo, B., 182–183
Daly, E. J., 9, 337
Darch, C., 281
Das, 402
Daub, D., 236
Davis, L. B., 302
Davis, W., 98
Daw, J. L., 239
DeGraff, M., 411
DeGruijter, D. N. M., 119
Del'Homme, M., 11–12, 455, 458
Demaray, M. K., 5
Deno, S. L., 291, 301
Derr, T., 237
Detterman, D. K., 4
Diamond, C. M., 411
Dodd, J. M., 9, 18
Doll, E. A., 414, 416
Doll, E. J., 237
Donnells, L., 472
Dool, E. J., 9
Drasgow, E., 41, 335, 336, 337
Dumond, R., 411
Dunn, L. M., 275
Dunst, C. J., 441, 442
DuPaul, G. J., 366, 367, 369

Eagle, J. W., 70, 71*n*
Eaves, R., 98, 281
Eckert, T., 366
Education, U.S. Department of, 4, 5, 6, 30, 54, 72, 74, 77, 184, 464
Ehrhardt, K. E., 365
Ehri, L. C., 460
Eliason, M. J., 368
Elliott, J. L., 185, 189, 366
Elliott, S. N., 5, 184, 188, 189, 324, 349
Engiles, A., 79
Englesson, I. L., 368
Erickson, D., 281
Ervin, R. A., 365
Evans, L. D., 237, 415
Evans, S. S., 297, 345
Evans, W. H., 297, 345

Faison, L., 412
Fan, X., 411
Feldt, L., 147, 150
Felix, B. C., 367
Fewell, R. R., 455
Field, S., 466
Figueroa, R. A., 406–407
Flanagan, D. P., 239, 385
Flaugher, R., 73
Ford, L., 41, 335
Foreman, A. L., 5
Forgan, J. W., 78
Forness, S. R., 4, 11–12, 74, 368, 382
Foster-Gaitskell, D., 414
Fowler, D. B., 236, 237
Fox, J., 337
Fradd, S., 73
Fromme, C., 79
Fuchs, D., 12, 74, 180, 300, 301, 302, 315, 380, 413
Fuchs, L. S., 74, 180, 238, 291, 300, 301, 302, 315, 324, 380
Fugate, D. J., 12
Fugate, M. H., 411
Fujiura, G. T., 30

Gable, R. A., 337
Gallegos, A., 182–183
Garcia, E., 326
Garcia, S. B., 12
Gardner, H., 380, 381–382, 406
Gartner, A., 74, 75, 77, 78
Gentry, N., 239
German, D., 202
Giannuli, M. M., 236
Gilkey, C. M., 442
Gillis, M., 316
Gilman, C., 413
Gindis, B., 31
Giordano, G., 182–183
Glascoe, F. P., 452
Glaser, R., 296
Glatthorn, A. A., 324
Goff, W. H., 492
Golden, L., 413
Goldenberg, D., 453, 454
Goldstein, S., 70
Gonzalez, M., 455, 458
Good, R., 290, 302
Goodman, J. F., 441, 442
Gopaul-McNicol, S., 12, 406
Gordon, M., 364
Goudena, P. P., 368
Graden, J. L., 12, 14, 17, 27, 98, 442
Graham, M., 439
Graham, S., 324
Greenspan, S. I., 445
Greenstein, J., 281
Gresham, F. M., 76, 338, 345, 349
Gridley, B. E., 412
Grimes, J. P., 385
Gronna, S., 189
Guerin, G. R., 320, 321, 322, 357, 358
Gulley, V., 365
Guthrie, D., 368
Gutkin, T. B., 12, 381
Guy, B., 466, 472

Habedank, L., 301
Haber, J., 367
Hagan, K. M., 12
Hagen, E. P., 397
Halgren, D. W., 12
Hall, J., 411
Hallman, C., 73
Hamby, D., 441, 442
Hamill, D. D., 273
Hamlett, C. L., 300, 301, 302
Hammill, D. D., 272, 273, 278, 279, 349, 352, 402, 403, 407
Handler, M. W., 366

Hansford, S. J., 326
Harrell, J., 70
Harris, D. B., 360
Harris, K., 324
Harrison, P. L., 414, 449, 450
Harry, B., 30
Hart, K. E., 296
Harvey, V., 11
Hasazi, S. B., 76
Hayeslip, P., 472
Heller, K., 154, 379
Hendrickson, J. M., 337
Hermansen, J., 472
Herrnstein, R. J., 380
Heshusius, L., 302
Hewett, J. B., 202, 237, 238
Higgins, M. M., 369
Hintze, J. M., 302–303
Hishinuma, E. S., 412
Hobbs, R., 326
Hoeppner, J. B., 368
Holtzman, W., 154, 379
Hopkins, B. R., 379
Hopkins, K. D., 379
Horn, E., 402, 413
Horn, J. L., 410
Horner, R. H., 336, 337
Horton, W., 74
House, A. L., 4, 189
Hover, S. A., 441, 442
Howell, K. W., 302, 311, 314, 315, 318, 319
Hoy, M., 484
Hresko, W. P., 273
Huebner, E. S., 76, 98, 183
Huefner, D. S., 62
Hughes, C., 290
Hultquist, A. M., 236, 290–291
Hunt, J., 445
Hurvich, M. S., 362, 363
Hynd, G. W., 367

Ikeda, M. J., 301–302
Ilmer, S., 449, 450

Jackson, G. D., 74
Jaeger, R., 281
Javorsky, J., 366
Jedrysek, E., 412
Jenkins, A., 189
Jenkins, J., 383
Jensen, A. R., 402
Johanson, C., 442
Johnson, B., 202
Johnson, C. B., 369, 441
Johnson, J., 383
Johnston, A. P., 76

Kamphaus, R., 415
Kasari, C., 11–12
Katsiyannis, A., 70
Katz, K. S., 439, 441, 442, 458
Kaufman, A. S., 170, 213, 214, 216, 217, 220, 223, 238, 291, 379, 385, 387, 388, 389, 390, 400, 401, 404, 410, 449, 452, 469
Kaufman, Alan, 450
Kaufman, J. C., 410
Kaufman, J. L., 410
Kaufman, N. L., 170, 213, 214, 216, 217, 220, 223, 238, 291, 400, 401, 404, 449, 450, 452, 469
Kaye, H. S., 466
Keith, T. Z., 411
Keogh, B. K., 4
Kerr, M. M., 343, 344
Klein, R. M., 368–369
Klinger, J. K., 78
Knoff, H. M., 360, 369
Knutson, N., 299–300, 301
Konold, T. R., 411
Koppitz, E., 360
Kozleski, E., 5, 189
Kranzler, J. H., 411
Kratochwill, T. R., 188, 189
Kroon, N., 368
Kubicek, F. C., 77
Kubick, R. J., 335
Kurait, S. K., 299
Kush, J. C., 411

LaGrow, S., 201, 202
Lambert, N. M., 484–485
Larsen, S. C., 272, 273, 279
Lasky, B., 70
Laurent, J., 411
Lavin, C., 411
Law, J. G., 412
Leak, D., 406
Leal, D., 382, 460
Lee, H., 78
Lee, S. W., 366
Lehmann, I., 139
Lehner, L., 239
Leigh, J. E., 425
Lenk, L. L., 76
Lennon, J. E., 460
Lentz, F. E., 442
Leonard, F., 472
LeResche, D., 79
Levine, P., 472
Levinson, E. M., 464, 466
Lewis, R., 171, 172, 182
Lewis, R. B., 379, 420
Lidz, C. S., 382
Liedtke, W., 318
Liggett, A. M., 76
Lillis, W. T., 238
Lindsey, P., 466, 472
Lipsky, D. K., 74, 75, 77, 78
Livingston, R., 411
Loiser, B. J., 368–369
Lopez, E. C., 73, 74
Lopez, R., 382
Lorber, R., 368
Lowe, P. A., 73, 381
Lueke, B., 78
Lusting, D. D., 296
Luther, J. B., 238
Lutz, J. G., 302–303

Maccow, G., 411
Macmann, G. M., 442, 458
MacMillan, D. L., 4, 74, 76, 382
Macready, T., 76
Maier, A. S., 320, 321, 322, 357, 358
Maller, S. J., 412
Mandelbaum, L., 74
Mann, L., 281
Mardell-Czudnowski, C., 410, 453, 454
Markwardt, F. C., 212
Marsh, T. Y., 31
Marshall, J., 301, 366
Marso, R. N., 307, 308
Marston, D., 291, 301
Martens, B. K., 9, 415

Martin, J., 466, 472
Martin, S., 237
Mastropieri, M. A., 78
Matavich, M. A., 412
Mather, N., 202, 236, 396
Mattison, R. E., 367
Maxam, S., 21, 21*n*
May, K., 119
Mayes, L. C., 445, 473
Mayes, S. D., 367
McArthur, D. S., 364
McCaffery, L. K., 410, 412
McCaughy, S. H., 367
McCauley, R. J., 296
McConaughy, S. H., 349, 354
McEntire, E., 262
McGoey, K. E., 366
McGrath, P. J., 368–369
McGrew, K. S., 201, 202, 236, 239, 385, 396, 410
McIntosh, D. E., 412
McIntyre, L., 11
McLaughlin, M. J., 72
McLean, J. E., 410
McLoughlin, J. A., 99, 171, 172, 182, 379, 420
McMurray, M. B., 369
McNeish, T. J., 360, 361–362
McNutt, G., 74
Mehrens, W. A., 139, 302, 303
Merrell, K. W., 236, 411
Messick, S., 14–15, 154, 379, 380
Metzke, L. K., 236, 290–291
Michael, J., 339
Michael, W. B., 239
Mick, L., 379
Miller, R., 466
Millman, J., 296
Minke, K. M., 441, 442
Mirkin, P. K., 301
Moats, L. C., 273
Moore, D., 281
Morehead, M. K., 302, 311, 314, 315, 318, 319
Morgan, S. K., 237
Morsink, C. V., 76
Moses, P., 79
Mueller, F., 369
Muenz, T. A., 238
Mulick, J. A., 11
Mullen, E. M., 446
Murphy, S., 410
Murray, C., 380

Nagle, R. J., 411
Naglieri, J. A., 360, 361–362
National Association of School Psychologists, 10
Nell, M., 367
Nelson, C. M., 343, 344
Nelson, J. R., 4, 9, 18, 189, 301, 366
Newcomer, P. L., 278
Newton, J. S., 336, 337
Nicewander, W. A., 119
Nicholson, C. L., 413
Nielsen, M. E., 12
Noell, G. H., 337
Nolet, V., 299–300
Norford, B. C., 368
Northup, J., 365
Nourse, S. W., 472
Noyce, R., 281
Nunes, S. R., 460
Nunnally, J., 149

Oats, R. G., 12
Oesterheld, J. R., 367
Office of Special Education and Rehabilitative Services, 186, 187
Office of Technology Assessment, 324
Olson, M., 316
Olson, T. K., 368
O'Neill, R. E., 336, 337
Orenstein, A., 79
Ouchi, B. Y., 238
Overton, T., 357
Owings, M. F., 72

Paget, K. D., 455, 457
Palomares, R. S., 368
Paratore, J. R., 326
Parker, L. D., 412
Patton, J., 27, 75, 467, 469, 471
Pearson, N. A., 273, 407
Perry, J. D., 335
Phillips, J. S., 366
Phillips, N. B., 301, 302
Phillips, S. E., 12
Pianta, B., 11
Pigge, F. L., 307, 308
Piper, A. L., 365
Plante, T. G., 412
Podell, D. M., 11
Poling, A., 365
Ponti, C., 12
Poon-McBrayer, F., 12
Portes, P. R., 31
Potter, M., 98
Powell, G., 281
Power, T. J., 367
Pratt, C., 414
Prewett, P. N., 236, 237, 238, 410, 412
Prifitera, A., 238
Prochnow-LaGrow, J., 201, 202
Prout, H. T., 360
Psyh, M., 17

Radford, P. M., 365
Rae, W. A., 368
Rafferty, J., 360
Rankin, R. J., 411
Reavis, K., 9, 18
Regan, R., 98
Reid, R., 366, 367
Reinehr, R. C., 369
Reinert, H. R., 343
Reschly, D. J., 5, 11, 14, 147, 150, 189, 379, 385, 413–414, 426
Retish, P., 484
Reynolds, C. R., 73, 291, 380, 381, 382, 411
Ricco, C. A., 367, 411
Richards, S. B., 380
Richey, L., 27, 98
Richman, L. C., 368
Rispens, J., 368
Roberts, G. E., 364
Roberts, M. L., 301, 366
Rodden-Nord, K., 301
Roe, B. D., 315–316, 317
Rogan, P., 466, 472

Rogers-Adkinson, D., 367
Rorschach, H., 365
Rosenfield, S., 299
Ross, C. M., 411
Rothlind, J., 369
Rotter, J., 360
Ruddell, M. R., 326
Rueda, R., 326
Ruehl, M. F., 75
Rynders, J., 449, 450

Sabers, D., 147, 150
Saenz, A. L., 73, 381
Salend, S. J., 71
Salvia, J., 143, 149, 150, 281, 290, 380
Sapp, G. L., 74, 239
Sattler, J. M., 397
Saura, K. M., 296
Scales, W., 472
Schatschneider, C., 5
Schattman, R. A., 76
Schaughency, E. A., 369
Schellinger, T., 296
Schmid, R. E., 345
Schneider, M., 202
Schrank, F. A., 410
Schulte, A. G., 188, 189
Schumm, J. S., 78
Schuster, B. V., 460
Scott, K., 439
Scott, M. M., 441, 442
Scruggs, T. E., 78
Scuitto, M. J., 296
Sena, R., 368
Serna, L. A., 12
Shadrach, E. A., 411
Shaklee, B. D., 326
Shanahan, T., 460
Shank, A., 382, 406
Shank, M., 460
Shapiro, E. S., 237, 290, 291, 297, 302–303, 320, 324
Shepard, L., 98
Shepherd, M., 74, 99
Sheridan, S. M., 70, 71*n*
Shinn, M. R., 299–300, 301–302
Shriner, J. G., 281, 336
Shull-Senn, S., 237
Silver, S., 41
Sinclair, E., 455, 458
Skinner, C. H., 338, 345
Slate, J. R., 239
Slesinski, C., 460
Smith, C. R., 75, 337
Smith, D. J., 9, 18
Smith, D. K., 413
Smith, J. J., 442
Smith, S., 382, 406, 460
Snider, V. E., 460, 462
Snyder, P., 443
Soodak, I. C., 11
Sparrow, S. S., 416, 417, 419, 420, 421, 422, 449, 450
Spenciner, L. J., 455, 456, 457
Spigelman, A., 368
Spigelman, G., 368
Spodak, R. B., 236
Sprague, J. R., 336, 337
Stanford, L. D., 367
Stanley, J. C., 379
Stevens, M., 411
Stile, S., 182–183
Stone, C. M., 442
Stoneman, Z., 70
Stoner, G., 301–302
Storey, K., 336, 337
Strain, P., 281
Strawser, S., 413
Strickland, B., 70, 78
Sugai, G., 9
Swanson, H. L., 343, 379
Swanson, J. M., 368
Sykora, C., 412
Symons, F. J., 4

Tannehill, R., 237
Taylor, H. G., 5
Taylor, L., 9, 18, 71
Taylor, R. L., 325, 379, 380, 386
Tharinger, D. J., 484–485
Thoma, C. A., 466, 472
Thomas-Presswood, T., 12, 406
Thompson, L. A., 4
Thorndike, R. L., 397
Thurlow, C. R., 5, 413
Thurlow, M. L., 5, 11, 14, 74, 185, 189, 201, 202, 465
Tindal, G., 291
Tochterman, S., 185
Trivette, C. M., 441, 442
Trommer, B. L., 368
Tucker, J., 379
Turnbull, A. P., 70, 78, 382, 406, 460
Turnbull, H. R., 78, 382, 383, 406, 460

Untiedt, S., 239
Urbina, S., 166, 200
Uzgiris, I. C., 445

Valcarce, R., 99
Valencia, R. R., 411
Valles, E. C., 12, 74
Vance, R., 281
Vaughn, S., 70, 78
Vig, S., 412
Vogel, S. A., 236, 472
Vygotsky, A., 31

Walker, D., 367
Walsh, B., 139
Ward, M., 466
Ward, S. B., 76
Ward, T. J., 76
Warren, S. F., 4
Watson, B. L., 379
Watson, T. S., 338, 345
Weatherly, M., 237
Weber, J., 70
Webster, R. E., 202, 238
Wechsler, D., 379, 390, 392, 393, 402, 447
Wehmeyer, M., 466
Weine, A. M., 366
Weiss, L. G., 238
Weller, C., 413
Wendling, B. J., 202
Werder, J. K., 202
Whemeyer, M. L., 466, 472
Whinnery, K., 302
Whitaker, J. S., 382
White, J. L., 184
White, R., 26, 27

Wiebe, M. J., 402
Wiederholt, J. L., 155, 270, 273, 279, 407
Wiener, J., 311, 312, 313
Wilkinson, G. S., 152, 202, 228, 232, 233, 234
Williams, R., 146–147
Willis, J. O., 411
Willows, D. M., 460
Wilson, C. P., 12
Wilson, V. L., 183, 411
Wise, L., 70
Wisnieswski, J. J., 11
Witt, J. C., 9, 337, 415
Witta, E. L., 411
Wolery, M., 445, 456
Wood, F., 383
Woodcock, R. W., 201, 202, 263, 265, 267, 291, 396
Worchel, F. F., 368
Worthen, B., 99
Worthington, C., 201
Yaghoub-Zadeh, Z., 460
Yakmaki, K., 30
Yell, M. L., 41, 63, 70*n,* 77, 78, 335, 336, 337
Ysseldyke, J. E., 4, 5, 11, 14, 27, 74, 98, 143, 149, 150, 185, 189, 201, 202, 380, 383, 465

Zern, D., 180
Zimmerman, D., 146–147
Zins, J., 12, 70

SUBJECT INDEX

AAMR. *See* American Association on Mental Retardation (AAMR)
ABI. *See* Adaptive Behavior Inventory (ABI)
Academic engaged time, 335
Academic knowledge, 207
Accommodations, 185
  in high-stakes testing, 187–188
Acculturation, 380
Achievement tests, 200, 201–239
  defined, 200
  Kaufman Test of Educational Achievement (K-TEA), 201–202, 213–224
  Mini-Battery of Achievement, 202
  Peabody Individual Achievement Test-Revised (PIAT-R), 201, 209–213
  research and issues, 236–239
  selecting academic, 239–240
  Wechsler Individual Achievement Test II, Second Edition (WIAT-II), 202, 224–228
  Wide Range Achievement Test-Revision 3 (WRAT3), 202, 228–230
  Woodcock-Johnson-Revised Tests of Cognitive Ability (WJ III), 201, 202–209
  Woodcock-McGrew-Werder Mini-Battery of Achievement, 234–235
Adaptive behavior, 378, 426–428
  assessing, 413–416
Adaptive Behavior Inventory (ABI), 424–426
  reliability of, 424, 426
  strengths of, 428
  validity of, 426
  weaknesses of, 428
Adaptive behavior scales, 200, 416
  AAMR Adaptive Behavior Scale-School, Second Edition (ABS-S2), 423–424
  Adaptive Behavior Inventory (ABI), 424–426
    Vineland Adaptive Behavior Scales, 416–423
    Interview Edition Expanded Form, 418, 420
    Interview Edition Survey Form, 417–418
    Technical Data for the Classroom Edition, 420–423
    Technical Data for the Expanded Form, 420
    Technical Data for the Survey Form, 418
AERA. *See* American Educational Research Association (AERA)
African Americans
  intelligence testing of, 379, 411
  nondiscriminatory assessment and, 72
  referral for disability services for students, 11
Age
  chronological, 167, 171–174, 378
  mental, 378
Age equivalents, 61
AGS Early Screening Profiles, 449–451
Alternative assessments, 6, 188–189
Alternative forms of reliability, 137
Alternative planning, 28
American Association on Mental Retardation (AAMR)
  Adaptive Behavior Scale-School, Second Edition (ABS-S2)
    reliability of, 423
    strengths of, 428
    validity of, 424
    weaknesses of, 428
  classification system, 116
American Educational Research Association (AERA), 23, 79
Analysis
  error, 6, 305, 315, 318
  factor, 154, 391
  functional behavioral, 336
  phonemic, 460
  task, 304–306, 318
Anecdotal recording, 337, 339–342
Animal pegs, 448
Annual goals, 61
Antecedents, 338–339
APA Standards, 153, 182
Apperception tests, 362–364
  Children's Apperception Test (CAT), 362–363
  Roberts Apperception Test for Children, 364
Applied problems, 205
Aptitude tests, 200
Arena assessment in infant and early childhood assessment, 456
Arithmetic, 448. *See also* Mathematics
Asian American students, referral and assessment practices of, 12
Assessment(s). *See also* Evaluation(s); Test(s)
  alternative, 6, 188–189
  arena, in infant and early childhood assessment, 456
  authentic, 324
  of behavior, 335–369, 488
  continuous, 5–9, 23–27
  criterion-referenced, 6, 291–299

criterion-related, 6
curriculum-based, 5, 200–201, 294, 299–303, 366
defined, 4
designing plan, 20–23
dynamic, 6, 382
early childhood, 444, 456–458
ecological, 14, 348, 349, 357–359
of functional academics, 469–472
functional behavioral, 336, 337–347, 365, 366
high-stakes, 184–189
importance of, in teaching, 4–5
of infants, 444–446
informal, 8–9, 290–326
intellectual, 380–382, 488
language, 274–280
methods of early childhood, 444
nondiscriminatory, 46–53, 72–75
performance, 6, 324, 325
portfolio, 6, 325–326
projective, 359–364
psychoeducational, 98–99, 137
reading, 155, 237, 239, 263–272, 281, 302, 311–318, 461
reliability and validity in, 129
research and issues related to transition planning, 472–476
special considerations in, 437–476
of students with disabilities, 5
testing as form of, 4
of toddlers, 446–455
of transition needs, 466–467
of whole child, 29–32
of young children, 446–455
Assistive technology, 188
At risk for developmental delay, 439
Attention deficit disorder, 54
computerized assessment of, 364–365
Attention deficit hyperactive disorder (ADHD), 54
behavior assessment for children with, 368–369
Attention disorders, meeting needs of persons with, 54–55
Audiologist as member of Individual Education Program team, 57
Authentic assessment, 324
Autism, 24
Average performance, 103–110
Basals, 175–178, 202–203
BASC. *See* Behavior Assessment System for Children (BASC)
Baseline, 338
Bayley Scales of Infant Development-II in infant assessment, 445
Behavior(s)
adaptive, 378, 413–416, 426–428
assessment of, 335–369, 488
checklists and rating scales for, 348–354
computerized, 364–365
ecological, 357–359
functional, 337–347
IDEA Admendment requirements, 335–337
projective techniques, 359–364
research and issues on, 365–369
sociograms, 355–356
structured classroom observations, 347–348
replacement, 336
target, 338
Behavioral consultant as member of Individual Education Program team, 56
Behavioral intervention plan, 335–336
Behaviorally stated short-term objectives, 484
Behavior Assessment System for Children (BASC), 351–352, 367
Behavior Rating Profile-2, 352, 366
Benchmarks, 484
Bias
curriculum, in norm-referenced assessment, 290–291
item, 154
in nondiscriminatory assessment, 72–73
Bidialectal environments, 406
Bilingual education, 12
Bimodal distribution, 105
Biological risk factors, 439
Birth health history in infant assessment, 444–445
Block design, 389, 448
Bodily-kinesthetic intelligence, 382
Brigance Inventories, 292
Brigance Diagnostic Inventory of Basic Skills, 293
Brigance Diagnostic Inventory of Early Development-Revised, 292–294
Brigance Diagnostic Inventory of Essential Skills, 293
Brigance Screens, 452–453

Calculation, 205
California Achievement Test (CAT), 234
California Test of Basic Skills (CTBS), 234
Capitalization, 207–208
Case studies, 506–544
background and referral information, 507–508, 513, 519, 523, 526–527, 532, 538–539
classroom observation and teacher interview, 508
classroom observation and teacher ratings, 513
Individual Education Program, 522, 531
parent conference, 513–514
parent interview, 520–521
play evaluation and home visit, 520
recommendations, 511, 517, 521, 526, 530, 536–537, 543
summary, 510, 517, 521, 525, 530, 536, 542
team meeting, 511–512, 517–518, 521–522, 530, 537–538, 543–544
test interpretations, 510
test results, 508–510, 514–516, 519–520, 523–525, 527–529, 532–536, 539–542
CAT. *See* California Achievement Test (CAT)
Caucasian students, referral for disability services, 11
CBCL. *See* Child Behavior Checklist (CBCL)
CEC. *See* Council for Exceptional Children (CEC)
Ceiling, 178, 202–203
Checklists, 6, 310, 348. *See also* Child Behavior Checklist (CBCL)
in assessing behavior

Child Behavior Checklist: Parent, Teacher, and Youth Report Forms, 349–351
Child Behavior Checklist: Semistructured Clinical Interview, 354
preferral, 15, 16–20
teacher-made, 6, 310
Child Behavior Checklist (CBCL), 349, 366, 367
in assessment of toddlers and young children, 446
Direct Observation Form, Revised Edition, 347–348
Parent, Teacher, and Youth Report Forms, 349–351
Semistructured Clinical Interview, 354
Children's Apperception Test (CAT), 362–363, 369
Child study committee, 9
in comprehensive evaluation, 27
Chronological age (CA), 167, 378
calculating, 171–174
Cloze in reading assessment, 311
CLT. *See* Cognitive Levels Test (CLT)
Code of Fair Testing Practices in Education, 23, 383
Coding, 388
Coefficient alpha, 139–140
Cognitive Levels Test (CLT), 281
Collaborative peer problem solving in prereferral, 9
Compliance, 41
Comprehension, 448
Comprehensive evaluation, 27–29, 44
Comprehensive Scales of Student Abilities, 273
Comprehensive Test of Basic Skills, 262
Comprehensive Test of Nonverbal Intelligence (CTONI), 273, 407–409, 413
reliability of, 408
strengths of, 427
validity of, 408–409
weaknesses of, 427
Concurrent validity, 151–152
Confidence interval, 144
Conners Continuous Performance Test, 365, 367
Conners Rating Scales-Revised, 352–353, 369
Conners Teacher Rating Scale, 367
Consent form, 45
Consistency
internal, 139
internal measures, 139–140
Construct, 153
Construct validity, 153–154
Content validity, 152–153
Continuous assessment, 5–9, 23–27
Continuous performance test, 364–365, 368
Convergent and discriminate validation, 154
Correlation, 129–136
negative, 133–134
no, 134
with other tests, 154
positive, 130–132, 138
Correlation coefficient, 130
Council for Exceptional Children (CEC), 23, 79
Standards of Practice set out by, 79–82
Criterion-referenced assessment, 6, 291–299
teacher-made, 294–299
Criterion-related assessment, 6
Criterion-related validity, 151–152
CTBS. *See* California Test of Basic Skills (CTBS)
CTONI. *See* Comprehensive Test of Nonverbal Intelligence (CTONI)
Cultural considerations in assessment, 29–32
Curriculum-based assessment, 5, 201, 294, 299–303, 366
standardized norm-referenced tests versus, 200–201
Curriculum bias in norm-referenced assessment, 290–291

Deaf-blindness, 24
Deafness, 24
Decision-making process, multidisciplinary team and, 75–76
Decoding skills in reading, 315
Derived scores, 102
obtaining, 183
Descriptive statistics, 97, 101–102
Detroit Tests of Learning Aptitude-4 (DTLA-4), 386, 402–404
reliability of, 403
strengths of, 427
validity of, 403
weaknesses of, 427
Developmental changes, 154
Developmental delays, 439
in infant assessment, 444
Developmental Indicators for the Assessment of Learning-Third Edition (Dial-3), 453–455
in assessing phonemic awareness, 461
Developmental version, 164
Diagnostic instruments, 250
Diagnostic tests, 200. *See also* Standardized diagnostic testing
educational achievement and, 491
Dial-3. *See* Developmental Indicators for the Assessment of Learning-Third Edition (Dial-3)
Diana v. State Board of Education, 383
Differential Ability Scales, 227
Digit span, 388
Direct measurement, 250, 294, 299–303
Direct observation, 337, 338
Disabilities
multiple, 25
perceptual, 58
specific learning, 25, 53–54
Dispersion, measures of, 110–116
Distribution
bimodal, 105
frequency, 103
multimodal, 105
negatively skewed, 117
normal, 102, 115–116
positively skewed, 117
skewed, 117–118
Domain, 164, 251
Draw-a-Person, 360
Screening Procedure for Emotional Disturbance, 361
Drawing tests, 360–362

DSM-IV (*Diagnostic and Statistical Manual*, 4th Edition), 353
DTLA-4. *See* Detroit Tests of Learning Aptitude-4 (DTLA-4)
Due process, 66–67, 78–79
  impartial hearing for, 67–68
  procedures for, 43
Duration recording, 337, 345
Dynamic assessment, 6, 382

Early childhood assessment
  methods of, 444
  techniques and trends in, 455–458
Early childhood education, legal guidelines of, 438
Early neonatal health history in infant assessment, 444–445
Ecobehavioral interviews in infant and early childhood assessment, 458
Ecological assessment, 14, 348, 349, 357–359
Educable mentally retarded (EMR), 383
Education, U.S. Department of, 4, 5, 30, 54, 77
Educational accountability, 4–5
Educational achievement and diagnostic test results, 491
Educational and Psychological Testing, Standards for, 80
Educational decisions, interpreting test results for, 485–487
Educational diagnostician as member of Individual Education Program team, 56
Educational objectives, writing, 500–503
Educational planning, 484
Education for All Handicapped Children Act (1975) (PL 94–142), 41–42, 413
Education for the Handicapped Act Amendments (PL 99–457), 42, 438
  differences in implementation of, 442
Eligibility, determining, for students with disabilities, 58–60
Eligibility decisions, 484
Eligibility meeting, 27
Emotional disturbance, 24
Employment, supported, 466
English as a Second Language (ESL), 12
Environmental influence, 380
Environmental risk factors, 439
Equivalent forms reliability, 137–138
Error, 143
Error analysis, 6, 305, 315, 318
ESL. *See* English as a second language (ESL)
Establishing operation, 339
Estimated true scores, 149–150
Ethics and standards, 79–84
Evaluation(s). *See also* Assessment; Test(s)
  assessment procedures and, 439–441
  of children with specific learning disabilities, 53–54
  comprehensive, 27–29, 44
  independent educational, 67
  Individual Education Program team, 55–58
  initial, 43–44
  play, 456, 520
Event recording, 337, 342–343
Experimental interventions, 154
Expressive language, 275

Factor analysis, 154, 391
Factual knowledge, 235
Family-centered program, 442
Family-focused program, 442
Field test, 164
Fluency, 315
  math, 205
  reading, 204–205
  writing, 205
Frequency counting, 342
Frequency distribution, 103
Frequency polygon, 105
Functional academics, Kaufman Functional Assessment Skills Test in assessing, 469–472
Functional assessment interview, 338
Functional behavioral analysis, 336
Functional behavioral assessments, 336, 337–347, 365, 366
  anecdotal recording, 339–342
  antecedents, 338–339
  direct observation techniques, 337, 338
  duration recording, 345
  event recording, 342–343
  interresponse time, 345–347
  interval recording, 343–344
  latency recording, 345
  time sampling, 343

Geometric designs, 448
GORT-4. *See* Gray Oral Reading Tests-Fourth Edition (GORT-4)
Grade equivalent, 61
Gray Oral Reading Tests-Fourth Edition (GORT-4), 270–271
  constructs underlying, 155
  reliability of, 271
  technical data, 270–271
  validity of, 271
Group tests
  high-stakes assessment, 184–189
  intelligence, 378

Hearing, impartial, 78–79
  due process, 67–68
Hearing impairment, 24
High-stakes testing, 6, 184–189
  accommodations in, 187–188
  issues in, 189
Hispanic students, intelligence testing of, 379
Hitting, 342
Home-school coordinator as member of Individual Education Program team, 57
Home Situations Questionnaire, 457
House-Tree-Person, 360
Human-Figure Drawing Test, 360

IDEA. *See* Individuals with Disabilities Education Act (IDEA) (PL 101–476)
IEP. *See* Individual Education Program (IEP)
IFSP. *See* Individual Family Service Plan (IFSP)
Impartial hearings, 78–79
  due process, 67–68
  officer at, 67
Independent educational evaluation, 67

Individual assessment plan, 21
Individual Education Program (IEP), 14, 335
  developing, 61–64
Individual education program team, 27
  evaluation, 55–58
  meeting results, 500–501
Individual Family Service Plan (IFSP), 28–29, 60, 440
Individuals with Disabilities Education Act (IDEA) (PL 101–476), 23, 41–43, 153, 154, 169, 171, 182
  1997 Amendments, 6, 9, 41, 60, 185–186
    on assessment, 4, 20
    authorization of funding for special-needs children, 438
    Congressional goals in passing, 42
    on cultural considerations, 29
    on educational equity and reform, 32
    emphasis on general curriculum, 5
    on evaluation and assessment procedures, 439–441
    on impartial due process hearing, 67–68
    on Individual Education Program team, 55–58
    on informed consent, 68
    initial assessment and reevaluation of students on, 51
    on parental consent, 44–45
    on parental involvement, 70
    procedural safeguards, 45
    regulations, 47–51
    requirements of, 335–336
    on transition services, 65
  assessment and, 43–53
  determining eligibility for services for students with, 58–60
  differences between Section 504 and, 68, 69–70
  disabilities defined in, 24–25
  implementation of, 30
  intelligence assessment and, 378
  provision for educational intervention at age 3, 438
  research and issues concerning, 68–71
  training of testors and, 74
  validation of tests and, 74
Infants
  assessment of, 444–446
  eligibility for services, 439
  issues and questions about serving, 441–443
  techniques and trends in, 455–458
Inferences, 129
Informal assessments, 8–9, 290–326
  authentic, 324
  Brigance Inventories, 292
    instruments, 292–294
    technical data, 294
  criterion-referenced assessment, 291–299
  curriculum-based assessment and direct measurement, 299–303
  defined, 290
  interview or questionnaire method, 311
  of mathematics, 318, 319
  performance, 324, 325
  permanent products, 311
  portfolio, 325–326
  of reading, 311–318
  of spelling, 318, 320
  task analysis and error analysis, 304–306
  teacher-made checklists, 6, 310
  teacher-made tests, 307–310
  work samples, 311
  of written language, 320, 324
Informal instruments, 250
Informal Reading Inventory-Third Edition, 315–318
Information, 448
Informed consent, 44
Initial evaluations, 43–44
Innate potential, 380
Instructional level, 250
Intellectual assessment, 488
  alternative views of, 380–382
Intelligence, 378
  adaptive behavior test results and, 490–491
  bodily-kinesthetic, 382, 411
  interpersonal, 382
  intrapersonal, 382
  linguistic, 381
  logical-mathematical, 381
  measuring, 378
  musical, 382
  research on measurement of, 410–413
  spatial, 381
Intelligence Quotient (IQ), 378
  nondiscriminatory assessment and tests, 74–75
  scale, 100
Intelligence testing
  of African Americans, 379, 411
  of Hispanic students, 379
  litigation and, 382–384
  of Native Americans, 411
Intelligence tests, 426–428
  Detroit Tests of Learning Aptitude-4 (DTLA-4), 402–404
  group, 378
  Kaufman Adolescent and Adult Intelligence Test (KAIT), 404–405
  Kaufman Assessment Battery for Children (K-ABC), 400–402
  Kaufman Brief Intelligence Test (KBIT), 405
  litigation and, 382–384
  meaning of, 378–380
  special considerations for students from culturally and linguistically diverse environments, 406–409
    Comprehensive Test of NonVerbal Intelligence (CTONI), 407–409
    nonverbal measures of intellectual ability, 407
    Test of Nonverbal Intelligence-Third Edition (Toni-3), 409
  Stanford-Binet Intelligence Scale-Fourth Edition (Stanford-Binet IV), 397–400
  use of, 385–386
  Wechsler Adult Intelligence Scale-Third Edition, 391–395
    subtests, 391–393
    technical data, 393
  Wechsler Intelligence Scale for Children-Third Edition (WISC-III), 386–391

interpreting scores of, 390–391
performance subtests, 388–390
technical data, 390
verbal subtests, 387–388
Woodcock-Johnson-Revised (WJ-R) Tests of Cognitive Abilities, 395–397
Interactive strategies in infant and early childhood assessment, 457
Interindividual interpretation, 487
Internal consistency, 137, 139, 154
measures of, 139–140
Interpersonal intelligence, 382
Interpolation, 166
Interpretation
interindividual, 487
intra-individual, 487
test, 488–489
Interrater reliability, 139–140
Interresponse time, 345–347
Interval recording, 337, 343–344
Interval scale, 100
Intervention, prereferral, 15–16, 18
Intervention-Based Multifactored Evaluation, 442–443
Interviews, 311, 348, 349, 353–354
ecobehavioral, in infant and early childhood assessment, 458
functional assessment, 338
parent, 488
teacher, 508
Intra-individual interpretation, 487
Intrapersonal intelligence, 382
Iowa Test of Basic Skills, 262
IQ. *See* Intelligence Quotient (IQ)
Item bias, 154
Item pool, 164

K-ABC. *See* Kaufman Assessment Battery for Children (K-ABC)
KAIT. *See* Kaufman Adolescent and Adult Intelligence Test (KAIT)
Kaufman Adolescent and Adult Intelligence Test (KAIT), 277, 404–405, 410, 412
reliability of, 405
validity of, 405
Kaufman Assessment Battery for Children (K-ABC), 224, 386, 400–402, 410–411, 427
in assessment of toddlers and young children, 446
reliability of, 402
strengths of, 427
validity of, 402
weaknesses of, 427
Kaufman Brief Intelligence Test (KBIT), 277, 410, 412, 413
reliability of, 405
validity of, 405
Kaufman Functional Assessment Skills Test (K-Fast), 239, 469–472
Kaufman Survey of Early Academic and Language Skills (K-SEALS), 452
in assessing phonemic awareness, 461
Kaufman Test of Educational Achievement (K-TEA), 170, 201–202, 209, 213–224, 236, 237, 238, 239
brief form, 221
strengths of, 240
weaknesses of, 240
comprehensive form, 213–214
strengths of, 240
weaknesses of, 240
reliability of, 220–221, 224
scoring brief form, 222
scoring comprehensive form, 214–218
technical data for comprehensive form, 218–221
technical for brief form, 222–224
validity of, 221, 224
KBIT. *See* Kaufman Brief Intelligence Test (KBIT)
KeyMath-Revised, 147, 239, 251–262, 263, 281, 291
reliability of, 262
scoring, 254–261
subtests, 251–261
technical data, 261–262
validity of, 262
K-FAST. *See* Kaufman Functional Assessment Skills Test (K-Fast)
Kinetic Family Drawings, 360
K-SEALS. *See* Kaufman Survey of Early Academic and Language Skills (K-SEALS)
K-TEA. *See* Kaufman Test of Educational Achievement (K-TEA)
Kuder-Richardson (K-R) 20, 139–140

Language
achievement tests for, 206, 207–208
expressive, 275
receptive, 275
written, 275, 320, 324
language, diagnostic testing of, 274–280
Language assessment, 274–275
Peabody Picture Vocabulary Test-Third Edition (PPVT-III), 275–277
Test of Adolescent and Adult Language-Third Edition (TOAL-3), 279–280
Test of Language Development-Intermediate: Third Edition (TOLD-I:3), 278–279
Test of Language Development-Primary: Third Edition (TOLD-P:3), 277–278
Larry P. v. Riles, 49, 383
Latency recording, 345
Learning disabilities, 58
evaluating children with specific, 53–54
Least restrictive environment, 63, 76–78
Legal guidelines of early childhood education, 438
Letter number sequencing, 391
Letter-word identification, 204
Linguistic intelligence, 381
Listening comprehension, 226
Litigation, intelligence testing and, 382–384
Logical-mathematical intelligence, 381
Long-term goals, 484
Lora v. New York City Board of Education, 383

Mainstream assistance teams in prereferral, 9
Manifestation determination, 335

Mathematics
  achievement tests for, 205, 207, 210, 213, 214, 221, 225, 230–231, 235
  diagnostic testing of, 251–263
  informal assessment of, 318, 319
  standardized diagnostic testing of, 251–263
Math fluency, 205
Matrix reasoning, 391
Mazes, 311, 389–390, 448
MBA. *See* Mini-Battery of Achievement (MBA)
Mean, 108–109
Mean differences, 117
Measurement
  curriculum-based, and peer tutoring, 302
  direct, 250, 294, 299–303
  importance of, 98–99
  of intelligence, 378, 410–413
  standard error of, 143–149
Measures of central tendency, 102–103
Measures of dispersion, 110–116
Median, 106–107
Mediation, 66
Mental age (MA), 378
Mental handicap, 58
Mental retardation, 24, 58
Metropolitan Achievement Tests, Eighth Edition, 227
Mini-Battery of Achievement (MBA), 202, 239
Minority overrepresentation, 72
  in special education, 72–73
Mode, 104
Mullen Scales of Early Learning: AGS Edition, 446–447
Multidisciplinary team
  decision-making process and, 75–76
  in prereferral, 9
Multimodal distribution, 105
Multiple disabilities, 25
Musical intelligence, 382

National Association of School Psychologists, 10, 23, 79, 80, 82–83
National Council on Measurement in Education, 23, 79
Native Americans, intelligence testing of, 411
Needed evaluation data, determination of, 52–53
Negative correlation, 133–134
Negatively skewed distribution, 117
Neonatal Behavioral Assessment Scale in infant assessment, 445
No correlation, 134
Nominal scale, 100
Nondiscriminatory assessment, 46–53, 72–75
Nonverbal measures of intellectual ability, 407
Normal distribution, 102
  standard deviation and, 115–116
Norm group, 164
Norm-referenced tests, 27, 100, 164–189, 201
  adapting, to represent criterion-referenced testing, 291–292
  basic steps in test administration, 169–183
    administering tests, 180–183
    beginning, 170–171
    calculating chronological age, 171–174
    calculating raw scores, 174–175
    determining basals and ceilings, 175–178
    obtaining derived scores, 183
    using information on protocols, 178–180
  construction of, 164–169
  group testing, high-stakes assessment, 184–189
  problems of, 290–391
  representation of reading curricula in, 290
  standardized, versus curriculum-based assessment, 200–201
  types of scores, 183–184
Numbers, getting meaning from, 99–100
Numerical operations, 225
Numerical scales, 100–101

Object assembly, 389, 447
Objectives
  educational, 500–503
  short-term, 61
    behaviorally stated, 484
Observations
  direct, 337, 338
  in infant and early childhood assessment, 457
  structured classroom, 347–359
Obtained score, 143
Occupational therapist as member of Individual Education Program team, 56
On-task time, 345
Oral and Written Language Scales, 277
Oral comprehension, 206
Oral expression, 226
Ordinal scale, 100
Orthopedic impairment, 25
Other health impairment, 25
Overidentification of special education students, 12

Paraphrasing in reading assessment, 311
Parent, surrogate, 44
Parental consent, 44–46
Parental permission, 488
Parent interview, 488
Parent participation, 60
Parents' rights booklet, 45
PASE v. Hannon, 383
Passage comprehension, 205
Peabody Individual Achievement Test-Revised (PIAT-R), 201, 209–213, 236, 238, 239, 263
  reliability of, 213
  scoring, 210–212
  strengths of, 240
  subtests, 209–210
  technical data, 212–213
  validity of, 213
  weaknesses of, 240
Peabody Picture Vocabulary Test (PPVT), 224
Peabody Picture Vocabulary Test-Revised (PPVT-R), 224
Peabody Picture Vocabulary Test-Third Edition (PPVT-III), 227
  reliability of, 275
  validity of, 275–277
Pearson's *r,* 136–137

Peer tutoring, curriculum-based measurement and, 302
Percentile ranks, 119–120, 183, 184
Perceptual disability, 58
Performance assessment, 6, 324, 325
Performance tests, 386
Permanent products, 310, 311
Phoneme blending, 460
Phoneme categorization, 460
Phoneme deletion, 460
Phoneme identity, 460
Phoneme segmentation, 460
Phonemic analysis, 460
Phonemic awareness, 459–464
Phonemic isolation, 460
Phonemic synthesis, 460
Physical therapist as member of Individual Education Program team, 56
Physician's assistant as member of Individual Education Program team, 57
Picture arrangement, 389
Picture completion, 388, 448
Picture vocabulary, 206
Play evaluations in infant and early childhood assessment, 456
Portfolio assessment, 6, 325–326
Positive correlation, 130–132, 138
Positively skewed distribution, 117
PPVT. *See* Peabody Picture Vocabulary Test (PPVT)
PPVT-III. *See* Peabody Picture Vocabulary Test-Third Edition (PPVT-III)
PPVT-R. *See* Peabody Picture Vocabulary Test-Revised (PPVT-R)
Practice effect, 137
Predictive validity, 152, 154
Prenatal health history in infant assessment, 444–445
Prereferral, 9–20
  checklists in, 15, 16–20
  interventions in, 9, 11, 12–13, 15–16, 18
Presentation format, 153
Probes, 250, 292
Procedural safeguards, 66
Projective assessment, 359–364
  apperception tests, 362–364
  drawing tests, 360–362
  sentence completion tests, 359–360
Protocols, 170
  using information on, 178–180
Pseudoword decording, 225
Psychoeducational assessment
  importance of, 98–99
  traits measured, 137
Psychophysiological disturbances in infant assessment, 444
Public Law 94–142. *See* Education for All Handicapped Children Act (1975) (PL 94–142)
Public Law 99–457. *See* Education for the Handicapped Act Amendments (PL 99–457)
Public Law 101–476. *See* Individuals with Disabilities Education Act (IDEA) (PL 101–476)
Punctuation, 207–208

Quantitative concepts, 207
Questionnaires, 310, 311, 348
  interviews and, 353–354
  rating, 349
  situational, in infant and early childhood assessment, 457
Questions, answering, in reading assessment, 311

Range, 111
Rating questionnaire, 349
Rating scales, in assessing behavior, 348–354
  Behavior Assessment System for Children (BASC), 351–352
  Behavior Rating Profile—2, 352
  Conners Rating Scales—Revised, 352–353
Ratio scale, 101
Raw score, 99–100, 174–175
Reading
  achievement tests for, 204–205, 206, 209–210, 213, 214, 221, 224–225, 230, 231–235
  decoding skills in, 315
  diagnostic testing of, 263–272
  fluency in, 315
Reading assessment
  answering questions in, 311
  cloze in, 311
  curriculum-based measurement in, 302
  Gray Oral Reading Tests-Fourth Edition (GORT-4), 155, 270–271
  informal, 311–318
  Informal Reading Inventory-Third Edition, 315–318
  maze in, 311
  paraphrasing in, 311
  sentence verification in, 311
  story retelling in, 311
  Test of Reading Comprehension-Third Edition (TORC-3), 271–272
  vocabulary in, 311
  Woodcock Reading Mastery Tests, 237, 461
  Woodcock Reading Mastery Tests-Revised (WRMT-R), 239, 263–270, 281
Reading fluency, 204–205
Receptive language, 275
Recording
  anecdotal, 339–342
  duration, 345
  event, 342–343
  interval, 343–344
  latency, 345
Reevaluations, 503
Regular education teacher as member of Individual Education Program team, 57
Regulatory disturbances in infant assessment, 444
Regulatory patterns in infant assessment, 445
Rehabilitation Act (1973), Section 504 of, 54, 68
Related services, 59
Reliability
  of AAMR Adaptive Behavior Scale-School, Second Edition (ABS-S2), 423

of Adaptive Behavior Inventory (ABI), 424, 426
of AGS Early Screening Profiles, 451
alternate forms, 137
in assessment, 129
of Brigance Screens, 453
of Comprehensive Test of Nonverbal Intelligence (CTONI), 408–409
correlation and, 129–136
of Detroit Tests of Learning Aptitude-4 (DTLA-4), 403
of Developmental Indicators for the Assessment of Learning-Third Edition (Dial-3), 454
for different groups, 141–142
equivalent forms, 137–138
evaluating, 140–142
of Gray Oral Reading Tests-Fourth Edition (GORT-4), 271
interrater, 139–140
of Kaufman Adolescent and Adult Intelligence Test (KAIT), 405
of Kaufman Assessment Battery for Children (K-ABC), 402
of Kaufman Brief Intelligence Test (KBIT), 405
of Kaufman Functional Assessment Skills Test (K-Fast), 472
of Kaufman Survey of Early Academic and Language Skills (K-SEALS), 452
of Kaufman Test of Educational Achievement (K-TEA), 220–221, 224
methods of measuring, 136–140
of Mullen Scales of Early Learning: AGS Edition, 447
of KeyMath-Revised, 262
of Peabody Individual Achievement Test-Revised (PIAT-R), 213
of Peabody Picture Vocabulary Test-Third Edition (PPVT-III), 275
split-half, 139–140
of Stanford-Binet Intelligence Scale-Fourth Edition (Stanford-Binet IV), 399
of Test of Adolescent and Adult Language-Third Edition (TOAL-3), 280
of Test of Language Development-Intermediate: Third Edition (TOLD-I:3), 279
of Test of Language Development-Primary: Third Edition (TOLD-P:3), 277
of Test of Mathematical Abilities-2 (TOMA-2), 263
of Test of Nonverbal Intelligence-Third Edition (TONI-3), 409
of Test of Reading Comprehension-Third Edition (TORC-3), 272
of Test of Written Language-3 (TOWL-3), 273
of Test of Written Spelling-4 (TWS-4), 274
test-retest, 137
of Transition Planning Inventory (TPI), 469
validity versus, 155
of Vineland Adaptive Behavior Scales, 418, 420
of Wechsler Adult Intelligence Scale-Third Edition, 393
of Wechsler Individual Achievement Test II, Second Edition (WIAT-II), 227
of Wechsler Intelligence Scale for Children-III (WISC-III), 390
of Wechsler Preschool and Primary Scale of Intelligence-Revised (WPPSI-R), 449
of Wide Range Achievement Test-Revision 3 (WRAT3), 234
of Woodcock-Johnson III Tests of Cognitive Abilities, 397
of Woodcock-Johnson-Revised Tests of Cognitive Ability (WJ III), 209
of Woodcock-McGrew-Werder Mini-Battery of Achievement, 235
of Woodcock Reading Mastery Tests-Revised (WRMT-R), 269
Replacement behaviors, 336
Response mode, 153
Risk factors
biological, 439
environmental, 439
Roberts Apperception Test for Children, 364, 368
Rotter Incomplete Sentence Blank, 360

Samples, 164
work, 310, 311
Scale(s)
adaptive behavior, 200, 416–426
interval, 100
nominal, 100
numerical, 100–101
ordinal, 100
rating scales, 348–354
ratio, 101
Scaled scores, 386
Scattergram, 130–131
School counselor as member of Individual Education Program team, 56
School nurse as member of Individual Education Program team, 56
School psychologist as member of Individual Education Program team, 56
School Situations Questionnaire, 457
School social worker as member of Individual Education Program team, 57
Scientific Research Associates (SRA) Achievement Series, 263
Scores
derived, 102, 183
estimated true, 149–150
obtained, 143
raw, 99–100, 174–175
scaled, 386
standard, 61, 102
stanine, 184
T, 184
true, 143
estimated, 149–150
Z, 119–120, 183, 184
Screening, 20
for sensory impairments or physical problems, 488

Screening committee in comprehensive evaluation, 27
Screening tests, 200
Section 504, 28
  differences between Individuals with Disabilities Education Act (1990) (IDEA) and, 68, 69–70
Sentence completion tests, 359–360
Sentences, 449
Sentence verification in reading assessment, 311
Setting events, 338–339
Short-term objectives, 61
  behaviorally stated, 484
Similarities, 448
Situational questionnaires in infant and early childhood assessment, 457
Skewed distributions, 117–118
Social/environmental disturbances in infant assessment, 444
Sociograms, 348, 349, 355–356, 366
Sound awareness, 207
Spatial intelligence, 381
Special considerations for students from culturally and linguistically diverse environments, 406–409
  Comprehensive Test of NonVerbal Intelligence (CTONI), 407–409
  nonverbal measures of intellectual ability, 407
  Test of Nonverbal Intelligence-Third Edition (Toni-3), 409
Special education
  curriculum-based measurement in placements, 301
  effectiveness of earlier programs, 4
  overidentification of students, 12
  overrepresentation of minorities in, 72–73
  services, 59
Special education supervisor as member of Individual Education Program team, 56
Special education teacher as member of Individual Education Program team, 56
Specific learning disability, 25
Speech impairment, 25
Speech-language clinician as member of Individual Education Program team, 57
Spelling
  achievement tests for, 205, 207, 210, 213–214, 216–217, 221, 225, 230
  diagnostic testing of, 273–274
  informal assessment of, 318, 320
  Test of Written Spelling-4 (TWS-4), 273–274
Split-half reliability, 139–140
Standard deviation, 110, 113–115
  normal distribution and, 115–116
Standard error of measurement, 143–149
  applying, 146–149
Standardized diagnostic testing, 249–282
  appropriate uses of, 250–251
  Gray Oral Reading Tests-Fourth Edition (GORT-4), 270–271
  KeyMath-Revised, 251–262
  language assessment, 274–275
    Peabody Picture Vocabulary Test-Third Edition (PPVT-III), 275–277
    Test of Adolescent and Adult Language-Third Edition (TOAL-3), 279–280
    Test of Language Development-Intermediate: Third Edition (TOLD-I:3), 278–279
    Test of Language Development-Primary: Third Edition (TOLD-P:3), 277–278
  research and issues, 281–282
  selecting, 281
  Test of Mathematical Abilities-2 (TOMA-2), 262–263
  Test of Reading Comprehension-Third Edition (TORC-3), 271–272
  Test of Written Language-3 (TOWL-3), 272–273
  Test of Written Spelling-4 (TWS-4), 273–274
  Woodcock Reading Mastery Tests-Revised (WRMT-R), 263–270
Standardized tests, 27
Standard scores, 61, 102
Standards for Educational and Psychological Testing, 23, 79, 80
  5.1, 84
  5.7, 84
  10.1, 84
  10.12, 84
  11.3, 84
  11.20, 84
  12.11, 84
  13.10, 84
  13.13, 84
Stanford Achievement Test (SAT), 234
  Ninth Edition, 227
Stanford-Binet Intelligence Scale-Fourth Edition (Stanford-Binet IV), 386, 397–400, 412
  composite score, 236
  reliability of, 399
  strengths of, 427
  in transition planning assessment, 466
  validity of, 399–400
  weaknesses of, 427
Stanine scores, 184
Statistics, descriptive, 97, 101–102
Story recall, 205, 206
Story retelling in reading assessment, 311
Structured classroom observations, 347–348
  checklists and rating scales, 348–354
  Child Behavior Checklist: Direct Observation Form, Revised Edition, 347–348
  ecological assessment, 357–359
  questionnaires and interviews, 353–354
  sociograms, 355–356
Students from culturally and linguistically diverse environments, assessment of, 406–409
Students with disabilities
  assessment of, 5
  determining eligibility of, for services, 58–60
Subskill, 293, 310
Subtasks, 304

Supported employment, 466
Surrogate parent, 44
Symbol search, 389

Talking out, 342
Target behaviors, 338
Task analysis, 318
  error analysis and, 304–306
Teacher(s)
  special education, as member of Individual Education Program team, 56
  use of continuous assessment, 5
  visiting, as member of Individual Education Program team, 57
Teacher assistance team, 8–9
  in prereferral, 9
Teacher interviews, 508
Teacher-made checklist, 6, 310
Teacher-made tests, 307–310
  criterion-referenced, 294–299
Teacher Report Form, 349
Teaching, importance of assessment in, 4–5
Test(s). *See also* Assessment; Evaluation(s)
  achievement, 200, 201–239
  apperception, 362–364
  aptitude, 200
  basic steps in administration of, 169–183
  criterion-referenced, 6
  diagnostic, 200, 491
  drawing, 360–362
  group, 184–189, 378
  intelligence, 378–431
  interpretation of, 488–489
  norm-referenced, 27, 100, 164–189, 201, 291–292
  performance, 386
  screening, 200
  sentence completion, 359–360
  standardized, 27
  standardized diagnostic, 263–271
    teacher-made, 307–310
  criterion-referenced, 294–299
  validity of, versus validity of test use, 154–155
  verbal, 386
Testing
  defined, 4
  high-stakes, 6, 184–189
    accommodations in, 187–188
  intelligence, 379, 382–384, 411
  standardized diagnostic, 249–282
Test manual, 169
Test of Adolescent and Adult Language-Third Edition (TOAL-3)
  reliability of, 280
  validity of, 280
Test of Language Development-Intermediate: Third Edition (TOLD-I:3)
  reliability of, 279
  validity of, 279
Test of Language Development-Primary: Third Edition (TOLD-P:3)
  reliability of, 277
  validity of, 278
Test of Mathematical Abilities-2 (TOMA-2), 262–263
  reliability of, 263
  technical data, 263
  validity of, 263
Test of Nonverbal Intelligence-Third Edition (TONI-3), 409
  reliability of, 409
  validity of, 409
Test of Reading Comprehension-Third Edition (TORC-3), 271–272
  reliability of, 272
  technical data, 271–272
  validity of, 272
Test of Written Language-3 (TOWL-3), 272–273
  reliability of, 273
  technical data, 273
  validity of, 273
Test of Written Spelling-4 (TWS-4), 273–274, 281
  reliability of, 274
  technical data, 274
  validity of, 274
Test results
  art of interpreting, 487–491
  case study, 492–500
  educational achievement and diagnostic, 491
  intelligence and adaptive behavior, 490–491
  interpreting, for educational decisions, 485–487
  writing, 491–492
Test-retest reliability, 137
Tests of Cognitive Abilities in transition planning assessment, 466
Test validity, 151–155
Time on task, 342
Time sampling, 343
TOAL-3. *See* Test of Adolescent and Adult Language-Third Edition (TOAL-3)
Toddlers
  assessment of, 446
    AGS Early Screening Profiles, 449–451
    Brigance Screens, 452–453
    Developmental Indicators for the Assessment of Learning-Third Edition (DIAL-3), 453–455
    Kaufman Survey of Early Academic and Language Skills (K-Seals), 452
    Mullen Scales of Early Learning: AGS Edition, 446–447
  eligibility for services, 439
  issues and questions about serving, 441–443
TOLD-I:3. *See* Test of Language Development-Intermediate: Third Edition (TOLD-I:3)
TOLD-P:3. *See* Test of Language Development-Primary: Third Edition (TOLD-P:3)
TOMA-2. *See* Test of Mathematical Abilities-2 (TOMA-2)
TONI-3. *See* Test of Nonverbal Intelligence-Third Edition (TONI-3)
TORC-3. *See* Test of Reading Comprehension-Third Edition (TORC-3)
TOWL-3. *See* Test of Written Language-3 (TOWL-3)
TPI. *See* Transition Planning Inventory (TPI)

Transition needs, assessment of, 466–467
Transition planning, 464
  research and issues related to, 472–476
Transition Planning Inventory (TPI), 467–469
Transition services, 64–66, 464–469
Traumatic brain injury, 25
True scores, 143
  estimated, 149–150
T scores, 184
TWS-4. *See* Test of Written Spelling-4 (TWS-4)

Uzgiris-Hunt Ordinal Scales of Psychological Development in infant assessment, 445

Validation
  convergent, 154
  discriminate, 154
  of tests, 74
Validity, 151
  of AAMR Adaptive Behavior Scale-School, Second Edition (ABS-S2), 424
  of Adaptive Behavior Inventory (ABI), 426
  of AGS Early Screening Profiles, 451
  of Brigance Screens, 453
  of Comprehensive Test of Nonverbal Intelligence (CTONI), 408–409
  concurrent, 151–152
  construct, 153–154
  criterion-related, 151–152
  of Detroit Tests of Learning Aptitude-4 (DTLA-4), 403
  of Developmental Indicators for the Assessment of Learning-Third Edition (Dial-3), 455
  of Gray Oral Reading Tests-Fourth Edition (GORT-4), 271
  of Kaufman Adolescent and Adult Intelligence Test (KAIT), 405
  of Kaufman Assessment Battery for Children (K-ABC), 402
  of Kaufman Brief Intelligence Test (KBIT), 405
  of Kaufman Functional Assessment Skills Test (K-Fast), 472
  of Kaufman Survey of Early Academic and Language Skills (K-Seals), 452
  of Kaufman Test of Educational Achievement (K-TEA), 221, 224
  of Mullen Scales of Early Learning: AGS Edition, 447
  of KeyMath-Revised, 262
  of Peabody Individual Achievement Test-Revised (PIAT-R), 213
  of Peabody Picture Vocabulary Test-Third Edition (PPVT-III), 275–277
  predictive, 152, 154
  reliability versus, 155
  of Stanford-Binet Intelligence Scale-Fourth Edition (Stanford-Binet IV), 399–400
  test, 151–155
  of Test of Adolescent and Adult Language-Third Edition (TOAL-3), 280
  of Test of Language Development-Intermediate: Third Edition (TOLD-I:3), 279
  of Test of Language Development-Primary: Third Edition (TOLD-P:3), 278
  of Test of Mathematical Abilities-2 (TOMA-2), 263
  of Test of Nonverbal Intelligence-Third Edition (TONI-3), 409
  of Test of Reading Comprehension-Third Edition (TORC-3), 272
  of Test of Written Language-3 (TOWL-3), 273
  of Test of Written Spelling-4 (TWS-4), 274
  of tests versus validity of test use, 154–155
  of Transition Planning Inventory (TPI), 469
  of Vineland Adaptive Behavior Scales, 418, 420
  of Wechsler Adult Intelligence Scale-Third Edition, 393–394
  of Wechsler Individual Achievement Test II, Second Edition (WIAT-II), 227
  of Wechsler Intelligence Scale for Children-III (WISC-III), 390
  of Wechsler Preschool and Primary Scale of Intelligence-Revised (WPPSI-R), 449
  of Wide Range Achievement Test-Revision 3 (WRAT3), 234
  of Woodcock-Johnson-Revised Tests of Cognitive Ability (WJ III), 209, 397
  of Woodcock-McGrew-Werder Mini-Battery of Achievement, 235
  of Woodcock Reading Mastery Tests-Revised (WRMT-R), 270
Validity coefficient, 151
Validity of test use, 154–155
Variability, 110
Variance, 110
Verbal tests, 386
Vineland Adaptive Behavior Scales, 416–423
  in assessment of toddlers and young children, 446
  Interview Edition Expanded Form, 418, 420
  Interview Edition Survey Form, 417–418
  reliability of, 418, 420
  strengths of, 428
  Technical Data for the Classroom Edition, 420–423
  Technical Data for the Expanded Form, 420
  Technical Data for the Survey Form, 418
  validity of, 418, 420
  weaknesses of, 428
Visiting teacher as member of Individual Education Program team, 57
Visual impairment, 25
Vocabulary, 206, 311, 387, 448

WAIS-III. *See* Wechsler Adult Intelligence Scale-Third Edition (WAIS-III)
Wechsler Adult Intelligence Scale-Third Edition (WAIS-III), 386, 391–395

reliability of, 393
strengths of, 427
subtests, 391–393
technical data, 393
in transition planning assessment, 466
validity of, 393–394
weaknesses of, 427
Wechsler Individual Achievement Test II, Second Edition (WIAT-II), 202, 209, 224–228, 239
in assessing phonemic awareness, 462
reliability of, 227
scoring, 226
strengths of, 240
subtests, 224–226
Supplement for College Students and Adults, 224
technical data, 226–228
in transition planning assessment, 466–467
validity of, 227
weaknesses of, 240
Wechsler Individual Achievement Test II, Second Edition (WIAT-II) Screener, 239
Wechsler Intelligence Scale for Children-Third Edition (WISC-III), 277, 386–391, 411–412, 412
interpreting scores of, 390–391
performance subtests, 388–390
reliability of, 390
technical data, 390
in transition planning assessment, 466
validity of, 390
verbal subtests, 387–388
Wechsler Intelligence Scales for Children, 236
Wechsler Preschool and Primary Scale of Intelligence-Revised (WPPSI-R), 386, 447–449
Whole child, assessment of, 29–32
WIAT-II. *See* Wechsler Individual Achievement Test II, Second Edition (WIAT-II)
Wide Range Achievement Test, 202, 224
Wide Range Achievement Test Revised (WRAT-R), 227, 236, 238, 263
Wide Range Achievement Test-Revision 3 (WRAT3), 152, 201–202, 228–230, 239
reliability of, 234
scoring, 231
strengths of, 240
subtests, 230–231
technical data, 231–234
validity of, 234
weaknesses of, 240
WISC-III. *See* Wechsler Intelligence Scale for Children-Third Edition (WISC-III)
WJ-R. *See* Woodcock-Johnson Psycho-Educational Battery-Revised (WJ-R)
Woodcock-Johnson III Tests for Achievement
in assessing phonemic awareness, 461
strengths of, 427
in transition planning assessment, 466
weaknesses of, 427
Woodcock-Johnson Psycho-Educational Battery-Revised (WJ-R), 386, 410
Woodcock-Johnson-Revised Tests of Cognitive Ability (WJ III), 201, 202–209, 236, 237, 395–397
in assessment of toddlers and young children, 446
extended battery, 206–208
reliability of, 209, 397
standard battery, 203–206
strengths of, 240
technical data, 208–209
Total Achievement Cluster, 209
validity of, 209, 397
weaknesses of, 240
Woodcock-McGrew-Werder Mini-Battery of Achievement, 234–235
reliability of, 235
scoring, 235
strengths of, 240
subtests, 234–235
technical data, 235
validity of, 235
weaknesses of, 240
Woodcock Reading Mastery Tests, 237
in assessing phonemic awareness, 461
Woodcock Reading Mastery Tests-Revised (WRMT-R), 239, 263–270, 281
reliability of, 269–270
scoring, 265–269
subtests, 264–265
technical data, 269–270
validity of, 270
Word attack, 206
Work samples, 310, 311
WPPSI-R. *See* Wechsler Preschool and Primary Scale of Intelligence-Revised (WPPSI-R)
WRAT3. *See* Wide Range Achievement Test-Revision 3 (WRAT3)
WRAT-R. *See* Wide Range Achievement Test Revised (WRAT-R)
Writing
achievement tests for, 205, 206, 210, 225, 235
diagnostic testing of, 272–273
Written expression, 225
Written language, 275
informal assessment of, 320, 324
WRMT-R. *See* Woodcock Reading Mastery Tests-Revised (WRMT-R)

Young children
assessment of, 446
AGS Early Screening Profiles, 449–451
Brigance Screens, 452–453
Developmental Indicators for the Assessment of Learning-Third Edition (DIAL-3), 453–455
Kaufman Survey of Early Academic and Language Skills (K-Seals), 452
Mullen Scales of Early Learning: AGS Edition, 446–447
considerations in assessing very, 458–459
eligibility for services, 439
Youth Self-Report, 351, 366

Z scores, 119–120, 183, 184